Political Sociology: Canadian Perspectives

Edited by Douglas Baer

OXFORD
UNIVERSITY PRESS

OXFORD
UNIVERSITY PRESS

70 Wynford Drive, Don Mills, Ontario M3C 1J9
www.oupcan.com

Oxford University Press is a department of the University of Oxford.
It furthers the University's objective of excellence in research, scholarship,
and education by publishing worldwide in

Oxford New York

Athens Auckland Bangkok Bogotá Buenos Aires Cape Town
Chennai Dar es Salaam Delhi Florence Hong Kong Istanbul Karachi
Kolkata Kuala Lumpur Madrid Melbourne Mexico City Mumbai Nairobi
Paris São Paulo Shanghai Singapore Taipei Tokyo Toronto Warsaw

with associated companies in Berlin Ibadan

Oxford is a trade mark of Oxford University Press
in the UK and in certain other countries

Published in Canada
by Oxford University Press

National Library of Canada Cataloguing in Publication Data

Main entry under title:
Political sociology: Canadian perspectives
Includes bibliographical references and index.
ISBN 0-19-541109-9
1. Political sociology. 2. Political culture–Canada–History–20th century.
3. Canada–Politics and government–20th century.
I. Baer, Douglas Edward, 1951–

JA76.P58 2001   306.2'0971   C2001-900940-2

Cover design: Brett J. Miller
Cover art: *Unity Rally III, Montreal,* 1996, by Evangeline Murray, Westmount, Quebec.

1 2 3 4 - 05 04 03 02

This book is printed on permanent (acid-free) paper ∞.
Printed in Canada

Contents

Contributors

Douglas Baer, Department of Sociology, University of Victoria.

Edward Bell, Brescia College, University of Western Ontario.

William K. Carroll, Department of Sociology, University of Victoria.

James E. Curtis, Department of Sociology, University of Waterloo.

Claude Dennis, Faculté Saint-Jean, University of Alberta.

Elisabeth Gidengil, Department of Political Science, McGill University.

Edward G. Grabb, Department of Sociology, University of Western Ontario.

Trevor W. Harrison, Department of Sociology, University of Alberta.

Alan Jeffrey, Department of Sociology, University of Western Ontario.

William A. Johnston, Department of Sociology, University of Alberta.

Tom Langford, Department of Sociology, University of Calgary.

Julia S. O'Connor, Director, National Economic and Social Council, Dublin, Ireland. Formerly in the Department of Sociology, McMaster University.

Maurice Pinard, Department of Sociology, McGill University.

Lorne Tepperman, Department of Sociology, University of Toronto.

Norine Verberg, Sociology and Anthropology, St Francis Xavier University.

Chapter 1

Political Sociology: An Overview

Douglas Baer

As Brym and Fox note (1989), Canadian political sociology has made efforts since the 1970s to differentiate itself from American political sociology. The Marxist legacy has always been stronger in Canadian sociology, and social class is far more routinely employed in the analysis of politics in Canada, even among non-Marxist scholars.[1] Like their American counterparts, though, Canadian scholars have made frequent use of survey research methods, something that distinguishes them from their British cousins, whose studies of political phenomena often employ methods of textual analysis, though increasingly surveys have become important in Britain as well.

Canadian political sociology has also rejected the 'behavioural' approach (Faulks 1999: 12) or the 'cultural/institutional' perspective (Brym and Fox 1989: 57). While these two terms are not exactly synonymous, they refer to the idea that shared political values determine how a society operates its political system. From this perspective, common norms and values also explain how societies differ. Why are some nations social democratic with large welfare structures and why are some 'liberal democratic'?[2] They also predict the success or failure of certain types of political institutions. Why is it that Canadian politics is different than American politics? This perspective finds reasons in the 'political culture' of the two countries and seeks to explain how the political

cultures may have developed differently. In Part A, Chapter 2 by Tepperman provides an extensive definition of 'political culture'; in simple terms, it refers to personality or individual 'character' attributes held in common by most individuals within a given society but that differentiate societies from one another. Thus, it refers to the social psychology of individuals, but only insofar as their values, political preferences, and belief systems are widely shared with others in the same society (see King 1986: 9; Welch 1993). An example of this can be found in the Lipset thesis. According to Lipset, Canada is seen as having a political culture where citizens have a tendency to be more respectful of authority than other countries, most notably the United States.

How does a political culture arise? Lipset puts it all down to the 'founding moment' of American society: the migration to Canada in 1776 of those Americans who did not wish to be part of the new society created by the American Revolution, and the subsequent influences this group had on shaping distinctively Canadian political values. Grabb and Curtis discuss the Lipset thesis in extended detail in Chapter 3, arguing it is flawed in many respects. Their criticism is part of a thread in Canadian political sociology that rejects the explanations of an older generation of American political sociologists. So, too, is the criticism that Tepperman provides of the

Inglehart thesis, another, but different, 'political culture' explanation—this time explaining how countries around the world are changing rather than how countries such as Canada and the United States are different from each other.

In a broader sense, the 'cultural/institutional' perspective tends to place a great emphasis on shared values and norms, in many senses focusing on *social cohesion* while disregarding *social conflict*. As Faulks (1999: 13) comments, '[this perspective sees] the success of liberal political systems [as] due to the maintenance of a distinct civil society characterised by value consensus, a common citizenship, and the wealth created by capitalist enterprises.' But this assumption of and emphasis on consensus has hardly been integrated into the thinking of Canadian political scientists over the last decades. In Chapter 4, Baer examines the different ways in which political sociologists have dealt with political beliefs, and the changing use of the term *ideology* to characterize these beliefs. He also examines how the social cohesion question, recently re-popularized with the work of Robert Putnam under the label *social capital*, ties in with an earlier literature concerned with the legitimacy of systems of governance. Through this discussion there is an important thread: Does ideology matter? This, as the chapter discusses, is related to some fundamental questions in sociological theory as well as the observations of political sociologists on the nature of contemporary social reality.

The study of the *state* has long been a concern for political sociologists. The relationship between formal political processes (legislatures, legal apparatuses) and actors (politicians) on the one hand and the bureaucracy and interest groups attempting to influence government policy on the other has concerned sociologists ever since Marx and Weber, the key figures in 'classical' sociology, wrote about these topics.[3] At the end of the 1980s, Brym and Fox (1989: 57) argued that 'less progress' has been made in the area of studies of the state in Canada, and this largely remains the case, though authors such as Myles (see Myles and Pierson 1997) have devoted some attention to the comparative development of the welfare state in Canada and other countries. Part B of this book presents some theoretical explorations of issues regarding the study of the state.

While the worldwide influence of large, multinational corporations has long been of concern to political economists, especially in Canada, the end of the 1990s saw an increased interest on the part of sociologists in questions and issues related to *globalization*. Globalization refers to two sets of concomitant processes that make it more difficult for democratic governments to exercise autonomy, that force a sort of cultural sameness on the world, and, in some variants of the theme, that promote capitalism. The first process is that of economic integration. Trade barriers have fallen around the world, with the development and extension of the European Union, the Free Trade Agreement between Canada and the United States, and the worldwide General Agreement on Tariffs and Trade. The second process is that of cultural integration, as the mass media distribute cultural products (largely American) around the world with great efficiency. In Chapter 5, Jeffrey, borrowing from Ritzer (1996), refers to this process as McDonaldization.

The 'radical' version of the globalization thesis, which argues that we are evolving into a single global economy with almost complete cultural homogeneity, is disputed on a number of fronts (see Faulks 1999: ch. 2). The 'one world' thesis is overblown, both in terms of the claim that we are heading toward a world in which states will no longer possess authority and in terms of the claim that there is an increasing degree of cultural homogeneity in the world. Jeffrey discusses the latter, pointing out that forms of 'local resistance' have made this image of a single world where all children drink Coca-Cola, wear Nike running shoes, and live as good consumers only one (very partial) vision of the future of the political world. It is by no means clear that a homogeneous world culture has emerged.

Although the reduction in trade barriers affected the freedom of action of the state, the state remains the primary site for political decision-making (see Faulks 1999: 67–70; Weiss 1997). Large corporations, to be sure, play a major role in the construction of policies and the governance of most countries, but this takes the form of struggles at the level of the state itself (in legislatures, policy bureaucracies, and in the legal system) rather than 'around' the state. Free trade agreements may have altered the balance of power in particular instances; corporations can now threaten other interest groups with pulling their operations out of the country and moving factories to the Third World if a government does not lower taxes and provide them with various grants and other 'investment incentives'. But, some would argue, this threat is never as total as it seems. Even though individual corporations may be able to engage in 'capital flight', and while the threat of doing so is a factor in the ongoing power negotiations that take place in the governance of Western countries, this option is not available to all forms of economic enterprise, and is difficult, expensive, or risky in others (see Faulks 1999: 62–5). Much of the globalization debate is not over whether increased economic integration is inconsequential (clearly, it has consequences), but over the extent of its impact.

In Chapter 6, O'Connor examines struggles around the welfare state. The term *welfare state* makes specific reference to government intervention in the economic marketplace in many capitalist societies with an orientation toward the redistribution of wealth to those who are in need. Welfare state programs include health care, various benefit schemes for unemployed individuals (including those on what we call 'welfare' programs), public childcare, and perhaps even the provision of other public services such as public transportation. Sometimes the definition is extended to include government regulation in the economy (marketing boards to set prices, regulations to restrict environmental damage) since these measures often have a redistributive effect.

Sometimes, the term *welfare state* refers to countries with high levels of state involvement in the economy, or at the very least strong redistributive policies that provide poorer citizens with a social 'safety net' (guaranteed income or some significant welfare provision). The countries that immediately come to mind here are the Scandinavian countries, especially Sweden. But the term *welfare state* can be applied to redistribution, even in countries such as the United States that have relatively low levels of welfare provision.

Although it can be traced to the 1960s work of T.H. Marshall, a recent development in the discussion of the welfare state is the literature on *citizenship* (see Turner 1987; Nash 2000: ch. 4). O'Connor discusses this in detail, introduces important debates in the area, and links this discussion to developments in feminist scholarship.

There is a longstanding theoretical tradition in sociology dealing with the 'crisis' tendencies of the welfare state (Habermas 1976; O'Connor 1973, 1984; Offe, 1984, 1994). Writers in this tradition argue, in various forms, that the welfare state 'compromise' is inherently unstable and crisis-prone, and that the balance of power makes it impossible for government, in the long run, to sustain the forms of expenditure necessary for the provision of welfare. Arguably, world free trade and the globalization of economic markets have made this situation worse. This theme appears throughout the chapters in this text, not only in Part B (The State), but also in Johnston's chapter appearing later in Part E.

Studies of the Canadian state have taken on a different complexion than studies in many other countries given the decades-long threat that Canada, as a political entity, might be broken up by the departure of Quebec from Confederation. Jeffrey introduces the topic indirectly, by locating the 'Quebec question' within a context of global transformations. In Chapter 7, Turpel extends this discussion by raising questions of political sovereignty and self-government not only in the context of Quebec but also in the context of First Nations citizens. How do aboriginals fit into the constitutional arrangements of either a united Canada or a separate Quebec? Since questions regarding the treatment of native Canadians tie in very closely to questions of social justice and social inequality, long the concern of Canadian political sociologists, we might expect more attention to this.

Across the Western world, but especially in Europe, political sociologists have been paying increasing attention to organizations outside the formal political system within what is termed *civil society*. There is not complete agreement on what, exactly, this term means. Most definitions agree that *civil society* represents activity outside the immediate auspices of the state, but disagree whether it includes the 'economy' as well, that is, capitalist economic enterprises (Faulks 1999: 2). Another definition places it between the state and the economy (see Cohen 1982; Cohen and Arato 1992; Janoski 1998). Organizations in civil society, according to Faulk (1999: 2) 'enjoy various degrees of autonomy from the state . . .[and] can act as counterpoints to the power of the state and are themselves political actors.'

For other theorists, organizations in civil society are not just autonomous from the state. They are also insulated from the economic marketplace by donations and other non-market forms of income. What does this mean from the standpoint of political discussion and debate? The argument here is that the organizations in civil society play, or at least have the potential to play, a crucial role in social change because of their independence from the dominant institutions of society. Some authors would argue that this sort

of autonomy occurs within the marketplace, as well. So, whereas Faulks would include business organizations in this list representing civil society, Cohen would not. In both cases, *social and political autonomy* is at issue, but in the second case this autonomy is wider because it is not itself constrained by the need to stay in business using the criterion of profitability.

Contemporary theories of civil society agree that social transformation is no longer likely to occur along class lines; if society is to 'emancipate' itself, some basis other than a violent revolution by a militant working class will need to be found for the transition to a better society (see Cohen 1982: 5ff). Although this view might seem to be distinctively anti-Marxist, social class is not always rejected as one of the markers for conflict in contemporary society. Much of this theorizing points in the same general direction as Marxist sociology: the idea here is to envisage conditions under which positive social transformations eliminating existing 'oppressions' might occur. In this regard, much emphasis is given to activities, associations, and ways of thinking that are outside the conventional restrictions of the formal political system. It is in this light that some prominence has been given to what have come to be called New Social Movements (NSMs). These groups are seen to play a leading role—at least potentially—in future social transformations.

What is the nature of social transformation in the contemporary period? The use of the term *postmodern* to describe the contemporary period gained much currency in the late 1980s through the 1990s. As Carroll points out in Chapter 8, other terms also describe the passage from 'modernity' into some new form of capitalism. These include *post-Fordism* and *disorganized capitalism*. Key attributes include the apparent demise of class conflict; a reorganization of the occupational structure, at least in advanced Western countries, away from the focus on commodity production; new types of social protest; the expansion of the mass media and technology; and a widespread cynicism regarding old forms of thought about the social world.[4] Perhaps in response to the crisis in Marxism, new social movement theories have begun to play a prominent role in political sociology, though these theories are hardly unitary. Some, as Carroll notes, attempt to reconstruct historical materialism, whereas others make a more explicit break from the Marxist tradition. In both cases, however, NSMs play roles in the redefinition of social and political values that are disproportionate to the actual size of the movements.

We can expect, then, to see more emphasis on voluntary association, non-profit sector, or social/new social movement organizations in the political sociology of the early twenty-first century. In this book, Carroll puts the study of social movements and new social movements in broad theoretical perspective in Chapter 8; in Chapter 9 Curtis and Grabb use survey data to examine the relationship between voluntary associations that do and voluntary associations that do not constitute new social movement associations. Both chapters ask the question, Are supporters of 'new' voluntary organizations more likely to engage in political protest and be critical of society? Briefly, Curtis and Grabb's research suggests that the distinction between 'old' types of voluntary associations and 'new' ones may have been overstated. In part, though, this consists in the finding that most people who are members of 'new' associations also tend to be members of other types of voluntary associations. Survey research is not the only means by which social movements can be studied, of course, and we will expect to see a variety of methods, including participant observation, historical research, and even textual analysis used to assess ideas concerning the role and development of new social movements.

There is always a tension between social movements—outside the formal political system—and political movements (that is, political parties). At one level, the very critical power of NSMs arises, by the standard of some theorists, from their autonomy from the state (including political parties). Yet, as Faulk (1999: 103) so aptly notes, NSMs face a dilemma: inasmuch as they retain their 'purity' (separation from formal politics), their ultimate ability to influence change is circumscribed. More to the point, the dividing line between 'social movements' and 'political movements' is somewhat arbitrary. In this book, Pinard's chapter on Quebec separation is in Part D on Political Movements, even though the discussion centres on support for separation much more than support for the political party (the Parti Québécois). And, of course, the separation discussed here entails a very narrow definition of *political* (formal political parties); we must realize that both types of organizations deal with issues that are fundamentally political in the sense that they affect public policy choices. In Chapter 13, Pinard studies the dynamics of the support for separation in the province of Quebec, returning us to an issue discussed indirectly earlier in the book in Chapters 5 and 6 where Jeffrey and Turpel discuss Quebec in the context of the analysis of the state in the Canadian context.

Part D, then, deals with formal political parties. One notable recent feature in the development of party politics in Canada has been the rise of the Reform Party (and its successor, the Canadian Alliance Party). The policies of this party can be referred to as *neo-liberal*; an important question in Canadian political sociology, or indeed in the political sociology of almost any of the advanced Western societies is, How do we account for the rise of neo-liberalism? First, though, an important clarification is required. In scholarly discourse, the terms *liberal* and *conservative* are not always consistent with the use of these terms in everyday language. If Canadians were asked if they were liberal or conservative, they would undoubtedly associate being liberal with supporting policies promoting social welfare, and being conservative as representing opposition to government intervention. In England at the time of the Industrial Revolution, however, conservatism referred to resistance to the newly emerging capitalist (or 'free enterprise') system, and liberalism referred to support for it. So, the term *liberal*, especially when referring to liberal democracy or neo-liberalism, actually refers to states with very little government involvement in the economy and minimal provisions for social welfare, and to support for the elimination of social programs. The terms *neo-liberalism* and *neo-conservatism* are almost interchangeable.[5]

Neo-conservatism has, of course, been on the ascendancy in the Canadian political scene. The rise of the Alliance Party, initially as the Reform Party in the provinces of Alberta and British Columbia but now forming alliances with neo-conservatives throughout English Canada, has changed the Canadian political landscape in the last decade. The election of Mike Harris to power in Ontario in 1995 and again in 1999 confirms that neo-conservatism has taken hold outside Western Canada (or, more specifically, Alberta). In Chapter 10, Harrison pays particular attention to the rise of the Reform Party, which, along with its successor the Alliance Party, has been the carrier of neo-conservative beliefs on the federal political scene in Canada.

Having no parallel in American politics, the New Democratic Party has garnered a fair amount of attention in Canadian political sociology, despite the fact that it now plays an insignificant role in federal politics in Canada. Its role in western provincial governments in Saskatchewan, Manitoba, and British Columbia has been a bit more pronounced, though, and the presence of a social democratic party like European social democratic parties (though with far less national influence) has been a feature that has distinguished Canada from the United States.

The New Democratic Party is discussed in this book in two different contexts in Part D. First, in Chapter 11, Bell asks why, if both had their roots in Prairie populist protest, the NDP was ascendant in Saskatchewan while the Social Credit (now the provincial Conservative Party and the federal Reform/Alliance Party) took hold in Alberta. He carefully outlines the historical developments that led to two different paths in the two provinces, pointing to key events that marked turning points or, perhaps more appropriately, forks in the road. Then, in Chapter 12, Denis challenges the conventional assumption that the NDP never had a chance to be an effective force in the province of Quebec, arguing that at one point it was close to a breakthrough in that province. Instead of capitalizing on some initial successes, though, the party defeated itself with poor strategies.

Part E deals with the role of social class in Canadian political sociology. The study of class divisions in political attitudes has usually involved the use of survey research method, and there is a body of literature detailing the extent to which individuals in different social classes display different voting patterns and political attitudes (Johnston 1995; Johnston and Ornstein 1985; Lambert et al. 1987; Langford 1986, 1992, 1996; Ornstein and Stevenson 1999; Pammett 1987). In Chapter 14, Gidengil places the study of the NDP within the context of a long research tradition in Canadian sociology: the study of 'class vote'. Her research suggests that class voting—the tendency of working-class people to vote for a different political party than upper/middle-class people—is not particularly strong in Canada. In Chapter 16, Langford also finds fairly 'small' effects of class on political attitudes, but suggests that class remains a fruitful variable when we study political phenomena. He also draws attention to some issues of conceptualization. We are reminded that there remains what Langford calls a 'patterning' of attitudes along social class lines.

In Chapter 15, Johnston ties together the

question of globalization and the role of the welfare state—also discussed in Part B (see, especially, Chapter 6 by O'Connor)—with social class. He extends the earlier discussion by examining the size of the welfare state in terms of the power of social classes within a historical context. At the same time he returns us to a question raised earlier, in Part D: How do we account for the rise of neo-liberalism?

Chapter 17 by Verberg provides an example of the sorts of additional directions Canadian sociologists have taken when they have examined the relationship between political attitudes and social class. For Verberg, home ownership is a class-related mechanism by which political attitudes come to be structured, and the survey data she employs speak to this question.

Taken together, the chapters in this book convey the breadth of work that has been done in the area of political sociology in Canada. Sociologists in Canada have debated the theoretical terms under which the discipline defines its work; critically assessed and engaged in pointed, often empirically based critiques of the works of American political sociologists; employed survey data to examine Canadian voting patterns and political attitudes; detailed the historical moments leading to the development of social movements, political movements, and/or the development of Canadian political institutions; and engaged in debates over the political future of the country. Each of these approaches is represented, in different ways, in the chapters found in this book.

Notes

1. There has been a recent increase in the use of class analysis in mainstream American sociology, though. See, for example, Brooks and Manza (1997a; 1997b).

2. Liberal democracy is a term that is usually employed with reference to states that adopt a policy of promoting free enterprise (capitalism) and attempt to restrict or reduce the influence of government regulation or taxation/redistribution policies on private enterprise.

3. For a basic introduction to the writings of Marx and Weber from the standpoint of their political sociology, see Chapters 2 and 3 of Orum (1989), Chapter 1 of Nash (2000), or Chapter 1 of Washburn (1982).

4. Social theorists would add to this list the 'death', or at least widespread rejection, of 'essentialism' or 'foundationalism'—any form of social theorizing that posits absolutes—in the humanities and social sciences. For a mixture of proponents and critics, see Dickens and Fontana (1994); Bologh (1994); Ilter (1994); Murphy (1989). As Jeffrey points out in Chapter 5, the modernism that postmodernists reject includes: (1) individualism, (2) a belief in linear progress and absolute truths, (3) rational planning, (4) an expansion of instrumental reason, and (5) the standardization of knowledge and of production (whether all of these form a coherent whole or not is arguable).

5. For a complete discussion of neo-liberalism, see Faulks (1999: ch. 4).

References

Bologh, R. and L. Mell. 1994. 'Modernism, Postmodernism, and the New World (Dis)order: A Dialectical Analysis and Alternative', *Critical Sociology* 20(2): 81–120.

Brooks, C., and J. Manza. 1997. 'Social Cleavages and Political Alignments: US Presidential Elections, 1960 to 1992, *American Journal of Sociology* 62(6): 937–46.

———. 1997. 'The Social and Ideological Bases of Middle-Class Political Realignment in the United States, 1972 to 1992', *American Sociological Review* 62(2): 191–208.

Brym, R., and F. Fox. 1989. *From Culture to Power: The Sociology of English Canada* (Toronto, Oxford University Press).

Cohen. J. 1982. *Class and Civil Society: The Limits of Marxian Critical Theory*. Amherst, MA: University of Massachusetts Press).

———, and A. Arato. 1992. *Civil Society and Political Theory* (Cambridge, MA: MIT Press).

Dickens, D., and A. Fontana. 1994. 'Postmodernism in the Social Sciences', *Postmodernism and Social Inquiry,* eds D. Dickens and A. Fontana (London: Guilford Press), 1–22.

Faulks, K. 1999. *Political Sociology: A Critical Introduction* (New York: New York University Press).

Habermas, J. 1976. *Legitimation Crisis.*

Ilter, T. 1994. 'Postmodernism and Radical Sociology', *Critical Sociology* 20(2): 51–80.

Janoski, T. 1998. *Citizenship and Civil Society: A Framework of Rights and Obligations in Liberal Traditional Social Democratic Regimes* (Cambridge, MA: Cambridge University Press).

Johnston, W. 1995. 'Social Divisions and Ideological Fragmentation', *Canadian Journal of Sociology* 12(4): 315–30.

———, and M. Ornstein. 1985. 'Social Class and Political Ideology in Canada', *Canadian Review of Sociology and Anthropology* 22(3): 369–93.

King, R. 1986. *The State in Modern Society* (London: Macmillan).

Lambert, R., J. Curtis, et al. 1987. 'Social Class, Left/Right Political Orientations, and Subjective Class Voting in Provincial and Federal Elections', *Canadian Review of Sociology and Anthropology* 24(4): 526–49.

Langford, T. 1986. 'Workers' Subordinate Values: A Canadian Case Study', *Canadian Journal of Sociology* 11(3): 269–92.

———. 1992. 'Social Experiences and Variations in Economic Beliefs among Canadian Workers', *Canadian Review of Sociology and Anthropology* 29(4): 453–87.

———. 1996. 'The Politics of the Canadian New Middle Class: Public/Private Sector Cleavage in the 1980s', *Canadian Journal of Sociology* 21(2): 153–83.

Murphy, J. 1989. *Postmodern Social Analysis and Criticism* (Westport, CT, Greenwood Press).

Myles, J., and P. Pierson. 1997. 'Friedman's Revenge: The Reform of "Liberal" Welfare States in Canada and the United States', *Politics and Society* 25(4): 443–72.

Nash, K. 2000. *Contemporary Political Sociology: Globalization, Politics, and Power* (Malden, MA: Blackwell).

O'Connor, J. 1973. *The Fiscal Crisis of the State* (New York: St Martin's Press).

———. 1984. *Accumulation Crisis* (Oxford: Basil Blackwell).

Offe, C. 1984. *Contradictions of the Welfare State* (London: Hutchinson).

———. 1994. 'Structural Problems of the Capitalist State: Class Rule and the Political System. On the Selectiveness of Political Institutions', *The State: Critical Concepts*, ed. J. Hall (London: Routledge), 1: 104–29.

Ornstein, M., and H.M. Stevenson. 1999. *Politics and Ideology in Canada: Elite and Public Opinion in the Transformation of the Welfare State* (Montreal: McGill-Queen's University Press).

Orum, A.M. 1989. *Introduction to Political Sociology: The Social Anatomy of the Body Politic* (Englewood Cliffs, NJ: Prentice-Hall).

Pammett, J. 1987. 'Class Voting and Class Consciousness in Canada', *Canadian Review of Sociology and Anthropology* 24(2): 269–90.

Ritzer, G. 1996. *The McDonaldization of Society: An Investigation into the Changing Character of Contemporary Social Life* (Thousand Oaks, CA: Pine Forge Press).

Turner, B. 1986. *Citizenship and Capitalism* (London: Allen & Unwin).

Washburn, P.C. 1982. *Political Sociology: Approaches, Concepts, Hypotheses* (Englewood Cliffs, NJ: Prentice-Hall).

Weiss, L. 1997. 'Globalization and the Myth of the Powerless State', *New Left Review* 225: 3–27.

Welch, S. 1993. *The Concept of Political Culture* (New York: St Martin's Press).

Part A

Political Beliefs and Political Culture

Theoretical perspectives that speak about the assumptions and beliefs people hold about the social world around them have had a controversial history in North American social science. These controversies sometimes centre on different ideas regarding the nature and importance of *political culture*. In Chapter 2, Tepperman provides a definition of political culture; briefly, it refers to patterns of beliefs and assumptions ordinary people have about the world around them (as these pertain to politics). He distinguishes it from ideology, but the two are linked in that both refer to broad sets of beliefs and attitudes. In the case of political culture, these are more diffuse, not associated with the interests of any particular group seeking political or economic advantage, and do not involve proposed 'solutions' to social problems. In the case of ideology, beliefs are explicit, contain sets of solutions for identified problems, and are often associated with particular groups seeking to secure advantages or at least having some sort of a stake in the outcome. In Part A, two of the chapters deal with political culture and one deals with ideology. The chapter on ideology encompasses some discussion of one particular approach to political culture (the 'social capital' thesis).

Three prominent theories of political culture enjoy current circulation in the fields of sociology

and political science, although two were presented to social scientists over two decades ago. The first of these, Ron Inglehart's postmaterialist (PM) thesis, is discussed in detail by Tepperman. The second, Seymour Martin Lipset's thesis regarding differences in political culture between Americans and Canadians, is the subject of the chapter written by Grabb and Curtis. A third perspective, Robert Putnam's thesis on the decline of social capital, is discussed briefly as part of Baer's chapter.

From the standpoint of Canadian sociology, Lipset's thesis is perhaps of most interest because it directs itself at Canada and asks questions about the evolution of Canadian society. In a nutshell, Lipset argues that the American Revolution constituted the 'founding moment' for both countries, and that the subsequent political cultures have been defined by the exodus of individuals faithful to the British Crown from the United States into Canada. The net outcome of this is that Canadians are seen as more deferential to authority and more willing to accept government intervention in the economy (Grabb and Curtis elaborate on this in Chapter 3). The thesis has had considerable play in the Canadian news media, and, if Lipset himself is not seen frequently being interviewed on this subject, journalists or even other academics will frequently invoke this conceptualization to explain or describe how

Canadians are different from Americans. Grabb and Curtis outline earlier work that seeks to explode this myth and, in the process, construct a more complex outline of how Canadian distinctiveness evolved and what it consists of. They also present some new evidence, taken from survey data, that has a bearing on the Lipset thesis.

Inglehart's thesis has enjoyed less currency in Canadian sociology or Canadian political science, but has certainly been the subject of much discussion in the United States (Bennett 1998; Easterlin and Crimmins 1997; Inglehart 1977, 1997; Inglehart and Abramson 1994; Rempel and Clark 1997; Van Snippenberg and Scheepers 1991). Inglehart has been involved in cross-national research projects, most notably the World Values Study (which has covered over 30 countries), and Canadian scholars (for example, Nevitte 1996) have been involved in this project. The postmaterialist scale has played a role in the Canadian publications associated with this project, although it has not been the centrepiece of this work, which has generally involved issues other than those directly associated with the PM thesis (Inglehart, Nevitte, and Basáñez 1996; Nevitte 1996). Because the theory is concerned with lifestyle changes and cultural orientations that might, if the thesis is correct, be broadly associated with (and supportive of) social movements, the theory's main influence has not been confined to the United States. Inglehart's thesis is rooted to some extent in the notion that there are diminishing marginal returns, from the standpoint of human happiness, to economic growth (hence the shift in value preferences to 'postmaterialist' values for those whose economic needs have been fulfilled).

Inglehart's thesis has been the subject of intense debate in American political science (see, for example, Brooks and Manza 1994; Duch and Taylor 1993), and this has now extended into sociology (Davis 1996). Tepperman's chapter systematically outlines the tenets of Inglehart's thesis,

and then outlines the criticisms of each of these. He clearly sides with the critics on each count, arguing that many of Inglehart's propositions lack empirical support. A careful distinction must be made, of course, between empirical support for a contrary position (which exists in some instances) and inconclusive evidence. In some instances— for example, the aspect of Inglehart's thesis that deals with childhood precursors to the postmaterialist orientation—longitudinal data would be extremely important in any empirical assessment, yet research criticizing Inglehart has employed cross-sectional data (Tepperman introduces some of both types of research to the discussion). At other points, interpretations of what constitutes a 'substantial' effect must be made, and this is always tricky in social science (especially when most social science models do not 'explain' large portions of variance in their dependent variables). For a response to some, but by no means all, of the criticisms raised by Tepperman, the reader may consult Abrahamson, Ellis, and Inglehart (1997), Abramson and Inglehart (1994), Abramson and Inglehart (1996), and Granato, Inglehart, and Leblang (1996). Still, Tepperman has made an important contribution by suggesting to us that the long-standing assumptions behind a well-known and well-received research tradition are not beyond challenge.

A third political culture perspective that is prominent at present can be found in the work of Robert Putnam (Putnam 1995, 1996). Putnam's thesis, like Inglehart's, speculates on long-term secular trends in value orientations, but, if correct, is far more sinister. Putnam argues that there has been a precipitous decline in social capital— the extent to which citizens are engaged in and attached to civil society—in the post-World War II period. The measures he uses are (a) 'trust in government' items on social surveys and (b) measures of voluntary association involvement. There has been considerable debate around the 'culprit' Putnam identifies—the mass media, or more specifically, television (Foley and Edwards 1997; Newton 1997; Norris 1996). Interestingly, little debate has followed on the core premise of Putnam's thesis that there has been a decline in public participation.[1] The social capital perspective is discussed to some extent by Baer in Chapter 4.

Usually political culture perspectives stand against structural perspectives for the explanation of social change. For Inglehart, the key dynamic is embedded in the postmaterialist ethos (that is, the transformation to postmaterialism). For Lipset, consistent with the conservative functionalist origins of his work, there is no dynamic: differences between Canada and the United States stand locked in time on the basis of 'founding moments'. But the driving force that keeps this stasis intact is cultural. Even though it is a political culture conceptualization, Putnam's perspective returns to the structural. For Putnam, the dynamic is a trend toward more anomic social relations associated with the decline of social capital. But he is not willing to stop there and speak of a political culture generating its own dynamic. Rather, he looks for 'causes'—factors that underlie values and attitudes. This search for causes is clearly structural:

What has changed in the structure of Western society? We now watch a lot of television.

The final chapter in this part, by Baer, deals with an important set of issues in a discussion of political ideology. Here, the question of whether people can be said to have coherent and consistent sets of beliefs about the political world and about public policy is analysed in the context of the 'dominant ideology' thesis and issues raised in the Gramscian perspective ('hegemony'). Perhaps as important, though, is the question of whether it makes sense to devote attention to political ideology. A critical perspective might argue (a) that ideology simply does not matter and never has from the standpoint of political outcomes; (b) that the importance of ideology has been subject to a secular decline such that, while once important, it is now inconsequential (the end-of-ideology thesis); or (c) that all ideologies have converged into a single form of 'truth' (which corresponds, roughly, to beliefs in democracy and capitalism—a variant of the end-of-ideology thesis). Whether ideology still matters, and what we are to make of end-of-ideology claims, is the final subject of Baer's chapter.

Note

1. Some work by Baer, Curtis, and Grabb (2000) using data from both the 1980 and the 1990 World Values Study dataset, suggests that this may not be correct, at least for the American case that Putnam refers to, when it comes to voluntary association involvement. The observed decline in 'political trust' does, however, seem to be present in both Canadian and American surveys.

References

Abrahamson, P., S. Ellis, and R. Inglehart. 1997. 'Research in Context: Measuring Value Change', *Political Behavior* 19: 41–59.

Abramson, P., and R. Inglehart. 1994. 'Education, Security, and Postmaterialism: A Comment on Duch and Taylor', *American Journal of Political Science* 38: 797–814.

———. 1996. 'Formative Security, Education, and Postmaterialism: A Response to Davis', *Public Opinion Quarterly* 60: 450–5.

Baer, D., J. Curtis, and E. Grabb. 2000. 'Has Voluntary Association Activity Declined? A Cross-National Perspective', paper presented to the Annual Meeting of the American Sociological Association, Washington, D.C., August.

Bennett, W.L. 1998. 'The UnCivic Culture: Communication, Identity, and the Rise of Lifestyle Politics', *Political Science and Politics* 31: 741–62.

Brooks, C., and J. Manza. 1994. 'Do Changing Values Explain the New Politics? A Critical Assessment of the Postmaterialist Thesis', *Sociological Quarterly* 35: 541–70.

Davis, J. 1996. 'Review Essay: Value Change in Global Perspective', *Public Opinion Quarterly* 60: 322–31.

Duch, R., and M. Taylor. 1993. 'Postmaterialism and the Economic Condition', *1993* 37: 747–79.

Easterlin, R., and E. Crimmins. 1997. 'American Youth are Becoming More Materialistic', *Citizen Politics in Post-Industrial Societies*, eds T. Clark and M. Rempel (Boulder, CO: Westview).

Foley, M., and B. Edwards. 1997. 'Escape from Politics? Social Theory and the Social Capital Debate', *American Behavioral Scientist* 40: 550–61.

Granato, J., R. Inglehart, and D. Leblang. 1996. 'Cultural Values, Stable Democracy, and Economic Development: A Reply', *American Journal of Political Science* 40: 680–96.

Inglehart, R. 1977. 'Values, Objective Needs and Subjective Satisfaction among Western Publics', *Comparative Political Studies* 9: 429–58.

———. 1997. *Modernization and Postmodernization: Cultural, Economic and Political Change in 43 Countries* (Princeton, NJ: Princeton University Press).

——— and P. Abramson. 1994. 'Economic Security and Value Change', *American Political Science Review* 88: 336–54.

Inglehart, R., N. Nevitte, and M. Basáñez. 1996. *The North American Trajectory: Cultural, Economic, and Political Ties among the United States, Canada, and Mexico* (New York: Aldine de Gruyter).

Nevitte, N. 1996. *The Decline of Deference: Canadian Value Change in Cross-national Perspective* (Peterborough, ON: Broadview Press).

Newton, K. 1997. 'Social Capital and Democracy', *American Behavioral Scientist* 40: 575–86.

Norris, P. 1996. 'Does Television Erode Social Capital? A Reply to Putnam', *Political Science and Politics* 29: 474–79.

Putnam, R. 1995. 'Bowling Alone: America's Declining Social Capital', *Journal of Democracy* 6: 65–78.

———. 1996. 'The Strange Disappearance of Civic America', *American Prospect* 24: 34–48.

Rempel, M., and T. Clark. 1997. 'Post-Industrial Politics: A Framework for Interpreting *Citizen Politics Since the 1960s*', *Citizen Politics in Post-Industrial Societies*, eds M. Rempel and T. Clark (Boulder, CO: Westview), 9–54.

Van Snippenberg, L., and P. Scheepers. 1991. 'Social Class and Political Behavior During a Period of Economic Stagnation: Apathy and Radicalism in the Netherlands, 1985', *Political Psychology* 12(1): 41–63.

Chapter 2

The Postmaterialist Thesis: Has There Been a Shift in Political Cultures?

Lorne Tepperman

Introduction

Theories of political thought and behaviour have changed since the 1960s, and this volume discusses many of these changes. Yet, in important ways, theorizing about political *culture* has stayed the same, drawing on a mixed bag of American social science elements that is decades old. A prime example is the theory of 'culture shift' developed by Ronald Inglehart, a political scientist at the University of Michigan.

This paper will discuss Inglehart's theory at length. The theory merits attention since it continues to influence social scientists in many countries. One major result is sets of national surveys in many nations, conducted in 1981–2 and 1991–2, which Inglehart has coordinated to test his theory.

However, the culture shift theory also shows just how little has changed in studies of political thought and behaviour. What's traditional about Inglehart's theory is, that like other work by American social scientists, it is America-centred. It views worldwide changes as imitating American changes. Also, it tries to connect economic, social, and cultural forms of modernization. In this respect, culture shift is merely the shift beyond modernism to postmodernism. Finally, like earlier work, the theory is based on an analysis of large cross-national surveys. Thus, it reminds us of the cross-national survey analyses by Lerner (1958), Lipset (1960), Almond and Verba (1963), and Inkeles and Smith (1974), among many others, three decades ago.

This means that a few words about the history of *political culture* are necessary. Gabriel Almond (1956) first introduced the term in his article 'Comparative Political Systems'. There he argued that the term improved on such earlier notions as 'national character', 'custom', and 'modal personality'. Their meanings were 'diffuse and ambiguous', he believed, and had failed to 'give proper weight to the cognitive and evaluative factors' in human behaviour.

What all these terms—*political culture* included—have in common is the goal of explaining how and why 'formally similar institutions operate in radically different ways' in different societies (Almond 1970: 19). To provide such an explanation preoccupied theorists of the postwar period. Then, considerable research was also devoted to understanding why bureaucracies worked differently in different countries even though they might have the same *formal*, that is organizational, properties. The answer: because actors brought radically different assumptions about life and work into these structures. The same is true of political life. To understand how politics works, one must understand the point of view of all the political actors.

So, for example, Almond and Verba studied the values and attitudes of people in many countries to find the characteristic beliefs that would make stable democracy more or less likely. Underlying this was the belief that, if one knew the conditions that led to a stable democracy, one could create these conditions—through education, literacy, public media, and so on—and thus spread democracy throughout the world. In the end, social science would bring about order, justice, prosperity, and peace.

From this standpoint, political culture includes a variety of beliefs and assumptions ordinary people make about the world which, ultimately, shape political behaviour. Students of political culture study popular views and values, even those held by people who are relatively inarticulate and lack a clearly thought-out point of view. Then, given these views and values, researchers try to make sense of why people vote or act (or don't act) as they do.

A society can have one or more political cultures. For example, it is entirely plausible that Canada has a problem of national unity because French and English Canadians have different and opposed political cultures. They cannot envision Canadian society, or the Canadian state, in similar ways. They cannot hold similar goals. They cannot find ways to trust one another. And in these respects, Canada is not the only society with multiple political cultures. On the other hand, some societies may become, effectively, members of another political culture, taking over the key political values and assumptions of that society. Then the state is in danger of disappearing as one society is subsumed by another.

A closely related concept, much discussed in this book, is *ideology*, which also refers to assumptions and beliefs about the world. Ideology differs from political culture, however, in several ways. First, an ideology is more likely to be explicit—conscious and stated outright—than is a political culture. Second, an ideology is often associated with a particular group of people who strive energetically to achieve a particular

political outcome. Third and related to this, an ideology generally contains a blueprint for the solution to society's problems. By contrast, a political culture is more likely to see no problems or provide no blueprints.

And this brings us to a fourth and, in some respects, crucial feature of political culture: its absence of commentary about social conflict. Generally, people who write about political culture see social change coming about through means other than conflict—whether through social differentiation, technological change, more education or literacy, cultural diffusion, demographic shifts, and so on. By contrast, people who write about ideology see change coming about through class conflict, gender conflict, ethnic conflict, imperial conflict, or another form of conflict.

In short, theories about political culture have little to say about conflict as a force for social change. More than that, they signify that the theorist holds an evolutionary view of history.

For several decades after the Second World War, evolutionary theories were very popular in American social science. More important, such views were very useful. Marxist and other conflict theories were decidedly unpopular—even dangerous—given the McCarthyite efforts to discover Communist subversives in the universities. And, many theorists who had formerly embraced Marxist theories of change through ideology and conflict no longer found it possible to do so. Stalin's grotesque experiments in the USSR, and successes of the welfare state in the West, took much of the gloss off Marx's and Lenin's abstract formulations.

As we will see, methodologically and ideologically Inglehart's culture shift theory is a descendant of 1950s and 1960s American social science. However, the theory is also different. Most particularly, it bears the mark of the baby boom generation. For example, it examines and celebrates anti-establishment, grassroots politics and skepticism about material progress. Because the theory centres on baby boomers, it emphasizes the effect of generational change on cultural change. In that sense, culture shift theory projects on to the big screen of global change earlier ideas (see, for example, Chamberlain 1970; Jones 1980; Kettle 1980) about the tradition-smashing role of the 'big generation' born between 1948 and 1963.

In this chapter I will briefly note key aspects of this theory; then, in each instance, I will examine supporting and opposing evidence. In the end, we will be better able to judge whether the culture shift theory has truly increased our understanding. The theory discussed here is found in Inglehart's two major works, *The Silent Revolution* (1977b) and *Culture Shift* (1990), and in a variety of published papers cited below. The essence of this theory is as follows:

1. **Childhood Socialization** People who grow up in prosperous and secure conditions develop high personal and social goals. They include the goals of belonging, self-esteem, and self-actualization. Throughout the Western world, the postwar generation grew up with these goals.
2. **Generational Replacement** Over time, this postwar generation replaces earlier generations as voters and in élite positions of influence. In the West the result is a new political culture. The new generation's goals increasingly come to define the political agenda of Western democracies.
3. **Postmaterial (PM) Culture** The new political culture links a variety of political, social, and economic views. As a result, it represents a new outlook on life. It is 'postmaterialist' (PM) in the sense that it places little importance on personal wealth, economic development, and economic determinants of social life. In this respect the new outlook is also 'post-Marxist'.
4. **Political Outcomes** The new PM culture contains political attitudes and potentials for action. It encourages more political involve-

ment, and more protest, than the materialist culture did. However, much of this activity is outside the framework of elections and traditional political parties.

Let's now consider each of these components of the theory. In what follows, we review the theory, examine the supporting evidence, and look at criticisms that have been levelled against the theory.

Examination of the Theory

1. CHILDHOOD SOCIALIZATION
The Theory
The theory assumes that people who grow up in security and prosperity develop high personal and social goals—particularly, goals of belonging, self-esteem, and self-actualization. Inglehart believes that, throughout the Western world, the postwar generation grew up with these goals.

To fully understand this reasoning, we must recall psychologist Abraham Maslow's (1954) influential 'hierarchy of needs', to which Inglehart refers. Maslow's theory holds that every person strives for self-actualization, the complete fulfillment of his or her unique potentiality. Gaining such fulfillment is the ultimate, basic human need. Such fulfillment will bring a person the greatest possible satisfaction with life.

The most distinctive feature of Maslow's theory is that it is a 'stage theory'. It proposes that people must pass through successive stages of fulfillment. They must satisfy needs for survival, security, belonging, and esteem before they can reach, or even seek, total 'self-actualization'. A failure to complete one stage prevents the person from moving on to the next. Thus, for example, a person must attain physical security before seeking acceptance or belonging, and must attain belonging before seeking esteem. People must pass through these stages in order and they must satisfy all the lower needs before self-actualization is possible. Only people who have passed through all the lower stages of fulfillment can hope to reach self-actualization.

More generally, people must satisfy their *material* needs first. Only after people have satisfied their basic needs for food and shelter, health and security, can they achieve satisfaction with any kinds of *postmaterial*—social and cultural—goals. No one will attain significant nonmaterial goals without first having satisfied their material needs. Conversely, satisfying one's material needs almost guarantees a move in the direction of satisfying nonmaterial needs. These latter needs are a step closer to the pinnacle of self-actualization, the goal of all human life.

This is where the Inglehart theory really begins. It sees the current interest in world peace and environmental protection, for example, as evidence of satisfied material needs and a striving for (higher) postmaterial goals. These are the goals that pull the new, big generation forward politically, he believes.

Supporting evidence

An early publication (Inglehart 1971) states that many Western Europeans have already satisfied their needs for physical safety and economic security. Younger, more affluent people give top priority to fulfilling their needs for belonging and intellectual and esthetic development, Inglehart argues. These needs remain secondary for older, less affluent people raised under less secure, less prosperous conditions.

Linked as they are to preferences for specific political issues and parties, these 'new' needs produce 'new' political behaviours—including shifts in goals and partisanship. Moreover postmaterialists (PMs), with higher reported levels of material satisfaction, are also more politically active than materialists (Inglehart 1978). Perhaps this is because they feel more personally and politically effective, the result of growing up in secure and prosperous households.

Because of these changes, the period between 1970 and 1985 saw a massive voting shift towards PM, with important political consequences (Inglehart 1986). Social class voting declined and Western electorates polarized around materialist versus PM values. Today, the large political parties are still linked to particular social classes and class interests. However, new social movements reflect a tension between materialist and PM goals. For example, the Moral Majority and right-to-life movements are a defence of traditional (materialist) values by a slowly dwindling part of the population. By contrast, the environmental movement embraces PM values held by a rapidly growing part of the population.

We can see evidence of similar changes throughout the West. For example, in Germany the new social movements have a PM orientation that favours alternative lifestyles. PM questions established beliefs—for example, the belief that technical progress emancipates people. It favours a new outlook—reflection and creativity versus logic and consistency. Such changes pose a challenge to educational theory and practice (Hornstein 1984), as well as to established political procedures.

Finnish surveys find that younger people, raised in prosperity and peace, hold different values from older people raised in war and reconstruction (Borg 1985). Similarly, Spanish survey research finds that younger respondents are less materialistic than older ones. There is also evidence that PM values provide support for Leftist ideology. Indeed, the support for PM grows from one survey to the next and suggests a cultural change that may be permanent, since it is based on generational change (Loriente 1989).

In the Netherlands, PMs display a more 'cultural' lifestyle and materialists, a more economic one. There is also evidence that parents directly transmit PM lifestyles to their children (De Graaf and De Graaf 1988b).

In sum, we find much scattered support for Inglehart's assertion that the swing to PM is a cultural change rooted in childhood experiences.

Criticisms

Yet despite such evidence, many researchers attack this aspect of Inglehart's theory, and the attacks grow more pointed with time.

An early critique by Lafferty (1976) notes that the use of Inglehart's PM scale works well in Norway to distinguish between materialist and postmaterialist values. It even correlates consistently with value-related issues Inglehart did not test. However, the data provide no evidence that need-satisfaction during childhood is what produces a PM outlook. We cannot rule out other possible explanations.

In Italy, education and age are better predictors of a respondent's values than are economic experiences between the ages of 10 and 18 (Nardi 1980). Professional goals influence students' values (i.e., materialism versus PM). So do class origins, which influence students' perceptions of urgent social problems (D'Alessandro 1990).

Data from eight nations show that, typically, children take on their parents' political values (Jennings 1984). This transmission of values affects children's position on the Left-Right continuum. Indirect transmission, via social class or religious institution, is less important. Overall, generational differences in attitudes seem to be a result of individual learning, not societal increases in prosperity. In the end, changes in family life and the educational system explain value changes better than economic development (Herz 1987).

Researchers may have also overestimated the extent of value changes among young people. What has occurred may be no more than a shift in a continuing value tradition. The values themselves may not have changed. Instead, their intercorrelations or relative popularity may have altered. Nor has PM resulted in a uniform younger generation. Instead, various 'carrier' groups have emerged, bearing different values and reflecting different learning experiences (Prisching 1986).

Research in the Netherlands finds no evidence that family background and childhood experiences influence values strongly. Instead, the association between age and values is largely because of educational attainment. Today, young people receive more education and a more liberal education. A large residual shows that there are strong unmeasured influences on socialization, another reason to doubt Inglehart's theory (De Graaf and De Graaf 1988a). At best, his theory is right but weak.

Survey data from eight Western European nations and the European part of the former USSR show that education and economic conditions at the time of the survey are better explanations of the variation in respondents' values than childhood economic conditions (Duch and Taylor 1993). As well, Austrian data show that political education continues to influence values (Gehmacher 1987). Thus, childhood experience has a limited importance in explaining adult values and behaviours.

Canadian data (Pfeiffer and Cote 1991) suggest that Inglehart has failed to consider how identity crises influence the development of values. In particular, he fails to distinguish between generational and life-cycle (or age) effects. Only by analyzing individual-level, longitudinal data could he validly assess generational value change and the influence of schooling, these authors believe.

Other Canadian research using Quality of Life survey data (Pfeiffer 1994) finds no relationship between values and childhood affluence. Beyond that, the ways in which values change in the panel data are consistent with an aging effect, not a generation effect. Demographic and social factors such as education and income prove to be weak predictors of values, compared with two personality measures—motivation and locus of control. None of these findings is congruent with Inglehart's thesis.

In short, the evidence that childhood prosperity leads to PM values in adulthood is weak. However, there is strong evidence that other factors also influence adult political values.

2. GENERATIONAL REPLACEMENT
The Theory
Recall that the essential argument here is that, gradually, the baby boom (postwar) generation has replaced earlier generations as voters and influen-

tial élites. Its goals have come to define the political and social concerns of Western democracies. The result is a new political culture in the West.

Supporting Evidence

The main work that supports this thinking is by Inglehart and his collaborator Abramson. It starts with an analysis of that major symbol-building enterprise, the construction of the European Union (EU), and a new, pan-European identity.

Inglehart (1977a) writes that, thanks to PM, mass support for political unification in Europe is increasing. PMs already make up more than 10 per cent of the population of Europe. Their number includes the best educated and most politically active people. It represents 40 per cent of the young, who grew up after the World Wars and Depressions that shaped the materialistic attitudes of older Europeans. These PMs value esthetic and intellectual goals over material and financial security. That's what allows them to embrace cosmopolitan ideas like political unification. Because people keep the values learned in their youth, the cosmopolitan PMs will continue to generate mass support for European integration.

Survey results also show more support for unification in the six original European Economic Community (EEC) countries, containing the largest percentage of young PMs, than in the three newer member-countries and the nonmember United States. Thus, the longer the time spent in the EU, the stronger people's loyalty is to supranationalism. This suggests that prospects for political unification of Europe are increasingly favourable.

Generational replacement, the mechanism that increases support for unification, increases support for postmaterialism too (Abramson and Inglehart 1986). Survey data reveal that, in West Germany, Great Britain, and the Netherlands, population replacement has not only contributed to the rise of PM. It has also neutralized short-term influences favouring materialism (because of economic recession) in France and partially offset them in Belgium and Italy.

Because of population replacement, between 1970 and 1985, the priorities of West Europeans shifted from materialist to PM (Abramson and Inglehart 1987). Projections suggest that value change will be slower during the rest of the century; that's because replacement will be slower (because of the 'baby bust'). However, replacement will continue to increase the level of PM throughout Europe and North America.

In the United States between 1952 and 1984, generational replacement caused the erosion of party loyalties among white voters (Abramson 1989). It also shrank the proportion of whites who identify with a political party and reduced class voting, especially among white party identifiers who said they were Republicans. Other changes because of generational replacement include a rise in the tolerance for ideological nonconformists. Replacement also slowed declines in political trust and feelings of political effectiveness.

The 1980s saw important shifts from materialist to PM values in Canada and Mexico, as in the United States (Inglehart 1992). Of 34 variables examined, 31 shifted toward PM. They include decreases in respect for authority, sexual restrictiveness, obedience, and confidence in public institutions, and a greater potential for unconventional political action. The correlation of these values with age suggests that intergenerational change is what causes social change.

Some analysts find Habermas's (1987) theory of the colonization of the life world—an alternative theory of value change—less simplistic than Inglehart's. They also believe it interprets survey results better. Nonetheless, as Inglehart would have predicted, generational differences do account for some observed value changes in Swiss-German data (Sacchi 1992).

Criticisms

Few studies have addressed this aspect of Inglehart's theory. One, by Jagodzinski (1985), notes that, if this theory is valid, values learned at an early age in life will remain in adulthood. The proportion holding a particular value within any generation will be constant over time. Finally, a value that gains acceptance among young people will diffuse into the whole society through generational replacement. But after a review of the literature, the author concludes there is little evidence of such intergenerational value changes toward PM.

In West Germany, the theory of generational replacement helps us to understand the attitudes of immigrants, who are more materialistic than native-born Germans (Boehnke et al. 1987). However, along with generational replacement, level of education attained also affects these values. As well, age and materialism are only associated for native-born Germans. Among immigrants, younger people prove to be even more materialistic than older ones—not what the theory would have predicted. This unexpected result may be because of changes in the origins of recent immigrants or decisions by older PM immigrants to return to their country of origin. Or it may result from the selection (or self-selection) of immigrants who hold particular values.

Cremer (1991) agrees with the emphasis Inglehart puts on young people as instruments of value change. However, he prefers a theory of Klages's (1986) that sees only a temporary and unique shift in values occurring in 1965–75. Klages believes that, then and only then, values of self-actualization briefly superseded values of duty and acceptance.

Similarly, data collected from American and German secondary school students reveal that the rise in PM values in Western societies in the late 1960s and early 1970s was a generational effect caused by the unique cultural outlook of the period. The persistence of PM values among the 'sixties generation' and their spread to younger people is a result of the development of institutional structures, especially political ones, that promote this orientation. The result is a very weak rela-

tionship between the positions of individuals on the need hierarchy and their value orientations. In general, economic conditions are not strongly related to either psychological needs or to values (Trump 1988).

Inglehart may also have given too little attention to differences within the middle class: for example, between employees in the public and private sectors. He also failed to examine differences in middle-class educational backgrounds. Knutsen (1983) concludes that, in Norway, the political significance of the PM middle class lies in their numerical strength within expanding sectors of the economy. It is not because of their strategic position in the decision-making process, as Inglehart believes.

Inglehart expects value change to produce a change in political and economic conditions. However this view ignores the role that social institutions play in shaping people's values (Pappi 1991). Ultimately, values may be the effect, and not the cause, of social changes Inglehart is discussing.

For example, a study of anti-American sentiment, fear of war, and support for NATO using Eurobarometer data finds little variation across generations and little variation according to value-preferences. During two Euromissile crises—in 1957–63 and 1979–84—public opinion in Britain, France, Italy, and Germany changed little. Scaminaci (1988) concludes that Euromissile crises are generated from above, by political, military, and intellectual élites, not by new (younger) generations that hold PM values.

In short, despite a correlation between age and political attitudes in many countries, the effect is weak and transient and, in any event, may not translate into politically important behaviour.

3. POSTMATERIALIST (PM) CULTURE
The Theory
Recall that the basic theory is that the new PM culture connects a variety of political views with social and economic views. To illustrate, Italy has seen the

emergence of a 'composite life ethic' among well-educated people concentrated in urban areas (Bovone 1983). Holders of this ethic express themselves more freely, give more attention to personal relationships, and want a freer organization of time than holders of the traditional Italian ethic. This change leads to a conflict between work and life ethics, changes in the sexual division of labour, and a precarious personal identity.

According to this theory, PM is a new type of culture or outlook on life. As we noted earlier, it is postmaterial in the sense that it places little importance on personal wealth, economic development, and economic determinants of social life. In this respect it is also 'post-Marxist'.

PMs are politically active and they vote for leftist parties as often as materialists, or more so. They are more involved in the peace and environmental movements than materialists. On the other hand, PMs attach little importance to traditional religion. The strongest followers of conventional religion are likely to be materialists, despite the nonmaterialist teachings of the Judeo-Christian religions (Inglehart and Appel 1989).

Supporting Evidence

As we have said, Inglehart's work has its roots in the American social science literature. PM's popularity among political scientists points to a renaissance in empirical value research in the social sciences (Suhonen 1985). Even Jurgen Habermas, the eminent German social philosopher, is now drawing extensively on empirical research. Therefore, we can criticize Inglehart's theory of a value revolution but it descends from a long line of research. Most important, it is engaging a wide variety of European social scientists in empirical debate.

Evidence shows that the growth of PM values reflects a decline in traditional values (Inglehart and Appel 1989). In the last few decades, materialist values that emphasize economic security have given way to PM values such as self-expression and belonging (Inglehart 1988). PM values

are also associated with religious agnosticism and with tolerance toward divorce and other traditionally stigmatized acts. In both Canada and the United States, the rise of PM values includes a growing support for the pro-choice position on abortion (Nevitte, Brandon, and Davis 1993). Accordingly, the spread of PM values leads us to expect the liberalization of abortion laws in the United States.

Other research supports the view that PM is a cluster of values that promote 'new politics'. Opp (1990) defines PM broadly as 'a set of preferences for a certain class of public goods'—for example, peace and clean air. In Canada, PM sentiment is expressed in more sympathy with Native peoples, more support for Native self-government, and more opposition to assimilation than in the past (Wohfeld and Nevitte 1990).

PM values and their connection with worries about the environment support the view that environmental concerns reflect a *general* change of values. Throughout the West, ecological concerns are growing. As well, many people report discussing environmental and climatic problems. Such exchanges of opinion and information are also important for the spread of environmental interest (Kastenholz 1993).

PM even seems likely to revolutionize work attitudes. Work will continue to play an important role in people's lives. However, it will no longer be as central to people's lives as it was in the past (Cesareo, 1987). In the future, work will become more flexible, some believe. It will adapt to the differing needs of individual workers and the increasingly complex demands of a postindustrial society.

The evidence on economic effects of PM is mixed, however. Research in Hong Kong finds that materialist values are associated (though weakly) with entrepreneurial characteristics. There, a value shift is taking place from materialist to PM values, with uncertain results for the economy. On the other hand, mainland Chinese are shifting from a belief that economic development is a social duty toward economic development for personal gratification (Ho 1986). This seems to contradict Inglehart's theory since, here, growing prosperity coincides with a shift from nonmaterial toward material satisfaction.

Criticisms

Data gathered in eight European countries in 1976 show that PMs give more weight to broad social and political issues, while materialists focus on things like income or housing quality. Group differences, however, are small and not always in the expected direction (Mastekaasa 1983). In short, not all empirical research supports Inglehart's position.

For example, Gehmacher (1987) says that the PM scale measures a set of 'values'—goals and ideas—that is long-term but not lifelong. This directly contradicts a study of two-wave panel data collected between 1974 and 1981 in the United States, West Germany, and the Netherlands, which reports that PM values are stable during adulthood (De Graaf, Hadenaars, and Luijkx 1989).

As PM theory would predict, values are influenced by economic well-being (as measured by income). However, political factors also influence social and political values. Beyond that, PM 'values' appear to change quickly. From this, Herz (1979) concludes that Inglehart has been measuring attitudes, not enduring values. American research also shows that individual values change throughout adolescence and early adulthood, in response to prevailing social and political conditions (Frankland, Corbett, and Rudoni 1980).

Inglehart and his colleagues ignore deep conflicts, such as those rooted in ethnicity and language. A study of multicultural Belgium and Canada shows that these cleavages override most other societal divisions, including the materialism-PM division. And for survey data from France and the United States, on which Inglehart did much of his research, a logit regression analysis finds little support for the PM thesis. Inglehart's findings only hold up when less powerful and less appropriate statistical tests are used (Paddock 1993).

Then there is the question of how many dimensions are needed to describe a political culture. Inglehart focuses on one: the materialism versus postmaterialism dimension. By contrast, Gehmacher (1987) says that we need a model of two distinct value systems that compete and modify one another. Inglehart may be oversimplifying when he counterposes 'acquisitive', or materialist, and 'postindustrial', or PM values (Leonardi 1983).

Some believe Inglehart's theory does not adequately deal with the complex nature of values. Herz (1987), for example, prefers five value dimensions that he derives from a theory of political conflicts. Other researchers would come up with other dimensions, even other *numbers* of dimensions. By this criterion, Inglehart's approach is surprisingly simple or naive.

In general, a one-dimensional view of political culture, which pits materialism against postmaterialism is too simple—indeed, inadequate (Hellevik 1993). By contrast, the theorist Klages thinks of values changing along two axes: on one axis, values of duty and acceptance, and on the other, values of self-actualization. Compared to Inglehart's, this model may be better grounded empirically, and takes more account of historical and economic conditions (Kadishi-Fassler 1993).

Other researchers question whether PM is really a new set of values at all. For example, Langer and Sagmeister (1983) write that what Inglehart labels PM are actually traditional socialist values. Socialism has always emphasized the importance of worker participation on the job and in society. If so, Inglehart wrongfully distinguishes between PM and (early) Marxism. In all historical periods, social movements have come and gone, often believing that their underlying goals are unique when they are not.

Some difficulties with PM theory are evident in relation to the topic of environment. For example, Inglehart led us to believe that environmentalism is a new and unique part of PM thinking. Yet PM and environmentalism are separate constructs in the minds of both Americans and Canadians (Steger et al. 1989).

One may also question the cross-national applicability of such ideas as PM. For example, Japanese attitudes to nature seem PM in the West, but they are part of the traditional Japanese value system. Therefore, the same values fulfill different functions in different cultures. This argues against using a single set of values—postmaterial values—to evaluate social change throughout the world (Trommsdorff 1983).

In the United States, materialist supporters of the new environmental paradigm (NEP) are deviant and distinct from both the non-NEP group and the PM pro-NEP group. In Japan, materialist supporters of the NEP are distinct in political and personal attributes from the PM supporters of the NEP. However, they are indistinct from materialist nonsupporters. In traditional Japanese culture, nature and humanity are one, a view that is also expressed in the NEP. Since the NEP is not new in Japan, NEP attitudes cut across other social and political belief patterns (Pierce et al. 1987).

The Soviet pattern doesn't fit conveniently into Inglehart's model either. In Russia the environmental movement dates back 30 years. The Soviet ecological movement always held PM values, opposed state bureaucracy, and operated through democratic methods. Unlike the Western environmental movement, the Soviet movement emerged when people lacked civil rights and experience with participation. Also, environmental pollution was chronic. This shows that, contrary to Inglehart's theory, the development of PM does not demand affluence, at least where environmentalism is concerned.

Effective international cooperation requires cross-cultural acceptance of common principles,

norms, and values, and some scholars believe that PM provides such a common meeting ground. It is intrinsically sympathetic to environmentalism. It also stresses quality of life issues such as belongingness, self-expression, and equality, as compared with earlier materialist emphases on economic and military security. However, there is an implicit contradiction between the universalistic, holistic demands of eco-protection and the pluralistic, individualistic thrust of postmaterialism (Pendergraft 1992). This leaves us wondering whether PM can serve as the basis for international environmentalism.

Even the true motivation behind environmentalism—whether selfishness or virtue—is far from certain. Some believe that environmentalism serves the interest of the new middle class. Others, like Inglehart, believe it lies in the 'new childhood' experienced by today's middle-class young adults (Eckersley 1989).

What is in question is the degree to which society has undergone a transition from a class-based ideological polarization to a new, value-based political division. American research (Carvalho 1992) finds that *neither* traditional liberal-conservative ideology *nor* Inglehart's materialist-PM value perspective can explain public attitudes toward economic development, environmental concerns, or trade-offs between the two. Both approaches provide limited insight into the variation in people's views. Further, the usefulness of each approach depends largely on how each theoretical approach is measured and what specific issue is examined.

Similar concerns arise in connection with the peace movement. Inglehart implies that the peace movement is a form of protest behaviour. However, increasingly, supporters of the peace movement are part of the 'establishment'. For example, people in Holland with PM values who support the peace movement are well integrated into such institutions as the Church and the private sector of the economy (Koopmans 1987).

Inglehart writes that PM extends into a variety of social spheres but the published support for this view is mixed. For example, women with PM values delay family formation, but they do not have fewer children (Klein 1990). In many spheres of life, value changes of the kind Inglehart describes do not cause significant behaviour changes.

And in many countries, even the values have not changed much. In thirteen Western countries, traditional views in the domains of marriage, family, sexuality, and education are still widespread (Halman 1991). Moreover, in the realm of values, the Western World—even Western Europe—is not homogeneous. Nation-specific traditions and conditions are too important to ignore. For example, some nations are more secular than others. This affects the rate, degree, and type of adoption of new values, despite economic development.

To summarize, researchers have raised many questions about the strength, generality, and durability of value changes. Everyone agrees that new attitudes or values have emerged in the West, but few are willing to concede that they constitute a coherent and important change in culture.

4. POLITICAL OUTCOMES
The Theory
Recall that the theory says the new political culture contains potentials for political action. The PM culture promotes more political involvement up to and including protest than the materialist culture. This is a view that directly opposes the Marxist position. Marxists would predict that poor people with a class-related plan for social change are more likely to take political action than highly educated middle-class people motivated only by abstract ideals.

Supporting Evidence
There is a presumption in Marxist, and much other, political writing that discontent is a necessary—though not sufficient—condition for polit-ical action. By contrast, Inglehart claims that discontent is largely irrelevant. If we want to explain political behaviour, we have to look for other sources. The reason: discontent is invariant over time and space, though political action is not.

For the most part, people's lives change slowly and so does their satisfaction. Because satisfaction varies so little, political action is unlikely to result from changes in satisfaction. That means political action and inaction must have other roots. So, for example, young Italians are politically inactive not because they are indifferent to politics or satisfied with their society, but because they distrust traditional modes of political participation (Armillei and Tirabassi 1992).

Within a given society, we see no difference in the subjective well-being—or life satisfaction—of materialists and PMs. The reason satisfaction varies so little is that most people achieve satisfaction by adjusting what they want to what they can get. A (downward) personal adjustment of aspirations to suit realities limits dissatisfaction, making it possible for most people to report being happy with their lives.

Throughout Europe, Andrews and Inglehart (1979) find similar structures of subjective well-being. This justifies a cross-national comparison of values and behaviours using identical instruments. (However, Borg et al. 1981 question and debate this comparability.)

Inglehart notes that the level of subjective well-being varies little between social groups with unchanging characteristics, such as sex (Inglehart and Rabier 1984a). That's because group members have had a long time to adjust their expectations to the realities of being male, or black, or tall, and so on. Subjective well-being varies more under the influence of such factors as income and marital status, but even these variations are modest. It varies most when people's income level or marital status changes. That's because these changes are often sudden and affect many areas of everyday life (Inglehart and Rabier 1984b).

On the whole, however, the invariance of discontent, and its lack of correlation with PM, leads Inglehart to conclude that discontent, or subjective well-being, is a useless variable.

The absence or presence of PM parties has a greater impact on voter turnout in 16 modern democratic industrial nations (Crepaz 1990). The opportunity to express political views, not their level of satisfaction, is what determines people's political behaviour. As Ogmundson has shown in Canada, people's beliefs about what particular parties or candidates represent are key to voting (and perhaps other political) behaviour.

Changes in values and a growing distrust of government both contribute to political disaffection. In the 1970s and 1980s, alienation from government and traditional politics had important electoral consequences in the United States—for example, the election of Ronald Reagan, who was seen as a political 'outsider' (Barnes and Mattioli 1982).

Changes in values also contributed to the decline of orthodox Marxist parties in Western Europe and a loss of belief in the ideology on which they are based. The result was a political realignment in advanced industrial societies—what Inglehart and Rabier (1986) call a shift from class-based politics to quality-of-life politics. Foremost among the factors behind this shift are changes in the structure of the workforce and changes in the goals of individuals. But the net result is a macro-structural shift in political partisanship.

On the other hand, changes in values gave support to new supranational organizations such as the European Union. Short-term economic decline increases the chance that people will vote like materialists—in this case, against the EU (Hendriks-Vettehen 1990). However, long-term influences dominate and the future of the European Union is secure. Attitudes to European unification have been overwhelmingly positive in the six long-established member countries. PM values contribute to strong public support for European integration (Inglehart and Rabier 1978, 1979).

Changes in values have produced a PM civic culture that increases the likelihood of political stability, rule of law, and democratic procedure. Between 1973 and 1987, the civic cultures of 22 societies varied widely. The variations included personal satisfaction with life, personal trust, and support for the existing order. However, as expected, countries that ranked high on this combination of attitudes also showed more support for stable democracy than did lower-ranking countries (Inglehart and Garcia-Pardo 1988).

Conversely, a shift in civic culture may produce political unrest. A gradual value shift was as important as worsening economic conditions in causing Poland's 1980 crisis, for example (Inglehart and Siemienska 1988). Survey data from Poland revealed strong desires for self-expression and participation in political decision-making. Well-educated, urban, and nonreligious respondents were least satisfied with the political order under communism. Poland's success in improving the economy promoted PM values, led to protest, and (in this way) caused the downfall of the state.

Something similar happened in the German Democratic Republic. There, some believe, the collapse of communism was brought about by individuation. The development of an apolitical civil society and the multiplication of social identities increased pluralism in society, by diversifying social groupings and categories. This increased pluralism promotes social tolerance and reduces social control. The multiplication of social groups presents people with a wide variety of ways to fulfill their social needs. In these ways, individuation produces a more democratic political culture. Authoritarianism loses its legitimacy and the chance for democracy increases (Hillhouse 1994).

In Austria, West Germany, the UK, and the US, the growth of PM increased the tension between party systems that are based on the Left-Right dimension and values that are not (Kaase and

Klingemann 1982). To outside observers, the 'old' Left seems more materialistic in the way it formulates its goals and more conservative in the means it uses to attain them. No wonder that the Socialists in France lost support among the PM-leaning population during the 1970s and 1980s (Ladrech 1989). The 'new' Left is more PM, progressive, and participatory than the old one.

As Inglehart's theory would predict, among young Spaniards social and moral attitudes have more effect on political ideas than do economic attitudes (Medrano, Garcia-Mon, and Nicolas 1989). It is because of the change in social and moral attitudes that political ideologies moved to the Left in the 1970s and 1980s. Especially with regard to energy and the environment, 'soft' values now prevail (Borg 1985). Similarly in Sweden, PM values have led to shifts in politics and social policies (Hoefer 1988).

Similarly, the development of PM values in France after 1968 gave ideological support to city-dwellers participating in rural (antinuclear and other) resistance movements. The recession has since weakened neopopulist thinking among urban radicals, endangering the success of rural antinuclear movements (Beach 1984).

PM values, as we have noted repeatedly, support environmental movements. Europeans (in Germany, France, Great Britain, and the Netherlands) give considerable support to environmental organizations. Most strongly related to environmental group support are PM values and the perception of a national pollution problem. In Germany and the Netherlands, environmentalism is the basis for new parties and puts pressure on the older ones. People who favour environmental groups are much more likely to support new or old Left parties. By contrast, in France and Great Britain environmental sentiments are only weakly linked to party choice. These findings suggest that environmentalism will continue to influence European public opinion and political parties in the future (Rohrschneider 1989, 1990).

National governments support international environmental agreements, such as the regulation of acid rain, as a result of many factors—new social movements, support for green or ecological parties, and domestic economic considerations, among others. Not to be ignored, however, is the role of PM values and value-holders (Sprinz 1993).

Even ethnic nationalist movements have gained strength from PM values. Scottish and Welsh survey data show that people who want more territorial autonomy often endorse PM values (Studlar and McAllister 1988). There is also evidence that a growth in PM values increases nationalist conflict and, even, illegal political actions.

It also increases protest behaviour. Student activism in Korea has increased in quantity and severity since the early 1980s, when the national economy first entered mature industrialization. Korean university students have a level of PM that is nearly as high as European young adults. They are change-oriented, Leftist, and sympathetic to protest. Compared to other students, Korean PM students are more likely to be involved in political protest, to have higher levels of political efficacy and more negative views of the existing system, and to prefer radical social change. However, the Left-Right ideological dimension still predicts the politicization of Korean students better than PM (Kim 1991).

Criticisms

Many researchers have criticized this portion of Inglehart's theory. For example, Niemoller and van der Eijk (1986) report that, in Holland, PM scarcely affects voting behaviour. PM is not an independent influence on political choice; voting depends mainly on the ideological (Left versus Right) outlook of the voter.

Nor does the PM dimension affect either the Leftist-Rightist or libertarian-authoritarian vote. When parties are arrayed along a Left-Right dimension, social class and Left-Right identification are the best predictors of voting. When they are arrayed along a libertarian-authoritarian dimension, religion is the best predictor (Middendorp 1989). In neither case is PM the best. Both the alignment and value models are poor at predicting Dutch voting patterns (Van Deth and Geurts 1989).

In Canada neither PM nor the Left-Right dichotomy is a strong predictor of policies and ideologies (Nevitte, Bakvis, and Gibbins 1989). At best, PM is only part of the political picture. Changes such as neoconservatism are largely a response of the capitalist welfare state to conditions of economic constraint, overload, and ungovernability (Hueglin 1987).

Likewise, in Germany the problems social-democratic parties like SPD face are not simply because of an inability to adjust to PM values and the decline of class voting. Difficulties in building a stable electoral coalition are also due to inconsistencies of postwar party policy, and particularly to inabilities of leaders to determine the SPD's proper role as a centre-left Volkspartei (Parness 1990).

The observed correlation between PM values and political behaviour may even be spurious, in the sense that a hidden third factor causes both. For example, in Scandinavia social class still has a large impact on interest-based values, support for the welfare state, party preference, and support for PM values (Hoel and Knutsen 1989). Sector of employment (private versus public) has begun to approach social class as an important political cleavage, while gender has only a small impact.

Are class divisions in politics weakening, compared to conflicts over nonmaterial issues? Using European data from 1973–85, Weakliem (1991) looks for a sign that segments of the middle class are joining the 'new PM' Left while working-class voters move to the Right. However, when education is controlled, he finds no evidence of changes in class support for PM. This suggests a similar shift in attitudes among all people with the same education. Perhaps educational change is the moving force in politics, not class or prosperity. As well, class divisions remain strong.

For this reason, special efforts must be made to build cooperation between labour and the (middle-class) peace and environmental movements. The conflict between them is because of working-class versus professional middle-class cultural differences, not narrow interests or PM values (Rose 1994). Class shapes people's perceptions of interests and ways of acting, even when goals are not explicitly stated in class terms. Coalitions depend on social relationships, trust, and bridge-builders who act as intermediaries, educators, and motivators. Participants in successful coalitions broaden their perspectives and develop a more inclusive understanding of issues.

Where political protest is concerned, data on the effects of PM are mixed. On the one hand, German interview data obtained from opponents to nuclear power show that PM has cumulative and multiplicative effects on the readiness for legal protest (Opp 1990).

On the other hand, Chinese survey data suggest that many factors—discontent with economic reforms, distrust of the government, aspirations for Western democracy, and disillusionment with communist ideology—all significantly increase protest. PM values may have no effect and may even have a negative effect by encouraging economic instead of political solutions to problems. So, PM values may promote political protest in the West but help to suppress it in China (Zhu and Rosen 1993).

In short, there is doubt that PM 'values' are the only or best explanations for change in political behaviour, or even that they lead to changes in behaviour.

Summary

Let us now spend a few moments reviewing what we have found out about postmaterialist theory and scholarly reactions to it.

Peace and Prosperity
The support for this portion of Inglehart's theory is more ideological than empirical. We are far

from having proved that 'the new culture', if it exists, is a result of childhood prosperity and a high level of need-fulfillment in childhood or adulthood. Research to date has failed to persuade us that new PM values are a result of peace and prosperity. Instead, such values may just as likely result from family- or class-based socialization, or changes of the educational system.

The underlying appeal of *this* portion of the theory may be its implicit endorsement of 1960s student activism. By implication, it says that 1960s activism really was a radical, new kind of politics, just as student protestors said at the time. Inglehart is living proof that new generations enter élite roles from which they spread new political ideologies. Inglehart's theory promotes the belief that, in the 1960s, middle-class students were truly radical. If we accept the entire PM theory, so were yuppies in the 1980s!

Second, the theory grows out of anti-Marxist 'end of ideology' writings associated with Daniel Bell (1956), Lipset and Clark (Clark and Lipset 1991; Clark et al. 1993) on the end of social classes, and others. In this respect, PM is the belief system underlying Bell's postindustrial society. Like Bell's, this is a self-congratulatory, nationalistic theory, which says that American social life is getting better and better. So is social life in other countries which are similar to—or model themselves upon—the United States.

Third, the theory grows out of life cycle and developmental literature, following Maslow (1954), Lewis (1961, 1966), and other culture of poverty theorists, Lipset (1960), who singled out working-class authoritarians, Inkeles and Smith (1974), who applauded 'modern', Westernized personalities, and Elder (1985, 1988) who studied Americans who grew up in the Depression. The common theme is that prosperity and economic development create 'better'—kinder, gentler, more open, and tolerant—human beings. Evil and conflict are because of poverty; economic growth makes poverty, hence evil, go away.

It is hard to resist the appeal of such a progressive, optimistic view of the future. However the data are far from conclusive in supporting it.

Generational Replacement

Inglehart's theory is on no firmer ground when it comes to the issue of generational replacement. Aside from the baby boom's self-conscious trend setting, we see little evidence of profound political changes over time. Again, given the mixed empirical support for Inglehart's theory, we need to consider its ideological underpinnings to understand the theory's appeal.

Several strong influences are in view. First, there is Kuhn's (1972) theory about scientific revolutions. It says that changes in thinking depend on changes in scientific personnel. Styles of thinking are rooted in and propagated by cliques, networks, and other social groups. As the power of social groupings rises and falls, so do the ideas they support. On this, see also the work on 'invisible colleges' (Crane 1974) and on networks of influence in academic and other communities (Mullins 1973a, 1973b).

Second, there is the common observation that the baby boom generation has had an enormous influence on modern culture. The key writers here include Richard Easterlin (1980). His theory about the flow of large and small generations through society cannot have served as a model for Inglehart's own thinking about generational replacement, but it reflects a demographic viewpoint that has been common ever since the 1960s. Another is Landon Jones (1980). He documented the great social changes the baby boom generation brought about as it passed from infancy to studenthood to work and marriage.

Generational replacement is the most interesting and potentially useful aspect of Inglehart's PM theory. If true, it makes possible political projection by means of demographic projection. If particular generations are permanent carriers of the ideas they adopted in childhood, then as their number in the population changes, so does the significance, or political potential, of these ideas. If this theory is valid, date of birth—an easily measured, unambiguous variable—becomes central to political forecasting.

But in the end, data have incompletely supported this theory of generational replacement. Researchers disagree about whether childhood experiences really mould permanent values and whether such influences are more important than current social and economic conditions. They also disagree about whether we are looking at a once-only or continuing generational shift in values. It is not yet clear whether Inglehart is only describing the baby boom generation, or Generation X and later generations too. Again, we must avoid being seduced by the elegant simplicity of the idea and the benefits we might obtain if it were valid.

A Real Culture Shift?

On the issue of whether postmaterialism constitutes a coherent cultural shift, we run into trouble. Again, we have to dig below the empirical findings and look at the ideology if we are to understand scholarly support for Inglehart's theory.

The 'post'-materialist aspect of the theory raises issues related to conceptualization, measurement, and even naming. What, we wonder, does Inglehart imply by calling the PM set of attitudes 'new'? Or calling PM a 'culture', instead of a set of attitudes? Or calling those attitudes postmaterialist instead of nonmaterialist? What if the baby boom generation comprises 'pre'-materialist people—people who are less willing than their parents to take responsibility for families, jobs, and traditional institutions!

Lumping Inglehart with other writers of the 1960s and 1970s, Rothman and Lichter (1978) deny that radical students were a 'psychologically liberated generation' or even, for that matter, possessors of healthy personalities. They criticize academics for whitewashing the student move-

ment and, by extension, glorifying PM. Along similar lines, Austrian data suggest that youth exhibit a skeptical attitude toward the adult world (Denz 1983). This skepticism shows up in apathy, alienation, and hazy frustration that fail to crystallize in either protest or self-actualization. This is far from the healthy, vigorous PM that Inglehart has led us to expect.

Then there are questions we can address to Maslow's work, to which Inglehart's thinking is related. What proof is there that the PM values are arrayed hierarchically, as Maslow and Inglehart believe? Or that people must satisfy the lower-order values before 'ascending' to the higher-order values? Such questions are briefly discussed in Tepperman (1994: ch. 1). There, the evidence shows that, above the very lowest levels of subsistence, people vary markedly in their values, desires, and behaviour.

Issues of measurement validity and reliability are central to PM theory, which claims there is an important, stable pattern of thinking around the world. But on the issue of stability, would Inglehart's measures consistently rate people materialist or PM if they were measured more than once? Or do the scores on this variable merely reflect social conditions at the time of the interview?

One can use the Inglehart data from 1981 and 1991—though they are not panel data—to shed light on this issue. So, for example, unpublished research by the author and James Curtis using Inglehart's data finds that between 1981 and 1991, surveyed Canadians, Americans, and Mexicans became slightly *less* tolerant of social and ethnic minority groups. This result is interpretable in terms of worsening economic conditions; it is uninterpretable in terms of PM theory. Said another way, if PM theory were valid, there would be no change or a change in the direction of *more* tolerance.

As well, many of the items Inglehart uses have little face validity. It is unclear what some questions mean to the respondent or to Inglehart's theory. For example, environmentalism is not self-evidently the highest stage of human development. We have no reason to think that support for the environmental movement is 'higher' than support for a trade union or political party. Or that the environmental movement has made a significant change in political life and political thinking.

Researchers have raised serious questions about the validity and applicability of the PM scale. We even have to wonder whether the spread of PM attitudes is important enough to justify calling it a 'value shift', much less a 'culture shift'.

New Political Behaviours

Finally, the problems in assessing change of political behaviour are not merely a matter of empirical disagreement: there are also questions of what we should be looking at. Should we examine political attitudes or political activities? If the latter, what kinds of political activities should we look at? And how should we evaluate these acts? What, for example, is the political significance of signing a petition for gay rights, compared with going out on strike at a meat-packing plant? Or of calling for stricter environmental standards, even at the cost of jobs or economic development? Without answers to these questions we cannot tell whether Inglehart's theory helps explain important political change or, even, that PMs are more politically active than materialists.

Evidence of the political effects of PM is mixed. There are signs that PM has had important effects on new social and political grassroots movements, such as environmentalism. However, we would be wrong to ascribe too much importance to PM. As we have seen, social class position and self-interest continue to exercise a powerful hold.

Ideology even influences which political behaviours we choose to look at as outcomes of the change process. It may well be that Inglehart attaches more importance to electoral politics and voting than conflict theorists, who would focus on interlocking directorships, élite lobbying, and upper-class connections.

Conclusion

The Inglehart-inspired survey data offer an incomparably rich source for testing a wide variety of hypotheses. For all its faults, the Inglehart culture shift theory continues to inspire and provoke research efforts around the globe. There are many reasons to doubt the validity of this theory. Yet, the theory remains important as a spur and an inspiration to further research on political culture.

No less than that, culture shift theory is also an artifact of North American political culture. The theory itself is a set of beliefs about modern life and the baby boom generation, about the future and social change. In all these respects, the theory is profoundly American and therefore profoundly optimistic. Finally, the theory is—like most influential theories in political culture—a proud descendant of earlier thinking. It marks the evolution of naive 1960s American thinking in a postrecessionary, post-Vietnam, postmodern, postmaterial world.

But the theory also carries the seeds of its own negation. If, after all, values and beliefs are a result of childhood experience and socialization, then this theory may be no more than the product (or record) of a prosperous and prolonged childhood—the wishful thinking of a pampered baby boom generation. Inglehart's theory may be valid or invalid today, and we have seen much evidence to question its validity. But even if it is valid today, much of the theory is unlikely to be valid tomorrow. Later generations—raised in periods of less prosperity, such as the 1970s and 1980s, or growing up in the turmoil of post-Soviet Europe—will carry a different political culture and produce different political theories about their own behaviour.

Beyond that, materialism may once again become attractive and seemingly progressive, as global competition puts everyone's material well-being, let alone self-actualization, into doubt. In the end, Inglehart's PM theory may be remembered as an enthusiastic belief that celebrated the future as American dominance passed into history.

I have attempted here, though sketchily, to show that in the study of political culture—indeed, in the study of sociology more generally—we see an interesting interaction. On the one hand, there are the beliefs we hold as members of a particular society at a particular moment in time. On the other hand, there are the universalistic requirements of social science, which specify the ways evidence must be brought to bear upon our beliefs. In the middle are the many institutions—journals, funding bodies, reviewers, universities, colleagues, and the like—that interpret and tilt the balance between these universal and particular tendencies. Perhaps it is only long after the fact that we are able, as scholars and students, to make sense of a particular theory like Inglehart's PM theory. As social science becomes more scientific, it may be easier to resist the ideological pressures of our own time.

Notes

I am grateful to Jim Curtis for thoughtful and painstaking comments on an earlier draft of this paper.

References

Abramson, P.R. 1989. 'Generations and Political Change in the United States', *Research in Political Sociology* 4, 25–280.

———, and Inglehart, R. 1986. 'Generational Replacement and Value Change in Six West European Societies', *American Journal of Political Science* 30 (1): 1–25.

———. 1987. 'Generational Replacement and the Future of Post-materialist Values', *Journal of Politics*, 49 (1): 231–41.

Almond, G. 1970 [1956]. 'Comparative Political Systems', Reprinted in *Political Development* (Boston: Little, Brown).

———, and S. Verba. 1963. *The Civic Culture: Political Attitudes and Democracy in Five Nations* (Princeton: Princeton University Press).

Andrews, F.M., and R.F. Inglehart. 1979. 'The Structure of Subjective Well-being in Nine Western Societies', *Social Indicators Research* 6 (1): 73–90.

Armillei, G., and A. Tirabassi. 1992. 'Apathy, Political Participation, Community Action: Young Italians During the 1980s', *Sociologia e ricerca sociale* 13 (37): 151–74.

Barnes, S.H., and F. Mattioli. 1982. 'US Politics and Public Opinion in the 1970s', *Sociologia e ricerca sociale* 3 (7): 61–85.

Beach, C.J. 1984. 'Out of the Dustbin of History: The Changing Meaning of Resistance to Development Projects in Rural Areas', *Social Alternatives* 4 (1): 31–4.

Bell, Daniel. 1956. *The End of Ideology* (New York: Free Press).

Boehnke, K., H. Merkens, F. Schmidt, and D. Bergs. 1987. 'Foreign Workers and Value Change: Is There a "Silent Revolution" among Immigrant Workers in West Germany?' *Kolner zeitschrift fur soziologie und sozialpsychologie* 39 (2): 330–46.

Borg, I., R. Bergermaier, F.M. Andrews, and R.F. Inglehart. 1981. 'Some Comments on "The structure of subjective well-being in nine Western societies"' *Social Indicators Research* 9 (3): 265–78.

Borg, O. 1985. 'The Revolution of Values—The Catch Phrase in Scientific and Social Debate', *Alkoholipolitikka* 50 (6): 325–30.

Bovone, L. 1983. 'Composite Life and New Values: Some Hypotheses of the Adult Generation', *Studi di sociologia* 21 (3): 281–92.

Carvalho, B.L. 1992. 'American Attitudes toward the Environment and Economic Development: A Comparison of Traditional Liberal/Conservative and the Materialist/Postmaterist Value Priorities Perspective'. Ph.D. diss. (Fordham University).

Cesareo, V. 1987. 'Italian Workers' Values and Needs', Studi di sociologia 25 (2): 111–22.

Chamberlain, N.W. 1970. Beyond Malthus: Population and Power (New York: Basic Books).

Clark, T.N., and S.M. Lipset. 1991. 'Are Social Classes Dying?' International Sociology 6 (4): 397–410.

Cotgrove, S., and A. Duff. 1981. 'Environmentalism, Values, and Social Change', British Journal of Sociology 32 (1): 92–110.

Crane, D. 1972. Invisible Colleges: Diffusion of Knowledge in Scientific Communities (Chicago: University of Chicago Press).

Cremer, G. 1991. 'Youth and Changing Values: Survey of the Literature 1980–1991', DISKURS 2: 56–62.

Crepaz, M.M.L. 1990. 'The Impact of Party Polarization and Postmaterialism on Voter Turnout: A Comparative Study of 16 Industrial Democracies', European Journal of Political Research 18 (2): 183–205.

D'Alessandro, V. 1990. 'Materialist and Postmaterialist Values in Higher-Educated Young People: An Empirical Inquiry in Two Roman Universities', Sociologia e ricerca sociale 11 (33): 65–94.

De Graaf, N.D., and P.M. De Graaf. 1988a. 'The Empirical Relation between Age and Postmaterialist Values', Sociologische Gids 35 (6): 397–417.

———. 1988b. 'Family Background, Postmaterialism, and Life Style', Netherlands Journal of Sociology 24 (1): 50–64.

De Graaf, N.D., J. Hadenaars, and R. Luijkx. 1989. 'Intragenerational Stability of Postmaterialism in Germany, the Netherlands and the United States', European Sociological Review 5 (2): 183–201.

Denz, H. 1983. 'Alienation and Value Shifts', Osterreichische zeitschrift fur soziologie 8 (4): 121–36.

Duch, R.M., and M.A. Taylor. 1993. 'Postmaterialism and the Economic Condition', American Journal of Political Science 37 (3): 747–79.

Easterlin, R.A. 1980. Birth and Fortune: The Impacts of Numbers on Personal Welfare (New York: Basic Books).

Eckersley, R. 1989. 'Green Politics and the New Class: Selfishness or Virtue?' Political Studies 37 (2): 205–23.

Elder, G.H., Jr. 1985. 'Linking Family Hardship to Children's Lives', Child Development 56: 361–75.

———. 'Economic Stress in Lives: Developmental Perspectives', Journal of Social Issues (44): 25–45.

Frankland, E.G., M. Corbett, and D. Rudoni. 1980. 'Value Priorities of College Students: A Longitudinal Study', Youth and Society 11 (3): 267–93.

Gehmacher, E. 1987. 'What Is Measured by the Inglehart Scale for Postmaterialism?' Osterreichische zeitschift fur soziologie 12 (1): 74–9.

Habermas, J. 1987. The Philosophical Discourse of Modernity: Twelve Lectures (Cambridge, MA: MIT Press).

Halman, L.C.J.M. 1991. Values in the Western World: An International Exploration of Values in Western Society (Tilburg: Tilburg University Press).

Hellevik, O. 1993. 'Postmaterialism as a Dimension of Cultural Change', International Journal of Public Opinion Research 5 (3): 211–33.

Hendriks-Vettehen, P.G.J. 1990. 'Postmaterialism and Voting', Mens en maatschappij 65 (2): 165–78.

Herz, T.A. 1979. 'Changing Value Conceptualizations in Western Industrial Societies', Kolner zeitschrift fur soziologie und sozialpsychologie 31 (2): 282–301.

———. 1987. 'Values, Sociopolitical Conflicts and Generations: A Test of the Theory of Postmaterialism', Zeitschrift fur soziologie 16 (1): 56–69.

Hillhouse, R.J. 1994. 'The Individual Revolution: The Social Basis for Transition to Democracy?' Ph.D. diss. (University of Michigan).

Ho, E. S-L. 1986. 'Values and Economic Development: Hong Kong and China' Ph.D. diss. (University of Michigan).

Hoefer, R. 1988. 'Postmaterialism at Work in Social Welfare Policy: The Swedish "case"', Social Service Review 62 (3): 383–95.

Hoel, M., and O. Knutsen. 1989. 'Social Class, Gender, and Sector Employment as Political

Cleavages in Scandinavia', *Acta Sociologica* 32 (2): 181–201.

Hornstein, W. 1984. 'New Social Movements and Pedagogics: On a Reconceptualization of Educational Theory Today', *Zeitschrift fur padagogik* 30 (2): 147–67.

Hueglin, T.O. 1987. 'The Politics of Fragmentation in an Age of Scarcity: A Synthetic View and Critical Analysis of Welfare State Crisis', *Canadian Journal of Political Science* 20 (2): 235–64.

Inglehart, R. 1971. 'The Silent Revolution in Europe: Intergenerational Change in Post-Industrial Societies', *American Political Science Review* 65 (4): 991–1017.

———. 1977a. 'Long Term Trends in Mass Support for European Unification', *Government and Opposition* 12 (2): 150–77.

———. 1977b. *The Silent Revolution: Changing Values and Political Styles Among Western Publics* (Princeton, NJ: Princeton University Press).

———. 1978. 'Value Priorities, Life Satisfaction, and Political Dissatisfaction among Western Publics', *Comparative Studies in Sociology* 1: 173–202.

———. 1986. 'Intergenerational Changes in Politics and Culture: The Shift from Materialist to Post-materialist Value Priorities', *Research in Political Sociology* 2: 81–105.

———. 1988. 'Cultural Change in Advanced Industrial Societies: Postmaterialist Values and their Consequences', *Revue internationale de sociologie* 3: 77–99.

———. 1990. *Culture Shift in Advanced Industrial Society* (Princeton, NJ: Princeton University Press).

———. 1992. 'Changing Values in Industrial Society: The Case of North America, 1981–1990', *Politics and the Individual* 2 (2): 1–30.

———, and D. Appel. 1989. 'The Rise of Post-materialist Values and Changing Religious Orientations, Gender Roles and Sexual Norms', *International Journal of Public Opinion Research* 1 (1): 45–75.

———, and N. Garcia-Pardo. 1988. 'Political Culture and a Stable Democracy', *Revista espanola de investigaciones sociologicas* 42: 45–65.

———, and J.R. Rabier. 1978. 'Economic Uncertainty and European Solidarity: Public Opinion Trends', *Annals of the American Academy of Political and Social Science* 440: 66–97.

———. 1979. 'Europe Elects a Parliament: Cognitive Mobilization, Political Mobilization and pro-European Attitudes as Influences on Voter Turnout', *Government and Opposition* 14 (4): 479–507.

———. 1984a. 'Aspirations Adapt to Situations: Intercultural Analysis of the Subjective Quality of Life', *Futuribles* 80: 29–57.

———. 1984b. 'On Happiness: Personal Feeling and Cultural Norm', *Futuribles* 81: 3–29.

———. 1986. 'Political Realignment in Advanced Industrial Society: From Class-based Politics to Quality-of-Life Politics', *Government and Opposition* 21: 456–79.

Inglehart, R., and R. Siemienska. 1988. 'Changing Values and Political Dissatisfaction in Poland and the West: A Comparative Analysis', *Government and Opposition* 23 (4): 440–57.

Inkeles, A., and D.H. Smith. 1974. *Becoming Modern: Individual Change in Six Developing Countries* (Cambridge, MA: Harvard University Press).

Jagodzinski, W. 1985. 'Is There an Intergenerational Change of Values Toward Postmaterialism?' *Zeitschrift fur socialisationsforschung und erziehungssoziologie* 5 (1): 71–88.

Jennings, M.K. 1984. 'The Intergenerational Transfer of Political Ideologies in Eight Western Nations', *European Journal of Political Research* 12 (3): 261–76.

Jones, L.Y. 1980. *Great Expectations: America and the Baby Boom Generation* (New York: Ballantine Books).

Kaase, M., and H.D. Klingemann. 1982. 'Social Structure, Value Orientations, and the Party System: The Problem of Interest Accommodation in Western Democracies', *European Journal of Political Research* 10 (4): 367–86.

Kadishi-Fassler, B. 1993. 'Changes in Social Values: A Comparison of the Theories of Inglehart and Klages', *Schweizerische zeitschrift fur soziologie* 19 (2): 339–63.

Kastenholz, H.G. 1993. 'Determinants of Environmental Action in a Swiss Mountain Region: An Empirical

Study with Regards to Climatic Risks'. Ph.D. diss. Eidgenossiche Technische Hochschule Zuerich.

Kettle, J. 1980. *The Big Generation* (Toronto: McClelland & Stewart).

Kim, K. 1991. 'The Impact of Post-materialism on Korean Students'. Ph.D. diss. (University of Nebraska-Lincoln).

Klages, H. 1986. 'Value Change Revisited', paper, International Sociological Association (ISA).

Klein, T. 1990. 'Postmaterialism and Family Formation Behavior', *Zeitschrift fur soziologie* 19 (1): 57–64.

Knutsen, O. 1983. 'Postmaterialism, the Middle Class, and Elite Groups in Norway', *Tidsskrift for samfunnsforskning* 24 (2): 123–54.

Koopmans, R. 1987. 'Value Change and the Potential of New Social Movements', *Acta Politica* 22 (3): 311–26.

Kuhn, T. 1972. *The Structure of Scientific Revolutions* (Chicago: University of Chicago Press).

Ladrech, R. 1989. 'Social Movements and Party Systems: The French Socialist Party and the Social Movements', *West European Politics* 12 (3): 262–79.

Lafferty, W.M. 1976. 'Basic Needs and Political Values: Some Perspectives from Norway on Europe's "silent revolution"', *Acta Sociologica* 19 (2): 117–36.

Langer, J., and G. Sagmeister. 1983. 'Job Images and the Future of Work', *Osterreichische zeitschrift fur soziologie* 8 (1): 26–38.

Leonardi, F. 1983. 'Values or Ethical-Social Stereotypes?' *Sociologia* 17 (1): 3–39.

Lerner, D. 1958. *The Passing of Traditional Society* (New York: Free Press).

Lewis, O. 1961. *The Children of Sanchez: Autobiography of a Mexican Family* (New York: Vintage Books).

———. 1966. 'The Culture of Poverty', *Scientific American* 215 (4): 19–25.

Lipset, S.M. 1960. *Political Man: The Social Bases of Politics* (Garden City, NY: Doubleday).

Loriente, M.T. 1989. 'The Materialist/Postmaterialist Dimension in Spain: Variables in Cultural Change', *Revista espanola de investigaciones sociologicas* 47: 227–54.

Maslow, A.K. 1954. *Motivation and Personality* (New York: Harper & Row).

Mastekaasa, A. 1983. 'Post-materialist Values and Subjective Satisfaction: Testing Ronald Inglehart's hypotheses', *Acta Sociologica* 26 (2): 141–59.

Medrano, J.D., B. Garcia-Mon, and J.D. Nicolas. 1989. 'The Meaning of Being Leftist in Today's Spain', *Revista espanola de investigaciones sociologicas* 45: 9–41.

Middendorp, C.P. 1989. 'The Meaning of Leftist-Rightist Self-Identification and its Effect on the Vote', *Mens en maatschappij* 64 (1): 66–79.

Mullins, N.C. 1973a. *Science: Some Sociological Perspectives* (Indianapolis: Bobbs-Merrill).

———. 1973b. *Theories and Theory Groups in Contemporary American Sociology* (New York: Harper & Row).

Nardi, R. 1980. 'Do Economic Conditions Influence Values? A Test of Inglehart's Hypothesis', *Revista italiana di scienza politica* 10 (2): 293–315.

Nevitte, N., H. Bakvis, and R. Gibbins. 1989. 'The Ideological Contours of "New Politics" in Canada: Policy, Mobilization and Partisan Support', *Canadian Journal of Political Science* 22 (3): 475–503.

Nevitte, N., W.P. Brandon, and L. Davis. 1993. 'The American Abortion Controversy: Lessons from Cross-national Evidence', *Politics and the Life Sciences* 12 (1): 19–30.

Niemoller, B., and C. van der Eijk. 1986. 'Left/Right, Postmaterialism, and Voting', *Mens en maatschappij* 61 (3): 251–69.

Opp, K.D. 1990. 'Postmaterialism, Collective Action, and Political Protest', *American Journal of Political Science* 34 (1): 212–35.

Paddock, E.M.H. 1993. 'Ethnolinguism and Post-materialism in Belgium, Canada, France and the United States'. Ph.D. diss. (University of Kansas).

Pappi, F.U. 1991. 'From the Silent Revolution to Cultural Upheaval: Is the Dramaticism of Value Change on the Increase?' *Soziologische revue* 14 (1): 21–26.

Parness, D.L. 1990. 'The SPD and the Challenge of Mass Politics: The Dilemma of the "Volkspartie"'. Ph.D. diss. (Georgetown University).

Pendergraft, C.A. 1992. 'Agents of Change: Political Culture, Environmentalism and the European Community'. Ph.D. diss. (Tulane University).

Pfeiffer, M. 1994. 'An Examination of Inglehart's Silent Revolution Thesis in Canada'. Ph.D. diss. (York University).

———, and J.E. Cote. 1991. 'Inglehart's Silent Revolution Thesis: An Examination of Life-Cycle Effects in the Acquisition of Postmaterialist Values', *Social Behavior and Personality* 19 (4): 223–35.

Pierce, J.C., N.P. Lovrich, Jr, T. Tsurutani, and T. Abe. 1987. 'Culture, Politics and Mass Publics: Traditional and Modern Supporters of the New Environmental Paradigm in Japan and the United States', *Journal of Politics* 49 (1): 54–79.

Prisching, M. 1986. 'Limits of Value Change: Continuity and Discontinuity in Processes of Cultural Change', *Schweizerische zeitschrift fur soziologie* 12 (1): 49–70.

Rohrschneider, R. 1989. 'The Greening of Party Politics in Western Europe: Environmentalism, Economics, and Partisan Orientations in Four Nations (France, Great Britain, Germany, The Netherlands). Ph.D. diss. (Florida State University).

———. 1990. 'The Roots of Public Opinion Toward the New Social Movements: An Empirical Test of Competing Explanations', *American Journal of Political Science* 34 (1): 1–30.

Rokeach, M. 1968. *Beliefs, Attitudes and Values* (San Francisco: Jossey-Bass).

Rose, F.R. 1994. 'Peace, Labor and Environmental Coalitions: Class Culture and Democratic Change'. Ph.D. diss. (Cornell University).

Rothman, S., and S.R. Lichter. 1978. 'The Case of the Student Left', *Social Research* 45 (3): 535–609.

Sacchi, S. 1992. 'Post-materialism in Switzerland from 1972 to 1990', *Schweitzerische zeitschrift fur soziologie* 18 (1): 87–117.

Scaminaci, J., III. 1988. 'The Second Euromissile Crisis'. Ph.D. diss. (Stanford University).

Smith, R.B. 1993. 'The Paradox of Gender Voting: An Exploratory Analysis', *Quality and Quantity* 27 (3): 271–89.

Sprinz, D.F. 1993. 'Why Countries Support International Environmental Agreements: The Regulation of Acid Rain in Europe'. Ph.D. diss. (University of Michigan).

Steger, M.A.E., J.C. Pierce, B.S. Steel, and N.P. Lovrich 1989. 'Political Culture, Postmaterial Values, and the New Environmental Paradigm: A Comparative Analysis of Canada and the United States', *Political Behavior* 11 (3): 233–54.

Studlar, D.T., and I. McAllister. 1988. 'Nationalism in Scotland and Wales: A Post-industrial Phenomenon?' *Ethnic and Racial Studies* 11 (1): 48–62.

Suhonen, P. 1985. 'Approaches to Value Research and Value Measurement', *Acta Sociologica* 28 (4): 349–58.

Tepperman, L. 1994. *Choices and Chances: Sociology for Everyday Life*, 2nd edn (Toronto: Harcourt, Brace).

Trommsdorff, G. 1983. 'Value Change in Japan', *International Journal of Intercultural Relations* 7 (4): 337–60.

Trump, T.M. 1988. 'Prosperity, Recession, and Value Formation: A Test of the Postmaterialist Explanation for Value Change'. Ph.D. diss. (University of Minnesota).

Van Deth, W., and P.A.T.M. Geurts. 1989. 'Value Orientation, Left-Right Placement and Voting', *European Journal of Political Research* 17 (1): 17–34.

Weakliem, D.L. 1991. 'The Two Lefts? Occupation and Party Choice in France, Italy, and the Netherlands', *American Journal of Sociology* 96 (6): 1327–61.

Wohfeld, M.J., and N. Nevitte. 1990. 'Postindustrial Value Change and Support for Native Issues', *Canadian Ethnic Studies* 22 (3): 56–68.

Yanitsky, O. 1991. 'Environmental Movements: Some Conceptual Issues in East-West Comparisons', *International Journal of Urban and Regional Research* 15 (4): 524–41.

Zhu, J.H., and S. Rosen. 1993. 'From Discontent to Protest: Individual-Level Causes of the 1989 Pro-democracy Movement in China', *International Journal of Public Opinion Research* 5 (3): 234–49.

Chapter 3

Comparing Central Political Values in the Canadian and American Democracies

Edward G. Grabb and James E. Curtis

Introduction

More than three decades ago the noted sociologist and political scientist, Seymour Martin Lipset, began a series of interesting and influential analyses that sought to identify 'the value patterns of democracy' in the English-speaking nations, especially the United States and Canada (1990, 1986, 1985, 1968, 1963a, 1963b). While acknowledging the considerable similarities and affinities between these two countries, Lipset has consistently stressed that, for historical and related reasons, both the meaning of democratic values and the exercise of democratic principles in Canada and the United States have differed in important ways.

Among the most prominent national differences that Lipset has suggested is the tendency for Canada's version of democracy to be more 'statist' than its Southern counterpart; in particular, the Canadian system of government is said to encourage less self-reliance among its people, and more dependence on state programs to provide for the everyday needs of its citizens. In a related way, Lipset also argues that Canadians are more 'élitist' than Americans; in other words, Canadians are more accepting of government leadership and more respectful or deferential toward the political and other élites that have authority over them. Similarly, Lipset contends that Canadians are less 'individualistic' and more 'collectivistic' than Americans; that is, Canadians are said to place a

lower value on such ideas as individual freedom, especially in those instances where personal liberties conflict with the collective good. More generally, these and other differences have meant that Canada has been 'a country more conservative than the United States' (1963a: 521), less likely to embrace a belief in progress and change or to take a more liberal or forward-looking outlook on political and other issues.

The purpose of this paper is to review and assess Lipset's explanations for why and how Canadians and Americans are supposed to differ in their political values and beliefs about democracy. We consider a range of historical and contemporary research dealing with Lipset's argument, especially regarding Canadian and American attitudes about politics and government, law and order, and the role of the individual citizen in a democracy. We also present some new evidence on differences in attitudes and beliefs in the two countries, using cross-national survey data from 1990–1. Finally, we conclude with an overview of our current knowledge about differences in democratic values in the two societies.

The Historical Case

The early histories of Canada and the United States have some clear parallels, the most important of which is the central role played by Britain in the founding of the two countries. The British influence can be easily identified in such examples as the predominant use of the English language in both nations. However, the shared British heritage is also reflected in less obvious ways, including elements of British common law that are evident in the legal and political systems of the two nations (see Zelinsky 1988). One example is the right to trial by jury, which is a basic principle in both the Canadian and American judicial systems.

Nevertheless, some observers have argued that, over time, the two societies moved in divergent directions from their common British roots. One of the leading proponents of this perspective is Seymour Martin Lipset. Lipset begins with an analysis of the contrasts in the so-called formative events of Canadian and American history. In his view, the United States is essentially the product of *revolution*, created out of a democratic struggle against British domination that ultimately led to American independence in the late 1700s. In contrast, Canada (especially, English Canada) is seen as growing out of an opposite process, or *counterrevolution*, in which the population rejected the fundamental changes advocated by the revolutionaries, remained loyal to the British monarchy, and sought to conserve their established, British-style institutions, values, and way of life (see, especially, Lipset 1968).

One prominent event that Lipset uses to demonstrate the historical divergence between Canada and the United States is the migration of the so-called United Empire Loyalists out of the American colonies and into Canada, both during and after the American Revolution. Estimates indicate that between 60,000 and 100,000 people moved into parts of what are now the Maritimes, Ontario, and Quebec, a number far larger than the group of about 15,000 English colonists already living in those regions (Bell and Tepperman 1979: 45; Thompson and Randall 1994: 15). Lipset argues that this pool of new set-

tlers brought with them both a strong opposition to the goals of the American Revolution and a clear affirmation of their British heritage. As a result, it is suggested, the Loyalists provided the historical core of English-Canadian culture, embracing most of the same British values, customs, and practices that the United States of America had rejected.

Some observers dispute the importance of the Loyalist migration in shaping Canadian and American value differences, at least beyond that specific historical period. These writers suggest that, apart from the Loyalist leaders themselves, many of the migrants into Canada were not strongly tied to a pro-British or anti-American outlook. For example, a large number were simply pioneers seeking new land; some were religious or ethnic minorities, including about two thousand African-American freedmen or former slaves; and more than a few were probably fugitives, criminals, or adventurers (see, for example, Bell and Tepperman 1979: 52–4; Errington 1987: 4–5; also Jones 1985; MacKinnon 1986; Thompson and Randall 1994; Upton 1967).

Nevertheless, many writers agree that the American Revolution played a part in establishing certain initial distinctions between the two nations (Archibald 1978; Clark 1975; Crysdale and Beattie 1973; Forcese and Richer 1975; Horowitz 1966; Horowitz 1973; Porter 1967; Thompson and Randall 1994). At the same time, however, some researchers also question the argument that the impact of this single set of events could sustain itself far beyond the original formative period, across more than two centuries of subsequent history (Baer, Grabb, and Johnston 1990a: 709; Grabb and Curtis 1988: 129; see also Nevitte and Gibbins 1990: 3). Such critics contend that important historical events since the Revolution produced significant changes in both nations, and probably also affected the pattern of value differences between the two populations.

Lipset himself mentions very few postrevolutionary historical events in his analyses. One exception is the opening of the western regions of both countries during the nineteenth century. In particular, Lipset notes the significant role played in the Canadian West by the Mounted Police, whom he sees as symbols of British-style peace, order, and widespread respect for the law in the population. The Mounties can be contrasted with the individualistic, unruly, and frequently lawless image of the American cowboy (Lipset 1964: 183; 1963a: 521, also 1990: 174–5, 1994: 15; see also Atwood 1972; Curtis and Tepperman 1990: 46; Hagan and Leon 1977). Lipset believes that these symbols of the Canadian and American Wests reflect the core value differences that existed when our two nations began. Central among these differences is the more statist nature of Canadian society, especially the more pervasive influence of government and stronger emphasis on control by state leaders in Canada compared to the United States.

However, various observers suggest that there are many other important elements in the historical record that Lipset has not adequately considered. First of all, it is not possible to fit the history of Quebec or French Canada into an argument based on the role of the American Revolution (see Smith 1994; Thompson and Randall 1994). In fact, only recently has Lipset referred to French Canada in his comparison of national values (1985: 158–9; 1990: 13, 119), and nowhere does he show how the political culture of this society, which he sees as quite distinct from that of both English Canada and the United States, can be understood with reference to the Revolution. Second, Lipset's focus ignores most of the conflict and dissension that is evident in Canadian history, especially the cases of popular rejection of government authority or state control. Among the most prominent and violent illustrations of such dissent and disobedience are the revolts in Upper and Lower Canada in the 1830s, the Red River and Riel Rebellions in the 1870s and 1880s

(Thompson and Randall 1994), and various cases of labour and union strife, such as the Winnipeg General Strike in 1919 (for a review, see Russell 1993, 1990). Finally, Lipset's emphasis on the Revolution clearly overlooks crucial aspects of American history, as well. Perhaps the most important omission is the American Civil War, which, according to many writers, was actually more significant than the Revolution for shaping contemporary American society (Foote 1989: 138; Reed 1982: 167, 1983: 24, 54, 85; for some discussion see also Thompson and Randall 1994).

Despite these counterexamples and subsequent changes in both countries since the formative events of the 1700s, Lipset maintains that the original differences have continued right up to the present day. In his own words, once the Revolution and its counterrevolutionary reaction 'had formed the structure of the two nations, their institutional character was set' (1968: 61). Thus, 'the two countries differ in their basic organizing principles', so that, even now, Canada 'is more class-aware, élitist, law-abiding, statist, collectivity-oriented, and particularistic (group-oriented) than the United States' (Lipset 1990: 8; see also Lipset 1985: 156, 1986: 146).

One point that seems consistent with Lipset's argument, and that few analysts would question, concerns the differences in the Canadian and American systems of government. Although both countries ultimately evolved into democratic nation-states, Canada's system developed along lines that are generally similar to the British parliamentary model and distinct from the American republican form in some respects. Partly because of these structural or organizational differences, Lipset and others have suggested that Canada's version of democracy involves a weaker commitment to such 'liberal' ideas as the priority of individual rights above all others (Pocklington 1985: 63, 115, 131). A related view, again paralleling Lipset's position, is that Canada's democratic institutions have tended to encourage more deference to élite authority than their American counterparts (Merelman 1991: 26–7).

Even so, a key question that needs to be addressed is whether such differences in the historical development of our national political structures correspond to differences in the two peoples themselves. Does it follow that structural differences of this sort necessarily translate into differences in the values and beliefs of citizens in the two countries? Lipset's answer to this question seems clearly to be in the affirmative. He contends that a different conception of the relationship between government and the individual arose, not only in the political systems and government leadership structures of the two societies, but also in the minds of the Canadian and American populations. Thus, Lipset argues that Canadians in general, compared to Americans in general, are more collectivist and less individualist, as well as more élitist and less egalitarian, in their views of democratic rights. These supposed differences mean, among other things, that Canadians are more likely to support the rule of law and order, even at the risk of restricting their own personal freedoms, and also are more accepting of established government authority and control of their everyday lives by the state (1963a: 525–6; 1963b: 211). In contrast, Americans are seen as relatively distrustful of government power, especially when it limits individual freedom. Instead, Americans prefer fewer state restrictions over people's actions, even if that means a more disorderly and unlawful society (Lipset 1968: 44, 49; 1985: 142, 144, 1990: 10).

In summary, the historical evidence suggests that Canada and the United States did have distinct beginnings, stemming in part from the two countries' different relationships with Britain. It appears, as well, that the systems of democratic government are different in certain respects, and that the state has played a larger role in Canada than in the United States in much of our history. What is not clear, however, is whether these his-

torical and structural differences between the two nations also promoted and entrenched important differences in the values and outlooks of the two populations, especially in the present day. The best way to assess this question is to look at recent evidence of the values of Canadians and Americans.

Contemporary Research on National Value Differences

Studies of national differences in values in recent years have been based largely on analyses of evidence of behaviour rates or attitude surveys. Researchers in this area generally assume that the things people do, say, or think about major social issues probably provide the best measures of their core values and beliefs. Many of the behavioural indicators that have been used to compare the two countries deal, in one way or another, with the topic of democratic values. Three types of measures that Lipset has emphasized are educational attainment, criminal behaviour, and involvement in voluntary associations.

BEHAVIOUR DIFFERENCES
Educational Attainment
One difference between the two populations over the years is that Americans, on average, have attained higher levels of education than Canadians. Lipset has interpreted this difference as evidence of a more democratic view of schooling among Americans, reflecting their greater stress on individual achievement and equal opportunity for all citizens. By comparison, the lower attainment of Canadians has been seen as indicative of a more élitist or British view in Canada, where the state encourages higher education among only a select few (Lipset 1963a: 523–5, 1964).

One shortcoming of this argument is that average educational attainment, at best, is only an indirect measure of commitment to equal educational opportunity, at least among the mass of the population. Such a difference may be partly or largely the result of factors unrelated to value differences. For example, Americans generally enjoy higher incomes and living standards, so that American families, on average, probably have more money than Canadians to cover the costs involved in providing higher education for themselves and their children (see Curtis et al.: 1989a, 1989b). In addition, alternative evidence suggests a different conclusion about how education is valued in both nations. Canada spends a larger proportion of government funds on education than the United States, suggesting that Canadians may actually place a relatively higher priority on educational opportunity than do Americans (Beauchesne, 1995). Finally, recent data indicate in any event that there is little or no difference between Canadians and Americans in educational attainment in the present day. Looking at 1989 data for all adults aged 25 to 64, Statistics Canada reported that the proportions of Canadians and Americans with at least some postsecondary education were only marginally different, at 31 per cent for Canada and 36 per cent for the United States (Canadian Press 1993). Other recent data, from the U.S. Census Bureau's National Center for Education Statistics, suggest that the difference may even have reversed, with 40 per cent of Canadians now holding a 'college degree or more', compared to 36 per cent of Americans (Hull 1995: 49).

Crime and the Law

A second area where significant national differences have been found is in criminal activity and the workings of the legal system. Especially prior to the institution of the Canadian Charter of Rights in 1982, Canadian courts and Canadian law seemed to place greater emphasis on crime control and maintaining social order, whereas the American system put relatively more stress on ensuring the individual rights of those accused of crime (Hagan 1986, 1991; Hagan and Leon 1977). However, as Lipset himself has observed,

since the early 1980s the Canadian legal system has taken major steps to 'Americanize itself', with greater recognition of personal rights and freedoms and more restrictions on government power (1990: 225; see also Cross 1992; Machado 1991). Moreover, there is, once again, the question of whether structural differences, this time in the legal systems, are an accurate reflection of value differences between the two peoples themselves. There appear to be many examples of laws in both societies that run counter to the strong preferences of the popular majority. To take one illustration, opinion polls have shown consistently that most Canadians favour the death penalty for certain kinds of homicide (see Grabb and Curtis 1988; Pocklington 1985: 403), yet the death penalty was abolished in Canada in 1976 and seems unlikely to be reinstated by the government. It is possible, then, that the laws created by a society are not the best indicators for assessing the values of its citizens, though they may be relevant as indicators of the preferences of the society's élites (see also Baer, Grabb, and Johnston 1990a: 695).

Criminal behaviour itself, as opposed to the laws that define such behaviour, is perhaps a more appropriate index of a people's values. Certainly, Lipset takes this position. He notes that crime rates have been consistently higher in the United States than in Canada and believes this pattern is indicative of fundamental differences in the two peoples' beliefs about the roles of government and the individual in a democracy. The greater criminality in the United States is seen by Lipset as an indicator or a consequence of the higher value that Americans place on personal liberty and freedom from state control (Lipset 1963a: 528, 1963b, 1964).

There is no doubt that rates for many types of crime have been and continue to be higher in the United States. Although the differences between the two countries are smaller for less violent and serious crimes, the differences are large and generally have increased over time in the case of crimes such as murder, rape, and aggravated assault (Hagan 1989a: 363–4, 1994: 22–3; also Cross 1992: 304; *Maclean's* 1989: 51; Malcolm 1985: 79; United Nations 1993).

Even so, the use of criminal behaviour is problematic as a measure of individualism, at least as individualism is normally defined in democratic societies. It is true that a fundamental tenet of American democracy is the belief in the individual's right to 'life, liberty, and the pursuit of happiness'. However, it seems inconceivable that the people who enshrined this idea in the American Declaration of Independence meant it to be used as a licence for the individual to satisfy any personal want or desire, even to the point of committing crimes against, and ignoring the rights of, other citizens. On the contrary, a convincing argument can be made that higher levels of crime are actually symptomatic of a weaker commitment by the population to the principles of democratic individualism. The classical sociologist, Emile Durkheim, recognized this point when he distinguished between 'egoism', by which he meant the unrestrained pursuit of personal self-interest, and true 'individualism', which requires each of us to recognize other people's rights in the quest for personal goals (Durkheim [1893] 1964: 203; [1902] 1964: 3–6; see also Baer et al. 1995).

There is also the question of whether higher crime rates in the United States stem primarily from fundamental value differences or from other influences, most notably such structural and historical factors as the more intense racial strife and the larger contrast between rich and poor in American society (see Davies 1993; Goar 1995). Overall, then, the relevance of differences in criminality for measuring the commitment to democratic values in the two populations is not completely clear.

Voluntary Association Activity

People's involvements in voluntary associations have also been used by Lipset and others to mea-sure commitment to democratic values. This approach is based on the reasoning that one of the hallmarks of democracy is the active participation of citizens in organized groups, freely associating in the pursuit of both collective and individual goals (Pocklington 1985: 4, 374–6). Some writers have suggested that Americans lead all other people when it comes to joining voluntary associations. The United States, it is argued, is a 'nation of joiners' (Hausknecht 1962), 'the association-land par excellence' (Weber 1911: 53), a place where people 'constantly form associations' (Tocqueville [1835] 1954: 141). Lipset concurs with this argument, asserting that, compared to Canadians, 'Americans are more likely to take part in voluntary efforts to achieve particular goals' and are less 'disposed to rely on the state' for such purposes (1985: 141; also 1986: 135; 1989).

The literature on voluntary associations does show that a relatively large proportion of Americans belong to such organizations. However, there have been few cross-national comparative studies that assess whether Americans are unique in this regard. A close examination of the available comparative studies raises some doubts as to whether Americans join associations more than all other populations, including Canadians. The first such study used representative cross-national sample data from the 1960s. This research revealed that Canadians were actually the most likely of the six populations considered to belong to at least one association, although Americans ranked about the same as Canadians if union memberships were excluded, and when multiple rather than single memberships were compared (Curtis 1971: 874–5).

A more recent analysis, based on data from 1981–3, found that Americans ranked the highest among fifteen national samples when asked if they belonged to at least one voluntary association (Curtis, Grabb, and Baer 1992; see also Grabb and Curtis 1992). However, this top ranking was largely due to the very high level of church or religious membership among Americans; with religious affiliations excluded, Canada and several other countries ranked as high as or higher than the United States (see also Curtis et al. 1989a; 1989b).

Another finding in this study was that Americans were more likely than other respondents to be members of associations but to take no active role in working for the organizations. In analyses that included only active memberships, Canadians and several other samples had higher levels of association involvement than the Americans (Curtis, Grabb, and Baer 1992: 146). In other words, then, to the extent that voluntary association membership is supposed to reflect a democratic emphasis on active participation in community organizations or institutions, the evidence fails to show that Americans surpass Canadians in their commitment to democratic values. This conclusion is especially appropriate when comparing Americans with English Canadians, as Lipset typically has done, because French Canadians are less involved in voluntary associations than either Americans or English Canadians (Curtis et al. 1989a; 1989b; Grabb and Curtis 1992).

PREVIOUS RESEARCH ON ATTITUDES AND BELIEFS

There is a growing body of research on the attitudes and beliefs of Canadians and Americans, although not all this work relies on representative national samples and only some of it deals with issues that pertain directly to the comparison of democratic values. Below we summarize some of the most recent and relevant examples of research based on national-level data.

Recall that, according to Lipset's interpretation, the American view of democracy involves greater support for individual rights and freedoms, as well as a greater opposition to élite authority and state control, than does the Canadian view. If this claim is true, we might

expect to find, for example, that, compared to Canadians, Americans are more in favour of equal opportunity for women, are less in favour of an authoritarian family structure, are less in favour of increased government spending on social services, and are less trusting of government power. In fact, though, research from the 1980s shows the opposite findings on each of these issues (Baer, Grabb, and Johnston 1990a, 1990b).

Given Lipset's thesis, especially his suggestion that Americans are less deferential to authority, we might also expect that, compared to Canadians, Americans should be more suspicious of situations where government leaders or other groups have power over them, and should be more willing to engage in acts of civil dissent or disobedience to oppose such situations. Once again, however, research based on the World Values Survey, a cross-national study from the early 1980s, indicates that Americans are significantly more likely than English or French Canadians to respect established authority, both as a general principle and in specific situations, such as in parent-child and employer-employee relationships (Baer et al. 1995). The latter analysis also shows that Americans are more likely than English or French Canadians to be highly confident in their government institutions (e.g., Parliament or Congress, the civil service, and the armed forces), although Canadians tend to show more confidence in the legal system and the police, and there are no differences in confidence concerning the education system. As for the exercise of civil dissent and disobedience, evidence in this study shows consistently that Canadians (especially English Canadians) are more willing to engage in such acts as signing petitions, joining boycotts, attending lawful demonstrations, and even occupying buildings for protest purposes. Thus, there is virtually no support in these analyses for the assumption that Canadians have more docile or passive attitudes about government power or authority in general than do Americans. A review of similar findings using more recent survey research led one analyst to conclude that, contrary to popular belief, it is Canadians and not Americans who 'are more likely to question, if not reject, traditional institutional authority, be it religious or secular' (Adams 1995).

A final illustration to consider concerns child-rearing values. Another study that was conducted using the 1981–3 World Values Survey looked at a checklist of qualities that people might believe are especially important for children to be taught at home. Some of these qualities are consistent with values that would typically be associated with a democratic value system: honesty, leadership, unselfishness, determination or perseverance, imagination, tolerance or respect for other people, independence, hard work, and a feeling of responsibility. An analysis of these data shows some differences between Americans and Canadians, but the patterns are mixed and virtually all of the differences are minor (Baer et al. 1995). Americans are slightly more likely than English Canadians to choose honesty and leadership as important, while English Canadians are somewhat more likely than Americans to choose unselfishness, determination, and imagination. There are no significant differences between the two groups in their ratings of tolerance, independence, hard work, or responsibility. The results vary somewhat when comparing French Canadians to Americans, but again the differences are small and inconsistent.

To summarize, then, the review of findings from a range of previous studies of beliefs and attitudes shows no basis for contending that Americans hold more strongly to democratic values than do Canadians. The results typically suggest only small differences and, where notable differences do occur, they tend to run counter to the patterns suggested by Lipset's thesis.

SOME NEW EVIDENCE ON ATTITUDES AND BELIEFS

Some recent data are now available that allow us to conduct additional comparisons of attitudes and beliefs in the two countries. A second version of the World Values Survey, conducted in 1990–1, provides data on a variety of issues that pertain to the question of democratic values.

In some cases, the 1990–1 survey repeats questions that appeared in the original survey for the early 1980s, thereby permitting some comparisons over time. Among the repeated questions are sets of items that deal with civil dissent and with childrearing values, although the list of items in each case has been reduced somewhat from the original survey.

Table 3.1 compares the responses of Americans, English Canadians, and French Canadians on these repeated questions. As with the findings reported earlier from the original World Values data, we see again that Americans are no more likely than English or French Canadians to indicate that they have engaged, or might engage, in various types of civil dissent or disobedience. In fact, tests of significance show that there are no differences among the three groups on signing petitions and on joining unofficial strikes; in the case of joining boycotts, attending lawful demonstrations, or occupying buildings, Americans are less likely than one or both of the Canadian groups to support such forms of protest.

The findings on the child value items shown in Table 3.1 are also generally consistent with the results from the original World Values data. Once more the differences in attitudes across the three groups tend to be few, mixed, and generally small. Americans are the most likely of all three groups to mention some of the qualities we might associate with a democratic value system, most notably hard work. At the same time, however, Americans and English Canadians are not significantly different from each other when it comes to preferring such values as independence, a feeling of responsibility, and determination or perseverance. Moreover, Americans are less likely than both of the Canadian groups to stress unselfishness and tolerance or respect for other people as important values for

Table 3.1   Attitudes about Civil Dissent and Preferred Qualities in Children for English Canadians (EC), French Canadians (FC), and Americans (US): National Survey Data, 1990–1.

(N) =	EC (1327–1332)	FC (378)	US (1831–1839)	Significance Tests		
				EC/US	FC/US	EC/FC
I. Civil Dissent						
% saying they 'have done' or 'might do' the following:						
1. sign a petition	90	92	90	-	-	-
2. join in boycotts	65	60	61	*	-	-
3. attend lawful demonstrations	61	67	57	*	*	*
4. join unofficial strikes	32	33	33	-	-	-
5. occupy buildings	20	32	18	-	*	*
II. Qualities in Children						
% mentioning:						
1. independence	49	25	52	-	*	*
2. hard work	33	41	49	*	*	*
3. feeling of responsibility	72	87	72	-	*	*
4. imagination	26	15	26	-	*	*
5. tolerance, respect for others	81	79	72	*	*	-
6. determination, perseverance	34	51	35	-	*	*
7. unselfishness	42	42	37	*	*	-
8. good manners	78	64	77	-	*	*
9. thrift	18	31	29	*	-	*
10. obedience	30	23	38	*	*	*
11. religious faith	30	29	55	*	*	-

*indicates the two groups are significantly different, p < .05.

NOTE: Ns vary somewhat due to different numbers of missing cases for some items.

children. Also interesting are the results for the items dealing with obedience and religious faith. These two values could be said to reflect deference and collectivism rather than individualism, and yet it is Americans rather than Canadians who are the most likely to mention them as preferred qualities in children. In general, then, these repeated items do not support the view that Americans place a higher priority than Canadians on individualism and related democratic principles.

Table 3.2 presents other data from the 1990–1 World Values Survey. The items in this table deal with a diverse array of other attitudes and beliefs that are relevant for assessing democratic values.

The first set of items in Table 3.2 concerns beliefs about the relationship between the individual and government. As discussed earlier, Lipset's thesis leads to the expectation that Canadians will be more accepting or trusting than Americans about the activities of the state. However, we find

Table 3.2   Attitudes about the Individual and Government, Jobs, and Change for English Canadians (EC), French Canadians (FC), and Americans (US): National Survey Data, 1990–1.

(N) =	EC (1272–1311)	FC (379–395)	US (1778–1811)	Significance Tests EC/US	FC/US	EC/FC
I. The Individual and Government						
% agreeing 'completely' or 'somewhat' that:						
1. our government should be made much more open to the public	91	91	83	*	*	–
2. if an unjust law were passed by the government I could do nothing about it.	37	49	30	*	*	*
II. Job Opportunities						
% agreeing that:						
1. when jobs are scarce, men have more right to a job than women	17	24	24	*	–	*
2. when jobs are scarce, people should be forced to retire early	26	48	16	*	*	*
3. when jobs are scarce, employers should give priority to (American/Canadian) people over immigrants	50	62	52	–	*	*
4. it is unfair to give work to handicapped people when able-bodied people can't find jobs.	7	11	10	*	–	*
III. Attitudes about Change						
Average score on a 10-point scale of support for:						
1. being 'cautious' about major changes in life (=1) versus acting 'boldly' to achieve (=10)	5.32	4.37	5.12	–	*	*
2. ideas that have 'stood the test of time' (=1) versus 'new ideas' (=10).	5.33	5.23	4.83	*	*	–
3. the belief that changes in life may cause 'difficulties' (=1) versus the belief that changes are 'welcome' as a new 'beginning' (=10)	6.49	6.42	5.91	*	*	–

* indicates the two groups are significantly different, $p < .05$.

NOTE: Ns vary somewhat due to different numbers of missing cases for some items.

instead that both English and French Canadians are more likely than Americans to believe that government should be more open to public scrutiny than it is, and also are more likely to believe that the individual can do nothing if the government passes an unjust law. Note, as well, that these results are consistent with earlier research reviewed above, in which Canadians were also found to be more suspicious of government than were Americans (Baer, Grabb, and Johnston 1990a).

The second set of items in Table 3.2 assesses people's attitudes about the rights of women, older people, immigrants, and the handicapped to have jobs 'when jobs are scarce'. We might assume from Lipset's thesis that, because Americans are said to be less élitist and more individualist than Canadians, Americans should be more likely than Canadians to emphasize equal employment opportunities for all people, even during hard times. However, there is little or no evidence that this is the case. Only a minority of respondents in all three groups agree that men have more right to a job than women in times of scarcity, but it is Americans (along with French Canadians) who are most likely to take this view, with English Canadians least likely to agree. Similarly, English Canadians are the least likely to think it is unfair for the handicapped to get jobs when the 'able-bodied' cannot find work, although very few people in any of the three groups agree with this statement. On the question of whether national citizens should get priority over immigrants in the job market, again it is English Canadians who voice the lowest level of agreement, with Americans about the same as the English in their level of agreement and French Canadians the most likely to accept job discrimination against immigrants. It is only on the question of forced retirement for older workers that Americans show a clear tendency to favour individual rights more than Canadians: only 16 per cent of Americans support forced retirement when jobs are scarce, compared to about one-

quarter of the English Canadians and almost one-half of the French-Canadian respondents.

The final three items in Table 3.2 deal with people's views on life changes of different kinds. They ask respondents to place themselves on 10-point scales between contrasting statements about their 'outlook on life'. First, is it better to be 'cautious about making major changes in life', or is it true that 'you will never achieve much unless you act boldly'? Second, are the best ideas those 'that have stood the test of time', or is it the case that 'new ideas are generally better than old ones'? Finally, when life changes occur, do they lead a person to 'worry about the difficulties they may cause', or should they be welcomed because of 'the possibility that something new is beginning'? Given Lipset's argument that Canadians are more conservative and less progressive in outlook than Americans, we would expect Americans to be the most likely to see change as desirable. However, while the differences are small, in all three cases, it is English Canadians who rank highest in support for change. Americans are not significantly different from English Canadians on the first item, dealing with 'caution' versus 'bold' action, but on the other two scales, the differences are statistically significant. On the latter two scales, the Americans rank lowest of all three groups in support for change, with French Canadians falling between the English Canadians and Americans.

In summary, then, the data in Table 3.2 lend virtually no support to Lipset's argument that Americans are more democratic or individualist in their values and beliefs than are Canadians. Contrary to Lipset's thesis, these results suggest that it is Americans who are more trusting of existing arrangements between the individual citizen and government. In addition, Americans, especially in contrast to English Canadians, tend to be somewhat less supportive of equal job opportunities for women and other disadvantaged groups, and also tend to have less favourable views about change.

Conclusions

We have now reviewed Lipset's thesis on Canadian-American differences in democratic values, and have assessed some of the major historical and contemporary studies of this topic. While there is much more to this subject than can be considered in one book chapter, we have been able to show how Canadians and Americans, both past and present, behave and think regarding various issues relevant to Lipset's thesis. In this concluding section, we summarize the main findings and offer some additional observations and speculations about the two nations and their peoples.

One important point to emphasize at the outset is that, although there are some notable differences between Canadians and Americans, we should be careful not to exaggerate or overstate them. This point is underscored by the generally small national differences in behaviours and beliefs we have found in most of the evidence reviewed here. Thus, despite the extensive literature that seeks to describe and explain the distinctions between the two peoples, we should not lose sight of their many striking and enduring similarities. As a number of analysts have indicated, including Lipset himself (1986: 114), there are probably no two countries or peoples in the world that have more in common. These similarities clearly extend to the two peoples' commitment to democratic values and beliefs.

Both nations, after all, are organized around similar principles of individual freedom and civil liberty, tempered by the rule of law. Both societies emphasize universal citizenship rights, which are enshrined in formal constitutions and protected by elaborate judicial systems, regular elections, and other mechanisms for restricting potential abuses of power by government. In both countries, educational opportunities are relatively extensive, enabling each population to achieve similarly high amounts of both educational attainment and material affluence. Finally, in both nations there is considerable freedom to associate with other citizens, as evidenced by the comparatively high levels of membership in voluntary organizations among both peoples. In short, then, both countries provide good examples of how democratic values have come to be embodied in contemporary societies.

We have also found that there are many similarities in the expressed attitudes and beliefs of Canadians and Americans, on issues ranging from preferred qualities in children, to beliefs about equal rights for disadvantaged groups, to attitudes about change. Where there have been differences in beliefs and opinions, they have been minor, for the most part, and often are in the opposite direction of what would be expected from Lipset's thesis. These kinds of results cast doubt on Lipset's arguments about Canadian and American differences, at least for describing the contemporary situation.

Many of the differences between Canada and the United States that we have discussed seem to involve variations on the same basic principles or characteristics (Bothwell 1992; Granatstein and Hillmer 1990; Gwyn 1985; Stuart 1992). Consider the issue of 'statism' or state power in both societies. As our review suggests, Lipset is probably correct to argue that the state has played a larger role in Canada than in the United States; this seems especially true in such areas as the provision of health care and social services to the population. In turn, the larger state role may have fostered a somewhat greater dependence on government by Canadians historically. At the same time, however, the government's activities in shaping and directing American society should not be underestimated, especially in the present day. Clearly, the government of the United States has become one of the most massive and complex in modern times, with a significant influence on the everyday lives of its citizens. The American system of government has also tended to become increasingly centralized in recent decades, particularly in comparison to the Canadian model, which is more diverse and regionally based than in the past (Baer, Grabb, and Johnston 1990a: 696; see Lipset 1985: 151–7). These patterns of change suggest that differences in statism within the two nations may now be relatively minor.

Crime is another area where Lipset has correctly pointed to differences between the countries. Based on the research we have reviewed, there is no doubt that serious crimes, especially violent offences, are less prevalent in Canada than in the United States. Nevertheless, here, too, some cautionary remarks are in order before deciding what this difference tells us about comparative values in the two societies. First of all, we should remember that the vast majority of citizens in both countries are basically law-abiding, so that the differences in crime are attributable to relatively small numbers of people in each population. Second, Lipset has contended that the lower crime rates in Canada reflect greater 'élitism' or acceptance of government control among Canadians; yet, as we have seen, there is no independent evidence of the latter two differences. In fact, the opposite pattern may well be the case, since Canadians express less trust in their politicians than Americans and also are more likely to support or engage in various forms of protest or civil dissent. Hence, although Canadians experience less crime than Americans, this does not mean that Americans are generally less respectful of the law, nor does it show that Canadians are more docile or deferential in the face of government power.

Recent events in Canadian history, such as the massive rejection of the Charlottetown Accord or the rise of the Alliance Party and other alternatives to the old-line political parties, serve to illustrate the considerable ambivalence felt by many Canadians toward established leaders and their policies. The negative reactions of many contemporary Canadians to government power raise doubts, as well, that there is some automatic correspondence between the values of Canada's leaders and the values of the Canadian people as a whole (see also Grabb 1994).

Current events in the United States indicate that some Americans also harbour distrust, disrespect, and, in a few cases, outright hatred for their government leaders. The most graphic illustration of the latter in recent years is the April 1995 bombing of US government offices in Oklahoma City, apparently by right-wing terrorists. The history of presidential assassinations in the United States also shows the unbridled enmity that sometimes confronts American politicians.

Lipset is among those writers who believe that, because cases of political violence are more common in the United States than in Canada, they provide proof that Americans have less regard for government or the law than do Canadians (Lipset 1990: 96). Again, however, it is important to recall that these incidents are quite rare, even in American society. In other words, such events, while alarming and horrific, are far too infrequent to demonstrate that Americans, in general, dislike their politicians or their form of government more than Canadians. It is probable, instead, that these episodes are rooted in the *extremism of a small minority* of Americans who, in cases of antagonism toward the government, are more willing than their Canadian counterparts to resort to outrageous acts against the state or its leaders. A similar interpretation might account for the higher levels of serious or violent crime in the United States noted earlier. That is, given that most people in both nations do not commit crimes, the higher American rates say more about the extreme tendencies of a narrow segment of the American population than they do about differences between Americans and Canadians as a whole.

Nonetheless, having argued that extremist behaviour in the United States originates with a relatively small number of citizens, it is difficult to deny that, in some ways, the United States is indeed a nation of more extremes and contrasts than is Canada. The historical fact of American slavery, for example, has contributed to problems of racial strife and injustice that are far more deep-seated than has ever been the case in Canada. Structurally, as well, the United States is a place of stark contrasts, where immense wealth lives alongside miserable poverty and where world-renowned universities co-exist beside ghetto schools and rampant illiteracy. By comparison, Canada is a society in which such differences, though present, are probably less pronounced. Most evidence indicates that the gap between the rich and poor in Canada is not as large as it is in the United States. Moreover, while Canada's educational institutions may lack the international reputation of the best American schools, Canadian schools rarely resemble the worst of American education either, occupying instead a solid middle ground in terms of both eminence and quality.

These and other contrasts make for interesting discussion and debate about Canada and the United States. We could also discuss the higher degree of religiosity that seems to exist in the United States, as well as the more overt and demonstrative national pride exhibited by Americans (Bibby 1987, 1994; Zelinsky 1988). In the end, however, it is arguable that the areas of convergence and common ground shared by the two societies are at least as notable. The long-standing economic and political linkages between Canada and the United States have helped to renew and reinforce these connections over time. Perhaps the most important force to promote similarity in the values of the two peoples is the pervasive influence of American culture in Canada. The impact of American tastes, outlooks, attitudes, and fashions is apparent in all of the popular media of communication, in television, films, music, books, magazines, and so on. As the noted British intellectual, Malcolm Muggeridge, once argued, 'a kind of cultural consensus has come to pass in the world, essentially American

in all its manifestations' (Muggeridge 1979). He went on to suggest that, for obvious reasons of geography, history, and language, Canadians are more susceptible to the American cultural influence than any other people. Possibly for this reason, some recent research has found that the Canadian-American border is not an important cultural dividing line, and that divisions within each nation may actually be more significant (Baer, Grabb, and Johnston 1993; Garreau 1981; Kahle 1986; Muller 1989).

The possibility that there may be more important differences within both countries than between them leads us to a final key issue: the distinctiveness of French Canada when drawing any comparisons of Canada and the United States. As some of the research reviewed in this chapter has shown, French Canadians often have rather different outlooks and behaviours than either English Canadians or Americans. While most differences are small, in some cases the gaps are significant. For example, we noted earlier that French Canadians have consistently been the least likely of the three groups to join voluntary associations.

Another difference that deserves comment concerns attitudes about immigrants and minorities. Some of the data we have presented in this chapter suggest that French Canadians are more likely than others to favour restricting the employment opportunities of immigrants when jobs are scarce. This finding is consistent with other research, over recent decades, that indicates somewhat more ethnocentrism, and even anti-Semitism, in French Canada than in the rest of the country (Brym and Lenton 1991; Lambert and Curtis 1982, 1983, 1984; Sniderman et al. 1992; see also Richler 1992). Such a pattern is puzzling in light of further evidence presented here and elsewhere showing that French Canadians are among the most likely to believe in equal rights and opportunities for many disadvantaged groups, especially women (see also Baer, Grabb, and Johnston 1990a). Why, then, would French

Canadians be more willing than other people to limit the rights of immigrants and minorities?

This outcome may result from the combined impact of the strong identity that French Canadians have with Quebec and the fear among some Quebeckers that their society could disappear as a distinct French 'nation', if the non-French population is allowed to flourish without restriction (see Grabb 1994). Quebec's limitations on the language and education rights of its English-speaking population, including the well-known Bill 178 outlawing English signs, illustrate how universal democratic principles can be undermined by such fears. In addition to restricting English rights, a few French Quebeckers have also argued that the descendants of the so-called *ancienne souche* (old branch) of French settlers, who arrived before the British conquest of Quebec in 1759, should be endowed with special rights and considerations denied to all others. Presumably these special rights are seen by some as a means to conserve the future of French Quebec and to make up for past injustices under English domination (see Richler 1992: 13, 103). Whatever the reasons behind such policies, they show that the concept of democracy has a different meaning for some French Canadians than for the majority of the Canadian population. The same is true for other groups, in both Canada and the United States, who define themselves as historically disadvantaged. In both countries, for example, organizations representing women, visible minorities, homosexuals, and the disabled have sought special considerations in recent years, in order to make up for the inequities of the past.

The question is whether, in the interests of trying to redress the genuine grievances of particular groups, some citizens should be granted rights and reparations that go beyond or override the rights of other citizens. Some people say yes to this question, in the interests of compensating for previous inequities; others, however, see this as a hazardous course to pursue, because of its potential for weakening the belief in equal treatment under the law, which has been fundamental to the democratic value system. If the argument for special rights is formally established and pervasively applied, then the traditional meaning of democracy could be radically altered, or lost. Ironically, perhaps, these pressures on the democratic system arise from another central tenet of democracy, which is that all citizens are free to lobby both the law courts and the lawmakers in the full pursuit of their own goals or interests.

Note

We gratefully acknowledge that our data source was made available by Ronald Inglehart and Neil Nevitte through the Inter-university Consortium for Political and Social Research. We also thank the Donner Canadian Foundation for their contributions to making the data available. Neither the original investigators nor the disseminating archive bear any responsibility for the analyses presented here.

References

Adams, M. 1995. 'Moralistic them, humanistic us'. *Globe and Mail*, 29 February.

Archibald, W.P. 1978. *Social Psychology as Political Economy* (Toronto: McGraw-Hill Ryerson).

Atwood, M. 1972. *Survival: A Thematic Guide to Canadian Literature* (Toronto: Anansi).

Baer, D., J. Curtis, E. Grabb, and W. Johnston. 1994. 'Respect for Authority in Australia, Canada, Great

Britain, and the United States'. *Sociological Focus* 28 (2): 177–95.

———. *North America Without Borders? Integrating Canada, the United States, and Mexico* (Calgary: University of Calgary Press), 303–6.

Crysdale, S., and C. Beattie. 1973. *Sociology Canada: An Introductory Text* (Toronto: Butterworths).

Curtis, J. 1971. 'Voluntary Association Joining: A Cross-national Comparative Note', *American Sociological Review* 36: 872–80.

———, E. Grabb, and D. Baer. 1992. 'Voluntary Association Membership in Fifteen Countries: A Comparative Analysis', *American Sociological Review* 57: 139–52.

Curtis, J., R. Lambert, S. Brown, and B. Kay. 1989a. 'Affiliating with Voluntary Associations: Canadian-American Comparisons', *Canadian Journal of Sociology* 14 (2): 143–62.

———. 1989b. 'On Lipset's Measure of Voluntary Association Differences between Canada and the United States'. *Canadian Journal of Sociology* 14 (3): 383–9.

Curtis, J., and L. Tepperman (eds). 1990. *Images of Canada: The Sociological Tradition* (Scarborough: Prentice-Hall).

Davies, J. 1993. 'The Distribution of Wealth and Economic Inequality'. In J. Curtis, E. Grabb, and N. Guppy (eds), *Social Inequality in Canada: Patterns, Problems, Policies* (Scarborough: Prentice-Hall).

Durkheim, E. [1893] 1964. *The Division of Labor in Society* (1st edn). (New York: The Free Press).

———. [1902] 1964. *The Division of Labor in Society. Preface to the Second Edition* (New York: The Free Press).

Errington, J. 1987. *The Lion, the Eagle, and Upper Canada* (Montreal and Kingston: McGill-Queen's University Press).

Foote, S. 1989. *Conversations with Shelby Foote* (ed. W.C. Carter) (Jackson, MI: University Press of Mississippi).

Forcese, D., and S. Richer (eds). 1975. *Issues in Canadian Society* (Scarborough: Prentice-Hall).

Garreau, J. 1981. *The Nine Nations of North America* (Boston: Houghton Mifflin).

Goar, C. 1995. 'Unequal Shares of the American Dream', *Toronto Star*, 14 May, F5.

Grabb, E. 1994. 'Democratic Values in Canada and the United States: Some Observations and Evidence from Past and Present'. In J. Dermer (ed.), *The Canadian Profile: People, Institutions, Infrastructure* (Toronto: Captus Press), 113–39.

Grabb, E., and J. Curtis. 1988. 'English Canadian-American Differences in Orientation Toward Social Control and Individual Rights', *Sociological Focus* 21 (2): 127–40.

———. 1992. 'Voluntary Association Activity in English Canada, French Canada, and the United States: A Multivariate Analysis'. *Canadian Journal of Sociology* 17 (4): 371–88.

Granatstein, J.L., and N. Hillmer. 1990. *For Better or Worse: Canada and the United States to the 1990s* (Toronto: Copp Clark Pitman).

Gwyn, R. 1985. *The 49th Paradox: Canada in North America* (Toronto: McClelland & Stewart).

Hagan, J. 1986. 'Crime and Deviance'. In R. Hagedorn (ed.), *Sociology* (3rd edn). (Toronto: Holt, Rinehart and Winston of Canada), 165–98.

———. 1989a. 'Comparing Crime and Criminalization in Canada and the U.S.A.', *Canadian Journal of Sociology* 14 (3): 361–71.

———. 1989b. 'Enduring Differences: Further Notes on Homicide in Canada and the U.S.A.', *Canadian Journal of Sociology* 14 (4): 490–1.

———. 1991. *The Disreputable Displeasures: Crime and Deviance in Canada* (Toronto: McGraw-Hill Ryerson).

———. 1994. *Crime and Disrepute* (Thousand Oaks, CA: Pine Forge Press).

———, and J. Leon. 1977. 'Philosophy and Sociology of Crime Control: Canadian-American Comparisons', *Sociological Inquiry* 47: 181–208.

Hausknecht, M. 1962. *The Joiners* (New York: Bedminster Press).

Horowitz, G. 1966. 'Conservatism, Liberalism, and Socialism in Canada: An Interpretation', *Canadian Journal of Economic and Political Science* 32: 143–71.

Horowitz, I.L. 1973. 'The Hemispheric Connection: A

Critique and Corrective to the Entrepreneurial Thesis of Development with Special Emphasis on the Canadian Case', *Queen's Quarterly* 80: 327–59.

Hull, J.D. 1995. 'The State of the Union', *Time* 145, 5 (February 6): 42–53.

Jones, E. 1985. 'The Loyalists and Canadian History', *Journal of Canadian Studies* 20 (3): 149–56.

Kahle, L.R. 1986. 'The Nine Nations of North America and the Value Basis of Geographic Segmentation', *Journal of Marketing* 50: 37–47.

Lambert, R.D., and J.E. Curtis. 1982. 'The French- and English-Canadian Language Communities and Multicultural Attitudes', *Canadian Ethnic Studies* 14 (2): 43–58.

———. 1983. 'Opposition to Multiculturalism among Québécois and English-Canadians', *Canadian Review of Sociology and Anthropology* 20 (2): 193–207.

———. 1984. 'Québécois and English-Canadian Opposition to Racial and Religious Intermarriage, 1968–1983', *Canadian Ethnic Studies* 16 (2): 30–46.

Lipset, S.M. 1963a. 'The Value Patterns of Democracy', *American Sociological Review* 28: 515–31.

———. 1963b. *The First New Nation* (New York: Basic Books).

———. 1964. 'Canada and the United States: A Comparative View', *Canadian Review of Sociology and Anthropology* 1: 173–85.

———. 1968. *Revolution and Counterrevolution* (New York: Basic Books).

———. 1985. 'Canada and the United States: The Cultural Dimension'. In C.F. Doran and J.H. Sigler (eds), *Canada and the United States*. (Englewood Cliffs, NJ: Prentice-Hall) 109–60.

———. 1986. 'Historical Conditions and National Characteristics', *Canadian Journal of Sociology* 11 (2): 113–55.

———. 1989. 'Voluntary Activities: More Canadian-American Comparisons—a reply', *Canadian Journal of Sociology* 14 (3): 377–82.

———. 1990. *Continental Divide* (New York: Routledge).

———. 1994. 'The Social Requisites of Democracy

Revisited'. *American Sociological Review* 59 (1): 1–22.

Machado, P. 1991. 'A Comparative Analysis of the Exclusion of Illegally Obtained Evidence in American and Canadian Criminal Law', paper presented at the Facing North/Facing South Conference, University of Calgary, Calgary, Alberta, May.

MacKinnon, N. 1986. *This Unfriendly Soil: The Loyalist Experience in Nova Scotia* (Montreal and Kingston: McGill-Queen's University Press).

Maclean's. 1989. 'A North-South Dialogue', 3 July.

Malcolm, A. 1985. *The Canadians* (Markham: Fitzhenry and Whiteside).

Merelman, R. 1991. *Partial Visions* (Madison: University of Wisconsin Press).

Muggeridge, M. 1979. 'The Land That Time Forgot', *The Canadian Magazine* October/November: 2–7.

Muller, T. 1989. 'The Two Nations of Canada vs. the Nine Nations of North America: A Cross-cultural Analysis of Consumers' Personal Values', *Journal of International Consumer Marketing* 1 (4): 57–79.

Nevitte, N., and R. Gibbins. 1990. *New Elites in Old States* (Toronto: Oxford University Press).

Pocklington, T.C. 1985. *Liberal Democracy in Canada and the United States* (Toronto: Holt, Rinehart and Winston of Canada).

Porter, J. 1967. 'Canadian Character in the Twentieth Century', *Annals of the American Academy of Political and Social Science* 370: 48–56.

Reed, J.S. 1982. *One South: An Ethnic Approach to Regional Culture* (Baton Rouge: Louisiana State University Press).

———. 1983. *Southerners: The Social Psychology of Sectionalism* (Chapel Hill: University of North Carolina Press).

Richler, M. 1992. *Oh Canada! Oh Quebec! Requiem for a Divided Country* (Toronto: Penguin).

Russell, B. 1990. *Back to Work? Labour, State, and Industrial Relations in Canada* (Toronto: Nelson).

———. 1993. 'Working Class Resistance and Collective Action'. In J. Curtis, E. Grabb, and N. Guppy (eds), *Social Inequality in Canada: Patterns,*

Problems, Policies (2nd edn) (Scarborough: Prentice-Hall).

Smith, A. 1994. *Canada: An American Nation?* (Montreal and Kingston: McGill-Queen's University Press).

Sniderman, P., D. Northrup, J. Fletcher, P. Russell, and P. Tetlock. 1992. 'Working Paper on Anti-Semitism in Quebec' (Institute for Social Research, York University).

Stuart, R. 1992. 'Almost Americans', paper presented at the Canadian Sociology and Anthropology Association meetings, Charlottetown, June.

Thompson, J.H., and S. J. Randall. 1994. *Canada and the United States: Ambivalent Allies.* (Montreal and Kingston: McGill-Queen's University Press).

Tocqueville, A. de. [1835] 1954. *Democracy in America.* (New York: Knopf).

United Nations. 1993. *Human Development Report* (New York: Oxford Press).

Upton, L.F.S. (ed.). 1967. *The United Empire Loyalists: Men and Myths* (Toronto: Copp Clark).

Weber, M. 1911. 'Deutscher Sociologentag' (German sociology today), *Verhandlungen* 1: 39–62.

World Values Study Group. 1994. WORLD VALUES SURVEY, 1981–1984 AND 1990–1993 Computer file. ICPSR version. Ann Arbor, MI: Institute for Social Research producer, 1994. Ann Arbor, MI: Inter-university Consortium for Political and Social Research distributor, 1994.

Zelinsky, W. 1988. 'A Sidelong Glance at Canadian Nationalism and Its Symbols', *North American Culture* 4 (1): 2–27.

Chapter 4

Political Ideology

Douglas Baer

Introduction

The definition of ideology, and the question of whether ideology is important in contemporary society, is highly contested in political sociology. Ideology is the study of beliefs and values that organize the way people think about politics. The study of ideology probably originated with the French philosopher de Tracy, who proposed a new science of ideas that would be like physical science and would produce a 'rational investigation of ideas, free from religious or metaphysical prejudice' (Giddens 1979: 163; McLellan 1995: 5; Rosen 1996: 170). De Tracy's conceptualization was positive—ideology was a good thing—but the concept quickly became used negatively as will be discussed below.[1]

What is an *ideology*? The 'grand narratives'[2] stemming from the rivalry between the Soviet Union and the United States between the end of the Second World War to the early 1990s—*capitalism* versus *socialism*—manifest the struggle between the two major ideologies of the twentieth century.[3] In this sense, the competing ideologies are views of the world as it exists and of how it *ought* to exist. As Adams (1993: 4–5) notes, any ideology will have a conception of an ideal society—that is, the 'morally best kind of society for human beings to live in'. For instance, socialism supports a conception of a utopian society. It usually entails a set of beliefs about human nature—for example, the idea that people are inherently

cooperative—and a set of beliefs about what types of (socialist) institutions are possible. Conversely, support for capitalism usually entails a belief that people are inherently greedy and competitive and it incorporates a utopian vision of society in which state involvement in the economy is minimized. Sometimes, models of history are incorporated within these world views. For example, for some Marxists, socialism is seen as an *inevitable* outcome in history, just as for some supporters of capitalism liberal democratic capitalism is seen as the *end of history* (Fukuyama 1992). How society is to view *social inequality* plays a prominent role in any ideology. Thus, socialism is said to place a high value on absolute social equality. Support for capitalism is said to tolerate or even support social inequality with certain qualifications; that is, inequality is acceptable as long as everyone is given an equal chance to succeed, as long as there is *equality of opportunity*.

For a few social scientists, then, ideology can be reduced to the duality of capitalism versus socialism. Even here, though, there are variants of each. Socialism for some includes models that posit a strong democratic socialist state, but others see a 'withering away of the state' under socialism. Likewise, support for capitalism might include an élitist conception of how the society should be governed or one in which formal democracy plays an important role.

As Adams (1993) points out, until recently, most of the usage of the term *ideology* has been in a negative sense.[4] Thus, ideology is reserved for the pronouncements of one's political opponents, and represents something that is self-serving and perhaps even deceitful. Ideology comprises a set of arguments whose primary function, if not deliberate intention, is to promote the interests of one group—usually a social class, but possibly an ethnic or national group—over those of another. Finally, whether by intention or otherwise, ideology is seen to obscure the truth. This latter view—ideology as distortion—is best known under the framework of Marxist perspectives employing the concept of 'false consciousness' (McLellan 1995: 9–30).

Ideology as Distortion or False Consciousness

In it simplest form, the Marxist notion of false consciousness implies that an ideology exists justifying capitalism, and that this ideology distorts the 'true' nature of relations between human beings or, specifically, between capitalists and workers. The image here is one of an inversion: social reality does not appear to be as it really is, and as a result beliefs about society are distorted or mistaken. The metaphor used most frequently is that of a *camera obscura*, which was a medieval artist's aid to reproducing scenes but that inverted them at the same time (Cormack 1992: 10). Ideology is seen as connected to conflict between social classes. Capitalist social relations—the ownership of productive property by some and the disenfranchisement of others, the unequal distribution of resources, the so-called alienation of human beings from the products of their labour—are made to seem just and natural, whereas in fact (according to this perspective) they are not.

Marx himself seemed to have different views of the relations between ideology and the material world. His earlier writing, such as *The German Ideology*, is often contrasted with his later writings (Cohen 1982: 43–6; McLellan 1995: 16; Therborn 1980: 3–8). As recent writers have pointed out, Marx's later writings do not examine the truthfulness or falsity of ideology. In capitalist society, the description that the ideology provides of the existing reality is correct, but the reality itself is 'false' (Cohen 1982: 43; Cohen and Arato 1992), when judged against a utopian vision (communism) under which human potential can be better realized. The notion of false consciousness received considerable play in Marxist writings throughout the 1960s and 1970s to explain why a working-class (revolutionary) consciousness had not developed (Aronowitz 1973; Portes 1971; Wolpe 1968). Even at that time, though, the concept referred more to beliefs and values supportive of the capitalist class than it did to specific (empirically verifiable) untruths.[5]

The notion of false consciousness, especially in its more recent expressions, does not just refer to the telling of lies and untruths. Newspapers and television documentaries are full of examples of individuals who overcame lower-class parental backgrounds to achieve economic success. These presentations reinforce the view that *anyone* can get ahead in capitalist society. This view is correct: while the odds may be considerably different for someone with a poor background (and even lower for someone of aboriginal descent), they are not zero. In other words, everyone *does* have a chance to get ahead, even though this chance may be very, very small in some cases. Since social inequality is far more palpable if everyone at least has a chance to get ahead, the portrayal of entrepreneurial 'heroes', and the concomitant absence of portrayals of individuals who made heroic efforts but failed against insurmountable odds, serve to reinforce views that, in turn, either support the status quo or defuse criticism of it. Does this represent false consciousness? No false statements or empirical claims have been made, but the mass media have selectively emphasized some aspects of social reality and de-emphasized others, thus creating impressions that are, generally, supportive of the status quo.

Dominant Ideology

The term *false consciousness* seems to have fallen out of favour, even among scholars identifying themselves with Marxism or progressive (left) political movements. Perhaps the term is simply too loaded with presuppositions, such as the built-in idea that the social scientist employing the term is able, somehow, to make a determination between correct and incorrect forms of thinking for particular groups. Even if it were possible for the analyst to make the proper determination of, say, who belongs in what social class—a matter over which there has been considerable recent debate within the general framework of class analysis (Crompton 1996; Eder 1993; Grusky and Sorensen 1998; Wright 1985, 1989)—it seems almost arrogant to suggest that the calculation of what best serves that group's interests and how these interests are affected by ideology is easily calculable and historically invariant. Much of the writing under the broad rubric of *dominant ideology* does not invoke the concept of 'false consciousness', even though this same writing usually recognizes that the dominant ideas in any society do not serve the interests of the individuals at the lower end of the income distribution.

The term *dominant ideology* was first popularized in sociology with the writings of Parkin (1971: 80–102). Parkin distinguished among three meaning systems associated with any system involving social stratification. The *dominant value system* defined the society's reward system in deferential or aspirational terms: either individuals' orientation toward the ideas embodied in this system of values was marked by a nonreflexive respect for authority, or individuals were in the

process of attempting to achieve mobility under the terms offered by the social system, or both.

The *subordinate value system* might be described as grudging and cynical acceptance of the status quo. Parkin himself used the phrase 'accommodative responses' to refer to this orientation. Individuals whose ideology could be described as subordinate have a clearly defined sense of difference between themselves (as members of the subordinate class) and those in the dominant class. There is some sense of solidarity with other workers, but this is largely confined to the realm of the 'personal' (in bars and taverns, in social meetings, in the tendency of people to interact, socialize, and even marry within their own class) and does not extend into any form of political organization. Action, both at the individual and at the collective level, is largely *instrumental*. Labour unions, for example, are not leading edges of a movement to change society, but rather seek narrowly to get as much as they can in the way of immediate income or related improvements for members. A fatalistic pessimism may underlie the instrumental orientation: lower-class members may accept the dominant value system's portrayal of the world of social inequality as 'natural' and 'inevitable' even though they simultaneously reject the further claim that this state of affairs is morally superior to any other possible outcome. In other words, they may not like what they see, but they do not feel it is possible to change things. In this context, Parkin's final category is the *radical value system* and involves a more wide-ranging and 'fundamental' opposition to the institutions of capitalism, combined with a wider connection to political movements and a party that expresses working-class interests (Parkin 1971: 97).

Parkin's approach to the classification of beliefs is closely paralleled by similar conceptualizations in other writers, who, for example, distinguish between class identification, oppositional consciousness, and class consciousness involving a conception of an alternative social order (Giddens 1973; Johnston and Baer 1993; Mann 1970).[6] The correspondence is not, of course, exact: while an orientation to alternative societies clearly corresponds with Parkin's 'radical' value system, oppositional consciousness and simple class identification *both* fit into the subordinate type.

Both Parkin and the various Marxist perspectives define class, or more specifically the dividing line between classes, as the primary axis around which ideologies are structured. It is in relation to a system of class inequality and class division, and the oppositions of interests associated with this division, that ideologies are formed. Other forms, such as religious division, or gender differences, are of lesser importance, if they are important at all. Implicit, then, is the view that class represents the salient division point for both present and future social conflict in contemporary capitalist societies. This view is challenged in a debate now occurring in contemporary sociology (Crompton 1996; Eder 1993; Grusky and Sorensen 1998; Pakulski and Waters 1996; Svallfors 1995). Some authors go so far as to suggest that the entire notion of class is outdated, though most take the view that class remains relevant but other, cross-cutting forms of social cleavage must be considered (equally) in any theory of ideology.[7]

Parkin's conceptualization also raises some important issues that cut across the Marxist and non-Marxist scholarship. While his 'dominant' and 'radical' types seem to fit the definition of ideology, it is not clear that this is the case with the subordinate value system. Parkin describes the 'accommodative' response of the subordinate value system as one which contains beliefs that do 'not call into question the values underlying the existing reward structure' (Parkin 1971: 91). At a broader level, this meaning system is characterized by 'normative ambivalence', which stands in contrast to the clear sense of an ideal society that forms the basis for either the dominant or the radical meaning-systems. For the individuals within the subordinate value system, an attachment to the status quo—or at least the absence of strong and violent opposition—is secured by the instrumental attachments provided in the workplace and in the consumer world beyond: the ability of the social system to 'deliver the goods' by providing workers with material possessions and in some sense encapsulate them in a common consumer culture.

This theme—the notion that it is an instrumental attachment to the political system rather than the presence of a coherent ideology that holds the system together—is elaborated and extended by others (Abercrombie, Hill, and Turner 1980; Bocock 1986; Giddens 1973: 211). The idea in turn raises a very important question in the study of political ideology: Does ideology matter? This is more than just a question of whether people have consistent or coherent views about the world. Do democracies actually function as systems that are responsive to expressions of public will? One view is that ideology is important even in the operation of dictatorships. While, in the short run, popular beliefs and ideas are clearly insufficient to stop the rumbling of tanks and the ping of army bullets, as Simon (1982) and Torstendahl (1992) and others point out, even in dictatorships it is difficult to secure by coercion alone all of the different forms of compliance required to make a society run. A contrary view would suggest that policy formation occurs 'above the heads' of individual citizens, because it is developed by an isolated élite (Domhoff 1972, 1983) or, even more seriously, dictated by 'system principles' that render the viewpoints of individuals, even those in the élite, irrelevant (Luhmann 1995).

Hegemony

The work of Gramsci (1979) has had a considerable influence on Western Marxist thinking in the twentieth century, an influence that extended past

Gramsci's death after years of imprisonment in the hands of the Italian Fascists at the onset of World War II. His key concept, *hegemony*, was widely used by 'cultural studies' scholars examining the mass media in the 1980s (Bennett 1986; Hall, Lumley, and McLennon 1977), but the term applies much more widely to the way in which the state interacts with *civil society* and the various mechanisms by which ideological domination takes place. Civil society represents the ensemble of institutions that have some independence from the state, such as churches, labour unions, and schools, as differentiated from institutions that are more directly connected to the state, such as the courts, the army, and the police. Roughly, the distinction is between institutions that focus on coercion and institutions that might be considered primarily 'ideological'. In many conceptualizations, the idea of civil society extends into the realm of ideology even further inasmuch as it represents not so much an ensemble of particular institutions but rather the intellectual 'space' within which a society's ideas are formed and critically examined (Benhabib 1996; Cohen 1982; Cohen and Arato 1992; Hall 1995; Keane 1988).[8]

Hegemony refers to a state of ideological domination. In a hegemonic condition, the state-civil society relation is reduced so that the distinction between the two becomes lost (Abercrombie, Hill, and Turner 1980: 13; Bobbio 1988; Bocock 1986: 28; Femia 1981: 27). Society's 'intellectual leadership' becomes incorporated into the dominant regime, and the *cultural integration* of subordinate groups ensues. As little more than agents for the dominant class, intellectuals diffuse the dominant world views, even to the point where these views take on a naturalistic (that is, 'common sense') appearance (McLellan 1995: 27). Even trade unions become mere instruments of the political order, as class conflict is 'domesticated' (Femia 1981: 35). Ideology is also fused with coercion and repression, although this will vary from society to society. In some cases, such as

pre-World War II Fascist states, with which Gramsci had the most familiarity, or capitalist dictatorships in Third World countries, the coercion component will be much stronger. In liberal democracies with 'freedoms' of association, repression may be limited to the coercion that occurs in the marketplace as individuals must seek employment to keep alive and as employers seek to hire 'cooperative' workers, and ideology will play a more important role.

Hegemony could be misunderstood to apply to a situation where there is widespread acceptance of a dominant ideology, but, as Abercrombie and colleagues point out (1980: 14-15), working-class *incorporation* can consist in 'moral and political passivity', and this may be sufficient to sustain the social order. The essential characteristic of a hegemonic state is the 'capture' by the dominant class of the mechanisms by which counterideologies might develop and the effective incorporation of the intellectual leadership of the society into the perspective of the dominant group.

Gramsci's view of hegemony in capitalist states was not deterministic. That is, it did not contain a picture of some inevitable and unalterable historical movement away from freedom or opportunities for positive social change. Indeed, he called for the working class to establish its own form of hegemony. Most important, Gramsci's perspective stood in counterdistinction to the view that ideas do not matter. Against this (vulgar) Marxist view, Gramsci suggested that any revolution initiated by the economic forces pushing workers to seek a better life would be doomed to failure unless its agents sought control of the intellectual life of society—that is, established a hegemony of their own.[9]

Instrumental Rationality and the Retreat from Ideology

From the 1950s onward, the idea that, in any Western society, there would be massive and revolutionary change brought about as a result of class conflict seemed increasingly remote. Well before this time, while most countries in the North American and European capitalist world were still undergoing an economic recession in the 1930s, the Frankfurt School theorists were in the process of developing a critique of approaches taken by some of their contemporaries on questions of social class, revolution, and political consciousness. The social world had changed greatly since the turn of the century, and some of the suppositions that underwrote Marxist theories of social change no longer seemed to hold true. Most notably, the thesis that the fate of the working class would become less and less tolerable over time in a downward spiral of misery and injustice, seemed less tenable. While working-class life in the 1930s was by no means without peril, the dark, dangerous, and polluted factories that characterized the onset of the Industrial Revolution in Britain and the United States were gradually being replaced by workplaces with some modicum of safety, with more reasonable working hours, with institutionalized mechanisms for the protection of worker rights (in the form of unions, government health and safety regulator apparatuses, et cetera) and with better relative wages. Though the evolution was by no means constant and linear, these trends continued and indeed were accelerated through the 1950s and 1960s.

Other important phenomena attended the change from what would later come to be described as the transition from early to late capitalism (Keane 1984; Norton 1995; Woodiwiss 1978). First, rather than disappearing, the 'middle classes' expanded enormously. The proportion of the workforce that fell into the category of the industrial proletariat declined over time.[10] As Przeworski and Sprague (1986) were later to argue, the optimum time point for a democratic overthrow of capitalism, when working-class consciousness combined with a sufficient proportion of the population being located within the working class, had already been reached in most countries without ever having attained the critical ratio necessary for a democratic transition to socialism. Second, the expanding role of the state meant that the 'reserve army'—unemployed individuals—faced at least a modicum of welfare support programs rather than outright starvation. Moreover, this was accompanied by distribution forms that helped exercise a degree of social control that would not otherwise be possible (Esping-Andersen 1989; Friedland 1980; Gough 1979).[11]

Third, the mass media—first radio and movies and then television—were playing an increasing role in the definition of a 'common culture'. The mass media displaced activities at the sites of traditional working-class culture—in the taverns, for example, where some local songs had a distinctively antisystem orientation—that took form in working-class communities at the onset of the Industrial Revolution. The widespread incorporation of the working class into the *consumer culture* of Western societies, while never complete, had an enormous impact. By the 1960s, some social scientists had declared that the working class had already undergone a process of *embourgeoisement*—that is, cultural incorporation into the middle class.[12]

These factors were all under consideration when Horkheimer, Adorno, Marcuse, and others wrote in the 1930s and again when they continued this work in the 1950s.[13] Like Gramsci, the *Critical School* authors were concerned with the possibility that ideology and social structure could combine in a 'totalizing' fashion to create a world in which very little intellectual space existed for debate and deliberation. This in turn was related to the *instrumental rationality* that was seen not only as an emerging orientation in the second part of the twentieth century, but also as a dominating pattern of thought that pushed aside other, more humanistic, ways of thinking. In some cases, this totality was seen to manifest itself in authoritarian states that exercised extreme control over the mass media and over the definition of culture; after all, the Critical School theorists had just barely escaped the Holocaust.[14] But liberal democracy was not exempt from criticism either. Almost 50 years later, a second-generation critical theorist, Claus Offe, would make a distinction between *formal democracy* and *substantive democracy* (Offe 1983, 1984). Formal democracy exists where the political parties go through the motions of popular sovereignty but where the elections themselves are cynical exercises in marketing and strategic manipulation while citizens have relatively little, if any, individual or collective control over matters that affect their lives. Substantive democracy, on the other hand, meets the real test of whether a state is democratic or not: the system is structured in a way that would permit real (and extensive) public deliberations on matters of public concern.[15] While the early Frankfurt School theorists had not developed nearly so extensive a critique of the limitations of the forms of liberal democracy now present in Western countries, it was nonetheless the case that they regarded this form of government with skepticism.

The concept of *instrumental rationality* is a fairly complex one, having to do not only with the way people think but also with the way in which social theorists conceptualize the objects of their study.[16] A simplification of this concept would suggest that, by discarding human values (goals, ends) and relegating them, at best, to the realm of 'personal preference', contemporary societies banish the all-important discussions of social values from everyday discourse. At the absurd extreme, for example, Nazi engineers engage themselves in debates over how to construct an efficient rail system so that Holocaust victims can be more efficiently eliminated in death camps in a society where discussion and action is limited to questions of how it can best be done, as opposed to the most important (value) question of *whether* it should be done. To be sure, this example may distort the concept slightly, and its application to contemporary democratic states may be remote. But the image of a society where people's thinking is dominated by questions of how to (most efficiently) engineer their lives and their contact with the natural environment as opposed to questions of, 'What sort of a human society do we want to see?' is at least consistent with the general description of instrumental reasons provided by the Critical School theorists.

While social class and class conflict is not removed entirely from the thinking of the early Critical School theorists, it hardly plays the same sort of central role as it does in most other accounts of ideology. In some senses, a strong reliance on models of science and technology even in application to matters of human interaction, and the insistence that empirical facts be separated from social values, becomes an ideology. In other senses, ideology—that is, matters pertaining to human goals—is in the process of disappearing entirely from human society.[17] Although they recognized the need for technological advancement to secure survival in the natural environment, the Critical School theorists argued that social thinking is now so thoroughly dominated by a perspective generated by this form of thinking that society has lost its sense of what it is to be human (and, correspondingly, its ability to respond with anything other than manipulated or 'false' needs). Human beings have, in the words of one of these writers, become 'one dimensional' (Marcuse 1964).[18]

Habermas: The Colonization of the Lifeworld

As with previous Critical School writers, Habermas had a concern about the ability of Western societies to engage in critical debate on public issues (see Calhoun 1992). For democracy to be realized, and, indeed, for humanity's capacity for self-improvement to be achieved, it is essential that citizens all have the capacity to critically evaluate and debate any matter of public concern through free and open discourse with other citizens. While Habermas saw hurdles in the path of this progressive movement toward a more open society, the impression left by his earlier work is that he did not share the profound pessimism of Horkheimer or Adorno about the likelihood that various 'pathologies' could be overcome.

One central concern shared by Habermas and the broad tradition of Western Marxism is the notion of *reification*. Technically, this concept is usually employed with reference to social relations associated with the capital-labour division; that is, it is of direct application to the Marxist class problematic (Burawoy 1990; Larrain 1979). More broadly, though, the concept refers to the notion that social relationships come to be regarded by human subjects as if they were 'natural', that is to say, inevitable and beyond the capacity of human agents to change. Is there something in 'human nature' that makes it impossible for us to exist in a society other than a capitalist society? Is there something that makes religion inevitable? For an extreme structuralist, the answer to either or both of these questions might be 'yes'. For a sociologist having an action/agency persuasion, including those sociologists who describe their analysis as dealing with the 'social construction' of reality (Berger and Luckmann 1967), the answer is negative.[19]

The agency versus structure division cuts across the line dividing Marxist from non-Marxist, left-wing from right-wing, and progressive from conservative scholarship. Some Marxist perspectives are heavily structuralist, and regard human action as the inevitable outcome of larger forces operating on the society at large. Others provide ample room for the conscious interaction of human agents and the possibility that the outcome of any social struggle is always contingent upon historical circumstances and the will of the human beings engaged in this struggle. Althusser

represents a classic, though unsuccessful, example of an attempt to straddle the two extremes (Anderson 1983: 38–9 et passim; Larrain 1989; Outhwaite 1987: 111ff). For him, ideology or the 'superstructure' had an autonomy of its own and was not fully 'determined' by the economic structure. At the same time, he argued that 'in the last instance', economic structure represented the determining factor. It is as if, having on one hand declared that human beings are free to define their own destinies, he erases this freedom with the claim that, ultimately, social relations boil down to the play between larger social structures beyond the power of any individual. Like theorists before him, Habermas had to confront the dual problem of how to acknowledge that human beings are not left totally free by the circumstances they find themselves in but at the same time are not totally bound by these circumstances either. A child of unemployed parents cannot simply declare herself wealthy and assume the services of an expensive mansion with a large staff of attendants. But neither is it the case that, as a member of a collectivity (whether consisting of individuals in the same situation or of society at large), this person is unable, through her actions as a future voter, as a potential member of a social movement, or as someone engaged in the same community of discourse as others with considerably more wealth, she will be totally unable to affect the circumstances under which poverty is reproduced from generation to generation.

For Habermas, social outcomes are not predetermined. There is no master plan containing an inevitable evolution towards either a utopian or a dystopian state. But there are human potentials and human tendencies that tend to lead to motion, generally in the direction of a re-invigorated public sphere. In his later writings, Habermas refers to the sphere of action in which communicative activity takes place or could take place as the 'lifeworld'. This stands in contradistinction to the 'system' which, roughly, refers to the elements of social structure that take place across society and beyond the conscious intentions of individuals. The particular systemic features that are of concern to Habermas reside in the economic and administrative systems of contemporary capitalist societies (Baxter 1987; White 1988). Habermas connects the concept of reification with the *colonization* of the lived experiences of individuals as structured by human communication (roughly, the lifeworld), a concept he employs to make reference to the suggestion that money and power have begun to displace communication in key spheres of action.[20] When arguments are settled by the imposition of power and coercion, the lifeworld has been degraded, and the human capacities and potentials Habermas sees as possible outcomes of human interaction have not been achieved.

In a related fashion, Habermas expresses a concern about the development of cultures of experts and the ability of these expert cultures to remove important decisions from the realm of discussion accessible to the average citizen.[21] This problem is referred to as 'cultural impoverishment', and it has profound implications for the study of ideology. The fragmentation that occurs means that the sort of global or 'grand' meaning-systems usually implied with the term *ideology* can no longer be sustained. In part, though, this occurs as a result of the increased rational scrutiny (and skepticism) being turned on such large-scale belief systems (White 1988: 116–7). One could label this as an 'end point' for ideology, but not in the sense of the displacement of ideology by simple instrumentalism ('I do not care if it is right or wrong; I am just here for the money') or non-thinking human action, and not in the sense that all debates over end-states have ended. Analytically, it may make sense to separate out the two parallel processes—increased expert control and increased public skepticism—since, while interrelated, these two processes might not work in the same direction vis-à-vis the future of argu-

mentation and discourse in the public sphere.

As an aside, in both Habermas's earlier and later writings, the possibility of an orientation that is very similar to pure instrumentalism throughout an entire society is not dismissed completely. In earlier writings, Habermas spoke of two related syndromes—*civil privatism* and *familial privatism* that worked against the emancipatory reconstruction of society (Habermas 1975: 76 et passim; Held 1982: 185; McCarthy 1978: 369). These concepts bear some relation to instrumentalism, and refer to the syndromes under which members of the public devote themselves to their careers and to their families, but not to public life.

Overall, what are the implications of the issues Habermas raises for the legitimacy of democratic regimes, and the sorts of public debates and challenges that are likely to occur in Western polities? And what are the future possibilities for a 'discursive democracy' (Dryzek 1990) that moves beyond the formal play-acting exhibited in the political arenas of many Western democracies? Habermas might be signalling an 'end of ideology', if ideology is defined in the broader sense suggested at the beginning of this chapter.[22] But, in the narrower sense, where ideology encompasses debates over social values, over conceptions of human nature, and so forth, this may not be the case, as long as the definitions of ideology do not *necessarily* entail strong pronouncements that do not leave room for human reinterpretation of what is possible, natural, or necessary.[23] In other words, discursive or communicative action, involving discussions of what should be done and what is possible continue to be part of social life; its status is a function of the interplay between human actors and the structural problems identified by Habermas (colonization and cultural impoverishment). In this sense, an end of ideology only entails an end to the sorts of grand narratives recited in the past by religions and sustained by tradition; tradition no longer has the power to 'turn off the switch' of discursive scrutiny (Habermas 1975, 1979)[24].

Legitimation

Can contemporary regimes survive without being seen as legitimate in the eyes of citizens? In the context of this discussion, the term *regime* refers not to a particular party in power, but to the system of governance that is in place. The term *survival* might, of course, be a bit strong. It comes from functionalist thinking that was once the mainstream of sociological theorizing, with well-known advocates such as Merton and Parsons (Ritzer 1992). Now, though, the idea that, for a system of governance to survive, certain requirements (or 'functions') must be met has largely been left behind in the development of sociological theory, and functionalism is frequently not taught as part of theory curricula in Sociology departments. Habermas's thinking reintroduces some concepts that have a distinctly functionalist bent. His use of functionalism always includes a notion of the contingent, though; for example, while governments' response to scrutiny on the part of citizens seems to be on a secular upward trend, there are circumstances where this 'requirement' might not exist. That is, we might still see a society in which people are unwilling or unable to engage in political debate, but which instead forces their concentration exclusively on their jobs and their families.

At a certain level, the idea of the 'functional prerequisite' must have seemed absurd to social scientists critical of the concept. One cannot talk about the death of a social system or a system of governance in the same way that one talks about the death of a biological organism. Social systems—including systems of government—constantly evolve. At what point can we say that the changes are large enough to signify the emergence of a new system, presumably on the ground that the functional requirements of the previous system could not be met? This would be the case, for example, with the idea that there is a disjuncture between early and late capitalism, or even with the idea of constructing 'late capitalism' as a distinct type (Hussain 1977; Keane 1984).

The end of the Soviet Union and the dismemberment of formerly socialist regimes in Eastern Europe might, of course, be a sobering antidote to the claim that the concept of survival has no meaning. Still, it is difficult to imagine massive transformation in the Western democracies that would signify that survival needs had not been met and that the system had collapsed. Even socialist thinkers are inclined to think about democratic transitions rather than abrupt revolutions (Stevens 1979; Wright, Levine, and Sober 1992). Does this mean that we should discard the concept of legitimacy altogether?

For one thing, the question of the outcome of a loss of legitimacy can be asked in a less grandiose fashion. Rather than speaking of 'survival', it might be possible to speak of the implications for systems of governance if mass legitimacy is not secured. It may be possible to govern without legitimacy, but the conditions under which this could occur and the implications for systems of governance may be worth studying. The withdrawal of the legitimacy of a particular political party in a democracy is, of course, unproblematic. Indeed, the voting into office of a political alternative may strengthen the overall legitimacy of the *system of government* (periodic mass elections providing a modicum of choice, at least insofar as determining political leaders is concerned). For this reason, it is probably incorrect to refer to the unpopularity of a particular government as a *legitimacy* issue, since legitimacy refers more widely to people's beliefs and attitudes about the *system of governance* (in Western societies, liberal democracy). This question is thorny because research methods employed to assess questions of legitimacy (survey questions such as 'How much do you trust government?') may, in fact, simply measure attitudes towards a particular incumbent political party.

The concept of legitimacy implies something akin to mass loyalty for the political system. Lipset would equate legitimacy with the presence of a common culture or value system (Alford and Friedland 1985: 69; Lipset 1981). Here, the concept of a relatively all-embracing *political culture* becomes important.[25] But is the adherence to the dominant value system necessary? To return to Parkin's typology, is legitimacy a problem when a large proportion of the population fit the category of the *subordinate* value system? Much depends on how much active involvement or support is required from those who, while rejecting the dominant ideology, at least do not subscribe to a radical ideology which directly challenges the status quo. While not dealing directly with questions of the legitimacy of political regimes, Burawoy's discussion of the relationship between workers and employers is instructive: this author makes the distinction between *consent*, which may be sufficient for system stability in the absence of organized opposition, and *legitimacy* (Burawoy 1979: 27). Similarly, Crouch (1979) points out that Western capitalist democracies, which are based on pluralism at the level of élite interaction, require *political apathy* more than anything else to function properly.

The view that forms of consent not requiring active political involvement or debate are sufficient to secure the stability of institutional structures and relations is not a matter of consensus, though. In the 1980s, Schaar (1984: 106) suggested that social science had failed to appreciate the precariousness of legitimate authority and authors such as Wolfe (1977: 263, 308) and Habermas (1975: 62–3) spoke of the *repoliticization* of social life. This notion can be best understood in relation to its concomitant, *depoliticization*. The latter term refers to the process by which a large body of decisions taken in capitalist society is removed from the purview of politics by virtue of the way in which capitalism makes a separation between the economy, which is gov-

erned by principles of the marketplace, and the polity, which is governed by principles of participatory democracy and the formal equality of citizens (Giddens 1973; Held 1980; Himmelstrand et al. 1981; Keane 1984; Offe 1984). In a pure market economy, almost no decisions are made by politicians, because the government's role is reduced to enforcing contracts, perhaps preventing fraud, preserving property, and repelling external military force. Inasmuch as the dominant ideology justifying this relationship holds sway, almost all of the important decisions affecting people's lives have been removed from public debate. Owners of property are, in other words, free to make use of this property as they see fit, even if it affects the lives of other people. This represents the extreme forms of depoliticization.

In Western states in the twentieth century, late capitalism now entails a heavy degree of state involvement in the economy in the form of social welfare provisions, regulation of commerce, the physical construction of transportation and related infrastructure and the education of citizens, among other things.[26] In his early writing Habermas (1975, 1979) argues that instability of the capitalist market, as well as its dysfunctional consequences, gave rise to *economic* crisis potentials, perhaps similar to those envisaged by Marx. But capitalist societies have adapted to this threat by transforming into social systems where these problems are dealt with. Wild peaks and swings in the markets are smoothed out by government intervention ('Keynsianism'). Chronic money circulation problems are ameliorated by government expansionary spending, and investment is promoted through various forms of government involvement (including, but not limited to, government spending in the education of the workforce). Some of the more obvious negative consequences of market interaction are countered by government regulation (extreme forms of pollution, for example). And the welfare state ensures that it is *not* the case that those who are unemployed have nothing to lose if they engage in violent insurrection.

But the welfare state has problems of its own. The ability of the state to raise taxes to support programs necessary for the forms of intervention described above is related to the problem of legitimacy, as was amply demonstrated by the movements on the part of neoconservative political parties in the Reagan era to slash government programs during the 1980s and beyond.[27] Even if the state is able to overcome its chronic inability to avoid huge financial deficits which in turn create funding crises (in extreme form, the inability to sell government bonds to fund the deficits without the payment of large interest premiums), it becomes obvious to citizens that the notion of a 'free market' hardly applies to existing society. Because so much of what is done involves, in some way, the state, it is increasingly the case that public scrutiny is applied to decisions of all sorts. This in turn creates the potential for crisis, because there is no overarching political rationale that forms an acceptable justification for political decision-making: it can no longer be argued that citizens have no business in debates over how to allocate resources, because the 'free marketplace' justification for their exclusion from the debate no longer holds intellectual force. The extension of the state into more and more areas of economic and social life saw to this (Connolly 1984: 13).

The idea that capitalist states faced a crisis in legitimacy was extremely popular in the sociology of the state in the 1970s and 1980s (Aronowitz 1981; Bowles and Gintes 1982; Habermas 1975; Hussain 1977; O'Connor 1973, 1984; Wright 1978). Much of the writing was produced, or became popular, at the time of the drastic altercations in the oil market associated with embargoes and supply curtailment on the part of Third World oil-exporting states, and the economic recession of the late 1970s and early 1980s. If, on the one hand, the stability of society needed to be secured by ideological loyalty, then the

increased involvement of the state in the economy rendered support for old anti-interventionist ideologies problematic. If, on the other hand, social stability was obtained through mechanisms that ensured the instrumental attachment of those less well off to the social system, the problems faced in securing the reproduction (continuation) of the social system were even more severe: these very instrumental attachments depended on certain long-standing features of the prolonged economic expansion that characterized Western democracies since the end of the Second World War. As Giddens (1973: 211) observed, the pragmatic acceptance of the status quo implied by instrumentalism was contingent upon features such as steadily rising incomes.

But the massive economic retrenchments in states such as Canada in the 1990s, involving declines in the real wages of all but the wealthiest of groups in society, the retreat of the state from the provision of health-care and welfare services, and the increase in the level of economic disparity (following decades during which the trend was the opposite) have not exactly led to the development of overt threats to the stability of the social system in Canada or the United States. Whether there exists some latent but unrealized tendency toward disequilibrium remains to be seen. As White points out (1988: 122), some side effects may be present in the form of increases in *individualized* responses such as tax evasion and, at a wider level, the development of the underground economy. But it is hard to imagine these developments playing more than an ephemeral role in the long-run evolution of Western liberal democratic states, since noncompliance with taxation demands occurs only within narrow parameters having to do with the ability of individuals to successfully evade notice.

A more pronounced indication might be the expansion of the so-called New Social Movements, which, by some accounts, represent a rejection of the conventional politics of political parties and contain the seeds for the evolution of new forms of social organization (Carroll and Ratner 1996; Eder 1993; Johnston, Larana, and Gusfield 1996; Laclau and Mouffe 1985; McAdam 1996).[28] At the same time, the deliberate noninvolvement of these organizations in formal political affairs (except for the Greens, they hardly constitute themselves as political parties) may impose self-limitations on the potential for change (Dryzek 1996).[29] One question that tends not to get asked is whether the continuities—similarities between the New Social Movements with long-standing forms of voluntary association—overshadow the discontinuities.

Social Capital

The sociological concern over the ability of systems of governments to sustain the loyalty, or at least the compliance, of citizens is paralleled in American political science with a literature dealing with *social capital* (Edwards and Foley 1997; Newton 1997; Putnam 1995, 1996; Teachman, Paasch, and Carver 1997). Interest in sociology in questions of system legitimacy were not as salient in that discipline after the 1980s, while the developments in political science are more recent. The term is most frequently associated with the work of Putnam, who acknowledges previous uses by J. Coleman and geographer/planner J. Jacobs (see Putnam 1995: 66 and fn. 4). It refers to the strength of the 'norms and networks of civic engagement', with the implication that strong ties—that is, high levels of social capital—improve the performance of governments by providing them with the social trust that 'facilitate[s] coordination and cooperation for mutual benefit' (Putnam 1995: 67).

Putnam uses a variety of indicators to assess levels of social capital; these include voluntary association memberships, voter turnout, and trust in government items commonly used in American academic election surveys asking questions such as, 'Do you feel the government can be trusted to do what is right?'[30] The latter is, of course, seen as the *outcome* of the extent to which a polity has dense networks of social and political interaction. Putnam himself added a more generalized question about trust of one's fellow citizens to this list, and subsequent authors have made suggestions for the list's expansion (Minkoff 1997).

In a functional sense, the concept of social capital plays a role very similar to the role played by legitimacy in the earlier sociological literature. The loss of social capital, or of legitimacy, entails a withdrawal of the social supports necessary for governments to engage in the act of effective governance. The parallel does not end there. The actual content of the 'trust in government' survey *measures* used by Putnam can be interpreted as indicators of the extent to which government, indeed, a political system, is seen as legitimate (Baer 1987; Weil 1989). Other highly correlated survey items in the same content domain and that are generally included in election studies have wordings that attempt to determine if respondents feel that the democratic promise has been fulfilled—that is, if government is seen as responsive to, rather than remote from, the wishes of the people. The items ask whether respondents feel governments are run 'for the benefit of a few big interests looking out for themselves or for the benefit of all the people', how much attention the government pays 'to what people think when it decides what to do'.[31]

Given the similarities, Putnam's observations, especially those from social surveys, have a bearing on issues raised both by the literature that he pioneered (the social capital literature) and on the earlier literature on the legitimacy of systems of government. Earlier studies, using data up until the 1970s, had suggested that, overall, Americans' levels of trust had, while being subject to fluctuations in conjunction with economic events (economic expansion or recession), demonstrated an upward trend (Citrin 1974; Citrin and Green

1986; Lipset and Schneider 1983). In contrast to this, Putnam observes dramatically declining levels of political trust during the period from the mid-1970s through the mid-1980s. For example, the proportion of Americans who reply that they trust government only 'some of the time' or 'almost never' rose from 30 per cent in 1966 to 75 per cent in 1992 (Putnam 1995: 68). Canadian levels of trust for government were consistently lower than those exhibited in the United States in 1984 (Baer, Grabb, and Johnston 1990), and have remained low through 1997.[32] Taken together, these data hardly suggest a reservoir of legitimacy or broad social support for the political system. Less understood is the extent to which this absence of legitimacy might affect the ability of governments to enact policies. One might argue, for example, that the withdrawal of legitimacy is accompanied by heightened degrees of volatility in voter support and identification, as a cynical electorate becomes increasingly willing to switch party and party leader allegiances. Rather than legitimating the democratic process by convincing voters that they have a say (that is, they can actually effect changes in governments), this process may lead to spirals of cynicism, as voters take the view that nothing much changes despite the fact that a previous administration has been thrown out of office.

Although it talks a bit about the withdrawal of mass publics from the deliberative processes accompanied by involvement in 'civic culture', Putnam's perspective deals less explicitly with ideology than did the earlier perspectives on the legitimacy problems faced by the contemporary nation-state. One could argue that the social capital perspective emphasizes social interaction and perhaps even affective (interpersonal) ties as the basis for politics, rather than a culture of discourse and deliberation. People might be drawn to civic involvement because of the social need to be with other people, yet do little in the way of democratic deliberation once they participate in the various civic associations. Yet, Putnam's work has a sense about it that is distinctively familiar to theorists concerned with the legitimacy of democratic governments. His complaint about the 'privatizing or individualizing' of leisure time (Putnam 1995: 75) may be less complicated than the earlier Habermasian complaint about 'civil privatism', but it clearly bears an affinity with the issues raised earlier. And his criticism of the mass media harkens to the earlier critique provided by the first generation of Critical School theorists (Agger 1992; Held 1982). While this literature does not directly address questions of the importance (or irrelevance) of political beliefs, many of its concepts overlap with those seen elsewhere in the study of political ideology.

Rethinking Left and Right

For most of the twentieth century, any discussion of ideology centred on the binary opposition between the grand project of the political left—the vision of a future socialist or communist society—pitted against the equally grand project of a capitalist society unaffected by anything other than minimal state involvement and intervention. This binary opposition played itself out as the world military contest between the United States and the former Soviet Union, even though neither came close to representing the 'pure type' theorized by capitalist free market exponents on the one hand or socialist writers on the other. Caught somewhere in the middle was the Western welfare state, especially of the sort observed in Scandinavian countries. While clearly capitalist—the fundamental organizing principle *was* the private ownership of the means of production—these societies were often characterized as being to the 'left' of countries with a more pronounced 'free enterprise' orientation. Thus, on a continuum, with unrealized and utopian capitalist and communist/socialist states falling at either end, actually existing societies could be located according to their degree of adherence to free market principles (on the right) as opposed to the centralized state planning (on the left).

Whether the use of this continuum makes sense in the contemporary period, either as a description of ideological orientations or as a way to parsimoniously summarize policy orientations of political actors, is the subject of debate in political sociology (Bobbio 1996; Giddens 1994; Kitschelt 1995). From a broader, philosophical perspective, too, the postmodern critique of ideology (Dickens and Fontana 1994; Hindness 1996; Ilter 1994; Larrain 1994) suggests that the all-encompassing way of thinking about the social world, as embodied by the extremes of left and right—that is, by ideologies—puts unacceptable constraints on conceptions of human nature and encapsulates a 'theory of history' that is unacceptably deterministic (Schwarzmantel 1998: 189).[33] This latter point is of particular importance, because of the increased skepticism on the part of contemporary social scientists for any theory that speaks of the 'inevitability' of social outcomes. While this criticism has been applied most frequently to Marxist theorists postulating an ineluctable movement toward socialism, it can apply equally to those who would argue that capitalism (with perhaps a democratic state structure) represents the 'end of history'. There is insufficient space here to provide an elaborate discussion of the postmodern critique of ideology, but this critique can be summarized as representing a criticism of anything remotely resembling a 'grand narrative', and the story told by the reduction of political ideology to the polarity of left and right probably constitutes one such narrative (if not, the belief structures said to reside at either pole—Marxism/socialism and free market/liberal capitalism, most certainly do).

Does the distinction between 'left' and 'right' have any applicability to contemporary politics? Bobbio (1996: viii) argues that the 'suppression' of the distinction in intellectual discourse is to

some extent a function of power differences in society: inasmuch as the discourse of left and right is linked to the discussion of social inequality, it stands to reason that the exercise of power in the formation of structures of inequality will be promoted if people do not conceptualize political activity on a continuum that places a lot of emphasis on this issue. In simplistic terms, the left-right distinction is an equality-inequality dimension; this construction probably distinguishes the policy preferences of individuals and groups in contemporary society, even if it does not constitute the *only* dimension along which social differences are constructed. For the inequality end of the spectrum, other notions of fairness, such as equity (outcomes are unequal because inputs—hard work, achievement, et cetera—are different) and equality of opportunity are not precluded.

In popular parlance, liberals are on the political left and conservatives are on the political right. As Giddens (1994: 9) points out, however, this does not correspond to the historical use of the terms in political theory. In fact, *liberalism*, following from writers such as Locke, implied attachment to free market principles. At the time of the Industrial Revolution, liberals promoted an opening of society from its feudal past, and this involved the introduction of markets. Liberal philosophy entailed adherence to free market principles. Conservatism implied support for the status quo. While the conservativism of the times also entailed economic inequality—an inequality determined by feudal privilege—liberalism by no means implied state intervention and policies to ameliorate inequality, as the term is now sometimes employed. Contemporary writers sometimes use terms like 'Lockean liberalism' or 'possessive individualism' to make it clear that they are using the conventional, and not the popular, form of the term. Indeed, Giddens calls for a return to the conventional use of the terms, suggesting that the so-called neoconservative politicians—Margaret Thatcher, Ronald Reagan (and, one might add, Ontario's Mike Harris)—should be called neoliberals and not neoconservatives (Giddens 1994: 28–36).

If described as a simple continuum between policy preferences for more social equality versus policy preferences for less social inequality, the left-right continuum becomes more benign than it was when it described one's position in relation to adherence to the grand ideologies of socialism and capitalism. Still, it is difficult to stop with such a simplistic construction, if only because of the linkages between these preferences and issues of the relationship between the state and capitalist firms: To what extent will the operation of these firms be subjected to some form of state control? For the political right, the marketplace represents the real centre of democracy: regardless of the possibility that constraints on the use of capital might come about as an outcome of elections, democracy is subverted when (wealthy) individuals are unable to exercise their 'property rights' as they see fit.

Recently, a variety of writers has argued that, while the left-right continuum still makes sense, there is another, distinct, dimension that needs to be considered. For Inglehart (1997), this dimension represents the materialism-postmaterialism distinction (see Chapter 2 of this text). Postmaterialists are said to place a value on certain quality-of-life issues and to, in some senses, move beyond the struggles over material possessions as was characterized in political and ideological struggles associated with the distribution of physical wealth (capitalism versus socialism, left versus right).[34] For a growing number of scholars (mostly European), this second dimension consists in the distinction between support for individual liberty as opposed to 'authoritarianism' (Bobbio 1996; Kitschelt 1995). It should be made clear that the libertarian end of the spectrum applies to the state's orientation toward *individual* as opposed to corporate freedoms, and does not

preclude the imposition of extensive controls on the use of capital by corporations. Libertarians are concerned with civil liberties and stand in opposition to the regulation of people's personal lives. Thus, they would oppose legal structures that, in almost any way, attempt to enforce 'family values' (for example, by outlawing homosexual acts between consenting adults), to limit free speech and assembly (including forms of public protest), or to otherwise regulate *individual* preferences. In contrast, authoritarians would place a strong emphasis on the use of the state to enforce the traditional (heterosexual) nuclear family as the preferred mode of cohabitation and sexual activity, the criminalization of hallucinogenic drugs, the suppression of due process and individual rights if these ever come in conflict with the ability of the police to wage war on 'crime' and, usually, an amplified use of the prison system (including long sentences, the use of capital punishment, etc.) to enforce the individual values it promotes.

In the political sociology literature of the 1960s and 1970s (Lipset 1981), equality was often posed in opposition to freedom. Indeed, in the social psychology of the time, social values were assessed with surveys that asked respondents to make a choice between equality and freedom, constructing these two as opposing values (see Rokeach 1973). In this context, Kitschelt's observations about political alignments in Europe are of some considerable significance: contrary to Lipset and Rokeach, Kitschelt observes that, while conceptually liberalism versus authoritarianism and left versus right constitute two distinct axes, in practice, they coalesce around a single axis created by the polarity between left-libertarian versus right-authoritarian (1995: 134). In other words, parties on the political right tend to take authoritarian orientations toward individual freedoms and liberties, while parties on the political left to be the opposite position. Although one might still use the left-right shorthand, it makes more sense, as a description of the political policies advocated by different parties, to make it clear that it is not only the equality/inequality dimension that is being described. Left parties and movements today, Kitschelt argues, are as concerned with individual (and social) autonomy and freedom as they are with economic equality. This helps to explain the linkages between new social movements and more formal political parties emanating from the old political left.

All of this suggests that the terms *left* and *right* might still be usefully employed, but in a much more restrictive and qualified sense than has been the case in the past. It is interesting to note that the terms themselves seem to generate, and may always have generated, confusion in the minds of mass publics in Western societies. When asked where they would locate themselves on a left-right continuum, large proportions of respondents decline to answer the question (see, for example, Lambert et al. 1987, 1988). It is not clear that this term has very much salience, even among respondents who provide consistent answers on social policy questions having to do with the distribution of wealth. This, of course, does not preclude the use of the left-right shorthand by social scientists, but should impose some discipline on those who would seek consistent patterns in the subjective responses of people who respond to survey questionnaires.[35]

Conclusion

DOES IDEOLOGY MATTER?

Contemporary political sociology has turned away from the problematic of ideology, but it has not stopped the study of political consciousness. There is increased skepticism toward conceptualizations that posit a utopian future, and with it see attitudes and values as pre-determined and not worth discussing. With an increased theoretical attention to democracy and the need for 'discursive justification' in political sociology, the contrary view—that political beliefs are important—remains active in theoretical debates (see (Dryzek 1990, 1996; Giddens 1994). Sometimes ideology is seen as a relatively small element in the exercise of power, because 'disciplinary practices' in everyday life are regarded as important components of power relations (Foucault 1977). For the most part, though, the study of political consciousness has not discarded the project of attempting to map, and then perhaps critique, systems of political belief. What constitutes a system, indeed, use of terminology of this sort in the first place, is of course under investigation. Overall, the perspectives are now less essentialist, and the approach to ideology more nuanced than they were in the past, when political preferences were discussed within the confines of a single left-right continuum and the class politics said to underlie it. But issues of inequality have not simply disappeared, and they remain salient in many of the contemporary discussions, even as these same discussions refocus the debate to include forms of inequality, such as gender inequality, not located along the social class divide. This having been said, it remains to be seen whether, in the face of rising levels of social inequality through the 1990s in most Western societies but especially Canada, new perspectives can adequately capture the new demands being placed on them without giving up entirely on the impetus that carried the notion of 'ideology' through the social sciences in the twentieth century.

Notes

1. A few years later, Napoleon used the term negatively in an attack on his political enemies (McLellan 1995: 5).

2. The concept of 'grand narrative' is a term employed by postmodern social theorists in critique of the previous 'modernist' mode of thinking (Dickens and Fontana 1994; Kaplan 1988; Murphy 1989; Shapiro 1992).

3. See Schwarzmantel (1998) for a view that sets this duality as accompanying 'modernity'. The question of a possible distinction between 'modern' and 'postmodern' beliefs will be discussed in more detail later.

4. See also Thompson (1990: 54ff); Larrain (1979: 14, 1989: 92). McLellan (1995 :1) suggests that the term is still mostly used in the 'pejorative' sense.

5. The idea that truth applies only to phenomena that are physically (empirically) verifiable is debated by writers in the Critical School, including Adorno, Horkheimer and, later, Habermas. To these authors, restrictions that pretend to separate facts and values and that make the claim that only facts can be assessed as truth-claims is limited.

6. Parkin is not generally considered to be a Marxist scholar. The parallel conceptualization of identity/opposition/alternative more closely relates to the Marxist problematic that establishes progressive stages of class consciousness.

7. See, for example, the earlier work of Abercrombie et al. (1983: 64) arguing that nationalism and not just beliefs regarding the superiority of capitalism 'qualifies (albeit uneasily) as part of the dominant ideology of late capitalism, at least in Britain'.

8. Civil society is usually conceptualized as not being directly connected to the economic marketplace (and hence subject to its dictates, at least direct), too (Cohen 1982: 48ff.).

9. Marxism is often associated with the view that ideas do not matter and that economic forces blindly push workers into an inevitable social revolution. This extreme 'materialist' view is a disputed reading of Marx himself (Callinicos 1987; Larrain 1989), and probably represents the perspective of only a small portion of the varied perspectives in late-twentieth-century Marxism. This issue will be discussed in additional detail later.

10. Contemporary Marxist writers such as Wright (1994, 1985, 1989) attempt to solve this problem by defining most middle-class workers as members of an extended proletariat or by arguing for a revised examination of the 'interests' of the middle class in a way that might see a political coalition between this group of workers and the traditional blue-collar proletariat.

11. See also the discussion by O'Connor on the welfare state in Chapter 6 in this text. The argument is that state welfare programs keep recipients in line by (a) maintaining surveillance on them, (b) imposing conditions on the receipt of benefits that tend to reduce the likelihood of collective action (job search requirements, workfare requirements, re-schooling, etc.), and (c) converting a 'we have nothing to lose' situation into something different for the less privileged members of the workforce.

12. This perspective is most frequently associated with Goldthorpe et al. (1968) in the 1960s, although a careful reading of the work of these authors suggests that the description is a bit more nuanced than that which would be implied by a simple notion of cultural incorporation.

13. The work of the Frankfurt School was interrupted by the War, although most of the scholars managed to emigrate from Germany to New York before the War broke out. Some of the original school remained in the United States (for example, Marcuse), while Horkheimer and Adorno returned to Germany.

14. Most of the members of the Frankfurt School were Jewish. One member of the school, Walter Benjamin, died trying to escape from Nazi Europe.

15. Dryzek employs the term *discursive democracy* to describe this (Dryzek 1990).

16. For an extended discussion, see Held (1980). It bears a strong affinity with, and indeed can trace its intellectual origins to, Weber's concepts of

zweckrationalitat and wertratinalitat (instrumental or means-rationality and value-rationality, respectively).

17. Here, then, there is some similarity between the early Critical School theorists and the later 'end of ideology' theorists which will be discussed later, with an important qualification: while the former looked at this development with dread and trepidation, the latter celebrated its arrival.

18. The discussion of the relationship between science and technology on the one hand and instrumental rationality on the other is tied in with a critique of positivism, which will not be detailed here. See Held (1980): 160–74 et passim. Of special concern is the analytic attempt by writers of this opposing persuasion to separate facts (which are said to be accessible to empirical scrutiny) and values (which are said to be inherently subjective). Critical School theorists would argue that the forms of knowledge embodied in values need to be subjected to scrutiny by the collective community affected by them.

19. More generally, this perspective is shared by symbolic interactionism, phenomenology, and ethnomethodology among others. For a more complete discussion of the agency-structure polarity in sociology, see Giddens (1979).

20. See White (1988: 109–10). The term *mediatization* is employed in this context.

21. As White (1988: 116) points out, this is not a new claim. For an extensive and highly critical discussion of the role of 'credentialization', see Collins (1979). Habermas does not necessarily go as far as Collins in arguing that much credentialization is totally functionally unnecessary.

22. White raises this issue in his discussion of the role of expert cultures in Habermas (White 1988: 116).

23. The form of argument being dispelled here is *essentialism*, which has long been associated with both the Marxist critique of capitalism on the one hand and the economist's justification of the marketplace on the other (Keat and Urry 1982: 41ff.).

24. Ironically, Habermas, who never actually uses the term, is himself accused of constructing a theoretical 'grand narrative' by postmodernists such as Derrida.

25. See Chapter 2 by Tepperman in this text for an extended discussion of the term and its implications.

26. It may, of course, be arguable that anything resembling a 'pure' market state ever existed, and that the stage referred to as early capitalism differed from late capitalism mostly in terms of the employment of technology, forms of élite interaction, the comparative size of the monopoly as opposed to the competitive sectors, and so on. In Canada, for example, massive levels of government support in the form of subsidies and land grants accompanied the nineteenth-century expansion of railroads, and government military spending undoubtedly provided a basis for much economic activity.

27. Even as European publics elected slightly more moderate governments in the mid-1990s, the Reagan legacy continued in Canada with the election of Mike Harris in Ontario in 1995 on a neoconservative political platform.

28. See Chapter 8 by Carroll in this text for a detailed review of the literature dealing with New Social Movements.

29. See Butler (1998) for a contrary perspective.

30. Similar survey items have been included in most federal election studies done in other countries, including Canada.

31. In political science, some of these items were originally formed as part of 'political efficacy' scales. For a discussion and critique of the 'efficacy' conceptualization, see Baer (1987: 110–4).

32. In 1984, 61 per cent of those responding to the Canadian National Election Study felt that they had 'no say' in the running of government and a similar percentage (60 per cent) felt that the government did not care about 'what people like me think'. In the 1997 National Election Study, these percentages were 63 per cent and 68 per cent respectively.

33. The term used here is *essentialism*. This term does not quite reduce neatly to 'conceptions of human nature' as might be suggested by the (simplified) argument employed here.

34. See Tepperman's Chapter 2 in this text for an extended discussion of Inglehart's work.

35. Despite these concerns, left-right scales are still sometimes used in Canadian political sociology to describe public policy orientations in relation to social inequality. Nakhaie and Brym (1998), for example, make claims about the 'liberalism' of university professors on the grounds of a comparison of their positions on the left-right scale against those of the Canadian public at large. The problem with this analysis is that, while higher educated persons in the 1984 survey were less supportive of positions taken by the political left (taxing the rich, reducing income disparities, etc.), they were slightly more likely to see themselves as 'left'. So self-placement on left-right scales is not consistent with policy preferences.

References

Abercrombie, N., S. Hill, and B. Turner. 1980. *The Dominant Ideology Thesis* (London: Allen and Unwin).

———. 1983. 'Determinacy and Indeterminacy in the Theory of Ideology', *New Left Review* 142: 56–66.

Adams, I. 1993. *Political Ideology Today* (Manchester: Manchester University Press).

Agger, B. 1992. *Cultural Studies as Critical Theory* (London: Falmer Press).

Alford, R. and R. Friedland. 1985. *Powers of Theory: Capitalism, the State and Democracy* (Cambridge: Cambridge University Press).

Anderson, P. 1983. *In the Tracks of Historical Materialism* (London: Verso).

Aronowitz, S. 1973. *False Promises: The Shaping of American Working Class Consciousness* (New York: McGraw-Hill).

———. 1981. *The Crisis in Historical Materialism: Class, Politics and Culture in Marxist Theory* (New York: Praeger).

Baer, D. 1987. 'Social Class, Legitimacy and the Canadian State', Ph.D. Diss. (University of Waterloo, Waterloo).

———, E. Grabb, and W. Johnston. 1990. 'The Values of Canadians and Americans: A Critical Analysis and Reassessment', *Social Forces* 68: 693–713.

Baxter, H. 1987. 'System and Life-World in Habermas's Theory of Communicative Action', *Theory and Society* 16: 39–86.

Benhabib, S. 1996. 'Toward a Deliberative Model of Democratic Legitimacy'. In *Democracy and Difference: Contesting the Boundaries of the Political*, ed. S. Benhabib (Princeton, NJ: Princeton University Press), 67–94.

Bennett, T. 1986. *Introduction: Popular Culture and the 'Turn to Gramsci'. In Popular Culture and Social Relations,* ed. T.M. Bennett, C. Mercer, and J. Woollacott (Philadelphia: Open University Press).

Berger, P.L. and T. Luckmann. 1967. *The Social Construction of Reality: A Treatise in the Sociology of Knowledge* (Garden City, NY: Anchor Books).

Bobbio, N. 1988. *Gramsci and the Concept of Civil Society*, ed. J. Keane (London: Verso).

———. 1996. *Left and Right: The Significance of a Political Distinction,* trans. A. Cameron (Chicago: University of Chicago Press).

Bocock, R. 1986. *Hegemony* (London: Tavistock).

Bowles, S., and H. Gintes. 1982. 'The Crisis of Liberal Capitalism: The Case of the United States'. *Politics and Society* 11(1): 51–93.

Burawoy, M. 1979. *Manufacturing Consent: Changes in the Labour Process Under Monopoly Capitalism* (Chicago: University of Chicago Press).

———. 1990. 'Marxism as Science: Historical Challenges and Theoretical Growth', *American Sociological Review* 55(6): 775–94.

Butler, J. 1998. 'Merely Cultural', *New Left Review* 227: 33–44.

Calhoun, C. 1992. 'Introduction: Habermas and the Public Sphere'. In *Habermas and the Public Sphere*, ed. C. Calhoun (Cambridge, MA: MIT Press), 1–48.

Callinicos, A. 1987. *Making History: Agency, Structure and Change in Social Theory* (Oxford: Polity Press).

Carroll, W. and R. Ratner. 1996. 'Master Frames and Counter-Hegemony: Political Sensibilities in Contemporary Social Movements', *Canadian Review of Sociology and Anthropology* 33: 407–35.

Citrin, J. 1974. 'Comment: The Political Relevance of Trust in Government', *American Political Science Review* 68: 973–88.

———, and D. Green. 1986. 'Presidential Leadership and the Resurgence of Trust in Government', *British Journal of Political Science* 16: 431–53.

Cohen, J. 1982. *Class and Civil Society: The Limits of Marxian Critical Theory* (Amherst, MA: University of Mass. Press).

———, and A. Arato. 1992. *Civil Society and Political Theory* (Cambridge, MA: MIT Press).

Collins, R. 1979. *The Credential Society: An Historical Sociology of Education and Stratification* (New York: Academic Press).

Connolly, W. 1984. 'Introduction: Legitimacy and Modernity'. In *Legitimacy and the State*, ed. W. Connolly (London: Basil Blackwell).

Cormack, M. 1992. *Ideology* (London: B. Batsford).

Crompton, R. 1996. 'The Fragmentation of Class Analysis', *British Journal of Sociology* 47 (1): 56–67.

Crouch, C. 1979. 'The State, Capital and Liberal Democracy'. In *State and Economy in Contemporary Capitalism*, ed. C. Crouch (New York: St Martin's Press), 1–54.

Dickens, D., and A. Fontana. 1994. 'Postmodernism in the Social Sciences'. In *Postmodernism and Social Inquiry,* ed. D. Dickens and A. Fontana (London: Guilford Press), 1–22.

Domhoff, G.W. 1972. *Fat Cats and Democrats: The Role of the Big Rich in the Party of the Common Man* (Englewood Cliffs, NJ: Prentice-Hall).

———. 1983. *Who Rules America Now?: A View for the '80s* (Englewood Cliffs, NJ: Prentice-Hall).

Dryzek, J. 1990. *Discursive Democracy: Politics, Policy and Political Science* (Cambridge: Cambridge University Press).

———. 1996. *Democracy in Capitalist Times: Ideals, Limits and Struggles* (Oxford: Oxford University Press).

Eder, K. 1993. *The New Politics of Class* (Newbury Park, CA: Sage).

Edwards, B. and M. Foley. 1997. 'Social Capital and the Political Economy of Our Discontent', *American Behavioral Scientist* 40: 669–78.

Esping-Andersen, G. 1989. 'The Three Political Economies of the Welfare State', *Canadian Review of Sociology and Anthropology* 26 (1): 10–36.

Femia, J. 1981. *Gramsci's Political Thought: Hegemony, Consciousness and the Revolutionary Process* (Oxford: Clarendon Press).

Foucault, M. 1977. *Discipline and Punish: The Birth of the Prison* (New York: Panthean).

Friedland, R. 1980. 'Class, Power and Social Control: The War on Poverty'. In *Classes, Class Conflict and the State*, ed. M. Zeitland (Cambridge, MA: Winthrop), 193–216.

Fukuyama, F. 1992. *The End of History and the Last Man* (New York: Free Press).

Giddens, A. 1973. *The Class Structure of Advanced Societies* (London: Hutchinson).

———. 1979. *Central Problems in Social Theory: Action, Structure and Contradiction in Social Analysis* (Berkeley. CA: University of California Press).

———. 1994. *Beyond Left and Right: The Future of Radical Politics* (Stanford, CA: Stanford University Press).

Goldthorpe, J., D. Lockwood, F. Bechhofer, and J. Platt. 1968. *The Affluent Worker in the Class Structure* (Cambridge: Cambridge University Press).

Gough, I. 1979. *The Political Economy of the Welfare State* (London: Macmillan).

Gramsci, A. 1979. *Letters from Prison* (London: Quartet Books).

Grusky, D. and J. Sorensen. 1998. 'Can Class Analysis Be Salvaged?' *American Journal of Sociology* 103: 1187–234.

Habermas, J. 1976. *Legitimation Crisis* (Boston: Beacon Press).

———. 1979. *Communication and the Evolution of Society.* (Boston: Beacon Press).

Hall, J. 1995. 'In Search of Civil Society'. In *Civil Society: Theory, History, Comparison,* ed. J. Hall (Oxford: Blackwell), 1–31.

Hall, S., B. Lumley, and G. McLennon. 1977. 'Politics and Ideology: Gramsci'. In *Center for Contemporary Studies On Ideology.* (London: Hutchinson), 45–76.

Held, D. 1980. *Introduction to Critical Theory: Horkheimer to Habermas* (Berkeley, CA: University of California Press).

———. 1982. 'Crisis Tendencies, Legitimation and the State'. In *Habermas: Critical Debates,* eds J. Thompson and Held (Cambridge, MA: MIT Press), 181–45.

Himmelstrand, U., G. Ahrne, L. Lundberg, and L. Lundberg. 1981. *Beyond Welfare Capitalism: Issues, Actors and Forces in Societal Change* (London: Heinemann).

Hindness, B. 1996. *Discourses of Power: From Hobbes to Foucault* (Oxford: Blackwell).

Hussain, A. 1977. 'Crises and Tendencies of Capitalism', *Economy and Society* 6(4): 436–80.

Ilter, T. 1994. 'Postmodernism and Radical Sociology', *Critical Sociology* 20(2): 51–80.

Inglehart, R. 1997. *Modernization and Postmodernization: Cultural, Economic and Political Change in 43 Countries* (Princeton, NJ: Princeton University Press).

Johnston, H., E. Larana, and J. Gusfield. 1996. 'Identities, Grievances and New Social Movements'. In *New Social Movements: From Ideology to Identity,* eds E. Larana, H. Johnston, and J. Gusfield.

Johnston, W. and D. Baer. 1993. 'Class Consciousness and National Contexts: Canada, Sweden and the United States in Historical Perspective', *Canadian Journal of Sociology and Anthropology* 30: 271–95.

Kaplan, E.A. 1988. 'Introduction'. In *Postmodernism and Its Discontents* (London: Verso).

Keane, J. 1984. *Public Life and Late Capitalism: Toward a Socialist Theory of Democracy* (Cambridge: Cambridge University Press).

———. 1988. *Civil Society and the State: New European Perspectives* (London: Verso).

Keat, R. and J. Urry. 1982. *Social Theory as Science* (London: Routledge and Kegan Paul).

Kitschelt, H. 1995. 'A Silent Revolution in Europe?' In *Governing the New Europe,* eds J. Hayward and E. Page (Cambridge: Polity Press), 123–65.

Laclau, E. and C. Mouffe. 1985. *Hegemony and Socialist Strategy: Toward a Radical Democratic Politics,* trans Winston Moore; Paul Cammack (London: Verso).

Lambert, R., J. Curtis, S. Brown, and B. Kay. 1987. 'Social Class, Left/Right Political Orientations, and Subjective Class Voting in Provincial and Federal Elections', *Canadian Review of Sociology and Anthropology* 24(4): 526–49.

———. 1988. 'The Left-Right Factor in Party Identification', *Canadian Journal of Sociology* 13(4): 385–406.

Larrain, J. 1979. *The Concept of Ideology* (Athens: University of Geogia Press).

———. 1989. 'Ideology and Its Revisions in Contemporary Marxism'. In *The Structure of Modern Ideology,* ed. N. O'Sullivan (Edward Elgar: London), 91–121.

———. 1994. 'The Postmodern Critique of Ideology', *Sociological Review* 42(2): 289–314.

Lipset, S. 1981. *Political Man: The Social Bases of Politics* (Baltimore: Johns Hopkins University Press).

———, and W. Schneider. 1983. *The Confidence Gap: Business, Labour and Government in the Public Mind* (New York: Free Press).

Luhmann, N. 1995. *Social Systems* (Stanford, CA: Stanford University Press).

Mann, M. 1970. 'The Social Cohesion of Liberal Democracy', *American Sociological Review* 35(3): 423–39.

Marcuse, H. 1964. *One-Dimensional Man* (Boston, MA: Beacon Press).

McAdam, D. 1996. 'Culture and Social Movements'. In *New Social Movements: From Ideology to Identity* (Philadelphia: Temple University Press).

McCarthy, T. 1978. *The Critical Theory of Jurgen Habermas* (Cambridge, MA: MIT University Press).

McLellan, D. 1995. *Ideology* (Buckingham, England: Open University Press).

Minkoff, D. 1997. 'Producing Social Capital: National Social Movements and Civil Society', *American Behavioral Scientist* 40: 606–19.

Murphy, J. 1989. *Postmodern Social Analysis and Criticism* (Westport, CT: Greenwood Press).

Nakhaie, R., and R. Brym. 1998. 'Political Ideology of the University Professoriate in Canada', paper presented to the Annual Meetings of the Canadian Sociology and Anthropology Association, Ottawa, Ontario.

Newton, K. 1997. 'Social Capital and Democracy', *American Behavioral Scientist* 40: 575–86.

Norton, B. 1995. 'Late Capitalism and Postmodernism: Jameson/Mandel'. In *Marxism in the Postmodern Age: Confronting the New World Order,* eds A. Callari, S. Cullenberg, and C. Biewener (New York: Guilford), 59–70.

O'Connor, J. 1973. *The Fiscal Crisis of the State* (New York: St Martin's Press).

———. 1984. *Accumulation Crisis* (Oxford: Basil Blackwell).

Offe, Claus. 1983. 'Competitive Party Democracy and the Keynesian Welfare State: Some Reflections on their Historical Limits'. In *The State, Class and the Recession,* eds S. Clegg, D. Dow, and P. Boreham (New York: St Martin's).

———. 1984. *Contradictions of the Welfare State,* ed. J. Keane (London: Hutchinson).

Outhwaite, W. 1987. *New Philosophies of Social Science: Realism, Hermeneutics and Critical Theory* (London: Macmillan).

Pakulski, J., and M. Waters. 1996. *The Death of Class* (Thousand Oaks, CA: Sage).

Parkin, F. 1971. *Class Inequality and Political Order: Social Stratification in Capitalist and Communist Countries* (New York: Holt, Rinehart, and Winston).

Portes, A. 1971. 'On the Interpretation of Class Consciousness', *American Journal of Sociology* 77(2): 228–43.

Przeworski, A., and J. Sprague. 1986. *Paper Stones: A History of Electoral Socialism* (Chicago: University of Chicago Press).

Putnam, R. 1995. 'Bowling Alone: America's Declining Social Capital', *Journal of Democracy* 6: 65–78.

———. 1996. 'The Strange Disappearance of Civic America', *American Prospect* 24: 34–48.

Ritzer, G. 1992. *Contemporary Sociological Theory* (New York: McGraw Hill).

Rokeach, M. 1973. *The Nature of Human Values* (New York: Free Press).

Rosen, M. 1996. *On Voluntary Servitude: False Consciousness and the Theory of Ideology* (Cambridge: Polity Press).

Schaar, J. 1984. 'Legitimacy in the Modern State'. In *Legitimacy and the State,* ed. W. Connolly (Oxford: Blackwell).

Schwarzmantel, J. 1998. *The Age of Ideology: Political Ideologies from the American Revolution to Postmodern Times* (New York: New York University Press).

Shapiro, M. 1992. *Political Theory as Textual Practice* (Minneapolis: University of Minnesota Press).

Simon, R. 1982. *Gramsci's Political Thought* (London: Lawrence and Wishart).

Stevens, J. 1979. *The Transition from Capitalism to Socialism* (London: Macmillan).

Svallfors, S. 1995. 'The End of Class Politics? Structural Cleavages and Attitudes to Swedish Welfare Policies', *Acta Sociologica* 38: 53–74.

Teachman, J., K. Paasch, and K. Carver. 1997. 'Social Capital and the Generation of Human Capital', *Social Forces* 75: 1343–59.

Therborn, G. 1980. *The Ideology of Power and the Power of Ideology* (London: Verso).

Thompson, J. 1990. *Ideology and Modern Culture: Critical Social Theory in the Era of Mass Communications* (Cambridge: Polity Press).

Torstendahl, R. 1992. 'Introduction: State, Society and History'. In *State Theory and State History,* ed. R. Torstendahl (Newbury Park, CA: Sage).

Weil, F. 1989. 'The Sources and Structure of Legitimation in Western Democracies: A Consolidated Model Tested with Time-Series Data in Six Countries Since World War II', *American Sociological Review* 54(5): 682–706.

White, S.K. 1988. *The Recent Work of Jürgen Habermas: Reason, Justice, and Modernity* (Cambridge: Cambridge University Press).

Wolfe, A. 1977. *The Limits of Legitimacy: Political Contradictions in Contemporary Capitalism* (New York: Free Press).

Wolpe, H. 1968. 'An Examination of Some Approaches to the Problem of Development of Revolutionary Consciousness', *Telos* 1: 113–44.

Woodiwiss, T. 1978. 'Critical Theory and the Capitalist State', *Economy and Society* 7: 175–92.

Wright, E. 1994. 'Class Analysis, History and Emancipation', *New Left Review* 202: 15–36.

———. 1978. *Class, Crisis and the State* (London: NLB).

———. 1985. *Classes* (London: Verso).

———. 1989. *The Debate on Classes* (London: Verso).

———, A. Levine, and E. Sober. 1992. *Reconstructing Marxism: Essays on Explanation and the Theory of History* (London: Verso).

Part B

The State

The concept of 'the state' is central to the study of political sociology. Yet, as with many constructs in sociology, the landscape in which debates take place is highly contested terrain. There is no consensus on what this seemingly simple term implies, and there is certainly no agreement on its boundaries. As Pierson (1996: 2) remarks, 'one-line definitions of the state have not generally fared well'.

State, Nation, and Territoriality

When we think of the state, we usually think of a set of institutions and practices. The term *governance* immediately comes to mind, in its democratic or nondemocratic form. As Oommen (1997: 23) suggests, definitions used by contemporary Western social science disciplines incorporate the notion of political sovereignty, that the state operates alone—it does not compete with other state institutions. One also sees the idea, from Max Weber, that the state is the only institution (some would say 'complex of institutions') with a monopoly on the legitimate use of force—the ability to raise and employ an army and to use police forces to apply physical restraints on individuals. Finally, the state has the formal authority to make almost every other human action conditional upon its assent. This authority reaches into every crevice of human action, from the exercise of property rights (property can be taxed, expropriated, even confiscated) to human sexual relations (many states define acts such as adultery or homosexuality as illegal, and some impart severe sanctions). Chodak (1989) coins the term *etatization* to refer to the increasing role played by the state in contemporary societies, arguing that, as a result, centralized state systems become more and more complex. This seemingly absolute power is, of course, always contingent (someone must follow the orders to use force if the state is to assert its authority against an unwilling populace) and frequently contested (not all citizens obey the law and some actually organize themselves in oppositional structures including organized crime).

These definitions of the 'state' would appear to be uncontroversial, yet there are caveats. For example, in some states, individuals are dual citizens—and not just because they are immigrants from a foreign country who retain rights from their countries of origin. Also, in countries such as the United States, Great Britain, Germany, Switzerland, and Canada, federal and state governments have jurisdiction over different matters—neither has a monopoly (see Oommen 1997: 50). In the United States, this division even extends to criminal law, where state and federal laws compete with each other in the same physical territory. The idea of equating the 'state' with 'unitary administration' can, of course, be salvaged if one argues that both federal and state authority exist under a single overarching legal structure (usually a formal constitution), but it is still clear from these examples that the terrain of governance might increasingly involve cohabitation and not single parenthood. As Jeffrey will argue in Chapter 5 in this part, it is also the case that, in the contemporary environment of global capitalism, extranational structures (international trade organizations, military alliances, some forms of business enterprise spanning national borders) also impinge on this image of a unitary state having absolute authority over the domain it is said to govern (see also Johnston in Chapter 15 in Part E).

The term *state*, referring to the set or cluster of institutions of governance, might be usefully set aside from a broader term, the *nation-state*, which is used to refer to the collectivity (or society) that is subject to the governance of state institutions. As sociologists such as Giddens (1984, 1995) and Tilly (1975) have remarked, the notion of a society based on a 'single legitimating structure' (Pierson 1996: 11) is a relatively recent phenomenon associated with the transition from early feudalism in European societies. With this transition came a gradual, but never complete, centralization of the use of lethal weapons in the hands of agencies of the state. At the same time, the state sponsored new forms of surveillance and control emanating from the state (in the contemporary period, these would include police, all sorts of regulatory authorities, and, depending on the theorist, institutions such as the education system). In his chapter on the state, Jeffrey makes some provocative suggestions with respect to the extent to which this 'pacification' of society can be seen as complete and final. Looking at the ethnic fragmentation of states around the world, he asks whether, in a global society where one mo-

ment's combatants can become next week's airline saboteurs, this idea really applies.

The connection between state and nation is important when examining the stability of state structures across time. Not all nations split apart under conditions of violence, as witnessed by the peaceful separation of Czechoslovakia into two countries. To be sure, a discussion of the stability of multiethnic states could occupy an entire chapter, but can only be examined briefly here. When one thinks of the concept of 'nation', a single ethnic group comes to mind or, at the very least, a single language group in a geographic territory with an autonomous governing structure.[1] State and nation are, in other words, co-terminous. Yet, as Oommen (1997: 47) notes, the conflation of state and nation works against a full understanding of how state structures interact with linguistic and ethnic groups in the contemporary world.

It is, of course, useful to distinguish between settler nations, such as Canada and the United States, and countries in the so-called Old World.[2] In the nations constituting a population of immigrants, linguistic homogeneity might arise from the slow introduction of these groups into a dominant language culture. The requirements of day-to-day living, including employment, make necessary the use of this language and the absence of 'institutionally complete' structures for the 'old' language lead to disuse after two or three generations.[3] But in countries where settlers have never constituted more than a small fraction of the country's population, one must ask what sort of a relationship exists between nation and country. Oommen (1997: 47) suggests that political sociologists have given insufficient attention to what he calls the 'multinational state'—a state that contains a number of populations, each of which might otherwise meet the conditions of nationhood (including a separate language and settlement in a distinct and more or less contiguous geographic region). Examples he provides include England (constituting initially separate nations of Ireland, Scotland, and Wales), France (containing Alsatians, Basques, Catalans, Corsicans, and Flemings).[4] Such initial linguistic differences do not always lead to the ultimate disintegration of the state.

But does the amalgamation of different nations under the umbrella of a single state inevitably lead to the dissolution of linguistic and cultural differences (in favour of a single, dominant culture)? This fear has, of course, occupied much of the discourse within Quebec surrounding the separatist movement; it lays claim to the need for a separate nation-state on the basis of the expected disappearance of French language and culture if a separate sovereign state is not established.

Linguistic-cultural minorities do not always seek a completely autonomous state, however (for example, the Catalans in Spain). Moreover, Quebec is an example where the federal state has either condoned or purposefully ignored aggressive local policies aimed at the preservation of the minority language and culture.[5] And, whether through cultural incorporation or a long-standing coexistence of multiple cultures, many European examples of successful multiple-nation states exist to balance the scales against the obvious instances of failure (the Sudeten Germans in Czechoslovakia, the relations between Serbs and Croats in Yugoslavia, the Czechs and Slovaks). In other words, there is no single, predetermined outcome (as yet) to situations such as the presence of a geographically contiguous French minority in Canada.

The uneasy relationship between Quebec and the rest of Canada means one can expect to see a different sort of discussion about the state in Canadian political sociology, emphasizing issues that are not nearly so pronounced in the United States. Both Jeffrey's Chapter 5 and Turpel's Chapter 7 deal with the definition of the Canadian state and the constitutional problem that arises when the creation of a separate coun-

try is contemplated. Jeffrey locates this issue within the wider context of global pressures on many nation-states around the world, and mentions in passing the paradox created for the native Cree population in Quebec. Turpel focuses on the situation in Quebec and its relationship to struggles by Native people in Canada, bringing historical detail to the discussion.[6] Self-determination, as she points out, is rarely a simple matter, either constitutionally or practically.

State and Society

A very different set of concerns informs the extended literature dealing with a core question in political sociology: Do state structures in Western capitalist societies exhibit *state autonomy* or are they a function of the features of the society around it?

The debate over state autonomy is connected to the long-standing dualism in sociological theories between those that are *voluntaristic*—that is, providing room for the actions of individuals who can construct the patterns of social interaction within which they operate—and those that have a more *deterministic* cast. In sociological parlance, the difference is between action and structure, but in everyday language it is better described as the distinction between 'free will' and 'inevitability' (not dictated by a religious deity or 'fate' but rather in the sense that social structures give rise to patterns of human interaction). Debates between structuralists (encompassing, for example, many variants of Marxism but also the conservative functionalism of Parsons or Merton) and voluntarists (for example, symbolic interactionists) faded after the 1960s and 1970s as theorists declared that, at the extremes, neither approach was adequate and called for new approaches to incorporate both action and structure into their work (see Giddens 1979, 1984, 1993). Marxist sociology also saw debates over the appropriate role of free will and social constraint in its explanations.

Marxist Theories of the State

As Jessop (1990: 25) notes, Marx did not offer an extended analysis of the capitalist state as part of his discussion of social relations in the three volumes of *Kapital*. Nonetheless, a considerable amount of attention and debate within Marxist sociology has dealt with the role of the state in relation to the capitalist class, and much of this debate has centred around the extent to which *state autonomy* does or does not exist. Are state bureaucrats, politicians, and officials pawns either of the capitalists or of larger historical processes that so constrain what they can do that they have no independent role in the development of social futures? Or do they play an important, discretionary role in initiating (or refusing to initiate) policy that will have a major impact not only on the lives of citizens but on class relations (structuring, for example, the manner in which struggles might take place)?

In its early form, the debate within Marxism over the state autonomy question was exemplified by the well-known debate between Miliband and Poulantzas in the *New Left Review* (Miliband 1970; Poulantzas 1969).[7] This debate pitted the *instrumentalist* approach of scholars such as Miliband, Domhoff, and Kolko against the *structuralist* approach of Poulantzas. The instrumentalist approach placed attention on the manner in which corporate connections with politicians and with the state bureaucracy could influence policy outcomes to the benefit of the capitalist class. In the Canadian context, it can be seen in the early work of Wallace Clement (1975). Instrumentalists focus much of their attention on documenting dense corporate networks and the ties between these networks and the state (see Barrow 1993: 14–47), and generally argue that the causal relationship is one way (that is, the capitalist class influences the actions of the state to its benefit, and not vice versa). Critics of this approach refer to it as 'class reductionist' (Hanneman and Hollingsworth 1992:

39), but these writers at least refocused the attention of Marxist scholars, who had hitherto not given the state much attention (see Mahon 1991).

The structuralist approach would allow for some independent effects of the state, and argue that its actions display a 'relative autonomy' from any given social class. Politicians and bureaucrats are not mere 'agents' of the capitalist class, but are social and political actors in their own right. Still, the dominant leitmotif of writers such as Poulantzas is that there are clear limits on this autonomy and the actions of the state in capitalist societies are largely determined 'in the last instance' by the character of class relations. One obvious form of limitation is that the main productive 'engine' in capitalist societies—the wealth-generating organizations—are constrained to take the form of private (usually for-profit) entities. Inasmuch as the state relies on these entities, acquiring its resources through taxation, its power and autonomy of action entails at least some limits. In the extreme form, capitalists have an enormous lever that can be held over the heads of state actors—the ability of capital to simply pull its investment from a given country (a phenomenon referred to as 'capital flight'). This issue is discussed extensively in Chapter 15 in Part E; the increasing *globalization* of the economic structure of countries has been the subject of much scholarly discussion over the past decade.

Authors such as Hanneman (1992: 39) would label instrumentalist approaches as 'class reductionistic'; the claim that a theoretical perspective is reductionistic is the argument that it (inappropriately) restricts social explanations to a single factor or class of factors when more complicated explanations are required. Hanneman links instrumentalists with their non-Marxist political opposites—structural functionalists—who 'placed considerable emphasis on other forces . . . [such as] ethno-cultural diversity, the level of economic development, etc.' Each, in its own way, plays down the autonomous role that the state is seen to play (at least by authors competing with both perspectives).

More recent writers in the Marxist perspective—Nicos Poulantzas, J. Hirsh, James O'Connor, and Fred Block—adopt what Hanneman has referred to as a 'weak' version of the 'class-centred' view, allowing that the state may be relatively autonomous from particular social classes. Still, as Hall (1994: 2) notes, there is a tendency in many Marxist perspectives to give the state a limited causal role that, while moving beyond the naive view that state structures are merely 'epiphenomenal' (see Jessop 1990), stops short of treating the state as a set of collective agents in its own right.

In Chapter 6, O'Connor touches on this issue, and discusses in more detail the relationship between Marxist structuralist explanations and their putative polar opposites, mainstream structural-functional explanations. While O'Connor's chapter focuses on the development of the welfare state, much of what she outlines in the way of theories of the welfare state has broad application. Her discussion of the question of the compatability of capitalism and the welfare state includes an important and useful outline of theories of 'crisis' and 'contradictions' of the state. O'Connor extends this discussion to an examination of the interrelationship of a liberal democratic political system and capitalist economic system in the context of welfare state policies. Later, she outlines the notion of 'welfare state regimes', distinguishing between social democratic, liberal, and corporatist (or status-based) systems, following Esping-Andersen's work. 'Liberal' here implies the dominance of private market mechanisms—something quite different from its use in popular parlance where, if anything, people associate the term with *more* government involvement in the provision of welfare and in the control of the economy.[8]

The Power Resources Model

What is the relationship between the level of welfare rights accorded to citizens and the struggles under which these evolved? O'Connor examines this question in Chapter 6. She outlines and discuss the power resources model, a perspective that will reappear elsewhere in the discussion of social movements (Chapter 8) and in the discussion of politics and social class (Chapter 15).

The O'Connor chapter in this part and the Johnston chapter in Part E both discuss what might be described as the rise of neoconservatism in Western societies. The names of leaders such as Margaret Thatcher and Ronald Reagan immediately come to mind, with some obvious (and some perhaps less than obvious) Canadian counterparts, including Brian Mulroney and provincial leaders such as Ralph Klein in Alberta and Mike Harris in Ontario. Each successfully promoted policies that involved radically reducing the size of the civil service, cutting government welfare expenditures (here, 'welfare' is seen in broad terms to include medical and even educational spending) and concomitantly reducing taxation (especially for corporations and wealthy taxpayers). As Johnston notes, the break with the long-standing 'accommodation' of the post-World War II period could hardly be more complete; whereas once the dominant political discourse centred around the assumed desirability of a welfare state compromise between the interests of the wealthy and the interests of the poor marginalized radical market-oriented approaches (including privatization of public assets, the elimination of universal programs, et cetera), the reverse is now the case. The political left has had difficulty countering the assault of the free market proponents with anything closely resembling a coherent strategy or a coherent discourse.

In different ways, Chapters 10 and 12 have some relevance to the questions raised on a theoretical level in this part. In Part D, 'Political Movements', Trevor Harrison discusses the rise of the Reform Party, precursor to the contemporary Alliance Party, in Canada. And Claude Denis outlines how the progressive social program of the

federal NDP party failed to lead to electoral success in the province of Quebec as a result of
assumptions and approaches taken by those making party strategy decisions in the late 1980s.

State-Centred Theory

No discussion of the state in contemporary society would be complete without reference to the
extensive literature following the work, in the
mid-1980s, of Theda Skocpol and her colleagues
(Evans et al. 1985; Skocpol 1979). This work has
dominated much of the attention given to the
state within the context of American political
sociology. It can be seen as a direct intellectual
assault on Marxist approaches, which are sometimes labelled 'society centred' inasmuch as these
perspectives are said (by Skocpol and her colleagues) to accord little causal priority to the
actions of the state (politicians and bureaucrats)
and most causal priority to 'societal' factors (most
notably social class).

The 'state-centred' perspective drew on two
initial forms of analysis: a comparative study of
revolutions in France, Russia, and China, and an
extensive analysis of the formation of New Deal
policies in United States (mostly federal) government agencies following the Depression of the
1930s. From the first of these arose the claim that
revolutions came about as a result of a crisis in
state systems rather than as a result of class antag-
onisms (Jessop 1990: 281–2). Similarly, the examination of the development of New Deal policies in the United States in the area of agriculture
(the US National Recovery Administration and
the Agricultural Adjustment Administration) led
to the conclusion that state factors (as opposed to
society factors) were key in the explanation of the
form that state policy took. The role of 'innovation' on the part of state policy-makers was seen
as particularly important in the United States,
and factors pertaining to the structure of the organization of the state itself were seen to account for

differences between Sweden and the United
States in terms of the national government's
'capacities to plan, coordinate and administer'
(Weir and Skocpol 1994: 371–3, 375–6).

It may not be surprising, then, that some of
the debate in the literature over the initial writings of Skocpol and her colleagues addresses two
questions: (a) Was Skocpol's account of the US
state during the period she studied correct—that
is, did she properly handle the 'empirical data'
(historical accounts) that she used? and (b) Does
the examination of other cases (different agencies
in the US state or state processes in other countries) validate or contradict the 'single case' findings pertaining to US agricultural policy? Here,
the reviews have been mixed (see Barkey and
Parikh 1991; Hooks 1990; McCammon 1994).
And Skocpol's work appears to have motivated
historical analyses seeking to demonstrate the
antithesis: that class mattered (see, for example,
McNall, Levine, and Fantasia 1991). More telling,
though, has been the criticism that her theoretical
conceptualization is too 'dualistic'.

Through the 1990s, the emerging response to
the idea of 'state-centred theory' has been an
uneasiness with the extreme form of this argument, and not with its admonition that theorists
should not simply disregard any historical
processes undertaken by human actors within the
confines of what can be called the state. As Jessop
(1990: 387) and others (Mahon 1991: 123)
argue, the state-centred perspective may rest on a
'straw man' account of the previous literature
(especially Marxist literature) of the state, some of
which contains a more nuanced and qualified
account of the interplay between society and state
factors, between class explanations and those
seeking to look for causal factors elsewhere, and
indeed between voluntarism and determinism
(what is inevitable given the class structure of a
society and what is changeable given the willful
action of human factors). As Barkey and Parikh
(1991: 525) state, a variety of empirical investiga-

tions may point to 'a more moderate version of the state's role by embedding it in its societal context' (see also Das 1996).

Skocpol (1992) seems to have backed off from the strong versions of her 'neo-institutionalist' claim, and conceded that her thinking had evolved into a 'policy-centred' approach in a book on the development of military pensions. What persuaded her was the ability of women outside the state to have an influence on government policies. One of her harshest critics, Domhoff, responded by claiming that she had 'in effect pronounc[ed] her own theory dead' (Domhoff 1992: 103) and that the new theoretical perspective appeared to be little more than 'old-fashioned pluralism'.[9] It may thus be the case that the intense debate over state-centred theory has and will continue to recede in prominence from the discipline of sociology, replaced by a more synthetic approach which argues, basically, that there was a kernel of truth in both sides of the argument (Gilbert and Howe 1991; Weiss 1997, 1998).

A DECLINE IN INTEREST IN THE STATE?
Writing 13 years after the publication of the book that generated the debate over state-centred theory, Weiss (1998: 1–2) argues that English social scientists, who in the 1980s wrote considerably more about the state than their American counterparts, seem to have left the field of study and gone elsewhere. 'Who reads "Bringing the State Back In" these days?' she asks, identifying broad trends and concerns in political sociology as having moved away from the state itself. These concerns include: (a) discussions about 'civil society', (b) the 'postmodernist turn' in contemporary social science, and (c) economic globalization and the transnational market.

It is certainly the case that the attention of many political sociologists has turned to issues associated with 'civil society' (Cohen 1982; Cohen and Arato 1992) and involved the often-enthusiastic discussion of the role of new social

movements (NSMs) in contemporary Western societies. *Civil society* is usually defined as encompassing those organizations and movements that stand between capital (the economy) and the state, including voluntary associations, social movements, and, depending on the conceptualization, families and churches.[10] Whether this academic inquiry should supplant the thorough theoretical and empirical investigation of the role of the state in capitalist societies is, however, another matter. A thorough discussion of the theoretical importance of civil society for sociological inquiry can be found in Part C (and, specifically, in Chapter 8). One promising direction for this sort of work would be to re-integrate the study of political processes and the state with the study of social movements, so that the state is not merely an empty vessel having no relevance to the path to be taken by social movements seeking to transform the 'culture' of contemporary society through attention to environmental issues, minority rights, and even social inequality in general.

Postmodernism as a theoretical orientation takes on many guises, so it is difficult to outline the implications this perspective has for a theory of the state. It has led to the widespread abandonment of some earlier perspectives, especially those with structural overtones, within the cohort of Canadian sociologists where this orientation is most prominent. Postmodernism imported analytic forms from other disciplines into sociology (for example, textual analysis) and applied them to the study of the social (Bromley 1991; Dickens and Fontana 1994; Hindness 1996; Murphy 1989; Shapiro 1992). Much of the initial impetus for the perspective came from its critique of Marxism as a 'grand narrative'. But the move away from formalistic, structural analyses of the state to those that incorporated notions of historicity, contingency, and the role of willful human action had already been well underway—even within 'neo-Marxist' perspectives—by the time postmodernism arrived on the scene (see, for example, the work of Korpi (1983, 1987a, 1987b, 1989; Korpi and Shalev 1980). It remains to be seen how extensive the postmodern orientation will become in Canadian political sociology over the next decade, and what sort of an influence it will have, ultimately, on the study of the state.

The question of the relationship between globalization and the state has now begun to capture the attention of political sociologists (Horsman and Marshall 1994; Laxer 1995; Piven 1995; Ruccio, Resnick, and Wolff 1991; Weiss 1997), and is likely to continue to do so in the future. In Chapter 5, Jeffrey also discusses globalization in considerable detail. The chapter bears some affinity with postmodernist theorizing and discourse, and emphasizes changes that have occurred (and the implications of these changes) in the transition from the 'modern' period. Perhaps this chapter takes an extreme view of globalization. As discussed in Chapter 1, the strong or radical version of the globalization thesis posits an unstoppable set of processes driven by technological change and the power of global capitalist enterprises acting in at least a partially concerted fashion to render irrelevant the rule of democratically elected governments. In many senses, it constitutes a *deterministic* argument, of the sort that postmodernist thinking would eschew—simple cause-effect structures representing social processes that cannot be changed by willed or conscious human intervention. This extreme version is discussed extensively by Faulks (1999: 55–67), whose useful overview of the literature suggests that some of the claims of the extreme version of the globalization thesis are exaggerated. There is, he argues, no global culture, though we cannot deny the fact that elements of US culture have found their way into local cultures around the world (often, though, expropriated and used quite differently than in the United States). And the term *internationalization* is probably more appropriate than *globalization* to describe the world economy; large companies are still 'overwhelmingly multinational rather than transnational, relying as they do on the political and legal frameworks provided by states' (Faulks 1999: 69). So, many writers have argued that there remain important avenues for the state to exercise power in the face of global forces that extend beyond its boundaries (Weiss 1997).

Notice, though, that Jeffrey, while describing in bleak detail the possible consequences of a homogeneous, globalized world, does not take on a determinist frame. In other words, his chapter speaks of globalization as a set of pressures on the state, rather than a set of inevitable process. And it posits some alternative futures, placing the chapter clearly in the camp (now ascendant in political sociology) where human actors are not hapless victims to inevitable processes (the 'momentum of history' or the inevitability of conflict) but at least have the potential to discuss and act on the problems that they have identified.

All the chapters in this part point to the continued importance of conceptualizations of the state in political sociology. Debates still take hold of the imaginations of political sociologists, and the variety of perspectives seen here suggests an ongoing vitality in this important topic of discussion.

Notes

1. See Gellner (1983, 1986), who suggests that language forms the basis for the construction of nations.

2. Oommen (1997: ix) makes the useful observation that, using the standard of whether or not a country is a settler nation, Africa and Asia qualify as part of the 'Old World'.

3. This formulation is, to be sure, a bit too simplistic. First, some countries such as Canada will have had more than one single 'founding' language around which practices and institutions developed initially. Secondly, there is at least some evidence of the retention of language and institutions—although under conditions of strong contestation—where the immigrant population is large enough and entered fast enough to (a) establish its own institutions and (b) act with a critical mass under which the use of the 'host' country's language can be avoided. This may be the case with the Spanish language in California.

4. Oomen (1997: 138) notes that, in 1789, half of the population in France did not speak French.

5. Specifically, in Quebec, with language laws preventing immigrants from receiving schooling in English.

6. The Turpel chapter was originally written in 1992.

7. See also Miliband 1973; Poulantzas 1976; Poulantzas 1978.

8. In any discussion in political science or political sociology, one must be careful of the term *liberalism*, for, more often than not—especially outside of the context of American scholarship—it implies a political orientation towards *minimalist* government (reductions in government), not the opposite (see Hyland 1995; Habermas 1996).

9. Pluralism is the perspective that argues that no one group has power. Thus, while multiple élites may govern a society, there is no one dominant group. Sometimes, this is extended with the argument that the overall public interest is thus safeguarded and protected (against, for example, the abuse of monopoly power) by the competitive interplay of these groups. Domhoff's strongest attack can be found in *The Power Elite and the State* (1990).

10. In some but by no means all formulations, education systems are not construed as part of this more or less autonomous domain.

References

Barkey, K., and S. Parikh. 1991. 'Comparative Perspectives on the State', *Annual Review of Sociology* 17: 523–49.

Barrow, C. 1993. *Critical Theories of the State: Marxist, Neo-Marxist and Post-Marxist* (Madison, WI: University of Wisconsin Press).

Bromley, S. 1991. 'The Politics of Postmodernism', *Capital and Class* 45: 129–50.

Chodak, S. 1989. *The New State: Etatization of Western Societies* (Boulder, CO: Lynne Rienner).

Clement, W. 1975. *The Canadian Corporate Elite: An Analysis of Economic Power* (Toronto: McClelland & Stewart).

Cohen, J. 1982. *Class and Civil Society: The Limits of Marxian Critical Theory* (Amherst, MA: University of Massachusetts Press).

———, and A. Arato. 1992. *Civil Society and Political Theory* (Cambridge, MA: MIT Press).

Das, R. 1996. 'State Theories: A Critical Analysis', *Science and Society* 60: 27–57.

Dickens, D., and A. Fontana. 1994. 'Postmodernism in the Social Sciences'. In *Postmodernism and Social Inquiry*, eds D. Dickens and A. Fontana (London: Guilford Press), 1–22.

Domhoff, G.W. 1990. *The Power Elite and the State: How Policy is Made in America* (New York: A. de Gruyter).

———. 1992. 'The Death of State Autonomy Theory: A Review of Skocpol's Protecting Soldiers and Mothers', *Critical Sociology* 19(2): 103–16.

Evans, P.B., D. Rueschemeyer, T. Skocpol, Social Science Research Council (US), Committee on States and Social Structures, Joint Committee on Latin American Studies, and Joint Committee on Western Europe. 1985. *Bringing the State Back In* (Cambridge: Cambridge University Press).

Faulks, K. 1999. *Political Sociology: A Critical Introduction* (Edinburgh: Edinburgh University Press).

Gellner, E. 1983. *Nations and Nationalism* (Ithaca, NY: Cornell University Press).

———. 1986. *Culture, Identity and Politics* (Cambridge: Cambridge University Press).

Giddens, A. 1979. *Central Problems in Social Theory: Action, Structure and Contradiction in Social Analysis* (Berkeley, CA: University of California Press).

———. 1984. *Constitution of Society* (Los Angeles: University of California Press).

———. 1993. *New Rules of Sociological Method: A Positive Critique of Interpretative Sociologies* (Stanford, CA: Stanford University Press).

———. 1995. *A Contemporary Critique of Historical Materialism* (Stanford, CA: Stanford University Press).

Gilbert, J., and C. Howe. 1991. 'Beyond "State vs. Society": Theories of the State and New Deal Agricultural Policies', *American Sociological Review* 56(2): 204–20.

Habermas, J. 1996. 'Three Normative Models of Democracy'. In *Contesting the Boundaries of the Political*, ed. S. Benhabib (Princeton, NJ: Princeton University Press), 21–30.

Hall, J. 1994. *Coercion and Consent: Studies on the Modern State* (Cambridge: Polity Press).

Hanneman, R., and J. Rogers Hollingsworth. 1992. 'Refocusing the Debate on the Role of the State in Capitalist Societies'. In *State Theory and State History*, ed. R. Torstendahl (Newbury Park, CA: Sage), 38–61.

Hindness, B. 1996. *Discourses of Power: From Hobbes to Foucault* (Oxford: Blackwell).

Hooks, G. 1990. 'From an Autonomous to a Captured State Agency: The Decline of the New Deal in Agriculture', *American Sociological Review* 55(1): 75–91.

Horsman, M., and A. Marshall. 1994. *After the Nation-State: Citizens, Tribalism and the New World Disorder* (London: Harper Collins).

Hyland, J. 1995. *Democratic Theory: The Philosophical Foundations* (Manchester: Manchester University Press).

Jessop, B. 1990. *State Theory: Putting the Capitalist State in Its Place* (Cambridge: Polity Press).

Korpi, W. 1983. *The Democratic Class Struggle* (London: Routledge).

———. 1987a. 'Political and Economic Explanations for Unemployment: A Cross-National and Long-Term Analysis', *British Journal of Political Science* 21: 315–48.

———. 1987b. 'Power, Politics and State Autonomy in the Development of Social Citizenship', *American Sociological Review* 54(3): 309–28.

———. 1989. 'Power, Politics and State Autonomy in the Development of Social Citizenship: Social Rights During Sickness in Eighteen OECD Countries Since 1930', *American Sociological Review* 54: 309–28.

——— and M. Shalev. 1980. 'Strikes, Power, and Politics in the Western Nations, 1900–1976', *Political Power and Social Theory* 1: 301–34.

Laxer, G. 1995. 'Social Solidarity, Democracy and Global Capitalism', *Canadian Review of Sociology and Anthropology* 32(3): 287–314.

McCammon, H. 1994. 'Disorganization and Reorganizing Conflict: Outcomes of the State's Legal Regulation of the Strike since the Wagner Act', *Social Forces* 72(4): 1011–49.

McNall, Scott, R. Levine, and R. Fantasia. 1991. 'Introduction'. In *Bringing Class Back In: Contemporary and Historical Perspectives* (Boulder, CO: Westview Press).

Mahon, R. 1991. 'From "Bringing" to "Putting": The State in Late Twentieth Century Social Theory', *Canadian Journal of Sociology* 16(2): 119–44.

Miliband, R. 1970. 'The Capitalist State: A Reply to Nico Poulantzas', *New Left Review* 59.

———. 1973. *The State in Capitalist Society* (London: Quartet Books [1969].

Murphy, J. 1989. *Postmodern Social Analysis and Criticism* (Westport, CT: Greenwood Press).

Oommen, T.K. 1997. *Citizenship, Nationality and Ethnicity: Reconciling Competing Identities* (Cambridge: Polity Press).

Pierson, C. 1996. *The Modern State* (London: Routledge).

Piven, F. 1995. 'Is It Global Economics or Neo-Laissez-Faire?' *New Left Review* 213: 107–14.

———. 1969. 'The Problem of the Capitalist State', *New Left Review* 58.

———. 1976. 'The Capitalist State: A Reply to Miliband and Laclau', *New Left Review* 95.

———. 1978. *State, Power, Socialism*, trans. P. Camiller (London: NLB).

Ruccio, D., S. Resnick, and R. Wolff. 1991. 'Class Beyond the Nation-State', *Capital and Class* 43: 25–41.

Shapiro, M. 1992. *Political Theory as Textual Practice* (Minneapolis: University of Minnesota Press).

Skocpol, T. 1979. *States and Social Revolutions: A Comparative Analysis of France, Russia, and China* (Cambridge: Cambridge University Press).

———. 1992. *Protecting Soldiers and Mothers: The Political Origins of Social Policy in the United States* (Cambridge, MA: Belknap Press of Harvard University Press).

Tilly, C., G. Ardant, and Social Science Research Council (US). Committee on Comparative Politics. 1975. *The Formation of National States in Western Europe* (Princeton, NJ: Princeton University Press).

Weir, M. and T. Skocpol. 1994. 'State Structures and Social Keynesianism: Responses to the Great Depression in Sweden and the United States'. In *The State: Critical Concepts*, vol. 2, ed. J. Hall (London: Routledge).

Weiss, L. 1997. 'Globalization and the Myth of the Powerless State', *New Left Review* 225: 3–27.

———. 1998. *The Myth of the Powerless State: Governing the Economy in a Global Era* (Cambridge: Polity Press).

Chaper 5

Globalization and the Late-Modern State

Alan Jeffrey

> The individual must be studied in the state, and the state in the individual.
> Rousseau (1712–78)

Introduction

For hundreds of years, the nation-state has constituted the major institutional-level influence on individual lives. At the same time, the nation-state is undergoing radical changes that will continue to affect individual lives. The following chapter assesses the changing role of the state in terms of multiculturalism, tribalism, natural resources, borders, and violence, and examines its future prospects.

Our starting point for tracking changes is *modernity*, a term used by sociologists and political scientists as a marker for the ending of the traditional world and the beginning of the modern world. In broad terms, 'traditional' societies exist in oral-religious cultures where the social hierarchy is based on birth (ascription) and there is little chance of social mobility. Custom and accepted practices guide people's actions, extended families exist in face-to-face communities (*Gemeinschaft*), and change is viewed negatively. In a 'modern' society, the culture tends to be literate, secular, and scientific, achievement affects the social hierarchy, actions are legitimated in terms of 'progress', and social mobility is high. The categories of 'family' diversify within an impersonal society (*Gesellschaft*) and change is viewed positively.

Modernism involved such phenomena as urbanization, secularization, industrialism, capitalism, and a progressive development of 'mass' life. It also includes: individualism, a belief in linear progress and absolute truths, rational planning, an expansion of instrumental reason, and the standardization of knowledge and of production. There is a concentration of administrative resources in modern states that control increasingly sophisticated means of using military strength and making war. With the evolution of modernity came an increasingly interdependent global system of industrialized societies, an integrated global division of labour, accelerated social change, and rapid technological innovation, including computerization and robotics.

Today, there is another transition taking place as we move away from the industrial base of the Western modern state into a world social and economic order that takes on a different form. In this new world, globalization is more important, and there is less emphasis on industrial production in First World countries. Commentators speculate about various social and economic forms that will supersede the industrial base in a 'postindustrial society'. Drucker (1993), for instance, suggests a 'knowledge base'. The current experiences of modernity may be considered a transition-in-progress. Whereas the label *Postmodernity* may suggest a completed transition, terms such as *High Modernity*, *Radical Modernity* or *Late Modernity*, capture the 'in-process' nature of the changes taking place.

In this transitional period, the late-modern state is experiencing pressures that are changing its functions, its abilities, and its role. The first and catalytic pressure is globalization, which from one perspective is an attempt to Americanize the cultures and economies of the world. The second is a series of low-level wars, spread throughout the world, waged against facets of modernity. The third is the depletion of natural resources and the increases in population that are intertwined with the fourth, the weakening of national borders, and the fifth, the increased potential of the movement of disadvantaged peoples of the Third World into First World late-modern nation-states.

In the Western world, the state is progressively changing because of outside forces that appear in the minds of observers to be beyond control. The state's provision of democratic participation in the form of public decision-making seems to be waning whereas the private decision-making that goes on in corporate boardrooms and offices has increasingly more influence. Some see corporations as 'corpora nations'.

Globalization has produced international agencies and contracts, such as the free trade agreement, that control and sometimes overrule aspects of the state, and hence affect the circumstances of everyday life. It has brought benefits for some, disasters for others, effected a general sense of uncertainty, and set forces in motion that, left unchecked, may bring about opposite effects, such as regionalism and tribalism. From an 'American perspective', globalization, especially 'free trade', is positive and is the culmination of a process leading to cultural homogeneity and a one-world civilization—some name it 'the Enlightenment project'. Capitalism, organized in the form of global enterprises (multinational corporations), is the engine of 'progress' and of the 'pregress' of the current pressures on the state.

The changing of cultures to the American brand-name consumer culture provides new markets. Recently, Coke achieved a market in every country in the world. However, one could argue that some worldwide violence may be a series of religious struggles by certain cultures against the 'immorality of modernism' that has been unintentionally sparked and sustained by the global reach and content of American videology such as MTV.

Another pressure on the late-modern state has been the result of the expansion of capitalism on a global basis, through its hold over cultures, states, and economies, and the resulting exploitation, and consequent depletion, of natural resources. When such depletion is coupled with increasing overpopulation and a decreasing access to the essentials to sustain life, the necessities become more inaccessible to the majority of people in the world. As access to natural resources (the necessities for life) decreases, violence in the name of accessing those essentials increases. In parts of the world, such as the Gold Coast of Africa, scarce resources have increased the intensity of forms of tribal warfare that include a return to warlords. All the while, the forces of capitalism continue to deplete those resources.

The above pressures, linked to an ecologically borderless world, are poised to crumble the borders of the late-modern state. We are now able to look upon many borders between countries as the marking of 'property' of those involved in the expansion of European culture throughout the world. The European colonizers, equipped with 'modern' cartography, constructed many of the borders between countries, in not only Europe itself but also elsewhere. The resulting map has been described as a ledger book of capitalism. With the ending of colonialism, these capitalistic borders, which many peoples were either unaware of, or resented, are being tested, disputed, ignored, changed, or overrun. The map of colonization had suppressed ancient ethnic grievances, which are bursting forth throughout the world as the artificial borders disappear. These pressures on borders also culminate in what is, and will increasingly be, points of confrontation. First World borders are becoming more permeable as witnessed by the increasing flow of illegal immigrants (sometimes called 'human cargo') into First World states.

Multiculturalism and monoculturalism are about borders and there are opposing views about the societal value of the former. Many see multiculturalism as a way to open up borders and to include. In a mirrorlike fashion, certain Canadian writers claim multiculturalism is a form of resistance by visible minorities against the borders created and sustained by racism. That negative view of multiculturalism may remove one set of borders but can set up the ever-regressive increase of borders required by monoculturalism. The resistance against the borders of racism in Canada is linked, by certain commentators (see Allahar and Côté 1998), to Fanon's (1963) writings about the liberation of Algeria from the yoke of colonialism. In resistance to colonialism and to multiculturalism, the extreme form of resistance is violence.

There are deep human tendencies, such as the 'in-group out-group' syndrome, that are brought to light in a discussion of multiculturalism. The in-group/out-group syndrome, when coupled with the acknowledgement of certain war historians that violence is a 'joy' to many people, may well turn the First World into a 'guarded Palace'. Further, several commentators believe that if the pressures that we have discussed so far are not alleviated, there is an almost unthinkable scenario that First World states may use the violent means at their disposal to prevent a flood of stateless, starving, thirsty, and emaciated Third World populations from crossing the borders into the lands of plenty.

RELATING THE PROBLEM TO CANADA: THE QUEBEC CASE

The 'Quebec situation' provides a local case to explore the above pressures on the late-modern nation-state. The focus will be a counterfactual question: 'What happens when Quebec secedes from Canada?' The Quebec situation involves the coexistence of the material benefits of modernism and the 'identity politics' manifest in the need for a separate national-cultural identity. Identity politics is a means of achieving power through identity and is often tied to multicultural, multiethnic, and multiracial concepts that grew out of the policy of integration, rather than assimilation. Further, Hughes (1993) views late-modern society as 'therapeutic' and therapeutic politics of identity are the cornerstone of the 'Culture of Complaint'. He sees that in a culture of complaint, set within a therapeutic late-nation-state: 'Identity politics has come to serve as a substitute for religion'.

The Quebec situation brings into focus the identity politics of indigenous peoples within the identity politics of Quebec, the control over natural resources, the changing of borders, especially those between Canada, Quebec, and the United States, and the power of the latter over the other two.

We can look at relationships between Canada and Quebec from two viewpoints. The Enlightenment view may see progress and mutual understanding in the future of Canada and Quebec. From an antimodernist view, the future prospect conjures the probability of violence. We will return to this very important question for Canadians after first examining some prevailing conceptions in political sociology regarding the relationship between individuals and society, and between free will and 'constraint'. Sociologists refer to this as the question of agency and structure.

Agency and Structure

Transformations in self-identity and globalization . . . are the two poles of the dialectic of the local and the global in conditions of high modernity.

Giddens (1990)

A person's ability to act freely is sometimes contested. When we ask: 'To what degree is the individual formed by the structure of society, the institutions of the state, or to what degree are those institutions and structure constituted, sustained, or changed by people'—we are dealing with the interrelationships between psychological structures and social structures. The debate over the relationships between society (structure) and individual action (agency) involves three basic positions (see Archer 1989).

In the first relationship, an individual or dominant group forms or changes structural properties, which, in turn, affect the individual. We might look at the example of the Nazi regime in Germany in the 1930s and 1940s, where a dominant group changed the social structure, which in turn affected (or effected) changes in individuals. This view does not treat 'structure' as given or static: real human beings (the dominant group) are agents in its creation. The view thus involves an agentic active bottom-to-top, then top-to-bottom, use of structure. However, for most individuals outside of the dominant groups, it appears as structure influencing individuals, with little 'negotiation'.

The second relationship involves an extension in time of the first, which results in a passive, downwards pressure on individuals. The agentic actions that had culminated in existing structures or central value systems fade from consciousness and both the core and periphery groups (see Baldus 1977) no longer notice the forces that keep the power structures in place. This is achieved through socialization, especially in the school system, which is seen as a neutral institution even by those who put it in place to serve their interests, and whose interests it still serves. The school illustration can be compared to the forces that buttressed, for an extended period, the 'traditional' society we have discussed.

In the third relationship, structure and agency are co-constitutive. The position allows for little intervention of time, and 'odd' words are used to describe that lack. For instance, a school and students 'instantiate' each other—school (structure) requires students (agents) to be a school, and students (agents) require a school (structure) to be students (agents). The co-constitutive relationship may be conceived in the question: 'If someone organized a war and no one came would there be a war?' Giddens (1984) claims that an individual exists within, and at the same time reconstructs, relationships and institutions—he calls this middle position, 'structuration' theory.

There are many theories concerning the reasons and causes for social change, and the ways in which it is brought about. None of the above positions on the structure/agency debate is clear on the matter. However, Elias (1978: 225) focuses on social change, a topic central to this chapter, and presents an explanation of change that involves the interconnections and the 'acts' of people. It is a more explicitly agentic position than the three positions we have discussed. The interconnections are between individual psychological structures (personality structures) and figurations (social structures). The latter comprise groups of interdependent individuals. Individual psychological structures and figurations are different, but inseparable, planes of the universe formed by people (individuals) and society—related to different yet inseparable aspects of the same human beings—both involved in a structural transformation.

Bearing in mind the above conceptions of the interrelationships between the individual and the state (society), we can turn to a sociologist who 'prefigured' the forms of the interrelationships involved in current changes involved in globalization. In 1959, Mills (1967) discussed the ways in which the freedom of the individual to exercise 'will' (*agency*) can diminish because of changes in the *structure* of continentwide societies. That diminution of agency, if left unchecked, may intensify as globalizing 'forces' increasingly overrule the power of the late-modern state. For an individual to navigate through the uncharted waters of structural changes, Mills advocates the use of the 'sociological imagination'. As that imagination allows individuals to become aware of, and to contextualize, larger issues, space is provided for them to act (exercise their agency) in a world in which the late-modern state is in a process of transformation and in which uncertainty reigns.

ISSUES AND TROUBLES

In any case, no man with a weak stomach and insomnia has any business investigating his own kind.

Quoted in Erikson (1964: 23)

Mills uses the terms *issues* and *troubles* to make more human the sociological terms of macro/micro and structure/agency. Issues transcend the local environments of the individual. Issues, such as the movement of North America's industry to offshore, are known. However, they are often unknown to the individual, or are presented on the infotainment news from a viewpoint conducive to the interests of certain groups. Many observers note that corporations generally control the press and television networks (see Aronowitz 1992).

Initially, issues may have little impact on the individual's outer or inner life. However, they may well become troubles. Troubles exist for, and within, the individual, her immediate relations with others, and the surroundings that frame her personal experience. The issue of globalism and the consequent movement of sections of North America's industry to offshore sites may lead to the troubles of the disappearance of her job, the social and personal identities that the job once provided, and will perhaps bring about poverty and/or forced mobility. The issues raised by globalism and the Americanization of cultures threatens value systems and intensifies the change in structures such as the once traditional institutions as the community, the family, sustained employment, and the particular type of support they each provided.

It is obvious that the issue of globalization and the consequent changing role of the late-modern state lead to personal troubles for some (but advantages to others). The impact of the combined issues on the individual depends, to great extent, on the individual's knowledge (as the adage says 'advance knowledge wins the war'). It also depends, in part, on the evolving role of the late-modern state and the individual's agency, to contribute to changes in the larger issue, or her ability to adapt, or not, as the situation changes. Again, knowledge of the interactions of globalization and the late-modern state allows action to begin. Globalization, then, raises this question: As the late-modern state changes under the pressures bearing upon it, and those it provokes, to what degree can the individual control her or his future?

There are those that are assured that somehow their faith in science and technology will save the world from a situation that a misuse of science and technology are creating. However, while the Enlightenment vision sees a progress toward the one-world culture and civilization, the actuality may be a future rife with violence stemming from, and ending in, the desolation of nature. Again, a stance toward the future is influenced by one's beliefs about the relative powers of agency and structure. Among possible future scenarios, there are two major opposing visions.

WHO SHALL INHERIT THE EARTH?

Mills saw the macro-level changes taking place and wondered about the 'types of human beings' that will prevail (1967: 158). We can approach that question using Weber's 'ideal types'. 'Ideal' denotes the essential, rather than the best, features involved in a typology. Ideal types serve as a shorthand for describing macro-level properties of two major types of human beings. One is the Americanized brand-name consumer. The expression *consumer*, while common in sociological texts, requires some getting used to. Although it includes the everyday meaning of eating, it also means to buy, to watch, and to listen to, various tangible and intangible products. A useful contrast is provided by production. As we move away from producing, and identifying ourselves with our job, we move toward consuming and identify ourselves with where we live, the things we wear, the types of entertainment we enjoy, etc. In fact, in an Americanized society we often identify and are identified with our particular 'consumer lifestyle'. The Americanized consumer is educated by the media and achieves self-identity by consuming standardized, brand-name images/products.

The other orientation is antimodernist, and is one in which individuals may achieve a sense of self-identity as 'cultural warriors', often inculcated by fundamentalist identity politics. The warrior, in the name of deep-rooted beliefs, attacks the degradation inherent in modernity.

THE AMERICANIZED BRAND-NAME CONSUMER

Taylor (1991) claims that the first source of worry in the age of modernity stems from the Enlightenment's cult of individualism. In many senses, that cult may be seen to generate similarities rather than differences. Americanized culture now requires individuals who believe, think, and act as if they were independent people. In doing so, nothing stands between the market forces and the individual. Consumerism undermines skeptical inquiry, autonomous judgment, and knowledge of how to resist manipulation.

There is a possible consequence of individualism, namely a rootlessness that Durkheim (1966) called *anomie*, which is an orientation to the world resulting from discrediting traditional rituals and norms that once met the universal human need for certainty. Weber (1956) similarly describes a 'disenchantment of the world' in which the individual loses a sense of a higher purpose. This negative side of individualism, centring on the self, diminishes the scope and meaning of our lives and results in less concern for others or society, a shutting out, or unawareness, of the greater issues or concerns that transcend the self. Durkheim claimed that *anomie* results from a lack of societal guidelines and may be a base for suicide—a theory that might well be tested with today's youth.

Americanized culture, via media, reaches most of the world and the images presented have been called those of 'McWorld' (Barber 1996) and 'McDonaldization' (Ritzer 1996). 'McCulture' aims at changing *interdependent* cultures into a culture of supposedly *independent* individuals. MTV's worldwide reach has 'McColonized' many native cultures. People in many divergent parts of the globe listen to, watch, and 'consume' similar brand-name clothing and accessories as they are imageered (by the illusion of individual choice) into a one-world Americanized culture. Oddly, people strive to be themselves but do so by adopting new modes of conformity that are marketed as 'different'.

Such a world and worldview contributes to the uncertainty of late-modernity. Arendt (1959: 83) notes that the reality and reliability of the human world rest primarily on the fact that things are more permanent than the activity by which they are produced. Conversely, in a world of disposable commodities, either such permanence is under threat, or it has gone. The production and appreciation of lasting artifacts has been replaced by disposable objects, the value of which lasts until the next shift in consumer trends. As Marx portended, all that is solid melts in air. Such is the milieu and make-up of the 'Ideal' Americanized brand-name consumer.

THE ANTIMODERNIST CULTURAL WARRIOR

Interdependent people have customs and rituals that, if McWorld has not taken over, it has either strengthened or created. Americanized enculturation is a two-edged sword. Those same media, replete with aspects of postmodernism(s), are

Table 5.1   A Comparison between the 'Ideal' Basic Attributes of Cultural Warriors and Those of Americanized Brand-Name Consumers

Jihad	McWorld
Identity by race.	Identity by consumerism.
Re-tribalization.	Integrate nations.
Narrow faith.	Secular faith or no faith.
Against interdependence of states.	Against independence of states.
For uniformity at tribal level.	For uniformity at world-wide level.
Anti-modern.	Modern.
Held together by exclusion, hatred, and tyrannical paternalism or consensual tribalism.	Held together by consumerism, communications, information, entertainment, and commerce.

SOURCE: Barber (1996)

enculturating parts of the world. However, they reach and offend certain fundamentalist cultures. These 'antimodernist' cultures, in the name of the purity of their religious and/or ethnic and/or cultural identities wage *Jihads*, violent holy wars, often through terrorist acts against the Western corruption manifest in modernism (Barber 1996).

These warriors exist in many cultures and many countries, including parts of America, and hold strict views concerning the appropriate conduct of the individual and the group. Using 'identity politics' such as race, ethnicity, religion, and fundamentalist ideologies, 'identifiable groups' seek, recover, or invent tribal identities under which to war against the American paradigm (and, often, each other). The Hutu or Bosnian Serb identity is less a matter of real historical memory than of media propaganda. The global media provides local culture with a medium, an audience, and a 'controlled' way of making known its aspirations and, increasingly, its differences and the 'rights' entailed by those differences.

There is a chronic incommensurability between the two cultures and consequent world views. The present 'solution' appears to be a series of propaganda and/or physical confrontations.

AGAIN: THE INTERRELATIONSHIPS BETWEEN PSYCHOLOGICAL STRUCTURES AND SOCIAL STRUCTURES

There is a late-modern belief that markets ultimately defeat ideology.[1] Consequently, Americanized consumers, often unaware and mesmerized, belonging to an 'unconscious civilization' (Saul 1995), move to the one-world civilization envisaged by the Enlightenment project.[2] On the other hand, some cultural warrior groups seek to maintain or establish an ethnically cleansed nation-state, as the recent events in the Balkans and Africa attest. Their mission is to establish a 'true' nation-state. Tilly (1990) notes that *national states* govern multiple contiguous regions and their cities by means of centralized, differentiated, and autonomous structures. These contrast with nation-states whose people share a strong linguistic, religious, and symbolic identity. These 'true' nation-states contribute to ever-multiplying borders.

Globalism's conjuring of violence against the late-modern state brings to light the state's 'legitimate' control of violence. The use of violence gave birth to the state and the state maintains its position by the threat or use of physical coercion. There is symmetry between the violence of present-day *Jihads* directed against the late-modern state and the violence that culminated in the birth of the nation-state.

AMERICA: THE LAST BASTION OF THE ENLIGHTENMENT PROJECT

O'Brien (1994: 151) states that: 'The United States is the heart and soul of the Enlightenment tradition, it being the only country committed to that tradition emotionally as well as intellectually'. That America apparently leads the Enlightenment project is evidenced by its influence on worldwide culture, its worldwide corporatism, and by its military power. Gray (1999: 101) provides a perspective on America's role in globalization as an extension of the Enlightenment project, when he states: 'Only in the United States is the Enlightenment project of a global civilization still a living political faith'.

From the Enlightenment's view, all peoples share a common human nature but each nation and age has unique characteristics. Consequently, all have the right to human fulfillment, to think freely, to publicly express personal opinion, and to realize their individual goals though political thought and action. These require the presence of equality, justice, and legal changes to extend rationalistic theories as the bases of law, social peace, and just order. However, O'Brien cautions that such a rosy view does not fully account for the range of human nature.

The Americanized Enlightenment project continues through the efficiency of American-style production/service provision, which when coupled with techniques of advertising and videology offers an image of a theme-parklike world filled with unlimited consumption. It has been, in many ways, successful, and its global reach extensive. When viewed from the American Enlightenment perspective it is 'progress' (a relatively recent and a much-used American term) toward an Americanized world civilization. However, to paraphrase Marx, it may well be pregnant with the seeds of its own destruction.

THE FREE(?) MARKET

A major constituent of the Enlightenment project, as discussed above, is the concern for individual freedom. The Enlightenment concern for freedom, mixed with a gross misunderstanding of Darwin's observations about the survival of the fittest, resulted in a *laissez-faire* (from the French 'leave it alone') ideology. Such economics seek to prevent governments from manipulating the economy because the 'law' of supply and demand stabilizes the economy (for example, in Canada, provincial governments in Ontario and Alberta are run by political parties that claim to be in favour of 'less government').

Free market ideology is far from new. Spencer was the first commentator to discuss natural selection's disposal of the unfit, and Social Darwinists, equipped with a perverse interpretation of Darwin's evolutionary law of the survival of the fittest, transposed it from its biological origin into the sociocultural arena. Social Darwinism became a part of the free market faith that brought England rapid material progress. To many capitalists, the withering of weak companies in a *laissez-faire* economy was the working out of a law of nature and a law of God. If people starved because they could not get sufficiently well-paying jobs in the job market, this too was 'natural' and governments should not be expected to intervene on their behalf.

Britain gave birth to the free market. It never was free; it resulted from savage governmental action. State power transformed common land into private property; the repeal of *Corn Laws* established agricultural free trade. *The Poor Law Act* set the level of subsistence lower than the lowest wage set by the market. In England, industrial transformation and the establishment of the market (labour markets especially, where workers buy and sell their 'labour power' to employers) weakened the institution of the mutual aid of the family and community and shifted it onto the individual, who was solely responsible for her or his own welfare. In the human species, social relations no longer embed the economy: the economic system embeds social relations. The free market is an Anglo-Saxon phenomenon and the first attempt survived until its collapse in the Great Depression. The devastation of the Depression gave rise, once again, to the communal assistance for the individual that free trade had wiped away.

Laissez-faire, anachronistically and strangely, returned to political life in the 1980s and 1990s. Sixty years after the first failure, proponents of the second free trade movement are again removing mutual assistance. It is as if the worldwide Depression of the 1930s had never occurred. Many commentators despair about the historical amnesia in Western populations and their governments. A pre-eminent historian writes:

> Those of us who lived through the years of the great slump still find it almost impossible to understand how the orthodoxies of the pure free market, then so obviously discredited, once again came to preside over a global period of depression in the late 1980s and 1990s. . . . Still, the strange phenomenon should remind us of . . . the incredible shortness of memory of both the theorists and practitioners of economics (Hobsbawm 1994: 103).

Those who are attempting the resurrection of free trade assume that the economic life of every nation can resemble that of America. However, capitalism is not following the American model in many other countries. The deregulated market in late-modern societies has engendered, in other cultures, new varieties of capitalism. For instance, in China and the Soviet Union, there are varieties of postcommunist anarcho-capitalism. The first utopia of a single global free market failed. According to Gray (1999), the second attempt has already failed.

GLOBALIZATION AND THE DIMINUTION OF THE LATE-MODERN STATE

The subservience of the late-modern state is to the ever-present shadow 'control' of international finance. Out of the shadow, it appears that corporations rule the state. Many hold to the futility thesis that asserts that neither individual nor collective action is worth undertaking against the corporate world since it will eventually prove incapable of redressing current inequity; McQuaig (1999) calls such a capitulation 'the cult of impotence'. The futility thesis is a mind-set born of the interrelations between psychological structures and social structures. It acquiesces to the power of structure over agency. The cult is an example of downward pressure by an existing structure or central value system—in the present case, corporatism—that imposes itself on cultural life. Many accept it through socialization and act and think as if there were never agentic actions behind the structure/agency situation. It is a Wizard of Oz scenario.

STRUCTURE, AGENCY, AND THE MALLEABILITY OF HUMAN NATURE

As we explored the interrelationships among individual psychological structures and figurations, psychological structures and social structures, the first question that arose was about the 'types of people' likely to develop. A parallel question is, 'How malleable are people in adapting to the structural changes "imposed" on them?'

We noted that it is important to understand the past with regard to gaining a fuller picture of the late-modern state (and the foolishness of not doing so with regard to free trade). The changes wrought by modernity not only produced the nation-state; they also introduced disciplines that examine change, such as psychology and sociology. Human nature was inimically involved with early sociological views on the state.

HUMAN NATURE AND PRESENT-DAY POLITICS

> I do not see how, at the level of theory, sociologists can fail to make assumptions about

human nature. If our assumptions are left implicit, we will inevitably presuppose a view of man that is tailor-made to our special needs. . . . Sociologists need to develop a more complex, dialectical conception of human nature instead of relying on an implicit conception that is tailor-made for special sociological problems (Wrong 1961).

Mills was concerned about the nature of human nature in the context of the worldwide changes that are taking place. Different views regarding the role of the state are built on concepts about the nature of the individual and about the nature of human nature. These opposing views gave rise to conceptions of different societies, each corresponding to a particular view about human nature, and a consequent view of the interrelationships between individual psychological structures and figurations.

For conservatives, human beings are imperfect and because human nature is faulty, no one can devise a perfect social system.[3] The negatives of existence cannot be eliminated but can be controlled in a society that is just and fair. Because many people will not exert themselves and motivation is lost, the levelling of classes will lead to a stagnant society. Change should take place slowly and with a respect for the precedents of the past. Some people are poor and some fail; and these unfortunate facts represent the natural diversity of human nature and the social system.

For a social democrat, human nature is such that all people are equal and deserve equal treatment.[4] Humans are not naturally good but they can be bettered through social policies (such as the fight for civil rights legislation). Changing laws will eventually produce changes in attitudes and everyday practices. Consequently, a strong government can be a good government.

The main political force behind and at play in the globalized, individualized, *laissez-faire* world is libertarianism. For the libertarian, there is an assumption of a discoverable, essential, human nature that is rational and operates in a free world equipped with a set of rights. The individual is an autonomous, discrete self. There is equality of opportunities, rather than equality of outcomes. Consequently, there is a support of the Protestant work ethic whereby people are successful because they educate themselves and apply themselves to work. Individuals are largely responsible for their own actions (we can see the libertarian influence in dismantling social supports during both attempts at *laissez-faire* markets). Through reason and utilitarianism (where everyone tries to maximize his or her happiness, without infringing on the rights of others) individuals can successfully live together. Because the individual is the centre of the social universe and individual freedom and individual rights are the highest values, the use of coercion is anathema. Libertarianism is liberal about social issues and allows any act that does not directly harm another person. There is a fundamental right to property and support for *laissez-faire* economics, and a call for a minimalist government.

It is clear that both pre- and postrevolutionary development of theories of the state rest on conceptions of human nature. The question of innate human goodness is political; it affects the linkage between views of human nature, ideologies, and forms of states. The question of the malleability of human nature is important in the context of the state's ability to socially engineer human beings, the types of people that can be 'produced', and the limits to such engineering. However, the form, nature, or the existence of human nature is problematic in the majority of present-day social sciences.

NEO-DARWINIANISM

We are potentially moral animals but we are not naturally moral animals. To be moral animals, we must realize how thoroughly we are not.

Wright (1994)

Neo-Darwinianism supports the idea of a common genetic basis for behaviour that applies to all humans of whatever culture. Perhaps the greatest contribution neo-Darwinianism can make to the late-modern state is to reveal, and to take into account, aspects of, and limitations to, human nature when implementing or altering state institutions. While taking into account human nature, neo-Darwinians acknowledge that the most radical differences among people are traceable to environment. They support the claim that alterations of the environment can alter most manifestations of human nature. Consequently, to say something is a product of natural selection is not to say that it is unchangeable.

A neo-Darwinian theory has implications in that a workable public policy must consider the limitations of human nature if it is to be effective. If people are selfish, then asking some to contribute to the good of the whole while some do not is an imposition and will be a policy difficult to sustain. On the other hand, as Swiss cantons prove by their long existence, humans can work for the good of the whole. Blanc's dictate, 'from each according to her ability, to each according to her need' aligns with the mutual aid that is important in natural selection's survival of the fittest (see Kropotkin 1989).

NEO-DARWINIANISTIC THEORY APPLIED TO INSTITUTIONS OF THE LATE-MODERN STATE

An example of policy changes that take into account genetics, and are already in effect in state institutions, can be found in the judiciary. Law rests on the assumption of free will. However, if a behaviour rests on chemistry, such that low serotonin levels encourage crime, a case can be made for diminished responsibility. Lawyers have argued a number of cases based on a person's chemical composition. They include the proposition that junk food produces diminished capacity to think clearly, and that full premeditation of a

crime is thus impossible. Those people who experience the 'action-addict syndrome' will seek higher levels of endorphins. Consequently, because the accused can satisfy the craving through committing a crime, a case can again be made that a lack of free will removes the action from the criminal jurisdiction.

The above in-place law practices suggest an overhauling legal doctrine where free will has served as the centre for justice. If the importance of free will continues to diminish in the eyes of the law, we could decide to 'restore' it and void the notion that biochemical conditions have a bearing on volition. An opposite course of action involves downplaying volition and adapting ourselves to utilitarian criteria for 'appropriate' punishment. Whatever course is taken between these extremes, it is vital to know of the hitherto unacknowledged aspects of our selves and of the limits to controlling them.

Neo-Darwinianism seeks to explain the similarities between people that underlie and support various cultures. Such knowledge may enhance a late-modern state's policy of assimilation, and the adoption of a multiculturalism that both celebrates 'difference' and encourages a state policy of integration. However, as I have mentioned, there is also a negative view of multiculturalism that neo-Darwinianism is also capable of casting some light upon. That view seeks to erect rather than take down borders. Again, neo-Darwinianism does not aim to provide solutions; it offers knowledge of the basic nature of human beings and the inclusionary and exclusionary aspects of people.

Multiculturalism

The origins of, and reasons for, multiculturalism in Canada are open to several interpretations. Some see multiculturalism, as an attempt to right social wrongs. Allahar and Côté (1998: 74) claim: 'Ideologically, at the level of law and government policy, official multiculturalism, as embodied in the Canadian Multiculturalism Act, implicitly acknowledges the racism of the wider system and seeks to implement programs to rectify past wrongs.' The authors see multiculturalism as a strategy that visible minorities use against racism in Canada. Meanwhile, Gairdner (1994: 107) sees multiculturalism as an act that encourages racism. He notes that in '1963 Pearson's government specifically directed the commissioners (of the Royal Commission on Bilingualism and Biculturalism) to change the basic character of this single nation and establish it as a union of two equal, racially defined nations'.

Multicultural, multiethnic, multiracial are concepts that grew out of the policy of integration (rather than assimilation). These policies of social diversity (pluralism) were developed with respect to minority groups and in Canada multiculturalism is a mandated part of public education, the major institution for promulgating governmental mandates. The positive view of multiculturalism sees it as a part of education that enriches the social fabric and knowledge of other cultures. However, others claim that 'multiculturalism threatens the future of public, as opposed to private schools . . . the idea of public education depends absolutely on the existence of shared narratives and the exclusion of narratives that lead to alienation and divisiveness' (Postman 1993: 17).

MULTICULTURALISM ON THE WORLD STAGE

Barber (1996) sees a great danger, as multiculturalism in the late-modern state becomes globalized. What begins as a simple search for a local identity has, in some cases, developed into identity politics, and may end as *Jihad* and the ethnic divisions of states. Recently, the Owen-Vance map for the partitioning of Bosnia multiplied boundaries as it attempted to accommodate ethnic communities, creating a multiculturalistic anarchy. Such divisions of divisions may become the rule,

not the exception. It has been predicted that the next 50 states likely to come into existence will all be defined by civil war due to ethnic conflict (Djilas 1993). Each of the states, perhaps as a form of resistance against racism, will itself become racist, self-determined, and monocultural. As national dismemberment enhances ethnic membership, it is a conceivable move from self-determination to multiple *Jihads*. As the late US secretary of state, Lansing, proclaimed: 'What a calamity that the phrase ("self-determination") was ever uttered! What misery it will cause' (cited in Barber 1996: 10). As the recent events in Bosnia testify, self-determination has at times resulted in 'Other' extermination in the name of ethnic 'purity'.

It must be borne in mind that the practices of the colonialists are at the bottom of a lot of the chaos and slaughter that is taking place over the divisions of states. They drew arbitrary lines on maps to satisfy the boundaries of acquisitiveness and the results of their implementation and rearrangement are still being endured throughout the former colonial world; and because of increased global interaction, the results affect many parts of the world.

Borders, Ecological Interdependence, Overpopulation, and the Depletion of Natural Resources

We are not in charge of the environment and the world is not following us. It is going in many directions. Do not assume that democratic capitalism is the last word in human social evolution.

Vlahos (1996)

States, since their beginnings, have crossed borders, created borders, and surrounded themselves with borders. However, how do you know that you have crossed a 'border' if there is no state apparatus where you cross? You do not, unless you read, use, and believe in a map. Cartography, map-making, orders the way we view the world and 'know' where borders are situated. The Western map of the world is a result of the invention of modern scientific techniques of measurement. War, nationalism, and the rise of nation-states in Europe over two centuries, have redrawn the political map of the world and divided it between nation-states.

COLONIAL CARTOGRAPHY: AN ACCOUNTANT'S BOOK OF MERCANTILE CAPITAL

In the world, the real players are not nations but tribes, many at war. They aim to redraw boundaries to divide nations (many of which were drawn up after the Second World War).
Barber (1996: 8)

The maps of European colonialism classified and 'fixed' the frontiers of 'new nations'. They introduced the concept of a 'frontier', a modern concept, and one that is important to the mythology of the American nation-state. Colonial cartography enabled colonialists to think of their particular 'holdings' as entries in a ledger book of mercantile capital which were represented within the map of the world.

With the collapse of colonialist cartography, as we have discussed, sectionist interests arise. 'In-groups' fight for their 'own boundaries' and the consequent 'right' of 'ownership' of lands and the 'control' of peoples inhabiting them, and the 'determination' of who will inhabit them. The rights of in-groups are often based on historical criteria that are often selective, revisionist, and focused on a specific point in time suitable to the group's purposes. The new cartography, like the colonial cartography, often seeks to encompass land containing valuable resources. Further, like all cartographies, it includes and excludes, leaving some populations to exist without defined borders.

There are sections of the world where there are borderless populations that live without the borders provided by Western cartography. For instance, the Kurds did not receive a state in the post-First World War peace treaties. A consequence of the 1991 Gulf War was that a Kurdish enclave was established in northern Iraq. In addition to Iraq, the Kurds live in Turkey, Iran, Syria, and the former Soviet Union. Their borderless presence has had a destabilizing effect on Iraq. States that do not offer them adequate living space may themselves suffer destabilization. Their situation is a reminder that if late-modern states do not involve themselves in the 'issues' of First World populations, they may well experience the result of destabilizing 'troubles'.

ENVIRONMENTAL AND DEMOGRAPHIC STRESSES, AND TRIBAL VIOLENCE

Ecology makes a mockery of state borders. Canada's forests are being destroyed by acid rain, some of it home-grown and some composed of toxins from 'over the border'. The fallout from a nuclear power disaster in the former Soviet Union took no account of the world's borders. All late-modern states are threatened by environmental stress and the diminishment of essential resources. As environmental degradation proceeds, the size of the potential social disruption increases. Over the next 50 years, the Earth's population will likely increase from 5.5 billion to more than 9 billion with 95 per cent of the population increase taking place in the poorest regions of the world.

Marx believed that the industrial world (read First World) would hold up a mirror of the future for the so-called 'underdeveloped' (a contentious word) countries. As a mirror reverses images, so the Third World may be presenting an image of the future for the First World. In the Third World, increasing populations, the increasing spread of borderless disease and ecological degradation may well force mass migrations and, in turn, incite group conflicts. In the twenty-first century, water will be in dangerously short supply and disputes over this most vital resource may fuse with the rising power of identity groups. Wars driven by scarcity and refugee flows engendering tribal strife may be the future of the Third World, and if no intervention takes place, the image may become reality.

In the developing world, as people move to seek resources, they redefine their identities in terms of similarities of religions, tribes, and ethnicities; the groups and the movements of these groups to access vital resources will not coincide with the borders of existing states. Around the globe, *Jihads* create and defend ethnic borders and particularist identities of peoples. Increasing identity bonding, tribalism, and the violence used to access scarce resources makes the late-nation-state borders extremely vulnerable.

THE WORLDWIDE IN-GROUP/OUT-GROUP SYNDROME

There are analogies—scenarios of a possible future in terms of the issues that we have discussed. One scenario is that the current world situation is a replay of a past before the birth of modernism, especially in the wars in medieval Europe. Using different implements of war, today's armed conflict may well turn into struggles between re-primitivized people. Warrior societies, in an overpopulated world, may be forced to fight for their place and share of the scarce resources. People's 'sameness' and 'differences' in a nonmulticultural world may gain importance as the in group/out group syndrome is re-invigorated.

Analogies have been forwarded of possible futures of the worldwide in-group, the First World, and of the out-group, the 'Other' occupying the rest of the planet. For those living in privileged First World countries the analogies include 'a guarded palace' and 'a lifeboat' (O'Brien 1994) and a 'stretch limousine' (Homer-Dixon 1999). Each keeps the outsiders out, sometimes with extreme violence. The palace guards against the incursion of Third World countries. The stretch limousine keeps those inside comfortable as they pass through a decimated world. The lifeboat saves the occupants from capsizing in a world of scarcity, ecological degradation, and personal violence. However, before exploring alternatives to possible futures, let us return to our test case, Quebec, and examine its possible future trajectories in light of the matters we have so far discussed. These matters are seldom, if ever, discussed in terms of the 'Quebec situation'.

A Sovereign Quebec Inside Canada?

We started with a counterfactual question: What happens when Quebec separates from Canada? The Québécois are nearly 8 million francophone Canadians (one million of whom live outside the Province of Quebec). As a French diaspora in North America, their struggle for cultural autonomy differs from that of the indigenous people who were 'conquered' and/or absorbed.

The separatists regard themselves as an internal colony. Rioux (1978) claims that the Quebeckers are among the oldest colonized people in the world and they are attempting to free themselves from the colonial yoke. McRoberts (1988: 424) notes that Quebec's political modernization has involved state building. He gives instances of that province's neonationalism and its efforts to develop a national consciousness. He views '*in-dépendantisme* as part of a *rejection* of traditional French-Canadian civilization rather than angst over its loss [and there] is no inherent reason why a viable Quebec identity must be based on the myth, let alone the reality, of a traditional society' (1988: 436–7). Coleman, (1984: 221) sees the indépendantiste movement as: 'A cry of fright from . . . a people that remember having some sense of self and of being a community and that feels that both are now virtually gone'.

Rioux (1978: 3–4) indicates that the 'coexistence with the "Other" in an environment saturated with the "Other" creates between them and the "Other" a sociological distance that would be abolished if they could escape from this environment.' There is an infinite regress entailed in altering the map of Quebec to allow an escape from 'this environment'. And, of course: 'The most inconvenient fact about the world for nationalist theorists or propagandists is that the number of communities and cultural groups far exceeds the number of states that either exist or could reasonably be established' (Birch 1989: 7).

THE OTHER 'OTHERS' IN QUEBEC

Quebec's separatism creates dilemmas for the native Cree Indian population, and a million or so nonseparatist, non-Québécois Canadian French who rely on Quebec for their status in Canada. In the 1995 referendum on Quebec's separation, the 'No' side survived. It was followed by the 1987 Meech Lake Accord, the first tenet of which posed difficulty because it recognized Quebec as a distinct society.

One of the dilemmas of the proposed accord became apparent when New Democrat Elijah Harper, a Cree, while holding an eagle feather for spiritual strength, stood in the Manitoba legislature and steadfastly refused to endorse any agreement that did not recognize special status of aboriginals. Should Quebec separate, the Native American Crees have their own case for separatism within Quebec. Their case has been greeted with a hypocritical lack of sympathy by Québécois who apparently see no similarity between their own suit against Canada and that of the Cree against them. They also appear unaware of the built-in regress caused by the entangled ethnic populations involved in Quebec or the issues for the francophone Canadians living outside of Quebec when it separates. (See note 5 for examples of the above absurdities in a separate Quebec that appears to embrace economic modernism even as it rejects the multicultural nation-state.)[5]

QUEBEC SECESSIONIST AMBITIONS SEEN FROM AFAR

> Canada, like most late-modern states, contains ethnic or cultural minorities that are only imperfectly integrated into the national society.
>
> Birch (1989: 3)

Several writers have forwarded opinions, advice, warnings about a Canada divided by a separate Quebec. Quebec is fitted into certain classification schemas. For instance: 'Often, sub-state nationalist movements formed by cultural or ethnic minorities proliferate demands for political autonomy. Movements as seemingly diverse as the Kurds, Basques, and *Québécois* are based on nationalistic urges' (Birch 1989: 12 [my emphasis]). Another schema points out that: 'Claims to independent statehood include those made by groups that do not come from distinct states, inhabitants of former colonies, and minorities within old, established Western states such as those in Quebec. If they all acquire their own territories, the 160-odd recognized states will become thousands of state-like entities, most of them tiny and economically unviable' (Ross and Trachte 1990).

Some commentators see the proliferation of states, which would include Quebec, in a positive light. From an economic stance Drucker (1993: 153–4) claims that 'bigness no longer confers much advantage and there has been success of small countries such as Austria and Finland, and in Canadian Quebec. A small country can now join an economic region and thus get the better of two worlds: cultural and political independence and economic integration.'

Following the above line of thought, and in an almost tongue-in-cheek manner, Barber (1996: 177) notices that an 'ambivalence can be found across the Atlantic among the Québécois separatists, where federal Canada faces a Quebec province whose separatist leanings have actually been magnified by its recent economic successes. Quebec would seem to want it both ways: "a sovereign Quebec inside a united Canada" as the telling quip goes.'

Canada's artfully constructed image as a peacekeeper has other people concerned by Quebec's attempt to separate. For instance, Fine (1996) comments: 'Even our peaceful northern neighbor, Canada, has recently gone through the wrenching process of observing Quebecois deciding by the smallest of majorities to remain within Canada. No doubt, this is an issue that will not pass.' Other commentators issue oblique warnings about separation.

> I would not include Canada in the number of disintegrating polities. But I would advise thoughtful Québécois, pondering a future referendum option, to visit Bratislava and hear the second thoughts of many Slovaks who formerly supported the decision to break up Czechoslovakia and set up an independent Slovakia (O'Brien 1994: 68).

Along similar lines, Gairdner (1994: 91) suggests 'in Canada, if we wish to avoid the fate of Ireland, Yugoslavia, and other divided nations that have devoured themselves over lines on the map, we have a duty to ask the right questions.'

An Approach to Providing Alternative Futures: A Higher Level of the Macro/Micro Interconnections

Thus far, we have traced the outlines of the pressures on the late-modern state. The future looks bleak. I believe there are alternatives; however, their implementation may be quite difficult. In order to examine these alternatives we will follow the contours of the chapter because some of the answers lie within those contours.

Alternative futures centre on the agency/structure debate, but now in a more macro sense. The original debate was set in terms of the late-modern state as the structure, and the individual as the agent. The model we adapted to account for change was that supplied by Elias (1978). If we take licence, globalization may be seen as the structure, and the late-modern state as the agent. Both aspects must be involved in the necessary structural and a personal transformation in order to bring about states that are interconnected on a global level and are capable of harnessing the power and benefits of the globalized corpora nation.

Human agency lies at the bottom of change. As detailed at the start, one of the first keys to exercising agency is to gain knowledge of what is happening in the globalized world and the interactions that effect and/or affect those happenings. Individual human beings must use the sociological imagination to gain knowledge of their state and interconnected states and their globalized interactions. That knowledge provides the spaces in which the agent (individual and/or state) can use or create.

INDEPENDENT OR INTERDEPENDENT FUTURES?

Mills's question about the 'types of people' that will rise in the future, coupled with his use of 'issues' and 'troubles' frame possible alternative futures. We have discussed possible 'types of people' that may come into being, and we centred on the *Jihad* warrior and the Americanized consumer. However, the point of concern with regard to the future is the difference between the *independent* and the *interdependent* types of people and societies. The independent person was a prerequisite of the original Enlightenment project. The consumerized, 'act as if' you are an independent person is incapable of seeking an understanding of much beyond the parameters of the 'imageered' self. The *Jihad* warrior is also unlikely to seek an understanding of much beyond the parameters of the imageered self.

Perhaps if the independent person gained knowledge of history and if the current and upcoming globalized issues became apparent, two results might occur. The first would be an agentic discontinuation of the current deformation of the Enlightenment project. The second is that we must accept that we are interdependent and consequently depend on each other and are dependent on nature.

The interdependence of the fundamentalist is only interdependence within an in-group. Knowledge of the ecological destruction underway, the free movement of chemical disasters across borders, the increasing scarcity of vital resources coupled with an increasing world population, and a consequent increase in violence that will make present-day *Jihad* pale before it, may bring about an understanding that the *Jihad* centre will not hold. It may become more apparent as the scarcities develop pockets of other groups equally prepared to die for a cause, in this case access to the necessities of life. The borders that enclose a group of people, and in some cases have generated wealth, such as oil, will have little value when there is no water to drink. Those borders may burst open by the 'Other' in search of a particular resource or they may have to break down their own ramparts, to get a drink of water.

In order to halt an approach environment that is conducive to the distortion of the Enlightenment project and unbridled capitalism, a working knowledge of human nature must be available. In order to bring about change in destructive fundamentalism, or in unbridled exploitative capitalism and increasing brand-name consumption a working knowledge of human nature must be available. Taking the neo-Darwinian view of human nature into account, we can bring the 'in-group/out-group' syndrome into public view as we can the built-in excesses of both capitalism and fundamentalism. Ortega y Gasset (1961) claims that the natural state of humans is drunkenness and

that claim supports the aspect of human nature that drives capitalism.[6]

The selfish bent of human nature also raises difficulties in the nurturing of affirmative multicultural societies. In an interdependent world, those societies must be nurtured. However, the greatest issues of all remain the increasing scarcities of essential resources and the ever-widening gap between the 'haves' and 'have nots'. The greed inherent in human nature may be a fountain of the disparities we have examined. The answer, in part, follows Aristotle's dictum that we must first know what it is we are dealing with before we deal with it.

WHAT IS THE DEAL?

The difficulty of the members of a consumer society actively 'knowing' is discussed by Saul (1995), who concludes that we are an 'unconscious civilization'. The unconsciousness manifests itself in 'manufactured consent' obtained not just by misinformation, but also by a lack of trust in the sincerity of the political body (see Gergen 1991). Lack of access to vital knowledge stems from the fact that the educational system is not geared to develop critical thinking; the media are largely capitalist-oriented and hold the government on a short leash. To know requires agentic effort, a commodity not readily available in a passive consumer society. Even for those who exercise their will to know, Chomsky (1972) cautions about the time and training necessary to access the necessary information to 'know'.

However, if we do not know and do not become 'conscious' we may be unaware that selfishness, greed, and violence are aspects of the human being to be taken into account. To change matters we must dialogue; again Aristotle's dictum holds—we must first know with what we deal, proclaim it, and then collectively deal with it. However, therein lies the rub: Are we agentic? The 'we' is, in the present context, both the individual and the aggregate of individuals comprising the late-modern state.

Conclusion

AGAINST THE FUTILITY THESIS

When I was young, nothing could hold me back. It took me a hundred years to figure out I can't change the world. I can only change Bessie. And, honey, that ain't easy, either.

> Bessie Delany, at the age of 101 (1993)

Earlier we discussed the futility thesis that asserts that neither individual nor collective action is worth undertaking against the corporate world since it will eventually prove incapable of redressing current inequity and such a capitulation is 'the cult of impotence'. Though Bourdieu, the progenitor of the futility thesis, pictures the social world as highly structured, he disagrees with the idea that it evolves 'according to immanent laws, which human actions are impotent to modify'. Social laws are temporally and spatially bound regularities that hold as long as the institutional conditions that underpin them are allowed to endure (Bourdieu and Wacquant 1992). In addition, we are free to alter the institutional conditions. Berger (1963) assures us that all social systems were created by humans, and it follows that humans can change them. Even as society defines us, we also define society. There is no total power in society, as there is no total impotence.

A POSSIBLE BUT PARTIAL DIRECTION

If we exercise our potency, a world-level arbitratory system might be put in place. It, on a utilitarian basis, would deal with the pressures on the late-modern state that we have discussed. Would it work? It would have to reach a compromise with the exploitation of certain aspects of capitalism and with the moral outrage *of Jihad*. As we have said, following Mills's advice, information is needed; perhaps ensuring that worldwide media move from infotainment and provide knowledge of the issues and problems we have discussed. It would have to recognize the non-obvious (Collins 1992) fact that there will always be criminal activity. However, by instituting and following a utilitarian judicial system that accounts for both the environment and human nature, a workable system might be possible. Again, would it work? It might, but what are the alternatives?

Notes

1. See Chapter 4 in this text for a more complete discussion of this issue.

2. The Enlightenment project is a search for certainty (Toulmin 1990), which is linked to development of Western society in the form of what is sometimes called a Grand Narrative whereby Western culture, using science as the guiding metaphor, describes its journey through time. The narrative is about progress, continuous upward movement, improvement, conquest, and achievement. The narrative leads to a single form of culture, or government, or economic system, or worldwide civilization that might finally solve humanity's problems. The project dispenses with traditions and cultures of the past. Its base is reason and involves a search for the elusive truth, for certain knowledge that moves toward an essence, a fundamental thing-in-itself. The methods of the project involve skepticism, rationality, observation, reason, progress, and essentials.

3. The term *conservative* arose from French political thought during the Napoleonic era and refers to a guardian of the principles of justice and the nation's civilized heritage. It is in opposition to the radical changes brought about by the French revolution. Nisbet (1994) suggests that sociology stems from such conservative political thought—especially the care for community, order, and authority.

4. Social democracy is a blend of contemporary liberalism, welfare-state economics, democratic socialism, and progressive democracy. There is a commitment to democracy and to a strong, involved, positive government. Unlike the conservatives, private institutions such as religion and the family have no special position and the government should allow the full flowering of lifestyles. Morality is a matter of individual choice and has no special place in society. It is unwarranted that some groups suffer discrimination because of differing beliefs and practices.

5. The million or so non-Québécois francophones may lose their equal place in Canada, including the 300,000 Acadians of New Brunswick who survived the 1755 dispersal by the English. Now after nearly four hundred years, they face Quebec's tribalism imperilling their own Canadian status. The Cree have a comparative right to leave Quebec. Anglophone villages can leave Quebec. Anglophone villages can opt out of a self-determining Cree nation. Francophones residing in predominantly English villages in the predominantly Cree region of predominantly French Quebec can. . .

6. From a purely pragmatic point of view, it must be obvious that if capitalists do nothing to prevent the future scenarios we have examined, they break one of the first laws of capital, the need for consumers.

References

Allahar, A.L., and J.C. Côté. 1998. *Richer and Poorer: The Structure of Inequality in Canada* (Toronto: Lorimer).

Archer, M.S. 1989. *Culture and Agency: The Place of Culture in Social Theory* (Cambridge: Cambridge University Press).

Arendt, H. 1959. *The Human Condition* (Garden City, NY: Doubleday).

Aronowitz, S. 1992. *The Politics of Identity: Class, Culture, Social Movements* (London: Routledge).

Baldus, B. 1977. 'Social Control in Capitalistic Societies', *Canadian Journal of Sociology* 2(3).

Barber, B.R. 1996. *Jihad vs. McWorld* (New York: Ballentine Books).

Berger, P. 1963. *An Invitation to Sociology* (Garden City, NY: Doubleday).

Birch, A.H. 1989. *Nationalism and National Integration* (London: Unwin Hyman).

Bourdieu, P., and L. Wacquant. 1992. *An Invitation to Reflexive Sociology* (Chicago: University of Chicago Press).

Chomsky, N. 1972. *Language and Mind* (New York: Harcourt Brace Jovanovich).

Coleman, W. 1984. *The Independence Movement in Quebec: 1945–1980* (Toronto: University of Toronto Press).

Collins, R. 1992. *Sociological Insight: An Introduction to Non-Obvious Sociology* (Riverside: University of California).

Delany, S., A.E. Delany, with A.H. Hearth. 1993. *Having Our Say: The Delany Sisters' First 100 Years* (New York: Kodansha International).

Djilas, A. 1993. 'A House Divided', *The New Republic*: 38.

Drucker, P.F. 1993. *Post-Capitalist Society* (New York: Harper Business).

Durkheim, E. 1966. *Suicide: A Study in Sociology*, ed. G. Simpson, (New York: Free Press).

Elias, E. 1978. *The Civilizing Process: The Development of Manners: Changes in the Code of Conduct and Feeling in Early Modern Times* (New York: Urizen Books).

Erikson, E.H. 1964. *Insight and Responsibility: Lectures on the Ethical Implications of Psychological Insight* (New York: W.W. Norton).

Fanon, F. 1963. *The Wretched of the Earth* (New York: Grove Press).

Fine, G.A. 1996. *Talking Sociology* (London: Allyn and Bacon).

Fukuyama, F. 1992. *The End of History and the Last Man* (New York: Free Press).

Gairdner, W.D. 1994. *Constitutional Crack-up: Canada and the Coming Showdown with Quebec* (Toronto: Stoddart).

Gergen, K.J. 1991. *The Saturated Self: Dilemmas of Identity in Contemporary Life* (New York: Basic Books).

Giddens, A. 1984. *The Constitution of Society: Outline of the Theory of Structuration* (Berkeley, CA: University of California Press).

———. 1990. *Consequences of Modernity* (Stanford, CA: Stanford University Press).

Gray, J. 1999. *False Dawn: The Delusions of Global Capitalism* (London: Granta Books).

Henshel, R.H. 1990. *Thinking about Social Problems* (New York: Harcourt Brace Jovanovich).

Hobsbawm, B. 1994. *Age of Extremes: The Short 20th Century 1914–1991* (London: Abacus).

Homer-Dixon, T.F. 1999. *Environment, Scarcity, and Violence* (Princeton, NJ: Princeton University Press).

Hughes, R. 1993. *Culture of Complaint: The Fraying of America* (Oxford: Oxford University Press).

Jessop, B. 1990. *State Theory: Putting the Capitalist State in Its Place* (Cambridge: Polity Press).

Kaplan, R.D. 2000. *The Coming Anarchy: Shattering the Dreams of the Post Cold War* (New York: Random House).

Kropotkin, P. 1989. *Mutual Aid: A Factor in Evolution* (Montreal: Black Rose).

McQuaig, L. 1999. *The Cult of Impotence: Selling the Myth of Powerlessness in the Global Economy* (Harmondsworth, UK: Penguin).

McRoberts, K. 1988. *Quebec: Social Change and Political Crisis* (Toronto: McClelland & Stewart).

Mills, C.W. 1967. *The Sociological Imagination* (New York: Oxford University Press).

Nisbet, R. 1996. *The Sociological Tradition* (New York: Basic Books).

O'Brien, C.C. 1994. *On the Eve of the Millennium* (Concord, ON: House of Anansi).

Ortega y Gasset, J. 1961. *The Revolt of the Masses* (London: Allen & Unwin).

Postman, N. 1993. *Technopoly: The Surrender of Culture to Technology* (New York: Vintage).

Rioux, M. 1978. *Quebec in Question* (Toronto: Lorimer).

Ritzer, G. 1996. *The McDonaldization of Society: An Investigation into the Changing Character of Contemporary Social Life* (London: Pine Forge Press).

Ross, R.J.S., K.C. Trachte. 1990. *Global Capitalism: The New Leviathan* (Albany: State University of New York Press).

Saul, J.R. 1995. *The Unconscious Civilization* (Concord, ON: House of Anansi).

Taylor, C. 1991. *The Malaise of Modernity* (Toronto: Anansi).

Tilly, C. 1990. *Coercion, Capital, and European States, AD 990–1990* (Oxford: Basil Blackwell).

Toulmin, S.E. 1990. *Cosmopolis: The Hidden Agenda of Modernity* (New York: Free Press).

Vlahos, M. 1986. *Strategy, Defence and the American Ethos: Can the Nuclear World Be Changed?* (Boulder, CO: Westview Press).

Weber, M. 1956. *From Max Weber: Essays in Sociology*, eds H.H. Gerth and C.W. Mills (New York: Oxford University Press).

Wright, R. 1994. *The Moral Animal: Evolutionary Psychology and Everyday Life* (New York: Free Press).

Wrong, D. 1961. 'The Oversocialized Conception of Man in Modern Sociology', *American Sociological Review* 26: 188–92.

Chapter 6

Understanding The *Welfare State and Welfare States: Theoretical Perspectives*

Julia S. O'Connor

Introduction

The essence of the welfare state is government-protected minimum standards of income, nutrition, health, housing, and education, assured to every citizen as a political right, not as a 'charity'.

Wilensky (1975: 1).

Welfare states are ensembles of social practices and strategic understandings designed to resolve historically specific problems of harmonizing the production of wealth and its distribution.

Myles (1989: 74).

These two quotations capture the essential elements of welfare states: welfare states have been developed in response to problems of production and distribution and these responses are reflected in social rights to certain minimum standards. While *the* welfare state as defined in the above quotations is a phenomenon of advanced capitalism and as such all developed capitalist economies can be identified as welfare states, it is important to recognize variation in the types of welfare states developed. This reflects the fact that different political choices have been made in different countries in response to the problems of reconciling production and distribution. These differences are reflected in differences in the scope and quality of social rights. One of the key

arguments of this chapter is that the range and quality of these social rights varies cross-nationally and that welfare state analysis must explain this variation. Our understanding of any particular welfare state is enhanced by understanding how and why it varies from other welfare states.

The welfare state as we know it today in Western developed capitalist countries has been developed primarily in the post-World War II period, but the roots of many of the contemporary programs were planted between the 1880s and 1920s in Western Europe (Flora and Alber 1981), and state intervention in social policy type activity—as a protection against the ravages of the market—goes back several centuries. In the next section, I briefly trace these roots and outline the characteristics of contemporary welfare states. The second section of the chapter is devoted to discussion of key aspects of several theoretical perspectives on the welfare state. First, I consider how analysts have explained the development, functions, and crises of the welfare state. Then I outline how analysts have explained differences amongst welfare states, in particular, why some welfare states are better than others in terms of social protection. This is followed by a brief discussion of the neo-institutionalist approach. The final section includes an outline of key arguments relating to the welfare state regime concept and the issue of citizenship, including the relationship between citizenship and social class and the critique of this approach by gender sensitive analysts. The final part of this section links these critiques to earlier arguments made by feminist analysts of the welfare state.

The Welfare State and Welfare States

THE ROOTS OF THE WELFARE STATE

The earliest published use of the term *welfare state* is in a 1932 German publication, although the origin of the term is frequently linked to a British clergyman, Archbishop Temple, who in 1941 contrasted the British 'welfare state' to the German 'warfare' and 'power' state (Flora and Heidenheimer 1981: 19). The term first became widely used to refer to the post-World War II package of reforms introduced in Britain, for which eligibility was based primarily on citizenship rather than class and which was considered the antithesis of the *Poor Law* concept of 'less eligibility'. The *Poor Law* system in England dates from 1601 and refers to a system of help for the destitute administered and funded by local taxation. In 1834 a major modification was introduced that divided the country into Poor Law Unions administered by locally elected Boards of Guardians but acting under centrally established principles, the most important of which was the concept of 'less eligibility'. This meant that able-bodied people were offered a level of assistance that was less than the lowest-paid worker could earn. This principle was implemented through the 'workhouse test', that is, those seeking help were forced to enter the workhouse where conditions were very severe. The reason for the 1834 change is important in that it illustrates state intervention not only in terms of social assistance but also in the formation of markets. It was a reaction against the existing system that had been developed in response to severe distress in Speenhamland, in Berkshire in 1795, and spread to other areas. The system guaranteed a basic level of subsistence linked to the price of bread, 'so that a minimum income should be assured to the poor *irrespective of their earnings*' (Polanyi 1957: 78). This Speenhamland system was a barrier to the development of labour markets since it prevented the transformation of labour into a pure commodity. It removed the incentive to employees to work for very low wages but provided an incentive to employers to lower wages (1957: 79). The 1834 change abolished the right to subsistence and forced the commodification of labour; that is, it forced people to depend on the labour market for their survival or to depend on assistance based on the less eligibility principle. But labour is not a commodity like others—the assumption that land, labour, or money are commodities like any other, is a 'fiction' (1957: 72–3). Workers need to reproduce if the system is to survive. If wages are pushed below subsistence by the operation of the free market, survival and, in particular, reproduction of the labour force will not be possible. Consequently, the state had to introduce measures to protect society from free market forces by introducing factory laws and social legislation (1957: 83). In other words, it had to introduce measures to de-commodify labour, that is, to protect it from the market system. The welfare state is to a large extent about de-commodification or protection from total dependence on the labour market for survival.

Poor law legislation was enacted in Nova Scotia in 1763 and in New Brunswick in 1786, but not in any other province. Yet, while not formally followed in Canada, the principle of less eligibility 'pervaded the administration of public assistance to the poor from the outset, resulting in meagre subsistence-level handouts' (Guest 1985: 36). This public assistance was administered on an emergency basis by municipalities or private charities acting as their agents and was referred to as 'outdoor relief', that is, people were not forced to enter institutions to obtain assistance. In contrast to the other provinces, there was heavy involvement of religious orders in the administration of programs to assist the poor in Lower Canada (Quebec).

The dominant characteristic of the *Poor Law* type provision was its discretionary characteristic. Individuals did not have a *right* to assistance, but had to prove destitution. The distinguishing characteristic of the welfare state is that at least for some programs there is a categorical right to services, that is, once one falls into a particular category one is eligible for services. The extent to which this type of categorical citizenship right is the principle on which services are based varies by welfare state (see sections on citizenship and welfare state regimes later).

WELFARE STATES: CHARACTERISTICS AND CROSS-NATIONAL VARIATION

The term *welfare state* is usually used to refer to expenditure on health, education, personal social services, and income maintenance programs such as pensions, unemployment insurance, and welfare or social assistance. This is the narrow definition of the welfare state and the social programs referred to exist to varying degrees in all Western capitalist countries. Increasingly, it is recognized that there is considerable variation across welfare states. Some welfare states are characterized by a high degree of coordination of social and economic policies; in particular, they incorporate labour market policy as an integral part of their social policy framework. The term *welfare state* is sometimes used in an even broader sense to characterize all post-Second World War Western capitalist interventionist states. This is illustrated in Claus Offe's (1984) use of the term interchangeably with *Keynesian welfare state*. This refers to states in which governments intervene in the economy in a counter-cyclical way as advocated by John Maynard Keynes (1973). Keynes was a British economist who advocated this approach in the 1920s and 1930s but it was not adopted on a widespread basis until the late 1930s. The most

significant aspect of Keynes' argument was the recognition that economies were not automatically self-correcting and they could reach equilibrium at less than full employment. A countercyclical approach implies stimulation of the economy in times of recession through unemployment insurance and public works programs and the dampening down of demand through taxation and control of the money supply in times of potential inflation.

Irrespective of whether a narrow or broad definition of the welfare state is used, a comparative focus indicates major differences across welfare states—differences in the scope and quality of social programs and social citizenship rights and in the extent of state action in relation to employment. A historical focus indicates that while the countercyclical activity is a phenomenon of the post-World War II era, the origins of some welfare state programs, most notably in Germany and to a lesser extent in the United Kingdom and France lie in the late nineteenth century. The first Canadian national level social program—old age pensions—was not established until 1927, although mothers' allowances were introduced in some provinces earlier. As indicated above, there were some limited municipal programs for the poor and indigent by the late nineteenth century (Armitage 1988: 270–1) although most activity at this period was voluntary and relatively limited.

In the next section I consider how analysts have explained the development of the welfare state and variation amongst welfare states.

Perspectives on the Welfare State

In this section I consider the most influential theoretical perspectives on welfare state analysis over the past three decades: functionalist explanations, both mainstream and Marxist, crises theories which emphasize crisis tendencies within capitalism, theories emphasizing the significance of mass mobilization as a spur to welfare state development, the power resource mobilization explanation, and the neo-institutional approach. In the next section I consider recent developments in welfare state research, in particular the analysis of welfare regimes and feminist analyses.

FUNCTIONALIST EXPLANATIONS

Up to the mid-1970s, convergence interpretations of the development of the welfare state, in particular those interpretations that downplayed or ignored political factors, were dominant (Cutright 1965; Wilensky 1975). Harold Wilensky's work was especially influential and it continues to be central because of the number of studies undertaken and the variations in emphases evident over time. His 1975 study of 60 countries is regarded as a classic statement of the convergence explanation, which implies increasing similarity in social provision across countries associated with increasing industrialization. Industrialization is associated both with economic growth and the emergence of new needs, such as a dependent population over the age of 65. Wilensky holds that welfare policy and expenditure are a response to these needs and are facilitated by additional resources associated with economic growth. This is a functionalist explanation based on a logic of industrialism view of social change (Kerr et al. 1964). The logic of industrialism argument is that all industrializing countries, irrespective of political system, will evolve toward a common model resulting from economic growth and technological development. Wilensky's approach is based on the view that the state functions as a mechanism for solving objective and universal problems—for example, the growth of a population of dependent people over the age of 65. Public welfare policy and expenditure are not regarded as class issues. Rather, they are interpreted as a response to need. The appropriate policy response is administered by a class-neutral state. Party politics is not considered relevant since the state is seen as a reflection of the general will of the population. In later work focusing on developed capitalist countries, Wilensky recognized the influence of democratic corporatist structures and political party configuration on the size of social security expenditure (Wilensky 1976, 1981).

Mainstream structural-functional explanations of social phenomena, such as the logic of industrialism explanation of welfare state development, are usually regarded as polar opposites of Marxist structuralist explanations of the same phenomena. Yet as Anthony Giddens has pointed out, *structural functionalism* refers to a logical form of argument found in both Marxist and non-Marxist theories; what distinguishes the two traditions is to be found in the substantive content of the theories in question (Giddens 1976). In explaining welfare policy the structural Marxist explanation centres on the logic of capitalism in contrast to the logic of industrialism focus of mainstream structural functionalism.

The implications of the Marxist structuralist position are that there are structural constraints that set the upper limits on what can be done by the state in terms of welfare effort. This type of explanation draws on the early work of Nicos Poulantzas (1976), in which the capitalist state is interpreted as relatively autonomous from the capitalist class but as acting as a factor of cohesion for that class. The relationship between the capitalist class and the state is systemic, not instrumental (Poulantzas 1972: 245). The functions of the state are broadly determined by the economic structures of the society rather than by the people who occupy positions of state power and thus use the state as an instrument of domination. The structuralist sees the welfare state as contributing to the accumulation of capital and the reproduction of capitalist social relations. While the state may respond to the demands of workers this is a partial response and public policies are constrained within limits that are compatible with the capitalist mode of production.

Within the structuralist perspective the role of the state but not of politics is considered central. The action of trade unions, political parties, and groups that dominate the bureaucracy are considered unimportant in the final analysis. Exclusive structuralist explanations of public policy downplay the struggles that have been undertaken to attain political and welfare rights. This is not justifiable in view of the historical development of the welfare state.

CONTRADICTIONS AND CRISES OF THE WELFARE STATE

Several Marxist analysts focus on the contradictions and crises of the welfare state. For example, James O'Connor (1973), an American economist, in *The Fiscal Crisis of the State* identified a contradiction between the accumulation and legitimation functions of the capitalist state:

> A capitalist state that openly uses its coercive forces to help one class accumulate capital at the expense of other classes loses its legitimacy and hence undermines the basis of its loyalty and support. But a state that ignores the necessity of assisting the process of capital accumulation risks drying up the source of its own power, the economy's surplus production capacity and the taxes drawn from this surplus (1973: 6).

O'Connor argues that the costs of legitimation accompanied by the private accumulation of profits create a fiscal crisis, or a gap between state expenditure and state revenues. This fiscal crisis is intensified by the pressure of special business interests, organized labour, and the unemployed and poor who make claims for various types of investment and expenditure (1973: 9). These struggles 'impair the fiscal capacity of the system and potentially threaten the capacity of the system to produce surplus' (1973: 10).

Most Marxist works on the welfare state do not adopt a pure structuralist approach. For example, Ian Gough (1979) in *The Political Economy of the Welfare State* incorporates both a structural view of the economy and a conflict theory of class struggle and the interrelationship between the two in an explanation of the welfare state. He characterizes the welfare state as 'the use of power to modify the reproduction of labour power, and to maintain the non-working population in capitalist societies' (1979: 44–5) but accepts that reforms can be achieved that benefit the working class. He argues that the experience of periods of social reform generates an ideology of the welfare state that is premised on a harmony of interests between social classes, but that in the final analysis senior state officials are always working for the maintenance of the stability of the existing system and thus in the interests of the capitalist class, which benefits most from this stability. Writing at the end of the 1970s Gough was pessimistic about the ability of the state to reconcile the conflicting demands of capital and labour in an era of low or no economic growth. He sees the development of the welfare state as essentially contradictory and the source of further contradictions (1979: 152). He argues that its development reflects the changing nature of advanced capitalist society but imposes new economic and political strains on the system, simultaneously limiting both capital accumulation and political freedom.

Claus Offe, a German sociologist, has written extensively on the 'crises' and 'contradictions' of the welfare state. This issue is of considerable importance at present in view of the critiques of the welfare state, by both the New Right and some on the left of the political spectrum. For different reasons these critics have found some common ground in asserting the incompatibility of capitalism and the welfare state. The label New Right refers to at least two strands of opinion: 'a liberal tendency which argues the case for a freer, more open, and more competitive economy, and a conservative tendency which is more interested in restoring social and political authority throughout society' (Gamble 1988: 29). Both elements are hostile to the welfare state because of its interference with the freedom of the market, its purported denial of choice, and ineffectiveness in eliminating poverty (Gamble 1988: 27–60 as cited in Pierson 1991: 41). At the opposite end of the political spectrum, the critique by some of the left is that the welfare state is ineffective and inefficient; it is repressive and generates a false understanding of social and political reality by suggesting that effective change is possible in the absence of structural transformation. The welfare state is seen as 'a device to stabilize, rather than a step in the transformation of, capitalist society' (Offe 1984: 154).

Offe conceives of late-capitalist society as consisting of three interrelated subsystems: the economic, the political administrative (the state), and the normative (legitimization) systems. The state is interpreted as relatively autonomous to the degree that the political administrative system becomes the 'independent' mediator of the class struggle inherent in the capitalist accumulation process. The purpose of the welfare state is to manage the structures of socialization and the economy; it is not just a provider of social services, but is defined by the goal of 'crisis management', that is, the regulation of the processes of legitimation/socialization and capital accumulation. Contradictions arise from the various mediating roles of the state. Offe's *political crisis theory* 'enlarges the field of vision of traditional economic crisis theories in so far as it no longer traces the origins of crises exclusively to the dynamics of the sphere of production. Instead, it explains crises with reference to the inability of the political system [and the welfare state, in particular,] to prevent and compensate for economic crises' (1984: 61). This is associated with fiscal, administrative, and mass loyalty problems. Despite this, as Offe points out, the 'contradiction is that while capitalism cannot coexist *with*, neither can it exist *without*, the welfare state' (1984: 153). He points

out that in the absence of state-subsidized housing, public education and health services, as well as social security schemes, the operation of an industrial economy would be inconceivable.

THE WELFARE STATE AND MASS MOBILIZATION

The theorists most closely identified with the mass mobilization approach are Frances Fox Piven and Richard Cloward (1971, 1977). In their 1971 book entitled *Regulating the Poor: The Functions of Public Welfare*, they argue that the intent of public welfare in the United States has always been to regulate the poor; that significant improvements in public welfare have been granted in response to mass mobilization, as reflected in widespread protest over social issues such as poverty; and that cutbacks take place when the threat of mobilization is no longer present. In particular, they argue that the process of relief-giving during the Great Depression fits this pattern. Further, they argue that the function of relief once political crises subside is to enforce work, especially very low-wage work. They support this argument by analysis of Aid to Families with Dependent Children, one of the major welfare programs for women and children in the United States, in the 1940–60 period—'the years of stability' (1971: 123–80). Similarly, they argue that the welfare expansion of the 1960s was a response to a 'turbulent black constituency' who had migrated to northern US cities from the 1930s on because of the modernization of southern US agriculture (1971: 281). The expansion of the US welfare state in the 1960s is explained in terms of 'economic disruption, large-scale migration, mass volatility, and electoral responses—a sequence of disturbances leading to a precipitous expansion of the relief rolls' (1971: 338).

OUTSTANDING ISSUES

The unifying difficulty of all the approaches considered so far is the tendency to downplay or ignore one or the other of the twin pillars of the welfare state: a liberal democratic political system and a capitalist economic system. As Flora and Heidenheimer point out (1981: 22), the works of de Tocqueville, Weber, Marx, and Durkheim imply agreement on the proposition that 'in the context of European history, the growth of the modern welfare state can be understood as a response to two fundamental developments: the formation of national states and their transformation into mass democracies after the French Revolution, and the growth of capitalism that became the dominant mode of production after the Industrial Revolution.' Despite the agreement implied in the classical analyses, most studies on the welfare state do not provide a balanced analysis of both elements.

There is a failure in the logic of industrialism explanation, as put forward by Wilensky (1975, 1976, 1981) to acknowledge the impact of the capitalist economic system on political decision-making: the conception of the state is class-neutral, the view of power is one-dimensional and voluntaristic (Lukes 1974: ch. 2). For their part, Marxist structuralist analyses pay insufficient attention to the transformation of the liberal state of the nineteenth century into the liberal democratic state of the twentieth century (Macpherson, 1966).

Why is the dual focus on democracy and capitalism essential? There is a fundamental difference between the economy and the state, in terms of political participation (relative power). The key point of difference is identified by Myles, in his study of pension policy, as 'contradictory rather than complementary principles of social participation and distribution' (1989: 4). The differing principles of social participation are class and citizenship. In terms of distribution, the economy and the political system are based on opposing logics. One grants rights to property and income earned in the market, thus confirming market distribution—the greater one's economic resources the greater one's power to purchase

goods in the marketplace. The other grants equal rights to citizens as voters, thus distributing values equally irrespective of property and/or income. These dual rights are not only distinct; they are in potential conflict. For example,

> The principle of free association of the workers is in direct opposition to the principle of free individual contract. Principles of anti-discrimination, which claim that all citizens have the right to equal treatment by employers or potential employers, constrain the free exercise of property rights. The right to employment, minimum health and safety conditions, due process, and democratic control in the accumulation process is contrary to any notion of a private sphere beyond the reach of the popular exercise of rights in persons (Bowles and Gintis 1982: 62).

This is not meant to imply that there are not limitations on the exercise of rights because of private property in the means of production. However, the economy and state not only interact along common boundaries, each thereby setting limits on the actions of the other; practices in one site can also bring pressure for change in the other (Bowles and Gintis 1982: 63). For example, equal rights as citizens vested in persons in the liberal democratic state may lead to demands for greater participation in decision-making in the work situation, which is characterized by inherently unequal relations (Carnoy and Shearer 1980). Such participation is reflected in developments such as works councils and other examples of labour-management cooperation in decision-making. Important implications are associated with the dual elements of liberal democratic capitalist societies, in particular, with the non-independence of the two elements, that is the interdependence of the political and economic levels. Firstly, an increase in citizenship rights is likely to have implications for power relations in the labour market, for example, entitlement to sickness benefits, unemployment insurance, or pensions as citizenship rights increase the bargaining power of labour in the labour market; similarly, entitlement to family allowances payable to the caring parent has implications for power relations within families. Secondly, the dual focus points to the fact that social expenditure is essentially an element of societal distribution of resources. Thus, in considering measures of inequality cross-nationally both market and non-market distribution must be considered. Thirdly, 'welfare states' can be distinguished on the basis of the mix between class and citizenship, a principle of inequality and a principle of equality, as bases for welfare entitlements. Some welfare states rely heavily on means and/or income testing as a basis for access to benefits and services, that is access is linked to socioeconomic status, which is linked to class location. In contrast, other welfare states rely heavily on universal access to services: access is granted as of right to all citizens irrespective of social and/or economic location. Because of the contradictory nature of the logics involved, welfare entitlements may differ markedly in terms of their class implications.

A double focus on the interrelationship of a liberal democratic political system and a capitalist economic system is clearly evident in the work of that group of theorists of the welfare state who have variously been identified under the headings 'new political economy' (Hollingsworth and Hanneman 1982), 'political class struggle' (Stephens and Stephens 1982), 'social democratic model' (Shalev 1983), and 'mobilization of power resources' analysts (Korpi 1983).

MOBILIZATION OF POWER RESOURCES AND WELFARE STATES

The power resources/class politics approach explicitly acknowledges the role of politics, both parliamentary and extraparliamentary, in influencing public policy formation and implementation. This is not a denial of structural factors but a recognition of the dual character of western capitalist societies, that is the coexistence of a liberal democratic political system and a capitalist economic structure.

The essential argument of the class politics approach is that strong reformist trade unions and social democratic parties can achieve substantial reforms of the capitalist system: that substantial reforms have been achieved in some countries, notably Sweden; and that the welfare state is the essential element of the compromise with labour on the part of the capitalist class (Korpi 1978, 1983; Stephens 1979). In direct contrast to the logic of industrialism approach, the welfare state is interpreted as (a) a class issue, (b) the formation and growth of which are political processes. In contrast to structural Marxist approaches the relative autonomy of politics is acknowledged. The prospects for systemic change are seen as a function of the balance of class power at the political as well as at the economic level.

Walter Korpi, a Swedish sociologist, proposes a 'power difference model of conflict'. Power resources are defined as 'characteristics which provide actors—individuals and collectivities—with the ability to punish or reward other actors' (1983: 15). Two types of power resources are central in capitalist societies: (a) capital and the control over the means of production and (b) human capital (labour power, education, occupational skills). Korpi argues that the distribution of these power resources varies in different countries and that this variation has implications for (a) the distributive processes in society and the degree of inequality, (b) the social consciousness of the citizens, (c) the level and pattern of conflict, and (d) the shaping and functioning of social institutions. From this perspective, change in the distribution of power resources between different collectivities is assumed to be of central importance for social change. This entails a rejection of the pluralist conception of the distribution of power resources as potentially equal.

In view of the inequality in power resources inherent in capitalism, the extension of political democracy is crucial to the enhancement of the power resources of the working class. The numerical superiority of the working class may lead to political power that may partially offset the economic power of capital. Politics is interpreted as an expression of the democratic class struggle, that is, 'a struggle in which class, socio-economic cleavages and the distribution of power resources play central roles' (Korpi 1983: 21). Conflicts of interest continuously generate bargaining, conflict, and settlements. Some of these settlements are the outcome of important changes in the distribution of power resources and significantly affect patterns of conflict and institutional arrangements and strategies of conflict for long periods of time. These 'historic compromises' are associated with change in the patterns and conceptions of 'normal politics'—for example, in the right of workers to unionize, universal suffrage, the separation of political power from economic power that resulted from the accession to power of the Social Democrats in Sweden in 1932, and the post-Second World War settlement in Britain which included the National Health Service and the 1944 Education Act; a similar settlement was reached in Canada in the post-World War II period (Muszynski 1985). All of these settlements or social contracts between capital, labour, and the state reflect a shift in the basis of social rights from class to citizenship.

In the power resources mobilization approach, politics is interpreted as an expression of the democratic class struggle. The principal power resources of the working class are the right to vote and the right to organize for collective action (Korpi 1989: 312). These power resources, expressed through trade union membership and labour or social democratic political party strength,

may be used in coalition with other social forces, such as farmers or the middle class, to lead to political power that may partially offset the economic power of capital (Esping-Andersen 1989).

Much of the early power resources work has been criticized for its 'Swedo-centrism', its linear approach to class analysis, and its concentration of attention on working-class power resources to the virtual exclusion of analysis of capitalist class strength and composition (Shalev 1983; Olsen 1991). It is now acknowledged by most analysts that political choices are not just influenced by more or less working-class strength, that political coalitions and 'the institutionalization of class preferences and political behavior' that has emerged from past reforms must be taken into account (Esping-Andersen 1990: 32). There is still little or no recognition that political mobilization is not just about class, that it is also about gender and in some states about race. Such mobilization cannot be captured by conventional political analysis (O'Connor 1993: 510–11). There is a move away from an exclusive focus on aggregate social expenditure measures 'to a focus on the multidimensional aspects of the development of welfare states, social rights and social citizenship' (Korpi 1989: 309). This is associated with a lively debate on social citizenship and on welfare state regimes. Before I discuss these issues, I will outline the key arguments of the state-centred/state autonomy/ neo-institutionalist analysis since some analysts adopting this approach have been strongly critical of the so-called society-centred approach of the power resource and other analysts (Orloff and Skocpol 1984).

STATE-CENTRED ANALYSIS/NEO-INSTITUTIONALISM

A significant body of research on the development of the welfare state, especially the US welfare state, emphasizes the importance of state variables such as state autonomy and capacity, the institutional context, and policy feedback in the development of welfare states. This approach was initially identified as the 'state-centred' approach by both advocates and others because of its emphasis on 'bringing the state back in' to the analysis of politics and its critique of what Orloff and Skocpol (1984) identified as society-centred approaches such as the logic of industrialism and working-class mobilization. The key arguments of the state-centred approach are that '[s]tates may be sites of autonomous official initiatives, and their institutional structures may help to shape the political processes from which social policies emerge. In turn, social policies, once enacted and implemented, themselves transform politics' (Skocpol and Amenta 1986: 131).

This approach is now more often identified as neo-institutionalism (Orloff 1993), the structured polity approach (Skocpol 1992), or historical institutionalism (Thelen and Steinmo 1992) and is characterized by a greater emphasis on state-society interactions. While there may be some variation in emphasis associated with these various headings there is a common emphasis on the importance of institutional context for the 'structuring of politics' (Steinmo, Thelen, and Longstreth 1992) and the development of policy. The key concepts identified by Orloff (1993) are state capacity, institutional context, and policy feedbacks. State capacity refers to capacity to plan, administer, and extract resources and is a precondition for the emergence of social programs; the institutional context refers to 'the character, capacity, and structure of the state and political institutions' which 'affects élite and popular political organization, capacities and orientations, and the formation of cross-class political coalitions' (Orloff 1993: 83). Policy feedbacks refer to the ways in which existing policy enhances administrative capacities, informs new policy debates and facilitates and encourages the formation of interest groups and coalitions. The analysis of policy feedbacks takes into account unintended consequences of past legislation that may be important barriers to, or facilitators of, future policy options. In addition to stressing institutional structures and their impact, some analysts put considerable emphasis on potential autonomy of the state and the role of professionals within state agencies in policy development (Orloff 1993; Skocpol 1992).

While there are significant differences between analysts who stress state-centred and society-centred approaches, few analysts now argue for an either/or approach. For example, Skocpol emphasizes that 'several aspects of politics and state-society interactions' are included in her analysis of the US welfare state (Skocpol 1992: 569 fn. 90). Most welfare state research activity emphasizes institutional and society-centred variables with recognition that these are not mutually exclusive. For example, Bo Rothstein (1992) uses insights from both institutional analysis and power resource theory to explain why some countries are more unionized than others. As Hattam (1992: 171–2) argues, the appropriateness of the state-centred approach varies across societies and time periods. A similar argument can be made about a society-centred approach. It is probable that in most situations the optimum approach will involve theoretically coherent insights from both perspectives, the relative emphasis varying by the question being considered and the historical context.

Welfare State Regimes, Citizenship, Class, and Gender

WELFARE STATE REGIMES AND CITIZENSHIP

Citizenship rights, in particular social citizenship rights, are central to welfare states. The development of welfare states can be seen as a process of the transition from access to services and benefits entirely on the basis of class position and associated resources to access to certain categories of services and benefits, for example health care in Canada, on the basis of citizenship. Most contemporary discussions of citizenship take as their source the essay 'On Citizenship and Social Class' presented by T.H. Marshall in 1949 (1964: 65–122). On the basis of British history, Marshall divided the development of citizenship into three stages. Civil citizenship, relating to liberty of the person and property rights, is dated from the eighteenth century with the development of the judicial system and legal rights. Political citizenship, relating primarily to the right to vote and to organize, for example in trade unions, is dated from the nineteenth century. Social citizenship, which relates to rights to economic welfare and security, is dated from the twentieth century with the extension of the educational system and the development of the welfare state. None of these rights just evolved naturally, but each was achieved through collective struggle. In the case of social rights, this collective struggle was possible because of the existence of civil and political rights. This analysis and periodization relates to the British situation and it is problematic even when applied there because of its assumption of a universal category of citizens, all of whom equally benefit from achieved citizenship rights. The timing of political citizenship rights is different for women and men and the ability to exercise citizenship rights is influenced by class position (Barbalet 1988). Despite these limitations Marshall's analysis provides major insights into citizenship and provides the background for the conception of citizenship embodied in much of the welfare state literature, in particular, the comparative analysis literature.

The welfare state regime concept is not new— Richard Titmus identified three models in the 1970s (1974: 30–1). However, the recent interest has been sparked by the work of Gosta Esping-Andersen (1989, 1990), especially in his book *The Three Worlds of Welfare Capitalism*. Citizenship rights are central to his welfare state regime concept. Welfare regimes refer to clusters of more or less distinct welfare state types in terms of the principles of rights and bases of stratification on which the welfare state is built. The three worlds or welfare regimes are the social democratic as exemplified by the Scandinavian countries, liberal as exemplified by the welfare states in the United States and Canada, Australia and Britain, and corporatist or status-based as exemplified by Germany, France, and Italy.

De-commodification, or protection from total dependence on the labour market for survival, is central to the welfare state project and the associated historical struggles. Commodification of labour refers to the situation where the individual's ability to sell her/his labour solely determines her/his access to resources while de-commodification reflects a level of insulation from the pressures of the labour market and contributes to the ability of workers to resist these pressures. In other words, the citizenship entitlements reflected in social security payments and public services, which to varying degrees in different countries and at different time periods in individual countries are independent of class position, facilitate resistance to the pressures of the market. Consequently, the level of de-commodification is central to the welfare state project (O'Connor 1989) but must be linked to the quality of social rights. The welfare regimes concept goes beyond comparison of countries on the basis of more or less expenditure on services, such as health and education, and on benefits, such as pensions and unemployment insurance, to examine the criteria for eligibility and access and the range of conditions covered, that is the quality of social citizenship rights. It also recognises that the welfare state is a mechanism of social stratification, that it is 'an active force in the ordering of social relations' (Esping-Andersen 1990: 23) and that the characteristics of social provision reflect, and are reflected in, state, family, market relations.

The quality of social rights and the issue of social stratification revolve around the criteria for access to, and duration of, benefits. These criteria are means and/or income testing, social insurance contributions, and citizenship. All welfare states make use of the three criteria of eligibility but the dominance of one criterion or another differentiates welfare states. In the social democratic welfare state, the citizenship criterion is dominant, as is reflected in the strong emphasis on universality of access to services and benefits. The liberal welfare state is characterized by a strong emphasis on income and/or means-tested programs and the conservative welfare state regime is characterized by a variety of social insurance schemes linked to class and status. Each of these is reflected in a particular form of stratification. For example, means testing promotes social dualisms. A variety of social insurance programs, as in conservative welfare regimes, is likely to consolidate divisions along class and status lines. While in theory access on the basis of citizenship is the most egalitarian and least stratifying it may also promote dualism if the universal access is to a low level of benefit or services. In this instance the more affluent are likely to purchase private supplementary insurance (Esping-Andersen 1990: 24). Not only does this promote dualism, but it is also likely to weaken support for universal services.

Welfare state regimes also vary in the primacy they accord to the state, the market, and the family: the social democratic regime relies heavily on state provision to meet social needs, the liberal regime relies relatively heavily on the market, and the conservative regime relies heavily on the family. A good example of these differences is childcare, although there is variation within regimes. Taking Sweden and Denmark as exemplars of the social democratic regime, public childcare provision is high, facilitating high female labour force participation. In the liberal regimes of the United States and Canada, female labour force participation is also relatively high but the majority of working parents with childcare responsibilities are dependent on market solutions. In Germany,

an exemplar of the conservative regime, female labour force participation is low, reflecting the reliance on the family for childcare (O'Connor 1996; OECD 1988).

While the welfare regime concept as outlined by Esping-Andersen has inspired considerable innovative work on the comparative analysis of welfare states, it has also been the subject of some criticism, for example, in relation to the inclusion of countries within the liberal regime and the exclusion from consideration of several southern European countries (Castles and Mitchell 1992; Leibfried 1993). Olsen (1994) has pointed to the difference between Canada and the United States in relation to health care and argues that welfare regime analysts have paid insufficient attention to such services. The most well-developed critique of welfare state regime typologies, especially the Esping-Andersen version, has been made by scholars interested in a gender-sensitive welfare state analysis.

WELFARE STATE REGIMES, GENDER, CLASS, AND CITIZENSHIP

Gender refers to the socially constructed structural, relational, and symbolic differences between men and women. The concern of gender-sensitive analysis is with 'how gender is involved in processes and structures that previously have been conceived as having nothing to do with gender' (Acker 1989: 238). It is also based on the recognition that gender and class are produced within the same ongoing practices. 'Looking at them from one angle we see class, from another we see gender, neither is complete without the other' (1989: 239). Gender-sensitive welfare state analysis is built on the recognition of the *interaction* of gender and class and is linked to a more general critique of the dominant conception of citizenship that underpins welfare state research. The conception of the citizen as a worker, specifically an organized worker with entitlement rights achieved through his/her, though generally his, incorporation into the political process (through trade unions and political parties) is associated with a failure to recognise diversity amongst citizens. In particular, it fails to recognize the difference between formal citizenship rights and ability to exercise those rights. This ability may be constrained by class position but also by status within the family. For example, civil and political rights are universal in principle but may have a class bias in practice (Barbalet 1988). Social rights may also fall into this category and a gender and/or race bias may exist singly or in interaction with one another or in interaction with a class bias in relation to all elements of citizenship. This is not to suggest that the achievement of formal citizenship rights was not significant for both men and women, but class and gender neutrality in the realization in practice of formal citizenship rights cannot be assumed.

The concern with the citizen as worker is associated with an emphasis on de-commodification, or protection from total dependence on the labour market for survival, as the central element of the welfare state. While de-commodification, as reflected in pensions and unemployment insurance for example, is a central protection for both men and women in the labour force, it is important to recognize that before de-commodification becomes an issue it is necessary to be a labour market participant. The primary concern for many women is not de-commodification but commodification as reflected in labour market participation. Recognition of this fact implies a need to incorporate the relationship between unpaid and paid work into welfare state analysis. This means that analysis of de-commodification must be accompanied by analysis of services that facilitate labour market participation, such as childcare and parental leave. It is also important to recognize that the unpaid caring work in the home, generally done by women, facilitates the labour force participation of others, generally men. Recognition of these facts implies a re-

thinking of the state market family relations dimension to take into account the impact of status in the family on ability not only to participate in the labour market but to exercise the associated social citizenship rights (O'Connor 1993). Ann Orloff (1993) argues for an additional measure of state activity which would capture variation in the extent to which welfare states meet the needs of those with caring responsibilities who are not in the labour market, that is are noncommodified. The objective is to identify how benefits, for example those for single mothers, contribute to the capacity to maintain autonomous households, that is, 'to survive and support their children without having to marry to gain access to breadwinners' income' (1993: 319) and enhance women's power vis-à-vis men within marriages and families.

Jane Lewis (1992) also argues that the concept of welfare regime must incorporate the relationship between unpaid and paid work. Further, she argues that the idea of the male-breadwinner family model has historically cut across established typologies of welfare states and that the model has been modified in different ways and to different degrees in different countries. She proposes a typology of strong, modified, and weak male-breadwinner regimes. The male-breadwinner model is not found in its pure form in any country, that is women are not totally excluded from the labour market and totally dependent on male breadwinners for survival; yet all countries reflect elements of this ideology and some adhere relatively strongly to the model. Services facilitating the labour force participation of women are absent or very limited in strong male-breadwinner states, such as Britain and Ireland, whereas they are relatively well-developed in weak male-breadwinner models such as Sweden. This reflects the fact that weak male-breadwinner states are relatively successful in solving the issue of valuing caring work—women are compensated at market rates for caring work which is typically unpaid, or paid at very low rates, in strong male-breadwinner states. This difference is reflected in levels of public provision of childcare and care for other dependent people and also in the payment rates for those, mostly women, who carry out this caring within welfare states. The second major issue related to unpaid work, namely, its division between women and men has not been addressed in any welfare state.

Diane Sainsbury (1994) extends the male-breadwinner model by identifying a number of neglected dimensions of variation amongst welfare states and constructing contrasting ideal types—the breadwinner and individual models. The latter is characterised by access to services on the basis of individual rights rather than through the male breadwinner. She identifies ten dimensions of variation in these models; for example, family ideology, basis of entitlement, unit of benefit and contributions, whether employment and wage policies give priority to men or are aimed at both sexes, whether care is primarily private or has strong state involvement, and whether caring work is unpaid or has a paid component. Analysis based on these dimensions allows for recognition of greater variation amongst welfare states than does classification into strong, weak, and modified male-breadwinner models.

The gender-sensitive critiques of welfare regime typologies just outlined build on earlier feminist analyses of welfare states. I present a brief outline of these in the next section.

FEMINIST ANALYSES OF THE WELFARE STATE

There is no single feminist analysis of welfare states. Despite considerable theoretical variation amongst feminists, often paralleling traditional approaches, what is common to all feminist welfare state analysts is the recognition of gender as a fundamental structuring mechanism in contemporary societies and the recognition of gender as fundamental to understanding welfare states. The

particular aspect of gender difference that is emphasised varies by theoretical orientation (Williams 1989: Table 3.1).

Despite variation in the economic and social position of women in OECD countries (Norris 1987) there are a number of common themes evident in feminist analyses of the welfare state irrespective of country of origin. The centrality of women for the welfare state, not only as paid workers and unpaid community caregivers and also the centrality of the welfare state for women as clients and as employees has been demonstrated in numerous studies based on experience in several OECD countries with different kinds of welfare state regimes (see O'Connor 1996, ch. 1 for an outline of this literature). Despite this double centrality most mainstream analyses of welfare states not only ignore gender as an analytical category but also pay little attention to women as a distinct category. As a consequence, much of the feminist analysis concentrates on making women visible in welfare states. This includes a growing body of research on women's role as social activists in women's organizations and bureaucracies in influencing the development of welfare states (Andrew 1984; Gordon 1994; Skocpol 1992).

One of the major differences evident in feminist analyses relates to the conception of the welfare state vis-à-vis women. Some analysts conceive the welfare state as oppressive whereas others see it as a potential resource for women. The theme of the welfare state as oppressive and the stress on the limitations it imposes on women was strongly evident in the early work on women in welfare states. This work stressed the ideological bases of social policy and the issue of public partriarchy or the social control of women by welfare state bureaucracies. One of the earliest and most widely cited books analysing women in the welfare state is Elizabeth Wilson's (1977) *Women and the Welfare State*. It presents a historical analysis of the British welfare state stressing its ideological and social control aspects. Wilson argues that 'the Welfare State is not just a set of services, it is also a set of ideas about society, about the family, and—not least important— about women, who have a centrally important role within the family, as its linchpin' (1977: 9). Mary McIntosh (1978), also on the basis of British experience, has identified the role of the welfare state in the maintenance of a particular family form—the male-breadwinner nuclear family—that is oppressive to women. In a similar vein, many studies based on US and Canadian experience emphasize the oppressive and social control aspects of the welfare state for women (Dickinson and Russell 1986; Fraser 1989; Nelson 1984). In contrast, comparative studies and those based on Scandinavian experience, while recognizing marked gender inequalities even in well-developed welfare states, emphasize the possibility for empowerment of women through the welfare state (Borchorst and Siim 1987; Dahlerup 1987; Hernes 1987; Norris 1987; Ruggie, 1984). This difference may reflect differences in welfare state institutions across welfare state regimes. In liberal welfare states access to many benefits and services are income and/or means tested and the predominant encounter of many women with welfare state institutions is as social assistance clients whose benefits are relatively meagre. In contrast, the experience of women in the social democratic welfare state regime is more likely to be as employees and citizens with rights to services; this is reflected in a relatively optimistic view of state potential. For example, Helga Hernes, a Norwegian analyst, discusses the possibility of achieving a 'woman-friendly state', that is, 'a state where injustice on the basis of gender would be largely eliminated without an increase in other forms of inequality such as among groups of women' (1987: 15). Despite the overall relatively pessimistic view of the state that permeates work on women in liberal welfare states some analysts have identified the state as a resource for women and the possibility

that social policy may provide opportunities for significant positive developments under particular historical circumstances even in liberal welfare states (Piven 1984; Quadagno 1990).

Despite the variation in emphasis amongst feminist analysts, all are interested not only in making women visible in welfare state analysis, but also in incorporating gender, conceived in structural and relational terms, as a central analytical category in welfare state analysis. While much of the earlier research was in the 'women and the welfare state' mode, that is, making women visible, much of the more recent research has been explicitly directed to the second project. This has been accompanied by an emphasis not only on the interaction of gender and class, but also by a recognition of the importance of race, in interaction with both gender and class, in structuring some welfare states, most notably the United States (Gordon 1994; Quadagno 1994; Williams 1989). As with most of the feminist analyses of welfare states, this work has tended to be country-specific historical analysis. This is not surprising in view of the complexity of comparative work involving several key dimensions of difference. Recently, Fiona Williams (1995) has highlighted the absence of race in the analysis of welfare state regimes. She advocates an analysis of states' relationship through welfare states to the areas of family, work, and nation. The nation dimension includes analysis of systems of migration, colonialism, and imperialism and processes of inclusion and exclusion from the nation-state as reflected in citizenship rights. She argues that an analysis focused on all three areas is necessary to grasp the diversity of welfare settlements in different countries.

The feminist critique of welfare state research demonstrates that analyses that consider the development of social citizenship rights exclusively in terms of how they lessen the impact of social class position on ability to access social services does not capture the complexity of experience in welfare states. This complexity can only be captured by an analysis that recognizes the welfare state as a mechanism of stratification and that can simultaneously deal with structuring by class, race, and gender. Despite the difficulty of comparative analysis on such a multifaceted basis, the use of quantitative and qualitative historical and comparative approaches as reflected in welfare regime analysis provides some of the tools for such an analysis.

Conclusion

Divisions amongst analysts of the welfare state parallel the broader theoretical divisions amongst social theorists. This is associated with little acknowledgement of the value of the other's enterprise from strong proponents of positions based on mutually incompatible theoretical assumptions. At a more general level one can understand the variation in perspectives on the welfare state in terms of the nature of the welfare state. The welfare state is a politically contested concept. Consequently, it is not surprising that theorists are contesting the concept of the welfare state (Barrow 1993: 11).

In evaluating theories of the welfare state it is important to bear in mind that '[i]f a theory focuses upon a particular factor as historically important, then the empirical manifestations of that factor become important, and they are singled out for investigation' (Alford and Friedland 1985: 398); in this process other factors are excluded or glossed over. This may be true of political or economic factors, of state-centred or society-centred factors. It was almost universally true of gender and race until recently and these are still excluded from consideration in much mainstream work on the welfare state irrespective of theoretical orientation. In evaluating conclusion, it is important to bear in mind that seemingly different conclusions may arise because different questions are being posed. Some analysts are interested in the welfare state as a phenomenon of contemporary society, whether that be conceived as capitalist or industrialized, while others are interested in explaining variation across societies at broadly similar levels of economic development. Within each of these areas of interest it is obvious that the sets of questions pursued will vary depending on theoretical assumptions and 'the empirical manifestations' that will be singled out for investigation will vary. Yet the latter may also vary because the interest is in the historical development of the welfare state rather than variation amongst welfare states or vice versa.

References

Acker, J. 1989. 'The Problem with Patriarchy', *Sociology* 23(4): 235–40.

Alford, R., and R. Friedland. 1985. *Powers of Theory* (Cambridge: Cambridge University Press).

Andrew, C. 1984. 'Women and the Welfare State', *Canadian Journal of Political Science* 17(4): 667–83.

Armitage, A. 1988. *Social Welfare in Canada* (Toronto: McClelland & Stewart).

Barbalet, J.M. 1988. *Citizenship Rights, Struggles and Class Inequality* (Minneapolis: University of Minnesota Press).

Barrow, C.W. 1993. *Critical Theories of the State: Marxist, Neo-Marxist, Post-Marxist* (Madison: University of Wisconsin Press).

Borchost, A., and B. Siim. 1987. 'Women and the Advanced Welfare State: A New Kind of Patriarchal Power?' In *Women and the State: The Shifting Boundaries of Public and Private*, ed. A. Showstack-Sassoon (London: Hutchinson), 128–57.

Bowles, S., and H. Gintis. 1982. 'The Crisis of Liberal Democratic Capitalism: The Case of the United States', *Politics and Society* 11: 51–93.

Carnoy, M., and D. Shearer. 1980. *Economic Democracy* (Armonk, NY: M.D. Sharpe).

Castles, F.G., and D. Mitchell. 1992. 'Identifying Welfare State Regimes: The Links Between Politics, Instruments and Outcomes', *Governance* 5(1): 1–26.

Cutright, P. 1965. 'Political Structure, Economic Development, and National Social Security Programs', *American Journal of Sociology* 70: 537–50.

Dahlerup, D. 1987. 'Confusing Concepts—Confusing Reality: A Theoretical Discussion of the Patriarchal State'. In *Women and the State,* ed. A. Showstack-Sassoon (London: Hutchison), 93–138.

Dickinson, J., and B. Russell (eds). 1986. *Family, Economy and State: The Social Reproduction Process under Capitalism* (Toronto: Garamond).

Esping-Andersen, G. 1989. 'The Three Political Economies of the Welfare State', *Canadian Review of Sociology and Anthropology* 26(1): 10–36.

———. 1990. *The Three Worlds of Welfare Capitalism* (Princeton: Princeton University Press).

Flora, P., and J. Alber. 1981. 'Modernization, Democratization and the Development of Welfare States in Western Europe'. In *The Development of Welfare States in Europe and America,* eds P. Flora and A.J. Heidenheimer (London: Transaction Books), 37–80.

Flora, P., and A.J. Heidenheimer. 1981. 'The Historical Core and Changing Boundaries of the Welfare State'. In *The Development of Welfare States in Europe and America,* eds Flora, P. and A.J. Heidenheimer (New Brunswick, NJ: Transaction Books), 17–34.

Fraser, N. 1989. 'Women, Welfare, and the Politics of Need Interpretation'. In *Unruly Practices: Power, Discourse and Gender in Contemporary Social Theory,* ed. N. Fraser (Minnesota: University of Minnesota), 144–60.

Gamble, A. 1988. *The Free Economy and the Strong State: The Politics of Thatcherism* (London: Macmillan).

Giddens, A. 1976. 'Classical Social Theory and the Origins of Modern Sociology', *American Journal of Sociology* 81(4): 403–29.

Gordon, L. 1994. *Pitied But Not Entitled: Single Mothers and the History of Welfare* (New York: Free Press).

Gough, I. 1979. *The Political Economy of the Welfare State* (London: Macmillan).

Guest, D. 1985. *The Emergence of Social Security in Canada* (Vancouver: University of British Columbia Press).

Hernes, H. 1987. *Welfare State and Woman Power: Essays in State Feminism* (Oslo: Norwegian University Press).

Hattam, V.C. 1992. 'Institutions and Political Change: Working-Class Formation in England and the United States, 1820–1896'. In *Structuring Politics: Historical Institutionalism in Comparative Analysis,* eds S. Steinmo, K. Thelen, and F. Longstreth (New York: Cambridge University Press), 155–87.

Hollingsworth, J.R., and R.A. Hanneman. 1982. 'Working-Class Power and the Political Economy of Western Capitalist Societies', *Comparative Social Research* 5: 61–80.

Kerr, C., J.T. Dunlop, H.F. Harbison, and C.A. Myers. 1964. *Industrialism and Industrial Man* (New York: Oxford University Press).

Keynes, J.M. 1973 [1936]. *The General Theory of Employment Interest and Money* (London: Macmillan).

Korpi, W. 1978. *The Working Class in Welfare Capitalism* (London: Routledge & Kegan Paul).

———. 1983. *The Democratic Class Struggle* (London: Routledge & Kegan Paul).

———. 1989 'Power, Politics, and State Autonomy in the Development of Social Citzenship: Social Rights during Sickness in Eighteen OECD Countries since 1930', *American Sociological Review* 54(3): 309–28.

Leibfried, S. 1993. 'Towards a European Welfare State? On Integrating Poverty Regimes in the European Community'. In *New Perspectives on the Welfare State in Europe,* ed. C. Jones (London and New York: Routledge), 133–56.

Lewis, J. 1992. 'Gender and the Development of Welfare Regimes', *Journal of European Social Policy* 2(3): 159–73.

Lukes, S. 1974. *Power: A Radical View* (London: Macmillan).

Macpherson, C.B. 1966. *The Real World of Democracy* (Oxford: Oxford University Press).

McIntosh, M. 1978. 'The State and the Oppression of Women'. In *Feminism and Materialism: Women and Modes of Production,* eds A. Kuhn and A. Wolpe (London: Routledge & Kegan Paul), 254–90.

Marshall, T.H. 1964. 'Citizenship and Social Class'. In *Class, Citizenship and Social Development* (Westport, T: Greenwood Press), 64–122.

Muszynski, L. 1985. 'The Politics of Labour Market Policy'. In *The Politics of Economic Policy,* ed. G.B. Doern (Toronto: University of Toronto Press), 251–304.

Myles, J. 1989. *Old Age in the Welfare State: The Political Economy of Public Pensions* (Lawrence, KS: University Press of Kansas).

Nelson, B. 1984. 'Women's Poverty and Women's Citizenship'. In *Women and Poverty,* eds B. Gelphi, N. Hartsock, C. Novak, and H.M. Strober (Chicago: University of Chicago Press), 209–31.

Norris, P. 1987. *Politics and Sexual Equality: The Comparative Position of Women in Western Democracies* (Boulder, CO: Rienner and Wheatsheaf).

O'Connor, J. 1973. *The Fiscal Crisis of the State* (New York: St Martin's Press).

———. 1989. 'Welfare Expenditure and Policy Orientation in Canada in Comparative Perspective', *Canadian Review of Sociology and Anthropology* 26(1): 127–50.

———. 1993 'Gender, Class and Citizenship in the Comparative Analysis of Welfare State Regimes: Theoretical and Methodological Issues', *British Journal of Sociology* 44(3): 501–18.

———. 1996. 'From Women and the Welfare State to Gendering Welfare State Regimes', *Current Sociology* 44(2): 1–124.

Offe, C. 1984. *Contradictions of the Welfare State,* ed. J. Keane (London: Hutchinson).

Olsen, G.M. 1991. 'Labour Mobilization and the Strength of Capital: The Rise and Stall of Economic Democracy in Sweden', *Studies in Political Economy* 34: 109–45.

———. 1994. 'Locating the Canadian Welfare State: Family Policy and Health Care in Canada, Sweden,

and the United States', *Canadian Journal of Sociology* 19(1): 1–20.

Orloff, A.S. 1993. 'Gender and the Social Rights of Citizenship: The Comparative Analysis of Gender Relations and Welfare States', *American Sociological Review* 58: 303–28.

———, and Skocpol, T. 1984. 'Why Not Equal Protection? Explaining The Politics of Public Social Spending in Britain, 1900–1911, and the United States, 1880s–1920', *American Sociological Review* 49: 726–50.

Pierson, C. 1991. *Beyond the Welfare State: The New Political Economy of Welfare* (University Park, PA: The Pennylvania State University Press).

Piven, F.F. 1984. 'Women and the State: Ideology, Power, and the Welfare State', *Socialist-Feminism Today: IV:* 11–19.

———, and R.A. Cloward. 1971. *Regulating the Poor: The Functions of Public Welfare* (New York: Vintage Books).

———, ———. 1977. *Poor People's Movements: Why They Succeed, How They Fail* (New York: Pantheon Books).

Polanyi, K. 1957 [1944]: *The Great Transformation* (Boston: Beacon Press).

Poulantzas, N. 1972. 'The Problem of the Capitalist State'. In *Ideology in Social Science: Readings in Critical Social Theory,* ed. R.M. Blackburn (London: Fontana), 238–53.

Poulantzas, N. 1976 'The Capitalist State', *New Left Review* 95: 63–83.

Quadagno, J. 1990. 'Race, Class, and Gender in the U.S. Welfare State: Nixon's Failed Family Assistance Plan', *American Sociological Review* 55: 11–28.

———. 1994 *The Colour of Welfare: How Racism Undermined the War on Poverty* (New York: Oxford University Press).

Rothstein, B. 1992. 'Labour Market Institutions and Working-Class Strength'. In *Structuring Politics Historical Institutionalism in Comparative Analysis,* eds S. Steinmo, K. Thelen, and F. Longstreth (New York: Cambridge University Press), 33–56.

Ruggie, M. 1984. *The State and Working Women: A*

Comparative Study of Britain and Sweden (Princeton: Princeton University Press).

Sainsbury, D. 1994. 'Women's and Men's Social Rights: Gendering Dimensions of Welfare States', In *Gendering Welfare States,* ed. D. Sainsbury (London: Sage), 150–69.

Shalev, M. 1983. 'The Social Democratic Model and Beyond: Two "Generations" of Comparative Research on the Welfare State', *Comparative Social Research* 6: 315–51.

Skocpol, T. 1992. *Protecting Soldiers and Mothers: The Political Origins of Social Policy in the United States* (Cambridge, MA: The Belknap Press of Harvard University Press).

———, and E. Amenta. 1986. 'States and Social Policies', *Annual Review of Sociology* 12: 131–57.

Steinmo, S., K. Thelen, and F. Longstreth (eds). 1992. *Structuring Politics: Historical Institutionalism in Comparative Analysis* (New York: Cambridge University Press).

Stephens, E.H., and J. Stephens. 1982. 'The Labour Movement, Political Power, and Workers Participation in Western Europe', *Political Power and Social Theory* 3: 215–49.

Stephens, J. 1979. *The Transition from Capitalism to Socialism* (London: Macmillan).

Thelen, K., and S. Steinmo. 1992. 'Historical Institutionalism in Comparative Politics'. In *Structuring Politics: Historical institutionalism in Comparative Analysis,* eds S. Steinmo, K. Thelen, and F. Longstreth (New York: Cambridge University Press), 1–32.

Titmus, R.M. 1974. *Social Policy* (London: Allen and Unwin).

Wilensky, H. 1975. *The Welfare State and Equality: Structural and Ideological Roots of Public Expenditure* (Berkeley, CA: University of California Press).

———. 1976. *The 'New Corporatism', Centralization and the Welfare State* (London: Sage).

———. 1981. 'Leftism, Catholicism, and Democratic Corporatism: The Role of Political Parties in Recent Welfare State Development'. In *The Development of Welfare States in Europe and America,* eds P. Flora and A.J. Heidenheimer (London: Transaction), 345–81.

Williams, F. 1989. *Social Policy: A Critical Introduction: Issues of Race, Gender and Class* (Cambridge: Polity Press).

———. 1995. 'Race/Ethnicity, Gender, and Class in Welfare States: A Framework for Comparative Analysis', *Social Politics International Studies in Gender, State and Society* 2(2): 127–59.

Wilson, E. 1987. *Women and the Welfare State* (London: Tavistock).

Chapter 7

Does the Road to Quebec Sovereignty Run through Aboriginal Territory?

Mary Ellen Turpel

The problem here is a denial of the past, or a narrowness of vision that sees the arrival and then spread of immigrants as the very purpose of history.

Hugh Brody[1]

Québec's resources are permanent; we do not owe them to a political system, or to specific circumstances. They are a gift of nature, which has favoured us more than others in this respect by allowing us to play a more important economic role, thanks to our resources.

Government of Quebec[2]

It is important to respect the aspirations of Québécois to *self-determination*, if they act in accordance with international law.

At the same time, it is difficult to address in a totally dispassionate way the spectre of 'Quebec secession'. Every time I begin to write about the international legal and Canadian constitutional dimensions of Quebec separation or accession to full sovereignty from the perspective of aboriginal peoples'[3] status, one area of my so-called professional and personal 'expertise' as an aboriginal woman and law professor, I am confronted with my concern for the status and rights of those most marginalized in this discussion—the aboriginal peoples of Quebec.

The claim by Québécois for full sovereignty, as it has been conceived by many secessionists,[4] appears to rest on the erasure of the political status of aboriginal peoples and the denial of their most fundamental rights to self-determination. These are two most critical points, seemingly resisted by the main political parties in Quebec, and not taken seriously enough outside Quebec by Canadian politicians, intellectuals, or the academic community. I am cautious with terminology here because just writing the expression 'Quebec secession' poses a problem—it conjures up an image of a single territory and a homogeneous people setting up a new state. The point of this essay is to demonstrate that it is not this simple.

How can it be presumed that there can be an accession to sovereign status for Quebec without considering the pivotal matter of the status and rights of the aboriginal peoples in this scenario? What does it mean to 'consider' the status and rights of aboriginal peoples in a secessionist scenario? It is not a perfunctory matter, or an administrative decision considering how best to transfer a head of jurisdiction (Indians and lands reserved for the Indians)[5] from the federal authority to a newly independent Quebec state. It is more complex than this, in both a legal and political sense.[6] The political success of the secessionist movement will ultimately be judged on its democratic process, its respect for fundamental human rights and, in the end, its political legitimacy in the eyes of the international community. I believe that the relations with aboriginal peoples could prove to be the key to assessing that legitimacy and could well influence the international recognition and acceptance of any new Quebec state.

Who are the aboriginal peoples in Quebec? Most people know something about the Crees in northern Quebec because of their current opposition to the Great Whale hydro-electric project in the James Bay territory, or perhaps because of the *James Bay and Northern Quebec Agreement*.[7] However, it is not only the Crees whose homeland is captured in some sense by the provincial bounaries of Quebec. There are also Inuit, Naskapi, Mikmaq, Maliseet, Mohawk, Montagnais, Abenaki, Algonquin, Atikawekw, and Huron whose homelands are at least partially within geographical boundaries of the Province of Quebec. I say 'partially' because, using the Mikmaq as a case in point, the Mikmaq of Gaspé comprise one of the seven districts of the Mikmaq nation, Mikmakik, which extends into Nova Scotia, New Brunswick, Newfoundland, and Prince Edward Island. A District Chief from this region sits on the Mikmaq Grand Council, the traditional governing body of the Mikmaq people situated in Cape Breton, Nova Scotia. The administrative boundary of the Province of Quebec for Mikmaqs in the Gaspé is an arbitrary boundary unrelated to their identity, both territorially and spiritually.

To note this is nothing new for aboriginal peoples, given that all provincial boundaries are somewhat arbitrary from an aboriginal historical perspective. These provincial boundaries, internal to Canada, do not demarcate aboriginal homelands. Indeed, even certain international boundaries suffer likewise from a similar arbitrariness. I will use the Mohawks at Akwesasne as another case in point. Their community extends over two provincial boundaries (Ontario and Quebec) and an international boundary with New York State. Their sense of division is compounded by the existence of three boundaries

which in no way correspond to their own territorial, spiritual, or political identity as Mohawks or members of the Iroquois Confederacy. What about 'Quebec secession' for these First Nations? While some aboriginal peoples in Quebec do speak French, their culture and linguistic identities are first and foremost shaped by their own First Nations culture, history, and language.[8]

While the Province of Quebec is undoubtedly no worse than any other province in terms of its history of a strained relationship with aboriginal peoples (although I would argue this is not an appropriate threshold for assessment), the recent confrontation with Mohawks at Oka in 1991 and the ongoing battle with the Crees over further hydro-electric development in the James Bay territory seem to have particularly embittered relationships between aboriginal peoples and the provincial government. Not surprisingly, when a future is laid out by the secessionists which envisages a fully sovereign state, claiming to exercise complete jurisdiction over peoples and resources within the current provincial boundaries, aboriginal peoples express concern. Given the recent political history of Quebec, the impact of the change in political status of the province on aboriginal peoples' historic relationship with the Crown presents a chilling potential for a complete breakdown in the political relationship between aboriginal peoples and Quebec.

Open discussion, dialogue, and consideration of aboriginal peoples' status and rights need to begin immediately in Quebec, but they also require an *informed basis*, founded on principles of equality of peoples, mutual respect, and self-determination. There are basic human rights principles at issue in this debate and the legitimacy of the sovereignist movement may well stand or fall on how these principles are reconciled. The sovereignist government cannot continue as a virtual steamroller ignoring or denying aboriginal peoples' status and rights and still hope to be successful. Thus far, the secessionists have not presented a framework for dialogue which embraces basic principles of respect for aboriginal peoples and their status and rights. Instead, aboriginal peoples have been offered vague assurances that they will be treated well by a new Quebec state. When aboriginal peoples have articulated their concerns and set out some basic principles upon which to begin a dialogue with Québécois, they have been unjustifiably attacked and diminished. It seems that, on the part of the Quebec sovereignists, there is no genuine commitment to understanding the aboriginal perspective on full sovereignty for Quebec.

Self-Determination: The Competing Claims

The explosive political atmosphere encircling the debate over full sovereignty and aboriginal peoples was revealed when the National Chief of the Assembly of First Nations, Ovide Mercredi, appeared in 1992 before the Quebec National Assembly's Committee to Examine Matters Relating to the Accession of Quebec to Sovereignty.[9] The National Chief, appearing with Chiefs and Elders from a number of the First Nations in Quebec, told the Committee:

> There can be no legitimate secession by any people in Quebec if the right to self-determination of First Nations is denied, suppressed or ignored in order to achieve independence. Our rights do not take a back seat to yours. . . . Only through openness, of the mind and of the heart, can questions of such vital importance to your people and ours be reconciled. The alternative, which we do not favour, is confrontation . . .

The response to this, and other submissions, of both the Quebec media and some members of the Committee, was one of outrage. It was as if the sovereignists were wilfully blinded to the prin-

ciples articulated by aboriginal peoples in support of their rights. This is particularly frustrating given that, at many levels, the principles that aboriginal peoples advance for the basis of a political relationship with Canada or a sovereign Quebec are not very different from Quebec's position (self-determination, territory, identity). At least in some cases, I believe the aboriginal position could prove stronger legally and politically. Since the Lesage era in the 1960s, French Canadians have argued that they want to be masters of their own house (*maîtres chez nous*). Aboriginal peoples have asserted an equally powerful concept—self-determination or self-government.

Sovereignists seem to see threats only when aboriginal peoples articulate their own perspectives. The worrisome point in this fury over the National Chief's appearance before the Committee on Sovereignty is that he is a committed moderate. There were no threats of violence, only pleas for dialogue and for measures to prevent a confrontation over the competing positions. As Chief Mercredi stated: 'I, as National Chief, welcome constructive dialogue between First Nations and Quebecers on constitutional issues. We should build partnerships in support of our respective rights and not construct hierarchies of your rights over ours.' Nevertheless, there seems to be a powerful drive towards castigating aboriginal peoples for advocating aboriginal and treaty rights. For example, the National Chief was chastised by Claude Masson of *La Presse* for speaking 'exaggerated, insulting, and outrageous words' and said that the aboriginal leadership 'must behave like reasonable and responsible human beings and not like warriors or criminals with a right of life and death over everybody else'.[10] This utter misrepresentation of the basic principles advanced by the National Chief, a leader who has worked hard to build alliances and open dialogue with Quebec, demonstrates how wide the gulf is growing between sovereignists and aboriginal peoples. The era of disciplining aboriginal peoples for being different is over. Political support for the aspirations of Québécois will not be won in Canada or around the world with this type of denigration.

There has been an obvious strategic decision in the Quebec independence movement to view aboriginal issues as business for a later date—after the accession to full sovereignty. The executive of the Parti Québécois has recently adopted a resolution to this effect. There seems to be little priority placed on dealing with aboriginal peoples' status and rights before accession.[11] In response to aboriginal suggestions that the situation is critical in Quebec, there is a 'why only pick on us' sentiment in the secessionist movement's response to aboriginal peoples, which is ill informed. Aboriginal peoples have been vigorously advancing their right to self-determination, territory, and cultural rights at all levels in Canada and internationally. The *Delgamuukw* action in British Columbia is a case in point. This case, which is now before the British Columbia Court of Appeal, is an assertion of Gitksan and Wet'suwet'en political and territorial sovereignty against the federal and provincial Crown.

The movement for adequate recognition of aboriginal and treaty rights is not confined to Quebec. With or without the prospect of Quebec's secession, the rights will be advanced in that province, too. But in light of the sovereignist agenda, it is seen as critical here because the movement for full sovereignty calls into question aboriginal peoples' status and rights in a most immediate and far-reaching way—there will be a decision made about the future of all peoples in Quebec, in a referendum to be held by 26 October 1992. Issues relating to that referendum—self-determination, territory, and identity—are brought directly to the fore by the sovereignist agenda which, once engaged through Bill 150, is a veritable juggernaut. Aboriginal peoples cannot be expected to ignore what is coming at them full force.

Moreover, these issues deserve more than just passing consideration in the context of [a theoretical discussion] of negotiating with a sovereign Quebec. From a human rights perspective, could there legitimately be a fully sovereign Quebec without according equal consideration to the aspirations and choices of aboriginal peoples? To simply begin the discussion by sketching the contours of negotiations with a sovereign Quebec may be putting the cart before the horse. For aboriginal peoples, Québécois, and Canadians there is a great deal at stake. Either one legitimizes *a priori* the reduction of First Nations peoples to the status of ethnic minorities with no right of self-determination, or one recognizes that there would be several other potential sovereign entities with which the Quebec state would have to negotiate.

Negotiating with a sovereign Québec could only mean, for aboriginal peoples, a political relationship based on negotiating international treaties between emerging independent peoples. Existing treaties involving Canada, aboriginal peoples, and Quebec, such as the *James Bay and Northern Quebec Agreement*, would not have continuing validity, and Quebec would not be able to claim the benefits of such treaties. If full sovereignty is declared by Quebec, this would amount to a unilateral breach of that agreement. The *James Bay and Northern Quebec Agreement* was not only explicitly negotiated and ratified in a federal context, but also contained perpetual federal and provincial obligations that cannot be altered without the aboriginal parties' consent. A unilateral declaration of independence would be a clear breach of that agreement and Quebec could not claim the benefits of the agreement while not respecting its negotiated terms.

Aboriginal peoples are not simply a head of jurisdiction, as seems to have been presumed by many Québécois and others outside the province. The first peoples in Canada are political entities—'peoples' in the international legal sense. This means that as peoples (with distinct languages, cultures, territories, populations, and governments), aboriginal peoples have full rights of self-determination. For the purposes of discussions over sovereignty, aboriginal peoples must be seen to enjoy that status of peoples with a right to self-determination. This position is supported by both Canadian and international law. The International Bill of Rights (an instrument which I presume a fully sovereign Quebec would want to respect in order to gain entry into the international community) recognizes the right of *all* peoples to self-determination. By this it is meant that peoples should freely determine their political status and that this should not be determined for them by a state, or an external actor.

Aboriginal peoples are independent political entities with distinct languages, cultures, histories, territories, spiritualities, and governments. As such, they can choose or determine their future relationship with Canada or a sovereign Quebec. This should not be determined for them by other peoples or governments. At present, the position of many sovereignists does not embrace self-determination for aboriginal peoples. It presumes that aboriginal peoples are not peoples or are too insignificant and dispersed to be independent political actors.[12] As academics and intellectuals, we should not promote recognition for a fully sovereign Quebec if it means that aboriginal peoples' competing rights of self-determination will be compromised.

We need to recognize that when the political discourse shifts to Quebec's secession, it moves from the familiar realm of federalist considerations of distinct society and the recognition and protection of distinct identities to the less certain context of political and territorial sovereignty. With this shift, there is a different grid structuring the debate, one with far broader implications. Once basic concepts of control over territory and peoples are put so squarely on the agenda by people in Quebec, the struggles in which aboriginal peoples are engaged across Canada come sharply

into focus. The basic presumption which operates in the minds of many sovereignists is that they either have, or will automatically acquire, sovereignty *over* aboriginal peoples in Quebec. Flowing from this sovereignty, some Québécois believe that the French-Canadian majority in Quebec can decide what it wants to do with aboriginal peoples. But what is the source of their sovereignty over aboriginal peoples and territories? Is it the right of the French-Canadian nation in Quebec for self-determination?

It would seem clear that the French-Canadian people are faced with the competing rights to self-determination of aboriginal peoples. Moreover, the right to self-determination is not a right of the province of Quebec.[13] In international law, provinces do not enjoy a right of self-determination; peoples do. Consequently, other peoples who may have competing claims, especially to territory, cannot be ignored. Sovereignists in Quebec have, in effect, constructed their claims on the basis of the province of Quebec as the entity which will exercise the right of self-determination. However, this would unjustly efface the competing and legitimate rights of aboriginal peoples.

As this short discussion illustrates, the competing self-determination claims by French Canadians and aboriginal peoples need to be carefully examined before we can deal with referenda or territory in an equitable and mutually respectful manner. Indeed, these three issues—self-determination, referendum, and territorial claims—are critically interwoven in the current Canadian context. No single issue can stand alone without the others being considered. An independent Quebec state would not meet with international recognition if aboriginal peoples were not treated as peoples, with full enjoyment of human rights, including the right of self-determination. Self-determination for aboriginal peoples may well require that they be involved as full, equal, and independent participants in the decision about the accession of Quebec to full sovereignty. I emphasize 'independent' because aboriginal peoples must be dealt with as 'peoples', not 'minorities' subject to the political will of the province. As distinct political entities, aboriginal peoples must participate in that process through their leadership and not be presumed to be 'represented' by members of the Quebec National Assembly or the federal parliament.

The federal government also has obligations to recognize aboriginal peoples' right to self-determination. If there are to be negotiations with Quebec on secession, then aboriginal peoples cannot be treated as a head of jurisdiction along with monetary issues or other items. Aboriginal peoples must each decide their relationship with a new Quebec state. As United States President Woodrow Wilson stated in 1917, '. . . no right exists anywhere to hand peoples about from sovereignty to sovereignty as if they were property.'[14] Aboriginal peoples cannot be handed from one sovereign (the federal Crown) to another (an independent Quebec state) as if they were property. Yet this seems to be the presumption operating in Bill 150, the Allaire report, and the Bélanger-Campeau commission report, where aboriginal peoples are viewed as minorities, authority over which can be simply transferred to a sovereign Quebec.

The persistence of this mindset of viewing aboriginal peoples as minorities or of an inferior status to French or English newcomers goes to the very problem Hugh Brody identifies in the quotation set out at the beginning of this chapter: there is a narrowness of vision here which sees the arrival and spread of immigrants (whether they be French, English, or otherwise) as the very purpose of history, including Canadian history. It is this vision which selects immigrant political objectives as superior to and more compelling than those of aboriginal peoples. Aboriginal perspectives and political aspirations are treated as secondary within the immigrant vision. Yet the immigrant vision has been vigorously challenged.

Even some voices in Quebec have challenged it, although they seem to fall on deaf ears. For example, Professor Daniel Turp (Université de Montréal), a leading sovereignist academic frequently cited by the Parti Québécois, acknowledged, when he appeared before the Committee on Accession, that 'in my opinion [aboriginal peoples] constitute peoples who are self-identified as peoples . . . this would confer on them a right to self-determination at the same level as Quebec . . . the same rules apply to aboriginal peoples as to Québécois.'[15] This aspect of his opinion has been largely ignored by sovereignists who instead emphasize the right of the French in Quebec to self-determination.

We know that the Canadian constitution is premised on a privileged reading of history, or the immigrant vision of (only) two founding nations, and that it has marginalized or excluded aboriginal visions. Aboriginal peoples, Québécois, and other Canadians should strive to establish a more honourable and collaborative process. This entails fundamental changes to existing political processes and constitutional structures. Moreover, in the context of secession, it requires a full airing of opinions on aboriginal peoples' status and rights.

Territory

In 1992, David Cliche, the Parti Québécois 'native policy' adviser and a member of the executive of the Parti Québécois, argued that, upon secession, Quebec will naturally take the territory within the current provincial boundaries. This position was endorsed by the leader of the Parti Québécois, Jacques Parizeau. What it ignores is that aboriginal peoples have no say in the matter. The decisions over the control of aboriginal territories should be made by aboriginal peoples, not Quebec or the federal government. Cliche opposes this view and suggests that the sovereignists would offer the aboriginal people the best deal they could ever get. But this promise misses the point, because self-determination for aboriginal peoples is not about the prospects of a good deal some time in the future. It is about peoples deciding freely their political and territorial status now and not being forced into political arrangements without that independent collective decision.

The gulf in our respective understandings of the situation is a broad one. I believe that from an international legal perspective, and in terms of the political legitimacy of the sovereignist movement, only aboriginal peoples can decide their future status. This cannot be usurped by the sovereignists, just as French Canadians want to decide their future without this being unilaterally usurped by the federal government.

Much of the sovereignist argument on territorial claims has rested on a doctrine of international law called *uti possidetis juris*, which is offered to support the claim that they will enter independence with the territory they had before. In this case, the secessionists say the territory they had before is Quebec within the current provincial boundaries. They sometimes call this the principle of 'territorial integrity'. This doctrine is said to displace the ordinary principle of occupation as a basis for territorial sovereignty. The international law on whether *uti possidetis* is compelling is dubious at best, with the leading scholars in the field wondering whether the doctrine is even a norm of international law.[16] Even the International Court of Justice has cautioned that this doctrine is problematic, as it conflicts with a significant principle in international law— self-determination.[17] The sovereignist claim to take the territory within the current provincial boundaries is weak, internationally, especially given that much land in the province is subject to aboriginal claims which have yet to be resolved, and which are tied in to aboriginal self-determination. The secessionists will have to present other arguments that can satisfy international legal standards if they hope to be recognized as a legitimate state with the existing provincial boundaries as their territorial base.

Control over aboriginal peoples' territories has been essential for the prosperity of Quebec. This certainly was the experience following the boundary extensions of 1898 and 1912. It is clear that the secessionist position is rooted in a realization that these territories are of continued significance. Issues of control over territory are fundamental to the secessionists because mass development projects like James Bay II (Great Whale) are part of their economic plan. Aboriginal peoples have legitimate concerns about the territorial consequences of full sovereignty. Would this mean that a new Quebec state can unilaterally make development decisions? James Bay may be but a glimpse of what aboriginal peoples could face with Quebec secession and full claims to jurisdiction over their territories. It has been an enormous struggle, albeit increasingly successful, for the Crees to gain support for their opposition to further James Bay hydro-electric development. As Grand Chief Coon-Come reflects:

> Bourassa's dream [of hydro-electric development] has become our nightmare. It has contaminated our fish with mercury. It has destroyed the spawning grounds. It has destroyed the nesting grounds of the waterfowl. It has displaced and dislocated our people and broken the fabric of our society. And we have decided, knowing the behaviour of the animals, that we will not be like the fox who, when he sees danger, crawls back to his hole. We have come out to stop the destruction of our land.[18]

In this quotation notice that the Grand Chief says 'our' when he refers to the land and to the fish. This contradicts the view of the government of Quebec (excerpted at the outset of this chapter) that the land and resources of the province are a gift of nature to the people of Quebec, in which regard they are more favoured than others.

The territorial claims of the secessionists to the current provincial boundaries are legally and politically insecure. The territory was not given to Québécois as a gift of nature. It was a gift of the federal government in 1898 and 1912—a gift made without the consent of the owners, aboriginal peoples. French Canadians will have to support their territorial claim to the lands within the existing provincial boundaries with something other than erroneous theories about gifts of nature or *uti possidetis*.[19] No one can presume these are theirs to take when the original occupants of the land, aboriginal peoples, assert their rights. Voting in a referendum in support of this position is not enough either, legally or politically.

Referendum: The Who/Whom

In 1902, Lenin posited the critical question in politics as 'who/whom': who rules whom, who decides for whom? Bill 150 provides for a referendum sometime between October 12 and 26, 1992. The who/whom question is pivotal. Bill 150 states that if the results of the referendum are in favour of secession, they will 'constitute a proposal' that Quebec acquire the status of a sovereign state one year to the day from the holding of the referendum. What question will be put to voters, who will vote, and the weighing of the results are all unclear at this point. For aboriginal peoples in Quebec, the ambiguity of the referendum is threatening because if a vote is registered in favour of sovereignty, it could legitimize the appropriation of aboriginal territories and the assumption of authority over them. They would be the 'whom' ruled by the 'who' in a simple majority referendum.

Is a simple 50-plus-1 majority enough in these circumstances? If it was, this could mean that aboriginal peoples' self-determination rights would be overridden, as aboriginal peoples may simply be outvoted by larger populations in non-aboriginal regions of Quebec. This kind of a referendum could not be held up internationally as supporting accession to sovereignty because of its implications for aboriginal peoples. Referendums are numbers games and aboriginal peoples would be set up for exclusion unless double majorities or separate referendums are employed. Aboriginal peoples will have to insist on double majorities, or independent (traditional) means for expressing their views on accession to full sovereignty. They cannot be lumped into a general referendum if the result is to be accepted for any purposes as a legitimate mandate for statehood.

While concerns about the status and rights of aboriginal peoples are grave, it is nevertheless important to stress that this is a great opportunity for the sovereignists to lead the way on self-determination. There is a natural alliance which could be struck between aboriginal peoples and the secessionists whereby aboriginal self-determination could be respected as a priority. This requires an immediate dialogue with aboriginal peoples within a framework of respect for the equally compelling right of aboriginal peoples to self-determination. This dialogue cannot be informed by the 'trust us, we'll give you a deal later' attitude which seems so popular among sovereignists.

Such an alliance would be a historic event and could lead to interesting and innovative political arrangements with Canada and a new Quebec state. However, the basic principles for such an alliance, such as aboriginal self-determination, must be discussed and openly embraced by the sovereignist movement. This requires a reconsideration of elements of its vision of a new Quebec state. Particularly, the territorial integrity position would have to be revised to embrace at least the principle of shared and co-managed resources. Currently, there is no indication that this is happening and the responsibility is really on the sovereignist side to demonstrate a willingness to respect the right of aboriginal self-determination.

As the title of this essay would suggest, the road to full sovereignty for Quebec runs through aboriginal territory. There is no detour, no other path. There is only one road, and it must be a course of justice and respect for aboriginal peoples. The secessionists will be well advised to look carefully at the map of this road now that they have chosen the path of statehood. Should Québécois fail to deal with aboriginal self-determination, their movement stands to lose a great deal of legitimacy and support both in Canada and the international community.

Notes

Source: 'Does the Road to Quebec Sovereignty Run through Aboriginal Territory?' in *Negotiating with a Sovereign Québec*, Daniel Drache and Roberto Perin, eds (Toronto: James Lorimer & Company, 1992), pp. 93–106. Reprinted by permission of the publisher.

1. H. Brody, *Maps and Dreams* (Vancouver: Douglas and McIntyre, 1988), p. xiii.

2. Government of Québec, *Quebec-Canada: A New Deal* (Éditeur Officiel, 1979), p. 89. This is the official Parti Québécois publication circulated prior to the referendum on sovereignty-association in 1980.

3. Although my preferred expression is First Nations, I use the phrase *aboriginal peoples* throughout this paper because I want it to be clear that I am referring to both the First Nations (sometimes called 'Indians') and Inuit.

4. Here I am particularly mindful of the comments of the members of the Committee on the Accession of Quebec to Full Sovereignty, established pursuant to Bill 150 (An Act Respecting the Process for Determining the Political and Constitutional Future of Quebec).

5. Now section 91(24) of the Constitution Act, 1867.

6. Of course, law and politics are hardly distinct. Some of the detail of the legal argument, at least on the issue of territory, can be found in Kent McNeil, 'Aboriginal Nations and Québec's Boundaries: Canada Couldn't Give What It Didn't Have', in *Negotiating with a Sovereign Québec,* Daniel Drache and Roberto Perin, eds (Toronto: James Lorimer & Company, 1992). For a detailed and superb legal analysis of aboriginal peoples' concerns *vis-à-vis* full sovereignty for Quebec, see Grand Council of the Crees of Quebec, *Status and Rights of the James Bay Crees in the Context of Quebec's Secession from Canada,* Submission to the United Nations Commission on Human Rights, 48th Session, 21 February 1992.

7. This is a land claim agreement or modern treaty entered into in 1975 by Cree, Inuit, and the federal and provincial governments.

8. As Zebeedee Nungak, spokesperson for the Inuit Tapirisat of Canada and the Inuit in northern Quebec, rather graphically illustrated at the federally sponsored constitutional constituency assembly 'Identity, Values and Rights', he identifies as an Inuk first, a Canadian second, and a Québécois third (7 February 1992, Royal York Hotel, Toronto). I say 'graphically' because he held up a map of Quebec which divided the province into the north and south, arguing that (to paraphrase) 'the distinct society of the south cannot override the distinct society of the north'.

9. The National Chief of the Assembly of First Nations, Ovide Mercredi, appeared on 11 February 1992. A copy of his text is on file with the author.

10. From the translation, reprinted in *The Globe and Mail*, 18 February 1992, p. 19.

11. The sovereignists often refer to a 20 March 1985, National Assembly resolution as a starting point for engaging with aboriginal peoples on issues relating to full sovereignty. However, it is important to note that this resolution was unilaterally imposed on the First Nations of Quebec. As a unilaterally imposed document, it is not a basis for a relationship which respects self-determination for aboriginal peoples.

The Crees suggest, in their brief to the United Nations, that 'it is unacceptable for the National Assembly or government of Quebec to unilaterally impose policies on First Nations. The contents of an acceptable Resolution were in the process of being negotiated. Also, a prior commitment had been expressly made by the Premier of Quebec that he would not table any resolution on this matter in the National Assembly without aboriginal consent'. Submission of the Grand Council of the Crees of Quebec, p. 166.

12. The secessionist position has been articulated in detail by Professor J. Brossard in his text, *L'accession à la souveraineté et le cas du Québec* (Montréal: Les Presses de l'Université de Montréal, 1977). This text has been referred to by the Committee on the Accession of Quebec to Sovereignty as an accurate statement of the rights of French Canadians to self-determination.

13. Brossard acknowledges that the basis of the claim to accession is the rights of French Canadians to self-determination. He goes further to suggest that in theory it is only the French-Canadian nation that could participate in the decision on full sovereignty, thus excluding the anglophones. *L'accession à la souveraineté*, pp.

183–5. He admits that politically such an alternative is impracticable.

14. This is quoted in the Submission of the Grand Council of the Crees of Quebec to the United Nations Commission on Human Rights.

15. He appeared before the Committee on Accession on 9 October 1991.

16. See, for example, I. Brownlie, *Principles of International Law*, 4th edn (Oxford: Clarendon Press, 1989), p. 135.

17. *Frontier Dispute (Burkina Faso/Mali)*, 80 I.L.R. 440 at 554 (separate opinion of Judge Luchaire).

18. Quoted in H. Thurston, 'Power in a Land of Remembrance', *Audubon* 52 (Nov.–Dec. 1991): 58–9.

19. As the National Chief of the Assembly of First Nations stated in his presentation to the Committee on Accession, 'The Quebec government's proposed principle concerning the territorial integrity of Quebec is an affront to First Nations. It is obvious that territorial integrity serves to consolidate your legal position to the extreme prejudice of the First Nations.'

Part C

Social Movements

For political sociologists, the study of social movements and the organizations associated with them follows a long tradition that extends back to de Tocqueville's interest in the voluntary association activity in the United States. Recently, this interest has been renewed with writing that deals with a group of social organizations referred to as new social movements (NSMs). As Carroll notes in Chapter 8, this group comprises the student movement, feminism, the peace movement, homosexual liberation groups, and the ecology movement.

In what sense are new social movements 'new'? This is a matter of some contention; indeed, Curtis and Grabb hint in Chapter 9 that patterns of association involvement point to the unexpected conclusion that the continuities with 'old' associations are more pronounced than the literature would anticipate. From the perspective of the literature (Adam 1993; Carroll and Ratner 1994; Johnston, Larana, and Gusfield 1996; McAdam 1996; Scott 1990) what is (supposed to be) different is the orientation of these movements toward cultural change that does not fit into the old divisions of left versus right. To writers such as Dryzek (1996: 50), new social movements are much more concerned with 'identity formation' than they are with conventional politics; in fact, if there is any radicalism at all in these groups, it is

'self-limiting' because the organizations are not directly concerned with acquiring power in the way that, say, the socialist movements of the nineteenth and early twentieth centuries were. Yet, all the groups that have been identified in the literature are 'vaguely on the left', and no NSM theorist has included the religious right, fundamentalism, and the anti-abortion movement in the list (Calhoun 1994: 22). Thus writers speak more of the historical continuity between NSMs and, say, the movements of previous eras—such as the labour movement—than they do of the 'break' in orientation between new and old movements.

For writers on the political left, new social movements have become particularly important because of an admitted decline in class politics from the divisions observed in previous generations. Whether social class is indeed now 'dead' (Pakulski and Waters 1996) is a hotly contested question (Crompton 1996; Eder 1993; Grusky and Sorensen 1998; Morris and Scott 1996; Svallfors 1995), but there can at least be some agreement on a few fundamental dimensions of the issue. First, the physical size and thus the electoral strength of the traditional blue-collar working class has diminished during the postwar period (Przeworski and Sprague 1986), thus reducing the likelihood of a class-based transformation of society from capitalism (or 'advanced capitalism') into some other form. Secondly, the de-industrialization of some Western economies, that is, the replacement of industrial infrastructure (heavy manufacturing) with tertiary sector industry (computer software, knowledge industries, etc.), has led to a secular decline in the organization power and capacity of traditional blue-collar unions and the labour movement in general. In most Western countries, labour union membership as a proportion of the working population has declined—sometimes precipitously—in all areas except perhaps a few professions and the civil service (neither of which form part of the traditional working class). Finally, the ability of labour union leaders to influence members has been compromised by the widespread geographic dispersal of working-class families across the suburban landscape and away from homogeneous working-class communities, the disappearance of working-class cultural 'gathering places' (such as various clubs and, to a lesser extent, pubs), and the widespread penetration of television and Hollywood popular culture (see also Chapter 15 in this text).

So, what is left for academics with an interest in emancipatory politics? Some authors (Cohen 1982; Cohen and Arato 1992) take the view that the traditional Marxist notion of the working class as the 'emancipatory subject' was always problematic because of the sometimes explicit, sometimes implicit assumption that the politics of working-class liberation would transform itself into a universalistic ethos—somehow, magically—at the point of a social transformation (that is, a revolution). For these authors, the development of a truly egalitarian society can come only if the universalistic ethos is carefully constructed as

part of the process of social transformation, and not simply after it. The brutality of the guillotine in the French Revolution, or the cruel deaths suffered by thousands if not millions in the gulags of Siberia stand as testimony to the mistaken belief that such a transformation is unproblematic. So it may be the case that, for some writers, the study of new social movements represents a continuity and a shift: a continuity with old perspectives seeking a radically transformed society (although perhaps not through violent revolution) and a shift in the definition of the 'revolutionary subject', whose bearers are now the well-educated individuals situated (mostly) in 'semi-autonomous' occupations (professions, students) rather than members of the old proletariat.

This interpretation is, to be sure, one-sided. As Carroll points out in Chapter 8, there is no single unitary (theoretical) perspective on new social movements, although some perspectives seem to be better theoretical travellers than others (from the standpoint of theoretical adequacy). But one can see that the importance of new social movements to many sociologists extends beyond a simple study of a particular type of voluntary association.

New social movement participation is subject to a great amount of cross-national variation. Certain European countries, such as the Netherlands, Scandinavia, and perhaps Germany appear to have more activity than other countries, with the possible exception of the United States. As Grabb and Curtis tell us, Lipset would predict that Americans would be very highly involved in organizations of this sort; their analysis in Chapter 9, however, shows that there is very little difference between Canada and the United States in this regard.

References

Adam, B. 1993. 'Post-Marxism and the New Social Movements', Canadian Review of Sociology and Anthropology 30(3): 316–36.

Calhoun, C. 1994. 'Social Theory and the Politics of Identity'. In Social Theory and the Politics of Identity, ed. C. Calhoun (Oxford: Blackwell), 9–36.

Carroll, W., and R.S. Ratner. 1994. 'Gramsci and the New Social Movements', *Critical Sociology* 20(2): 3–26.

Cohen, J. 1982. *Class and Civil Society: The Limits of Marxian Critical Theory* (Amherst, MA: University of Massachusetts Press).

———— and A. Arato. 1992. *Civil Society and Political Theory* (Cambridge, MA: MIT Press).

Crompton, R. 1996. 'The Fragmentation of Class Analysis', *British Journal of Sociology* 47(1): 56–67.

Dryzek, J. 1996. *Democracy in Capitalist Times: Ideals, Limits and Struggles* (Oxford: Oxford University Press).

Eder, K. 1993. *The New Politics of Class* (Newbury Park, CA: Sage).

Grusky, D. and J. Sorensen. 1998. 'Can Class Analysis Be Salvaged?' *American Journal of Sociology* 103: 1187–234.

Johnston, H., E. Larana, and J. Gusfield. 1996. 'Identities, Grievances and New Social Movements'. In *New Social Movements: From Ideology to Identity,* eds E. Larana, H. Johnston, and J. Gusfield (Philadelphia: Temple University Press).

McAdam, D. 1996. 'Culture and Social Movements'. In *New Social Movements: From Ideology to Identity,* ed. E. Larana, H. Johnston, and J. Gusfield (Philadelphia: Temple University Press).

Morris, L., and J. Scott. 1996. 'The Attenuation of Class Analysis: Some Comments on G. Marshall, S. Roberts and C. Burgoyne, "Social class and the underclass in Britain and the USA"', *British Journal of Sociology* 47(1): 45–55.

Pakulski, J. and M. Waters. 1996. *The Death of Class* (Thousand Oaks, CA: Sage).

Przeworski, A. and J. Sprague. 1986. *Paper Stones: A History of Electoral Socialism* (Chicago: University of Chicago Press).

Scott, A. 1990. *Ideology and the New Social Movements* (London: Unwin Hyman).

Svallfors, S. 1995. 'The End of Class Politics? Structural Cleavages and Attitudes to Swedish Welfare Policies', *Acta Sociologica* 38: 53–74.

Chapter 8

Social Movements

William K. Carroll

Introduction

Like other central concepts in political sociology, the idea of social movements is very much associated with the phenomenon of 'modernity' and particularly with the consolidation of national states and liberal democratic politics in the 19th century. This is not to say that prior to the modern era aggrieved social groups did not resist domination in their own characteristically localized and episodic ways. The historical record is replete with examples of slave revolts in the ancient world and tax revolts against feudal tutelage. Collective resistance is as old a phenomenon as is social domination.

But as Tilly (1978) has emphasized, social movements in the contemporary sense are products of structural transformations that gave rise to modern national—and now increasingly global—politics. Urbanization, capitalist industrialization, and the creation of a democratic polity all played important roles in this transformation, as scattered rural populations became concentrated in cities, as small-scale agriculture and artisanry gave way to modern industry and its industrial proletariat, as the market relations of capitalism replaced paternalistic class relations with the 'cash nexus', and as national states moved to consolidate national markets and to grant some measure of citizenship to their subjects. In these new circumstances opportunities opened up for new forms of sustained resistance to domination. The

urban, industrialized setting, the creation of a national space for economic and political action, the liberal freedoms of speech and association, all enabled large urbanized populations to organize around their common interests in 'distributive justice': the redistribution of economic resources in the direction of meeting human needs rather than serving the capitalist class's thirst for profit and competitive advantage.

It is not surprising that *social movement* bore a rather unitary meaning in the century during which modern capitalist societies were consolidated in Europe and North America. When it entered political discourse in the nineteenth century, the term called attention not to a plurality of *movements*—of collective actors using extraparliamentary means to achieve or resist social change—which is roughly the contemporary meaning of *social movements*. Instead, the reference was to *one* social movement—the movement of the people against the state and the capitalist class, striving toward the goal of socialism.

It was not until the twentieth century, and mainly in American sociological discourse, that the notion of a plurality of social movements gained currency, and within American sociology the focus was primarily not on the emancipatory possibilities raised by movements but on the challenges that social movements raised to liberal democratic politics.

In the sociological literature of the 1930s and 1940s, two perspectives had influence. The first, pioneered by the symbolic interactionist Herbert Blumer, depicted movements as engaged in *collective behaviour*—actions, occurring typically in crowds, that transgress the routines of normal, institutionalized conduct. For Blumer (1939), and later for Turner and Killian (1957) the spontaneity of collective behaviour provides a context for the emergence of new norms that might entail a creative process of adaptive social problem-solving. The second approach, pioneered in 1942 by structural-functionalist Talcott Parsons, viewed movements as symptoms of societal dysfunctionality. In his analysis of the rise of fascism, Parsons (1969) emphasized the structural strains associated with the uneven impact of modernization processes on different social groups. This perspective reached its apogee with the comprehensive framework offered by Parsons's student Neil Smelser in a 1962 treatise entitled *The Theory of Collective Behavior*. For Smelser, social movements are the result of a cumulative combination of structural and psychological factors: 'people under strain mobilize to reconstruct social order in the name of a generalized belief' (1962: 385). On this basis, Smelser goes on to distinguish the various kinds of generalized beliefs (for example, hysteria, wish-fulfillment, and hostility) and the structural conditions (for example, the conduciveness of stock exchanges to panic trading) that lead to particular kinds of collective behaviours. For instance,

> panic will occur if the appropriate conditions of structural conduciveness are present, *and* if the appropriate conditions of strain are present, *and* if a hysterical belief develops, *and* if mobilization occurs, and if social controls fail to operate (1962: 385).

Since Smelser's statement, the theoretical framing of social movements in sociology has been radically rethought. The waning of structural-functional analysis was in part because of profound changes in the terrain of social movement politics. The rise (or re-emergence) in the 1960s and 1970s of the student movement, feminism, the peace movement, gay and lesbian liberation, ecology, and other 'new' movements significantly transformed political agendas, political culture, and social identities, so that analyses that relegated movements to the irrational margins of modern politics lost plausibility. Smelser's theory was the product of an intellectual practice that counselled objective detachment from the object of sociological analysis, but that typically represented movements as 'a threat to the existing order, an irrational form of "deviant" behavior' (Eyerman and Jamison 1991: 40). In contrast, many of the generation of sociologists that came of age in the 1960s and 1970s were themselves active in or at least sympathetic to the movements of the day. The sociological accounts they developed reflect the preponderance of the 'insider's perspective'— whether as 'movement intellectuals' whose analyses contribute insights as to how movements achieve political efficacy or as movement 'ideologists' whose analyses contribute to the developing world views of movements (1991: 40–2).

Two Paradigms

In place of structural-functionalism, two broad paradigms have informed sociological analysis of social movements since the 1970s. One strand— predominantly American—emphasizes the *rationality* of collective action; another—predominantly European—emphasizes the culturally innovative and *democratic* character of movements as collective agencies within a differentiated *civil society*. John Urry's (1981) analysis is helpful in encapsulating the context that an expanded and diverse civil society provides for movement activism in late modernity. Civil society can be thought of as a realm of activity distinct from the state and from the economy, in which many aspects of social and political identity—such as gender, sexuality, and ethnicity—are primarily grounded. Within capitalist democracies the terrain of civil society is vast; it includes institutions such as religion and the family, voluntary associations such as clubs and amateur sport, and a *social movement sector*: 'the configuration of individuals and groups *willing to engage in disruptive direct action* against others to achieve collective goods' (Tarrow 1988: 432). Like other aspects of civil society, movements are neither components of the state apparatus nor appendages of the capitalist economy. It is within this relatively autonomous sphere that movements articulate grievances and alternative visions—whether about family violence or homophobia or environmental degradation or poverty—and mobilize themselves as new collective agencies of change. Social movements thus politicize the issues and identities that are part of the texture of everyday life. Movement activism is distinct from the logic of both the capitalist economy and the party politics that surround the state, yet movements are often implicated in these more institutionalized dimensions of political economy. Or, put another way, '*civil society* has become the indispensable terrain on which social actors assemble, organize and mobilize, even if their targets are the economy and the state' (Cohen 1985: 682). On these points, various contemporary theories are in agreement. Compared to the Parsonian paradigm that preceded them, these theories provide a view of movements that is nonpejorative and often expressly sympathetic. But the European and American approaches differ from each other in many important respects. Grasping these differences is one key to understanding social movement theory today.[1]

At the outset, two distinctions between the paradigms can be drawn. First, resource mobilization theory (RMT)—the predominantly American approach—focuses primarily upon *how*

movements form and engage in collective action; the more European new social movement (NSM) formulations focus primarily on *why* particular forms of collective identity and action have appeared in late twentieth-century Euro-North American societies (Melucci 1989). By implication, RMT analyses tend to be sensitized to the specific situational context which facilitates or hinders a process of movement mobilization, while NSM theories are typically more sensitized to the broad, macro-sociological transformations of the late twentieth century that have provided new cultural, political, and economic contexts for collective-identity formation.

Second, RMT offers a conception of movement practice that emphasizes the *shared interests* that underlie the process of mobilization: in forming a movement a social group engages in the rational pursuit of its common interests. NSM theory, in contrast, views movements less as agencies of common interest and more as new forms of *collective identity*, which not only transform people's self-understandings but create cultural codes that contest the legitimacy of established points of view (Cohen 1985).

Resource Mobilization Theory

Mobilization is a process by which resources useful to a group's collective action are brought under collective control. It is this pooling of resources that enables a group to transform itself from a collection of political spectators sharing a common interest to a contending group able to pursue a shared goal (Tilly 1978)—a social movement. RMT analysts differ in describing the kinds of resources that are mobilized by movements, but any credible list would include labour (the active commitment of constituents to work for the movement), money, land or facilities (for example, an office and communications equipment), and technical expertise (the skills of key activists—whether in media relations, popular education, or political strategizing) (see Jenkins 1983: 533).

Bringing such resources under collective control, in turn, requires *social organization*, in two senses. First, pre-existing social networks and collective identities are prerequisite to mobilization. Indeed, the mobilization potential of a group is mainly determined by its degree of pre-existing social organization. Groups lacking such social networks and shared consciousness rarely mobilize: they have no practical means by which to pool resources. Conversely, groups sharing strong identities and dense interpersonal networks are highly organized, and can be mobilized rather readily (Tilly 1978: 62–3). Often, mobilization involves the cooptation of resources from pre-existing organizations in civil society, such as voluntary associations or churches. Second, social organization *results from* mobilization; that is, mobilization typically involves the construction of a *social movement organization* (SMO). Such organizations institutionalize the collective control of resources—the commitment of activists, the group's claim to other resources such as communications media (for example, a newsletter)—and thus maintain the movement in a more or less mobilized state. SMOs are thus 'the carrier organizations that consciously attempt to coordinate and mobilize supporters' (Zald and McCarthy 1987: 339).

McCarthy and Zald's Entrepreneurial Mobilization Model

Within the resource mobilization paradigm there are two distinctive schools of thought: namely, the professional organizer or entrepreneurial mobilization model (Jenkins 1983: 527) and the political process model (Pichardo 1988). The *professional organizer model*, developed primarily by McCarthy and Zald (1973, Zald and McCarthy 1987), draws on organizational theory and on Olson's (1965) rational-choice political theory. Rational-choice theory presents a model of instrumental rationality in which rational decision-makers base their choices on a calculus of costs and benefits. As applied to the issue of resource mobilization, the key insight is that *mobilization costs something*; that is, in pooling their resources to strive for a collective benefit, people forgo other pursuits: they commit their time, money or other resources to the common cause. From this premise, the *entrepreneurial mobilization model* constructs accounts of the technical and practical aspects of social movement formation. The costliness of mobilization makes the link between grievances (or shared interest) and collective action contingent upon creating the right combination of manageable costs and tangible benefits such that resources will be pooled and wielded effectively (Fireman and Gamson 1979: 9).

One consequence of focusing on the instrumental rationality of costs and benefits is a blurring of the distinction between movements and other modern forms of political contention—parties and pressure groups. Like other modern political organizations, social movement organizations will, in a cost-effective manner, tend to adopt organizational forms that routinize the flow of resources in order to ensure movement survival (McAdam, McCarthy, and Zald 1988: 697). This is not to say that SMOs necessarily evolve into bureaucracies. Rather, different organizational forms are appropriate for different tasks. A bureaucratic structure may promote technical expertise but may also be less effective at mobilizing the grassroots. A decentralized structure may be more effective at the latter task but less capable of making timely strategic interventions (Jenkins 1983: 542).

Another implication of rational-choice analysis has to do with recruitment and participation of activists. Each person is viewed as a rational actor who weighs costs and benefits and decides to participate when potential benefits outweigh expected costs (McCarthy and Zald 1977). Yet for resource mobilization theory, this account of the economically rational, egoistic individual immediately presents a 'free rider' problem. Collective action, if successful, generates collective goods such as improved wages or working conditions, or socialized health care, or stronger regulations on pollution. Such collective goods can typically be enjoyed by all members of the movement's constituency—*regardless of whether or not a particular person has participated in the movement*. Given the costliness of participation, it is most rational for each individual to ride free: to enjoy the collective benefits of movement mobilization without bearing any of the costs (Olson 1965: 11). Yet if all potential participants make this egoistically rational choice, no mobilization—thus no movement—occurs. From Olson on, the standard solution to the free-rider paradox has been to consider how SMOs distribute 'selective incentives' to activists, thus rationalizing their intense participation. A major means by which an SMO sustains a movement over time is through provision of selective incentives to *movement entrepreneurs*—'professional' organizers, specialized in the task of movement mobilization, who invest much of their time in the movement but also reap such selective benefits as salaries, prestige, and power. Overcoming the free-rider problem imposes organizational and technical imperatives on SMOs. To fund selective incentives such as salaries for professional organizers, external resources must be tapped: thus the search for funds becomes a major organizational preoccupation (Scott 1990: 112). The permanent and elaborate canvassing practices of SMOs such as Greenpeace come to mind.

Such organizational imperatives bring up a final claim of the entrepreneurial mobilization model, one based explicitly on McCarthy and Zald's (1973) reading of the 'trend of social movements' in the United States. They argue that before the post-World War II wave of prosperity, social movements were based in aggrieved populations that directly contributed their own necessary resources. The increased middle-class affluence of postwar American society brought a new situation in which movements could acquire many resources from 'conscience constituents'—supporters who do not stand to benefit directly from the movement's success (Zald and McCarthy 1987: 23). The rising affluence of the 1950s and 1960s thus furnished SMOs with an expanding pool of discretionary income. Movements of the 1960s and 1970s, then, mobilized an affluent conscience constituency (including university students) and coopted institutional resources from government agencies, private foundations—even corporations. In consequence, an important shift in social movements has taken place. The trend is *away from* classical SMOs with indigenous leadership, extensive membership, volunteer staff, resources from direct beneficiaries, and actions based upon mass participation, and *toward* professional SMOs 'with outside leadership, full time paid staff, small or nonexistent membership, resources from conscience constituencies, and actions that "speak for" rather than involve an aggrieved group' (Jenkins 1983: 533). It is especially in this changed context that movement leaders become 'social movement entrepreneurs', endeavouring to mobilize financial resources from conscience constituents and to manipulate 'images of relevance and support through the communications media' (Zald and McCarthy 1987: 374).

This reading of contemporary movements can be described as Weberian in its basic thrust. Several of the features of modernity emphasized by Weber—the predominance of instrumental rationality in human affairs, the increasing importance of professional expertise, the creation of efficient organizational forms—figure prominently in the professional-organizer model.

Tilly's Political Process Model

The second variant of RMT—the *political process model*—has intellectual roots closer to Marx than to Weber, and the historical grounds for its account come more from nineteenth- and twentieth-century Europe than from postwar American society. One distinguishing feature of this approach is its sensitivity to the importance of the state as a centre of modern political contention. Charles Tilly, the political process model's most influential exponent, defines a national social movement as 'a sustained challenge to state authorities in the name of a population that has little formal power with respect to the state' (1988: 1), and notes that such sustained challenges can occur only where states exist. In the modern era, the elaboration of a system of formally autonomous national states claiming to base their sovereignty at least partly on the consent of the governed, has set the terms for the collective actions of social movements. On the one hand, each state's claim to sovereignty on the basis of democratic consent renders it vulnerable to 'concerted public displays of numbers and commitment' by challenging groups (1988: 3); on the other hand, mobilization of such collective actors has typically occurred in nationally bounded contexts within which the state constitutes the political 'centre'.

A key insight in the political process model is that to create change, social movements need more than mobilized resources: they require an *opportunity to act*. Within the context of national states, changes in the *structure of political opportunities* can have telling impact on the ebb and flow of movement activism. At different places and times the state may be particularly receptive or vulnerable to organized protest by a given dissenting group (McAdam, McCarthy, and Zald 1988: 699). As Marx and McAdam note:

In one era, the political forces aligned against the challenger may make collective action a near impossibility. In another, shifting political alignments may create a unique opportunity for political action by, or on behalf of, the same group (1994: 84).

The configuration of mobilized social forces—both within the state and in civil society—provides the strategic context within which a social movement acts. Indeed, the political process model focuses on the *strategic interaction* between SMOs, the state, and other collective actors, organizations, and institutions. A good deal of strategic interaction involves various instances of *repression* and *facilitation*, as groups influence each other's costs of collective action, whether upwards (repression) or downwards (facilitation) (Tilly 1978: 100–1). For instance, in the 1980s the peace and anti-poverty movements in Vancouver were notably vibrant in part because the local labour council *facilitated* these movements by providing key resources to SMOs like End the Arms Race and End Legislated Poverty (Carroll and Ratner 1995). Conversely, the United States government's outlawing of the Communist Party (CP) during the Cold War was *repressive*: it raised the CP's cost of collective action by guaranteeing that its leaders would be jailed whenever it undertook visible collective action (Tilly 1978: 100). In 1999, many social movement organizations concerned about the élitist, nondemocratic character of the World Trade Organization (WTO) converged on its ministerial meeting at Seattle, and their collective action played a part in preventing a planned international accord from being reached. By working as a coalition that included human rights activists, environmentalists, trade unionists, and feminists, these groups facilitated each other's collective action. Simultaneously, their tactic of blocking access to the meeting venue repressed the WTO from doing its work, and the state's response—the use of riot police, tear gas, and pepper spray to disperse protestors—in turn repressed the anti-WTO coalition by raising its costs of collective action to prohibitive levels (see Bleyer 2000).

Over time, the changing structure of political opportunities shapes the social movement sector of each national state. In Canada, for instance, the move since the late 1970s 'from consent to coercion' in the state's approach to industrial relations has had a *repressive* impact on the labour movement, obliging unions to rethink their own strategies and to build mutually *facilitative* alliances with other progressive movements (Bleyer 1997; Carroll and Warburton 1995). It is well to note additionally that movements—as agencies of change—can affect their own opportunity structures. The cumulative impact of environmental activism in raising public awareness in the 1970s and 1980s has made states and corporations more vulnerable to the claims of environmentalists relating to wilderness preservation, industrial pollution, sustainable development, etc.

In the twenty-first century, the cumulative impact of protests against agencies of 'globalization from above'—the WTO, International Monetary Fund, and the like—may come to have a similar impact upon public consciousness and ultimately upon the opportunity structure that faces movements that press for a 'globalization from below' (Falk 1994).

Also subject to change is the *repertoire of collective action* available to a given group. Demonstrations, strikes, and petition campaigns are forms of collective action that emerged and developed with modernity. Strikes were the means by which artisans who were threatened with proletarianization retaliated by disrupting the production process and imperilling employers' profits. In the nineteenth century the strike became the primary means by which workers advanced *new claims* regarding wages, working conditions, and job security (Tilly 1978: 161). In the process, the strike became a core element in the modern working-class's repertoire of action. Yet, use of the strike depends on the structure of political opportunities:

at different times, political pressure, sabotage, demonstrations, and occupations of the workplace all become alternatives to striking. The workers' repertoire of collective action includes more items than the strike (Tilly: 166).

Much the same holds for other movements and for other forms of collective action.

A final aspect of the political process model, implicit throughout this discussion, is its emphasis upon endogenous organization and mobilization of resources (McAdam, McCarthy, and Zald 1988: 697)—in contrast to the entrepreneurial mobilization model's emphasis upon exogenous leadership and resources from conscience constituents. Studies by Morris (1984) and McAdam (1982) dispute McCarthy and Zald's claim that the primary impetus for recent movements in the United States came from white middle-class liberal and élite groups. Morris shows that resources crucial to the success of the civil rights movement came from within black communities, which took advantage of the pre-existing social organization afforded by black churches. Invoking a Marxist analysis of power and interests, proponents of the political process model also doubt the claim that élite groups form an important conscience constituency for contemporary movements. Within the societal structure of power and privilege, the interests of such affluent groups typically conflict with those of insurgent groups committed to social change. On this reading, to the extent that élite groups act to facilitate an SMO's mobilization or action, they are motivated not by an authentic sense of social conscience but by 'a desire to contain or control the impact of the movement or to exploit the conflict for their own gains' (Pichardo 1988: 101).

Notwithstanding these internal disputes, RMT presents a reasonably coherent perspective in which social movements are portrayed as deeply implicated in the social and political practices of modernity: in professionalization, in instrumental rationality, in formal organization, in distinctively modern repertoires of collective action, and in political opportunity structures that centre around the liberal democratic state but span outward to include other agents in civil society. RMT offers a serviceable means of conceptually map-ping the field of movement activism in *pragmatic* terms. It attends to mechanism rather than substance (Eyerman and Jamison 1991: 39), to the 'how' of contemporary movements—the practicalities of mobilization and strategic interaction in pursuit of collective goods.

Criticisms of RMT

A number of weaknesses and limitations have been noted by critics of RMT, and some of these critiques have inspired a rethinking of the paradigm in recent years. First, in spite of the virtues of an approach that recognizes the *rationality* of collective action instead of dismissing such action as governed by crowd psychology and panic, the particular model of rationality embraced by RMT—rational-choice theory and its corollary in the free-rider problem—has been vigorously criticized by numerous sociologists (Fireman and Gamson 1979; Ferree 1992; Schwartz and Paul 1992). There are several grounds for this first criticism, each of which casts doubt upon the importance of the free-rider problem:

1. in movement mobilization the cost/reward dichotomy becomes blurred so that collective action can be 'its own reward' in expressing the actor's deeply held values, including solidarity with others (Scott, 1990: 121);
2. in situations where people come to share a sense of group fate, free-rider logic can be overridden by a 'group logic' which holds that 'unless large numbers join the group effort, *nobody* will benefit—in which case free-riding becomes irrational' (Schwartz and Paul 1992: 214);
3. the rational-choice criterion at the centre of RMT uncritically reflects the consumerist and technocratic consciousness that predominates in corporate-capitalist society, yet movement activists—the principal critics of that consciousness and that society—make their choices *not* on the basis of anticipated person-

al gain but on moral grounds (Ferree 1992: 33). That is, for groups struggling for social justice the task of mobilization is not to make participation personally 'profitable' to individual constituents but to promote an alternative morality that questions the dominant calculus of selfish individualism.

RMT, then, falsely universalizes or *reifies* a certain form of rationality—the instrumental rationality of the socially isolated, profit-motivated individual—and misapplies this model to the sphere of movement politics.[2]

A second critique of RMT highlights a related reification. As Ferree notes, 'the prevalence of bureaucratically structured organizations and the individual utilitarian calculus in our society . . . can make being structured like a profit-making company appear natural' (1992: 47). In McCarthy and Zald's entrepreneurial mobilization version, the formal organizations that dominate the state and economy in late modernity are reified as models for social-movement organization. In this sense, RMT contains an organizational bias which implies that 'only formally organized bodies can act effectively' (Buechler 1993: 223). In contrast, contemporary feminism and other NSMs have been structured less around formal organizations than around 'social movement communities'—informally organized networks of activists, many of whom explicitly repudiate formal organization on ideological grounds and strive to create more egalitarian and participatory forms of organization (1993: 223). By the same token, the political process version of RMT has a built-in tendency to reify the state—a formal organization *par excellence*—as the focus of movement politics. In contrast, critics like Magnusson (1990: 535) point out that movement groups such as the Raging Grannies practise a lateral politics that not only avoids formal hierarchies among participants but concentrates less on the state and more on extending the political and cultural sensibilities of the movement to more and more people.

This brings up a third criticism of RMT: its deficient theorization of *consciousness*. A highly restrictive focus on tangible *resources* has led RMT analysts to neglect the *interpretive* factors associated with mobilization (Benford and Hunt 1995: 85), which take in the whole spectrum of human experience from psychology to ideology and culture. In recent years, RMT analysts have themselves been active in attempting to broaden the paradigm to take account of the social-psychological 'micro-mobilization contexts' within which movements form and act (McAdam, McCarthy, and Zald 1988).

A particularly important development in this regard is the notion of 'framing'. Snow and Benford (1992) define collective-action frames as emergent action-oriented sets of meanings and beliefs that inspire and legitimate movement campaigns and activities. Simply put, such frames are interpretive schemata through which movements define certain conditions as unjust, attribute responsibility for the injustice, and enunciate alternatives that might be achieved through collective action (1992: 137). By analysing the frames through which social movement organizations and activists define their political situations, one can gain insight into the psychological and cultural dimensions of mobilization. An integral aspect of mobilization involves a process of 'frame alignment' (Snow et al. 1986) as SMOs strive to establish a congruence between their definitions of the situation and those of their constituencies. Without such a discursive and psychological alignment, very few members of the constituency are likely to participate. That is, the human resources crucial to any movement cannot be pooled unless a collective will to participate is created, and such a collective will requires a common interpretive understanding of issues, goals, and strategies. Recent research on collective-action frames has explored the various kinds of 'frame disputes' that occur between SMOs in a single movement (Benford 1993) and the role of 'master frames' in coordinating mobilization across diverse movements (Carroll and Ratner 1996a, 1996b; Gerhards and Rucht 1992).

Despite the hopeful development of frame analysis as a means of extending the paradigm, a fourth limitation of RMT concerns its insensitivity to emergent features of social movement activism—features that may point away from the modernist practices of professional organization, state-centred campaigns, and a given repertoire of collective action. As Ingalsbee (1994: 140) observes, 'even though it was developed to explain the actions of post-War movements, RM theory has had no sense of the alternative oppositional forms of consciousness and action being created by contemporary social movements'. This deficiency of RMT brings us to the alternative paradigm of new social movement theory, which can be read as a series of attempts to understand the particular kinds of movements—such as environmentalism, gay and lesbian liberation, and feminism—which have emerged (or, in the case of feminism, re-emerged) in the advanced capitalist democracies since the 1960s.

New Social Movement Theories

Various versions of NSM theory were worked out in France, Italy, and Germany in the 1970s, as theoretical responses to two historical developments. In the first place, it has become increasingly evident that Western capitalism entered a new era in the 1960s and 1970s, variously described as postindustrial, post-Fordist, postmodernity, high modernity, disorganized capitalism, and programmed society. These appellations are not entirely interchangeable, but they do highlight common themes concerning the diminution of bipolar class conflict, the expansion of cultural, consumption, and leisure activities, the growth of tertiary sectors, and especially the new types of social protest (Ray 1993: 60). In the second place, the events of May 1968—when students in France took the lead in mass protests while workers and Communists played a cautiously conservative role—unsettled the thinking of many European intellectuals whose commitments to an influential tradition of Marxist theory and working-class struggle were thereby placed in question (Wallerstein 1989). The NSM theories that emerged out of this matrix seek to account for the changed character of movement politics in the closing decades of the twentieth century while responding to the crisis of Marxism, either by endeavouring to reconstruct historical materialism (Habermas, Hirsch) or by explicitly breaking from Marxism and its problematic of capitalism, the state, and emancipation through collective action (Melucci).

Melucci's Theory of Collective Identity

Alberto Melucci's theory of social movements and collective identity provides the clearest example of a clean theoretical break from the Marxist tradition. Influenced by his former teacher Alain Touraine (1981, 1988)—who coined the term *new social movement*—Melucci's (1989) *constructivist* theory depicts contemporary movements as 'nomads of the present' forging temporary spaces and identities for themselves within the complex societies of late modernity. For Melucci, the rise of complex society has brought a displacement of material production (and with it, class) from the centre of social life, and its replacement with the 'production of signs and social relations' (1989: 45). By implication, power is no longer concentrated in a materially dominant class; it is dispersed across the diverse fields of the social and increasingly is located in symbolic codes and forms of regulation. Melucci views social movements not as unified collective actors strategically pursuing their rational interests, but as variegated 'networks of meaning' (1989: 58) whose collective identities are little more than tentative products of ongoing practices submerged in everyday life.

New social movements do not contest political power, as did old movements such as the labour left; their concern has 'shifted towards a non-political terrain: the need for self-realization in everyday life' (1989: 23). Rather than adopt the modernist, state-centred quest for power, NSMs strive to *reveal and expose* 'that which is hidden or excluded by the decision-making process. Collective protest and mobilization bring to light the silent, obscure or arbitrary elements that frequently arise in complex systems decisions' (Melucci 1994: 185). In exposing power, movements mount 'symbolic challenges that overturn the dominant cultural codes' (Melucci 1989: 75). At the same time, the ongoing construction of collective identity within social movement networks is also the ongoing creation of new cultural practices. From the circulation of alternative media to psychotherapy, 'recovery', and consciousness-raising, these everyday practices provide individuals with alternative self-understandings and ideological frames while furnishing the movement with a basis for solidarity and collective identity (Scott 1990: 124).

In challenging dominant codes, in constructing new identities such as the 'out' gay or the independent woman, new social movements open public spaces free from control or repression, wherein questions surrounding ecology, gender, sexuality, and so on are rendered visible and collective. The upshot is a 'democracy of everyday life' which, through movement activism, has the potential to become globalized:

Social movements can prevent the system from closing upon itself by obliging the ruling groups to innovate, to permit changes among élites, to admit what was previously excluded from the decision-making arena and to expose the shadowy zones of invisible power and silence which a system and its dominant relations inevitably tend to create. By their action, they are already contributing to making visible the planetary challenges and to establishing a new trans-national political arena in which people and governments can take responsibility for the dramatic choices that human beings are facing for the first time (Melucci 1992: 73).

As important as Melucci's insights regarding symbolic contestation and collective identity are, his theory has been criticized by Bartholomew and Mayer (1992) on two telling grounds (see also Mooers and Sears 1992). First, in his effort to overcome the 'political reductionism' he discerns in formulations like RMT, Melucci falls prey to a 'cultural reductionism' which distinguishes too sharply between political action (which NSMs supposedly eschew) and collective identity formation (which NSMs supposedly embrace). Citing examples from the American civil rights and women's movements, Bartholomew and Mayer contend that the construction of collective identity depends in part on present and past political engagements with the state. In reality, the cultural and political aspects of social movement formation are interdependent, yet Melucci's singular focus on everyday life, culture, and symbolic challenges blinds his analysis to this interdependence.

Second, unlike other concepts invoked to comprehend the present era, such as disorganized capitalism (Offe 1985a) and post-Fordism (Ely 1993), Melucci's complex society fails to specify any structural relations of hierarchy and unequal power, eventuating in 'an analysis which treats codes/regulation as neutral in the sense of lacking inscription of relations of inequality and domination' (Bartholomew and Mayer 1992: 148). Such a view informs Melucci's assertions that NSMs do not challenge power but merely render it 'visible', and that 'conflicts no longer have winners, but they may produce innovation, modernization and reform' (Melucci 1989: 76–8). In parting company with the historical legacy of Marxism, Melucci cedes the possibility of locating

NSMs within the admittedly complex but deeply inegalitarian orders of contemporary capitalist democracies, in which political and economic power is substantially concentrated within clearly identifiable state and corporate hierarchies.

Both major shortcomings in Melucci's theory—his cultural reductionism and his deficient concept of complex society—are symptomatic of a lack of *political economy* in his understanding of the context within which social movements act. Other NSM theories to be considered presently address this inadequacy while maintaining an emphasis on the constructed and cultural character of social movement practice.

Habermas's Theory of System and Lifeworld

Jürgen Habermas, probably the most significant German social theorist since Max Weber, has written relatively little on social movements per se. His most widely cited discussion of this topic takes up barely six pages of his two-volume opus *The Theory of Communicative Action* (1987: 391–6). Yet Habermas's influence has been substantial, as theorists such as Arato and Cohen (1989), Eyerman and Jamison (1991), Ray (1993), and Eder (1993) have pursued the implications of his perspective for contemporary social movements. Habermas views late modernity or 'welfare-state capitalism' as a configuration of *system and lifeworld*—of macro-structures organized by markets and bureaucracies (system) and of meaningful everyday life within 'the relations and communications between members of a societal community' (lifeworld) (Hewitt 1993: 62).

Following Weber's lead, Habermas holds that the historical trajectory of the system has been toward *rationalization* in the very restricted sense of instrumental rationality—the capitalist's concern for maximizing profit and the bureaucrat's preoccupation with cost-benefit analysis being indicative of this tendency. The computer-programmed trading that in some degree drives contemporary capital markets and the obsessive concerns of most governments with eliminating state debts almost irrespective of the social consequences testify to the dominance of instrumental rationality in the economy and state, which are the central components of the 'system'. But unlike Weber—and unlike his own critical theory forebears—Habermas argues that throughout modernity a parallel albeit suppressed process of rationalization has partially transformed the lifeworld from a sphere of meaning and identity based upon unquestioned conventions to an increasingly post-conventional discursive formation, open to critical reason and democratic practice: that is, open to 'communicative rationality'. A rationalized lifeworld entails a distinctive morality based not on hierarchical authority and fixed traditions but on self-reflexive individuals able to take the standpoint of others, aware of the relativity of personal values, and committed in their interactions to free and open discussion. However, the central role that capitalism has played in the making of modernity has given dominance to system rationality over the communicative rationality immanent in the lifeworld; indeed, rationalization of the lifeworld has been suppressed in favour of its *colonization* by money and bureaucratic power issuing from the political-economic system. Even so, critical reason grounded in a partially rationalized lifeworld has continued to constitute modernity's counterculture—'a permanent opposition to the dominant forms of instrumentality' which has surfaced in such emancipatory social movements as socialism and feminism (Ray 1993: 81). Like Karl Marx, Habermas thus argues that the possibilities for emancipation are immanent in modernity itself, but instead of Marx's revolutionary proletariat, Habermas emphasizes the cumulative potential for releasing cognitive and moral learning processes within an increasingly rationalized lifeworld. 'The task for Critical Theory, then, is to locate those social movements which are potential carriers of new learning potentials, which offer the capacity for widening the scope for a critical politics whilst defending endangered ways of life against systemic encroachment' (1993: 81).

At this point, NSMs enter the Habermasian scenario. Since the 1960s, conflicts have developed in capitalist democracies that deviate from the institutionalized (and instrumentalized) pattern of electoral and trade-union struggle over material distribution. Indeed, the structures and practices of the welfare state—collective bargaining arrangements for unions and economic concessions to the disadvantaged—have muted the agency of old social movements such as the labour movement. The new conflicts appear in domains of social integration and cultural reproduction—in and around the lifeworld—and they are pursued not through statist channels of political representation but through the popular mobilization of protest. The new movements express a 'silent revolution' in values and attitudes—a shift from the old politics of social and economic security to the new politics of participation, quality of life, individual self-realization, and human rights. They seek no material compensation from the welfare state but have to do with 'the grammar of forms of life' (Habermas 1987: 392).

Such NSMs may be defensive—shielding particularistic features of the lifeworld (for example, local community) from the colonization by money and bureaucratic power—or they may be offensive—experimenting with new ways of cooperating and living together, based in a communicative ethics. The latter are exemplified for Habermas in the universalistic emancipatory concerns of feminism; in struggling against patriarchal oppression feminism strives to redeem promises of equality and justice anchored in modernity's unfinished project (Habermas 1987: 393). Such movements are offensive in attempting to extend the public sphere—to transform hierarchical and instrumentalized social relations in the direction of communicative reason, and thereby to democratize civil society.

One can point, as do Eyerman and Jamison (1991: 89–90), to the example of the student movement of the 1960s, which was fundamentally a defence of freedom of speech and expression and a refusal to participate in the instrumentally rational 'military-industrial complex', the experimentation with new forms of learning—the teach-in, the free school, the proliferation of alternative media—all under the banner of a movement for a 'democratic society'. Today, the same sort of democratic impulse informs many movements for participatory democracy and local decision-making. For example, Toronto's Metro Coalition for Social Justice (MCSJ) exemplifies 'a new political form that emerged over the last decade: the permanent, cross-sectoral, multi-issue social justice coalition' (Conway 2000: 45). Founded in 1992 in resistance to severe cuts to social services, much of MNSJ's 'movement building' efforts were focused on a continuing campaign for economic and political literacy (EPL) which at its peak in 1996 included community-based workshops on neoliberalism and popular-democratic alternatives to it, regular 'train-the-trainer events' at which democratic pedagogies and expertise were developed, and Advancing Knowledge seminars at which activists could take their political analysis to a higher level. Although limited organizational resources and internal factional divisions cut short the EPL initiative, the MCSJ's commitments to grassroots capacity-building, participatory knowledge creation, and democratic organizational development heralded in Conway's view 'the emergence of a new political praxis in a new political era, organically embedded in the microprocesses of a social movement coalition' (Conway 2000: 65).

The major weaknesses in Habermas's account of NSMs have been noted by Ray (1993), who goes on to present a more sociologically adequate

Habermasian formulation. First, like all the formulations presented in this chapter, Habermas's has a Euro-North American centricity and takes as its object the nation-state. Yet the system of money and power is increasingly a global one, and likewise, networks of communicative action (including SMOs themselves) often traverse national borders (Thiele 1993). Second, in asserting that NSMs are primarily concerned with symbols and identity—with the 'grammar of social life'—Habermas veers some distance toward a cultural reductionism not unlike Melucci's:

> Not only is it difficult to separate symbolic from material objectives, but identity politics can involve a privatization of political questions into subcultural movements which eschew engagement with the state and thereby conspire in their own marginalization (Ray 1993: 177).

Conversely, the claims of 'offensive' movements like feminism clearly concern more than a 'border dispute' between system and lifeworld: they point toward structural transformation of economic, state, and interpersonal relations (Ray 1993: 177).

Neo-Gramscian Theory

Like Habermas, neo-Gramscian theory retains the Marxist critical analysis of capitalism; indeed, Antonio Gramsci was a founder of 'western Marxism' and a political leader of the Italian left in the 1920s, who spent his last dozen years in a fascist prison writing his extensive notebooks on culture and politics. In the 1970s, translation and wide distribution of selections from Gramsci's *Prison Notebooks* (1971) inspired an extensive neo-Gramscian literature on the culture and politics of late capitalism, much of which has relevance to contemporary social movements.

But if both Habermas and Gramsci share a Marxist concern with not only *analysing* the social world but consciously participating in its emancipatory *transformation*, they differ from each other in other respects. Whereas Habermas's analysis turns on his dual conception of *rationalization* (of system and lifeworld), Gramscian thought emphasizes the duality of *hegemony*. On the one hand, under the conditions of modern capitalist democracy 'formal freedoms and electoral rights exist alongside the class inequalities of the bourgeois state; therefore relations of domination need to be sustained with the consent of the dominated' (Carroll and Ratner 1994: 5). Hegemony in this first sense refers to the practices, cultural codes, and social relations through which that consent is organized and the 'system' thereby stabilized. The bourgeoisie does not rule directly and singularly but participates as a leading social force in an ensemble of alliances involving other groups, including intellectuals such as journalists and liberal economists who articulate perspectives that tend to be consonant with the interests of capital. This ensemble of alliances constitutes a hegemonic bloc that governs by presenting its interests as universal while selectively dispensing material concessions to pre-empt the unification of opposition from below. In this way, a 'general interest' or collective identity is constructed that unites dominant and subordinate alike as members of the same political community—as in the notion of the 'national interest'. Nor is hegemony merely or even primarily a matter of state control. In Gramsci's analysis, power is both concentrated in the state and diffused throughout the organizations of civil society such as the school, the church, the family, and other agencies of socialization and culture which diffuse hegemonic world views into daily life (Caroll and Ratner 1994: 6). To the extent that this prevailing consciousness is widely internalized as reflecting the natural order of things it becomes a politically momentous aspect of 'common sense'. Where hegemony gains this kind of self-evident validity it fulfills a role that direct coercion can never perform: it mystifies power relations and public issues; it encourages a sense of fatalism and passivity toward political action; it justifies every type of system-serving deprivation and sacrifice. In various ways, then, hegemony works 'to induce the oppressed to accept or "consent" to their own exploitation and daily misery' (Boggs 1976: 40).

Yet for Gramsci and neo-Gramscians, the crises and contradictions of capitalism limit the lifespan of any hegemonic order. As the material basis for consent deteriorates, opportunities open for constructing hegemony in a second sense; namely, an alternative hegemony that unites various subaltern groups into a counterhegemonic bloc of oppositional forces committed to an alternative social vision. Such a vision frames social justice not in terms of one or another group's immediate interests but 'through a conception of the world attentive to democratic principles and the dignity of humankind' (Holub 1992: 6). Counterhegemonic politics involves both an engagement with capital and the state and a cultural politics in the realm of civil society and everyday life to create popular support for a radically democratic order.[3] Building an alternative hegemony thus entails what Gramsci termed a protracted 'war of position' in which a coalition of oppositional movements wins space and constructs mutual loyalties in civil society, in the state, and in the workplace, thereby disrupting and displacing the hegemony of the dominant class and its allies.

Neo-Gramscians claim that the NSMs of the late twentieth century express alternative visions that are both symptomatic of a weakening or crisis in the post-World War II hegemonic order and imbued with the potential for counterhegemony. The postwar era of the late 1940s and early 1970s witnessed the consolidation of what Gramsci presciently termed *Fordism*. In this form of capitalism, mass production and mass consumption coincided in a unionized workforce whose soaring affluence cemented its support for a welfare-state capitalism. In turn, this guaranteed near-full employment and social benefits such as medicare and unemployment insurance. Hence,

> Fordism was based on the centrality of industrial labor as producer and consumer. Male workers were relatively well-paid, and the welfare state propped up consumer demand during slack periods. The social movement sphere was monopolized by the official labor movement, centralized and bureaucratized labor unions; closely connected were social-democratic or labor parties engaged in neo-corporatist relations with employers' organizations and the state (Steinmetz 1994: 192).

Yet while the labour-capital accord and welfare state served to organize consent to this hegemonic order, Fordism also engendered new areas of conflict as it developed. NSMs emerged as key voices of dissent—whether to the enforced conformism of the male-dominated nuclear family (feminism, gay/lesbian liberation), to the unbridled domination of nature in the mass-production system (ecology), or to the authoritarian, disabling ways in which the welfare state ascertains and serves people's needs (movements of welfare-state clients, citizens' movements for participatory democracy) (Steinmetz 1994: 193–4). According to this interpretation, NSMs are not so much responses to the system's colonization of the lifeworld. Instead, they emerge to a considerable extent among constituencies that were *left out* of Fordism's hegemonic bloc of white, male established workers and managers (Cox 1987). As Hirsch (1988: 50) argues,

> The new social movements are the real products of the social and political form of Fordist capitalism, Taylorism, mass consumption, social disintegration, normalized

individualism, excessive exploitation of nature, and bureaucratization and state control. Their aim is, in sum, individual emancipation, the recovery of civil society, freedom from bureaucratic control and suppression, self-fulfillment, and 'the good life.'

This is not to say, however, that NSMs articulate a coherent social vision that might sustain a counterhegemonic bloc. New social movement politics is framed within a complex array of ideological discourses that include radical-democratic collectivism, civil-libertarian liberalism and romantic conservatism (as in deep ecology's critique of industrialism (Bookchin 1988)). There is a political and ideological vagueness to these movements that, however, also suggests a capacity to produce new radical political concepts: 'The new social movements are a contradictory battlefield in the struggle for a new hegemony' (Hirsch 1988: 51).

Offe (1985b) has suggested that in the advanced capitalist democracies, the prospects for effectively advancing an alternative social and political paradigm hinge on the nature of the alliances forged between NSMs, the traditional left, and the traditional right. In view of the diverse constituencies of NSMs, any of three scenarios is possible. If traditional middle-class elements gain influence in framing NSM politics, the probable alignment will be with the traditional right; thus, for example, environmentalism can be reframed within a discourse of ecocapitalism, sustainable development, and green consumerism which poses no challenge to existing power (Adkin 1992); or feminism can be re-cast within a 'new conservative' frame that emphasizes equitable co-parenting without confronting institutionalized structures of male dominance (Stacey, 1983). If the so-called peripheral groups gain influence in framing NSM politics, the likely alignment will be between traditional left and right—that is, a renewal of the labour-capital accord in which NSM claims are marginalized as sectarian.[4] This scenario has been played out in the squatters' movements of urban Germany and the Netherlands (Offe 1985b), but the 'ecoterrorism' practised by some direct-action environmental groups and the separatist or 'disengaged' politics of radical feminism might provide other examples (Adamson et al. 1988). Finally, if the new middle-class elements— white-collar employees particularly in the state sector—are influential in shaping the NSM agenda, the likely alignment will be with the left—with the labour movement and with political parties like Canada's NDP. Such an alliance, which according to Offe is 'the only one of the three which could possibly lead to an effective and successful challenge of the old paradigm of politics' (1985b: 868), would require a reframing of collective identities on both sides of the NSM/labour divide. As Adkin remarks in the context of environmentalism,

> a counter-hegemonic discourse is formed by the rearticulation of elements of existing identities, values, and conceptions of need. For example, it is when the 'environmentalist' confronts the crisis of livelihood of the 'worker', and when the 'worker' confronts the destructive impacts of her livelihood that alternatives to the hegemonic model begin to be not only thinkable, but necessary. . . . As a consequence, the definition of conflict changes from 'environmentalists versus workers' to 'those who defend the conditions for a possible and desirable life versus those who defend practices and relations that make impossible such a life (1992: 136).

There is some evidence that a confluence of labour and NSMs into a potentially counterhegemonic bloc is more than an abstract possibility. In Canada, the Canadian Labour Congress's turn toward 'social unionism' and its sponsorship of the Action Canada Network—a coalition of labour and NSM organizations—is suggestive (Bleyer 1997), as is Carroll and Ratner's (1995) finding that many labour activists in Vancouver show the same sensibilities as NSM activists regarding the importance of a politics of everyday life and of alternative culture. In fact, a number of scholars have challenged the claim that the political sensibilities and practices of NSM activists are qualitatively different from those of 'old' movements such as the labour movement (see Calhoun, 1993; Plotke, 1990; Scott, 1990). According to Adam (1993), the particularistic politics of autonomy, identity, and lifestyle constitute only one face of NSMs. The other face is a socialist one, showing a universalistic concern for social justice produced out of the practices of new social movements themselves:

> This other face of new social movement mobilization includes a great many participants who understand their praxis within a comprehensive worldview which recognizes and supports subordinated people wherever they exist. There already exist complex linkages among feminist labour activists, gay third-world solidarity activists, black ecologists, diasabled peace activists, and so on, working in organizations of more than one movement. In addition to overlapping participants, the movements have tremendous influence upon each other in terms of analyses, strategies, and self-criticism. These workers for social justice often understand themselves as socialists and represent a potential source of renewal generally ignored both by Marxism and new social movement theory (Adam 1993: 330).

Yet even if such commentaries invite us to entertain the possibilities of a confluence of movements around shared commitments to social justice, the challenges of building a counterhegemony are formidable.

Although one can point to coalitions of social movements, viewed over time, such coalitions seem inherently unstable and ephemeral. To what

extent are such coalitions vehicles for a Gramscian 'war of position' and to what extent are they
mere mechanical assemblages of convenience that
decompose at the next political conjuncture, with
shifts in the structure of opportunities (Carroll
and Ratner 1989)? Put another way, to what
extent does coalition politics bring a transformation of particularistic and instrumental 'discourses of interests' into a universalist 'discourse of
rights' that can inform and inspire counterhegemonic practice (Hunt 1990: 310)?

Moreover, the pursuit of counterhegemony—of
a coherent practical and ethical alternative—always
carries with it the possibility of creating *new injustices*. By presenting their interests as the most universal, some movements can play a leading role that
relegates others to the margins; yet other groups
can be left out of the 'grand coalition' altogether,
through exclusionary practices that may not even
be evident to coalition activists themselves
(Michaud 1992). This conundrum has prompted
some political theorists to endorse a 'politics of difference' which takes NSMs' struggle for autonomy as
the archetype in validating the specific claims of a
plurality of aggrieved groups (Young 1990). Yet a
politics of difference tends to *fragment* the social
movement sector into many incommensurable
units, an eventuality whose unintended consequence may be to reinforce the existing hegemony
(Carroll and Ratner 1994). There is no definitive
solution to this quandary. Recalling Habermas's
analysis of communicative rationality, however, we
can suggest that pursuit of social justice within a
counterhegemonic bloc requires a continuing
reflexivity about the extent to which communicative practices foster truly equitable participation.

Conclusion

A final issue to be considered concerns the lack of
attention in virtually all social movement theories
to the political contexts and social movements of
the periphery of the world system. Do these theories say anything of relevance to the four-fifths of
the world's population who live outside the core
formations of advanced capitalism—a billion of
whom live in abject poverty?

It is well to note first that the specific political
economies of former colonies present distinct problems to NSMs on the periphery. There, the issue of
development is central to virtually all movements,
yet the *meaning* of development is increasingly an
object of political contention. The hegemony of ruling élites in the Third World has been built upon
their claim to be the agents of national development
for the common good (Escobar 1992), yet NSMs
and labour movements challenge this assertion by
pointing to the failure of capitalism and its devel-
opmentalist state to meet social and ecological
needs. Parajuli (1991: 181) observes that in India,
as in Europe 'a critique of growth is increasingly
linked with the criteria of livability.' But unlike the
tendency for NSMs in Europe and North America to
be mainly concerned with the quality of life and
less concerned with the distribution of economic
benefits, 'the basic thrust of India's ecological and
women's movements is to stop the monopolistic
control of the rich over their natural resources'
(1991: 181). On the periphery, feminist, ecological,
and other NSM struggles intersect with struggles for
economic justice, and this confluence has led to an
alternative concept that links development with
participatory democracy:

> successful development is viewed as a
> process of human development, a process of
> social transformation in which people are
> both the subject and object. In such a
> process the people participate at all levels of
> decision-making in matters affecting the
> totality of their lives and through this
> process of empowerment a more democrat-
> ic process is initiated (Wignaraja 1993: 27).

The second point to make is a neo-Gramscian
one. Since the 1970s the crisis of Fordism—the

decline of the link between mass production and mass consumption, of full-employment Keynesian policy, of the welfare state, and of the capital-labour accord—has become increasingly acute in the advanced capitalist democracies. What has replaced Fordism is a regime of globalized capitalism in which workers compete more directly against each other in a new international division of labour, in which states are primarily concerned with securing competitive advantage rather than maintaining domestic employment and social entitlements, and in which globalized capitalist organizations—the 'SMOs' of the ruling class such as the International Monetary Fund and the Trilateral Commission—form the nucleus of a neoconservative hegemonic bloc (Gill 1989). An important aspect of this new hegemony is the tactical retreat of the state—the attempt to convert statist regulation of social life into rule through the depoliticized mechanisms of the global market (Ray 1993: 83–5). If this development has meant the demise of the Fordist bloc and of the postwar consensus politics in the core of the world system, on the periphery (where the legacy of colonialism has limited the formation of democratic institutions while depressing living standards) the obstructions to class formation may give way even more easily, because 'social and political structures are less solid' (Cox 1987: 390).

All this raises the possibility—indeed, the necessity—for social movements to build counterhegemony on a global basis. It is too soon in the process of globalization to say exactly what this might mean, but some scholars have provided a few provisional thoughts. Waterman, for instance, discerns an emerging 'social movement unionism' on the periphery (and potentially at the core of the world system) in which labour movements are becoming 'intimately articulated with other non- or multiclass democratic movements (base movements of churches, women's,

residents', ecological, human-rights, and peace movements, etc.)' (1993: 267). In conjunction with this we can note a tendency for capitalist globalization to be met by what Richard Falk (1994) calls a 'globalization from below'. Social movements, including the labour movement, are increasingly forming coalitions that span national boundaries, and such transnational social movement organizations offer the promise of redefining concepts of community or security, or social justice itself, in a more inclusive way (Thiele 1993). For instance, the Action Canada Network—mentioned earlier as a Canadian example of coalition-formation between labour and NSMs—has been extended hemispherically under the 'Common Frontiers' initiative, as the free trade agenda has grown to include Mexico and other Latin American countries. Similarly, the 1999 Seattle mobilization against the WTO marked an important convergence of diverse movements and activists from North and South:

> In Seattle, activists from every continent and every sector didn't just come together, they worked together, they shared experiences and perspectives, they attended teach-ins, they sat on panels and they took part in workshops. In Seattle, diversity wasn't about splendid isolation, it was about working to achieve a meaningful unity. North and South, old and new, labour and environment all shared a path of 'convergence' (Bleyer 2000: 28).

As globalization proceeds, the lives and welfare of people 'elsewhere'—for example, in Mexico or Chile—become directly implicated in the lives of people 'here', and as our fates become increasingly intertwined, the need and the ability to extend social movements globally become more evident.

Notes

1. Comparative discussions of the two approaches can be found in Cohen (1985), Klandermans (1986), and Canel (1992).

2. The tendency in RMT to reify instrumental rationality contrasts sharply with the use of an alternative concept of 'communicative rationality' in Habermas's version of NSM theory, discussed below. On this point Cohen (1985) offers a useful comparison.

3. The task of building an alternative hegemony affords an instructive comparison between neo-Gramscian theory and RMT. One major practical barrier to counterhegemonic formation is the permanent scarcity of resources with which oppositional groups must cope, which (as RMT emphasizes) leads each SMO to prioritize the immediate concerns of its constituency in its work. On this score, RMT illuminates one side of the relationships between social movement organizations—the *competition* for resources and strategic advantage (McCarthy and Zald 1987;

Marx and McAdam 1994: 102–4). So long as interests are defined sectorally, this dynamic will tend to be operative, and cross-movement coalitions will tend to have an opportunistic, instrumental, and unstable character (Carroll and Ratner 1989: 46). It is only by consciously promoting broadly resonant counterhegemonic discourses and practices that factional strife can be significantly reduced if not overcome. By the same token, it is only by promoting a compelling alternative vision to the hegemonic ideology of liberal individualism that oppositional movements can overcome the barrier to mobilization posed by egoistic rational-choice logic. It is precisely in circumstances where liberal individualism is hegemonic that the 'free-rider problem' is, indeed, a big problem for oppositional groups.

4. Peripheral groups are, namely, 'de-commodified' categories on the margins of social and political participation such as the unemployed, youth, and students (see Offe 1985b).

References

Adam, B. 1993. 'Post-Marxism and the New Social Movements', *Canadian Review of Sociology and Anthropology* 30: 316–36.

Adamson, N., L. Briskin, and M. McPhail. 1988. *Feminist Organizing for Change: The Contemporary Women's Movement in Canada* (Toronto: University of Toronto Press).

Adkin, L.E. 1992. 'Counter-Hegemony and Environmental Politics in Canada'. In *Organizing Dissent,* ed. W.K. Carroll (Toronto: Garamond Press), 135–56.

Arato, A. and J. Cohen. 1989. *Civil Society and Democratic Theory* (Cambridge, MA: MIT Press).

Bartholomew, A. and M. Mayer. 1992. 'Nomads of the Present: Melucci's Contribution to "New Social Movement" Theory', *Theory, Culture & Society* 9: 141–59.

Benford, R.D. 1993. 'Frame Disputes within the Nuclear Disarmament Movement', *Social Forces* 71: 677–701.

———, and S.A. Hunt. 1995. 'Dramaturgy and Social Movements: The Social Construction and Communication of Power'. In *Social Movements: Critiques, Concepts, Case-Studies,* ed. M.L. Stanford (London: Macmillan), 84–112.

Bleyer, P. 1997. 'Coalitions of Social Movements as Agencies for Social Change: The Action Canada Network'. In *Organizing Dissent* (2nd edn), ed. W.K. Carroll (Toronto: Garamond Press).

———. 2000. 'The Other Battle in Seattle', *Studies in Political Economy* 62: 25–33.

Blumer, H. 1939. 'Collective Behavior'. In *An Outline of Principles of Sociology,* ed. R.E. Park (New York: Barnes & Noble).

Boggs, C. 1976. *Gramsci's Marxism* (London: Pluto).

———. 1986. *Social Movements and Political Power* (Philadelphia: Temple University Press).

Bookchin, M. 1988. 'Social Ecology Versus Deep Ecology', *Social Review* 18(3): 9–29.

Buechler, S.M. 1993. 'Beyond Resource Mobilization? Emerging Trends in Social Movement Theory', *The Sociological Quarterly* 34: 217–35.

Calhoun, C. 1993. '"New Social Movements" of the Early Nineteenth Century', *Social Science History* 17: 385–427.

Canel, E. 1992. 'New Social Movement Theory and Resource Mobilization: The Need for Integration'. In *Organizing Dissent*, ed. W.K. Carroll (Toronto: Garamond Press), 22–51.

Carroll. W.K., and R.S. Ratner. 1989. 'Social Democracy, Neo-Conservatism and Hegemonic Crisis in British Columbia', *Critical Sociology* 16(1): 29–53.

————. 1994. 'Between Leninism and Radical Pluralism: Gramscian Reflections on Counter-hegemony and the New Social Movements', *Critical Sociology* 20(2): 3–26.

————. 1995. 'Old Unions and New Social Movements', *Labour/le travail* 35: 195–221.

————. 1996a. 'Master Frames and Counter-hegemony: Political Sensibilities in New Social Movements', *Canadian Review of Sociology and Anthropology* 33: 407–35.

————. 1996b. 'Master Framing and Cross-Movement Networking in Contemporary Social Movements', *The Sociological Quarterly* 37(4): 601–25.

————, and R. Warburton. 1995. 'Capital, Labour and the State: The Future of the Labour Movement'. In *Social Issues and Contradictions in Canadian Society* (2nd edn), ed. B. Singh Bolaria (Toronto: Harcourt Brace), 336–57.

Cohen, J. 1985. 'Strategy or Identity: New Theoretical Paradigms and Contemporary Social Movements', *Social Research* 52: 663–716.

Conway, J. 2000. 'Knowledge, Power, Organization: Social Justice Coalitions at a Crossroads', *Studies in Political Economy* 62: 43–70.

Cox. R.W. 1987. *Production, Power, and World Order* (New York: Columbia University Press).

Eder, K. 1993. *The New Politics of Class* (Newbury Park, CA: Sage).

Ely, J. 1993. 'Post-Fordist Restructuring in Germany: What Role for the New Social Movements?' *New Political Science* 25: 145–73.

Escobar, A. 1992. 'Imagining a Post-development Era? Critical Thought, Development and Social Movements', *Social Text* 32: 20–56.

Eyerman, R. and A. Jamison. 1991. *Social Movements: A Cognitive Approach* (University Park, PA: Pennsylvania University Press).

Falk, R. 1994. 'From Geopolitics to Governance: WOMP and Contemporary Political Discource', *Alternatives* 19: 145–54.

Ferree, M.M. 1992. 'The Political Context of Rationality: Rational Choice Theory and Resource Mobilization'. In *Frontiers in Social Movement Theory*, eds A.D. Morris and C. McClurg Mueller (New Haven: Yale University Press), 29–52.

Fireman, B., and W.A. Gamson. 1979. 'Utilitarian Logic in the Resource Mobilization Perspective'. In *The Dynamics of Social Movements*, eds J.D. McCarthy and M.N. Zald (Cambridge, MA: Winthrop), 8–44.

Gerhards, J., and D. Rucht. 1992. 'Mesomobilization: Organizing and Framing in Two Protest Campaigns in West Germany', *American Journal of Sociology* 98: 555–95.

Gill, S. 1989. *American Hegemony and the Trilateral Commission* (Cambridge: Cambridge University Press).

Gramsci, A. 1971. *Selections from the Prison Notebooks* (New York: International Publishers).

Habermas, J. 1987. *The Theory of Communicative Action* (vol. 2) (Cambridge: Polity Press).

Hewitt, M. 1993. 'Social Movements and Social Need: Problems with Postmodern Political Theory', *Critical Social Policy* 13(1): 52–74.

Hirsch, J. 1988. 'The Crisis of Fordism, Transformations of the "Keynesian" Security State, and the New Social Movements', *Research in Social Movements, Conflicts and Change* 10: 43–55.

Holub, R. 1992. *Antonio Gramsci: Beyond Marxism and Postmodernism* (New York: Routledge).

Hunt, A. 1990. 'Rights and Social Movements: Counter-hegemonic Strategies', *Journal of Law and Society* 17: 309–28.

Ingalsbee, T. 1994. 'Resource and Action Mobilization Theories: The New Social-Psychological Research Agenda', *Berkeley Journal of Sociology* 38: 139–55.

Jenkins, J.C. 1983. 'Resource Mobilization Theory and the Study of Social Movements', *Annual Review of Sociology* 9: 527–53.

Klandermans, B. 1986. 'New Social Movements and Resource Mobilization: The European and the American Approach', *Journal of Mass Emergencies and Disasters* 4: 13–37.

McAdam. D. 1982. *Political Process and the Development of Black Insurgency: 1930–1970* (Chicago: University of Chicago Press).

———, J.D. McCarthy, and N. Zald. 1988. 'Social Movements'. In *Handbook of Sociology,* ed. N.J. Smelser (Beverly Hills, CA: Sage), 695–737.

McCarthy, J.D., and M.N. Zald. 1973. *The Trend of Social Movements in America: Professionalization and Resource Mobilization* (Morristown, NJ: General Learning Corporation).

———. 1977. 'Resource Mobilization and Social Movements: A Partial Theory', *American Journal of Sociology* 8: 1212–41.

Magnusson, W. 1990. 'Critical Social Movements: De-centring the State'. In *Canadian Politics: An Introduction to the Discipline,* eds A. Gagnon and J.P. Bickerton (Peterborough: Broadview Press), 525–41.

Marx, G.T. and D. McAdam. 1994. *Collective Behavior and Social Movements* (Englewood Cliffs, NJ: Prentice-Hall).

Melucci, A. 1989. *Nomads of the Present: Social Movements and Individual Needs in Contemporary Society* (Philadelphia: Temple University Press).

———. 1992. 'Liberation or Meaning? *Social Movements, Culture and Democracy',* *Development and Change* 23 (23): 43–77.

———. 1994. 'Paradoxes of Post-industrial Democracy: Everyday Life and Social Movements', *Berkeley Journal of Sociology* 38: 185–92.

Michaud, J. 1992. 'The Welfare State and the Problem of Counter-hegemonic Responses within the Women's Movement'. In *Organizing Dissent,* ed. W.K. Carroll (Toronto: Garamond Press), 200–14.

Mooers, C., and A. Sears. 1992. 'The "New Social Movements" and the Withering Away of State Theory'. In *Organizing Dissent,* ed. W.K. Carroll (Toronto: Garamond Press), 52–68.

Morris, A. 1984. *The Origins of the Civil Rights Movement* (New York: Free Press).

Offe, C. 1985a. *Disorganized Capitalism* (Cambridge: Polity Press).

———. 1985b. 'New Social Movements: Challenging the Boundaries of Institutional Politics', *Social Research* 52: 817–68.

Olson, M. 1965. *The Logic of Collective Action* (Cambridge: MA: Harvard University Press).

Parajuli, P. 1991. 'Power and Knowledge in Development Discourse: New Social Movements and the State in India', *International Social Science Journal* 43(1): 173–90.

Parsons, T. 1969. *Politics and Social Structure* (New York: Free Press).

Pichardo, N. 1988. 'Resource Mobilization: An Analysis of Conflicting Theoretical Variations', *The Sociological Quarterly* 29: 97–110.

Plotke, D. 1990. 'What's So New about New Social Movements?' *Socialist Review* 20(1): 81–102.

Ray. L. 1993. *Rethinking Critical Theory: Emancipation in the Age of Global Social Movements* (Newbury Park: Sage).

Schwartz, M., and S. Paul. 1992. 'Resource Mobilization versus the Mobilization of People: Why Consensus Movements Cannot be Instruments of Social Change'. In *Frontiers in Social Movement Theory,* eds A.D. Morris and C. McGlurg Mueller (New Haven: Yale University Press), 205–23.

Scott, A. 1990. *Ideology and the New Social Movements* (Boston: Unwin Hyman).

Smelser, N.J. 1962. *The Theory of Collective Behavior* (London: Routledge).

Snow, D.A. and R.D. Benford. 1992. 'Master Frames and Cycles of Protest'. In *Frontiers in Social Movement Theory,* eds A.D. Morris and C. McClurg Mueller (New Haven: Yale University Press), 133–55.

———, E. Burke Rochford, Jr., S. Wordon, R. Benford. 1986. 'Frame Alignment Processes,

Micromobilization, and Movement Participation', *American Sociological Review* 51: 464–81.

Stacey, J. 1982. 'The New Conservative Feminism', *Feminist Studies* 9: 559–83.

Steinmetz, G. 1994. 'Regulation Theory, Post-Marxism, and the New Social Movements', *Comparative Studies in Society and History* 36: 176–212.

Tarrow, S. 1988. 'National Politics and Collective Action: Recent Theory and Research in Western Europe and the United States', *Annual Review of Sociology* 14: 421–40.

Thiele, L.P. 1993. 'Making Democracy Safe for the World: Social Movements and Global Politics', *Alternatives* 18: 273–305.

Tilly, C. 1978. *From Mobilization to Revolution* (Reading, MA: Addison-Wesley).

———. 1988. 'Social Movements, Old and New', *Research in Social Movements, Conflicts and Change* 10: 1–18.

Touraine, A. 1981. *The Voice and the Eye: An Analysis of Social Movements* (Cambridge: Cambridge University Press).

———. 1988. *The Return of the Actor* (Minneapolis: University of Minnesota Press).

Turner, R., and L. Killian. 1957. *Collective Behavior* (Englewood Cliffs, NJ: Prentice-Hall).

Urry, J. 1981. *The Anatomy of Capitalist Societies* (London: Macmillan).

Wallerstein, I. 1989. '1968, Revolution in the World-System', *Theory and Society* 18: 431–49.

Waterman, P. 1993. 'Social Movement Unionism: A New Model for a New World Order?', *Review* 16(3): 245–78.

Wignaraja, P. 1993. 'Rethinking Development and Democracy'. In *New Social Movements in the South,* ed. P. Wignaraja (London: Zed Books), 4–35.

Young, I.M. 1990. *Justice and the Politics of Difference* (Princeton, NJ: Princeton University Press).

Zald, M. and J.D. McCarthy. 1987. *Social Movements in an Organizational Society* (New Brunswick, NJ: Transaction Books).

Chapter 9

Involvement in the Organizational Base of New Social Movements in English Canada and French Canada

James E. Curtis and Edward G. Grabb

Introduction

A voluntary organization (VO) is a formally organized collectivity of people who voluntarily lend their time, energy, financial contributions, and sentimental support to the organization, in order to aid the pursuit of its goals. These organizations are formal rather than informal and are often quite bureaucratic, with hierarchical decision-making structures. However, what sets them apart from many otherwise similar formal organizations is that they generally are not places of paid work, unlike the workplaces in many private and public bureaucracies. That is, most of their members are *volunteers*, ranging from highly active people who give considerable amounts of time and energy to the organization, to 'nominal' members who simply pay dues, make contributions, or lend their identities and sentimental support to the organization. Many organizations contain some full-time or part-time paid administrative and leadership staff, but these personnel are in a small minority compared to the volunteer members (Curtis et al. 1989a, 1952; Grabb and Curtis 1992; Hausknecht 1962; Knoke 1986; Smith 1975).

Voluntary organizations generally are quite large in terms of numbers of participants and the geographic distribution of members, at least when all levels of the organizations are taken into account. Such organizations usually involve local community groups, provincial-level and national-level organizations, and, sometimes, international-level bodies. Some examples of voluntary organizations are: trade unions, political action groups, environmental conservation organizations, and women's interest groups.

As these examples suggest, voluntary organizations often take on as their major tasks the work of *social movements* of the past or present. Social movements are collective efforts to promote some new way of doing things in society. Sometimes the organizations call for changes to improve the lot of a group that is seen by organization members as unfairly disadvantaged. For example, workers' interests have long been promoted in the labour union movement; women's interests are currently being pursued in the women's movement; and the rights of unborn children are presently at issue for the Right to Life movement. At times, a new social value is promoted by participants in the social movement. A good example of new value promotion is how participants in the environmental and ecology movements have sought to elevate the conservation of nature to a higher priority. Participants in these movements also argue that we should abhor wasteful consumption. In each of the other three examples of social movements just mentioned—social movements working on the behalf of labour, women, and unborn children—the members of the movement argue that the value, 'social equality', should be applied more universally—that certain rights should be extended to groups that do not yet enjoy them fully (see Curtis and Lambert 1994).

Social movements usually begin from the view that something is quite wrong with the current arrangements in society, and that these should be changed. Sometimes the social change called for is a return to old ways of doing things, such as the Right to Life argument that abortion should be made illegal in this country. Another example is the call for large cutbacks in expenditures on social welfare and medicare by some conservative political groups. At other times, the views and values of the movement point instead to an as yet unrealized social arrangement; illustrations include calls for full gender equality by groups in the women's movement or requests for guaranteed minimum incomes for all people by some advocates of the poor.

The term, *new social movement* (NSM), refers to a social movement that has come into being in the last few years, or that has become comparatively strong again after a period of little or no support in the population. In these cases, the movement's activities and demands for action have only recently gained popular momentum and attention to its interests (Carroll 1992; Larana, Johnston, and Gusfield 1994).

There is considerable agreement across social commentators and social researchers concerning what are the major new social movements currently in North America. Most would list the following among the central new movements: the ecology and environmental conservation movements, the Right to Life movement, the peace movement, the gay liberation movement, the women's movement, and the animal rights movement.

We have indicated that voluntary organizations are central to the work of social movements, including NSMs. For example, the environment movement today is carried forward by such groups as Greenpeace, Friends of the Earth, Earth First, and the Sierra Club. Most organizational

vehicles used by social movements are non-governmental organizations such as these. The government may provide funding for some of their activities, but the organizations generally accept such support only if it comes with 'no strings attached'. Many voluntary organizations associated with social movements try to stay relatively independent of government influence, because their agendas generally include trying to force government to change policies and laws. Such movements do not want to be beholden to government; instead, they want to remain completely free to exert whatever legitimate influence upon government it takes to make changes occur.

Within any social movement there are likely to be many different types of voluntary organizations, not all of which are confrontational. While some groups protest loudly and sometimes even see their members go to jail for civil disobedience, other groups carry on milder forms of protest, such as collecting signatures on petitions. Also, there are usually some groups that limit themselves to rather uncontroversial projects. For example, the peace movement included some groups that simply arranged for their cities to be 'twinned' with cities in Communist Eastern Europe and then organized cultural visits between the cities. These visits were also the occasions for local discussions of the need for better understanding of other cultures and the importance of pursuing world peace.

The sociological literature does not provide specific terms to distinguish between those voluntary organizations that work in the interest of new social movements and voluntary organizations that are associated with older social movements or institutionalized activities (for example, religious groups associated with churches, or political groups associated with political parties and government). For present purposes, let us call examples of this first type of organization *new voluntary organizations* (NVOs). Below, we present a procedure for measuring involvement in NVOs.

PREVIOUS STUDIES OF SUPPORT FOR VOs, NVOs, AND NSMs

The study of who gets involved with voluntary organizations, broadly defined, has received quite a bit of attention in Canada and the United States. However, the category of NVOs has not been singled out for separate consideration or for comparisons with other categories of voluntary organizatons. These tasks are among the central concerns of this chapter.

Much of the relevant Canadian research in the area of voluntary organization activity in general has been by Seymour Martin Lipset, or by other writers responding to his research. Lipset has concluded that Americans are more likely than Canadians to join voluntary organizations (Lipset 1985: 141ff., 1986: 135; see also Lipset 1990: 147ff., 1996: 278–80). This view is based on his longstanding argument that there are fundamental differences in the values and institutions of Canada and the United States (Lipset 1963; 1964; 1968). Lipset contends that because of the United States' origins in the American Revolution (versus Canada's origins in counterrevolution), Americans have developed a political culture that promotes a much greater commitment to individual democratic action than is found in Canada. The commitment to democratic action is said to manifest itself in higher levels of involvement in voluntary organizations and public protest. Combined with this Canadian-American difference, according to Lipset, is a pattern of lesser respect for authority and more questioning of politics and politicians on the part of Americans.

While research over the years has suggested that there is relatively extensive voluntary organization activity in the United States (Babchuk and Booth 1969; Bell and Force 1956; Curtis 1971; Hausknecht 1962; Hyman and Wright 1971; Olsen 1982; Verba and Nie 1972), little of this work has directly compared Canada with the United States. One study (Curtis 1971) for the 1960s found higher levels of voluntary organiza-tion membership in the United States than in four other countries: Great Britain, West Germany, Italy, and Mexico. However, in contrast to Lipset's conclusions, this study showed that Canadians were equal to or higher than Americans in voluntary organization involvement (Curtis 1971). Some more recent analyses of data for the 1980s (see Curtis et al. 1989a; 1989b; Curtis, Grabb, and Baer 1992; Grabb and Curtis 1992) also suggest that Canadians and Americans are similar in their levels of voluntary activity, if forms of voluntary organization beyond church or religious memberships are considered and if active organizational memberships, as opposed to only nominal memberships, are examined. In many comparisons, in fact, Canadians appear to be significantly more involved in voluntary organizations than are Americans.

In commenting on these analyses, Lipset has maintained that his original view on Canadian and American differences in voluntary organization involvement is still very plausible, but he concedes that the available evidence now makes the answer less clear, that 'the tentative verdict in this case must be the Scottish one: not proven' (Lipset 1989b: 382).

The present chapter will further consider the question of Canadian-American differences in voluntary organization activity, this time using new data for the 1990s. The research will also address two problems in previous work. The first problem is that most research does not adequately take into account the fundamental linguistic duality of the Canadian population. A second difficulty is that the part played by NVOs in the pattern of overall voluntary organizational involvement in the two countries has not been adequately explored. Each of these issues requires some elaboration.

In his general comparisons of Canada and the United States, Lipset acknowledges the importance of distinguishing between Canada's French and English subcultures. For example, he has incorporated this distinction into some of his analyses of the value differences between Canadians and Americans (Lipset 1990: chs 5 and 6). However, none of his research on voluntary organizations has included the French-English distinction. This distinction may be crucial because, as Curtis and colleagues (1989a; 1989b; Grabb and Curtis 1992) have shown, French Canadians are less likely than English Canadians to join voluntary organizations of various kinds, and the differences in voluntary activity between Americans and English Canadians, by themselves, do not conform to Lipset's claims. This research finds, for sets of national survey data from the two countries in 1982 and 1984, that English Canadians are about as likely to join various types of voluntary organizations as are Americans. The only major exception is a much higher level of American involvement in churches and religious organizations.

A second problem with the literature we have mentioned is the lack of specific attention to patterns of involvement in NVOs. These organizations have not been studied comparatively, across types of voluntary organization, or across Canada and the United States. Some relevant research has looked at the social characteristics of people who support NVOs (for several relevant studies of particular social movements and NVOs, see the edited collections by Carroll 1992; Larana, Johnston, and Gusfield 1994). A review of such studies suggests that NVOs and NSMs are supported by groups of people that are different from those supporting traditional voluntary organizations. Support for NVOs is said to come more often from disaffected people, such as the poor, women, and the young, than is the case for other forms of voluntary organizations. Also, the research suggests that, compared to other people, supporters of NVOs participate more in protest activity and also think more critically about their society. However, as we have said, direct comparisons between members and nonmembers of NVOs and other

forms of voluntary organizations are required to substantiate these conclusions, and such comparisons have yet to be conducted.

Prevailing theoretical views on NVOs and NSMs are expressed in different terms by liberal and Marxian political sociologists, yet virtually all of these views lead to the same hypotheses. These theories hold that the 'old' politics, characterized by the conflict between classes in capitalist societies, is being replaced by a 'new', 'postmodern', and 'postmaterialist' politics based on nonclass identities (Inglehart 1977; Laclau and Mouffe 1985; see also Giddens 1994). This shift is said to be a consequence of the 'decomposition' of increasingly heterogeneous social classes in 'disorganized' late capitalist societies (Dalton, Flanagan, and Beck 1984; Habermas 1973; Offe 1985a). The new patterns of exploitation and domination to which the NSMs and NVOs have responded are believed to cut across class cleavages, leading to a 'dealignment' of the traditional class base of political parties and electoral politics (Dalton, Flanagan, and Beck 1984; Nevitte, Bakvis, and Gibbons 1989; Offe 1985b, 1987). Of great significance to theorists of NSMs is the idea that NSMs have transcended traditional patterns of political participation. The new social movements are thought to have mobilized otherwise demobilized citizens to support a substantial critique of the political status quo. NSMs are also said to have organized mass political activity outside the limits of conventional electoral politics (Pizzorno 1981; Magnusson and Walker 1988; Magnusson 1990). NSMs are seen as society's new agents of political change, reform, and even revolution (Giddens 1984, 1994; Laclau and Mouffe 1985).

Previous studies of voluntary associations in general have consistently shown the following outcomes concerning the social background correlates of voluntary association involvement: social class levels are positively correlated with involvement; community size is negatively related to involvement; education level and being employed are both positively related to involvement; males are somewhat more likely to be involved than females; married people are somewhat more involved than unmarried; and age is curvilinearly related to involvement, with the middle-aged being the most likely to join organizations, followed by older people and then younger people (Curtis 1971; Curtis, Grabb, and Baer 1992; Hausknecht 1962).

WORKING HYPOTHESES AND RESEARCH QUESTIONS

These theoretical views, and the relevant studies to date, suggest certain expectations or hypotheses about what we will find concerning support for NVOs and NSMs. First, we expect a comparatively weak social class or socioeconomic status (SES) base to the support for NVOs, with the social class base being weaker than that for non-NVOs. In a related way, we expect a weaker effect of class background on support for NVOs compared to the effects of other social background factors, such as gender, age, marital status, employment, education level, and community size. Second, we expect to replicate findings from earlier studies of voluntary organizations concerning the relationships of social class, gender, age, marital status, education, and community size on the one hand and organizational involvement on the other hand. Third, we should find a relatively stronger 'ideological' component in the support for NVOs compared to that for other VOs. That is, we expect participants in NVOs to have a more critical approach to society, and a greater distrust of government, than people who are nonmembers or who are supporters of other voluntary organizations. Fourth, we expect to see greater political protest activity among those participating in NVOs than we find among other people.

What expectations should we have concerning the involvement of Americans and Canadians in NVOs? Taking our lead from Lipset's work (1963, 1985, 1986, 1990), we should find that Americans are higher in involvement in NVOs than either English or French Canadians. Americans are supposed to be lower in deference to authority and higher in voluntary association activity in general than Canadians. For these reasons, Americans may also be expected to be more involved in NVOs than Canadians. However, the contrary findings for American-Canadian differences in voluntary association activity in the earlier work of Curtis and colleagues would argue against any quick extrapolation to national differences in NVOs membership based on Lipset's theory. There is also evidence for the 1980s that contradicts Lipset's claims of lower deference to authority in the United States (Baer et al. 1995). It is necessary, then, to see what the comparative data show.

The above working hypotheses will be tested by answering these separate research questions in the analyses that follow: (1) What is the extent of involvement in NVOs, as well as VOs in general, among English Canadians and French Canadians? (2) Are English Canadians and French Canadians relatively less involved (i.e., compared to Americans) in NVOs and in VOs generally? (3) Who supports NVOs and are they different people from those who support VOs in general? (4) Are supporters of NVOs more likely than others to engage in political protest and to be critical of society?

Assuming that there will be reasonably high levels of multiple organization membership, we expected it to be uncommon for people who have NVO memberships to have no other VO memberships. In other words, we expected the majority of NVO members to have other VO memberships, as well. This fifth research question will be answered in the analysis as well. If our expectation is supported, it will be important to do comparisons across four different groups: that is, those who are members of NVOs only, members of other VOs only, members of both types of organizations, and members of no organizations of any kind. These comparisons will allow us to determine whether there is some uniqueness to the social background characteristics and political activities of NVO members compared to other organization joiners.

Data Source and Procedures

DATA SOURCE
Our data were gathered through surveys of national adult samples from Canada and the United States. These and other samples were collected as part of the larger World Values Survey of 1991–2, an international survey of more than 40 countries that was conducted by Ronald Inglehart and associates. In each country, a nationally representative sample of adults aged 18 and over was interviewed, with essentially the same questionnaire used in each nation (see Inglehart et al. 1994).

The Canadian respondents were divided into two groups, based on whether they indicated English or French as their first language. Our analyses were limited to people aged 21 or older in each nation, to ensure that all respondents were old enough to be able to join most associations. The working samples included 227 French Canadians and 1,350 English Canadians (there were 1,625 Canadians overall because 48 respondents had other first languages). As we have indicated, some comparisons also are made with the sample of Americans, which had 1,735 respondents. Table 9.1 shows the results.

Measures of Organization Membership
The basic measure of voluntary organization membership was the number of memberships reported by each respondent when asked the question,

> 'Which, if any, of the following do you belong to?' Respondents were presented a checklist of 16 possible organization categories: charities and social welfare, churches or religious organizations, education or

arts groups, trade unions, political parties or groups, community action groups, human rights organizations, conservation or environmental groups, animal welfare groups, youth work groups, sport and recreation organizations, professional associations, women's groups, peace groups, health organizations, and 'others'.

The analysis was conducted, first, using the total number of reported memberships and, second, with church memberships excluded. As well, analyses were done in which only memberships in NVOs were considered. This measure included human rights, environment and conservation, women's groups, peace, and animal rights organizations. Another analysis, shown in Table 9.2, looked at the proportions of people with memberships in NVOs only, compared to memberships in VOs other than NVOs, and compared to memberships in both types of organizations combined.

Additional measures were based on a second question that asked, '*And do you currently do any unpaid voluntary work for any of them?*' These measures, which are referred to here as 'working memberships', were also employed based on a total count, a count with church memberships excluded, and a count for NVOs only (see Table 9.3). Because very small proportions of people had more than two memberships on most measures, each of the measures was recoded into three categories: no membership, one membership, and two or more memberships.

For each type of organization membership, then, we can distinguish memberships that are nominal—formal but essentially inactive involvements—from those that are genuinely active, working memberships. This distinction is important to consider, of course, if we are to obtain assessment of voluntary organization *activity*, as opposed to support through nominal identification, membership fees, and, perhaps, financial contributions.

We also had available and report on informa-

Table 9.1   Percentages of People with Voluntary Organization Memberships (All Memberships and Working Memberships) among English Canadians and French Canadians, National Sample, 1991–2

Memberships	English Canadians % (N=) (1,350)	French Canadians % (227)	All Canadians % (1,625)
All Memberships			
Including Church-related Groupsa			
None	35.0	41.4	35.9
One	19.9	24.2	20.8
Two or more	45.1	34.4	43.3
Excluding Church-related Groups			
None	39.7	46.7	40.9
One	22.2	22.5	22.9
Two or more	38.1	30.8	36.8
New Voluntary Organizations Only			
None	79.7	80.2	79.8
One	14.7	13.7	14.3
Two or more	5.7	6.2	5.8
Working Memberships			
Including Church-related Groups			
None	56.5	57.3	56.7
One	19.7	22.9	20.1
Two or more	23.8	19.8	23.1
Excluding Church-related Groups			
None	60.9	61.2	61.0
One	20.9	21.6	20.9
Two or more	18.2	17.2	18.1
New Voluntary Organizations Only			
None	89.0	86.3	88.5
One	7.9	7.8	8.0
Two or more	3.1	5.9	3.5

a This English-Canadian–French-Canadian difference is statistically significant at < .05; the other results are not statistically significant.

Table 9.2   Patterns of Memberships Considering Separately New Voluntary Organizations (NVOs) and
Other Voluntary Organizations (VOs) among English Canadians and French Canadians

Membership Pattern[a]	English Canadians %	French Canadians %	All Canadians %
None	35.1	41.9	36.1
NVOs Only	1.7	2.2	1.8
Other VOs Only	46.6	41.9	46.0
Both Types of VOs	16.6	14.1	16.1

[a] The pattern of English-Canadian–French-Canadian differences is statistically significant at < .05.
'Other' organizations are excluded from the analysis because it is unclear which are NVOs versus other VOs.

Table 9.3   Percentages of People with Voluntary Organization Memberships (Nominal and Working for
Different Categories of Organizations) Comparing English Canadians, French Canadians, and
Americans, National Samples, 1991–2

Memberships	English Canadians %	French Canadians %	Americans %
All Memberships			
Member Including Church-related [a,b,c]	65.0	58.6	71.4
Member Excluding Church-related [b,c]	60.3	53.3	57.2
Member New Voluntary Org. Only	20.3	19.8	21.3
Working Memberships			
Member Including Church-related	43.5	42.7	47.2
Member Excluding Church-related	39.1	38.8	34.7
Member New Voluntary Org. Only	11.0	13.7	10.9

[a] Statistically significant differences at p < .05 between English Canadians and French Canadians.
[b].....between English Canadians and Americans.
[c].....between French Canadians and Americans.

tion on respondents' *expressed approval for each of six social movements*, whether they were a member of organizations working for the movement or not. Respondents were asked:

There are a number of groups and movements looking for public support. For each

of the following movements which I read out can you tell me whether you approve or disapprove of the movement. . . . Use 'approve strongly'; 'approve somewhat'; 'disapprove somewhat'; or 'disapprove strongly': ecology movement or nature protection, antinuclear energy movement; disarmament

Table 9.4   Social Background Predictions and Patterns of Involvement in NVOs and VOs in General among Canadians

		Memberships %			
	None	NVOs Only	Other VOs Only	Both Types of VOs	(N)
SES[a]					
Upper Class	25.8	2.1	50.9	21.3	(287)
Middle Class	32.3	2.3	47.3	18.1	(558)
Mid-Low Class	41.0	1.5	45.0	12.5	(522)
Lower Class	51.8	0.6	37.3	10.2	(166)
Occupational Status Level					
Employer/Manager of 10+ Employees	29.8	2.1	42.6	25.5	(47)
Employer/Manager of < 10 Employees	34.9	1.6	57.1	6.3	(63)
Professional	17.3	1.7	57.7	24.2	(289)
Middle Level Nonmanual	35.0	2.1	46.2	16.8	(143)
Lower Level Nonmanual	34.6	2.6	47.6	15.2	(191)
Foreman	44.1	5.1	33.9	16.9	(59)
Skilled Manual	38.5	0.9	52.1	8.5	(117)
Semiskilled Manual	45.7	1.3	41.5	11.5	(234)
Unskilled	43.4	1.3	43.5	11.8	(228)
Farm Owner, Employer	31.6	1.3	43.0	24.1	(79)
Employment Status[a]					
Full-time	31.1	1.6	52.6	14.7	(875)
Part-time	25.2	0.8	49.6	24.4	(131)
Housewife	47.1	1.6	35.8	15.5	(187)
Other	44.9	2.3	36.1	16.7	(432)
Education[a]					
Up to 14 years	51.2	2.4	35.2	11.2	(125)
15–18 years	43.0	1.7	42.4	12.9	(721)
More than 18 years	27.1	1.7	51.8	19.6	(749)
Age[a]					
21–29	40.6	1.9	46.1	11.4	(308)
30–39	34.4	0.9	48.6	16.2	(457)
40–49	29.5	2.2	49.8	18.4	(215)
50–59	30.4	1.0	53.6	15.0	(207)
60–69	39.3	3.1	39.8	17.8	(191)
70+	50.3	2.0	27.2	20.4	(147)

		Memberships %			
		NVOs	Other VOs	Both Types	
	None	Only	Only	of VOs	(N)
Sex[a]					
Males	35.1	1.0	50.7	13.3	(807)
Females	37.2	2.4	41.4	18.9	(818)
Marital Status[a]					
Married	34.8	1.7	46.8	16.7	(1163)
Divorced/Separated/Widowed	43.8	2.1	38.3	15.7	(235)
Single	34.5	1.3	50.4	13.7	(226)
Community Size[a]					
< 2000	32.6	2.0	44.9	20.6	(399)
2–10,000	44.4	1.5	36.3	17.8	(135)
10–20,000	34.3	1.0	50.0	14.7	(102)
2–100,000	39.0	0.7	47.5	12.8	(141)
100–500,000	33.2	1.6	54.7	10.5	(190)
500,000+	37.1	2.0	45.3	15.7	(658)

[a] Statistically significant at $p < .001$.

movement; human rights movement (at home and abroad); women's movement; anti-apartheid movement.

Measures of Respondents' Social Background Characteristics

Seven social background characteristics were used in the analysis. *Social class* or SES was measured using interviewer evaluations of the socioeconomic status of the respondents. Four categories were employed by the interviewers: (1) upper and upper middle class; (2) middle class, nonmanual workers: (3) mid- to lower-level manual workers who were skilled and semi-skilled: and (4) lower manual unskilled workers and the unemployed. The respondent's report of his or her *occupational status*, in terms of 1 of 10 categories (see Table 9.4), also was used as a measure of social class. *Employment status* was categorized as full-time work, part-time work, housewives, and others. *Educational level* was measured as respondent's age at completion of schooling. The categories were less than age 15, 15 to 18, and 18 and older. *Sex* was male versus female. *Age* was grouped into six categories: 21–29, 30–39, 40–49, 50–59, 60–69, and 70 or older. *Marital status* was divided into married (or common law), divorced/separated/widowed, and single. Finally, *community size* was coded into seven categories: less than 2,000; 2,000–10,000; 10,000–20,000; 20,000–100,000; 100,000–200,000; 200,000–500,000; and 500,000 or more.

Measures of Protest Activity and Critical Evaluation of Society

We had five measure of *Public Protest Activity*, based on responses to questions that were asked as follows:

Now I would like you to look at this card. I'm going to read out some different forms of political action that people can take, and

Table 9.5   Membership in New Voluntary Organizations (NVOs) and Other Voluntary Organizations (VOs) and Involvement with Types of Public Protest Activities among Canadians

Have Done This Form of Protest One or More Times	None	Memberships %		
		NVOs Only	Other VOs Only	Both Types of VOs
Signed a Petition[a]	64.0	78.6	83.6	88.5
Joined a Boycott[a]	12.9	15.4	27.7	38.6
Attended Demonstrations[a]	13.2	15.4	23.0	36.3
Joined a Strike[a]	4.3	2.0	9.0	9.9
Occupied Building, etc.[a]	1.6	2.0	2.6	7.2

[a] Statistically significant at $p < .001$.

I would like you to tell me, for each one, whether you have actually done any of these things, whether you might do it, or would never, under any circumstances, do it: signing a petition, joining a boycott, attending lawful demonstrations, joining strikes, or occupying buildings or factories.

Three measures of *Critical Evaluations of Society* were provided by other questions asked in the survey. First, a set of questions on *Views on Required Societal Change* was asked of respondents:

On this card are three kinds of attitudes toward the society we live in. Please choose which best describes your own opinion: (1) the entire way our society is organized must be radically changed by revolutionary action; (2) our society must be gradually improved by reform; (3) our present society must be valiantly defended against all subversive forces.

The first response, of course, is the most critical of society; the last response is least critical (see Table 9.6).

The second measure used responses to a question where the sample was asked, 'Why are there people in this country who live in need? Here are four possible reasons. Which one reason do you consider to be most important?' Respondents could choose one of the four possible reasons: (1) 'because they are unlucky'; (2) 'because of laziness and lack of willpower'; (3) 'because there is injustice in our society'; and (4) 'because they are an inevitable part of modern progress'. Then the respondents were asked, 'Which reason do you consider to be the second most important?' If 'injustice in our society' was cited as most important, a score of two was assigned; a score of one was assigned if this option was chosen as the second most important reason. Other responses were given a score of zero. This procedure produced a measure of *Blames Society* with scores ranging from 0 to 2.

A third measure of being critical of the society was provided by a question on *Trust/Distrust of Government* (see Table 9.8). 'How much do you trust the government in Ottawa to do what is right? Do you almost always? Most of the time? Only some of the time? Almost never?'

Table 9.6   Membership in New Voluntary Organizations (NVOs) and Other Voluntary Organizations (VOs) and Views on Required Changes in Society among Canadians

Views on Required Changes in Society	None	Memberships %		
		NVOs Only	Other VOs Only	Both Types of VOs
Revolutionary Change	5.8	7.7	3.5	4.9
Gradual Change	79.1	84.6	82.8	84.8
Maintain Society As Is	15.1	7.7	13.7	10.2

Not statistically significant.

Table 9.7   Membership in New Voluntary Organizations (NVOs) and Other Voluntary Organizations (VOs) and Blaming Society for People Being in Need among Canadians

Blame Society Scale	None	Memberships %		
		NVOs Only	Other VOs Only	Both Types of VOs
Low	47.7	53.6	47.1	39.7
Medium	24.0	25.0	21.4	19.8
High	28.3	25.4	31.6	40.5

Statistically significant at $p < .05$.

Table 9.8   Membership in New Voluntary Organizations (NVOs) and Other Voluntary Organizations (VOs) and Trust in Government among Canadians

Trust in Government	None	Memberships %		
		NVOs Only	Other VOs Only	Both Types of VOs
Almost Always	29.1	11.1	25.7	23.4
Most of the Time	51.1	85.2	53.8	60.2
Only Some of the Time	16.1	3.7	17.2	15.2
Almost Never	3.2	0.0	3.4	1.2

Statistically significant at $p < .05$.

RESULTS

What Is the Extent of Involvement in NVOs and VOs in General?

As Table 9.1 shows, about 65 per cent of English Canadians and 59 per cent of French Canadians are involved in one or more voluntary organizations, including church-related associations. The figures drop to 60 per cent for the English and 53 per cent for the French Canadians when church-related associations are excluded. English Canadians are also more likely than the French to have multiple memberships, 45 per cent compared to 34 per cent. A little over 40 per cent of the English and French had working memberships with all types included, and somewhat less with church groups excluded. For working memberships there were no significant English-French differences.

When we look at membership in NVOs only, we find that only 20 per cent of both English and French Canadians have such memberships, and only about 10 per cent have working memberships in NVOs.

To What Extent Are Members of NVOs Also Members of Other VOs and Vice Versa?

Table 9.2 shows that the vast majority of those having NVO memberships are also members of other VOs. A remarkably low 2 per cent of both English and French Canadians have memberships in new voluntary organizations alone. Seventeen per cent and 14 per cent of English Canadians and French Canadians, respectively, had memberships in both NVOs and other VOs. The most frequent category of respondent, though, was those who had membership in other VOs only—47 per cent of English Canadians and 42 per cent of French Canadians. The overall patterns of differences between the language groups is statistically significant.

Are Canadians Comparatively Low in Involvement Levels?

Table 9.3 compares the organization memberships among English and French Canadians with those

for the American sample. If we look at all VOs combined, we find results that are similar to those reported by Curtis and colleagues (1992) for the 1980s. That is, Canadians from each linguistic community are less involved than Americans, so long as church-related memberships are included. However, when church-related organizations are excluded, English Canadians are just as likely to be involved, if not more so, while French Canadians are slightly lower in involvement than both of the other two groups. It is also notable that, if NVOs alone are considered, there are no significant differences across all three groups in their levels of organizational membership.

The results for working memberships, too, show no statistically significant American-Canadian differences. Once nominal memberships and religious organizations are excluded, Americans are no more likely to be involved in voluntary associations than either of the two Canadian groups, whether for work in NVOs or in other VOs.

Who Supports NVOs and Are They Different Types of People from Those Who Support VOs in General?

Table 9.4 looks at the way membership patterns relate to respondents' social background characteristics. We present findings for French Canadians and English Canadians combined because of the low numbers of cases for NVOs when the two language groups are kept separate. Further analysis (not reported here) when the language groups were considered separately showed essentially the same patterns of social backgrounds correlates of membership as in Table 9.4 for the language groups combined.

We find that the interviewer's social class evaluation of respondents is a comparatively strong predictor of organization involvement. Whether for NVOs, other VOs, or both, the higher the SES, the greater the involvement. The same pattern occurs for the respondents' reported occupational status levels; the higher the status, the greater the involvement, of each type. Employment status and educational status are also positively related with memberships of each type. We find, further, the expected curvilinear relationship between membership involvement and age across the types of associations. Contrary to expectations, however, marital status and community size are not related to our membership measures. Consistent with expectations from the literature on new social movements, women are more involved than men when we look at NVOs alone, and when we look at NVOs in combination with other organizations. Men, however, are more involved than women when organizations other than NVOs are considered separately. Further analysis shows that the greater female involvement in NVOs still holds even if women's groups, which have primarily female members, are excluded from the NVO category, although the gender differences in involvement are reduced by this exclusion.

Are Supporters of NVOs More Likely than Others to Engage in Political Protest and to Be Critical of Society?

Table 9.5 shows that people who are members of NVOs only, as well as those who are members of VOs only, differ from others in their levels of involvement in five types of protest activity. These activities include signing a petition, joining a boycott, attending lawful demonstrations, joining a strike, and occupying buildings and other premises. People involved with VOs tend to protest more than those in the other categories. However, people who are involved in both types of VOs are considerably more likely than other respondents to have participated in each type of protest activity. The people who are least involved in these forms of protest are those who have no memberships in VOs of any type, whether they were NVOs or others.

As might be expected, involvement in strikes and building takeovers, which are quite infre-

quent events in the society, are not very common among the respondents, either for members of NVOs or for members of other VOs. Nonetheless, even in the case of these more extreme protest activities, VO members are more frequently involved than are nonmembers.

Next, Table 9.6 looks at the respondents' assessments of society by type of voluntary organization involvement. There are no statistically significant differences in people's views on the need for social change across the different categories of organizational involvement. Only a very small minority of each category of members wants 'revolutionary change' to occur (under 8 per cent), and the vast majority (79 per cent or more across all groups) wants to see gradual change occur.

In Table 9.7 we find, using a different measure of 'society criticism', that the tendency to blame society for people being in need is most pronounced among those respondents who are involved both in NVOs and in VOs. This tendency is least evident among those with NVO memberships only.

Further, moving to a third measure, distrust of government is comparatively low among people with only NVO memberships, and is about equally high (with about 20 per cent saying they trust government 'only some of the time' or 'almost never') among respondents who have no memberships, only non-NVO memberships, or both NVO and non-NVO memberships (see Table 9.8).

Conclusion

The preceding results, using new data for the 1990s, contribute further to answering the question of whether or not Americans are bigger 'joiners' than Canadians when it comes to voluntary organization involvement. When looking at results that do not distinguish among different types of involvement, we find support for Lipset's conclusion, as well as that of Curtis and associates, that Canadians are less involved overall than

Americans. However, as in the earlier research by Curtis and colleagues, our findings here indicate that English Canadians do not differ from Americans once church-related organizations are excluded from consideration, whereas French Canadians are slightly less involved than both of the other two populations. Another important finding is that the greater overall involvement of Americans is largely because of their higher level of *nominal* membership in VOs. When we focus on active *working* memberships, Canadians (whether English or French) do not differ significantly from Americans. Moreover, the results for involvement in NVOs also show no substantial differences among English Canadians, French Canadians, and Americans, a finding that is contrary to what we might have expected from Lipset's theory of national differences. About 20 per cent of each group has one or more NVO memberships overall, and just over 10 per cent in each case has one or more working memberships.

If asked to offer interpretations for the *similarities* we have found in voluntary organization membership and activity across the three groups, we would hypothesize that the similarities probably stem from the comparable processes of urbanization, industrialization, and role specialization operating in all three populations. The social differentiation and complexity that are concomitant with these processes promote considerable diversity in the occupational, family, and leisure experiences of all three groups. In such a diverse and varied social context, numerous opportunities should arise for people who share common experiences to organize and meet around their joint interests. Prevailing democratic norms, as well as the considerable leisure time that many people have in all three settings, also facilitate high levels of activity. Because the United States, English Canada, and French Canada are not very different in these respects, it is not surprising that their populations differ very little from each other in levels of voluntary organization involvement

(Curtis 1971; Curtis et al. 1989a; Curtis, Grabb, and Baer 1992; Grabb and Curtis 1992).

Any notable differences in involvement among the three populations seem to be restricted primarily to the specific case of religious organizations. This observation suggests a second avenue of interpretation. As Curtis and colleagues (1989a; cf. Bibby 1987) have argued, the greater level of religious group involvement of Americans compared with the two Canadian populations is probably related to the greater differentiation among churches and faiths and, hence, the greater competition for attracting church members in the United States. As Bibby (1987) suggests, there appears to exist a more fully developed 'marketplace' for religion in the United States, in which a larger and more aggressive 'sales' force is able to reach a much greater proportion of religious consumers than is possible in Canada and most other nations. In other words, the higher levels of church affiliation among Americans may have little to do with a greater American propensity for individualism and democratic participation, and more to do with how religious leaders more vigorously sell their organizations in a highly competitive religious marketplace. This interpretation applies to both the American-English Canadian and the American-French Canadian differences we have found in levels of religious group involvement.

It is also possible that voluntary organizations in the United States frequently are able to employ more effective strategies for membership recruitment (such as direct mail), because they are larger and have more financial resources than their Canadian counterparts. This would help account for why Americans are higher on levels of nominal membership, but not on levels of working membership. However, as we have shown, these differences do not extend to memberships excluding church-related organizations, nor do they apply to memberships in NVOs.

When we look at *who* joins and works for voluntary organizations we find support for some of the hypotheses drawn from the general literature on voluntary organization involvement. People with higher occupational status and higher education are considerably more involved than others. These findings extend to involvement in NVOs, particularly to involvement in NVOs in conjunction with other memberships. Contrary to the expectation from the literature on new social movements, however, the participants in NVOs do not have different social background profiles. SES does not appear to have a different relationship to involvement in NVOs than it does to involvement in other types of organizations. Rather, people with higher SES are more likely to belong to both NVOs and other VOs.

Surprisingly, given the previous literature, some social background factors—community size and marital status—have weak and nonsignificant relationships with involvement in organizations in our results. Women do have more involvement in NVOs than do men, a result that is consistent with the literature on NVOs and NSMs.

When we turn to the issue of the political protest activity of participants in voluntary organizations, the results suggest that organization participation leads to greater protesting, regardless of the patterns of organization membership considered; that is, whether we consider participants in NVOs only, other VOs only, or both types of organizations. In all cases, we find that the more involved people are, the more they protest. Thus, NVOs do not appear to be unique among voluntary organizations in promoting protest.

Similar patterns occur for the relationship between organization involvement and 'blaming society'. Non-NVO participants, as well as those who participate in both NVOs and other organizations, are more likely to blame society for people's problems than are those involved only in NVOs. And, there are parallel patterns for 'distrust of government' and 'calling for societal reform'. Those involved in organizations of both types are less trustful of government and more interested in seeing society reformed.

How should we account for these departures from the expectations that we should draw from the social movements literature? Part of the answer lies in our finding that few people are members of NVOs alone. In the two large national samples we have considered, less than 2 per cent of respondents are in this circumstance, and a very large percentage of members of NVOs are also members of other organizations. Thus, most members of NVOs are also 'plugged into' and influenced by what goes on in other community organizations. At the same time, most members of NVOs are not strongly disaffected people who have not been recruited by other organizations as well.

Another interpretation that requires consideration is that the NVO members who are most 'into' political protest and critical thinking about society—those with both NVO and other VO memberships—are probably more likely to be *multiple members* than people in the NVOs-only and non-NVOs-only categories. Some individuals in these two categories will have multiple memberships, but probably not as many as in the group who have combined NVO and non-NVO memberships. This suggests that what makes the people in the latter category more critical and more likely to protest is their greater organizational activity compared to other individuals. Such a possibility will have to be explored in further research, where the separate effects of multiple membership, and of NVO and other VO involvements, are assessed using multivariate analysis.

We should conclude by noting that nearly all voluntary organizations, not just the new ones and their attendant social movements, have some interest in influencing or promoting change in society. When members of most associations get together to interact, or when they are contacted by their organizations through the mails, regular discussions of change and ways of protesting current arrangements are likely to take place. Our results for the organization types that we were able to study suggest that voluntary organizations in general contain people that are 'into' criticizing society, looking for social change, and protesting, certainly as compared to those not involved in such organizations. Some of their calls for change may be modest, but even this level of interest distinguishes them from those who have no involvement in organizations of any type. The extent to which these patterns result from the 'teaching' that occurs in voluntary organizations, as we have suggested above, or from selective recruitment of already critical and change-oriented people by voluntary organizations, is something that remains unclear. Likely both processes occur. This should be studied in further, longitudinal, research.

Note

We gratefully acknowledge that our data source was made available by Ronald Inglehart, University of Michigan, and Neil Nevitte, University of Calgary, through the Inter-university Consortium for Political and Social Research. We also thank the Donner Canadian Foundation for their contributions to making the data available. Neither the original investigators nor the disseminating archive bear any responsibility for the analyses presented here. Terry Stewart, University of Waterloo, provided very helpful assistance with our data analysis.

References

Babchuk, N., and A. Booth. 1969. 'Voluntary Association Membership: A Longitudinal Analysis', *American Sociological Review* 34: 31–45.

Baer, D.E., J.E. Curtis, E.G. Grabb, and W.A. Johnston. 1995. 'Respect for Authority in Canada, the United States, Great Britain, and Australia', *Social Focus* 28: 177–95.

Bell, W. and M. Force. 1956. 'Urban Neighborhood Types in Participation in Formal Associations', *American Sociological Review* 21: 25–34.

Bibby, R.W. 1987. *Fragmented Gods: The Poverty and Potential of Religion in Canada* (Toronto: Irwin).

Carroll, W., ed. 1992. *Organizing Dissent: Contemporary Social Movements in Theory and Practice* (Toronto: Garamond Press).

Curtis, J. 1971. 'Voluntary Association Joining: Cross-National Comparisons', *American Sociological Review* 36: 872–80.

———, E.G. Grabb, and D.E. Baer. 1992. 'Voluntary Association Membership in Fifteen Countries: A Comparative Analysis'. *American Sociological Review* 57: 139–52.

Curtis, J. and R. Lambert. 1976. 'Voting, Political Interest, and Age: National Survey Findings for French- and English-Canadians', *Canadian Journal of Political Science* 9: 293–307.

———, 1994. 'Ideology and Social Change'. In *The Social World* (2nd edn), ed. L. Tepperman (Toronto: McGraw-Hill Ryerson).

Curtis, J., R. Lambert, S. Brown, and B. Kay. 1989a. 'Affiliating with Voluntary Associations: Canadian-American Comparisons', *Canadian Journal of Sociology* 14: 143–61.

———.1989b. 'On Lipset's Measure of Voluntary Association Differences Between Canada and the United States', *Canadian Journal of Sociology* 14: 383–89.

Dalton, R.J., S.C. Flanagan, and P.A. Beck (eds). 1984. *Electoral Change in Advanced Industrial Democracies* (Princeton: Princeton University Press).

Giddens, A. 1984. *The Constitution of Society* (Berkeley: University of California Press).

———. 1994. *Beyond Left and Right: The Future of Radical Politics* (Stanford: Stanford University Press).

Grabb, E.G., and J.E. Curtis. 1992. 'Voluntary Association Activity in English Canada, French

Canada and the United States: Multivariate Analyses', *Canadian Journal of Sociology* 17: 371–88.

Habermas, J. 1973. *Legitimation Crisis* (London: Heinemann).

Hausknecht, M. 1962. *The Joiners* (New York: Bedminster Press).

Hyman, H.H., and C. Wright. 1971. 'Trends in Voluntary Association Memberships of American Adults: Replication Based on Secondary Analysis of National Sample Surveys', *American Sociological Review* 36: 191–206.

Inglehart, R. 1977. *The Silent Revolution* (Princeton, NJ: Princeton University Press).

———, et al. 1994. *World Values Surveys, 1991–92: Individual and Aggregate Level Codebook* (Ann Arbor, MI: University of Michigan, Institute for Social Research).

Knoke, D. 1986. 'Associations and Interest Groups', *Annual Review of Sociology* 12: 1–21.

Laclau, E. and C. Mouffe. 1985. *Hegemony and Socialist Strategy* (London: Verso).

Larana, E., H. Johnston, and J. Gusfield (eds). 1994. *New Social Movements: From Ideology to Identity* (Philadelphia: Temple University Press).

Lipset, S.M. 1963. *The First New Nation* (New York: Basic Books).

———. 1964. 'Canada and the United States: A Comparative View', *Canadian Review of Sociology and Anthropology* 1: 173–85.

———. 1968. *Revolution and Counterrevolution* (New York: Basic Books).

———. 1985. 'Canada and the United States: The Cultural Dimension'. In *Canada and the United States*, eds C.F. Doran and J.H. Sigler (Englewood Cliffs: Prentice-Hall), 109–60.

———. 1986. 'Historical Traditions and National Characteristics: A Comparative Analysis of Canada and the United States', *Canadian Journal of Sociology* 11: 113–55.

———. 1990. *Continental Divide: The Values and Institutions of Canada and the United States* (New York: Routledge).

———. 1996. *American Exceptionalism: A Double-Edged Sword* (New York: W.W. Norton).

Magnusson, W. 1990. 'Critical Social Movements'. In *Canadian Politics: An Introduction to the Discipline*, eds A. Gagnon and J.P. Bickerton (Peterborough, ON: Broadview Press).

———, and R. Walker. 1988. 'Decentering the State: Political Theory and Canadian Political Economy', *Studies in Political Economy* 26: 37–72.

Nevitte, N., H. Bakvis, and R. Giggons. 1989. 'The Ideological Contours of "New Politics" in Canada: Policy, Mobilization and Party Support', *Canadian Journal of Political Science* 2, 475–503.

Offe, C. 1985a. *Contradictions of the Welfare State* (Cambridge, MA: MIT Press).

———. 1985b. *Disorganized Capitalism* (Cambridge: Polity Press).

———. 1987. 'Challenging the Boundaries of Institutional Politics: Social Movements since the 1960s'. In *Changing Boundaries of the Political*, ed. C.S. Maier (Cambridge: Cambridge University Press).

Olsen, M.E. 1982. *Participatory Pluralism: Political Participation and Influence in the United States and Sweden* (Chicago: Nelson-Hall).

Pizzorno, A. 1981. 'Interests and Parties in Pluralism'. In *Organizing Interests in Western Europe: Pluralism, Corporatism and the Transformation of Politics*, ed. S. Berger (Princeton, NJ: Princeton University Press).

Smith, D.H. 1975. 'Voluntary Action and Voluntary Groups', *Annual Review of Sociology* 1: 247–70.

Verba, S. and N.H. Nie. 1972. *Participation in America: Political Democracy and Social Equality* (New York: Harper & Row).

Part D

Political Movements

Canadian politics is different from American politics because our political system supports 'third parties' and Canadian sociologists have focused on this in their political analyses. Thus, questions of how leadership images affected electoral choices for the two federal mainstream parties that dominated the scene prior to 1993 (the Liberal Party and the Conservative Party) have been left to the sister discipline of political science, with the possible exception of the study of the role of charismatic leadership in third parties. Of course, third parties have, from time to time, come into power in provincial governments, and are thus of some importance to a political scene that includes extensive federal-provincial negotiations and the general divisions of the responsibilities of government between these two levels. More important, third parties always threaten to have an impact on the political system that far outweighs their initial or present size. In minority federal governments, the NDP had an impact on the development of social welfare provisions in the 1960s and 1970s. And the policies of the Parti Québécois, the dominant provincial party in Quebec politics over the past two decades, have the potential for profoundly affecting the Canadian political environment. The Alliance Party (then the Reform party) was discussed as a third party prior to the 1990s, yet it is now the Official Opposition in the Parliament of Canada. Indeed, the demise of the Conservative Party as a major political force on the federal scene in the Canadian federal elections since 1993 suggests that the characterization of Canadian federal politics as a 'two-party' contest with various minor third parties may no longer be appropriate. Instead, we might talk about new political parties or, better yet, *political movements*. Usually, these take the form of new political parties (the NDP in its day, the Parti Québécois, the Reform, and then the Alliance Party), but sometimes they take the form of major political shifts within existing political parties—the neoconservative 'revolution' in the Conservative Party of Ontario under Mike Harris, for example.

Political movements threaten to disrupt the 'normal politics', that is, the competitive but stable system in which parties (usually two of them) vie for power within a more or less shared framework of political expectations and beliefs but with major differences on some substantial policy concerns. It is perhaps for this reason that the Reform Party and its successor, the Alliance Party, with its supposedly radical neoconservative agenda, some strong ideas about 'participatory democracy', and its sometimes restrictive view with respect to social liberty issues (abortion, childcare, homosexual rights, etc.) has attracted the attention of sociologists, including Harrison, who writes about them in Chapter 10. Harrison details the historic evolution of the party, tracing its popularity, ironically, to the large electoral victory achieved by the Conservatives in 1984. The irony occurs in the sense that the conservatives then became the 'establishment' party and, unable to counter Western alienation and discontent, left the field open for the Reform Party to pick up support from dissent against the political mainstream. Harrison also discusses the composition of the party—who its supporters are. Here, we find that dominant groups play an important part, but Harrison suggests that status threat and status decline may have played a role.

Both Harrison and Bell ask, in different ways, the question of why so-called populist movements originating in Western Canada took on a left-wing as opposed to a right-wing form. Certainly, the nature of coalitions between labour, farmers, and small business have been different in Canada than they were in, say, Sweden (Clement 1990; Johnston and Baer 1993; Korpi 1987; Przeworkski and Sprague 1986), where postfeudal alliances established a political program and a base of support for left political parties. Harrison suggests that ethnic homogeneity (in Europe) might play a role too; although he may overstate the case (for a discussion of the extent to which European states are linguistically and ethnically heterogeneous, see Oommen [1997] or the Introduction to Part B in this text), it is certainly the case that the Scandinavian countries fit this description.

Especially from the standpoint of federal parties, the development of political movements must be seen in the context of the electoral system under which Canada operates. Canada's electoral system is a constitutional system; the phrase 'first past the post' is sometimes used to describe this form. As Keane (1988: 23) notes, this has implications, sometimes profound implications, for the development of political parties and systems. In constituency democracy, minority parties are underrepresented. A party could easily obtain 30 per cent of the popular vote, yet have no seats in the legislature because it did not gain the most votes in any single riding. Conversely, where more than two parties are contenders of any sort, the plurality required for election in each riding falls, since the system does not allow for 'run off' votes. In a close race, a candidate can win a seat with 35 per cent of the vote, as long as the remaining votes are split with something like 32.5 per cent for each of the other two candidates. In a four-party race, the percentage of votes required to win in each riding can be even smaller. In 1990, the Ontario NDP came to power with only 37 per cent of the popular vote—yet they achieved a majority of the seats in the legislature. Similarly, the Mike Harris government came to power in 1995 with somewhat less than 50 per cent of the popular vote.[1]

In other countries, different systems deal with this problem. Another democratic form, proportional representation (PR), exists in many European countries, although sometimes as a modified version that includes regular constituencies. Proportional representation usually involves the election of representatives from countrywide lists of candidates instead of the election of local representatives. Each party submits an ordered list of potential representatives. As a voter, one chooses between the federal political parties. If a party gets 20 per cent of the vote, then the top 20 per cent of its 'list' gets sent to the legislature. A vote distribution of 45 per cent, 35 per cent, 20 per cent would lead to *exactly* the same distribution in seats in the legislature, whereas in the 'constituency democracy' system that Canada has, the party with 45 per cent is most likely to win a majority government and the party with 20 per cent of the vote may, depending on regional distributions, get shut out of Parliament entirely or at least have far fewer seats than its 20 per cent support would warrant. Although often associated with instability (one can think of Israel or

Italy), long, stable regimes have existed in countries such as Germany operating under PR. Interestingly, the re-election of the Liberal Party in 2000, with a majority government despite the general unpopularity of its leader, has led to an increased expression of interest in the PR form of governance among individuals from both ends of the political spectrum (political left and political right) in Canada.

Canada's 'constituency democracy' system has the implication not so much of blocking the development of parties of dissent, but of channelling this dissent. Divisions and conflicts that take on territorial form—that is, *regional* divisions—are more likely to provide emerging political movements with electoral success in the Canadian system. A political party with 20 per cent of the vote across the country will find itself unrepresented in Parliament, but if that same 20 per cent of the vote is concentrated in one or two provinces, the party can make a substantial impact on the political map. In the past, this factor contributed to the ability of the NDP to emerge, but it channelled its political form. Much of the NDP's parliamentary strength was based on election outcomes reflecting regional grievances and disaffection from the political mainstream. The story, then, of political movements in Canadian society has largely been a story of regional alienation and the political response to this alienation.

In the two neighbouring Prairie provinces of Saskatchewan and Alberta, very different political parties have emerged. The 'Why right in Alberta and left in Saskatchewan?' question has had a long legacy in Canadian social science (Lipset 1971; Macpherson 1970), with a variety of explanations being provided. Bell examines this question in Chapter 11, placing an emphasis not so much on 'structural' factors but on the confluence of historic events and decisions taken by the actors involved in the political movements in the respective provinces. Thus, the fact that Alberta is

richer in oil and gas deposits (which has major implications for the province's economy)—a structural factor—takes a back seat to issues such as the timing of electoral victories, the strategies of the movement leaders, and the responses of the (mainstream) governments of the day to the political challenge.

For a time, when one spoke of third parties in Canada, one meant the NDP. Now, the NDP's chances of playing a major role in the federal government appear to be negligible, and the party seems to be on a downward spiral from which anything more than a nominal recovery seems unlikely. One could, perhaps, examine the decline of the NDP with an examination of the *structural* factors that may have contributed to this decline. Sociologists such as Giddens (1994) would argue that the 'old style' socialist project is no longer relevant given the collapse of the Soviet Union and the development of a globalized (capitalist) economy, but the NDP's policies rarely entailed anything close to a socialist project. Structural explanations might also include changes in population structures (for example, changes in the regional base of the party), in occupational structure (the decline in the absolute size and relative proportion of the blue-collar working class), and in terms of the economic 'muscle' opposing parties can bring to bear (no major Canadian newspaper publicly supports the NDP).

But structural explanations rarely tell the whole story. In Chapter 12 Denis focuses on one seemingly small but ultimately very significant aspect of the NDP's history: its attempt to attract voters in the province of Quebec in the late 1980s. Why should this matter? Denis argues that the NDP was on the verge of making an important breakthrough in that province, but threw away its opportunity through a series of decisions and actions which, ultimately, doomed the party in Quebec. Denis might have overstated—only slightly—the strength of 'post-structuralist' explanations against a simple structural explanation. The latter would proceed as follows: the party was doomed in Quebec because of the nature of its support base elsewhere in Canada. Given its Western Canadian base, and given the nature of Western Canadian grievances toward the rest of Canada, *including* Quebec, the NDP would have inevitably fractured one way or the other. Still, one cannot dismiss the impact of key decisions taken by NDP party leaders, and Denis's discussion of how the NDP's platform was received in Quebec—how the *narrative* was constructed and then how it fell apart—represents an important lesson in the study of politics.

The Quebec separation movement—and its political manifestations—is a political movement like no other in Canada. In Chapter 13, Pinard provides an extensive outline of the dynamics of support for separation in Quebec, and situates this discussion within some theoretical frames that can be used to examine the ethnolinguistic division between Quebec and English Canada. The chapter provided here was written in late 1997 and reflects upon the situation in Quebec at that time. In the succeeding years, the Parti Québécois has appeared to drop its plan for another referendum because of the (slightly) diminished popularity of the separation option, although the possibility of a change in plans always looms in the minds of individuals concerned with the relationship between Quebec and the rest of Canada.

As Pinard points out, in 1980, a referendum on separation garnered 40.4 per cent support for this option: 15 years later, in 1995, the future of Canada was decided by the slimmest of margins (50.6 per cent versus 49.4 per cent). Pinard's discussion ties in with some of the themes and issues discussed earlier in Part B (see Chapter 5 by Jeffrey and also the Introduction), but the interrelationship among ethnic grievances, ethnic segmentation, ethnic identification/nationalism, and élite regulation add important dimensions to this discussion.

Pinard provides a careful detailing of the nature of public opinion in Quebec, and outlines how opinion varies with 'how the question is asked' in the referendum. Few Quebecers prefer the federalist status quo, but few also want outright separation as their first choice. How the rest of Canada and its political leaders respond to the aspirations of Quebecers for more autonomy within Canada will play an important role in determining whether Canada remains intact through the next century. There is, of course, an irony here: the very federal nature of the government in Canada has facilitated the development of institutions (specifically, the provincial government) around which the political movement of separatism was able to develop. This having been said, no retreat to the status quo is likely to lead to a permanent, stable solution.

Pinard reports a slight decline in support for separatism after the 1995 referendum, and this decline seems to have continued into the opinion polls conducted early in 1999. Yet support for the status quo has, if anything, declined, with 44.5 per cent responding 'yes' to a question using the term *sovereign someday* in April of 1999.[2] In early 2000, this continued,[3] but by late summer of that year support for separation had increased. Pinard's Chapter 13 should be sobering for English Canadians, because it suggests that there is considerable leeway for a sovereignty movement to work with strategies, referendum question options, and approaches to negotiations with the federal government.[4] A misstep on the part of the federal government could, under this scenario, still lead to the dissolution of the country.[5] Jean Chrétien and the federal Liberals may have come very close to doing this in 1995 by their insistence on a 'status quo' option which, according to Pinard's analysis, received the support of only 19 per cent of the population. The Liberals were almost outflanked by the Parti Québécois, which moved to a compromise position in order to garner favour with voters who wanted something between the two extremes of the status quo and complete separation.

While the increase in Liberal Party support and the declines in Bloc Québécois support in the 2000 federal election might suggest to us that separatism is no longer a major issue in Quebec politics, this outcome may have simply been a result of discontent with certain provincial gov-

ernment policies (with the Bloc taking the punishment for voter discontent over the performance of its provincial counterpart). Pinard's work makes clear that the constitutional status of the province of Quebec and indeed its continued presence as part of the Canadian federation will remain issues in Canadian politics.

Notes

1. There are even instances, such as the first election of Grant Devine's Conservative government in Saskatchewan, where the party elected to power with the most seats in the legislature received *fewer* votes than the party that 'lost' the election.

2. *Globe and Mail,* 16 April 1999, p. A6.

3. *Globe and Mail,* 6 March 2000, p. A4.

4. Support for the 'status quo' may have declined, too, although the 14.5 per cent reported in the

Globe and Mail on 16 April 1999 may not have entailed exactly the same question as that reported by Pinard in his chapter.

5. The secession of Slovakia from the Czech republic was discussed earlier in Part B. The separation of the two countries came about largely as a result of the efforts of political élites in Slovakia, and not as a result of a popular vote with a clear ballot question.

References

Clement, W. 1990. 'Comparative Class Analysis: Locating Canada in a North American and Nordic Context', *Canadian Review of Sociology and Anthropology* 27(4): 462–86.

Giddens, A. 1994. *Beyond Left and Right: The Future of Radical Politics* (Stanford, CA: Stanford University Press).

Johnston, W., and D. Baer. 1993. 'Class Consciousness and National Contexts: Canada, Sweden and the United States in Historical Perspective', *Canadian Journal of Sociology and Anthropology* 30: 271–95.

Keane, J. 1988. *Civil Society and the State: New European Perspectives* (London: Verso).

Korpi, W. 1987. 'Power, Politics and State Autonomy in the Development of Social Citizenship', *American Sociological Review* 54(3): 309–28.

Lipset, S.M. 1971. *Agrarian Socialism: The Cooperative Commonwealth Federation in Saskatchewan: A Study in Political Sociology* (Berkeley, CA: University of California Press).

Macpherson, C.B. 1970. *Democracy in Alberta* (Toronto: University of Toronto Press).

Oommen, T.K. 1997. *Citizenship, Nationality and Ethnicity: Reconciling Competing Identities* (Cambridge: Polity Press).

Przeworkski, A., and J. Sprague. 1986. *Paper Stones: A History of Electoral Socialism* (Chicago: University of Chicago Press).

Chapter 10

Populism: The Rise and Transformation of the Reform Party of Canada

Trevor W. Harrison

Introduction

Under its founder, Preston Manning, the Reform Party of Canada emerged within the short space of ten years (1987–97) to become Canada's Official Opposition party. Three years after the 1997 Canadian federal election, and in time for the 2000 election, the party transformed itself into the Canadian Alliance Party and chose a new leader in a bid to break out of its Western political base.

The success of Reform and its Alliance successor are not unique in Canadian history. Rather, they fit within a long line of populist parties, stretching back to the Grangers of the nineteenth century, the Progressives of the 1920s, and the Social Credit and Cooperative Commonwealth Federation (CCF) of the 1930s.

This chapter examines the remarkable rise of the Reform Party and subsequent transformation within the context of the notion of *populism*. Specifically, the chapter examines the conditions under which populist parties arise; and the manner in which populism has changed over time. The chapter begins with a discussion of the contentious notion of populism itself.

What Is Populism?

Populism is an ambiguous concept. Journalists frequently use the term as shorthand for a leadership style that appeals to 'the common person'. On this basis, writers have referred to such his-torical figures as Benito Mussolini, Juan Peron, and Louis Riel as populists. More recently, the same label has been given to Ralph Klein, Ross Perot, and Ronald Reagan. Defined simply as style, the term covers a lot of ground and thus no particular ground at all. The notion of populism can be made more analytically useful if we examine a few key elements that all so-called populist movements seem to hold in common.

First, all populist movements and parties appeal to a mass audience. Central to this mass appeal is the notion of 'the people', a group defined by its historic, geographic, and/or cultural roots. Second, this appeal is made urgent by the perception of a crisis threatening 'the people'. Third, the source of this threat is a group (a power bloc) viewed as physically or culturally external to 'the people', typically (from a left-wing perspective) capitalism or 'big business' or (from a right-wing perspective) 'big government' (Conway 1978; Laclau 1977; Patten 1993; Sinclair 1979). In short, *populism can be defined as a mass political movement, mobilized around symbols and traditions congruent with the popular culture, which expresses a group's sense of threat, arising from powerful outside elements, and directed at their perceived 'peoplehood'.*

It is important to note that both 'the people' and the power bloc are contested concepts. That is, neither concept exists 'naturally'. Rather, they are socially constructed in the course of real political struggles between competing leaders and organizations attempting to mobilize support and build coalitions. This constructed nature of the people/power bloc antagonism explains, in part, the rise of various types of populist movements.

Types of Populism

Several attempts have been made to classify various types of populism. Until recently, one popular classification schema has seen populist movements labelled as either 'progressive' or 'reactionary'. Unfortunately, this schema is much too value-laden to be of much use. One person's reaction might be another's progress—and vice versa.

Canovan (1981: 8) distinguishes two broad types of populism. Agrarian populism is defined by 'a particular kind of socioeconomic base (peasants or farmers), liable to arise in particular socioeconomic circumstances (especially modernization of one sort or another), and perhaps sharing a particular socioeconomic program'. By contrast, political populism is defined as a 'particular kind of political phenomenon where the tensions between the élite and the grass roots loom large'.

More typical, however, have been attempts to situate populist movements along a traditional right-left continuum. Seminal in this regard is Richards' (1981) characterization of populist movements in Canada. Specifically, Richards notes, historically, left populist movements in Canada have tended towards class (farm-labour) alliances; to present a general critique of corporate capitalism; to demand a greater role for the government and state in countering the power of the corporate sector; and to spring from rural cooperative organizations. In contrast, right populist movements have tended to mobilize along regional rather than class lines; to restrict their critique to the power of banks, the money supply, and credit; to view big government as the primary enemy; and to downplay participatory democracy in favour of plebiscites. Richards' typology was subsequently applied by Finkel (1989) to his examination of the Social Credit Party in Alberta, and expanded by David Laycock (1990) into four categories—social democratic populism, radical democratic populism, plebiscitarian populism, and crypto-Liberalism—in his examination of past populist movements in Western Canada.[1]

It is one thing to classify movements. It is another thing to explain them. What factors underlie the rise of populist movements?

Traditional Explanations of Populist Movements

Ever since American journalists first coined the term *populism* in the 1890s, historians and social theorists have tried to define and explain the rise of populist parties. This section examines five prominent explanations.

Economic explanations typically argue that populist movements arise out of the cyclical problems and uncertainties of hinterland or regional economies. The structure of unequal exchanges between the hinterland and a more prosperous centre is viewed as the catalyst for local anger directed at the power of outside economic interests, such as bankers, financiers, and industrialists. One implication of economic explanations is that the more volatile the economy, the greater likelihood of populist unrest. This hypothesis is congruent with relative deprivation theory (see McGuire 1981).

As with economic explanations, *political* explanations contend that populist movements are most likely to arise in hinterland regions. Likewise, economic issues are seen as playing an important role in populist discontent. Nonetheless, the emphasis in political explanations is on powerlessness and alienation: economic issues are merely a consequence of structural inequities in the political realm. Finally, political explanations also typically contain a social-psychological component; that is, populists are viewed as rebelling against a colonial relationship imposed on them by dominant outside interests (see Brodie 1990).

While economic and political explanations of populist movements typically treat them sympathetically as progressive efforts at asserting democratic control, *class* explanations have tended to take a less benign view. Class explanations of populism are drawn initially from Marx and Engels' (1977 [1848]) theory of class conflict as first outlined in *The Communist Manifesto*, and later elaborated on by Lenin (1960, 1970). Class explanations have tended to view populist movements as, first, products of a particular class—the petite bourgeoisie—and, second, as inherently reactionary and nostalgic in attempting to resurrect a mythical utopian past. Until recently, this argument has continued as a staple of much political theory regarding populist movements (see Bell 1993).

Cultural explanations view populist movements as stemming from a disturbance of 'the people's cultural or symbolic order'. A chief proponent of cultural explanations was the historian Richard Hofstadter (1955) who contended that the American agrarian movements of the nineteenth century were irrational, regressive, anti-intellectual, and paranoid. From his descriptions, it is clear that Hofstadter viewed populist movements as motivated largely by nativism. Nativism is a belief forged from a conjunction of nationalism with ethnocultural, religious, and/or racial prejudice, arising during periods of social, political, and/or economic crisis, that tends to focus on an imaginary threat posed by various minority groups (see Palmer 1982). Thus, from a cultural perspective, populist movements might be predicted to arise during periods of rapid demographic and economic change.

More recently, populist movements have been explained from the perspective of *resource mobilization theory* (see McCarthy and Zald 1987; Tilly 1978). This theory notes that discontent is always present in every society. Whether or not a populist alternative arises is determined by the capacity of a leadership to mobilize such resources as people, money, and materials. (See Chapter 8 for more on resource mobilization theory.)

Finally, what is the fate of populist parties? History suggests three—not exclusive—theoretical possibilities. First, the initial passion or circumstances giving rise to a populist party may dissipate (see Zakuta 1975) or the party may disintegrate from internal discord (example: various Western separatist parties). Second, the populist party's ideas and supporters may be co-opted by an existing party (for example, the National Progressives by the Liberals). Third, the populist party may be transformed into a traditional party much like the others (for example, the CCF's change into the New Democratic Party).

Each of these theories offers important insights into the causes and trajectory of populist parties. Most of these ideas also have found a place in studies of populist movements in Canada.

Studies of Populist Movements in Canada

Many exponents of populist politics in Canada borrowed their ideas early on from the American experience. Similarly, many of the early explanations for populist movements also followed those developed in the United States. Thus, economic arguments that viewed American nineteenth-century populism as a regional agrarian response to the increasing scarcity of free land under advanced settlement and the growing power of eastern-based monopoly interests (Buck 1913, 1920; Hicks 1931), resonated subsequently in analyses of Canadian populist movements.

In the federal election of 1921, the newly founded Progressive Party took 65 seats, second only to the victorious Liberals under Mackenzie King. William L. Morton's (1950) later classic study of the Progressives showed that the party's support base was primarily rural, largely Western, and particularly strong in wheat-growing areas. Morton's explanation for this support followed several well-developed models. Economically, Western agrarians in 1921 were upset by the decline of wheat prices following the First World War and the end of subsidies to which they had grown accustomed. Politically, this discontent arose against a backdrop of perceived colonization by central Canada, and a political culture increasingly infused by populist notions imported from the United States.

Like Morton, Seymour M. Lipset's (1950) study of the CCF in Saskatchewan contended that its creation in 1933 and eventual rise to power (in 1944) could be explained by the uncertainty of regional hinterland economies, a resultant sense of regional alienation, and the development of a populist political culture. But Lipset also examined empirically the class, ethnic, and religious bases of CCF support, as well as the role of existing social organizations, particularly the farmers' cooperatives, in mobilizing discontent.

Macpherson's (1953) study of Social Credit in Alberta combined Marxist class theory with political-regional explanations. Specifically, Macpherson contended that Social Credit's meteoric rise to power in 1935 under the leadership of the charismatic William ('Bible Bill') Aberhart could be explained as the reaction of a particular class—the petite bourgeoisie—located in a regional hinterland, whose economic situation during the Depression was growing increasingly bleak. Despite recent refutations of much of Macpherson's class analysis (see Bell 1993), his book nonetheless remains a seminal work in Canadian studies of populism.

More recently, Maurice Pinard (1971) also combined class analysis with declining economic conditions in studying the sudden success of Social Credit's Quebec counterpart, the Créditistes, during the federal election of 1962. According to Pinard, the Créditistes were a rural-based party that appealed primarily to small businesspeople, farmers, and workers, all of whose class position had declined precipitously, relative to the province as a whole, during the recession of the early 1960s. But Pinard also emphasized two other factors important to the rise of a 'third party'. First, Pinard contended that economic and social strains alone are insufficient to result in the rise of a third party; the social and political situation also must be conducive to a third party's emergence. Frequently, this means the weakness of existing parties. Second, Pinard also emphasized the importance of organization and resources in mobilizing the existing discontent, points often noted in passing by previous theorists (see Lipset 1950) but not sufficiently emphasized.

As stimulating as these studies were, however, by the late 1970s, North American debates about populism had reached an impasse. Either explicitly or implicitly, most theorists seemed to regard populist movements as a historical and largely agrarian phenomena, rapidly disappearing under the sway of modern, postindustrial life (Sinclair 1979).

In the 1980s, however, the notion of populism underwent a kind of resurrection in North America. In the United States, Ronald Reagan rode the right-wing populist slogan of 'getting government off the backs of the people' to the presidency in 1980 and again in 1984; while the Newt Gingrich-led Republicans harnessed a similar, albeit short term, appeal in achieving their congressional successes in 1994. Meanwhile, in Canada, a political party also emerged that paid even more explicit homage to the populist past, the Reform Party. What specific factors account for the rise of the Reform Party? To this question and others I now turn.

A Brief History of the Reform Party

Brian Mulroney's Conservatives were elected in 1984, taking a stunning 209 of 295 seats. The Tories had widespread support throughout Canada, but were particularly strong in Quebec and Western Canada, notably Alberta and British Columbia. Yet, within two years, much of this support dissipated, particularly in the West.

Throughout the fall of 1986, disgruntled Westerners—many of them former Tory supporters—met to discuss their grievances. As a result of these meetings, an assembly was held in Vancouver in the spring of 1987, attended by three hundred people, at which it was decided to launch a new political party. This was followed by a convention, held in Winnipeg in October of 1987, at which the party formally acquired its name—the Reform Party of Canada—and its first leader, Preston Manning, the well-known son of Ernest Manning, Alberta's former Social Credit premier.

The 1988 federal election saw Reform run candidates in a number of Western Canadian ridings. While the party failed to win any seats, it captured 275,767 votes and a respectable 8.5 per cent of the votes in ridings it contested.

Reform won its first parliamentary seat the following spring in a by-election. Later the same year, a Reform Party candidate, Stan Waters, won a seat in the senate in Canada's first election to that house. Reform's standing in public opinion polls continued to rise throughout 1990–91 bolstered by the party's opposition to such things as the Meech Lake Accord and the Goods and Services Tax (GST), and support for smaller government, debt reduction, and a tougher stance on crime.

The 1993 federal election saw Reform capture 52 seats, finishing third behind the victorious Liberals (177 seats) and just shy of the Bloc Québécois, which (with 54 seats) became Canada's Official Opposition party. Reform continued its remarkable rise in the 1997 federal election, garnering 60 seats (to the Liberal's 155 seats and the Bloc's 44), in becoming Canada's Official Opposition party.

While Reform obtained more seats in 1997 than in 1993, its total votes actually declined. More fundamentally, Reform had failed to make electoral inroads east of Manitoba. The percep-

tion that Reform had 'stalled' resulted in renewed efforts after 1997 to unite Canada's right wing. Thus, in early 2000, Reform disbanded in favour of the Canadian Reform Conservative Alliance Party. The Alliance Party's new leader, Stockwell Day, a prominent—if controversial—former Alberta politician, gave the party a younger, fresher image and immediately attracted increased corporate support. For many observers and long time Reformers, however, the new party seemed increasingly like the other parties, in policy and style. Though Alliance garnered a greater percentage of votes in 2000 than Reform had in 1997, increased its number of Parliamentary seats to 66, and maintained its Official Opposition status, the party once more found itself largely confined to Western Canada (Table 10.1).

No matter the eventual result of the Alliance 'experiment', Reform's rapid rise to political prominence during the 1990s was remarkable. How do we explain the party's success?

Explaining Reform's Rise

It seems correct that, during Reform's formative period, much of its appeal reflected public animosity directed at the then-governing federal Tories, particularly their leader, Brian Mulroney. The majority of Reform voters in 1993 were lapsed Tory supporters (Pammett 1994). Subjective factors, however, are insufficient to explain Reform's continued success in 1997 and thereafter. We need to look for deeper explanations.

Note that Reform's support was particularly strong in the West's two wealthiest provinces, British Columbia and Alberta. These provinces provided the majority of delegates to Reform's founding convention (Harrison 1995) and supplied the majority of Reform's MPs in both 1993 and 1997, as well as those of the Alliance Party in 2000. Two factors explain this geographically located support.

First, regional alienation has a long and deep history in both Alberta and British Columbia. In

Table 10.1 Number of Votes (000s), Percentage of Votes, and Members Elected, by Province, for the Reform and Alliance Parties, 1993, 1997, and 2000

Province/ Territory	1993 Votes	1993 % Vote	1993 Elected	1997 Votes	1997 % Vote	1997 Elected	2000 Votes	2000 % Vote	2000 Elected
Newfoundland	2.3	1	0	5.6	3	0	8.8	4	0
Prince Edward Island	.7	1	0	1.0	1	0	3.7	5	0
Nova Scotia	60.4	13	0	45.0	10	0	41.6	10	0
New Brunswick	32.6	8	0	52.2	13	0	60.2	16	0
Quebec*	0	0	0	10.9	0	0	212.4	6	0
Ontario	982.7	20	1	878.8	19	0	1048.8	24	2
Manitoba	120.9	22	1	112.3	24	3	148.3	30	4
Saskatchewan	132.6	27	4	157.8	36	8	206.0	48	10
Alberta	629.4	52	22	575.3	55	24	736.0	59	23
British Columbia	593.6	36	24	644.9	43	25	790.9	49	27
N.W.T./Nunavut**	2.0	8	0	2.4	12	0	2.3	11	0
Yukon	1.9	13	0	3.4	25	0	3.7	28	0
Canada	2,559.2	19	52	2,490.0	19	60	3,262.8	25	66

N* Reform did not run candidates in Quebec in 1993.

** Nunavut was created after the 1997 election. Reform did not run candidates in Nunavut in 2000. The totals for the Northwest Territories and Nunavut are combined, however, for ease of comparison over time.

SOURCE: Elections Canada, 1993, 1997, 2000.

both provinces, alienation also has a long history of attachment to right-wing politics through several Social Credit governments—a party linked by the Manning name to the Reform Party. Thus, when seeking out a political alternative, voters in these provinces feel more comfortable in selecting parties from this area of the political spectrum.

Second, as previously noted, volatile economies are likely to lead to volatile politics. While Alberta and British Columbia are wealthier than either Saskatchewan or Manitoba, their economies are also less predictable, more subject to the vagaries of 'boom and bust' cycles. In 1985–86, just prior to Reform's creation, Alberta's economy went into a recession (see Harrison 1995:

96–100; see also Krahn and Harrison 1992). When combined with the aforementioned sense of alienation, the result was a concoction with explosive consequences during the 1990s for the Canadian political system.

Further broadening Reform's appeal during this period was the influence of neoconservative Republicanism streaming across the border during the Reagan-Bush years. This influence was reflected in a growing disenchantment with the state and government, and a greater reliance upon 'free market' solutions. Neoconservatism found in Alberta a particularly hospitable environment (see Laxer and Harrison 1995), but was not exclusive to that province. Canadians as a whole were extremely concerned with their economic security, an unease intensified by the recession of 1990–92 and its aftershocks (see Harrison, Johnston, and Krahn 1996).

Adding to these economic worries were political concerns for the future of Canada. Continued demands by a succession of Quebec governments for greater autonomy and recognition of that province's cultural uniqueness were chief concerns, and increased hostility toward Quebec among non-Quebecers. But Quebec's demands also intensified the effects of an identity crisis faced by English-speaking Canadians in the wake of the erosion of Anglo-Canadian institutions, the heightened intrusion of American culture, and changes in Canada's ethnic-demographic profile due to immigration (Harrison 1995). Reform was able to tap into many of these insecurities felt by English-speaking Canadians.

As Pinard (1971) noted, however, discontent is a necessary but not sufficient cause for the rise of a populist party. Discontent must be channelled and organized. Reform's success proves the point. From the beginning, Reform was supported by highly influential members of Western Canada's political and business establishment. The party also had (at least unofficially) a 'party organ'—the *Alberta Report* and its magazine affiliates—with which to disseminate its message. In Preston Manning, the party also had a well-known and capable leader—one in fact steeped in the tradition of Canadian populist lore—able to call upon symbols that connected with the concerns of many Canadians (Flanagan 1995; Sharpe and Braid 1992). Over time, Reform became a fully modern political party, replete with advertising agencies, pollsters, media communications, and a large and active membership (see Harrison 1995: 190–9).

In summary, by the late 1980s, many English-speaking Canadians sensed that the country was in crisis. Furthering this sense was the perception that the existing political parties had failed to deal effectively with the crisis. As the latter became de-legitimated in the eyes of much of the public, a political space was created during the 1990s for an alternative party that could declare its solidarity with 'the people' of Canada (Harrison 1995).

A Profile of Reformers

No party truly represents all 'the people'. Reform, like all political parties, garnered its strongest support among a particular constituency. Reform supporters tended to be English speaking, older, well-educated, Protestant males, of Anglo-European descent, with moderately high incomes. A significant number of Reform delegates, general members, and supporters were farmers, while many others occupied technical and/or professional occupations, or owned small businesses. Reform attracted disproportionately few union members. Finally, while Reform was overrepresented by rural dwellers, the bulk of its support was urban (Harrison 1995).

Reform Party supporters also tended to be somewhat ideologically distinct, seeing themselves as far to the right of traditional parties in Canada. They held very specific ideas on certain issues. In general, Reformers—whether convention delegates, party members, or merely electoral supporters—tended to be strongly, distinctively, and unanimously anti-government (and very pro-free market), anti-social welfare (that is, the welfare state and assorted policies), and hostile to what they termed as 'special interests' (for example, women's groups, and ethnic minorities). They tended also to be strongly opposed to multiculturalism, bilingualism, current immigration policy, and the granting of 'distinct society' status to Quebec (see Archer and Ellis 1994; Harrison and Krahn 1995; Harrison, Johnston, and Krahn 1996; Laycock 1994; Patten 1994). More generally, Reform's ideology can be best described as combining traditional liberal economic beliefs and traditional moral conservatism (an amalgam often referred to as 'neoconservatism') with right-wing populism (see Dobbin 1991; Flanagan 1995; Harrison 1995; Sharpe and Braid 1992).

Following the proposition that a person's beliefs are at least partially grounded in their social circumstances, we can note a certain congruency between these beliefs and the background characteristics of many Reformers. For example, we can note that many Reformers were of Anglo-Saxon-Celtic or European background. The social status and power of these groups declined considerably after the 1960s relative to francophone Quebecers and visible minorities—two groups towards whom many Reformers tended to harbour particularly negative attitudes. Likewise, it is not surprising that many Reformers were opposed to such policies as multiculturalism and immigration from non-European countries.

Similarly, it has been noted that farmers, and rural voters in general, made up a disproportionate percentage of Reform support. It seems likely that the declining income and status of farmers, and the loss of the rural way of life in general, over the past 30 years resulted in the kind of rural revolt to which a populist party such as Reform might appeal. The decline of male status and position in Canadian society during the same period would seem also to explain the overrepresented number of males among Reform supporters and weak support among party supporters for policies of gender equality (see Harrison 1995: 207–8).

More broadly, Reform can be viewed as the product of a series of economic, social, and political crises that beset Canada's liberal-welfare state beginning in the mid-1970s. The failure of existing parties to address these crises in turn alienated many voters and finally broke down the long-standing system of electoral coalitions. Put another way, Canada's traditional political parties failed, in the midst of a series of crises, to fulfil their central functions of representing the demands of their constituents and thereby *containing* discontent. As the allegiance of various individuals and

groups to existing political parties loosened, the opportunity was created for a populist party such as Reform that proclaimed its mission to represent the Canadian 'people' (Harrison 1995).

Why, however, did a right-wing form of populism arise? In part, this can be explained by the fact there was already a left-wing party—the New Democrats. Because the NDP had never been in power federally, left-wing supporters were not disappointed in their performance and hence did not seek out another left-wing alternative. By contrast, Reform arose precisely because the Conservative Party had gained power in 1984, but thereafter disappointed its supporters as not being conservative enough.

But Reform's rise also must be viewed in the context of broader historical currents. These currents, involving a crisis of the postwar Keynesian welfare state, have washed over several Western industrialized countries in recent decades, resulting in similar policies of smaller government, free markets, and privatization. In calling for the implementation of similar policies, Reform touched a long tradition of populism in North America.

What is the basis of North American populism? In contrast to Western Europe, where right-wing populism is relatively an ineffectual movement populated by fringe elements (see Betz 1994), why is populism such a potent and recurrent force in North American politics?

The Foundations of North American Populism

I argue that the rise of the Reform Party can be traced to the gradual breakdown, after the mid-1970s, of the traditional political coalitions that had underpinned the Canadian political system since the Second World War. I want to further suggest that, more broadly, certain structural and political-cultural features make it more likely that political coalitions in North America are more likely to fragment than similar coalitions in Europe, and that this fragmentation predisposes the greater possibility of populist parties emerging.

Precisely, I argue that North American society—the United States even more than Canada—is highly individualized, with people bound less to traditional institutions than are Europeans. As a result, the benefits of allegiance to traditional parties are low, as are the costs of mobilizing against such parties, or against the political system as a whole. By contrast, the greater social solidarity of European society renders high both the benefits of continued allegiance and the consequent costs of opposition.

Several structural features predispose Europe's greater degree of social solidarity. By contrast with Canada and the United States, European countries are ethnically more homogeneous, though this is changing. Largely unhindered by ethnic cleavages, social conflicts in Europe historically tended instead to occur along either religious or class lines (Korpi 1983). With modernity, religious conflicts also began to abate, while the strength of Europe's working class, in solidarity with agrarians in several countries, resulted over time in the institutionalization of class conflict. This process of institutionalization in Europe occurred in three interrelated ways. First, high rates of unionization (see Krahn and Lowe 1998: 334–7) reduced conflicts within the working class. Second, the implementation of a corporatist, tripartite system of decision-making contained conflicts between labour and capital. Third, the creation of an elaborate system of welfare state provisions after the Second World War bound citizens as a whole, either as consumers or providers, to their respective states (see Esping-Andersen 1990; Keegan 1993).

By contrast, largely unrecognized regional, racial, ethnic, and gender differences in both the United States and Canada historically have fragmented social solidarity (Korpi 1983; Laxer 1989). These differences have further obscured—though not prevented—class conflict, and

thwarted the extensive level of union solidarity found in Europe (see Krahn and Lowe 1998). Furthermore, the kind of welfare state regimes that arose in Canada and the United States after 1945 were minimalist in both extent and intent (see Esping-Andersen 1990; Keegan 1993), and did little to bandage over the structural cleavages.

In brief, only the extreme fringe elements in Europe escape the intricate bonds that link the state and civil society. The characteristics of radical right-wing supporters in Europe prove the point (see Betz 1994). By contrast, in North America it is not only fringe elements who remain outside of the political 'centre', but also significant numbers of the working and middle classes. The strength of these classes provides the basis for the populist movements and parties that arise: note, for example, the high educational, income, and occupational statuses of most Reformers (Harrison 1995).

These social-structural differences underpin further differences in ideology that precondition the greater possibility of populist parties arising in North America. In general, North America's political culture can be said to differ from that of Western Europe along the following ideological dimensions: less deference to established authorities; a greater emphasis on individualism; a greater mistrust of the notion of government in general; and a greater belief in the desirability of a separation of political and economic spheres.

The connection between these ideological features of North American political culture and populism seems obvious. Low levels of deference to authority and an inherent mistrust of government increase the likelihood of populist actions against the state. Likewise, the belief that politics should be separate from economics limits what governments can do for people, even as they frequently get blamed when the economy goes wrong, hence, furthering the state's delegitimation. Finally, except in times of immediate threat (for example, war), the ethos of individualism reduces the state's collectivist appeal.

In short, certain structural and ideological features of North American society make it likely that people will become alienated from traditional institutions, that political coalitions will fragment, and that people will be attracted by political leaderships arising from outside the existing party system. Still, a question arises: If North American society is so prone to populist appeals, why do not more populist parties abound? Certainly, the notoriously low level of voting in American elections—barely 50 per cent in the 2000 presidential election, much lower among specific ethnic groups—supports the notion that a lot of that country's citizens are in fact politically alienated.

Two answers. First, the centralization of power in Washington, the entrenchment of the Republican and Democratic party machines in office, and the intrusion of excessive capital into the American political system (see Phillips 1994) make virtually impossible the creation of a meaningful 'third party' in that country. Only a committed and wealthy egotist (for example, Ross Perot) could hope to do so. By contrast, Canada's more decentralized political system and low limits of political spending have allowed for the rise of regional political parties, such as Reform. It is highly unlikely that Preston Manning could have gotten the Reform Party off the ground in the United States.

Second, the same individualism and social isolation that renders support for the state or political parties tenuous in North America also makes it difficult to mobilize opposition to them. For North American sociologists, conflict may have a social context, grounded in race, ethnicity, class, gender, etc. In much of the public consciousness, however, conflict remains at the level of the 'personal' (Mills 1961). In a sense, political and social stability at the macro-level in the United States, and to a lesser degree Canada, is a product not of the containment or resolution of conflicts, but rather their reduction to the level of individual encounters. Nonetheless, sufficient conditions of

alienation and fragmentation exist for populist parties to occasionally arise, and with force.

Traditional vs. Modern Populism: A Comparison

Preston Manning equated Reform to the great populist parties of the past, notably the Progressives (Harrison 1995; Manning 1992). In some ways, he was correct in doing so. Reform's appeal to many Canadians can only be understood in a context of long-held Western grievances. Likewise, Reform's articulation of Canada's problems borrowed heavily from populism in its defence of 'the people' against various threats. But modern populist parties, such as Reform, also differ from their historic counterparts in several important respects.[2]

First, traditional populist movements and parties were largely *gemeinschaft* in nature. People shared more or less similar lifestyles. They met frequently and habitually in face-to-face circumstances, often working and playing together. They shared a common history and culture.

By contrast, modern populist movements are of a *gesellschaft* type: large, impermanent, and formal. The number of members who will ever directly encounter each other is few. Indeed, to the extent modern populists constitute a community, it is what Benedict Anderson (1983) has referred to as an 'imagined community', connected by televisions, newspapers, and computers. The Reform Party's attempts at 'teledemocracy'—the holding of nationwide electronic town hall meetings—are archetypal of modern populist efforts to achieve an imaginary unity (see Barney 1995).

A related second difference between traditional and modern populist movements resides in their relation to the economy. The great populist movements of the past, whether industrial labourers or agrarians, were producer-based. In the manner suggested by Marx and Engels (1977), a consciousness of one's class and other interests emerged enabling political action against an identifiable group—frequently owners, bankers, and politicians.

Modern populist parties are instead consumer-based. In part, this fact proceeds from the gradual *embourgeoisment* and fragmentation of the working class, the eclipse of agrarian life, and the rise of new technologies. But it also reflects a change in cultural values. In contrast to traditional societies, people in modern societies are defined not by what they produce, but by what they possess (Macpherson 1962) or, more particularly, consume (Veblen 1979). This change has important consequences for political action. While production is necessarily social, consumption is necessarily individual.

This transformation from producer-populism to consumer-populism can further be viewed as a product of what is termed *globalization* and the erasure of state borders (Marchak 1993). Producer-populism is linked to collective notions of mutuality and citizenship; consumer-populism is linked to a series of individualizing identities—consumer, customer, client, taxpayer. Producer-populism, no less than citizenship, arises out of the state (Kincaid 1994: 78); consumer-populism reflects the state's declining importance in the lives of some elements—frequently well off—within modern Western society. Producer-populism is tied emotionally and otherwise to a 'territory'; consumer-populism recognizes allegiance to no territory. Consumer-populists want simply 'the best deal'. Their 'place of residence' could be a Wal-Mart store.

At the same time as globalization weakens the basis for collective action, however, it also increases peoples' sense of powerlessness and anxiety. The result has frequently been the rise of defensive communalism and 'tribalism' (Schlesinger 1997)—a resurrection of populist unrest against 'unseen' and ill-defined enemies.

This resurrection of populism in the time of globalization underscores a final, third difference

between traditional and modern populism: to wit, the change in the nature of the perceived 'enemy' identified in North American populist discourse. Traditionally, populist parties, whether of the right-wing or left-wing variety, spoke of the 'big interests'. In the case of the former, this frequently meant the banks, less often government; in the case of the latter, 'big interests' referred to businesspeople and corporations with, more generally, capitalism as the ultimate enemy.

In the 1960s, however, the New Left emerged, embracing new social groups—that is, not simply the Old Left's reliance on the working class—as the vanguard of social change. In response, the discursive terms used by right-wing populists also began to change. No longer do they speak of 'big interests'; rather, they condemn 'special interests', among them feminists, gays, public sector workers, and visible minorities. In the eyes of supporters of New Right parties, such as Reform (see Harrison, Johnston, and Krahn 1996; Laycock 1994; Patten 1994) and Alliance, 'special interests' have been able to garner public monies to advance causes to which, as individual taxpayers and consumers, they do not wish to contribute.

Conclusion

Like all populist parties, the Reform Party arose in response to a series of political, economic, and social crises that delegitimated the existing parties and fragmented their electoral coalitions. In putting together the new party, Preston Manning and the rest of Reform's leadership relied on a typically populist appeal to 'the people' of English-speaking Canada. This appeal found particular resonance among certain elements of Canadian society, notably Western Canadians and members of the middle class.

More broadly, Reform can be viewed as part of the wider economic crisis facing the postwar Western welfare states, a crisis reflected in rising unemployment and lowered profits. At the same time, however, this crisis did not result in Western Europe in the same degree of success for right-wing populist parties as found in North America. The reasons for the greater appeal of populism in North America are both structural and ideological, and relate to issues of social solidarity and political containment.

Finally, populism must be understood in its proper historical context. While modern populism bears similarities to traditional populism, it also differs in several important respects. Modern populism has been impacted by the same global changes that otherwise have occurred in society. These changes in turn have altered populism's methods and capacity for mobilization, the nature of its appeal, and the focus of its support.

Notes

1. Betz (1994) offers a further typological distinction between two types of right-wing populism in Europe today, neoliberalism, defined by a belief in individualism, free markets, and a minimal state; and national populism, which draws its appeal more from notions of a national culture, bordering on xenophobia. He contends that the agenda of most of the right-wing populist parties in Western Europe has moved over time from neoliberalism to nationalism.

2. Harrison (2000) details differences between traditional and modern populism in the specific case of Alberta.

References

Anderson, B. 1983. *Imagined Communities: Reflections on the Origin and Spread of Nationalism* (London: Verso).

Archer, K., and F. Ellis. 1994. 'Opinion Structure of Party Activists: The Reform Party of Canada', *Canadian Journal of Political Science* 27(2): 277–308.

Barney, D. 1995. 'Pushbutton Democracy: The Reform Party and the Real World of Teledemocracy', paper presented to the Annual Meeting of the Canadian Political Science Association, Montreal, June 4–6.

Bell, E. 1993. *Social Classes and Social Credit* (Montreal/Kingston: McGill-Queen's University Press).

Betz, H.-G. 1994. *Radical Right-Wing Populism in Western Europe* (New York: St. Martin's Press).

Brodie, J. 1990. *The Political Economy of Canadian Regionalism* (Toronto: Harcourt Brace Jovanovich Canada).

Buck, S. 1913 [rpt. 1965]. *The Granger Movement: A Study of Agricultural Organization and Its Political, Economic and Social Manifestations* (Lincoln: University of Nebraska Press).

———. 1920. *The Agrarian Crusade: A Chronicle of the Farmer in Politics* (Toronto: Brook and Company).

Canovan, M. 1981. *Populism* (New York: Harcourt Brace Jovanovich).

Conway, J.F. 1978. 'Populism in the United States, Russia, and Canada: Explaining the Roots of Canada's Third Parties', *Canadian Journal of Political Science* 11(1): 99–124.

Dobbin, M. 1991. *Preston Manning and the Reform Party* (Toronto: Lorimer).

Elections Canada. 1993. *Thirty-Fifth General Election: Official Voting Results* (Ottawa: Chief Electoral Officer of Canada).

———. 1997. *Thirty-Sixth General Election: Official Voting Results* (Ottawa: Chief Electoral Officer of Canada).

———. 2000. *Thirty-Seventh General Election: Preliminary Voting Results*. Online: http://www.elections.ca

Esping-Andersen, G. 1990. *The Three Worlds of*

Welfare Capitalism (Princeton, NJ: Princeton University Press).

Finkel, A. 1989. *The Social Credit Phenomenon in Alberta* (Toronto: University of Toronto Press).

Flanagan, T. 1995. *Waiting for the Wave: The Reform Party and Preston Manning* (Toronto: Stoddart).

Harrison, T. 1995. *Of Passionate Intensity: Right-Wing Populism and the Reform Party of Canada* (Toronto: University of Toronto Press).

———. 2000. 'The Changing Face of Prairie Politics: Populism in Alberta', *Prairie Forum* (special issue) 25(1): 107–22.

———, and H. Krahn. 1995. 'Populism and the Rise of the Reform party in Alberta', *Canadian Review of Sociology and Anthropology* 32(2): 127–50.

Harrison, T., W. Johnston, and H. Krahn. 1996. 'Special Interests and/or New Right Economics? The Ideological Bases of Reform Party Support in Alberta in the 1993 Federal Election', *Canadian Review of Sociology and Anthropology,* 33(2): 159–79.

Hicks, J. 1931. *The Populist Revolt: A History of the Farmers' Alliance and the People's Party* (Minneapolis: University of Minnesota Press).

Hofstadter, R. 1955. *The Age of Reform: From Bryan to F.D.R.* (New York: Alfred A. Knopf).

Keegan, W. 1993. *The Spectre of Capitalism* (London: Vintage).

Kinkaid, J. 1994. 'People, Persons, and Places in Flux: International Integration versus National Fragmentation'. In *Integration and Fragmentation: The Paradox of the Late Twentieth Century,* eds G. Laforest and D. Brown (Kingston: McGill-Queen's University Press).

Korpi, W. 1983. *The Democratic Class Struggle* (London: Routledge & Kegan Paul).

Krahn, H., and T. Harrison. 1992. '"Self-referenced" Relative Deprivation and Economic Beliefs: The Effects of the Recession in Alberta', *Canadian Review of Sociology and Anthropology* (special issue) 29(2): 191–209.

Krahn, H., and G. Lowe. 1998. *Work, Industry, and Canadian Society,* 3rd edn (Scarborough, ON: Nelson Canada).

Laclau, E. 1977. *Politics and Ideology in Marxist Theory: Capitalism—Fascism—Populism* (London: New Left Books).

Laxer, G. 1989. *Open For Business: The Roots of Foreign Ownership in Canada* (Toronto: University of Toronto Press).

———, and T. Harrison. 1995. *The Trojan Horse: Alberta and the Future of Canada* (Montreal: Black Rose).

Laycock, D. 1990. *Populism and Democratic Thought in the Canadian Prairies, 1910 to 1945* (Toronto: University of Toronto Press).

———. 'Reforming Canadian Democracy? Institutions and Ideology in the Reform Party Project', *Canadian Journal of Political Science* 27(2): 213–48.

Lenin, V. 1960 [1894]. 'The Economic Content of Narodism and the Criticism of Mr. Struve's book'. In *Collected Works* (Moscow: Foreign Languages Publishing House).

———. 1970 [1897]. 'The Heritage We Renounce'. In *Selected Works* (Moscow: Progress Publishers).

Lipset, S.M. 1950 [rpt. 1968]. *Agrarian Socialism: The Cooperative Commonwealth Federation in Saskatchewan* (Garden City, NY: Doubleday).

Macpherson, C.B. 1953. *Democracy in Alberta: Social Credit and the Party System* (Toronto: University of Toronto Press).

———. 1962. *The Political Theory of Possessive Individualism* (Oxford: Oxford University Press).

McCarthy, J., and M. Zald (eds). 1987. *Social Movements in an Organizational Society: Collected Essays* (New Brunswick, NJ: Transaction Books).

Manning, P. 1992. *The New Canada* (Toronto: Macmillan).

Marchak, P. 1993. *The Integrated Circus: The New Right and the Restructuring of Global Markets* (Kingston/ Montreal: McGill-Queen's University Press).

Marx, K., and F. Engels. 1977 [1848]. 'The Communist Manifesto'. In *Karl Marx: Selected Writings*. D. McLellan ed. (Oxford: Oxford University Press).

Mills, C.W. 1961. *The Sociological Imagination* (New York: Grove Press).

Morton, W.L. 1950 [rpt. 1978]. *The Progressive Party in Canada* (Toronto: University of Toronto Press).

Palmer, H. 1982. *Patterns of Prejudice: A History of Nativism in Alberta* (Toronto: McClelland & Stewart).

Pammett, J. 1994. 'Tracking the Votes'. In *The Canadian General Election of 1993*, eds A. Frizzell, J.H. Pammett, and A. Westall (Ottawa: Carleton University Press).

Patten, S. 1993. 'Populist Politics? A Critical Re-examination of "Populism" and the Character of [the] Reform Party's Populist Politics', paper presented to the Annual Meeting of the Canadian Political Science Association, Ottawa, June 6–8.

———. 1994. 'A Political Economy of Reform: Understanding Middle Class Support for Manning's Right-Libertarian Populism', paper presented to the Annual Meeting of the Canadian Political Science Association, Calgary, June 12–14.

Phillips, K. 1994. *Arrogant Capital: Washington, Wall Street, and the Frustration of American Politics* (Toronto: Little, Brown).

Pinard, M. 1971. *The Rise of a Third Party: A Study in Crisis Politics* (Englewood Cliffs, NJ: Prentice-Hall).

Richards, J. 1981. 'Populism: A Qualified Defence', *Studies in Political Economy* 5: 5–27.

Schlesinger, A. Jr. 1997. 'Has Democracy a Future?' *Foreign Affairs* 76(5): 2–12.

Sharpe, S., and D. Braid. 1992. *Storming Babylon. Preston Manning and the Rise of the Reform Party* (Toronto: Key Porter Books).

Sinclair, P. 1979. 'Class Structure and Populist Protest: The Case of Western Canada'. In *Society and Politics in Alberta: Research Papers*, ed. C. Caldarola (Toronto: Methuen).

Tilly, C. 1978. *From Mobilization to Revolution* (Reading, MA: Addison-Wesley).

Veblen, T. 1979 [1899]. *The Theory of the Leisure Class* (Markham: Penguin).

Zakuta, L. 1975. 'Membership in a Becalmed Social Movement'. In *Prophecy and Protest: Social Movements in Twentieth-Century Canada*, eds S.D. Clark, J.P. Grayson, and L.M. Grayson (Toronto: Gage).

Chapter 11

Prairie Politics: Why 'Right' in Alberta but 'Left' in Saskatchewan?

Edward Bell

Introduction

An enduring paradox of Canadian society is the predominance of 'right-wing' politics in Alberta while the 'left-wing' variety prevails in Saskatchewan. Why would these two provinces, which are ostensibly so alike, have such different politics? Why, for example, was the Social Credit movement able to come to power in Alberta but not Saskatchewan? What allowed the Co-operative Commonwealth Federation to form the government in Saskatchewan but not Alberta? Why is there at present a conservative government in Edmonton but a social democratic one in Regina? Although one runs the risk of oversimplification in searching for a single factor or group of factors that can answer all of these questions, the differences in the politics of these two provinces become more intelligible once a few key issues are explained.

The explanation of Alberta-Saskatchewan differences offered here will involve more than a discussion of the politics and history of two Canadian provinces. An important theoretical issue is also at stake: the role of human agency in the making of history, and the place of human agency in the theories of political behaviour that dominate the social sciences. For if these two provinces are similar in a number of key respects, yet are characterized by different political behaviour, theories of politics will have to go beyond a discussion of macro-sociological factors (such as those pertaining to class, ethnicity, and gender) and embrace the concept of human agency. That is, if different social outcomes arise from similar social conditions, it follows that there is a certain *indeterminacy* about social phenomena. This indeterminacy may be explained, at least in part, by human agency or will. This is not to say that the macro-sociological variables that social scientists traditionally use to explain social behaviour are of no value or, to paraphrase Margaret Thatcher, that society does not exist. It simply means that there may be more room for human agency in explaining politics and society than most theories acknowledge.

Another caveat is in order. Saying that human will can affect the course of history is not to say that we have the ability to mould history exactly as we please. As in everyday life, our chosen actions may indeed have real effects, but those effects, alas, may be very different from the ones intended.

The first task in explaining anything is providing a clear description of what is to be explained. Much of the discussion that follows is devoted to an examination of how the politics of these two provinces differ. Although that seems straightforward enough, the issue is in fact fraught with controversy and misunderstanding. The discussion will begin with an examination of the early political history of the two provinces.

Early History

The politics of Alberta and Saskatchewan were quite similar upon their creation in 1905. A Liberal government in Ottawa, through newly appointed lieutenant-governors, called upon prominent Liberals in both provinces to form the government until provincial elections could be held. This meant that the party controlled both federal and provincial patronage which it could dispense to bolster its public support. The Liberal party tended to be popular in the region even without the advantage of patronage, as it had organized the mass immigration that had brought most of the people to the area, and was more inclined than the Conservatives to favour lower tariffs for imported goods, a key issue in agrarian politics. The Liberals were elected to office in both provinces several months after province-hood had been achieved.

At the time of their creation, both Alberta and Saskatchewan were predominantly farming regions, with agrarian politics and organization figuring prominently in their early histories. In Alberta the dominant farm organization was the United Farmers of Alberta (UFA), which was formed in 1909 with the merging of two rival farm groups. The UFA was a powerful lobby group in Alberta politics; according to L.G. Thomas (1959: 206), the UFA convention had more influence in provincial affairs than the legislature.

The Saskatchewan Grain Growers' Association (SGGA) was the leading farm organization in that province. Like the UFA, the SGGA was a powerful lobby group that had considerable influence on the governing Liberals. It was successful in persuading the province to undertake a number of projects to assist farmers, including the establishment of a provincially owned telephone system (Lipset [1950] 1971: 73).

The agrarian groups in both provinces tried to convince federal governments of the day to improve the position of the farmer through ad-justments to freight rates and rail service, changes in grain marketing policies, and reductions in tariffs on imported goods. They also organized cooperative ventures such as grain companies to sell members' grain at the Winnipeg exchange, and farmer-owned grain elevators. Cooperative retail outlets for farm supplies and consumer goods were set up as well.

The first significant difference in the politics of the two provinces emerged in the relationship that the agrarian organizations had with the ruling provincial Liberals. In Saskatchewan there was a 'carefully cultivated tie' between the Liberals and the SGGA (Lipset ([1950] 1971: 76; see also Wood [1924] 1975: 340–1). Prominent SGGA leaders such as W.R. Motherwell, Charles Hamilton, J.A. Maharg, George Langley, and Charles Dunning were also Liberal cabinet members. Cooptation of agrarian leaders by both provincial and federal Liberal governments would characterize Saskatchewan politics until the election of the CCF in 1944.

In Alberta, by contrast, UFA leader Henry Wise Wood persuaded the agrarian movement in his province to reject any form of integration with the governing Liberals (Smith 1969: 19). His political philosophy maintains that each occupational group in society, for example, farmers, business, labour, etc., should have its own organizations to pursue the interests of the group, and that all groups should interact in a genuine spirit of cooperation. The group organizations should not form an allegiance to any party, as the party system, for Wood, compromises the group interests of the less powerful classes (Rolph 1950: 62–6; Sharp 1948: 143–7). This ruled out a close alliance with the Liberals. A provincial Liberal cabinet minister usually attended the UFA's annual convention to explain the government's position on the issues of the day, but that was the extent of the relationship.

Political factors concerning the Liberal Party in each province were to play a crucial role in generating interprovincial differences once the idea of independent political action on the part of farmers gained momentum some 10 years after the two provinces were formed. The farmers' organizations had improved the position of farmers, but unstable prices for wheat and repeated failures to convince the federal government to lower import tariffs led many in the agrarian movement to the conclusion that they would have to take control of governments themselves to make any further progress. They were inspired in this regard by the success of the Non-Partisan League, an agrarian movement formed in North Dakota in 1915 that captured the governor's chair and state legislature in dramatic fashion.

The push for an independent farmers' party brought about an important difference in the politics of Alberta and Saskatchewan. In the years immediately after World War I, agrarians across the country mobilized in both provincial and national organizations for direct political action. The first sign of success was the election of the United Farmers of Ontario in 1919. The United Farmers of Alberta were next, taking power in 1921; their victory was followed by that of the United Farmers of Manitoba in 1922. Nationally, the Progressive Party won 65 seats in the House of Commons in the election of 1921.

In Saskatchewan the outcome was different. Although the Progressives won 15 of 16 seats in the province in the 1921 federal election, the independent provincial farmers' party was stillborn. Reading the postwar situation well, the Liberal government implored SGGA members to reject the call for an independent party, telling them that the government was already controlled by farmers (Lipset [1950] 1971: 76–7). The 1920 association convention considered the issue of independent political action, but there was insufficient support to approve the proposal. The issue was brought up again at the 1921 convention, but again no consensus could be reached. Meanwhile, to distance his party from the federal

Liberal Party, which was falling out of favour, Premier Martin declared that the Saskatchewan Liberal Party was neutral in national politics. To further bolster the party's position, J.A. Maharg, a prominent SGGA leader, was appointed provincial minister of agriculture.

Martin called an election for June 1921, and was rewarded with a legislative majority. Maharg and George Langley, another prominent agrarian activist, were part of the new government.

That a Saskatchewan farmers' party would have indeed spelled the doom of the Liberals, and that the policy of cooptation was indispensable for the latter's survival, is suggested by the success of the 13 independent farmer candidates who ran without the cachet of the SGGA in 1921—all but one were elected.

The Liberal compact of 1921 in Saskatchewan soon began to fall apart. Langley resigned within a few months, while Maharg quit shortly thereafter, angry that Martin's professed neutrality in national politics did not prevent him from campaigning for federal Liberal candidates once his party was returned to power in Regina. Ironically, it was another well-known figure in the SGGA, W.R. Motherwell, running as a Liberal, whom Martin had supported. To complicate matters, Martin resigned before the mandate of 1921 expired, only to be replaced as Liberal premier by C.A. Dunning, another agrarian leader (Wood [1924] 1975: 340–1).

In response to what they viewed as Martin's duplicity in the federal election campaign, the SGGA in 1922 decided in favour of independent political action. The following year, Maharg led sixteen members of the legislature, most of whom had been independent farmer candidates, in opposition to Dunning. The spectacle of farm leader opposing farm leader threatened the unity of the SGGA; to avoid a terminal split in the association the 1924 convention voted to withdraw from provincial politics (Wood [1924] 1975: 341).

There was indeed a great deal at stake for the

Saskatchewan Liberals in the early 1920s. The provincial election of 1921 was held just a few weeks before the UFA defeated the Liberals in Alberta, and they would never recover from the loss—they have been out of power ever since. But the Saskatchewan Liberals, by coopting farmers, were able to dominate their province in the interwar period, losing only one election.

The absence of an independent farmers' party in Saskatchewan and the existence of one in Alberta would have important consequences for the two provinces, consequences that became manifest in the 1930s. One might also note that since Alberta had a class-conscious farmers' party in power in the interwar period, it was the more radical province of the day.

The 1920s were, by and large, prosperous years on the prairies. With a thriving economy, agrarian militancy declined. Politics in the two provinces was primarily concerned with administrative affairs; no fundamental changes in policy were contemplated. The Saskatchewan Liberals had secured legislative majorities in all five elections held from 1905 to 1921, and were re-elected with a majority in 1925. Their grip on power was not broken until 1929, when they were replaced by a Conservative-led coalition. The 1929 election was not fought on agrarian issues, however, as the Progressive movement was a spent force by this time. It was ethnoreligious tensions, exacerbated by a visit from Ku Klux Klan organizers, that toppled the Liberals that year (Archer 1980: 207–12).

Although no one knew it at the time, 1929 was the perfect time to lose an election. In short order, the Depression would set in, sending the region, and the rest of the world, into crisis. The party in power would have to answer for the ravages of poverty and unemployment which no provincial government could stop, but for which any sitting government could be blamed. Also to the Liberals' advantage was the fact that they had by no means been crushed in 1929; they retained

just under half the seats in the legislature.

The United Farmers of Alberta, who had been re-elected in 1926, faced an election in 1930. The Alberta Wheat Pool, a prized creation of the government, had lost a great deal of money with the recent decline in wheat prices, but Premier Brownlee guaranteed its debts and otherwise retained sufficient public confidence to win the election. It was the most disasterous electoral victory in Alberta history.

As the Depression deepened, the governments of Alberta and Saskatchewan faced increasingly hostile publics. Neither government could make any headway in combatting deplorable conditions. The Alberta farmers' party, with the advent of the Depression, affiliated with the CCF, as did the provincial labour party. By the time the 1935 provincial campaign was underway, many Albertans believed that the CCF had been in power for over two years and had done nothing to improve Depression conditions. To make matters worse, the UFA was seriously fragmented into socialist and social credit factions (neither of which was supported by the cabinet), and a personal scandal resulted in the premier's resignation. These events badly discredited the UFA and Labour parties, who were the core of the Alberta CCF. Ben Swankey, who was a Communist activist in Alberta in the 1930s, has remarked that 'to many people the UFA was the CCF in office and they wanted no more of it. The UFA helped to sully the meaning of the word Socialism in Alberta and the CCF never recovered from it' (1980: 35). Social Credit entered the field as the only powerful movement offering an alternative to orthodox government.

In Saskatchewan, the agrarian and labour organizations had the luxury of being on the political sidelines when the Depression struck, thanks to the practice of cooptation. The traditional vehicle for farmer protest, the Liberal Party, was also out of the picture, which meant that neither had been tainted by Depression conditions.

The existence of an unsullied Liberal Party made it difficult for the CCF to gain broad public acceptance in the provincial campaign of 1934. In the next election, the CCF had to outflank a growing Saskatchewan Social Credit movement which split the left vote, taking 16 per cent of the popular vote to the CCF's 19 per cent.

The Social Credit and the CCF movements would leave their signatures on Prairie and national politics. The former would be the first to be elected, in 1935; the latter would take power nine years later. As these two movements are commonly believed to have embodied crucial interprovincial differences, the philosophy and policies of each are considered below.

Social Credit in Alberta

It is often said that Social Credit's accession to power in 1935 and its 36-year tenure in government thereafter is indicative of a predisposition toward right-wing or conservative politics in Alberta. But what did Social Credit stand for in 1935?

The Alberta movement came to power in the midst of the Great Depression, claiming to have a program that could create prosperity in the province and even the world at large. The movement was founded on the ideas of Major C.H. Douglas, a British engineer. Douglas argues that recessions and depressions recur because there is never enough money in circulation to buy up all the goods and services available on the market. For Douglas, the problem with capitalist economies is not production—they are quite capable of producing enough to make everyone wealthy. The problem lies in *distributing* this vast wealth.

Distribution is severely curtailed, he claims, because the public is denied its rightful purchasing power. His A + B theorem maintains that the general public's income derives from 'A' payments, which all businesses make to individuals for things such as wages, salaries, and dividends.

All firms also have to make B payments, which go to other firms for raw materials, bank charges, and so on. It follows from this, he claims, that the value of all goods and services on the market is equal to the sum of all A and B payments, as this is what is paid to produce them. But a serious problem arises because consumers only have incomes totalling all A payments, and so can purchase only a small fraction of all the goods and services available. What is needed is an infusion of 'social credit' equal to all B payments to give consumers incomes equal to A + B, thus enabling them to buy up everything available.

Douglas would have the social credit distributed equally among all citizens. It could take the form of a regular amount issued to each person at fixed times, or it might be disbursed by giving it to businesses in order to allow them to charge a lower, 'just' price for their goods or services. However issued, social credit is not to be paid back or taxed. The credit is not a redistribution of funds acquired through taxation either; it derives from a country's ability to produce goods and services. Eventually, social credit would replace wages and salaries as the public's main source of income.

What separates the general public from a much higher standard of living via social credit are the people who control the banks and other financial institutions. In Douglas's view, these people use their influence to insure that the public remains ignorant of social credit ideas, and above all do their utmost to prevent the implementation of a social credit plan. Such financiers ultimately control the economy and the polity, and amass great fortunes by manipulating currency and credit in their favour. The general public is left to work long hours in meaningless jobs for low wages, never reaching their full potential as human beings. In addition, Douglas was an anti-Semite, often alleging that the pernicious bankers were Jews.[1]

The Alberta movement adopted various aspects of Douglasism, but rejected others and added some ideas and policies of its own. For example, they readily agreed with Douglas that financiers were primarily responsible for the Depression, but neither movement leader William Aberhart nor his successor Ernest Manning were anti-Semitic. (Manning received the National Humanitarian Award from B'nai B'rith in 1982.)[2] There were also social democratic elements in the Alberta program that were absent in Douglasism. For example, the Albertans promised each adult in the province $25 worth of social credit a month if elected (which was a substantial sum in the 1930s), but their explanation of where the money was going to come from differed markedly from Douglas's.[3] At one point, Aberhart claimed that 'there is an enormous spread in price between the producer's cost and the consumer's price. It is the intention under the Social Credit system to reduce this spread' (1935: 27). He promised to take the difference between the capitalist's costs and the consumer's price and distribute it to the public as social credit. This is a major departure from Douglasism, as the founder of the doctrine did not see excessive profits as a serious problem and did not claim that social credit was to be paid for through taxation.

The Aberhartite version of the just price also betrayed a social democratic bent. As Manning explained the policy in 1936, 'no group of consumers should be exploited by anyone having possession of goods, to charge prices that are unfair and excessive,' and the producers of goods 'must be protected from having to produce articles and place them on the market at so low a price that he cannot secure the cost of production, plus something to them for their work' (Manning 1936). For Douglas, prices for consumer goods were definitely too high, not because producers or merchants were exploiting consumers by overpricing and thus taking excessive profits, but because the existing monetary system did not put enough money into the hands of the public.

The movement's position on state medicine also suggests that it advocated left-reform policies that distinguished it from a pure Douglasite movement. The Alberta Social Credit League advocated a comprehensive government-run medical plan that would cover everyone in the province. The medicare program was approved by the Social Credit provincial convention in 1935, and reaffirmed at every convention from 1937 to 1940 (Finkel 1986: 76, 82).

The party's legislative record in its first term of office tells a similar story of support for social democratic policies. In 1936, the party enacted minimum wage laws for men in all occupations except farm and domestic labour. The Tradesmen's Qualification Act protected tradesmen from unqualified competition and the public from inferior workmanship; the Industrial Conciliation and Arbitration Act provided labour with collective bargaining rights; and the Industrial Wages Security Act guaranteed the payment of wages to coal miners (Hooke 1971: 128). These were controversial measures by 1930s standards and were quickly condemned by the Alberta Manufacturers' Association (Barr 1974: 91).

The Alberta Social Crediters were not concerned that their departures from Douglasism would contaminate their ideological purity. In fact they saw their social democratic additions and deletions as a strength rather than a weakness. Manning claimed that their plan to convert excess profits into social credit would belie 'the common hearsay abroad today that Social Credit simply means the socialization of financial credit advocated by various progressive reformers of our day' (*Alberta Social Credit Chronicle*, 10 August 1934: 1, 5). Manning's remarks suggest that in the 1930s, some people misconstrued the movement as one that simply stood for a reform of the financial system. Such misunderstanding was also to characterize many academic interpretations of Social Credit in subsequent decades.[4]

Most scholars share an even more serious misinterpretation of the movement, one that goes beyond being innocent of Social Credit's early social democratic leanings. This appears to stem from a misunderstanding of Douglasism. To be sure, Douglas did maintain that social credit dividends and just prices would rejuvenate the economy. But his vision of what the relations of production and distribution should be are very different from what one finds in the standard works on his thought, which tend to portray Douglasism as monetary tinkering designed to revive capitalism without altering capitalist relations of production.

According to Douglas, capitalist economies do not produce goods that people really need, but rather goods that ultimately make financiers rich. He complained of 'the tawdry "ornament", the jerry-built house, the slow and uncomfortable train service, the unwholesome sweetmeat,' which the current system produces (Douglas 1920: 78). To rectify this situation, he recommends that 'the community' be given the power to decide what is to be produced. The community is also to decide how much consumers will pay for each item (Douglas 1922b: 154). Moreover, the producers of the goods are to be subservient to the community. They are to stand 'fundamentally and unalterably on a basis of Service—it is their business to deliver the goods to order, not to make terms about them' (Douglas 1922a: 35–6). 'The chief owners, and rightful beneficiaries of the modern productive system,' Douglas claims, 'can be shown to be the individuals composing the community, as such' (1933: 50). '[T]he plant of civilization belongs to the community, not to the operators, and the community can, or should, be able to appoint or dismiss anyone who in its discretion fails to use that plant to the best advantage' (Douglas 1922a: 41–2).

What Douglas advocates is a decentralized command economy. The community is to decide what is to be produced and what the prices will be, and productive enterprises are to abide by its decisions. People would use social credit (which

is to be distributed equally and take the place of wages and salaries) to make purchases.

In a Douglasite social system, the formal ownership of all businesses, including the banks, is to remain in private hands. But as the above discussion indicates, businesses are to be strictly controlled by the community. In Douglas's words, there must be 'public control of economic policy through public control of credit' (1921: 91). As they are not free to decide what to produce and what to charge for their goods or services, and the wealth they produce is to be distributed equally through social credit, business owners, large and small, would have a status closer to civil servants than capitalists.[5]

Douglas was asked to explain his plan before an Alberta legislative committee in 1934. A member of the committee asked him 'how we can administer wealth which is privately owned? Does not . . . the Douglas system [entail] . . . social ownership?' Douglas replied, 'I am perfectly certain there is no difficulty whatever in distributing socially privately produced production.' Another committee member read a prepared statement claiming that Douglas is 'urging us to recapture complete constitutional and legal control over all the institutions that sell currency or credit so that the issue of the tickets by means of which, alone, goods and services can circulate, will be subject to public policies of general welfare rather than to considerations of private profit.' To this Douglas replied, 'Broadly speaking, subject to reading it carefully, I should agree with that statement' (Alberta 1934: 104, 106–7).

The Alberta Social Credit movement adopted these policies of Douglas, but with a twist: 'experts' acting in the public interest rather than 'the community' would be directing economic activity. Aberhart explained that his movement stood for '*controlled* individual ownership' of business (1935: 23 [emphasis added]). '[E]xperts would fix the minimum and maximum wage just the same as they could fix the price of goods' (p. 43). 'Alberta

Credit' would replace Canadian currency as the most common medium of exchange. All wages and salaries were to be paid, 'as now, but in credit, not money' (1935: 21). Gross inequalities in wealth were not to be tolerated: 'no one should be allowed to have an income that is greater than he himself and his loved ones can possibly enjoy, to the privation of his fellow citizens' (1935: 55).

Aberhart also promised to distribute 'temporary, supervised credit' to producers to allow them 'to serve the citizenship in the best possible way' (1935: 23). His explanation of how this would work provides an indication of how he wanted the economy to function and what part the state would play in directing economic activity. At the 1934 legislative hearings a committee member said to the Alberta leader, 'I gather from you the credit loans would not be fixed on any flat basis at all but be according to the requirements of the producer.' Aberhart interjected, 'The requirements of the *country or state*. The producer might say I am going to produce this but your control of policy is the same as that of the banks today. They control production by the amount of loans they are willing to give' (Alberta 1934: 74 [emphasis added]). After asking further questions in an attempt to clarify Aberhart's position, the committee member asked, 'Then we have to be the dictators as to the amount of credit any one man must have?' Aberhart replied, 'I think that is about the same position.' The questioner retorted, 'Then that is the same as Soviet Russia. To work out your plan then we have to put the state in a position where it is controlling the individual initiative of the man?' Aberhart answered, 'I would not so control the position of the individual man as much as the banks should do it today. The state should be a better advisor' (1934: 74–5).

That the movement envisioned a system that differed markedly from the existing capitalist one is suggested by the movement's pledge to do away with profits. 'Social Credit Science,' the movement claimed, 'proposes the removal of all profit in its

generally accepted sense and the granting of commission on turnover as a substitute' (Social Credit League of Alberta c1935: 7). While the 'commission on turnover' concept was never spelled out, people on commission normally do not enjoy the prerogatives of ownership such as the power to set wages or prices for the company as a whole, and they do not have a claim on the overall surplus wealth generated by the enterprise.

In their first term of office, the party took a number of steps that were consistent with the notion that production and distribution should be communal matters organized by the government. It printed 'Registration Covenants' that were essentially contracts stating that if the signatory cooperated with the government, he or she would be entitled to the benefits of the social credit system. Four types of covenants were issued. In the Citizens' covenant, for example, people agreed to cooperate with the government and their fellow Albertans 'in providing food, clothing and shelter for every one of us'. In return, registrants were promised 'a just rate of wages' payable in 'Alberta Credit,' and 'reasonable hours of labour.' The government also promised to issue 'monthly dividends'. The covenant for Manufacturers and Processors required that such people 'cooperate with the Alberta Government in planning the supply of goods and produce required for the Province'. For its part, the government agreed to issue Alberta Credit 'primarily for use in purchasing Alberta-made goods and services', as well as establish just prices for the same. The latter would provide manufacturers with 'a fair commission on the turn-over' (*Alberta Gazette*, 15 August 1936: 821–6).

In 1939 the Social Credit administration created a provincial marketing board through which the government could buy or sell any product. The board could also go into the business of manufacturing or distributing any product, and was given the power to purchase or otherwise acquire any land or property it required (Finkel 1986: 75).

Business groups felt threatened by what the Social Credit movement was proposing. The Edmonton Chamber of Commerce believed that Aberhart's plan 'threatens the ultimate mortgaging or confiscation of all private property' (Edmonton Chamber of Commerce 1935: 2); the Calgary Board of Trade feared that the movement's intervention in the economy would be disasterous, claiming that 'any attempt to fix just prices can only result in incredible confusion and paralysis of business. . . . The Social Credit proposals will isolate Alberta and render it impossible for either the farmer or businessman to buy or sell to advantage' (Calgary Board of Trade c1935). Labour groups feared that having 'experts' set wage rates would threaten collective bargaining and the union movement itself (Finkel 1986: 79).

Using the governing party as the criterion, once again it was Alberta that was the radical province of the time.

The CCF in Saskatchewan

Like Social Credit, the Co-operative Commonwealth Federation was a child of the Depression. Its founding conference was held in Calgary in 1932; its first national convention was held in Regina the next year. The organization was a true federation, bringing together diverse farmer, labour, and socialist organizations. Member groups declared their support for the *Regina Manifesto* of 1933, but were given considerable latitude to work out their own policies and progams. Provincial CCF organizations were also formed; they too enjoyed considerable autonomy, including a large measure of independence from the national organization.

In Saskatchewan, the provincial CCF was formed when the Farmer-Labour Group joined the federation. The Farmer-Labour Group had been created through a merging of the United Farmers of Canada (UFC) (Saskatchewan Section) and the Independent Labour Party (Sinclair

1973: 422), the latter being a small urban Fabian socialist party. The UFC itself had been formed in 1926 through the merging of the SGGA and the more militant Farmers' Union (Thomas 1981: 3).

The genealogy of the Saskatchewan CCF illustrates an important difference between it and the Social Credit party in Alberta. The former developed out of the existing agrarian and labour movements; it got its leadership and much of its program from pre-existing class organizations. The Social Credit movement, by contrast, did not spring from the existing politico-economic associations, but was mobilized instead by people who lacked close ties with the UFA and Labour Parties, and who for the most part had never been active in politics. One consequence of this was that in Alberta the Social Credit government had no organizational or ideological ties with the union movement; unions were viewed as one interest group among many, including business.[6]

The *Regina Manifesto* provided, in general terms, the program for the implementation of democratic socialism in Canada. The following excerpt exemplifies the nature and scope of the program:

> We aim to replace the present capitalist system, with its inherent injustice and inhumanity, by a social order from which the domination and exploitation of one class by another will be eliminated, in which economic planning will supercede unregulated private enterprise and competition, and in which genuine democratic self-government, based upon economic equality, will be possible (Young 1969: 304).

The evils of the existing system, the *Manifesto* reads, 'can be removed only in a planned and socialized economy in which our natural resources and the principal means of production and distribution are owned, controlled and operated by the people.' The most famous line of the document is the final one: 'No CCF government will rest content until it has eradicated capitalism and put into operation the full program of socialized planning which will lead to the establishment in Canada of the Co-operative Commonwealth.'[7]

The general terms of the *Manifesto*, like the purposes of the CCF itself, are subject to a number of interpretations. Some CCF supporters viewed their movement as a merging of the agrarian populism that had developed over the previous decades with the trade union movement; for others the CCF was a Canadian version of the British Labour Party; for a minority it was a means to implement Marxism (Richards and Pratt 1979: 35; Thomas 1981: 5).

For Tommy Douglas, who would carry the party to victory in Saskatchewan, the social ownership aspect of the program could take the form of federal, provincial, municipal, or cooperative ownership. But he did not take the view that any and every business enterprise should be socialized. Speaking in 1943 he explained that the CCF 'has never advocated government ownership of any industry in which there is sufficient competition but advocates government ownership only of those industries which have become monopolistic in character' (Larmour 1985: 161).

The Saskatchewan CCF's first attempt to put its program before the electorate came in the 1934 provincial election campaign. Part of the party's platform originated in a motion that had been passed at the 1931 UFC convention recommending that 'use leases' take the place of conventional ownership titles for farm land. Under a use-lease system, the ownership of farm land would be transferred to the provincial government, which would then lease it back to the farmer. The plan was designed to give farmers security of tenure on their land; devastated by depression conditions, many farmers were unable to pay their debts and feared that their farms would be seized by mortgage companies (Hoffman 1975: 54–5). Opposition parties and the press claimed that the use-lease system would be equivalent to

Stalinist collectivization. The party pleaded with the public that the measure was designed to save the family farm, not destroy it, and that farmers would carry on as they always had except that under use-lease no one would take their farms from them.

The policy was poorly understood, even by some of its advocates, and all the ramifications of the program had not been worked out (Hoffman 1983: 51–2). It proved to be such a political liability that the name of the program was changed to 'use-hold' to emphasize that it stood for security of tenure rather than collectivization. The terms of the system were changed as well, making use-hold optional rather than compulsory. Even the watered-down version met with such resistance that the policy was dropped after the 1934 provincial election (Sinclair 1973: 424–5).

The CCF received 24 per cent of the vote in 1934, a very respectable accomplishment for a new movement, but only 5 of 55 seats. Despite the promising showing, party activists were demoralized by the outcome, and became even more so after the party's poor showing in the federal election held the following year.

The CCF in Saskatchewan in 1934 had a much more difficult time getting the public to accept 'socialism' than Alberta Social Crediters had in getting the residents of their province to support 'social credit'. Socialism for many people meant dictatorship, atheism, confiscation, and the horrors of the Soviet experience. There was no equivalent failure of a social credit system that opponents of the Alberta movement could draw on, as no social credit scheme had ever been implemented. The Catholic Church in Saskatchewan implored its followers to reject socialism in 1934; no such admonishment was deemed necessary for potential Social Crediters in Alberta. Another indication of the greater stigma attached to socialism was the treatment CCF supporters were given in Saskatchewan in the 1930s. M.J. Coldwell was fired from his position as principal of a Regina school for his political activities; William Aberhart, also a school principal, was not. The CCF also had the difficulty of trying to get the public to endorse a rather nebulous concept: the cooperative commonwealth. It was much easier for people to relate to Social Credit's infinitely more tangible $25 a month.

The Saskatchewan CCF decided that in order to win greater public support, it would have to downplay its socialist objectives. It also adopted a policy of cooperation with other 'progressive political organizations', including Social Credit (Lipset [1950] 1971: 138–42; McLeod and McLeod 1987: 98–100). The new strategy doubled their seat count to 10 in the 1938 provincial election, but the party's popular vote percentage actually decreased.

After the 1938 election the 'united front' strategy was officially abandoned. Another change that occurred was that Tommy Douglas replaced George Williams as party leader. The CCF fought the 1944 campaign on a combination of specific left-reform policies and broad socialist principles. The former included prevention of foreclosures and evictions, debt moratoria, further development of the cooperative movement, compulsory collective bargaining, socialized health services, and increased old age pensions; the latter was to involve the 'planned development of the economic life of the province and social ownership of natural resources' (Thomas 1981: 9–10).

Social Credit and CCF Rule: A Comparison

The conventional right-left categorization of the two provinces begins to make sense after the CCF took power in Saskatchewan. By this time, Ernest Manning was defending private enterprise and spouting anti-socialist rhetoric in Alberta. This was in marked contrast to the party's position in the 1930s, which openly condemned the capitalist system. The *Alberta Social Credit Chronicle*, for

instance, had taken the view that 'the system of Social Credit can be traced back many thousands of years, but was unfortunately crushed by the capitalist system' (27 July 1934: 3). Also, rank and file Social Crediters had collaborated with socialists and even communists in the 1930s (Finkel 1986: 69, 77–9).

Why anti-socialism all of a sudden? For one thing, the CCF was extremely weak in Alberta in the 1930s and posed no threat to the Social Credit movement, making it pointless to denounce socialism at that time. But by the mid-1940s there was a surge of support for the CCF in Canada, making the provincial wing a viable threat to Social Credit dominance. Secondly, after the failure to implement a social credit plan in their first term of office, the Alberta administration had to choose another economic program to advocate. With the Depression in full retreat, conventional economic policies were the safest bet, and were in any case consistent with the original Social Credit policy of leaving the formal ownership of productive enterprises in private hands.

Also, once elected, radical politicians almost invariably become more conservative. Unforeseen or underestimated barriers to change are encountered, as in the disallowance of Social Credit legislation in their first term of office, and powerful sectors of society are usually unwilling to submit to radical changes.[8] There is also the process of bureaucratic conservatism whereby an organization, political or otherwise, seeks to perpetuate its existence and all the power, prestige, and material benefits that go with it, even if its principles or original purpose are compromised. In the case of Social Credit in Alberta, these factors were augmented by the death of the firebrand Aberhart in 1943 and his replacement by the more cautious Manning.

The CCF was also subject to conservative forces. A 'protest movement becalmed' tradition in the historiography of the CCF-NDP maintains that the organization was transformed from a 'movement' dedicated to fundamental social change into a 'party' primarily interested in holding power (Whitehorn 1992: 2).[9] Most of the Saskatchewan CCF's challenges to existing ways of doing things, with the exception of the medicare program launched in the early 1960s, were undertaken in its first term of office. Even Joe Phelps, who was one of the most radical socialists in the first CCF government, was not immune to the tendency to become more conservative. After only four years in office he adopted the view that labour is not always right in its demands, and that the employer is not always the 'big bad wolf' it once was (Lipset [1950] 1971: 335).

The strongest contrast in the politics of the two provinces existed in the mid-1940s. But in some ways it is a false comparison, as it juxtaposes a government that had grown conservative after a decade in power with a movement coming to power for the first time. The CCF's years in power would set it on a course that would become increasingly similar to the one taken by Social Credit, much reducing the differences between the two governments.

Ernest Manning's economic philosophy for the postwar era was tersely expressed in a comment he made in the legislature in 1954: 'Public ownership is bad in principle, worse in practice' (Richards and Pratt 1979: 67). One might paraphrase the Saskatchewan CCF's philosophy at this time as, 'Public ownership is good in principle, troublesome in practice.'

Natural resource development was a crucial issue at this time. Manning did his best to lure private investment into the province, and was largely successful. The natural gas and oil industries boomed under private ownership, albeit operating under labyrinthine government regulation. The revenues accruing to the government permitted the debts accumulated in the Depression to be paid off, and financed a level of government spending on social services that was often well above the national average (Long and Quo 1972: 6), although opposition parties claimed the oil companies were not contributing enough to the public purse and that labour legislation left much to be desired.

Manning's economic philosophy was flexible to some extent: he did not privatize the provincially owned telephone company or liquor stores, and his government sponsored a plebiscite in 1948 to decide whether privately owned power companies should be converted into a publicly owned utility. (He opposed the latter move and managed to convince a slim majority of Albertans to take the same position.)

The CCF in Saskatchewan also grappled with natural resource development, beginning in its first term of office. Unlike the Manning government, it seriously considered using Crown Corporations to do the job. But it soon became apparent that Crown development of the oil industry was not feasible. Like the Social Credit government of the day, the Saskatchewan government had little expertise in the industry and insufficient capital to invest in such an expensive and risky endeavour. It instead fostered private development of the resource, which in any case was not as abundant as in Alberta. Before long, a similar policy of encouraging private investment was enacted for potash development (Richards and Pratt 1979: 126–39).

The CCF under Douglas did establish a number of Crown Corporations, including a box factory, brick plant, shoe factory/tannery, woollen mill, bus company, sodium sulphate mine, insurance corporation, and a small airline. It also maintained and expanded the pre-existing publicly owned power and telephone companies. The shoe factory/tannery and woollen mill suffered heavy losses and had to be abandoned. The box factory had some successful years but eventually ran up large losses and also had to be closed. The sodium sulphate mine was a success; the airline and brick plant were privatized by the Thatcher Liberals, who defeated the CCF in 1964 and remained in office until 1971 (Richards and Pratt 1979: 111–18).

Recent Decades

There was a change in government in both Alberta and Saskatchewan in 1971. In the former province, the Lougheed Conservatives ended the 36-year reign of Social Credit, but the new government was quite similar in economic philosophy to the Manning regime.[10] The Alberta Conservatives have established a dynasty that is beginning to rival that of Social Credit, as they are now well into their third decade of uninterrupted rule.

The NDP was victorious in Saskatchewan in 1971, and introduced public ownership in both oil and potash through the establishment of Crown Corporations. The party also moved to expand medicare by abolishing user fees and subsidizing prescription drugs. The NDP was out of office again in 1982, being replaced by the Progressive Conservatives, who embarked on a comprehensive program of privatizing Crown Corporations (see Pitsula and Rasmussen 1990). The NDP showed its staying power in the province by winning the elections of 1991, 1995, and 1999.

Alberta-Saskatchewan differences in the postwar era may be summed up as follows. Alberta has had a centre-right government continuously since the mid-1940s. The pattern for Saskatchewan has been one of alternating centre-left and centre-right governments: 20 years of CCF rule, followed by two Liberal terms, followed by two NDP terms, followed by two Progressive Conservative terms, followed by three NDP terms. For the non-CCF/NDP years, Saskatchewan has had governments quite similar in outlook to those existing in Alberta.

Analysis

How can the Alberta-Saskatchewan differences sketched here be explained? Political phenomena, like any form of human behaviour, arise from the interplay of social conditions and human decision-making. Conditions and decisions have a reciprocal relationship: conditions affect decisions and decisions affect conditions. The absence of a farmers' government in Saskatchewan in the 1920s and early 1930s, it appears, was the outcome of astute political decision-making on the part of prominent Liberals. Without a policy of coopting farmers, and farmers' willingness to take this approach to government, it is quite likely that a farmers' party would have been elected in 1921. Conversely, without a Henry Wise Wood counselling against cooptation in Alberta, Liberal rule may well have been prolonged in that province.

The different paths taken in the 1920s largely determined which Depression-inspired movement would come to power years later. In Alberta, the farmers' party was emaciated and humiliated by five years of Depression rule, and could muster only a feeble defence of their realm when challenged by the Social Credit movement. But because of the practice of cooptation, in Saskatchewan the CCF-affiliated agrarian and labour organizations had not had the misfortune of governing during the economic crisis, and so could present themselves as political innocents. Other factors contributed to the Saskatchewan party's breakthrough, including Tommy Douglas's accession to the party leadership, the national surge in support for the CCF in the mid-1940s, and uncharacteristic blundering on the part of the provincial Liberals whereby they took their mandate beyond the five-year limit. That the CCF's victory came shortly before the largest economic boom in history helped as well.

Radical parties were elected in Alberta and Saskatchewan in the 1930s and 1940s. Since about 1944 no government to the left of centre has been in power in Alberta, while in Saskatchewan centre-left governments have alternated with centre-right regimes. How can this difference be explained?

From the late 1940s to roughly 1980, Alberta experienced extraordinary economic growth due primarily to the expanding oil and gas sector.

Manning's strategy to use private capital to develop these industries appeared to have worked—unemployment and taxes were low, wages were rising, and social services were improving. For a province that had been devasted by the Depression, the turnaround was remarkable. To experiment with democratic socialism at this time would have risked killing the goose that laid the golden egg. With a booming economy and expanding social services, there was not a great demand for a social democratic party. Manning's reputation as a sober, hard-working, no-nonsense premier contributed to Social Credit's success as well.

In Saskatchewan, the Douglas regime earned a reputation as a caring, prudent administration. This established the party's credibility and dispelled oft-stated fears that a CCF government would bring disaster. Success bred success; as a governing party it was able to attract established candidates and create an energetic public service. And CCF activists and supporters had good reason to believe that when the party was out of office, the chances of an eventual return were good. This expectation of success provided a crucial motivator that was absent among CCF/NDPers in Alberta.

Also, in Saskatchewan postwar economic growth was not as spectacular as in Alberta. This probably resulted in less marvelling at the ability of private enterprise to create general prosperity and a greater willingness to support social democratic policies.

Conclusion

A central purpose of this chapter is to identify how and why the politics of Alberta and Saskatchewan differ, and in the process clear up some misconceptions. Both human agency and social conditions are cited as determinants of these differences, with emphasis placed on the former. Human agency is highlighted here as a corrective to the tendency among political sociologists to focus too closely on social structure. The opposite problem—too much causal weight placed on human will—is sometimes found among historians and political scientists.

Notes

1. The preceding summary of Douglasism is based on C.H. Douglas (1920, 1921, 1922a, 1922b, 1931, 1933, 1934). Douglas's A + B theorem has been incontrovertably refuted: see Gaitskell (1933), Durbin (1934), Hiskett (1935), Lewis (1935), and Hiskett and Franklin (1939). For further discussion and a critique of Douglas's ideas, see Bell (1993a: ch. 4).

2. Manning did have to snuff out anti-Semitic elements in his party in the 1940s. See Barr (1974: 127–30).

3. As Barr (1974: 57) points out, in Alberta during the Depression eggs were sold for 5 cents per dozen, roasts for 75 cents, accommodation could be rented for 9 dollars a month, and men's made-to-measure suits cost about 25 dollars.

4. See Bell (1993a: chs 3–5).

5. Cf. Lenin's plan to have capitalists 'converted into employees' of the state ([1918] 1925: 132).

6. This did not prevent Social Credit from receiving a high level of electoral support from members of the working class. See Bell (1993a: ch. 6).

7. The *Regina Manifesto* is reprinted in Young (1969: 304–13).

8. See Mallory (1954) for an account of the disallowance of Social Credit legislation.

9. Whitehorn is critical of the 'protest movement becalmed' tradition. He sees the movement/ party dichotomy as problematic and argues that the CCF was closer to a political party than a movement from the very beginning (1992: 23–6).

10. For an account of the decline of Social Credit in Alberta, see Bell (1993b).

References

Aberhart, W. 1935. *Social Credit Manual: Social Credit as applied to the Province of Alberta* (Calgary).

Alberta. 1934. *The Douglas System of Social Credit: Evidence Taken by the Agricultural Committee of the Alberta Legislature, Session 1934* (Edmonton: King's Printer).

Archer, J.H. 1980. *Saskatchewan: A History* (Saskatoon: Western Producer Prairie Books).

Barr, J.J. 1974. *The Dynasty: The Rise and Fall of Social Credit in Alberta* (Toronto: McClelland & Stewart).

Bell, E. 1993a. *Social Classes and Social Credit in Alberta* (Montreal and Kingston: McGill-Queen's University Press).

———. 1993b. 'The Rise of the Lougheed Conservatives and the Demise of Social Credit in Alberta: A Reconsideration', *Canadian Journal of Political Science* 26(3): 455–75.

Calgary Board of Trade. c1935. 'Calgary Board of Trade Takes Stand on Social Credit', pamphlet.

Douglas, C.H. 1920. *Economic Democracy* (London: Cecil Palmer).

———. 1921. *Credit Power and Democracy* (London: Cecil Palmer).

———. 1922a. *The control and distribution of production* (London: Eyre and Spottiswoode).

———. 1922b. *These Present Discontents and The Labour Party and Social Credit* (London: Cecil Palmer).

———. 1931. *The Monopoly of Credit* (London: Chapman and Hall).

———1933. *Social Credit* (London: Eyre and Spottiswoode).

———. 1934. *Warning Democracy* (London: Stanley Nott).

Durbin, E.F.M. 1934. *Purchasing Power and Trade Depression: A Critique of Under-Consumption Theories* (London: Jonathan Cape).

Edmonton Chamber of Commerce. 1935. 'The Dangers of Aberhart's Social Credit Proposals', pamphlet.

Finkel, A. 1986. 'Alberta Social Credit Reappraised: The Radical Character of the Early Social Credit Movement', *Prairie Forum* 11(1): 69–86.

Gaitskell, H.T.N. 1933. 'Four Monetary Heretics'. In *What Everybody Wants To Know About Money*, ed. G.D.H. Cole (London: Victor Gollancz).

Hiskett, W.R. 1935. *Social Credits or Socialism: An Analysis of the Douglas Credit Scheme* (London: Victor Gollancz).

———, and J.A. Franklin. 1939. *Searchlight on Social Credit* (London: P.S. King and Son).

Hoffman, G. 1975. 'The Saskatchewan Farmer-Labour Party, 1932–1934: How Radical Was It At Its Origin?' *Saskatchewan History* 28: 52–64.

———. 1983. 'The 1934 Saskatchewan Provincial Election Campaign', *Saskatchewan History* 36: 41–57.

Hooke, A. 1971. *30 + 5: I Know, I Was There.* Edmonton: Institute of Applied Art.

Larmour, J. 1985. 'The Douglas Government's Changing Emphasis on Public, Private, and Co-operative Development in Saskatchewan, 1944–1961.' In *Building The Co-operative Commonwealth: Essays on the Democratic Socialist Tradition in Canada,* ed. J.W. Brennan (Regina: University of Regina, Canadian Plains Research Centre).

Lenin, V.I. [1918] 1925. *The State and Revolution* (London: Communist Party of Great Britain).

Lewis, J. 1935. *Douglas Fallacies: A Critique of Social Credit* (London: Chapman and Hall).

Lipset, S.M. [1950] 1971. *Agrarian Socialism* (Berkeley, CA: University of California Press).

Long, J.A., and F.Q. Quo. 1972. 'Alberta: One Party Dominance'. In *Canadian Provincial Politics* ed. M. Robin, (Scarborough: Prentice-Hall), 1–26.

McLeod, T.H. and I. McLeod. 1987. *Tommy Douglas: The Road to Jerusalem* (Edmonton: Hurtig).

Mallory, J.R. 1954. *Social Credit and the Federal Power in Canada* (Toronto: University of Toronto Press).

Manning, E. 1936. Speech at the meeting of Retail, Wholesale and Manufacturers' section of the

Edmonton Chamber of Commerce, 10 January. Provincial Archives of Alberta.

Pitsula, J.M. and K. Rasmussen. 1990. *Privatizing a Province: The New Right in Saskatchewan* (Vancouver: New Star Books).

Richards, J., and L. Pratt. 1979. *Prairie Capitalism: Power and Influence in the New West* (Toronto: McClelland & Stewart).

Rolph, W.K. 1950. *Henry Wise Wood of Alberta* (Toronto: University of Toronto Press).

Sharp, P.F. 1948. *The Agrarian Revolt in Western Canada* (Minneapolis: University of Minnesota Press).

Sinclair, P.R. 1973. 'The Saskatchewan CCF: Ascent to Power and the Decline of Socialism', *Canadian Historical Review* 54(4): 419–33.

Smith, D.E. 1969. 'A Comparison of Prairie Political Developments in Saskatchewan and Alberta', *Journal of Canadian Studies* 4(1): 17–26.

Social Credit League of Alberta. c1935. 'What Would Social Credit Do For Us?' Pamphlet.

Swankey, B. 1980. 'Reflections of a Communist: 1935 Election', *Alberta History* 28(4): 28–36.

Thomas, L.G. 1959. *The Liberal Party in Alberta* (Toronto: University of Toronto Press).

Thomas, L.H. 1981. 'The CCF Victory in Saskatchewan, 1944', *Saskatchewan History* 34(1): 1–16.

Whitehorn, A. 1992. *Canadian Socialism: Essays on the CCF-NDP* (Toronto: Oxford University Press).

Wood, L.A. [1924] 1975. *A History of Farmers' Movements in Canada* (Toronto: University of Toronto Press).

Young, W.D. 1969. *Anatomy of a Party: The National CCF 1932–61* (Toronto: University of Toronto Press).

Chapter 12

The New Democratic Party in Quebec Politics

Claude Denis

Introduction: The 1988 Turning Point

Studying the NDP in Quebec seems to be an odd research topic. For one thing, it is well known that the NDP has never succeeded in Quebec because it is centralist, anglophone, and does not understand the Québécois. So, why ask questions that have already been answered? Also, the NDP has been so marginal in Quebec that it has hardly deserved attention. Why not study something more important? This last question would seem all the more to the point given the result of the Fall 2000 federal election, in which the NDP barely hung on to official party status and was reduced to seeing these 12 seats as some kind of victory. Why not study something with more current relevance?

There are two short answers to all these questions: first, the odd and little-studied experience of the NDP in Quebec provides insight into both the party's overall fortunes and the Quebec/Canada relationship; second, the 1988 federal election marked a turning point for Canadian politics, and the NDP's campaign in Quebec and elsewhere was a key component of this sea change.

Indeed, the three federal elections after 1988 (in 1993, 1997, and 2000) have produced the same—new—result for the NDP and, more broadly, for Canada's federal party system: the NDP and the Progressive Conservative Party have hovered near electoral extinction, the Bloc Québécois and the Reform/Alliance Party have been strong,

respectively, in Quebec and the West, and the Liberal Party has been broadly popular across the country and dominant in Ontario. This chapter's contention is that this realignment of the party system is an outcome of the 1988 election and, to a surprising extent, of the NDP's performance in that election. (For the full analysis from which this chapter is adapted, see C. Denis 1994.)

The NDP had never appeared so strong, in Quebec and in all of Canada, as in the 18 months preceding the election of 21 November 1988. In the summer of 1987, the NDP was the first choice of Canadians, including Quebecers, in several opinion polls. Hopes were high among party activists and leaders that a breakthrough was about to happen. It did not, and failure in the wake of the highest hopes ever provides a dramatic test case for bringing to light the underpinnings of the NDP's historical experience in Quebec.

More broadly, the NDP experience in Quebec in 1988 provides surprising insight into the general dynamics of Canadian politics. Quebec's national discourse has indeed presented a specific problem for the NDP—as it has to Canada in general, at least in the last 40 years. And yet, in some profoundly important respects, the NDP's electoral practices and their consequences have been much the same in Quebec and elsewhere, accounting for much of the party's limited successes across Canada. Given the large role played by Quebec issues in pan-Canadian politics, more-over, even the challenge posed by Quebec nation-alism should be considered relevant to the New Democrats' overall 'life and times'; that is to say, any federal party that is consistently unable to establish some kind of *modus vivendi* with Quebec is doomed to remain at least somewhat marginal in Canadian politics.

A party's performance in Quebec, then, repre-sents an acid test on its pan-Canadian prospects. In the age of the Bloc Québécois, this is a state-ment that may sound bizarre. The statement was more self-evident when it could be said that fed-eral governments were 'made in Quebec'. For all these reasons, the NDP's Quebec experience can be understood as a particularly revealing example of the party's overall weaknesses. There is a seem-ing paradox, here, which seldom makes its way into the analysis of the Quebec-Canada relation-ship: even as political dynamics push it ever clos-er to a drive for sovereignty, Quebec remains best understood as a highly *Canadian* polity. State-ments about the ambivalence of Quebecers are a staple of pundits' conventional wisdom, but the more wide-ranging social correlates of such mixed feelings are generally beside the point of Quebec analysis. Thus, scholars have failed to answer the 'Quebec question' within its Canadian context with theoretical coherence. There is, of course, a large literature on Quebec by Quebec social scientists; but a signal feature of this litera-ture is that it tends to understand Quebec society as though it were largely unconnected to Canada (see Denis, 1993; Salée, 1982)—as though Quebec were already independent.

Although the NDP was never more than the third player in the federal political game, and especially so with regard to Quebec, its status as an established protest party gave it a key role in the stability of the whole party system. The peri-od leading to the 1988 election, in this respect, was particularly crucial: both the Liberals and the Tories were having serious difficulties in present-

ing credible leadership to the Canadian elec-torate, and as a result the NDP found itself poised to become one of the two leading parties. New Democrats, however, were unable to carry this support to the voting booth on 21 November 1988. On the morning after the election, it seemed like nothing had changed: the Tories were still in power and the NDP was still in third place. In fact, the party system that came out of the 1988 election was very fragile.

In this sense, the 1993 election, then, was at once the final stage in the destruction of the party system which had ruled Canada since the end of World War II and the beginning of something new. The postwar system prior to this was char-acterized by an electoral struggle between three major parties, supplemented for much of the period but with increasing irrelevance, by a fourth party, the Social Credit. In hindsight, it is clear that the party system was first undermined by two things: on the one hand, the 1981–2 con-stitutional renewal, of which the Quebec govern-ment was not a part, and on the other hand by the pro-Quebec change in leadership and outlook of the Progressive Conservative Party. This set the stage for the 1984 Conservative victory under the leadership of Brian Mulroney, which included massive support in francophone Quebec.

Commentators were unsure at the time whether this signalled the dawn of a new party system, or at least a new alignment within the system, with the Progressive Conservatives as Canada's new 'natural governing party': the Tory victory had been huge, but the new government quickly lost much of its popularity (see Penniman 1988). The 1988 election was expected to clear up the picture, and the Conservatives' second consecutive majority did appear to consolidate a new alignment, with the Liberals and New Democrats far weaker than the ruling party.

By November of 1988, however, the Meech Lake process of tying up the loose ends of the 1981 constitutional renewal had already begun to unravel and was going to take a major turn for the worse in 1989. The manner in which the three established parties acted through the developing constitutional crisis was a major contributor to the rise of both the Bloc Québécois and the Reform Party. In addition, dissatisfaction with the Conservatives, Liberals, and New Democrats was greatly enhanced by the economic difficulties that accompanied the implementation of the Free Trade Agreement with the United States. Each established party was attacked, in fact, by its own friends for failing to deal properly with some aspect of Canada's economic situation.

From our vantage point, the 1988 election can be seen as the last gasp of a failing party system—the system's last chance to adjust to its changing environment. This adjustment did not take place, and thus the 1988 election set the stage for what was to come five years later. The NDP's failure to break out of third-party status was a key element of this story, because as the established third party it was the first option of Canadians dissatisfied with the Conservatives and Liberals, as opinion polls showed from 1986 to 1988. By failing to displace one of the two major parties and by making common cause with them in the constitutional debate, the NDP actually opened the door to Reform, now the Alliance, and the Bloc. I am tempted to call this just departed party system *the New Democratic era*, first because the CCF/NDP's presence distinguishes the period from previous times also marked by Conservative-Liberal competition, and second because the CCF/NDP itself was the keystone to the stability of the whole system. In this perspective, the dynamics of the NDP's sociopolitical presence in Quebec say much about the Quebec-Canada relationship and about the state of federal politics in the 1990s.

After 1988, the federal NDP never really recovered, in Quebec as elsewhere. Its credibility as a protest party went from bad to worse at every turn of the constitutional debate. But even before, the NDP was a party in trouble: from 1979 to

1988, there was a three-election pattern of declining support for the NDP in several regions of English Canada—a pattern largely hidden from view by increased support in Quebec, going from 5 per cent in 1979 to 14 per cent in 1988, which was only 6 per cent below Ontario's stagnant NDP support. It is thus ironic, and not a little indicative of how political imaginations function in Canada, that the wrath of NDPers after 1988 focused on Quebec. In this sense, then, if Quebec was a drag on the party's cross-Canada popularity, it was less and less so as the 1980s advanced. It turns out, then, that the NDP was an established player in Canada's federal party system, but never a very stable one: so long as the two main parties retained a high level of legitimacy, the NDP was along for the ride, fitfully gathering a partly different one-fifth of the vote from one election to the other. Things changed after 1988. The political dynamics that flowed from the 'free trade election' brought about, on the one hand, the rebirth of Quebec's sovereignist movement; on the other hand, they led to economic policies that, combined with a deep economic crisis, made the Canadian electorate very angry.

A Poststructuralist Political Sociology

Asking what it is about the NDP as a political party that has kept most Quebecers from becoming NDP supporters, puts this chapter squarely within the field of political sociology. The manner in which I go about answering the question, however, is at variance with the main currents in the field: my construction of this object of study is organized by what is typically (and misleadingly) labelled *poststructuralist theory*.

I will quickly outline here some of the basic assumptions of this outlook, from which I have built the analytical procedures used below. The long-standing debate in the history of sociology between what one may call interpretivists and empiricists, has been recast in the last two decades by the arrival on the scene of several perspectives that focus on language and discourse. Interpretivists have long given primacy to 'human lived experience', and poststructuralists now shift the focus by replacing this primacy with that of the linguistic forms that allow experience to acquire meaning (Prus 1990: 359).

In this context, it is important to ask the question: What may we know? In other words, how is meaning constituted? David Carr, building on the work of French philosopher Paul Ricoeur, shows that the historical past *as it is socially known* is constitutive of the identities of 'ordinary persons' (as opposed to only professional historians): 'we are *in* history as we are *in* the world: it serves as the horizon and background for our everyday experience' (1986: 4). Knowing history, then, is knowing ourselves, and vice versa. Carr shows that the historical past's role in everyday life as horizon and background takes a particular form, or configuration: that of the narrative. And essential to narrative structure is the sense of a temporal configuration: the story has to have a beginning, a middle, and an end. Also necessary to this concept of the narrative is the presence of a storyteller and of an audience (1986: 46).

This means that for social actors, individual or collective, life is a narrative, a story: 'The actions and sufferings of life can be viewed as a process of telling ourselves stories, listening to those stories, and acting them out or living them through' (1986: 61). The study of social life, as a result, starts by listening to these stories, reading them, attempting to understand them. This is where *reader response theory* comes in, as the main direct source of the *voter response model*, which I have developed in order to study the NDP in Quebec. Derived from phenomenology, hermeneutics, and linguistics, reader response theory was developed by literary critics, starting from the principle that the constitution of meaning in literary texts is 'an experience resulting from the interaction between the text and its reader through the whole process

of reading' (Heidenreich 1989: 77). Transferred to the political field, reader response theory highlights the centrality of the *communication* that may or may not take place between the political party and the electorate. And the communicative social relationship between party and voters is grounded in the narratives that constitute the collectivity of voter identities—the stories with which people identify—as an *interpretive community*.

First, the voter-response model stems from the simple-minded principle that, for a person to consider voting for a given party, she or he needs to be provided with some knowledge of that party. For this to happen, the party must produce some form of text, and make it available to the voters, using its *knowledge-projection resources* (that is, the combination of its workers, organization, finances). Voters will then make sense of it according to the narrative(s) by which they are constituted; that is, the meeting between text and voter will occur on the terrain of a specific interpretive community. The text, then, may reach the voters in one of many states, depending on the way in which it is communicated to them; and it will be read differentially by the voters, according to their subject position. A whole range of meanings will then be produced. The voter-produced meanings will often be at variance with the party's actual discourse, for there is no reliable way in which a party can control the meaning-giving practices of voters. Yet it is on that basis that decisions will be made to vote for or against the party.

A second prerequisite for success is the existence of some institutional space being created in the polity for a new narrative. That is to say, in a situation where the narratives of the dominant parties correspond closely to the identities of the interpretive community, there is little if any chance of a third party displacing even one of the dominant parties. But voter dissatisfaction by itself is not enough to ensure the success of a 'new' party. Success would also depend on the party's actual work, aiming to achieve the integration of the party's narrative into the interpretive community. The voters must, in other words, be offered something that will count, for them, as *good reasons* to switch their vote to the (perhaps) emerging party. This is difficult to accomplish because such an attempt to *reformulate the interpretive community* would have to overcome resistance on the part of the established political agents, and ultimately from the established political identities themselves: the party's first task would be to develop *cooperative readers* (Eco 1990), so that voters would not tend to misread the party's text on the basis of long-established understandings and loyalties.

In most circumstances, the knowledge that voters have of a party will come from the media and to a lesser extent from party workers and adversaries. The exception is when, for instance, I attend a party meeting, at which I hear the leader's speech, get a sense of the size and enthusiasm of the crowd, and so on. But the party's overall campaign and the status of that campaign in the party's history are things that are beyond anyone's direct grasp; they are the object of a unifying interpretation by some authority (the authors of party literature, party workers, the media). But remember that no authority can ever have the final word on such things, and that voters are always *active* readers. The other way to look at the party-voter relationship is from the party's point of view. This second angle addresses the question of actual party resources, which to a large extent are either the sources of party knowledge, or the enabling apparatus that underlies these sources. Resources include people ('core partisans', party officials, strategists) and money. The party's narrative itself and what may be called the party's '"spin" and crisis management capability'—the party's ability to project its narrative so that it reaches the electorate in a positive manner—are also resources.

Several analytical procedures can be generated by this general model. This chapter will present

two such procedures, that account to a dramatic extent for the NDP's failure to break through—in 1988, in Quebec, and more generally across Canada and through the years. First, coverage of the NDP campaign in Montreal's three French-language daily newspapers will be analysed in order to see to what extent media readers (most of whom are also voters) were offered good reasons to support the NDP. Second, the electoral expenses of the three main parties will be analysed, across Canada and locally in four provinces (Quebec, Ontario, Alberta, and British Columbia). Expenditures will serve as indicators of the extent and use of each party's knowledge projection resources, in order to see whether there is something unique to Quebec voters in their resistance to the NDP's appeals.

Before we turn to these tasks, however, it will be useful to establish the context in which the 1988 elections occurred, and how the various parties had positioned themselves.

Decade of Turmoil: An Overview of the Years 1980–88

The period preceding the 1988 federal election was an extraordinary one in Canadian politics. For our purposes, we can consider it to have opened in 1980: with the return to power in Ottawa of Pierre Trudeau's Liberal Party, and the referendum on sovereignty-association in Quebec.

The period was marked by the renewal of the constitution and adoption of the *Canadian Charter of Rights and Freedoms*, by a deep recession starting in 1981, and by the dramatic arrival in power of Brian Mulroney's Tories in 1984; in Quebec, by a profound crisis of the sovereignist movement and the arrival in power of Robert Bourassa's Liberals in 1985; by the signing of the Meech Lake Accord in 1986 and of the Free Trade Agreement with the United States in 1987; and by the Mulroney government's severe loss of popularity in opinion polls, which put the Liberal

Party, and then the NDP, in first place across Canada in 1987.

This was a major turnaround for the NDP, which had appeared on the verge of extinction just before the 1984 elections: it was unpopular and riven with divisions, in midreflection on fundamental issues of social democracy, and in serious confusion on issues of Quebec and the constitution. The party was divided and demoralized—in no shape to present a convincing alternative to the Canadian electorate, it could barely hope to survive with the help of the 'ordinary Canadian' gambit hatched in desperation in the months before the election. Meeting to plan strategy on 27 May 1983, the members of the Election Planning Committee themselves could not come to agree on 'the themes and issues that party spokesmen ought to pursue' (Morley 1988: 127–8). A coping strategy was developed, involving 'a major effort to restore morale' by means of a pre-election campaign that would 'secure and reinforce the base in priority ridings' (1988: 127–8), and that would focus on what opinion polls said was the party's strength: its championing of 'the little guy'. Further polls and focus groups confirmed that this focus was the best chance of survival for the party. Nothing was guaranteed, however, as Gerald Caplan noted: 'We can avoid the apocalypse some predict for us, but it is by no means inevitable that we will' (quoted by Fraser 1989: 119). As it turned out, the NDP survived the elections, making the 'ordinary Canadian' strategy appear brilliant. One effect of the strategy to focus on priority ridings, however, was that Quebec was largely neglected in the party's campaign, at a time when Quebecers could have been responsive to its appeal: this was the first federal election after the 1980 referendum: the sovereignist movement was crippled; and a good number of nationalist social democrats were trying to 're-launch' the NDP within Quebec. But the party made no gains.

The years following the 1984 Conservative triumph were marked by a series of contradictory trends for the NDP: unprecedented popularity, in the middle of a severe identity crisis for social democracy around the world, and soon after it had been on the brink of catastrophe; electoral positioning torn between policy orientations and polling-driven populism; a stable public image, covering severe internal tensions. The run-up to the 1988 election would see all these trends crystallize into a roller-coaster ride of hope, disappointment, and finally bitterness as NDPers stepped out of the carts after the election.

After the 1984 election, and partly in the context of its rising popularity in *all* regions of the country, the NDP had worked at giving answers to the two unsolved problems of the 1981–4 period: What is social democracy in a neoliberal environment? and What is the role for Quebec in the NDP, and vice versa? By the spring of 1987, at its biennial federal convention, the party had provided itself with answers that it felt were workable. First, a task force given a wide consulting mandate produced policy ideas that, merged with the influence of European ideas of 'autogestion', gave birth in 1985 to a party-endorsed report, *Canada Unlimited*. This report 'emphasized decentralizing themes' and stressed 'the new role to be played by local and municipal governments in responding to community needs' (Bradford 1989: 101). Second, the party adopted a full-employment policy, to be implemented by means of 'new federal-provincial structures institutionalizing community input into national economic strategies' (1989: 102). This link between full employment and decentralization would allow considerable flexibility to the national economy, thereby solving social democracy's neoliberal or post-Fordist problem. At the March 1987 NDP convention, 'Ed Broadbent announced that the full-employment issue would be the cornerstone of the NDP's next election campaign' (1989: 103).

The 1987 convention also marked the launch of the NDP's so-called Quebec strategy, motivated by the NDP's rising popularity in that province, and the realization that it would be a pivotal electoral ground in the next elections (Caplan, Kirby, and Segal 1989: 90, 154). In a highly symbolic move, the party had chosen to hold the meeting in Montreal, for the first time in its history. And it planned to adopt policies it felt would appeal to the Quebec electorate. In the months before the convention, the NDP had also succeeded in improving its relations with the Quebec labour movement to the point that three of its leaders attended the convention and offered 'official welcomes' to the delegates. The Quebec labour leaders were thus establishing, in the present, new beginning- and end-posts for the NDP's presence on Quebec's narrative landscape. This story was beginning with their welcoming the NDP to Quebec—as though it had not previously been there—and its projected end was success at the next election. Also, because of who they were, these leaders were opening some institutional space for that new presence. The NDP's Quebec narrative was thereby being recast along two principal lines, transforming at the same time Quebec's own narrative: the party showed itself to be open to moderate Quebec nationalism in the policy field, and gathered the accolades of the Quebec labour movement, a collective actor holding a distinguished place in Quebec's national story since the Quiet Revolution. The resolutions that had been endorsed at the federal council were confirmed by the delegates. Thus was born the NDP's 'Quebec strategy'. Along with the focus on full employment and decentralization, it ensured that on the policy front, this time, the NDP would be prepared to meet the electorate and go for big gains.

How this whole policy overhaul would figure in the NDP's electoral campaign, however, remained to be seen. A lot of work would have to be done to widen the institutional space opened by the union chiefs' support. The aim of that work would be to achieve the integration of the

NDP's new narrative into the Quebec interpretive community: the NDP's story would have to become an integral part of the ways in which Quebecers' political experiences are organized on a continuing basis. But strategic planning for the elections would come to largely neutralize all the narrative thrusts of the convention by championing an essentially populist revisiting of the 'ordinary Canadians' approach. And reticences to Quebec nationalism at the centre of the NDP's campaign especially blunted the 'opening to Quebec'. Early signs of this were visible in the relationship between the Ottawa-based establishment and those who had tried to 're-launch' the party from within Quebec. This attempt, spearheaded by John Harney, had initially met with mixed results, but it continued after the 1984 Conservative victory. As summarized by Graham Fraser, Harney's effort had

> built the party from almost nothing to a group with a growing membership of several thousand. He had taken nationalist positions, and drawn into the party veterans of the union movement, left-wing splinter groups, and the Parti Québécois (1989: 122).

But Harney was a controversial figure in the party, after having run twice for the leadership against Ed Broadbent and a long history of trouble-making (Fraser 1989). The Québécois nationalism of Harney and his followers, in any case, went farther than what the party was quite willing to endorse. Thus, in January 1987, a federal council devoted to 'Quebec and the Canadian Constitution' endorsed, in the words of a *Globe and Mail* reporter, 'a resolution affirming Quebec's right to self-determination, and calling for recognition of Quebec's uniqueness in the preamble of the Constitution'. But it refused to endorse an *NPD-Québec* proposal to transfer all powers over language to the Quebec government. Six weeks after this federal council, Harney was pushed aside as the Quebec NDP's main spokesperson (1989). He then became increasingly marginalized, as the new leaders became more conciliatory on the 'national question' with the approach of the election (Lamoureux 1988). Although still quite nationalist, they chose an approach that was more careful of the NDP establishment's sensibilities.

The 'Quebec opening' and the populist approach inherited from 1984 were proceeding on parallel tracks, the controls of which were in the hands of the election planning committee. They cohabited rather uneasily, until a somewhat traumatic change in personnel resulted in amplifying both the party's populism and its effort in Quebec, which combined into putting a populist spin on the Quebec opening. The consequences of this would eventually lead to great disappointment. For all the hopes raised in Quebec by the 1987 convention, the Harney-led efforts, and the party's poll-expressed popularity, the 'Quebec strategy' as put into practice turned out to be a shallow one. As the election neared, it becamed identified with a focus on Ed Broadbent's popularity, calling for him to travel often to Quebec and to be the focus of the party's advertising campaign. A full half of the NDP's $3-million advertising budget was allocated to Quebec (Caplan, Kirby, and Segal 1989: 154–5). As NDP strategist Gerald Caplan and his two coauthors have written, the NDP's going in Quebec would be tough because 'few party organizers or strategists really had any idea of how the political process in the province worked'. As a result, 'there was no sense of a clear strategy for Quebec' (1989: 91).

But it was not only the Quebec strategy that suffered from the campaign's main thrust: while Ed Broadbent had announced that the full-employment issue would be at the core of the NDP's 1988 campaign, it too was pushed out of the limelight by the strategic planners' polling lessons. Campaign logistics were also lacking not only in Quebec, as strategists Bill Knight and Robin Sears later conceded: 'no one was prepared for what a challenge it would be to organize the resources and deal with the demands of a fully national campaign' (Fraser 1989: 130). We will now see the practical consequences of these strategic deficiencies.

Follow the Money

In the context of the voter-response model, party organization is to be analysed in terms of its ability to 'project' knowledge in a manner such that voters would become (or remain) inclined to vote for the party. The resources that fuel knowledge projection come down, ultimately, to (1) people and money (insofar as it is, so to speak, put to work); and (2) the ways in which money and people are made to relate to each other and are allocated.

This latter type of resources, which we may call *relations of knowledge projection*, brings into the picture not only the *quantity* of money and people available to a party, but also the *quality* of their allocation: it is on the basis of various kinds of *expertise* and decision-making that money will be well spent, and that party workers will be well used. This expertise, and the organization, or structure, it brings to a campaign, are very much among a party's resources. But it is not enough to look at amounts of money spent by a party and at how it allocates it. In a competitive environment, the ability of a party to spend *more* money than its adversaries is, other things being equal, an advantage. It is, then, important to study the relative spending of parties in order to gain a secure insight into the quantity and quality of their effort.

Dollar figures are, of course, only an imperfect proxy for measuring a campaign's effort. It is often said that the NDP has always been cash-poor and has relied intensively on the free labour of its militants (see, for instance, Whitehorn 1992). Witness its development of the 'canvassing' technique in the 1960s (see Brodie and Jenson 1988: 276–7). But in a society thoroughly penetrated by market relations, one can only go so far without using money. And political campaigns need to be able to rent office space, to have several telephone lines that serve to canvass potential supporters, to produce and print campaign literature, etc. All this, the NDP does. And in fact, as we will see below, in 1988 the NDP's 'national' campaign spent more money than the Liberal Party's did.

At this point, it is important to recall that knowledge-projection resources are only one factor in the determination of voter response. To put the matter in somewhat coarse terms, such resources have the triple task of carrying the party's message to the voter, of identifying the sympathetic voter, and of bringing him or her to the voting booth. The core message itself and the discursive environment within which the message is produced and communicated are analytically independent from the contribution of knowledge-projection resources, and they both are crucially important in modulating the impact of those resources on voter response. Still, we will now see that it is possible to bracket both message and environment, and to find that knowledge-projection resources have, on their own, a large part to play in party success. We will find that, indeed, money talks.

When we look at the pan-Canadian aggregate data of the three main parties' expenses in the 1988 federal elections, we find that the NDP fares surprisingly well: it reported expenses of $7,060,563, second to the Tories' $7,921,738 and *ahead* of the Liberals' $6,839,875. And yet, in their book *Election*, Gerry Caplan, Michael Kirby, and Hugh Segal note that the scope of the NDP's 'national campaign' was restricted by its limited access to such resources as 'private' polling, a very expensive enterprise which the Progressive Conservatives and, to a lesser extent, the Liberals were using extensively (1989: 93–4); this limitation would have been a considerable disadvantage for the NDP. What are we to make of this contradiction? First, with respect to the private polling issue raised by Caplan, Kirby, and Segal, which can largely be

accounted for under the 'professional services' heading of the parties' reports to the Chief Electoral Officer, it is clear that the Tories devoted a quantity of resources to probing the electorate, out of all proportion with the other two parties— not only the NDP, but the Liberal Party as well. Other polarities can be identified: the NDP was in a high-spending class by itself when it came to paying salaries and spending money on fundraising, while it dragged far behind in advertising and in purchasing broadcast time. The NDP also spent less than the others on the leader's tour, and more on administrative expenses. A pattern emerges, here, of an NDP commitment of resources quite different from those of the other parties, especially the Tories: the NDP commits very heavily to the administrative support apparatus of the campaign and much less to items that put the party in more direct contact with the voters.

Now, we must not lose sight of our basic goal, which is to acquire an understanding of the NDP's weakness *in Quebec*. And a focus on the 'national' campaign can do rather little to specify what is particular to Quebec, relative to the other provinces (or to the 'rest of Canada' as a whole). In addition to the expenses incurred by national campaigns, *local* candidates also spend large amounts of money in their attempt to get elected. They rent office space and telephone lines, buy advertising, pay salaries, etc. Parties may also spend money at the *provincial* level; but this is dwarfed by the other two levels. We will now look at the expenditures of local campaigns.

NDP candidates, as a group, were outspent by the candidates of at least one party in Quebec, Ontario, Alberta, and BC, the four provinces included in this analysis of electoral spending. Even in British Columbia, where the NDP won a majority of the seats, it was second in spending to the Tories (by the slimmest of margins). In Alberta, the NDP was also second to the Tories, but far behind, and just ahead of the Reform Party. In Ontario and Quebec, the NDP candidates were third in spending, far behind those of the two main parties. Overall, the higher the NDP's spending was in comparison to its competitors, the better were its electoral results as measured by percentage of the vote and number of seats. In Quebec, the NDP candidates did not run hard: they came up short when compared to the other parties' candidates in Quebec *and* to their NDP colleagues in other provinces. But this is a rather too general statement, based as it is on aggregate data. The fact is that some NDP candidates in Quebec spent quite a lot of money. Some others spent next to nothing. We can ask, then, what effect (if any) varying levels of local spending by NDP candidates had on the Quebec electorate. Were Quebec voters sensitive to the knowledge that was offered by the NDP in degrees proportionate to the intensity of that offer? Or were they impervious to even the strongest local NDP campaigns?

Before answering these questions, however, we need to look at what general relation (if any) exists between spending and winning—regardless, that is, of which party wins. What will interest us here is *which 'spender' wins*. This is important because while it is obvious that, generally speaking, a candidate has to run hard in order to win, it is not a foregone conclusion that the highest-spending candidate will always win. It turns out that, while it is indeed important to run hard, being the highest spender is far from ensuring victory: on average, 49 per cent of the winners were top spenders, and 42 per cent were second spenders; all four provinces were near these marks. This is not a large difference, which would appear to go against the expectations of the voter-response model. But there is more to spending than the total sum of money that a candidate poured into a campaign. For example: money used to print literature that will be delivered to voters' homes by a campaign volunteer is closer to the voter than money used to pay for the campaign office rent or heating, or for the campaign staff's salaries. Thus, the voter-response model

points to differences between types of expenses— finer distinctions than those based on aggregate sums of money. The Chief Electoral Officer's summary reports of each candidate's expenses allow for *some* analysis of this distinction, by separating expenses on advertising (subdivided between radio-TV and other) from office and travel expenses, salaries, and other expenses. In the terms set by the voter-response model, advertising expenses should have a larger impact on the electorate than other types of expenses, which by and large can be termed *bureaucratic expenses*.

With the striking exception of British Columbia, a 'first-advertiser privilege' was clearly affirmed in 1988—and especially so in Quebec and Alberta. Spending on advertising is spending on telling a story; and the higher the spending, the better the chance that the story will be heard. Behind the numbers, then, there are stories. And these stories are quite different from one province to the next. The unevenly successful insertion of party stories within an interpretive community is what constitutes in large part a political tradition. And it is, indeed, when considering the state of political traditions in these four provinces that we can make sense of their various patterns of rewarding party spending, and especially advertising spending. Thus, the pattern that combines a 'first-advertiser privilege' in three provinces *and* the BC exception can be largely accounted for by the relationship between Conservative (un)popularity and party systems with varying degrees of competitiveness.

With a few exceptions, there remained no old loyalties in Quebec, and no old exclusions; indeed, the fact that the Progressive Conservatives had been excluded from the Quebec scene for decades (with the shortlived Diefenbaker exception) was now ancient history, irrelevant. But the Tories were by no means in a safe position: they would have to fight hard if they were to win. At the same time, it seemed that some space had been opened for the NDP. Consequently, the election belonged to the party that spun the most appealing narrative in the here and now, that ensured it was successful in reaching the voters, and that monitored its supporters all the way to the voting booth. On the terms of the voter-response model, the election belonged to the party with the best and the largest amount of knowledge-projection resources.

Let us now look at local NDP spending. The pattern, which we found in the NDP's national campaign, of heavy bureaucratic spending and light advertising spending is reproduced by the party's local campaigns—and dramatically so. But on this count, Quebec candidates come out as somewhat less bureaucratic than others. Given the NDP's generally bureaucratic way of doing things, this is undoubtedly an indication of the weakness of NDP organization in Quebec, rather than smarter resource allocation on the part of Quebec candidates. Most strikingly, while the very strong BC NDP had 88 per cent of the province's 'first bureaucrats', it only had 16 per cent of 'first advertisers'. But the Ontario situation is more appropriate for a comparison with Quebec. While the Quebec NDP had 15 per cent of the province's 'first bureaucrats' and 0 per cent of 'first advertisers', the corresponding figures for Ontario were 38 per cent and 1 per cent. Viewed in this light, the fact that the NDP won less than 10 per cent of Ontario seats, while finishing third in 78 per cent of the ridings is brought into sharp focus, and is anything but surprising. This is better than the party's placing third in 91 per cent of Quebec ridings, but not a shining performance by any means.

The NDP's enormous proportion of third places in Quebec is largely attributable to its number of noncompetitive candidates (where competitiveness is indicated by the percentage of the allowed expense actually spent by the candidate). But if the proportion of noncompetitive NDP candidates in Quebec is staggering, with almost two-thirds of them spending less than 40 per cent of the limit, it is almost as high in Alberta (57.7 per cent) and far from negligible in Ontario (27.3 per cent). It

is only in BC, in fact, that NDP candidates were competitive on a massive scale.

It turns out that the situation of the NDP in Ontario in 1988 is remarkably similar to that in Quebec, when not taking into account the actual number of seats won. Indeed, these two provinces share some traits that are made all the more evident when they are compared with BC and Alberta. For our purposes, one crucial similarity between Quebec and Ontario is that in both these provinces the NDP is a third party in a three-way competition. One dimension of this is that in both Ontario and Quebec *the provincial composition of NDP spending* was generally detrimental to individual candidates' chances. In other words, the NDP's Quebec 'second advertisers' could not count on some indirect publicity from a number of NDP 'first advertisers' in the province, which could have contributed to increasing their vote. This is also the case in Ontario, although at a less extreme level, as we will now see with a quantitative approximation of the relationship between spending (on advertising) and success.

We can get a reasonable fix on this relationship, taking into account the provincial composition of NDP spending, with a calculation involving the following elements: the composition of the NDP candidates' advertising rankings, the percentage of NDP candidates who spent at least 60 per cent of the allowed limit, and the all-party percentage of second-advertising winners, first in Ontario and then in Quebec. Taking the NDP's *three* Ontario second-advertising victories as a benchmark and example, we come to the equation and expected seats presented in Table 12.1 for second-advertising winners and in Table 12.2 for third-advertising winners.

In the end, the Quebec-Ontario comparison produces an amazing result: the pattern of the NDP success in Quebec and Ontario is identical—Quebec voters behaved exactly as Ontarians did. Using Ontario as a benchmark, simulating a few third-advertising winners in Quebec, and assuming that nothing else (such as a weak message) intervened to

Table 12.1 Relationship between Spending (on Advertising) and Success in Ontario and Quebec for NDP 2nd advertisers, 1988 Federal Election

	# NDP 2nd Advertising Candidates	X	% all-party 2nd advertising winners	X	% party candidates with +60% expenses	Expected seats (Actual seats)
Ontario	20	X	28.3	X	51.5	2.9 (3)
Quebec	12	X	30.7	X	24.0	0.9 (0)

Table 12.2 Relationship between Spending (on Advertising) and Success in Ontario and Quebec for NDP 3rd advertisers, 1988 Federal Election

	# NDP 3rd Advertising Candidates	X	% all-party 3rd advertising winners	X	% party candidates with +60% expenses	Expected seats (Actual seats)
Ontario	64	X	15.2	X	51.5	5.0 (5)
Quebec	63	X	5.0 *	X	24.0	0.76 (0)

* This is a simulation. In Quebec, there were no third-advertising winners, from any party. This is in good part due to the (financially) very weak campaigns of many NDPers, such that a large number of races were in effect two-way contests. As a result, a calculation using 0% of third-advertising winners would be meaningless. For the sake of approximating expectations, therefore, I have simulated 5% of Quebec third-advertising winners.

dampen expectations, we arrive at the conclusion that the NDP's effort in Quebec was worth all of 1.66 seats. In other words, the NDP candidates in Quebec were able to count on an electorate that was supportive in proportion to their efforts, but they ran their campaigns in such a way as to be entitled to hope for, at the very best, one or two seats.

The NDP in the Newspapers: 'Je ne suis pas Québécois'

Keeping in mind that the two sources of knowledge about political parties and electoral choice are the parties themselves and the media, one of the subject positions of the collectivity of voters-readers is that of a *media audience* (Ang 1990). As the second prong in our analysis of the NDP's appeal to Quebec voters in the 1988 elections, we will now examine texts that were made available to them by the media. More specifically, we will look at Montreal's three French-language daily newspapers: *Le Devoir, La Presse*, and *Le Journal de Montréal*. Taken together, these three media sources reach directly 60 per cent of Quebec's population (Tremblay, 1990)—that is to say, around 70 per cent to 75 per cent of Quebec's French-speaking population, which was the primary target of the NDP's campaign.

We know that the NDP's strategists took the 1988 campaign in Quebec seriously: the party would spend a lot of money and dispatch many experienced out-of-province campaign organizers, in an effort to be in 'the big leagues', to be *seen* to be in the big leagues, and so to elect candidates for the first time. But strategists only had a vague idea of how to accomplish this, beyond capitalizing on Ed Broadbent's popularity in Quebec as elsewhere. The NDP's primary message to Quebecers had to be that Ed Broadbent belonged among them— that he and his party were not foreigners, out-siders—and that as such the NDP deserved con-sideration. Only once this was accepted could an ordinary electoral message be heard: since the other two leaders (and parties) were interchange-able and untrustworthy, Ed Broadbent and the NDP deserved the support of Quebecers. What became of this double-barrelled message in *Le Devoir, La Presse*, and *Le Journal de Montréal*?

One way to show that they belonged was for NDPers to emphasize issues that were thought important by Quebecers. The NDP opened its campaign with one such issue: the environment. And it got positive coverage from both *La Presse* and *Le Journal de Montréal*. But the environment soon lost its salience as a campaign issue, to be replaced at first in all three newspapers by the NDP's alliance with the Quebec Federation of Labour (QFL).

Now this, the relationship between labour unions and social democratic parties, is an issue whose importance is not limited to one electoral campaign or another. Compared to the situation of social democratic parties elsewhere, the NDP-Labour links in Canada (not only in Quebec) are quite weak (Archer 1990). But the prominence of the Labour connection is considered by NDP lead-ers as a mixed blessing at best, something made plain in the 1988 campaign by Ed Broadbent's downplaying the financial contribution of unions to the party (*Le Devoir* 14 Nov. 1988). The expe-rience of social democratic parties in other coun-

tries, however, shows that a strong Labour link is necessary to ensure a measure of success (Przeworski and Sprague 1986). Given the pre-sent limited popularity of unions in North America, a strong but low-profile link is probably what the NDP would most profit from. The NDP's 1988 Quebec campaign, however, produced a high-profile union link because unions are known to be a major Quebec institution. By showing an unusual degree of enthusiasm for the NDP, they gave it a chance to claim: 'We belong!'

Le Devoir's limited resources and its nationalist vocation combined to fashion a coverage of the NDP that was almost completely given over to the party's bid to be accepted within the Quebec national family. In this respect, it is clear that *Le Devoir* took seriously the NDP's professed intent of 'opening [itself] to Quebec' and its coverage was, in a sense, designed to ascertain whether the party's claim could be trusted—a concern perfectly sum-marized by the headline covering two letters to the editor, published late in the campaign: 'Can we trust the NDP?' (*Le Devoir* 14 Nov. 1988). But it cannot be said that *Le Devoir's* readers were either well or fully informed of the NDP's campaign: too many things were missing, and the emphasis on the QFL was exaggerated. It could be, however, that they were *usefully* informed: to the extent that they shared their newspaper's concerns and priorities about Quebec's national existence, *Le Devoir's* skewed editorial choices might have been their own. Readers were supplied the information that they were likely to find most important in making an opinion about the NDP, leaving the free trade issue in particular, in the background.

Although grossly misrepresentative of the com-plexity of the whole campaign, *Le Devoir's* fixation on the NDP's place in Quebec's grand narrative cor-responded to the kind of story the party hoped to convey to the Québécois electorate. Only a very strong and coherent campaign could have with-stood this kind of scrutiny, however, and the NDP was not up to the task. This is, very distinctly, the

NDP's failure and not a sabotage by *Le Devoir*, for the NDP's hopes of success rested on its ability to convince the skeptics; and *Le Devoir*'s stance was, quite legitimately, that of the skeptic. *Le Journal de Montréal*, which otherwise paid little attention to the issue of QFL involvement, first responded strongly to the 'national family' connection, then (informed by *Le Devoir*) skeptically to Labour's ability to deliver votes to the New Democrats; at best, the NDP could be considered a very junior member of the family. In this concern for the national family, the élite and the populist newspaper converged, each in its own way. *La Presse* ignored the 'family' theme, questioning instead the propriety, in a liberal democracy, of links between a political party and unions, and condemning such links. On the basis of its own liberalism, then, *La Presse* focused on what might be called the social democratic aspect of the NDP-Labour links, instead of their national aspect—bypassing the message that the NDP hoped to transmit and highlighting the dimension of those links that is often viewed, throughout Canada, as problematic.

The media's next prominent theme of the NDP's campaign, the quality of Ed Broadbent's French in the leaders' TV debate, erupted in *La Presse*, but not in *Le Devoir*, and only marginally in *Le Journal*. Three and a half weeks into the campaign, then, *La Presse* was getting involved in the grand narrative that the NDP had hoped to emphasize, that of its belonging in Quebec's national, French-language, community. Until then, *La Presse* had paid little attention to the 'We belong!' claim, but the leaders' debates brought it front and centre in the newspaper's coverage. And here it was emphatically denied: Ed Broadbent, and by extension his party, were strangers in Quebec. In a sense, *La Presse* was catching up to *Le Devoir*'s and *Le Journal*'s narration of the campaign, but in its own loud and insistent way—an insistence perhaps best understood as compensating for the delay in joining the national chorus accompanying the NDP's progress. In the English-language

debate, meanwhile, Broadbent was badly marginalized by the Turner-Mulroney pyrotechnics surrounding the Free Trade Agreement.

The debates thus proved to be disastrous for the NDP and its leader in the whole country. In this sense, Broadbent's counterperformance in French was merely the most obvious expression of the party's vulnerability. This development is worth insisting on, because it dramatizes a much more general NDP predicament, to which we will return: Broadbent's performance was clearly better in English than in the French-language debate, but this did not seem to matter since he was badly marginalized in both debates, as opinion polls in French Quebec and English Canada showed. The questions, specific and general, raised for the NDP by the outcome of the two debates can be put in a nutshell: how could the NDP be uniformly marginalized as a result of two vastly different performances by its leader? In what sense is there a Quebec electorate, separate and different from the English-Canadian electorate?

It is generally expected that Quebec is indeed a separate electorate within Canada, although the evidence is far from compelling (Johnston et al. 1992). The issue on which this expectation most obviously rests is the national question divide within the Canadian polity. Not coincidentally, this is an issue that has long bedevilled the NDP. In this campaign, the controversy that erupted within Quebec over the national question press conference by seven New Democratic candidates (dubbed the Group of Seven) was the first time that *Le Devoir* and *La Presse* both focused their coverage on the NDP's 'We belong!' claim. The press conference thrust front and centre the highly sensitive issue of the defence of Bill 101 versus the protection of minority rights, which had been dormant, awaiting a Supreme Court decision. The notwithstanding clause of the Constitution, which nationalists wanted to use as a foil to the anticipated striking down of Bill 101 by the court, was at the heart of the question. The whole issue was so sensitive that Caplan, Kirby, and Segal (1989) repeatedly state that the strategists of all three parties were terrified at the thought that the Supreme Court might release its decision on Bill 101's sign provisions before November 21. Pending the justices' decision, the parties would try hard to ignore the issue.

The text of the Group of Seven press release itself was submitted to the party's chief strategists, who approved it (Caplan, Kirby, and Segal 1989). Amazingly, they seemed to forget that this was a powder keg, and were unprepared for the reactions of opponents to Québécois nationalism, which were faithfully sought out and reported by the media. Instead of sticking to the party-approved position and consistently positioning themselves on the (moderate) nationalist side, Ed Broadbent and his strategists hedged and more or less disavowed the seven candidates. Then, Broadbent came up with a stance he could be comfortable with: a rather noncommittal support for Bill 101's goals of protecting the French language, and a disclaimer: Je ne suis pas Québécois. Although factually accurate, politically prudent, and superficially respectful of Québécois sensitivities, 'Je ne suis pas Québécois' was an astonishing denial of the 'We belong!' claim.

Broadbent's statement could be translated either as 'I am not a Quebecer' or 'I am not a Québécois', with markedly different consequences. In the first formulation, the French *Québécois* is taken to be merely descriptive, a resident of Quebec; this is what Broadbent intended, as the rest of his statement makes clear. But in Canadian political language, Québécois is often left untranslated in English, as in 'The Québécois nation . . .', indicating a particular allegiance to Quebec, and to its French character. In this connection, I want to argue that there is a larger political meaning to Broadbent's statement than the mere fact of his province of residence. If it is usually expected that a party speaks through its leader, then the disengagement stated in 'Je ne suis pas Québécois' can be understood as the NDP say-

ing 'I am not a Québécois'. Broadbent's personal origin, clearly, is not what mattered here, for the point in dispute was where NDP loyalties stood. By claiming that in fact, he did not belong, Broadbent failed to express his (and his party's) solidarity with Quebec's French majority, something that was supposed to be at the heart of the NDP's campaign. The NDP leader's final stand in this controversy did manage to put down a fire lit by his own troops, who had been using a page of the campaign's own instruction book in trying to appeal to Quebec's moderate nationalists. But Broadbent failed to enhance his party's commitment to its chosen constituency. And this can stand as the embodiment of the NDP's message to Quebec in 1988, the year when the NDP was supposed to make itself a home among the Québécois.

Conclusion: Re/established Narratives

In its attempt to become one of the two major players in Canadian federal politics, the NDP in 1988 used its resources poorly across the country, and offered a weak message to (at least) Quebec, one of its key targets. There is no mystery, then, as to why it failed, in Quebec as elsewhere. There ought to be no mystery, in particular, about why Quebecers did not respond more positively to the NDP. This brings up the issue of the reactions to the NDP's disappointing 1988 results.

Election after election since its creation in the early 1960s, the NDP has fielded candidates in Quebec ridings and has failed to get any of them elected. There are no in-depth social-scientific studies whose aim is to understand that failure, but assignment of blame has never been hard to come by, in the media, among political activists and commentators, and in social-scientific literature only marginally concerned with the issue. In 1988, the NDP's expected gains did not materialize on election night. Party officials, defeated candidates, and media analysts were quick off the mark in offering answers to the question 'Why not?' A party line emerged immediately—an 'official story'. On the very night of the election, party officials and defeated candidates said that the NDP had been marginalized by the free trade issue, which had turned the election into a referendum after the TV debates. But if this was so, *why* was the party marginalized by the free trade debate? Because, some NDPers said, in such critical situations people revert to familiar options—in this case, the Conservatives and the Liberals. Others, especially in the labour movement, blamed the party leadership for allowing the Liberals to steal the free trade issue.

The party line was meant to account for the NDP's failure to do better, indeed to supplant the Liberal Party, across Canada. It was supplemented in the Quebec arena by a bipartisan (Liberal and New Democrat) denunciation of Robert Bourassa and other provincial politicians who supported the free trade deal and, therefore, the Conservatives. By highlighting phenomena that are 'beyond the NDP's control', the party line appealed to the old NDP narrative, often activated in the wake of a defeat—in the 1962 Quebec provincial election, for example, when the nationalization of electricity issue caused the party to hitch a ride on the Liberal bandwagon (see Morton 1986).

At the same time as the official story was put forward, a set of alternative stories were offered by disappointed candidates and supporters, and by 'experts' and journalists, that focused on Quebec-specific phenomena. What is remarkable in both the official story and the alternative stories is how quickly they emerged—in fact, even before election day. Instant analysis, it is true, has become a required element of media coverage of 'breaking' events. On what were these instant assessments based? By and large, the Quebec-specific stories reproduced extant explanations of the NDP's historic 'absence' from Quebec. Sketchy as they are, existing interpretations of the CCF-NDP's failures in Quebec revolve around three interrelated but distinct axes, grounded respectively on a theory of 'Quebec society', a theory of the nature of the CCF-NDP, and a politics of the national question. Individual authors typically proceed to articulate at least two of the three axes and, depending on theoretical and political proclivities, switch the blame for NDP failures from one axis to the other.

The first theme refers to an alleged lack of a populist and/or labour tradition in Quebec, which could have provided the party with a constituency. Walter Young (1969: 210) thus wrote: 'French-Canadian society lacked the characteristics that would have led to more leftist voting.' The salience of this theme was at its highest for the period before the 1960s, but may live on when interweaved with the second theme, which holds that the NDP is essentially foreign to Quebec, that it has no roots there. Young continues: 'While the CCF did have an intellectual cadre in English Canada, it lacked an indigenous one in Québec.' Echoing Young, Jacques Rouillard has offered this characterization of Quebec's political culture up to and including the mid-1960s: 'contrary to English Canada, social democratic thought has almost no tradition in the francophone milieu. It will take long term work to establish the new party' (Rouillard 1989: 397 [my translation]).

The third theme, when interweaved with the previous one, has given rise to interpretations at both the societal and organizational level. At the societal level, the whole thrust of the Quiet Revolution is often believed to have undermined the NDP's potential in several decisive ways: it attracted to the Quebec government a battery of tools thought to be necessary to an activist federal government; by becoming a very large employer of unionized workers, the provincial government concentrated onto itself the attention and the ambivalent loyalty of labour federations; finally, the Quiet Revolution fuelled a nationalism that quickly gave rise to the Parti Québécois and made separatism hegemonic among the Left—

with the result that the PQ became a proxy for a Quebec-based social democratic party. This thesis describes well the sequence of events in Quebec since the 1960s, and it is often reproduced in various forms in literature where this history is relevant without being of central importance (see for instance Brym, Gillespie, and Lenton 1989). While adequate for such purposes, however, a good description is not an explanation.

These alternative stories, then, were reaffirming the validity of the old 'NDP in Quebec' narrative, against the new narrative that had attempted to establish itself in the previous two years. But where did it come from, this old narrative? What kind of knowledge about the NDP in Quebec was it made of? The first difficulty one encounters in the literature on the NDP is that so many NDP scholars also are, or have been, NDP activists. For such scholars, the task of standing outside or at the margins of the dominant NDP narrative(s) can be expected to be especially difficult. Desmond Morton's (1986) violent criticism of the Waffle in his history of the NDP, *The New Democrats, 1961–1986: The Politics of Change*, can be traced back to his participation as a mainstream NDPer in the Waffle debates. And the narrative rationale of André Lamoureux's work on the NDP in Quebec (1985, 1988, 1989) would seem to be geared more to the politics of the NPD-*Québec* than to some scholarly rationale—this being said in full consciousness of how fragile the distinction might be. The discursive territory covered by scholars such as Morton and Lamoureux is the very same one that is defined and inhabited by political agents themselves, thereby giving a veneer of 'learned' history to the categories of thought of 'national memory'. Scholars who situate themselves within the terms of the debate which they purport to study can only produce a knowledge of that which is already known through the social intercourse that ostensibly needs to be elucidated. As such, they condemn themselves to reproducing in their accounts the

patterns being analysed. A second difficulty of the literature on the NDP in Quebec is that, with the exception of Lamoureux's work, all published interpretations (which draw upon the three axes noted above), are fragmentary and anecdotal; and they often make their points implicitly.

What is missing from all those accounts is a sense of the overall work that was done by the NDP to attract votes, in 1988 and before. Our resulting knowledge of the NDP in Quebec is impressionistic, if not outright spurious. Accounts of the NDP's repeated failures abound, then, but they all rely on exceedingly narrow types of data, leaving in the dark key dimensions of social intercourse. Given that a contemporary electoral campaign happens at several levels, it is not enough for analysts to look at the national level—the leaders' tours, the party stars, and the official policies, all these the focus of the mass media's attention—in order to explain the results. If we think about the campaign from the voter's point of view, it is clear that how the media report the parties' efforts matters, as does the ground level action: the quality of the riding organizations in terms of campaign workers, candidates, and finances. We have just seen, indeed, that a large part of the NDP's experience in Quebec as elsewhere can be accounted for by its coverage in the media and its electoral expenses.

What may we conclude, then, from this analysis of the federal NDP's electoral practice in 1988, the year when it had its best-ever chance to break out of third-party status? First, that although the NDP claimed to be joining the major leagues, it was not at all equipped to do so—whether in Quebec, Ontario, or in most other provinces. But whatever the NDP did in Quebec in 1988, it worked to some extent—and it worked better than in Ontario, Manitoba, Nova Scotia, and New Brunswick, where NDP support declined compared with 1984. Having targeted Quebec's francophone voters, the NDP did attract more of them than in the past, but it was at the cost of alienating traditional, anglophone supporters who were horrified at the wooing of Quebec nationalists—no matter how weak-kneed that attempt was. Second, then, we can conclude that with regard to Quebec, the NDP's pan-Canadian pattern of weakness accounts to a large extent for its failure to break through to the Québécois; we have also seen, however, that the party was inept at communicating an attractive message to the Québécois.

In the end, Quebecers, like other Canadians, had a tendency to vote for NDP candidates in a degree proportionate to the strength of these candidates' local campaigns, no matter what the party's weak message. This conclusion goes strongly against the conventional wisdom of NDP weakness in Quebec, which ascribes everything to the national question. It is in accord, on the other hand, with the general expectations of poststructuralist literature, which is skeptical of the ability of grand narratives such as nationalism to account for social life. Rather, this literature puts the emphasis on the 'micro-practices' of everyday life which, in an electoral campaign, include the local campaigns. The confirmation of this expectation in our analysis of campaign expenses was not pre-ordained: we may have found that there was no particular relationship between patterns of local expenses and electoral success. That we did find this empirical confirmation does not mean, however, that the national question does not matter, or that the NDP was ever convincingly 'Québécois'. The NDP has not been convincingly Québécois, and the national question matters, but in a less concentrated way than is generally expected.

This is important because something like the conventional wisdom about the NDP in Quebec is not found only in academic textbooks: it is 'out there', in the media, among political activists—a component of interpretive communities. And, by being called upon to explain a disappointment like the NDP's 1988 electoral result, it contributes to exacerbating the national conflict in the Canada/Quebec relationship: NDPers in English Canada got angry at Quebecers when they might have recognized that in fact Quebec support kept overall NDP support from dropping; and Quebecers felt scapegoated, at a time when they had been more responsive than ever to the party. Thus, at the NDP's 1989 leadership convention, English Canadian NDPers were both critical of the attempted alliance with Quebec nationalism's left wing, and increasingly hostile to constitutional accommodation with Quebec. And not only was the Quebec delegation smaller than it might have been because a number of potential delegates had been put off by postelection criticism of Quebec, but those who did go felt embattled throughout the convention and rather less than welcome. The national question explains relatively little of the NDP's experience in Quebec in 1988; but when people automatically revert to the national grand narrative to explain failure, they make it a self-fulfilling claim by feeding subsequent conflicts *and* they hide from view the NDP's problems in English Canada. Only when we look past this all-too-convenient story can we begin to understand the NDP's cross-Canada debacle since then. But that is *another* story.

References

Ang, I. 1990. 'The Nature of the Audience'. In *Questioning the Media,* ed. J. Downing et al.

Archer, K. 1990 *Political Choices and Electoral Consequences. A Study of Organized Labour and the New Democratic Party* (Montreal and Kingston, McGill-Queen's University Press).

Baldus, B. 1990. 'In Defense of Theory: A Reply to Cheal and Prus', *The Canadian Journal of Sociology* 15 (4): 470–75.

Bradford, N. 1989. 'Ideas, Intellectuals, and Social Democracy in Canada'. In *Canadian Parties in Transition,* ed. Gagnon and Tanguay, 83–110.

Brodie, J., and J. Jenson. 1988. *Crisis, Challenge and Change. Party and Class in Canada Revisited* (Ottawa: Carleton University Press).

Brym, R.J., M.W. Gillespie, and R.L. Lenton. 1989. 'Class Power, Class Mobilization, and Class Voting: The Canadian Case', *The Canadian Journal of Sociology* 14(1): 25–44.

Caplan, G., M. Kirby, and H. Segal. 1989. *Election. The Issues, The Strategies, The Aftermath* (Scarborough, ON: Prentice-Hall).

Carr, D. 1986. *Time, Narrative and History* (Bloomington: Indiana University Press).

Denis, C. 1993. 'Quebec-as-Distinct-Society as Conventional Wisdom: The Constitutional Silence of Anglo-Canadian Sociologists', *The Canadian Journal of Sociology* 18(3): 251–69.

———. 1994. *False Hopes: The New Democratic Party of Canada in Quebec in the 1988 Federal Elections.* Ph.D. diss. Department of Sociology, University of Toronto.

Denis, R. and S. Denis. 1992. *Les syndicats face au pouvoir. Syndicalisme et politique au Québec de 1960 à 1992* (Ottawa, Les Editions du Vermilion).

Dufour, C. 1989. *Le défi québécois* (Montréal: L'Hexagone).

Eco, U. 1990. *The Limits of Interpretation* (Bloomington: Indiana University Press).

Fraser, G. 1989. *Playing for Keeps: The Making of the Prime Minister, 1988* (Toronto, McClelland & Stewart).

Gagnon, G. 1971. 'La gauche a-t-elle un avenir au Québec?' In *Essays on the Left. Essays in Honour of T.C. Douglas*, ed. Laurier Lapierre et al. (Toronto and Montréal, McClelland & Stewart).

Heidenreich, R. 1989. 'La problématique du lecteur et de la réception', *Cahiers de recherche sociologique* 12: 77–89.

Johnston, R., A. Blais, H. Brody, and J. Crête. 1992. *Letting the People Decide: Dynamics of a Canadian Election* (Montreal/Kingston: McGill-Queen's University Press).

Lamoureux, A. 1985. *Le NPD et le Québec. 1958–1985* (Montréal, Editions du Parc).

———. 1988. 'Le NPD de 1984 à 1988; la recherche d'un nouvel élan', *Politique* (Revue de la Société québécoise de science politique) 14: 83–118.

———. 1989. 'L'élection fédérale de 1988 et la défaillance du NPD', *Politique*, 15: 79–103.

Lipset, S.M. 1950. *Agrarian Socialism: The Cooperative Commonwealth Federation in Saskatchewan. A Study in Political Sociology* (Berkeley: University of California Press).

Macpherson, C.B. 1953. *Democracy in Alberta. The Theory and Practice of a Quasi-party System* (Toronto, University of Toronto Press).

Milner, H. and S.H. Milner. 1973. *The Decolonization of Québec: An Analysis of Left-Wing Nationalism* (Toronto: McClelland & Stewart).

Morley, J.T. 1988. 'Annihilation Avoided: The New Democratic Party in the Federal General Election'. In *Canada at the Polls, 1984,* ed. H. Penniman (Durham, NC: Duke University Press).

Morton, D. 1986. *The New Democrats 1961–1986: The Politics of Change* (Toronto: Copp Clark Pitman).

Penniman, H. (ed.). 1988. *Canada at the Polls, 1984: A Study of the Federal General Elections* (Chapel Hill: Duke University Press, for the American Enterprise Institute for Public Policy Research).

Postgate, D., and K. McRoberts. 1976. *Québec: Social Change and Political Crisis* (Toronto: McClelland & Stewart).

Prus, R. 1990. 'The Interpretive Challenge: The Impending Crisis in Sociology', *Canadian Journal of Sociology* 15(3): 355–63.

Przeworski, A. and J. Sprague. 1986. *Paper Stones: A History of Electoral Socialism* (Chicago: University of Chicago Press).

Rouillard, J. 1989. *Histoire du syndicalisme au Québec: des origines à nos jours* (Montréal: Boréal).

Salee, D. 1986. 'Pour une autopsie de l'imaginaire québécois: Regards sur la morosité postmoderne', *Canadian Journal of Political and Social Theory* 10(3): 114–23.

Taylor, C. 1991. 'Shared and Divergent Values'. In *Options for a New Canada,* eds Ronald L. Watts and D.M. Brown (Toronto: University of Toronto Press), 53–76.

Tremblay, G. (dir.). 1990. *Les industries de la culture et de la communication au Québec et au Canada* (Sillery et Sainte-Foy (Qué.): Presses de l'Université du Québec-Télé-Université).

Turner, B.S. 1990. 'Periodization and Politics in the Postmodern'. In *Theories of Modernity and Postmodernity,* ed. B. Turner (Newbury Park: Sage).

Weinmann, H. 1987. *Du Canada au Québec: Généalogie d'une histoire* (Montréal: L'Hexagone).

Whitehorn, A. 1992. *Canadian Socialism. Essays on the CCF-NDP* (Toronto: Oxford University Press).

Young, W.D. 1969. *Anatomy of a Party: The National CCF 1932–1961* (Toronto: University of Toronto Press).

Chapter 13

The Quebec Independence Movement: From Its Emergence to the 1995 Referendum

Maurice Pinard

Introduction

Most Western multicultural societies witnessed a surge of ethnoregional movements during the 1960s and early 1970s, but on the whole these movements have been on the decline since around the middle 1970s. The Quebec independence movement followed that pattern until recently. Although its decline came somewhat later, it also lost ground during most of the 1980s. Contrary, however, to its counterparts elsewhere, it began to re-emerge dramatically during the late 1980s, to attain levels of popular support unimagined even during its earlier heydays. It has now recently been going through a second phase of decline, although it remains stronger than in previous phases. This is most visible with regard to the separation or independence of Quebec, the most radical option of the Quebec movement. Until 1989, that option had never attracted the support of more than about one citizen in four, with much lower levels of support in the early 1960s and during the decline of the mid-1980s. But by 1990, it drew the adhesion of close to a majority, to decline again to a level of support of about one in three voters. How can the emergence and the various phases of growth and decline of this movement (or similar ones) be explained?

To answer at least part of this question, we will, in the first section, describe the four phases of the movement and in particular the sudden and spectacular shifts observed around 1990 in the options of Quebecers in the light of long-term trends. This will be done by focusing on three variants of the movement's constitutional options: first, the separation or independence of Quebec; second, sovereignty; and third, a less radical option, sovereignty-association.[1] Because of space limitations, we will not be able to present an analysis of all four phases in this paper, but we will, in the second section, consider the original upsurge, which will be analysed in theoretical and comparative terms.[2] Finally, a last section will consider a major recent episode, the 1995 Quebec referendum, the outcome of which will be briefly analysed.

The Four Phases of the Quebec Movement

SUPPORT FOR THE INDEPENDENCE OF QUEBEC

Quebec's current independence movement has now gone through four specific phases since its emergence around 1960: a first, relatively long phase of slow growth, which lasted until 1980 (I); a second, more rapid phase of demobilization, from 1980 to 1987 (II); a third phase of spectacular growth from 1988 to 1990 (III); and a new phase of rapid demobilization from 1991 to at least 1995, on the eve of the referendum of that year (IV). Although all these phases are, as we will see, most visible through data on the mobilization or demobilization of popular support for the movement's original option, the independence of Quebec, they could also (except possibly the last one) be observed clearly through an examination of trends in membership in the movement organizations, or trends in the monetary resources they have collected through fund drives (Millar 1997).

Since 1962, the support for independence or separation of Quebec has been repeatedly measured in polls, with either identical or relatively similar questions.[3] Summary trend data, based on 117 polls taken between 1962 and 1994, are presented in Figure 13.1.[4] (For details see Table 13.1.)

At the very beginning, during the early sixties, less than 10 per cent favoured independence, while about 75 per cent were opposed to it. Then the movement grew slowly during the first phase until it reached a peak in 1980, on the eve of the referendum held by the Parti Québécois government on its sovereignty-association option (all polls of that year were taken before the May referendum). By that time, about a quarter of the respondents favoured independence, but yet again no less than two in three were still opposed to it—usually *strongly* opposed to it, as data not presented here indicate (Pinard 1980: 159). The proportion undecided was also slowly decreasing. Overall, between 1962 and 1980, support increased by only 16 per cent—slightly less than one per cent per year on the average—while opposition decreased by only 12 per cent, and irregularly at that. Notice that most of the growth during that first phase took place before 1976, the year the Parti Québécois (PQ) came to power. It is as if, once it had been elected, many voters had become worried about its option so that no further mass mobilization took place.

In 1980, towards the end of its first term in office, the PQ lost a first referendum on a softer option, that is a simple mandate to negotiate sov-

ereignty-association, with a Yes vote of 40.4 per cent against a No vote of 59.6 per cent. This defeat signalled the beginning of the second phase, one of demobilization. While the PQ itself was re-elected for a second term in 1981, it was defeated in 1985. Meanwhile, as will be discussed later, it took increasingly more moderate constitutional stands until 1988, and membership and militancy within the party declined substantially; so did public support for independence, which gradually dropped to only 15 per cent by 1985. At the same time, opposition went back up to where it stood in the early sixties, at around 75 per cent.

A clear sign that by that time the issue itself had left the public agenda is that fewer and fewer poll measurements of the support for that option were being taken; indeed, none that we know of were carried out in 1986 and 1987.

As for the third phase, there is an indication from a few 1988 polls that the resurgence started at about that time.[5] The existence of a resurgence, and of a strong one at that, was confirmed during the second half of 1989, during which all polls of that year were carried out. Support for independence then reached the level of one in three respondents—a level never attained before—and opposition dropped to barely more than one in two. The new pronounced upward trend continued in 1990 when, for the first time, the proportions of supporters and opponents were about equal, at around 45 per cent. Indeed, the trend reached its peak in the last six months of 1990, following the formal demise of the Meech Lake Accord in June of that year: at that point, according to the two polls taken then, 56 per cent were in favour of independence and only 36 per cent were against it (see Table 13.1). All in all, in three years, support for the option had increased by some 30 percentage points above the 1985 low point or, on the average, 10 per cent per year, something spectacular, when compared to the growth of less than one per cent per year before 1980. Even if one assumes that, as in the past,

Table 13.1 Support for Independence in Quebec: 1962–95*

Phases	Polls	For (%)	Against (%)	Not Stated (%)
I 1962–65	2	8	76	17
1968–72	6	11	73	17
1973–74	2	16	69	15
1976	1	18	58	24
1977	10	19	69	13
1978	3	14	75	10
1979	6	19	71	10
1980	9	24	64	12
II 1981	2	23	65	12
1982	2	22	68	10
1983	2	20	74	7
1984	1	16	76	7
1985	1	15	74	11
III 1988	1	28	47	25
1989	3	34	53	13
1990	9	46	45	9
IV 1991	13	44	48	8
1992	12	35	53	12
1993	4	37	53	10
1994	28	36	55	10
1995 (to June)	11	37	54	9
Semiyearly Data				
1990 (Feb–April)	4	44	46	11
1990 (May–June)	3	43	49	8
1990 (Nov–Dec)	2	56	36	9
1991 (Feb–June)	7	44	46	9
1991 (Sept–Oct)	6	43	50	7
1992 (Feb–July)	5	38	51	11
1992 (Aug–Nov)	7	34	54	13
1993 (April)	1	37	50	13
1993 (Oct–Dec)	3	37	54	9
1994 (Mar–July)	12	38	52	10
1994 (Aug–Dec)	16	34	57	10
1995 (Jan–June)	11	37	54	9

* Percentages are unweighed averages of the polls conducted for each year or period considered. Questions varied from poll to poll, but referred to either the 'separation' or the 'independence' of Quebec, with respondents being asked whether they were favourable to it or not, or whether they would vote for it or not in a referendum. For more details on our data from 1962 to 1980, see Breton and Stasiulis 1980: 305–8; Hamilton and Pinard 1982 and other references listed therein; for subsequent data, contact the author.

Figure 13.1 Support for Independence in Quebec: 1962–94

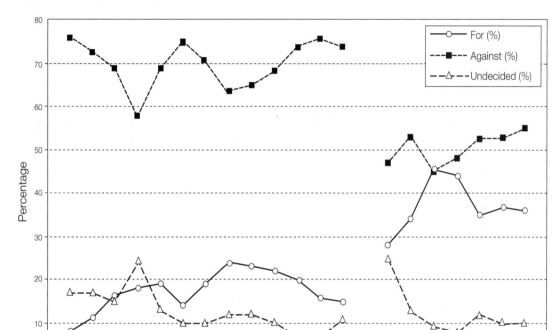

most of the undecided would disproportionately lean toward opposition, this would not change the observation that for all of 1990 close to a majority now declared themselves supporters of independence and that a clear majority appeared to be in favour of it by the fall of 1990.

But a countertrend was quick to develop, against the expectations of those who thought the turnaround of the third phase was a definitive one. This new phase, the fourth one, was marked by demobilization again. It started slowly in 1991, followed by a sharp drop in 1992, with barely more than a third (35 per cent) then favouring independence and a majority (53 per cent) being opposed to it. Support and opposition stabilized at around those levels until the eve

of the 1995 referendum. It is evident, however, that this new trough was higher than that observed around 1985. Indeed, the overall trend of the last 35 years or so is clearly an upward one, showing, as during the first phase, an average increase in support for independence of close to one per cent per year.

In what precedes, if instead of considering all Quebec respondents, one looked only at francophones, who constitute 83 per cent of the Quebec population, the proportions favourable to independence would have been about 4 per cent higher until 1985 and about 6 or 7 per cent higher since then. This meant that among francophones, supporters were in the majority during 1990 and 1991, but have been in the minority since then.

SUPPORT FOR THE SOVEREIGNTY OF QUEBEC

In 1987–88 the radicalization of the PQ, brought on by the return of the 'orthodox' wing to a dominant position in the party under Jacques Parizeau's leadership, marked a revival of the original option of the early 1960s. But instead of returning to *independence*, the term used at that time, the term *sovereignty* was adopted to refer to the party's option. This term, of course, came from René Lévesque's 'sovereignty-association' option, but with the association part of it now being relegated to a nonessential, indeed clearly secondary position. Political sovereignty was the goal, and the economic association, while seen as desirable, was no longer a prerequisite for the former. Pollsters followed suit and started using the single term *sovereignty* in their measures of support for the party's option. It yielded different results.

Indeed, while all three terms—separation, independence, and sovereignty—refer to the same reality, that is, the secession of Quebec from the rest of Canada, the levels of support and especially of opposition started to differ substantially according to the term used by pollsters, as if they were three different options, even though the leaders of the movement recognized that they were not. This was something new, as the use of the terms separation and independence, the only ones used previously, had hardly made a difference.[6]

The levels of support and opposition for these three variants of the secessionist option, between 1988 and 1994, are presented in Table 13.2.[7] First, in all three cases, the data of course show again the dramatic upsurge taking place between 1988 and 1990, and the decline that followed. But the differences in support or opposition between the three variants of the same option are no less striking, with sovereignty eliciting higher levels of support than independence, and independence higher levels than separation. Specifically, the data show that support for sovereignty exceeded support for independence by an average of 8 percent-

age points between 1989 and 1993, and the difference between sovereignty and separation averaged 11 points in favour of sovereignty during the same period. Even independence elicited greater support than separation, with a difference of about 7 per cent between 1990 and 1992. Inverse and even greater differences appeared in the case of opposition to these options. Opposition to separation was greater than opposition to sovereignty by an average of 15 points. Moreover, the percentage of those not revealing their choice increased slightly as we move from separation to sovereignty. It is no surprise, therefore, that federalists preferred the terms separation or even independence and that secessionists were campaigning under the sovereignist umbrella.

The data also reveal that lately, as support for these options has declined, the differences between them have been narrowing down. In particular, by 1994, support for sovereignty and independence no longer differed, as support for sovereignty dropped that year to the level of support independence had already reached two years earlier. As a result, by 1994, support for sovereignty, which had appeared to be a 'winning' option from 1990 to 1993, started lagging behind opposition to it; support now stood at 38 per cent, and opposition, at 48 per cent.[8] This situation continued to prevail in the spring of 1995 (see Table 13.3 for details).

What are the reasons for the differences we have just described? For one thing, there is still a great deal of confusion about the meaning of these terms. In addition, there may also be some misunderstanding about their implications.

First, the confusion. For many, these are not simply different terms, but different options. While the meaning of separation may be understood, the same is not true for sovereignty. In particular, many see it as maintaining *political* ties with the rest of Canada. Thus, according to a March 1992 CROP survey, among others, 31 per cent of respondents mistakenly believed, among other things, that a

Table 13.2 Support for Quebec Secession According to Terms Used in Polls: 1988–95

	Separation, Full Independence, Or similar terms	Independence or Independent country	Sovereignty or Sovereign country	Differences Col. 2 minus Col. 1	Differences Col. 3 minus Col. 1	Differences Col. 3 minus Col. 2
% Favourable						
1988	—	28	27	—	—	-1
1989	37	29	41	-8	+4	+12
1990	42	50	58	+8	+16	+8
1991	41	47	52	+6	+11	+5
1992	32	39	47	+7	+15	+8
1993	36	38	45	+2	+9	+7
1994	34	38	38	+4	+4	0
1995 (to June)	37	37	39	0	+2	+2
% Unfavourable						
1988	—	47	58	—	—	+11
1989	51	56	46	+5	-5	-10
1990	50	41	30	-9	-20	-10
1991	52	43	34	-9	-18	-9
1992	58	48	38	-10	-20	-10
1993	56	50	39	-6	-17	-11
1994	57	51	48	-6	-9	-3
1995 (to June)	54	53	50	-1	-4	-3
% Not Stated (No. of Polls)						
1988	—	25 (1)	15 (1)	—	—	-10
1989	13 (2)	14 (1)	13 (3)	+1	0	-1
1990	9 (4)	10 (5)	12 (7)	+1	+3	+2
1991	7 (7)	10 (6)	14 (12)	+3	+7	+2
1992	11 (6)	13 (6)	15 (17)	+2	+4	+2
1993	8 (2)	13 (2)	16 (12)	+5	+8	+3
1994	9 (19)	11 (9)	14 (28)	+2	+5	+3
1995 (to June)	9 (9)	11 (2)	11 (22)	+2	+2	0

NOTE: In the first column we give the results that use only the word *separation* or the words separation and *independence* together; also included are the results of questions referring to 'complete independence, both political and economic', or 'without formal ties with Canada' or referring to Quebec 'as remaining (or not) a province of Canada' and so on. The second column only contains results of questions that use the single word *independence* (of Quebec) or the term *independent country*, and the third column, *sovereignty* (of Quebec) or *sovereign state or country*. Each percentage is the unweighted average of the percentages in all polls that fell in one or the other of the categories that year. The number of polls involved for each item in the table is given in parentheses in the lower part of the table.

Table 13.3 Support for Sovereignty: 1988–95*

Phases	Polls	Favourable (%)	Unfavourable (%)	Not Stated (%)
III 1988	1	27	58	15
1989	3	41	46	13
1990	7	58	30	12
IV 1991	12	52	34	14
1992	17	47	38	15
1993	12	45	39	16
1994	28	38	48	14
1995 (to June)	22	39	50	11
Semiyearly Data				
1990 (Feb–June)**	3	57	33	11
1990 (June–Dec)	4	59	28	14
1991 (Feb–June)	6	53	34	14
1991 (Aug–Dec)	6	52	35	13
1992 (Feb–June)	9	48	37	15
1992 (Aug–Oct)	8	46	39	15
1993 (Feb–Jun)	5	45	41	14
1993 (Sept–Dec)	7	44	38	18
1994 (Jan–Jun)	8	43	44	13
1994 (Jul–Sept)***	9	36	52	12
1994 (Sept–Nov)	5	35	49	16
1994 (Dec)****	6	39	47	15
1995 (Jan–June)	22	39	50	11

*Questions varied from poll to poll, and referred to *sovereignty* or to a *sovereign country*, with respondents being asked whether they were favourable to it or not, or whether they would vote for it or not in a referendum. The averages are unweighted. Before 1994, questions on opinions (being favourable or not to the option) or on vote intentions did not make much difference, when any; in 1994 and 1995, vote intentions for sovereignty were respectively 6 and 8 percentage points lower than opinions favourable to it, so that part of the decline in those years is attributable to those differences.

**From February to June, before Meech official demise on June 24th.

***From July to September 12, date of the provincial election bringing the PQ to power.

****In December, after the PQ made public its first draft bill on Quebec's sovereignty.

sovereign Quebec 'would still be part of Canada', and 14 per cent did not know; similarly, 20 per cent thought that Quebecers 'would still elect members of Parliament to Ottawa', and 21 per cent did not know.[9] Another CROP survey (April 1992) revealed that no less than one-quarter of the respondents in favour of 'Quebec sovereignty' opted, in reply to another question, for Quebec 'to remain a province of Canada' rather than 'to become an independent country'.

With so much confusion, it is not surprising that in a 1992 study different results were obtained depending on the wording of the question on sovereignty (Blais and Gidengil 1993). When respondents were simply asked if they were in favour of or opposed to 'Quebec sovereignty', 47 per cent said they were in favour and 38 per cent opposed; when they were asked instead if they were in favour of or opposed to 'Quebec sovereignty, that is, Quebec is no longer a part of Canada', only 39 per cent said they were in favour and 55 per cent opposed (and those who were undeclared dropped from 15 per cent to 6 per cent). In short, by being specific that sovereignty means 'Quebec would no longer be part of Canada', support for that option dropped by 8 per cent and opposition increased by 17 per cent. These differences, incidentally, are very similar to those shown in Figure 13.1 and Tables 13.1 through 13.3. The authors further concluded, at the time, that 'the standard surveys in Quebec overestimate support for sovereignty by close to 10 percentage points'. (See also Johnston et al. 1996, ch. 8, in which the data, limited to francophones and to voters, reveal even greater differences.)

Observed differences also come from some misunderstandings. Many assume that an *economic* association would accompany not only sovereignty but also independence, even though the survey questions selected here are not measures of support for sovereignty-association as such. Support for the latter, as will be seen presently, is even higher.

As far as sovereignty proper is concerned, there may be no misunderstanding among those who support it, believing it probable, if not certain, that sovereignty will eventually be accompanied by an economic association. But there is misunderstanding among those who support sovereignty, if they think that it is only a short form for 'sovereignty-association', and that sovereignty will not occur if an economic association is not successfully established at the same time.

An April 1991 *Canadian Facts* survey supports this interpretation. It revealed that 58 per cent of Quebecers intended to vote for sovereignty and 31 per cent against it, if there was no constitutional accord in 1992. But only 51 per cent chose a sovereign country, while 44 per cent preferred to remain within Canada, when they thought that an agreement on an economic association could not be reached.

Similar data were obtained in several surveys concerning independence. An April 1993 SOM survey showed that 37 per cent of Quebecers would vote for and 50 per cent against the proposal that Quebec become an independent country. However, when faced with the specific scenario of Canada refusing an economic association with Quebec, only 31 per cent of respondents chose independence, compared to 55 per cent against.[10] In a more general way, when survey questions specify that independence means the absence of political and economic ties with the rest of Canada, support diminishes by 6 to 7 per cent.[11]

Finally, the differences we observe between support for separation and support for the other two variants of that option could, in some cases, be because of the fact that some supporters of independence refuse to state their preference when the term *separation* is part of the question, because the connotations of that term are too negative in their view.

SUPPORT FOR SOVEREIGNTY-ASSOCIATION

With polls in 1994 and early 1995 indicating that a new referendum could not be won on sovereignty alone, sovereignist leaders took a *virage* in April 1995 and realigned themselves on the original PQ option, that is, sovereignty-association, adding even a political component to the economic association envisioned in that option and renaming it 'sovereignty-partnership'. It is therefore important to examine the level of support for that option.

Sovereignty-association represents, of course, a much softer option than the three variants of the secessionist option just discussed. By including an economic association with the rest of Canada together with political independence, this option, as implied above, reassures many voters who would otherwise be afraid of the presumed economic costs of complete independence. Indeed, polls have often indicated that people expect lower economic costs from sovereignty-association than from independence (Pinard 1980: 169–71).

On the other hand, sovereignty-association, like sovereignty, also remains a confused notion. In 1980, as with sovereignty, many thought that under sovereignty-association, Quebec would remain a province of Canada and continue to elect deputies in Ottawa. Moreover, our analysis revealed that misinformed respondents were more likely to have voted Yes in the 1980 referendum than well-informed ones (Pinard and Hamilton 1984).

For these reasons, the level of support for sovereignty-association has always been higher than that for separation or independence, although the differences narrowed down around 1990. It has also been higher than support for sovereignty alone, except in 1989–90, when the two drew almost equal support.

The trend data on sovereignty-association are, however, less satisfactory, as data on that option are available for only one year (1970) prior to 1977. Moreover, the levels of support and opposition to sovereignty-association vary much more from one poll to the next than is the case with regard to the other options. This is due in part to the greater complexity of, and greater confusion about, sovereignty-association (meaning of the term *sovereignty*, certainty or uncertainty about the association, whether the two components of the option are divisible or not, etc.). These issues in turn are reflected in greater variations in the questions formulated by pollsters. Be that as it

may, during the first phase of the movement, support for that option appears to have grown only slowly, and irregularly at that (see Table 13.4). In 1970 about one in every three citizens of Quebec was in favour of sovereignty-association, whereas about one in two was opposed to it. By 1980, the level of support had increased to 42 per cent, while opposition had declined to 44 per cent.[12]

Here again, this was followed from 1981 to 1985, by a phase of decline. The decline was not however very pronounced, possibly because this is a less radical option. Yet the levels of support and opposition, in 1985, were almost identical to those of 1970.

Unfortunately, for the years 1986 to 1988, there are no *opinion* data like those which served to establish Table 13.4. Importantly, there are, however, *vote intention* data for February 1988, and they do not indicate a resurgence by then.[13] Only 30 per cent then reported they would vote for sovereignty-association in a referendum, with 48 per cent saying they would vote against it.

However, just as in the case of the other options, a reversal of the downward trend, for this option, was first registered in 1989, with four respondents in ten, as in 1980, supporting it; the proportion of those opposing sovereignty-association was only a few percentage points higher than the proportion favouring it. But, more importantly, the new trend sharply gathered momentum all through 1990 and, by the fall of that year, a new peak was reached with as many as two in three respondents (65 per cent) supporting sovereignty-association and with barely more than one in four (28 per cent) opposing it (see Table 13.4).

The 1991 level of support for sovereignty-association remained at about the same level as in 1990. But the semiyearly data of Table 13.4 show that, compared to the fall of 1990, the results of 1991 indicate a slight decrease all through that year in the support of it. The decline has subsequently continued, although at a slower pace than with the other

Table 13.4 Support for Sovereignty-Association: 1970–95*

Phases	Polls	Favourable (%)	Unfavourable (%)	Not Stated (%)
I 1970	2	32	51	18
1977	2	40	48	12
1978	2	37	49	14
1979	5	34	48	19
1980	8	42	44	14
II 1981	2	36	47	18
1982	2	38	52	11
1985	1	34	51	14
III 1989	1	40	44	16
1990	6	60	29	12
IV 1991	11	61	32	8
1992	4	56	35	9
1994	2	54	39	8
1995 (to June)	8	53	39	8
Semiyearly Data				
1990 (Mar–Apr)	2	53	33	15
1990 (May)	2	61	27	13
1990 (Nov–Dec)	2	65	28	8
1991 (Feb–June)	6	62	31	7
1991 (Sept–Dec)	5	60	32	8
1992 (Feb–June)	2	55	35	11
1992 (July–Aug)	2	57	36	8
1994 (May)	1	50	41	8
1994 (Dec)	1	57	36	7
1995 (Jan–June)	8	53	39	8

*Only *opinions*, not *vote intentions*, regarding this option are considered in this table. Vote intentions on that option (in hypothetical referendums) tend to be about five percentage points lower than simple opinions expressing whether one is favourable or not to the option. The averages are unweighted.

options, probably, once again, because sovereignty-association is a less radical option than the other ones. Indeed, by 1994, that option still retained the favour of a majority (54 per cent), while only 39 per cent were opposed to it. These results did not change in early 1995, as indicated presently. In short, while there were only relatively small variations between 1977 and 1988, the following two years witnessed a dramatic upsurge in support for sovereignty-association, followed by a new decline, the two paralleling the surge and decline in support for the other options.[14]

It should be noted at this point that *vote intentions* regarding sovereignty-association have always tended to elicit levels of support about 5 percentage points lower than *opinions* favourable to it, as if some people like the option in principle, but not its actual implementation. This has not changed. Thus, in the first six months of 1995, favourable opinions regarding this option stood, on the average, at 53 per cent, while 39 per cent held unfavourable opinions and 8 per cent were undecided. But the proportion intending to vote for it was at only 47 per cent, with the percentage of those intending to vote against it standing at 42 per cent, the others not revealing their preference (11 per cent). In either case, sovereignty-association appeared to receive support from a plurality of respondents on the eve of the 1995 referendum, when the PQ leaders returned explicitly to it, but with support leading by only five percentage points in the case of vote intentions.

It should be noted, however, that polls have practically always overestimated the strength of the sovereignist forces, either in terms of PQ support in elections or support for its position in the 1980, 1992 (Charlottetown Accord), and 1995 referendums.[15]

Moreover, support for sovereignty-association has always been in large part 'conditional' in the sense that it hinged on the assurance that the economic association would be successfully negotiated. During the 1970s, half of the support for that option was conditional on an economic association in that sense while the other half was unconditional (Hamilton and Pinard 1982: 218–19; Pinard 1980: 163). Question formulations in polls usually ignore that distinction, suggesting that the two components of the option are indivisible. This would not be a serious problem if the PQ, as in the 1980 referendum, were committed to consult the population in another referendum following the negotiations regarding the option. But this is no longer the sovereignist position; it now states that in the case of a Yes victory, sovereignty would be proclaimed even if an association could not be negotiated. However in a 1995 poll, a large majority of Quebecers (73 per cent) held an economic association to be 'essential to the success of a sovereign Quebec', while only 18 per cent held the contrary view (Paré 1995: 56). Another poll found that the proportion who would vote in favour of sovereignty-association if not certain of the association stood at only 31 per cent, while 59 per cent would vote against it under such a condition, with 9 per cent undecided. Conversely, 51 per cent said they would vote for, and 39 per cent against, sovereignty if assured that the latter would not take place without an economic association.[16] The voters' correct assessment of the unconditional nature of the current PQ proposal therefore remains a crucial element of the debate, not to mention their comprehension of the term *sovereignty*. Important as well is the 'conditional' sovereignists' assessment of the likelihood of a negotiated association should the sovereignists win a referendum on that option.[17]

The Quebec Ethnic Revival of the 1960s in Comparative Perspectives

Many determinants played an important role in the emergence of the Quebec independence movement in the early 1960s and in its growth during the first phase. These factors were not, however, very different from those involved in the emergence of other ethnoregional movements in Western Europe at about the same time. While many analyses have been focused on specific movements or on a limited number of factors, a more general theoretical and comparative account can be developed for these movements as well as for other similar ones. Only a brief sketch of our perspective can, however, be presented here as a fuller presentation is well beyond the scope of this paper.

In this theoretical sketch, the phenomena to be explained are, on the one hand, the mobilization of resources, seen from the angle of their delivery to a movement by group members, and on the other hand, the movement's collective action itself. As will be mentioned later, it is when seen from the angle of the efforts of a movement to control those resources and of its success in this regard that mobilization itself becomes a determinant of collective action. We do recognize, however, that it is often difficult to empirically distinguish mobilization from collective action (Rule 1988), but their analytical distinction remains important.

MOTIVATIONAL FORCES

The first set of factors to be considered concerns various motivational elements. Whichever approach one follows, the analysis of social movements always implies a motivation model. The latter, however, remains too often implicit or incomplete; ours represents an effort to be explicit and general.

We hold that in order to be motivated to participate in an ethnic movement—or in any other type of social movement—a person must be moved by three motivational forces that are all necessary: some internal motives, that is, internal states pushing them to act; some positive external incentives, that is, potential rewards 'out there' pulling them into action; and some expectancy of success in that action. Internal motives pushing

one to act are likely to be derived from all kinds of deprivations, grievances, or threats, especially relevant ones of an ethnic nature, but can also come from simple aspirations and/or can result from some sense of moral obligation that one ought to act in accordance with one's values. As for external incentives, they will be provided by collective goods in the case of altruistic participation, and by selective ones if the person is self-interested, or a mixture of the two in most instances (Pinard and Hamilton 1986: 229–32; for more details, see Pinard 1983).

In the case of the ethnoregional movements of the 1960s and 1970s, an analogous—but not similar—set of ethnic grievances was involved together with ethnic aspirations, the latter being much more important among leaders. The most important grievances usually resulted from ethnic stratification and involved the often historically rooted ethnic inequalities of various kinds: class-economic ethnic inequalities (some ethnic groups occupying lower socioeconomic positions in the class system), regional-economic inequalities (inhabiting poorer regions), ethnic status inequalities (being considered as an inferior group), and/or ethnic political inequalities. Various cultural and in particular linguistic threats or clashes were also often important.

Theorists have too often restricted themselves to only one of these dimensions. Hechter, for instance, insisted that the first two economic dimensions were the important ones, and that besides, they were related to one another; that is, regional inequality—internal colonialism—was engendering class inequality—a cultural division of labour. For Horowitz and for Taylor, the status dimension—the recognition of equal group worth—was the main factor involved (although Taylor also insisted on the recognition of cultural differences). Breton and Breton, on the other hand, placed the emphasis on the distribution of power, more specifically organizational power and the ethnic (or regional) barriers to its attainment. Others, such as van den Berghe, tended to lump all inequality dimensions indiscriminately together, as if they were all necessarily linked. Others yet, such as M.G. Smith, or Rabushka and Shepsle, argued that the conflicts were primarily rooted in the necessary cultural clashes generated by ethnic diversity and segmentation (Breton and Breton 1980; Hechter 1975; Horowitz 1985; Rabushka and Shepsle 1972; Smith 1969; Taylor 1992; van den Berghe 1981). Our argument is that, theoretically, any one of these grievances alone—or other ethnic grievances—could suffice and that none should be assigned an exclusive role, although empirically more than one and at times all of them have been involved.[18] But we also maintain that ethnic status grievances, when present, play a most important role, because of their consequences for collective and individual self-esteem (Gordon 1975: 91–7; note that Gurr [1993] discusses all types, except status ones).

In the case of Quebec, class-economic, status, and power grievances were all involved, but regional-economic grievances were not seriously at stake; cultural threats also played a role (Breton and Stasiulis 1980; McRoberts 1979; Pinard, Bernier, and Lemieux 1997: ch. 10; Pinard and Hamilton 1986). In the cases of relatively wealthier regions (for example, the Basque country and Catalonia in Spain, Padania in Northern Italy, Croatia and Slovenia in Yugoslavia), economic subjugation was obviously not involved, but power inequalities and at times cultural grievances were important, as well as feelings that they were contributing disproportionately in providing economic subsidies to poorer regions. (On this last point, see Horowitz 1985: 249–50). For Gourevitch (1979), economic domination coupled with political subordination is even considered the main factor of ethnic resurgences. Slightly different is the case of the Walloons in Belgium; new regional-economic, but clearly not status, grievances and political, but not cultural, threats were involved; for their Flemish counter-parts, old feelings regarding previous regional-economic grievances and persisting status, political, and cultural discontents all acted as motivating forces. All four of these elements also seemed relevant in, for instance, the case of the Bretons and Corsicans in France. Political and status grievances may have been the main ones in the Scottish and Welsh peripheries of Great Britain, together with less crucial economic and cultural problems. If class-economic, status, and political grievances all played a role in Northern Ireland, the latter appeared to weigh more heavily than the others.

Switzerland offers a revealing contrast here; at the national level, none of the types of grievances just discussed has developed between Switzerland's two main linguistic groups, the French- and German-speaking Swiss, and consequently a high level of harmony has been maintained between them.[19]

In addition to internal motives such as grievances and aspirations, external collective incentives—the gains and losses perceived to be linked to means and goals of political actions—and expectancy of success also play necessary motivating roles. In Quebec, for instance, the relative popularity of various constitutional options is very much determined by their expected costs and rewards, in particular the expected economic costs of independence and the expected cultural and status gains flowing from that option (Martin 1994; Meadwell 1993; Pinard 1980; Pinard, Bernier and Lemieux, 1997: chs 4 and 10; Pinard and Hamilton 1986).[20] Not enough attention has, however, been paid to these factors in theoretical work or in empirical research bearing on other movements (but see Horowitz [1985] and Esman [1977]).[21]

ETHNIC SEGMENTATION

But motivating forces will not alone give rise to ethnic movements and conflicts. Another very important determinant is found in the degree to which ethnic groups have developed, internally, a rich substructure of various kinds of organizations and associations of their own—a well-developed civil society of their own. This encapsulates them and keeps them externally isolated from their potential opponents. In the case of ethnic groups, this is mainly provided by extensive structural ethnic segmentation (or pluralism or polarization, as it is also labelled), a situation that largely prevails, although in different forms and degrees, for all the ethnoregional groups just mentioned.[22] Particularly important in this regard is the degree to which the political parties are themselves ethnically segmented.

Variations in degrees and forms of structural segmentation will account, together with the other factors, for variations in mobilization and conflict. Such segmentation generates large pools of potential ethnic leaders and followers who are less vulnerable to sanctions by their opponents and indeed could stand to profit from ethnic mobilization; it facilitates bloc rather than individual recruitment; it decreases the negative collective incentives which national integration and interdependence, its obverse, would otherwise foster; it facilitates the intensification and the sharing of feelings of grievances and the emergence and maintenance of strong ethnic identities, loyalties, and nationalist ideologies; it fosters strong ethnic aspirations and incentives among ethnic leaders; it increases the likelihood of rapid and sustained collective protest. In short, structural ethnic segmentation is highly conducive to ethnic mobilization and collective action (Oberschall 1973: ch. 4).

Structural ethnic segmentation can be accompanied by different degrees of cultural ethnic segmentation—in particular, language diversity—and by territorial ethnic concentration.[23] The latter will indeed tend to produce the first two, and all three will have the effects posited above. There is, however, one crucial exception in this regard: territorial ethnic concentration tends, during

peaceful periods, to prevent the development of political party segmentation in single-member plurality electoral systems. That is important because a combination of territorial concentration and ethnic party segmentation could otherwise prove fatal for the maintenance of a unified polity (Pinard 1976: 44–52).

Notice that according to our view, segmentation is not *the* cause of conflict through the value clashes it generates as in M.G. Smith's framework, but a condition that is conducive to the emergence and intensification of conflict, if the necessary motivating factors for it are present in the first place.

To be sure, ethnic segmentation can exert other effects. It can, for instance, reduce the likelihood of conflict when it is present in social domains in which unfair competition between groups would otherwise prevail. Conversely, it can increase the probability of conflict by its impact on the maintenance and further development of ethnic inequalities, discrimination, and the like (Breton 1978). All in all, however, the main impact of segmentation is the positive conducive role described above. From this perspective, it also follows that different degrees of ethnic segmentation or integration prevailing among various subgroups within an ethnic group will be important for the opposition and conflict within it (for instance, between French-speaking federalists and separatists within Quebec, or in a recent past, between unitarists and federalists within each linguistic group in Belgium). Indeed, conflicts can be more intense and acrimonious within than between ethnic groups (Brass 1985).

A possible dimension of segmentation that can exert a particularly strong influence is the degree to which ethnoregional groups have political institutions of their own, for instance, in federal systems or other systems allowing for some degree of regional ethnic autonomy. On the one hand, such decentralization involves the devolution of powers to ethnoregional groups and as such it can provide at least a partial solution to political grievances and a powerful means to act on other group problems. However, federalism and other forms of decentralization are not the panaceas they are often thought to be: witness the recent conflicts in Canada, in the former Yugoslavia, or in the former Soviet Union. Decentralization offers major political incentives to ethnic political leaders who are, to say the least, rarely devoid of compelling aspirations for such power. Decentralization also becomes the primary goal of ethnoregional groups in conflict simply because it is a solution more easily seen as legitimate and amenable to legislation than various solutions to economic inequalities (e.g., quotas) and, in particular, to status grievances (the recognition of status equality cannot easily be legislated). Decentralization is also a goal because political concession may symbolize status recognition.

In this regard, it is somewhat ironic to observe that when ethnic movements emerge in a unitary political system, their leaders tend to consider federalism or other forms of regional autonomy and devolution as solutions to their grievances (as, for instance, in Belgium, in Spain, or in Great Britain), but that when such movements develop in a political system that is already federal, the latter is seen as part of the problem and outright secession is then claimed to be the solution (as, for instance, in Canada). At any rate, as long as motives for conflict remain, decentralized political institutions are simply an additional form of political segmentation, one that can be extremely conducive to further ethnic collective action. These institutions provide, in particular, ethnoregional groups with an organizational basis, a leadership pool, and an alternative focus of political loyalty that can be quite crucial when a group mobilizes to press demands against other groups or the political centre. They also contribute to an increase in the group's self-confidence regarding its ability to be completely autonomous (Dion 1996: 280). Let us add that the federal structure

can also be conducive to the rise of strong ethnoregional parties; in Canada, for instance, it allowed the Parti Québécois to become one of the two major parties in Quebec, something it could not have done at the national level, and which Belgian (until recently) and British ethnoregional parties could not do under unitary political systems. This, together with the collapse of the Union Nationale, one of the two strong provincial parties in Quebec previously, largely explains why the Parti Québécois was much more successful than many other ethnoregional parties.

ETHNIC IDENTITIES, LOYALTIES, NATIONALISM, AND OTHER BELIEFS

A third important determinant of ethnic conflict is the emergence and development of strong ethnic identities and loyalties and especially of a well-developed nationalist ideology. Ethnic groups could mobilize without well-developed ethnic identities, beliefs, and sentiments (although in that case such elements would then tend to emerge), but their prior presence, something frequent within ethnic groups, should greatly enhance the likelihood of conflict and its intensification if the other conditions are present. Let us note that collective identity issues are increasingly at the centre of concerns among students of social movements in general (see, among others, Melucci 1988 and Gamson 1992).

Our approach does not, of course, imply an adherence to the primordial sentiments perspective held by such authors as Geertz (1963) and Isaacs (1975). The assertion that the central source of ethnic conflict lies with such sentiments and their immutable, unaccountable, uncontrollable, and irrational manifestations is in our view clearly unwarranted. Ethnic nonroutine collective action is not inherently any less rational than various forms of routine collective action, and ethnic beliefs and ideologies are often changing and remain fully accountable.

There are, however, many conflicting perspectives in the theories developed to account for ethnic loyalties and nationalism. A detailed discussion is beyond the scope of this paper; suffice it to mention that some consider ethnic loyalties and nationalism as very different in nature, the former being perennial, the latter, fundamentally modern. Thus Gellner (1983) sees nationalism as a political principle which holds that the political and the national unit should be congruent. Nationalism is not rooted in existing nations being awakened to self-consciousness, but invents nations altogether, although it does need some differentiating marks to start with. And nationalism, Hall (1993) argues, has no sociological moorings whatsoever; it only depends on strong political projects.

The foregoing claims are mistaken in our view. Ethnic loyalties (as simple feelings of attachment to the group and shared interests) and nationalism (as a fully developed ideology, taking different forms, be it cultural or political, in different circumstances) are both firmly rooted in social conditions. There need not be, to be sure, any specific common heritage, or shared language and culture, or some other traits or markers. Following Stinchcombe's (1975) views, we claim that what generates ethnic loyalty and nationalism is the presence of ethnic segmentation, as defined above, that is, made of structural, cultural, and geographical elements, mixed in different ways and degrees. Moreover, the ecological ranges of segmented institutions and cultures have greatly increased with modernization, so that over time loyalties and nationalism have become the appanage of ever-larger groups (Hannan 1979). If, in addition, such groups are stratified in economic, status, or power terms, or develop other grievances, loyalties and nationalism will tend to be intensified by such motivating elements (Stinchcombe 1975: 599–616).[24] In such cases, ethnic leaders do not simply invent sentiments that they then propagate; they rather articulate through such sentiments perceptions

and grievances which, among many, may not have exhibited much consciousness, but which were nevertheless firmly rooted in their social conditions and of which they were at least vaguely aware. Leaders can then intensify such sentiments and make use of them in the pursuit of their own political goals.

Put differently, ethnic beliefs and nationalism are in our view intermediate variables, mainly rooted in the segmentation and motivational forces discussed above; but once developed, those beliefs can exert strong effects of their own.[25]

This is not to deny the argument that nationalism, as a fully articulated ideology, could not develop before modern times, nor the argument that it involves important political components, as argued by those adopting instrumentalist perspectives.[26]

In such perspectives, nationalism is seen as an instrument used by political élites for the sole mobilization of masses behind the pursuit of their political interests. State building becomes the main determinant of the emergence of nationalism, and political élites aspirations the main implied motivating forces behind it (for example, Hall 1993: 1–5).[27] Although this tells part of the story, and only as far as the élites are concerned, it misses important elements. Without a set of substructural and cultural conditions and, specifically, without ethnic segmentation and grievances, involving both masses and élites—that is, without social moorings—the élites could not bring to consciousness feelings of ethnic loyalty and could not develop a nationalist ideology. Without such a substratum, they would have to use alternative ideologies altogether to mobilize the masses. There are, therefore, constant processes of awakenings and reawakenings taking place among the masses in each and every phase of mobilization by élites.

Nationalist sentiments have constituted the core ideology of French Canadians for at least two centuries, and they have provided a powerful cultural force during each new phase of ethnic conflict, in this or in the previous century. The same obviously could be said for most of the other ethnoregional movements mentioned above, and variations in the strength of pre-existing nationalist feelings could no doubt account for some of the variations in the strength of recent movements.[28] Again, ethnic beliefs and sentiments are only one of the determinants explaining ethnic conflict, and to make nationalism—even of a nonprimordialist variety—the key factor of such conflict implies a narrow perspective. Nationalism, for one thing, is too constant a phenomenon to alone explain great variations through time in levels of conflict.

There is another type of beliefs and values that must be considered as a fourth determinant in recent decades. In our view, the ethnic movements of the 1960s and 1970s, as well, for that matter, as the other so-called new social or new left movements of that period—ecology, women's, student movements—were all triggered at the time they were because the period was one of unusually rapid and long-lasting economic growth and prosperity. The unequalled affluence and security that this growth provided allowed many people to gradually shift their preoccupations from those of the usual materialistic economic type to postmaterialistic value priorities, such as those involved in styles and quality of life issues, status equality, ethnic self-realization and self-pride, and the like (Inglehart 1990) (see Chapter 2 of this text). This type of value change developed as a medium-term trend closely associated with the economic conditions of those decades. It came together—something not usually distinguished in the literature—with a long-term, indeed secular, trend toward more general liberal values on noneconomic issues; this trend was more closely rooted in increasing educational attainment, but it was greatly accelerated during the same period because of the educational revolution accompanying the economic growth of the period. In addition to the defence of basic freedoms, civil liber-

ties, and democratic rights, this liberalism also promoted secularization, tolerance, individual and collective equality, anticolonialism, and the principle of self-determination.

Changes in these two nonmaterial value dimensions, especially marked among the young and the well-educated, contributed to the emergence and strength of the ethnic (and other) movements of that period.[29] The first one in particular freed large numbers of people in the middle classes from more immediate economic constraints, and made them available for other concerns and causes. The little evidence that has been assembled indicates that postmaterialism and liberalism are both related to support for ethnic movements.[30]

Finally, let us briefly mention that social movements often emerge after the beneficiary group has experienced increases in collective self-confidence and in its sense of political efficacy. Indeed 'cognitive liberation' is, according to McAdam (1982: 48–51), one of the three determinants of social movements. That, in turn, affects some motivational dimensions such as the expectancy of success and the perception that the collective action entails only minimal costs. An increase in self-confidence is also important in that it helps to assuage the need for collective self-assertion in response to inferiority status feelings.

HUMAN AND MATERIAL RESOURCES

A fifth necessary determinant of great importance concerns the amount and nature of the material and especially human resources that are controlled by ethnic groups and that are made available for ethnic mobilization. The most important of these resources is no doubt the size of the group and hence its pool of human resources: many very small ethnic groups such as, for instance, the Saami (known as Lapps) in Norway, Sweden, or Finland, have been found to be unable to generate a high degree of mobilization, and the likelihood of mobilization of other groups was shown to increase with their size; indeed in his study of 46 minority linguistic groups in Western Europe, Allardt (1981) found the size of the group to be the most important resource factor.[31] Beyond that, the size of the intellectuals' stratum and more generally of the larger professional intelligentsia, especially their youth contingent, appear crucial since they provide the bulk of their leadership (Pinard and Hamilton 1989). Indeed, since the ethnic and the other new social movements are typically rooted in the middle classes, they can tap large pools of various resources unavailable to lower-class movements. It must be stressed that intellectuals and the larger intelligentsia, and especially their young members, were precisely the social strata most likely to espouse the new values just discussed (Inglehart 1990; Pinard and Hamilton 1989).

The possession of resources by a group must be differentiated from the mobilization of these resources, that is, the efforts that are made to ensure their delivery to a social movement. Let us only mention here, without elaboration, that the quantity and quality of these efforts—implying goals, discourse, recruitment, tactics, and strategies—are fundamental for the delivery of those resources. Proponents of the resource mobilization approach are fully justified to insist on these processes.[32]

DYNAMIC ASPECTS: SOME TRIGGERING FACTORS

Many of the factors we have so far mentioned have been present, in various degrees, for a long time—indeed long before the emergence of the 1960s ethnoregional movements. Although necessary, they were relatively constant and could not therefore have been the triggering factors of their emergence. This is generally so for the various types of ethnic grievances and other internal motives discussed above, as well as for the various components of ethnic segmentation and of nationalist beliefs we have mentioned. No doubt the mobilization that resulted from the actual triggering factors intensified the strength of some of the above factors, such as an increased sensitivity to grievances and to nationalist beliefs, but the latter could not, logically, be themselves the triggering factors, since they were the effects rather than the causes of that mobilization. More specifically, during the 1960s and 1970s, the dynamics of the movements did not result from an increase in grievances, as often claimed in classical approaches to the study of social movements (for example, Gurr 1970), but from other factors. In these instances, it must be recognized that the resource mobilization approach provides a better account of these phenomena (for more details, see Pinard and Hamilton 1986: 226–41).

But what were then the triggering factors of the ethnic (and other) movements of the 1960s and 1970s? Let us only briefly mention here that, in our view, two of the factors discussed above were involved: first, the major value changes we have described and, second, the immense growth in the size of the intellectual stratum and more generally the intelligentsia—both the results of massive economic growth and unsurpassed prosperity in the post-World War II period. In addition, in the case of ethnic movements, the growth of the state during the same period and its increasing involvement in its citizens' lives may also have triggered rising expectancies and aspirations and stimulated demands, but mainly among ethnic political élites, as implied by some recent literature on nationalism. However, the changes in human resources and values just mentioned must have been more important, as they account for the dynamics behind all new social movements, not just nationalist ones.

Finally, the era of prosperity and of social change of the postwar period also contributed to an increase in collective self-confidence, as mentioned above. This, in turn, facilitated an increase in the expectancy of success, as well as a perception that the collective costs of the action were not very important.[33]

ÉLITE REGULATION

Finally, a last determinant concerns the presence or absence of élite efforts toward ethnic conflict regulation. These problems have occupied a large place in the works of European political scientists bearing on ethnic and religious conflict (see, in particular, Lijphart [1977] and McRae [1974]; see also Nordlinger [1972]). In our view, many of the proponents of that approach have greatly exaggerated the ease with which political élites can engage in regulatory efforts as well as their ability, even when they try, to moderate such conflicts. In particular, a widespread sense of grievances within ethnic groups is likely to push large segments of their élites and, through reaction, of their opponents, toward conflict intensification rather than conflict regulation. Besides, these élites could only be responding to a polarization taking place among the masses in response to these grievances and to the ongoing conflict, as has been the case in Canada during the 1990s. It is because of these factors, among others, that until recently, despite the élites' efforts to devise various forms of accommodation, the process has been unsuccessful in Canada and that, in Belgium, the solutions that were gradually adopted always appear to be incomplete. The failures of the Meech and Charlottetown Accords in Canada recently are good cases in point.

This brief analysis of the emergence of the ethnoregional movements of 1960 is but a sketch that would require substantial elaborations for each of the factors examined, both theoretically and empirically, but unfortunately this cannot be attempted here. With regard to the three subsequent phases of the Quebec movement proper, an analysis has been presented elsewhere (Pinard, Bernier, and Lemieux 1997: ch. 4) and cannot be repeated here for reasons of space. Instead we will briefly summarize our analysis of the last major episode of that movement, the Quebec referendum of October 1995.

The 1995 Referendum

As mentioned before, the Parti Québécois, under the leadership of Jacques Parizeau, had planned, when it returned to power in September 1994, to hold a referendum bearing on sovereignty alone. When polls revealed that with such a radical option it could face a defeat as severe as the one it had experienced in the 1980 referendum, the party took a sharp *virage* in April 1995 and returned to its original option, sovereignty-association, now renamed sovereignty-partnership.

As we have seen, the popular support for that softer option was obviously greater and polls indicated in the following months that on the average 53 per cent would vote Yes to that option and 47 per cent would vote No (after a proportional reallocation of the undeclared vote intentions).

On September 7, 1995, the government of the Parti Québécois made public the referendum question; it essentially stated: 'Do you agree that Quebec should become sovereign, after having made a formal offer to Canada for a new economic and political partnership . . . ?'

Within about a week, the intended Yes support dropped to around 45 per cent, as presumably voters realized they would have to take an imminent, real decision. A few, however, soon returned to the Yes camp, but support for the Yes stood at only 47 per cent at the start of the official referendum campaign on October 1st, a level from which it did not move for almost two weeks. Then suddenly, within a week, support for the Yes side climbed back to 53 per cent, a level at which it remained for the last ten days of the campaign. But, as usual, polls had overestimated the support for the sovereignist side, and on referendum day (30 October), the sovereignists again faced a defeat, albeit by a very narrow margin this time: 49.4 per cent had voted Yes, as against 50.6 per cent who had voted No. (For more details on all this, see Pinard, Bernier, and Lemieux 1997: ch. 8; for the analysis which is briefly summarized below, see chs 9 and 10.)

What were the factors behind this improved showing of the sovereignist camp, when compared to its 1980 results—some nine points better? What were on the other hand the factors that yet allowed the federalist camp to be victorious again? Let us summarize our answers to these two questions. As will be seen, more of the factors that we have identified worked to the advantage of the Yes side than to that of the No side. In some cases, the factors exerted their impact in the short run, in others, over a longer-term period.

FACTORS FAVOURING THE GROWTH OF SOVEREIGNIST SUPPORT

Many recent analysts of nationalism and of social movements have insisted on the role of political forces, such as state-building and political opportunities, in the development of these phenomena. In the 1995 referendum, the political context was such that it created important opportunities for the sovereignist forces. In addition, the results revealed once more the very great impact that an extremely popular political leader, imbued with much charisma, can exert on the fate of a political movement.

The Bouchard Effect

Let us consider this last point first. It refers to what was identified as the 'Bouchard effect', an interpretation according to which the sudden upsurge of the Yes vote during the referendum campaign, more precisely in mid-October, was attributable to the popularity of Lucien Bouchard. The processes leading to this short-term effect started when the Yes camp decided to bank even more than before on Bouchard's popularity; on October 7, Jacques Parizeau, the official leader of the Yes forces, appointed Lucien Bouchard, Bloc Québécois leader and Leader of the Opposition in Ottawa's House of Commons, as chief negotiator of the planned partnership in the case of a Yes victory. From there on, Bouchard played an in-

creasingly important role in the Yes campaign, becoming for all practical purposes the *de facto* leader of the Yes forces. Within a few days, among men, and within about a week, among women, the Yes vote started to increase, to reach 53 per cent a week later. It is this very rapid gain of about six points that has been attributed to Bouchard's talents.

His high degree of popularity had indeed been well confirmed before in many polls. For instance, in a poll taken some seven months before the referendum, no less than 68 per cent said they had a great deal or some confidence in him, as compared to 46 per cent or less for five other important sovereignist and federalist leaders in Quebec.[34] His popularity was great not only among intending Yes voters, but also among intending No and, especially, undecided voters. Among the last two groups of voters, some admitted having been swayed by him when interviewed in an October poll.

Bouchard's popularity rested on many traits typical of charismatic leaders: he was an excellent speaker, using simple but very emotional language; he was highly convincing because he appeared utterly sincere and deeply convinced of the just character of his cause. Moreover, and this was important, he was highly reassuring because he appeared more moderate than Jacques Parizeau. His nomination as chief negotiator of the proposed partnership led to an increase in the proportion of voters who saw this partnership as a likely outcome in the event of a Yes victory and a decrease in the proportion of those who expected independence to be costly. By his populist appeals to traditional tenets of French-Canadian nationalism—domination, humiliation, etc.—he may also have contributed to enhanced feelings that independence would result in greater self-pride for the Québécois.

Political Opportunities

Bouchard's popularity was only one among the political factors working in favour of the Yes side.

Three other aspects of the political context represented increasing opportunities for the sovereignists. First, there was the record of repeated failures in the efforts of their opponents to renew federalism, most notably the failure of the Meech Lake Accord in 1990, which had been extremely damaging for the federalists, but also that of the Charlottetown Accord in 1992.[35] In particular, the failure of Meech had led to the creation of the Bloc Québécois and to renewed mobilization efforts on the part of the secessionist leaders, following the demobilization phase of the 1980s. On the whole, Quebecers had become more pessimistic about any possibility of reforms and sovereignist leaders made it a point to remind voters of these repeated failures; they insisted that the system could not be improved and repeatedly pointed to the fact that there were no proposals to reform federalism in the platform of the No camp. The medium-term effects of those failures may therefore have combined with short-term, campaign effects, leading more voters to conclude that sovereignty was the only viable alternative.

A second aspect of the political context was also important. One can represent the main constitutional options that have for long been considered in Quebec by the following diagram, in which the percentages indicate the preferences of Quebecers in early 1995, when asked to choose among these four options.

A	B	C	D
Status Quo	Renewed	Sovereignty-	Sovereignty
(19%)	Federalism	Partnership	Alone
	(36%)	(32%)	(9%)

But while the population preferred intermediate options (B and C),[36] the two camps, in early 1995, had positioned themselves at one of the extremes: the Parti Québécois was planning a referendum on sovereignty alone (point D), and the federalist forces were close to point A; while open to changes, they were not offering any specific proposal to renew federalism. The result of the referendum was therefore partly dependent on the movement—or the absence of movement—of each camp on the continuum of our diagram. As we have seen, the sovereignists soon moved squarely to point C, when they engaged in the *virage* of April 1995, a strategy that immediately improved their level of support. On the other side, the No camp did not move from point A until the last week of the campaign, when Prime Minister Chrétien made some limited overtures. That strategy was dictated by, among other things, an expectancy of victory and more importantly, by the presence of the same structural constraints that had led to the failures in reform efforts mentioned above, that is, the multiple cleavages within the larger federalist coalition in Quebec and the rest of Canada. The quasi-paralysis of the No forces created added opportunities for their adversaries and, indeed, almost led to a Yes victory.

Finally, on the eve of the referendum, the greater strength of the federal Bloc Québécois and the provincial Parti Québécois, when compared to their Liberal counterparts, also constituted an element of the political context conducive to an increase in sovereignist support.

Social-Psychological Factors

In addition to these political conditions, there were social-psychological factors which, on a longer-term basis, had led to an increase in sovereignist support. Some of these pertain to the motivational dimensions discussed earlier in the section on Quebec ethnic revival in the sixties.

There are first the ethnic grievances felt by the francophones in Quebec. To be sure, a detailed analysis shows that these grievances—be they of an economic, status, cultural, or political nature—had not been increasing over time. Therefore the increase in Yes support since, say, the first referendum could not be attributed to a more aggrieved electorate. But while grievances had not been increasing, it must be realized that they were already very high in 1980, being generally shared by a majority of the francophones. The difference between the two referendums is that, while the aggrieved had not all been mobilized in 1980, a larger proportion of them were in 1995; in addition, more of the nonaggrieved were attracted to the Yes side, given the other factors discussed.

It should be noted, incidentally, that the level of grievances remained high, despite great progress made in many areas by francophones in Quebec over the previous 35 years or so. But once grievances are articulated as part of a nationalist ideology, they become stereotypes that are quite resistant to reality checks and that continue to exercise political effects.

If the level of grievances did not change much, another motivational element did change, to the advantage of the Yes side. Again, although this cannot be presented here in detail, the analysis shows that over the previous 25 years there was a substantial decrease in the proportion of Quebecers who expected independence to be economically costly—a decrease from 63 per cent in 1970 to only 38 per cent during the last week before the 1995 referendum. This decrease in the anticipation of economic costs constitutes, in our view, a major factor of the long-term growth of sovereignist support in Quebec.[37] To the extent that the expectations of economic costs constituted one of the most important barriers to secessionist sentiments (Pinard and Hamilton 1986), a decrease in such expectations could only greatly facilitate one's adherence to such sentiments.

Two other social-psychological dimensions must also be mentioned. The first one pertains to some of the ethnic beliefs discussed in the second section of this paper, notably ethnic identities and attachments. With regard to identities, francophones in Quebec have increasingly come to identify themselves as Québécois rather than as French Canadians, in line with their adoption of sovereignist options. In addition, their attachment to

Quebec has been and remains extremely strong, with 90 per cent or more of them reporting that they 'feel profoundly attached to Quebec'. These are also components of their nationalism and they all provide important underpinnings for the growth of the independence movement.

The second dimension is of a different nature altogether. There is much evidence to indicate that many support the Yes option while not favouring the secession of Quebec. Some do it strategically, as a way to induce federalists to negotiate some form of renewed federalism. But many do it out of simple confusion, as discussed in the first section of this paper. They do not realize that sovereignty means an independent country, that the partnership offered does not simply involve a form of renewed federalism, or that secession would take place even if the negotiations regarding that partnership failed. In the end, both strategic and confused voters contributed to a strengthening of the Yes side.

A Generation Effect

Finally, a factor of a sociodemographic kind favouring the sovereignist camp over the long run is worth noting. From the beginning, the independence option has been disproportionately favoured by younger voters. Over time, two processes could have occurred: one, a life-cycle (or aging) effect, according to which sovereignist preferences would have been altered as one got older, with, say, new middle-aged voters adopting the views of previous middle-aged cohorts, rather than keeping the preferences that were theirs when they were young; second, a generation effect, according to which the preferences adopted by the members of a new generation of voters would have been maintained as they grew older. The available evidence indicates that, with regard to the independence option, a generation effect has largely prevailed in Quebec. As a result, support for the Yes side is no longer only a youth phenomenon, but in the last referendum prevailed almost equally in all age cohorts below the age of 45. Even the 45 to 54 age cohort was strongly pro-Yes. Only older voters, who largely entered the electorate before the emergence of the movement, remained disproportionately opposed to independence.

This has led some to conclude that, everything else being constant, there would soon be a majority supporting the Yes side. But everything else is not constant, and indeed preferences have been subject to period effects, whereby they manifested ups and downs over the last 40 years, in response to various political and other events. These can increase or depress the sovereignist preferences of all age groups; examples of such events are the economic conditions, the popularity of various leaders, successes or failures in renewing the federal system, or a harder question, to mention a few obvious instances. Moreover, it is in the nature of generational phenomena to witness the emergence of new generations that reject, rather than adopt, the preferences of the previous ones, in response to differences in formative experiences. So far, however, the generational effects observed and the lack of changes from one generation to the next constituted a condition very favourable to the sovereignist cause.

FACTORS CONTRIBUTING TO THE (SLIM) NO MAJORITY

There were fewer factors obviously favouring federalist preferences than those that could be related to sovereignist ones, but those that did were important. Let us consider first those that were of a social-psychological kind.

Let us mention that some of the factors so far discussed also worked in part to strengthen the support of the No side. Thus, if the fears concerning the economic costs of independence had been decreasing over time, those fears remained substantial and they motivated many to vote No. Similarly, the partnership envisioned by the sovereignists tended to alleviate those fears, but the uncertainty that remained regarding its successful negotiation held back potential Yes supporters.

Identities and Loyalties

With regard to people's identities and loyalties, one must realize that in multicultural societies these sentiments are generally dual, indeed multiple, rather than unique. In Quebec, if attachment to the province and its institutions is very strong and even often predominant, it remains that an attachment to Canada also prevails among the majority of its citizens. It may be less strong, less emotional, and more self-interested than the former, but it was still a very important dimension of the No vote. Indeed, about two-thirds of the Quebecers (and about 60 per cent of the francophones) expressed a profound attachment to Canada, and to a statement implying dual loyalties, that is, loyalties to both Quebec and Canada ('I am proud of being both a Quebecer and a Canadian'), no less than 80 per cent in 1995 expressed their agreement; among francophones, the proportion was 77 per cent.

If the attachment to Canada was stronger than the No vote, it is because this attachment was shared by many Yes voters. While practically all No voters (about 90 per cent) expressed an attachment to Canada, as many as about one in four Yes voters also expressed such an attachment. If high levels of ethnic segmentation and ethnic grievances foster strong Quebec loyalties, there remain many forms of national integration—particularly in the economy and the polity—which produce a strong attachment to Canada. These in turn sustain one's allegiance to it.

This is quite clearly shown by the importance so many attached to remaining a province of Canada, an attitude that at the time of the 1995 referendum prevailed among 60 per cent of the respondents. And indeed, a clear, unambiguous question in this regard produced results quite at odds with those of the official referendum question. Thus in a 1997 poll, in which respondents were asked how they would vote in a new referendum with a question asking them, 'Do you want Quebec to remain a province of Canada?' it was found that 67 per cent would vote Yes, and only 33 per cent would vote No (after a proportional reallocation of the undecided). Among francophones, the Yes stood at 62 per cent.

A last set of social-psychological factors may also have been involved. On the one hand, electorates tend to be quite conservative when faced with potential social or political changes, particularly if these are substantial in nature, as breaking Canada would be. This is particularly so when a group has not been experiencing drastic forms of domination or oppression. After all, francophones in Quebec have lived under a democratic system for a long time, and federalism, despite its shortcomings, has allowed them much political autonomy. Moreover, when compared to other countries, Canada has been faring very well in almost all respects.

Sociodemographic Dimensions

Aspects of the sociodemographic context also favoured the No vote. First and foremost, one must mention the quasi-unanimous No support that prevailed among anglophones and those whose mother tongue was neither French nor English: our estimate is that, overall, about 95 per cent of the members of these two groups voted No (97.5 per cent among anglophones, and 80 per cent among others). Add to this that on the whole the No vote was equally high (90 per cent) among members of aboriginal groups. As a consequence, the Yes vote had to reach at least 60 per cent among francophones for the Yes side to attain a majority in the total population.

Second, women have traditionally been more supportive of the No side than men, and this did not change in the referendum: on the average, women were 9 per cent more likely to vote No than men and they were more likely to vote No than to vote Yes. Moreover, the differences between

women and men did not decrease during the campaign, despite special efforts of the Yes camp to enlist women, and the Bouchard effect was slower to develop among them than among men.

Finally, changes in the class bases of the independence movement appear to have slowed down the mobilization of Yes support. For instance, the movement had traditionally been stronger among the more educated segments of the population and especially among the well educated who were young. This is no longer the case: at the time of the referendum campaign, the Yes side appeared to be strongest among those with an intermediate degree of education, and those who were both young and well educated were less likely to be Yes supporters than middle-aged or less-educated respondents. Indications are that as the movement is making gains among the lower socioeconomic strata, it is losing support in its traditional stronghold, the higher strata.

Conclusion

Five years have now passed since the 1995 referendum. At that time, the prognosis of many had been that soon there would be a majority in favour of the Yes option. During the rest of their term in office (1995–8), the leaders of the Parti Québécois promised that a third referendum would be held during their next term, if re-elected.

They did get re-elected in 1998, but with the more cautious promise that a new referendum would be held only when the 'winning conditions' were met. By the end of 2000, no referendum had been held and, barring some unforeseen crisis, none appears likely in the very near future, for one simple reason: the most important winning condition—a likely victory—is currently missing.

Indeed we have seen that support for all variants of the option declined from 1990 to the time of the 1995 referendum. Now regular polls carried out since then indicate that the decline has continued ever since. Thus support for complete independence, which stood at 37 per cent in 1995 (see Table 13.2), was at only 25 per cent in 2000. Similarly, support for the Yes option during the last week of the 1995 referendum campaign stood at 53 per cent, after a proportional redistribution of the undeclared vote intentions; it had declined, according to regular CROP soundings, to an average of 41 per cent by 2000. To be sure, those trends should not be read to imply the end of the independence movement. As we have seen, a major resurgence took place just before the 1990s and new phases of growth are certainly possible in the future. Unfortunately, political sociologists are not very good at forecasting them.

Notes

1. The original variant of the movement's option, until the creation of the Parti Québécois in 1967–8, was the complete independence of Quebec. At that time, that party, under the leadership of René Lévesque, adopted sovereignty-association as its option, that is, political independence accompanied by an economic association with the rest of Canada, although the stress on the two components of that option has varied greatly over time. Under the leadership of Pierre Marc Johnson (1985–7), 'national affirmation' became the immediate goal of the party. But when Jacques Parizeau assumed the leadership of the party in early 1988, sovereignty alone became the main option, with the association as a nonessential corollary. For the 1995 referendum, the party returned to a position placing a greater emphasis on the association part of that option, contemplating even the establishment of a political partnership together with the economic one. For greater details regarding support for these options in the pre-1980 period, see Pinard (1980).

2. For an analysis of the other three phases, see Pinard, Bernier, and Lemieux (1997, ch. 4).

3. As will be seen below, it can be observed that between 1990 and 1994, 'hard' questions using expressions like separation, complete independence, or the like, reveal a level of support about 5 per cent lower that 'soft' questions using expressions like independence or independent country.

4. Whenever there was more than one poll for a set of years (for the period 1962–74) or for a given year (from 1976 on), unweighted averages of the results of the various polls were calculated. To better assess a very rapidly changing situation, the data of the last six years are broken down into shorter periods in the second panel of some tables.

5. There are disagreements as to the beginning date of this third phase. Cloutier and his colleagues (1992: 59–62) see it as beginning in the fall of 1985, on the basis of a single PQ poll of October of that year; but they also write that they have no explanation for this presumed resurgence, and they mention that it would indeed have come at a time when the PQ itself was adopting a softer line. In addition, they have no other data for the three subsequent years. However, a SORECOM poll of November 1985 (see Tables 13.1 and 13.4) registered no increase in support for either independence or sovereignty-association; nor did an unpublished Environics poll of February 1986. The first signs of a weak resurgence appeared in a December 1987 Environics poll (again unpublished) and a March 1988 CROP poll on sovereignty (see Table 13.3), But even then, an Environics poll of March 1988 indicated only weak support for the PQ's new orientation: 68 per cent said that the PQ should either give up the independence idea (44 per cent) or put it in abeyance (24 per cent); only 25 per cent said it should promote it (*Le Devoir*, 25 April 1988: 1). As will be seen below, a SORECOM poll of February 1988 also indicated no increase in voting support for sovereignty-association. (Notice that in 1987 the late fall poll coincides with the re-emergence of the radical wing within the PQ under Jacques Parizeau's leadership, as discussed later.) By the fall of 1988 and the following year, the signs of a resurgence, however, became very clear.

6. But previously, some supporters of independence appeared to be 'soft' ones, since support for independence declined when respondents were pre-

sented with the prospect that there would be no economic association. Thus, in a 1980 poll carried out on the eve of the referendum, respondents who were favourable to independence (26 per cent) were asked in a follow-up question whether they would remain favourable to it if certain that no economic association would accompany it. The proportion in favour of independence then dropped to 15 per cent, while the proportion of those opposed increased from 64 to 71 per cent (from a CROP poll of April 1980 for the Canadian Unity Information Office).

7. The criteria used to classify survey questions under any one of these three variants are specified in a note to Table 13.2.

8. One reason for the sharp decline in support for sovereignty in 1994 is that vote intentions in favour of that option were some six percentage points lower than opinions favourable to it, something that was barely present during the 1990–2 period, but continued to prevail in early 1995. (Comparisons are not possible for 1993.) In any case, vote intentions and opinions regarding sovereignty dropped in 1994.

9. There is some indication from early 1995 polls that the confusion was finally decreasing concerning the fact that under sovereignty Quebec would no longer be a province of Canada. The same prevails with regard to the data presented in the next paragraph. See also Pinard, Bernier and Lemieux (1997, ch. 10).

10. Again, these findings were replicated with analogous data in early 1995.

11. This is why we have classified these 'hard' independence questions with those on 'separation'.

12. Notice that as with independence, support for sovereignty-association did not increase from 1976, when the PQ came to power, to 1979. The data would even indicate a decrease here. For a more detailed analysis of this in the pre-1980 period, see Pinard (1980: 160–4).

13. The data of Table 13.4 are based on questions asking respondents if they were favourable or not to sovereignty-association, not if they would vote for it or not; more on this below.

14. Support for an even softer version of this option, a simple mandate to negotiate sovereignty-asso-

ciation with the rest of Canada, which became a new variant of the sovereignty-association option during the years immediately preceding the 1980 referendum, drew even higher levels of support for those years. On the average, in 13 polls carried out between 1977 and 1979 (10 of which were conducted in 1979), 44 per cent declared they were favourable to giving such a mandate to the government of Quebec, while 38 per cent expressed their opposition and 18 per cent did not make a choice. (For an analysis of some of these polls, see Pinard [1980: 164–7].) The official referendum question in 1980 adopted that formulation and, in addition, contained the promise of a second referendum before any change in constitutional status could be implemented. The 19 polls carried out on that question from February to March 1980, preceding the referendum, showed, on the average, a level of support of 42 per cent for the Yes side, of 44 per cent for the No side, with 15 per cent not stating their preference. Taking only the eight polls of the official referendum campaign (April 15 to May 20), the corresponding percentages are 40, 43 and 17 per cent, respectively. In either case, if the 'undecided' are allocated proportionately, the polls anticipated a Yes vote of 49 per cent, as against a No vote of 51 per cent. As we have seen, only 40 per cent actually voted Yes and 60 per cent voted No, suggesting that practically all the 'undecided' moved to the No side. Regarding trends over time, a new referendum with the same question in 1983 would have seen, according to one poll, the Yes dropping as low as 23 per cent and the No reaching 61 per cent, with 16 per cent undecided. In sharp contrast, a 1990 referendum with that question would have yielded a Yes of 68 per cent, with only 21 per cent for the No side and 12 per cent undecided. (The 1983 poll is a SORECOM poll of September-October for *Le Soleil*; the 1990 one is an IQOP one of March for CJMS/Radio Mutuel.)

15. The PQ support and the independence option have been overestimated by an average of 3 per cent in polls carried out during election campaigns since 1970 and by an average of 6.5 per cent in the first two referendums. (The first average includes the cases of two elections [1973 and 1989] in which the PQ vote was underestimated by 1 per cent.) The Liberals' support and the federalist position have been underestimated in all

instances by an average of 4 per cent in elections, and 6.5 per cent in the first two referendums. In 1995, support for the Yes side was overestimated by 2 per cent during the whole referendum campaign, but by 4 per cent during the last 10 days. These phenomena have been attributed to the fact that the federalist vote tends to be concentrated among citizens less likely to participate in polling exercises or, if they do, to reveal their preferences; in particular, they are older, less educated and less interested in politics.

16. A Multi-Réso poll of March 1995 for The Council for Canadian Unity.

17. While polls usually report that a majority of Quebecers find it likely that an association would be maintained or established, a majority also think that in the case of a Yes vote, the rest of Canada will refuse to negotiate anything (see the February 1995 CROP poll for Radio-Canada and the Multi-Réso poll cited in the previous footnote).

18. It follows that one cannot deny, as Connor does (1984), the relevance of economic deprivations on the grounds that they cannot account for the ethnic movements of more well-to-do regions: Ethnic grievances of an economic kind are simply one possible type of deprivation, not a necessary one. It should also be clear that we do not hold that purely economic grievances, flowing from recessions, high unemployment rates, and the like, are important factors of ethnic movements. On this we agree with McGarry and O'Leary (1995). Our generalizations are not concerned either with individual, but with collective *ethnic* economic inequalities, and all the grievances just discussed are about collective ethnic goods. McGarry and O'Leary's position is not entirely clear in this regard and it leads them to greatly underestimate the role of ethnic inequalities of an economic kind.

19. The evidence supporting the points of the last two paragraphs can be found in the vast literature on each of these regions; see in particular Lorwin (1973) and McRae (1986) on Belgium; Rose (1971) and Urwin (1982) on Great Britain; Linz (1973) and Greenwood (1977) on Spain; Breton and Stasiulis (1980), Breton (1988) and Pinard and Hamilton (1986) on Canada; McRae (1983) and Bélanger and Pinard (1991: 454–5)

on Switzerland. Notice, however, that severe inequalities may impede ethnic collective action. In general, to act collectively, a group must be disadvantaged enough to share grievances, but also resource-rich enough to mobilize (Bélanger and Pinard 1991: 449).

20. It should be indicated, however, that the rational choice approach adopted in the papers by Meadwell and Martin overlooks the internal motives reviewed above.

21. As one moves from the motivations of simple adherents to those of participants making contributions to a movement, other motivating elements and, in particular, moral obligations and selective incentives, must also be considered, but this cannot be examined here. See Pinard and Hamilton (1986); Hechter (1985); Levi and Hechter (1985).

22. For some comparative data on many of these cases, see McRae (1974). Here again, McGarry and O'Leary (1995) are, we think, in error when they downplay the role of 'segregation' in various institutions, even though we agree with them that 'social mixing' is not necessarily a solution. As will be seen presently, it is in ways other than in simply preventing mixing that segmentation plays its most important role.

23. Let us add, however, that the greater the degree of subordination of an ethnic group, the less it tends to be territorially concentrated (Horowitz 1985: 29–30) and, more generally, the smaller its degree of segmentation. Highly underprivileged groups are therefore not only poor in resources (see note 19), but also short of the advantages provided by a high degree of segmentation.

24. Similar perspectives can also be found in Deutsch (1966), Barth (1969) and Hechter (1975). We do accept, however, that nationalism itself, as a fully blown type of ideology, is a rather modern phenomenon, just as articulated class ideologies are.

25. This view differs from both that of authors who see ethnic loyalties and nationalism as the sole important independent variable to explain ethnic conflict—as in the primordialist perspective—and that of others for whom both nationalism and ethnic conflict are fused into only one

dependent variable, as in many recent studies of nationalism. It must be stressed that nationalism can exist without much conflict, the former being much more stable overtime and permanent than the latter.

26. For an interesting comparison of contrasting perspectives, see Smith (1984). The redefinition of ethnic boundaries and of relevant ecological ranges is also a politically-driven phenomenon. For some data on this phenomenon, see for instance the description of changing identities in Quebec in Pinard, Bernier, and Lemieux (1997, ch. 4).

27. Ethnic grievances, by contrast, tend to occupy a marginal position in such theorizing; but see Hall (1993: 11, 15); Gellner (1983: 60–2).

28. On Belgium, for instance, the absence of long-standing grievances and ethnic nationalism in Wallonia and their presence in Flanders have no doubt been important factors of the greater Flemish mobilization during the 1960s and 1970s, not to mention earlier periods.

29. In Inglehart (1990), these two dimensions are fused into a single one, postmaterialism. We follow Flanagan (1987) who rightfully claims that postmaterialism should be distinguished from liberalism.

30. On the impact of liberal values in the Quebec movement, see Pinard and Hamilton (1978: 767–8) and other sources cited there; on the impact of postmaterialist values in ethnic movements in Western Europe, see Inglehart (1990, ch. 11; 1977: 234–43).

31. Allardt, however, conceptualizes too many elements as resources, which makes this factor lose much of its analytical power.

32. For an analysis of the impact of some of these efforts in the Quebec movement, see Pinard, Bernier, and Lemieux (1997: ch. 4).

33. A critical examination of the perspective according to which the triggering factors are first and foremost found in various aspects of the oppor-

tunity structure cannot be attempted here (Tarrow 1994). Let us only mention that many of these factors are *stable* (as for instance ethnic segmentation) and that they had been previously identified as elements of conduciveness (Smelser 1963). Moreover, this perspective either neglects other triggering factors or assimilates them to opportunities, which makes that concept, like that of resources, less analytically useful. (On these questions, see especially Gamson and Meyer 1996: also McAdam 1996.) The role of opportunity factors in the 1995 referendum is discussed below.

34. The other five leaders (and the proportions of respondents who expressed confidence in them) were: Jacques Parizeau (43 per cent), Mario Dumont, leader of a minority party, *L'Action démocratique du Québec,* backing the Yes camp (46 per cent), Jean Chrétien, Liberal prime minister (39 per cent), Daniel Johnson, Liberal leader of the opposition in Quebec's National Assembly and leader of the No forces (37 per cent), and Jean Charest, leader of the federal Progressive-Conservative party (34 per cent).

35. In addition to Meech and Charlottetown, one must also mention, among the unsuccessful attempts at reform, the Fulton-Favreau amending formula (1966), the Victoria Charter (1971), federal government proposals (1978), the repatriation of the Constitution without the consent of the Quebec government (1982), as well as the proposals of the Pépin-Roberts Commission (1979). Meech's failure was the most damaging because this was the only episode of constitutional negotiations in which the solutions were accepted by Quebec, but rejected in English Canada.

36. As had always been the case, the population also preferred the two federalist options (55 per cent) to the two sovereignist ones (41 per cent).

37. Let us add that the anticipation of costs was even lower with regard to sovereignty-partnership than with regard to independence alone.

References

Allardt, E. 1981. 'Ethnic Mobilization and Minority Resources', *Zeitschrift fur Soziologie* 10: 427–37.

Barth, F. 1969. 'Introduction'. In *Ethnic Groups and Boundaries*, ed. F. Barth (Boston: Little, Brown), 9–38.

Bélanger. S., and M. Pinard. 1991. 'Ethnic Movements and the Competition Model: Some Missing Links', *American Sociological Review* 56: 446–57.

Blais, A., and E. Gidengil. 1993. 'The Quebec Referendum: Why Did Quebeckers Say No?', paper presented at the Canadian Political Science Association meetings in Ottawa.

Brass, P.R. 1985. 'Ethnic Groups and the State'. In *Ethnic Groups and the State*, ed. P.R. Brass (London: Croom Helm), 1–56.

Breton, A., and R. Breton. 1980. *Why Disunity? An Analysis of Linguistic and Regional Cleavages in Canada* (Montreal: The Institute for Research on Public Policy).

Breton, R. 1978. 'Stratification and Conflict Between Ethnolinguistic Communities with Different Social Structures', *The Canadian Review of Sociology and Anthropology* 15: 148–57.

———. 1988. 'French-English Relations'. In *Understanding Canadian Society*, eds J. Curtis and L. Tepperman (Toronto: McGraw-Hill Ryerson), 557–85.

———, and D. Stasiulis. 1980. 'Linguistic Boundaries and the Cohesion of Canada'. In *Cultural Boundaries and the Cohesion of Canada*, eds R. Breton, J.G. Reitz, and V. Valentine (Montreal: The Institute for Research on Public Policy), 137–323.

Cloutier, E., J.H. Guay, and D. Latouche. 1992. *Le virage: L'évolution de l'opinion publique au Québec depuis 1960 ou comment le Québec est devenu souverainiste* (Montréal: Québec/Amérique).

Connor. W. 1984. 'Eco- or Ethno-Nationalism?' *Ethnic and Racial Studies* 7: 342–59.

Deutsch, K.W. 1966. *Nationalism and Social Communication* (2nd edn) (Cambridge, MA: MIT Press).

Dion, S. 1996. 'Why is Secession Difficult in Well-Established Democracies? Lessons from Quebec', *British Journal of Political Science* 26: 269–83.

Esman, M.J. 1977. 'Scottish Nationalism, North Sea Oil, and the British Response'. In *Ethnic Conflict in the Western World*, ed. M.J. Esman (Ithaca, NY: Cornell University Press), 281–6.

Flanagan, S.C. 1987. 'Value Change in Industrial Societies', *American Political Science Review* 81: 1303–19.

Gamson, W.A. 1992. 'The Social Psychology of Collective Action'. In *Frontiers in Social Movement Theory*, eds A.D. Morris and C.M. Mueller (New Haven, CT: Yale University Press), 53–76.

———, and D.S. Meyer. 1996. 'Framing Political Opportunity'. In *Comparative Perspectives on Social Movements*, eds D. McAdam, J.D. McCarthy, and M.N. Zald (New York: Cambridge University Press), 275–90.

Geertz, C. 1963. 'The Integrative Revolution: Primordial Sentiments and Civil Politics in the New States'. In *Old Societies and New States*, ed. C. Geertz (New York: Free Press), 105–57.

Gellner, E. 1983. *Nations and Nationalism* (Oxford: Basil Blackwell).

Gordon, M. 1975. 'Toward a General Theory of Racial and Ethnic Group Relations'. In *Ethnicity: Theory and Experience*, eds N. Glazer and D.P. Moynihan (Cambridge, MA: Harvard University Press), 84–110.

Gourevitch, P. 1979. 'The Reemergence of "Peripheral Nationalisms"', *Comparative Studies in Society and History* 21: 303–22.

Greenwood, D.J. 1977. 'Continuity in Change: Spanish Basque Ethnicity as a Historical Process'. In *Ethnic Conflict in the Western World*, ed. M.J. Esman (Ithaca, NY: Cornell University Press).

Gurr, T.R. 1970. *Why Men Rebel* (Princeton, NJ: Princeton University Press).

———. 1993. *Minorities at Risk: A Global View of Ethnopolitical Conflicts* (Washington: United States Institute of Peace Press).

Hall, J.A. 1993. 'Nationalisms: Classified and Explained', *Daedalus* 122: 1–27.

Hamilton, R., and M. Pinard. 1982. 'The Quebec

Independence Movement'. In *National Separatism*, ed. C.H. Williams (Vancouver: University of British Columbia Press), 203–33.

Hannan, M.T. 1979. 'The Dynamics of Ethnic Boundaries in Modern States'. In *National Development and the World System*, eds J. Meyer and M.T. Hannan (Chicago: University of Chicago Press), 253–75.

Hechter, M. 1975. *Internal Colonialism: The Celtic Fringe in British National Development, 1536–1966* (Berkeley, CA: University of California Press).

———. 1985. 'Internal Colonialism Revisited'. In *New Nationalism of the Developed West*, eds E.A. Tiryakian and R. Rogowski (Boston: Allen and Unwin), 17–26.

Horowitz, D. 1985. *Ethnic Groups in Conflict* (Berkeley, CA: University of California Press).

Inglehart, R. 1977. *The Silent Revolution: Changing Values and Political Styles Among Western Publics* (Princeton, NJ: Princeton University Press).

———. 1990. *Cultural Shift in Advanced Industrial Society* (Princeton, NJ: Princeton University Press).

Isaacs, H.R. 1975. *Idols of the Tribe* (New York: Harper & Row).

Johnston, R., A. Blais, E. Gidengil, and N. Nevitte. 1996. *The Challenge of Direct Democracy: The 1992 Canadian Referendum* (Montreal and Kingston: McGill-Queen's University Press).

Le Devoir. 1988. 'La relance de l'indépendance par le P.Q. rebute les Québécois'. 25 avril.

Levi, M., and M. Hechter. 1985. 'A Rational Choice Approach to the Rise and Decline of Ethnoregional Political Parties'. In *New Nationalisms of the Developed West,* eds E.A. Tiryakian and R. Rogowski (Boston: Allen and Unwin), 128–46.

Lijphart, A. 1977. *Democracy in Plural Societies* (New Haven, CT: Yale University Press).

Linz, J. 1973. 'Early State-Building and Late Peripheral Nationalisms Against the State: The Case of Spain'. In *Building State and Nations*, vol. 2, eds S.M. Eisenstadt and S. Rokkan (Beverly Hills, CA: Sage), 32–116.

Lorwin, V.R. 1973. 'Belgium: Religion, Class and Language in National Politics'. In *Political Opposi-*

tions in Western Democracies, ed. R.A. Dahl (New Haven, CT: Yale University Press), 147–87.

McAdam, D. 1982. *Political Process and the Development of Black Insurgency 1930–1970* (Chicago: University of Chicago Press).

———. 1996. 'Conceptual Origins, Current Problems, Future Directions'. In *Comparative Perspectives on Social Movements*, eds D. McAdam, J.D. McCarthy and M.N. Zald (New York: Cambridge University Press), 23–40.

McGarry, J., and B. O'Leary. 1995. 'Five Fallacies: Northern Ireland and the Liabilities of Liberalism', *Ethnic and Racial Studies* 18: 837–61.

McRae, K.D. 1974. 'Consociationalism and the Canadian Political System'. In *Consociational Democracy: Political Accommodation in Segmented Societies,* ed. K.D. McRae (Toronto: McClelland & Stewart), 238–61.

———. 1983. *Conflict and Compromise in Multilingual Societies: Switzerland* (Waterloo, ON: Wilfrid Laurier University Press).

———. 1986. *Conflict and Compromise in Multilingual Societies: Belgium* (Waterloo, ON: Wilfrid Laurier University Press).

McRoberts, K. 1979. 'Internal Colonialism: The Case of Quebec', *Ethnic and Racial Studies* 2: 293–318.

Martin, P. 1994. 'Générations politiques, rationalité économique et appui à la souveraineté du Québec', *Canadian Journal of Political Science* 27: 345–59.

Meadwell, H. 1993. 'The Politics of Nationalism in Quebec', *World Politics* 45: 203–41.

Melucci, A. 1988. 'Getting Involved: Identity and Mobilization in Social Movements'. In *From Structure to Action: Comparing Social Movement Research Across Cultures,* eds B. Klendermans, H. Kriesi, and S. Tarrow (Greenwich, CT: JAI Press), 329–48.

Millar, D. 1997. *Militancy During a Phase of Demobilization in the Parti Québécois.* Ph.D. diss. (McGill University).

Nordlinger, E.A. 1972. *Conflict Regulation in Divided Societies* (Cambridge: Harvard University, Center for International Affairs).

Oberschall. A. 1973. *Social Conflict and Social Movements* (Englewood Cliffs, NJ: Prentice-Hall).

Paré, J. 1995. 'Noui au Canada: Non à Ottawa', *L'actualité* 15 mars: 51–8.

Pinard. M. 1976. 'Pluralisme social et partis politiques: quelques éléments d'une théorie'. In *Partis politiques au Québec,* ed. Réjean Pelletier (Montréal: Hurtubise HMH), 37–52.

———. 1980. 'Self-Determination in Quebec: Loyalties, Incentives and Constitutional Options among French-Speaking Quebecers'. In *Resolving Nationality Conflicts,* eds W.P. Davison and L. Gordenker (New York: Praeger), 140–76.

———. 1983. 'From Deprivation to Mobilization', paper presented at the American Sociological Association Meeting, Detroit.

———, R. Bernier, and V. Lemieux. 1997. *Un combat inachevé* (Québec: Presse de l'Université du Québec).

———, and R. Hamilton. 1978. 'The Parti Québécois Comes to Power: An Analysis of the 1976 Quebec Election', *Canadian Journal of Political Science* 11: 739–75.

———. 1984. 'Les Québécois votent NON: le sens et la portée du vote'. In *Comportement électoral au Québec,* ed. Jean Crête (Chicoutimi, PQ: Gaëtan Morin Editeur), 335–85.

———. 1986. 'Motivational Dimensions in the Quebec Independence Movement'. In *Research in Social Movements, Conflict and Change,* ed. L. Kriesberg (Greenwich, CT: JAI Press), 225–80.

———. 1989. 'Intellectuals and the Leadership of Social Movements: Some Comparative Perspectives'. In *Research in Social Movements, Conflict and Change,* ed. L. Kriesberg (Greenwich, CT: JAI Press), 73–107.

Rabushka, A. and K.A. Shepsle. 1972. *Politics in Plural Societies* (Columbus, OH: Charles E. Merrill).

Rose, R. 1971. *Governing without Consensus: An Irish Perspective* (Boston: Beacon Press).

Rule, J.B. 1988. *Theories of Civil Violence* (Berkeley, CA: University of California Press).

Smelser, N.J. 1963. *Theory of Collective Behaviour* (New York: Free Press).

Smith, A.D. 1984. 'Ethnic Persistence and National Transformation', *British Journal of Sociology* 35: 452–61.

Smith, M.G. 1969. 'Some Developments in the Analytic Framework of Pluralism'. In *Pluralism in Africa,* eds L. Kuper and M.G. Smith (Berkeley, CA: University of California Press), 415–58.

Stinchcombe, A.L. 1975. 'Social Structure and Politics'. In *Handbook of Political Science,* eds F. Greenstein and N. Polsby (Reading, MA: Addison-Wesley), 557–622.

Tarrow, S. 1994. *Power in Movement: Social Movements, Collective Action and Politics* (Cambridge: Cambridge University Press).

Taylor, C. 1992. 'The Politics of Recognition'. In *Multiculturalism and the Politics of Recognition,* ed. C. Taylor (Princeton, NJ: Princeton University Press), 25–73.

Urwin, D.W. 1982. 'Territorial Structures and Political Development in the United Kingdom'. In *The Politics of Territorial Identity: Studies in European Regionalism,* eds S. Rokkan and D.W. Urwin (London: Sage), 19–73.

van den Berghe, P.L. 1981. *The Ethnic Phenomenon* (New York: Elsevier).

Part E

Politics and Social Class

Through the 1980s, social class played a prominent role in English-speaking Canadian sociology. Of the five major sections listed in the index of Brym and Fox's monograph on the sociology of English Canada, three either had the word *class* or contained subsections with the word *class* included (Brym and Fox 1989: vii–ix). This work continued into the 1990s. Although some of this work attended to structural properties and developmental dynamics of Canadian capitalism, much of it was devoted to the political impact of social class divisions. Two main sets of dependent variables were used in the series of empirical studies, using mostly survey data, undertaken during this time: (a) class voting (Brym, Gillespie, and Lenton 1987, 1989; Erickson 1981; Hunter 1982; Keddie 1980; Lambert, Curtis, Brown, and Kay 1986, 1988; Nakhaie 1992; Ogmundson 1980; Ogmundson and Ng 1982; Pammett 1987; Schreiber 1980) and (b) political attitudes (Apostle, Clairmont, and Osberg 1986; Johnston and Ornstein 1985; Langford 1986; Ornstein, Stevenson, and Williams 1978, 1980). The former entailed categorizations of political parties as 'working class' (or 'left') versus 'middle class' (or 'right') parties, while the latter concentrated on survey questions dealing with inequality, economic redistributions, subjective class identification and, less frequently, political alienation (or its converse, 'efficacy').

This work often took the form of multivariate statistical analysis, designed to separate out the effects of social class from those of other independent variables said to form competing explanations. The appropriateness of this strategy depended on the theoretical concern being raised and the variables being 'controlled' for. Does one, for example, control for income when assessing the impact of social class on political attitudes when social class is likely to be seen as causally antecedent? Does it even make sense to control for other variables if the issue is 'How strong are social group divisions?' (As opposed to, 'To what extent do factors related to class position give rise to—that is, "cause"—these divisions?') Because researchers tended to report findings both with and without statistical controls, and because most reported patterns tended to occur across variations in the use of statistical procedures, this issue is perhaps not as important as it might at first appear. In Chapter 14, Gidengil summarizes the findings in terms of the *class vote* literature and in Chapter 16 Langford summarizes the findings in terms of the literature dealing with *political attitudes*. The class vote findings suggest that class differences exist, but there has been some debate over whether these are particularly strong (see Gidengil's chapter for an extensive discussion of this issue). The political attitudes research suggests something similar, although it would appear that class differences are a bit more pronounced for attitudes than they are for voting behaviours.

The Canadian interest in social class was not necessarily matched by a similar interest in American sociology. Indeed, as Brym and Fox argue (1989: 57 ff.), both the study of Canadian politics and the study of the Canadian economy started with the importation of American-influenced interpretations but progressed to 'structural (especially class) bases . . . [as] the chief subject of attention'. In this regard, Canadian sociology perhaps more closely approximated British sociology, albeit with more attention to the use of survey data (a research method more prominent in American sociology than British sociology) and with less attention to questions of cultural interpretation as they related to class (the British 'cultural studies' approach of the 1980s; see Golding and Murdock 1978; Hall 1977, 1982, 1986; Thompson 1990).

Through the 1990s, serious questions about the appropriateness of social class as an explanatory variable were raised and a vigorous debate on this question followed (Adam 1993; Cohen and Arato 1992; Crompton 1996; Eder 1993; Grusky and Sorensen 1998; Lafferty 1996; McLennan 1996; Pakulski and Waters 1996; Turner 1986).[1] This debate is ongoing, and the vigorous response to critics from (mostly) American sociologists working in the paradigm suggests that class analysis is certainly not dead (Lembcke 1991; Morris and Scott 1996; Van Parijs 1987; Wright 1991, 1994, 1997). It is of relevance to Canadian sociologists because of the implicit and explicit claims of critics that social class (a) is declining in importance as a predictor of important (political) outcomes and (b) represents divisions that are better dealt with without recourse to the term *class* (for example, as social status, education, or income). In his chapter, Langford addresses the first of these questions and finds, interestingly, that there has hardly been any change in the nature of class divisions over the past

decade and a half on political attitude issues that were originally studied in the late 1970s. That is, divisions between the working class and other classes (especially) have remained.[2]

As the debate over the appropriateness of social class was debated internationally, Canadian sociologists continued to study questions of political attitudes and class-related voting behaviour into the 1990s (Johnston 1995, Langford 1992, Nakhaie 1992; Smucke and van den Berg 1991). While the study of social class is not likely to come to a halt in Canadian sociology, it is possible that some of the elements of the discussion and debate surrounding its appropriateness may inform future analyses. Minimally, the conceptualization of class has been influenced by the critique, especially around the definition of the 'middle class'. Langford's chapter anticipates some of this discussion by including (briefly) an examination of the divisions between public sector and private sector professionals and managers (see also Esping-Andersen 1993; Fairbrother 1989). This division may have been crucial in the dissolution of the alliance that brought the NDP to power in Ontario in 1990 with the strong support of public sector professionals and semi-professionals; heavily influenced by private sector union advisors in a time of fiscal crisis, only two years later the NDP government employed draconian labour measures on public sector workers and as a result saw the erosion of an important part of its support base.

Class analyses may also need to be more sensitive to the gender dimension, as Gidengil points out in her chapter. Some elements of class structuration are coincident with gender—according to Gidengil women are more likely now to be in the working class than men—and this may have profound future effects on the nature of class politics. This goes beyond the traditional view that gender is important and must be seen as a cross-cutting measure included in studies of class to suggest that gender is now implicated in the very definition of class itself. This plays out, especially, in the division between public sector and private sector workers.

The study of social class has also been extended into some areas not considered part of the traditional research design of class studies. A final chapter by Verberg in this section examines a variable that may be related to class politics but has not been examined as such previously: home ownership.

Regardless of the status of social class, issues of social inequality, which provide the impetus for most class studies, are likely to remain if not intensify in the minds of sociological researchers as pressures from the global economic system (see Chapter 15 by Johnston) affect occupational structures, a developing 'underclass' and patterns of economic inequality. Recently, there appears to have been a renewed interest in American sociology in the politics of class (Brooks and Manza 1997a, 1997b, 1997c), and it would appear that the declaration that class analysis is 'dead' (Pakulski and Waters 1996) is at least premature.

Class studies can take a variety of forms. Some employ survey research, while others construct broad historical comparisons between countries to discuss the relative power of social classes as they negotiated for formal and informal political power around the policies of the welfare state. Increasingly, comparative frameworks, comparing Canada with other countries, are becoming popular in the field.

Johnston raises some important issues about the relative power of the traditional working class, arguing that, after 20 years of post-World War II economic expansion, the environment under which class competition occurs has changed. The question of the relative power of capitalists can be framed with dependent variables that include the extent of universal welfare provision, the density of union memberships, the level of inequality in the wage structure, and the electoral and legislative power of formal political parties, especially 'social democratic' parties. The causal mechanism is not, of course, only in one direction; the density of union membership is not only affected by the balance of power (for example, legislation can make unionization more difficult, as we see in the case of the United States, especially the southern US), but has an effect on that power (stronger unions are better able to push their legislative agendas). Johnston examines these interrelationships both temporally (across time) and cross-nationally, making a particularly useful comparison between the cases of Sweden and Australia. Why, he asks, are some of the outcomes—especially those related to the welfare state—so different between the two countries when each appears to have now and has had in the past a strong labour movement? Here, historical explanations become important.

Notes

1. See also the debate over 'state-centred' versus 'society-centred' theories, discussed in the Introduction to Part B. The 'society-centred' theories under attack by Skocpol and others included class theories.

2. It is the case, though, that changes in the postindustrial workplace have led to declines in the numbers of individuals in the traditional working class, so the political importance of these divisions may have declined.

References

Adam, B. 1993. 'Post-Marxism and the New Social Movements', *Canadian Review of Sociology and Anthropology* 30(3): 316–36.

Apostle, R., D. Clairmont, and L. Osberg. 1986. 'Economic Segmentation and Politics', *American Journal of Sociology* 91(4): 905–31.

Brooks, C., and J. Manza. 1997a. 'Class Politics and Political Change in the United States, 1952–1992', *Social Forces* 76: 379–408.

———. 1997b. 'The Social and Ideological Bases of Middle-Class Political Realignment in the United States, 1972 to 1992', *American Sociological Review* 62: 191–208.

———. 1997c. 'Social Cleavages and Political Alignments: U.S. Presidential Elections, 1960 to 1992', *American Journal of Sociology* 62: 937–46.

Brym, R. and B. Fox. 1989. *From Culture to Power: The Sociology of English Canada* (Toronto: Oxford University Press).

Brym, R., M. Gillespie, and R. Lenton. 1987. 'A Reinterpretation of Class Voting in Canada', paper presented to the Annual Meeting of the Canadian Sociology and Anthropology Association, McMaster University.

———. 1989. 'Class Power, Class Mobilization, and Class Voting', *Canadian Journal of Sociology* 14(1): 25–44.

Cohen, J., and A. Arato. 1992. *Civil Society and Political Theory* (Cambridge, MA: MIT Press).

Crompton, R. 1996. 'The Fragmentation of Class Analysis', *British Journal of Sociology* 47(1): 56–67.

Eder, K. 1993. *The New Politics of Class* (Newbury Park, CA: Sage).

Erickson, B. 1981. 'Region, Knowledge and Class Voting in Canada', *Canadian Journal of Sociology* 6(2): 121–44.

Esping-Andersen, G. 1993. 'Post Industrial Class Structures: An Analytical Framework'. In *Changing Classes: Stratification and Mobility in Post-Industrial Societies,* ed. G. Esping-Andersen (Newbury Park, CA: Sage), 7–31.

Fairbrother, P. 1989. 'State Workers: Class Position and Collective Action'. In *Democracy and the Capitalist State,* ed. G. Duncan (Cambridge: Cambridge University Press).

Golding, P., and G. Murdock. 1978. 'Theories of Communication and Theories of Society', *Communication Research* 5: 339–56.

Grusky, D. and J. Sorensen. 1998. 'Can Class Analysis Be Salvaged?', *American Journal of Sociology* 103: 1187–234.

Hall, S. 1977. 'Culture Media and the Ideological Effect'. In *Mass Communication and Society,* eds J. Curran, M. Gurevitch, and J. Woollacott (London: Edward Arnold).

———. 1982. 'The Rediscovery of Ideology: Return of the Represses in Media Studies'. In *Society and the Media,* eds T.B. Michael Gurevitch, J. Curran, and J. Woollacott.

———. 1986. 'Popular Culture and the State'. In *Popular Culture and Social Relations,* eds C.M. Tony Bennett and J. Woollacott (Milton Keynes, UK: Open University Press).

Hunter, A. 1982. 'On Class, Status and Voting in Canada', *Canadian Journal of Sociology* 7(1): 19–40.

Johnston, W. 1995. 'Social Divisions and Ideological Fragmentation', *Canadian Journal of Sociology* 12(4): 315–30.

———, and M. Ornstein. 1985. 'Social Class and Political Ideology in Canada', *Canadian Review of Sociology and Anthropology* 22(3): 369–93.

Keddie, V. 1980. 'Class Identification and Party Preference Among Manual Workers: The Influence of Community, Union Membership and Kinship', *Canadian Review of Sociology and Anthropology* 17: 24–36.

Lafferty, G. 1996. 'Class, Politics and Social Theory: The Possibilities of Marxist Analysis', *Critical Sociology* 22: 51–66.

Lambert, R., J. Curtis, S. Brown, and B. Kay. 1986. 'Social Class, Left/Right Political Orientations and Subjective Class Voting in Provincial and Federal Elections', *Canadian Review of Sociology and Anthropology* 24(4): 526–49.

————. 1988. 'The Left-Right Factor in Party Identification', *Canadian Journal of Sociology* 13(4): 385–406.

Langford, T. 1986. 'Workers' Subordinate Values: A Canadian Case Study', *Canadian Journal of Sociology* 11(3): 269–92.

————. 1992. 'Social Experiences and Variations in Economic Beliefs among Canadian Workers', *Canadian Review of Sociology and Anthropology* 29(4): 453–87.

Lembcke, J. 1991. 'Class Analysis and Studies of the U.S. Working Class: Theoretical, Conceptual and Methodological Issues'. In *Bringing Class Back In: Contemporary and Historical Perspectives,* eds R. McNall, R. Levine, and R. Fantasia (Boulder, CO: Westview Press), 83–97.

McLennan, G. 1996. 'Post-Marxism and the "Four Sins" of Modernist Theorizing', *New Left Review* 218: 53–74.

Morris, L., and J. Scott. 1996. 'The Attenuation of Class Analysis: Some Comments on G. Marshall, S. Roberts and C. Burgoyne, "Social class and the underclass in Britain and the USA"', *British Journal of Sociology* 47(1): 45–55.

Nakhaie, R. 1992. 'Class and voting consistency in Canada: Analyses bearing on the mobilization thesis', *Canadian Journal of Sociology* 17(3): 275–300.

Ogmundson, R. 1980. 'Liberal Ideology and the Study of Voting Behaviour', *Canadian Review of Sociology and Anthropology* 17: 45–53.

————, R., and M. Ng. 1982. 'On the Inference of Voter Motivation: A Comparison of the Subjective Class Vote in Canada and the United Kingdom', *Canadian Journal of Sociology* 7(1): 41–60.

Ornstein, M., H.M. Stevenson, and P. Williams. 1978.

'Public Opinion and the Canadian Political Crisis', *Canadian Review of Sociology and Anthropology* 15: 158–205.

————. 1980. 'Region, Class and Political Culture in Canada', *Canadian Journal of Political Science* 13: 227–71.

Pakulski, J., and M. Waters. 1996. *The Death of Class* (Thousand Oaks, CA: Sage).

Pammett, J. 1987. 'Class Voting and Class Consciousness in Canada', *Canadian Review of Sociology and Anthropology* 24(2): 269–90.

Schreiber, E.M. 1980. 'Class Awareness and Class Voting in Canada: A Reconsideration of the Ogmundson Thesis', *Canadian Review of Sociology and Anthropology* 17: 37–44.

Smucke, J., and A. van den Berg. 1991. 'Some evidence on the effects of labour market policies on workers' attitudes toward change in Canada and Sweden', *Canadian Journal of Sociology* 16(1): 51–74.

Thompson, J. 1990. *Ideology and Modern Culture* (Cambridge: Polity Press).

Turner, B. 1986. 'Citizenship and Capitalism'.

Van Parijs, P. 1987. 'A Revolution in Class Theory', *Politics and Society* 15: 453–82.

Wright, E. 1991. 'The Conceptual Status of Class Structure in Class Analysis'. In *Bringing Class Back In: Contemporary and Historical Perspectives,* eds S. McNall, R. Levine, and R. Fantasia (Boulder, CO: Westview).

————. 1994. 'Class Analysis, History and Emancipation', *New Left Review* 202: 15–36.

————. 1997. *Class Counts: Comparative Studies in Class Analysis* (Cambridge: Cambridge University Press).

Chapter 14

The Class Voting Conundrum

Elisabeth Gidengil

Introduction

Almost 40 years have passed since Alford (1963) declared Canada a case of 'pure non-class voting.' His conclusion was based on a comparative study of class voting in the four Anglo-American democracies. Alford viewed a relationship between class position and voting behaviour as almost a given in Western democracies. Indeed, he considered that it would be remarkable if such a relationship were *not* found. He did anticipate differences in the degree of relationship, depending on variations in the intensity of class interests and the salience of crosscutting or reinforcing cleavages, and he expected class voting to be lower in Canada and the United States than in Britain or Australia. What he did not anticipate was the apparent lack of class voting in Canada.[1] He attributed this perverse (non)finding to the strength of cross-cutting cleavages in Canada, concluding that 'regional and religious cleavages supersede class almost entirely as factors differentiating the support for national parties' (x–xi).

Alford's findings have provoked three basic types of reaction among scholars who assert the relevance of class to electoral politics in Canada. Some scholars have accepted the validity of Alford's conclusion—and his rationale for it—and concentrated on uncovering evidence of higher levels of class voting where conditions are right. Other scholars refute Alford's claim, arguing that class voting only *seems* low because of faulty mea-surement. Still other scholars accept the fact of low class voting, but reject Alford's culturalist rationale in favour of more materialist explanations.

The Evolutionary Model of Class Voting

Alford anticipated a greater role for class in shaping Canadian electoral behaviour as industrialization and urbanization eroded parochial bases of political behaviour. This prediction was very much in the tradition of the evolutionary model of mass politics developed by Lipset and Rokkan (1967). The model's central idea is that different types of political cleavages tend to predominate during different phases of a nation-state's development. Lipset and Rokkan identify the two crucial cleavages as the territorial-cultural and the functional: 'In the one case the decisive criterion of alignment is commitment to the locality and its dominant culture: you vote with your community and its leaders irrespective of your economic position. In the other the criterion is commitment to a class and its collective interests: you vote with others in the same position as yourself whatever their localities' (1967: 13). The assumption is that territorial-cultural conflicts will be the norm in the early phases of nation-building, but they will give way to functional cleavages in the wake of industrial development.

Given the variation in levels of industrialization from province to province, it makes sense from an evolutionary perspective to look for evidence of class voting in Canada's most industrialized provinces. Using data from the 1974 federal election, Jenson (1976) classified the stage of development of each provincial party system according to the electoral cleavages she observed. She took the dominance of ethnic, linguistic, or religious cleavages to indicate a 'traditional' party system and the dominance of class cleavages to define a 'modernized' party system. The results were disconcerting. It was Saskatchewan, Canada's least industrialized province, which turned out to have the most 'modern' party system.[2] Conversely, in Canada's industrial heartland of Ontario, the 'traditional' cleavages of language and religion won out over social class.

Wilson (1974) encountered similar difficulties when he attempted to fit the Canadian provinces into a typology based on the Anglo-American historical experience. As a society evolves from the preindustrial or beginning industrial stage through the industrializing stage to the advanced industrial stage, he reasoned, its party system will change in terms of the cleavages that it reflects and the kinds of interests that it serves. His data consisted of two-party vote shares across time. Again, Saskatchewan emerged as Canada's sole example of a 'modern' party system, while Ontario's party system only qualified as 'transitional'.

Blake (1972) has provided the most comprehensive examination of this notion that socioeconomic conditions have to be 'right' before class voting will appear. His purpose was to determine whether urbanization and industrialization and heightened interregional contact have eroded regional idiosyncrasies in Canadian voting behaviour and made social class the major determinant of partisan choice. Studying elections between 1908 and 1968, he detected no apparent decline in the aggregate-level impact of region on major party support patterns. He did detect the emergence of cross-regional 'class cleavages', but these cleavages found both upper-status *and* blue-collar groups giving disproportionate support to the Liberals and blue-collar groups giving disproportionate support to the Conservatives as well. There are still no signs that territorial-cultural cleavages are weakening in Canada. Indeed, with the emergence of the Bloc Québécois and the regionalization of the vote in recent federal elections, these cleavages have arguably strengthened over the past decade (Gidengil et al. 1999; Nevitte et al. 2000: 11–14).

The failure of territorial-cultural cleavages to give way to a conventional class cleavage would not necessarily have surprised Lipset and Rokkan (1967). They did not see anything automatic about the evolutionary trajectory from territorial-cultural cleavages to functional cleavages. Archaic forms of political conflict may become institutionalized in a party system that endures long after the original conflicts have lost their salience. Or the conflicts of nation-building, if unresolved in the preindustrial era, may continue into later evolutionary stages.

Research in the Lipset-Rokkan tradition has tended to conceptualize the role of class and region in either/or terms: the rise of class cleavages is taken to imply the decline of regional cleavages, while the persistence of regional cleavages is taken to represent the failure of class to become salient. What gets overlooked in this approach is the possible interplay between class and region. Voters sharing the same social class membership may perceive their position differently and react to it differently depending upon the structural context in which they are located (see Gidengil 1989).

The Methodological Critique

Other critics have been less ready to accept the conclusion that class voting is weak in Canada. Myles (1979) has gone so far as to describe the

'Canadian exception' as a 'pseudofact', the result of theoretical and methodological shortcomings in Alford's analysis. The methodological critique has centred on three issues: the measurement of voters' own class positions, the classification of Canada's political parties, and the measurement of class voting itself.

MEASURING VOTERS' CLASS POSITIONS

Researchers elsewhere have found that 'research into the political effects of class is peculiarly dependent on the way in which classes are defined empirically; answers to the simplest questions . . . must depend on the operations by which the classes are separated' (Kahan, Butler, and Stokes 1966: 122). It turns out that Canada is an exception in this regard as well: however class position is measured, the level of class voting remains low.

Social class is typically measured either objectively, using indicators like occupation, income, or education, or subjectively, using self-reported class. Each of these measures has its limitations. Regional disparities complicate the use of income and education as surrogates for class. The social significance of a given level of income or schooling varies across Canada and interprovincial differences in the retentiveness of the school system and the number of years required for high school graduation make it difficult to come up with consistent categories (see Schwartz 1974: 589–90). On largely pragmatic grounds, Alford argued for occupation as the measure of choice. Occupational status is reasonably meaningful across regional and national boundaries and it tends to be the best predictor. However, critics have questioned the meaningfulness of Alford's dichotomization of occupation into manual versus non-manual occupations (Korpi 1972). Alford's rationale was that contrasts in lifestyles, education, and values between the working class and the middle class make the shift from a blue-collar to a white-collar job more significant—personally and socially—than a shift within these broad categories. The difficulty arises with lower white-collar occupations like sales and clerical workers whose economic circumstances and lifestyle may differ little from those of skilled blue-collar workers. When lower white collars are assigned to the working class instead of the middle class, however, the level of class voting actually appears to go down (Myles and Forcese 1981).

Income, education, and occupation cannot be used interchangeably. The intercorrelations among them range 'from modest to moderate' at best (Hunter 1982: 24; cf. Coburn and Edwards 1976). This is only to be expected: the weakness of the intercorrelations is an integral part of stratification in postindustrial societies. Social mobility and the erosion of class barriers mean that many people have 'contradictory' class attributes. Not surprisingly, the three class indicators frequently give disparate results. In fact, education and occupation turn out to be related to the NDP vote in *opposite* ways (albeit neither very strongly nor altogether consistently).[3]

Similarly, self-defined social class will not necessarily agree with more objective criteria. Pineo and Goyder (1973) found only moderate correlations between self-perceived class and education, income, and occupation. Subjectively defined social class 'should identify an individual's perception of where his [sic] class interests lie' (Kay 1977: 131). The problem is that respondents may identify with a social class simply to oblige an interviewer who has presented them with a list of class labels, even though they lack any real sense of what these labels mean (see Schreiber 1980). This is especially likely when reluctant respondents are pressed to make a choice. A different type of criticism sees the subjective approach as inadequate simply because so many voters believe that they belong to the middle class.

In fact, the percentage of respondents identifying with the middle class does generally tend to decline down the status hierarchy with all three of the conventional objective measures. Only with occupation, however, does a sharp cleft in subjective class identification occur between categories. The main division is between manual occupations and nonmanual occupations (Gidengil 1989; cf. Coburn and Edwards 1976). Moreover, there is a substantial gap in subjective status between the lowest nonmanual occupational category and the highest manual category, despite the fact that skilled manual workers tend to earn higher incomes than white-collar clerical and sales workers. This suggests that the manual-nonmanual distinction 'is much more than an analytical simplification of those who have studied social class' (Kahan et al. 1966).

Schwartz (1974a) has suggested that 'perhaps it is because such crude indicators of class have been used that we found so little class-based voting'.[4] Yet, with all their limitations, these same indicators do work in other countries, so we must still wonder, along with Schwartz, why they do not work in Canada. And even the use of more theoretically rigorous class categories turns out to provide only modest evidence of class cleavages in Canadians' political behaviour.

The 'class' measures discussed so far have all had a socioeconomic referent rather than a Marxist or neo-Marxist referent. In the stratification approach, the criterion is the individual's relative share of the *same* attribute, whether occupational status, income, education, or some combination of the three. In the Marxist conception, on the other hand, the criteria of class membership are *opposite* characteristics, conceived in terms of relationship to the means of production and control over the labour process (see Stevenson 1977). The Marxist approach views class in nominal terms, with the divisions between classes assumed to represent fundamental discontinuities. Similarly, class conflict is understood as a struggle not over consumption but about the fundamental relations of production that underlie differential market capacity (see Myles and Forcese 1981).

Ornstein and his colleagues (1980) have attempted to use a more theoretically rigorous, Marxist definition of class derived from Wright's (1976) class typology. That typology was based on the correspondence—or noncorrespondence—between ownership or control of the means of production, control over investment, and control over the labour process. The lack of correspondence among these three criteria defines three contradictory locations between the bourgeoisie, the petite bourgeoisie, and the proletariat. The typology requires very detailed information on people's work situations. Ornstein and his colleagues' analysis was conducted in two parts, first using three conventional indicators of class and then the Marxist class categories. Interestingly enough, the two parts produced quite compatible answers to their research questions, suggesting that the weakness of the class cleavage observed in other studies cannot be attributed simply to the theoretical inadequacy of the class measures used to tap it.[5] In their most recent work, Ornstein and Stevenson (1999) extend their class typology to examine the effects of manual/non-manual differences, supervision, and pay differences *within* classes. While they demonstrate that 'there are limited but significant differences in the attractiveness of different parties to segments of different social classes' (p. 247), they conclude that 'this analysis does not challenge the scholarly consensus on the nature of federal party support in Canada' (p. 268).

The use of other Marxist class typologies has produced similarly modest results. Proponents suggest that 'measures of class, developed along Marxist lines, provide some insights into the character of political ideology in Canada that are invisible to studies using conventional indicators of stratification' (Johnston and Ornstein 1985: 370). They are obliged, nevertheless, to concede 'the central fact that none of [sic] independent variables is a very strong predictor of political ideology'.

MEASURING THE CLASS POSITIONS OF POLITICAL PARTIES

Myles and Ogmundson have been the most force-ful proponents of the argument that the low level of class voting in Canada is more apparent than real. Part of their argument centres around the proper class placement of Canada's political par-ties. Alford's index of class voting involves sub-tracting the percentage of voters in nonmanual occupations voting for left parties from the per-centage of manual workers voting for left parties. In other words, his approach assumes a two-party system with a clear left-right dichotomy, or at least a system in which the political parties can be ordered on a left-right continuum. The question of how the political parties are to be classified into these two categories of left and right has proved a source of controversy in Canada.

Relying on the opinion of a respected academ-ic authority (Dawson 1954), Alford himself orig-inally defined the CCF-NDP and the Liberal Party as Canada's left parties and the Conservatives and the old Social Credit Party as the parties of the right. Critics (for example, Ogmundson 1975a, 1975b, 1975c; Myles 1979) have charged that Alford's left-right division of the two major feder-al political parties is highly misleading. Ogmundson cited academic opinion, aggregate voter perceptions, bases of electoral support, sources of funding, and the social origins of Members of Parliament to support his reclassifi-cation of the political parties in terms of a major-minor dichotomy. By these criteria, he argued, the Liberals, like the Conservatives, are clearly a party of the middle class, while Social Credit appeared almost as working class as the NDP.[6] Using this classification, the rate of class voting did increase, but only to a level that remained 'unusually low' by international standards.

Myles and Forcese (1981) counter that if by left party we mean a socialist or social democrat-ic party, the only appropriate left-right division is one that distinguishes between the NDP and all other parties. The fact that voters *think* a party is for the working class does not make it a left party and neither does the fact that it draws dispropor-tionate support from the working class. 'In Canada voting for or against the NDP is the most important test of class voting' (Fletcher and Forbes 1990). The NDP qualifies as Canada's only left party on several counts: its formal links with the trade union movement, its left-wing ideology, its membership in the Socialist International, and its history of making class appeals. In fact, in his later work, Alford (1967) did treat the NDP as the only party of the left, but he still could not detect much class voting.

MEASURING CLASS VOTING

The one revisionist strategy that has produced higher levels of class voting has involved chang-ing the measurement of class voting itself. This strategy has taken two forms. Myles (1979; cf. Myles and Forcese 1981) has 'standardized' Alford's index to remove the effects of skewed marginal distributions, while Ogmundson (1975b, 1975c; Ogmundson and Ng 1982) has pioneered the use of the subjective class vote.

Myles is critical of Alford's original index be-cause it is sensitive to the marginal distributions of the class and vote variables. When one or other of these is highly skewed, the index confounds the effect of class on vote with the overall level of left voting. Skewness becomes a problem when left voting is equated with a vote for the NDP. Myles' solution is to remove the effects of skew-ness using the Deming adjustment. With this adjustment, levels of class voting in Canada and the US become indistinguishable. Skewness should not be viewed as simply a statistical prob-lem, however. The fact that the NDP has never attracted more than 20 per cent of the vote in fed-eral elections is itself evidence of the weakness of class voting in Canada.

As measured by Alford, 'class voting' is simply a statistical relationship (see Johnston 1981). It does not take any account of voters' understandings or intents. People may be voting for 'their' class party for reasons that have nothing to do with class, simply because they like the candidate, say. So defined, 'class voting' need not imply any conscious intent to translate class interests into class action or even any consciousness of class. Ogmundson (1975b, 1975c; Ogmundson and Ng 1982) has attempted to develop a subjective measure of the class vote. It incorporates voter perceptions of political parties' class positions to take account of what voters *think* they are doing. These perceptions were derived from a semantic differential item included in both the 1965 and 1968 Canadian election studies which asked respondents to rate the federal political parties on a seven-point 'for the working class'/'for the middle class' scale. When individual perceptions were used to define the class orientation of the parties, the rate of class voting increased to a level that Ogmundson described as almost 'normal' in terms of international standards.

Lambert and Hunter (1979) have replicated Ogmundson's findings 'in almost every detail', using data from the 1968 Canadian election study (Ogmundson's data were drawn from the 1965 study). They were more cautious, however, in interpreting these findings. Noting that some small amount of class voting could be observed, they conclude that 'it was probably real enough, but relatively unimportant'. As for incorporating individual voter perceptions, they judged it 'a research tradition that might best be discontinued as unpromising' (1979: 302–3).

Kay (1977) raised further doubts about classifying political parties by individual perceptions with his perplexing finding that middle-class identifiers were actually more likely to vote for the two major parties if they perceived those parties to be favouring the 'working class', rather than their own middle class. Lambert and his colleagues (1987) subsequently changed the categories to read 'for the lower social classes' and 'for

the higher social classes', arguing that class conflict is more likely to be perceived in those terms. The evidence of class voting remained less than compelling. Nationally, income, occupation, and education only explained trivial amounts (1.5 per cent federally and 3.1 per cent provincially) of the variance in subjective class voting. Adding social class self-placements and left/right political orientations did increase the percentage of variance explained, but only to 6.8 per cent federally and 9.3 per cent provincially.[7]

Even when we do find that working-class identifiers are more likely to vote for a party perceived to be 'for the working class' or 'for the lower social classes', it remains a statistical association. We still lack direct evidence of any sort of intent to cast a class vote, as Ogmundson himself acknowledged. And there is the problem of misperception: Do we really want to count a working-class voter who perceives the Conservative Party as being for the working class or for the lower social classes as casting a class vote for that party?

Lambert and Hunter (1979; cf. Schreiber 1980) have also raised the possibility that class labels are simply academic abstractions that few Canadians understand well. This possibility was explored in the 1984 Canadian Election Study (Lambert et al. 1986). When asked whether the idea of social classes had any meaning to them, only a bare majority (55 per cent) of respondents answered positively, and of these respondents, only half (50 per cent) chose an economic criterion[8] as the most important difference between social classes. Those who said the idea of social classes had no meaning to them were even less likely to choose an economic criterion (26 per cent), opting instead for personal traits (44 per cent) like character and ambition. Blue-collar workers turned out to be the least likely to offer materialist definitions of social class. It is difficult to escape the conclusion that only a minority of Canadians understand the terms in the way that advocates of the subjective class vote seem to assume.[9]

From Culturalist to Materialist Explanations

If those labels are poorly understood, does this reflect the low salience of social class for many Canadians or the fact that 'the dominant ideology contains little in the way of a class analysis of Canadian politics generally, much less of parties in particular' (Lambert and Hunter 1979: 303)? This is the central argument of those critics who accept that the class cleavage is modest at best, but reject Alford's rationale for it. According to these critics, 'the main source of the anomaly associated with the Canadian case resides, not with the Canadians themselves, but with the nature of the electoral options presented to them' (Ogmundson 1975c: 506), options that reflect élite interests rather than mass desires. In other words, 'the apparent classlessness of our politics can best be explained, not by public opinion, but by the skill of the "bourgeois" parties in manipulating the situation to their advantage' (Ogmundson 1980: 47). A key element in this strategy of élite manipulation is said to be an exaggerated, even artificial, emphasis on regional cleavages. 'Regionalism,' Ornstein and his colleagues (1980: 227) claim, 'often diverts attention from the class character of Canadian society'.

Brodie and Jenson have argued forcefully that the weakness of the class cleavage at the voters' level should not be taken to mean that electoral politics is therefore devoid of class content.[10] Elections and partisan politics, they argue, in fact play a crucial role in the class struggle by defining politics in a way that protects and advances the interests of the dominant capitalist class, while suppressing those of the subordinate classes. They seek to show how the two 'bourgeois' parties have deliberately inhibited the growth of class-based parties and class voting by repeatedly emphasizing the twin themes of a bicultural Canada and the need for consensus amid diversity (cf. Horowitz 1968).

These alternative rationales for Alford's findings emphasize the nature of electoral options that make it difficult for working-class voters to express their class interests. According to Schreiber (1980), on the other hand, if the traditionally dominant parties have failed to differentiate themselves in class terms, this is because they are responding to the preferences of the modal Canadian voter. Ogmundson (1976, 1980) points to the salience of class-related economic issues in public opinion surveys to buttress his case that the problem lies at the élite rather than the mass level. Schreiber counters that these issues would only count as 'class' issues if there were clear differences in the way that people in different classes saw them. Ogmundson (1976, 1980) examines ideal party class images and shows that working-class respondents would prefer a party slightly favourable to the working class. Schreiber (1980) responds by questioning why, election after election, most fail to vote for the party that is perceived as being for the working class.

This is where the 'wasted vote' thesis comes in. Working-class voters are not voting their 'true' preference because they do not want to waste their vote on a party that has no realistic chance of forming a government. As Schreiber (1980) notes, if these voters are more concerned about 'wasting' their votes than furthering their class interests, those interests cannot be very salient. And if the traditionally dominant parties are seen as virtually interchangeable on the class dimension, why should a vote for one rather than the other be any less of a waste from the perspective of a class-conscious working-class voter?[11]

Ogmundson's 'wasted vote' thesis does receive some support from Zipp and Smith's (1982) finding that class voting is higher in areas of NDP strength.[12] Even in areas where the NDP was electorally viable, however, the effects were 'not overwhelming.' In any case, the explanatory status of electoral viability is ambiguous. The political context certainly places important constraints upon voting choice, but the viability or not of particular parties is itself a function of voters' prior choices (Schwartz 1974b: 165). In other words, there is an element of circularity to the argument: class voting is weak because the left party is weak, but the left party is weak because class voting is weak (see Brym et al. 1989).

Part of the problem seems to be that voters simply do not see very much difference between the parties in class terms. In the 1984 Canadian Election Study, only 16 per cent of respondents believed that their first- and third-choice parties were 'very different' in their class orientations (Lambert and Curtis 1993). Perceived choice does have an impact on class voting: the greater the perceived discrepancy among parties, the more class voting. However, the lack of perceived class difference necessarily limits the amount of class voting. Similarly, the more knowledgeable voters are about the parties' class positions, the more class voting, but, again, voters are not very knowledgeable (Erickson 1981). And it is manual workers who have especially low knowledge levels.

Conclusion: Whither the Class Voting Debate?

The class voting debate began with a simple statistical association (or, rather, lack of association) between social class and vote. Alford was only interested in the degree to which working-class voters and middle-class voters diverged politically. Whether voters were conscious or not of their class identity and whether they perceived political parties in class terms, Alford maintained, should be kept separate questions.[13]

These questions are now regarded as central to the study of class voting. Analyses have moved beyond the simple association between social class and vote to take account of a range of mediating variables. It is the very weakness of these mediating links, it turns out, that helps explain the weakness of the class-vote relationship in Canada. Canadians are simply not very class conscious. Pammett (1987) has provided the most damning evidence. Across a three-wave panel study over the 1974–79 period, only 3 per cent of Canadians maintained a spontaneous working-class identification. Even manual workers were more likely to have a middle-class identification than a working-class one, if they had a class identification at all. This low level of class consciousness and its middle-class character are the more basic puzzles.

Élite manipulation arguments, we have seen, point to the role of political leaders in obfuscating class issues. There are at least two problems with this.[14] First, it begs the question of why Canadian élites have been so much more successful at this than their counterparts elsewhere. Second, relying as it does, at least implicitly, on the notion of false consciousness on the part of the working class, it has to confront the puzzle: how and why does this false consciousness persist when 'continually confronted with the reality of daily life under capitalism' (Gold et al. 1975: 41)? Regional cleavages, for example, are not necessarily the result of 'false consciousness', but of very real differences in material conditions (see Gidengil 1989).

The political mobilization approach (Brym et al. 1989; Nakhaie 1992), on the other hand, points to the importance of subordinate class power in the process of transforming objective class position into subjective class action. Levels of union membership and left party strength are taken as indicators of subordinate class power because they are assumed to reflect the distribution of power resources among classes. And trade unions and a viable left party are considered vital organizational resources in themselves.

The proportion of the provincial population belonging to a union does have a significant effect on NDP voting, but the individual-level effects of union membership are modest (Archer 1985; Nevitte et al. 2000: ch. 9). This poses a problem for resource mobilization theory. The theory assumes that integration into an organization will have a socializing effect on individuals (see Nakhaie 1992). Union membership is supposed to have just this effect: 'the trade union, by emphasizing collective action and the existence of conflicts of interest between workers and management, may help to engender a sense of solidarity among workers' (Keddie 1980: 31). While union members are somewhat more likely to vote for the NDP than nonmembers, it turns out that this does not reflect a working-class consciousness on their part (Pammett 1987). In fact, union members are more likely to identify with the middle class than with the working class. And in the 1997 federal election, union members were more likely to vote for the Reform Party (20 per cent) than for the NDP (15 per cent).[15]

The socializing effect of union membership is problematic when trade unions narrow conflict to issues of wages and conditions and fail to challenge the basic structure of labour-capital relations. This 'business unionism' is unlikely either to crystallize subordinate class ideology or to legitimize class conflict in the eyes of workers (see Buttel and Flinn 1979). Myles and Forcese (1981) link this style of unionism to the larger issue of Canada's economic dependency on the United States. Dependent industrialization meant that 'In large measure, the capitalist class which developed and organized the Canadian industrial structure was the American capitalist class'. Along with American branch plants came the American industrial relations system and American methods for organizing the labour process.

The explanation for the weakness of class voting in Canada may indeed lie in the intersection of political sociology and political economy. There is a good deal of uncertainty about how to characterize the class structure of advanced capitalist societies. Indeed, given the disagreement among experts, ordinary workers can hardly be taken to task for failing to classify themselves

'correctly'. The Canadian situation is made even more complicated by Canada's ambiguous position in the international economic system (see Glenday 1989; Resnick 1989). Canada is an advanced capitalist country and yet economically dependent upon the US. At the regional level, structural relations of dependency among regions have been linked to variations in the nature and level of class voting. These same relations of regional dependency help explain the weakness of the national class cleavage in voting (Gidengil 1989). The implications of Canada's own dependency for class consciousness and class voting have yet to be examined.

We also need to pay more attention to the impact of production sector on class voting. Scholars have only just begun to explore this relationship. Blais and his colleagues (1990) have analysed the effect of public versus private sector employment on support for the NDP. They found that public sector workers were more likely to vote NDP than private sector workers. The production sector cleavage in left voting, though, proved to be weaker in Canada than in the United States. Similarly, Langford (1996) found that the public sector branch of the Canadian new middle class was more likely than the private sector branch to support the NDP. The difference in NDP support between the two sectors, however, dropped from 13 percentage points in 1982 to only five percentage points in 1988. And while public sector workers remained more likely to vote NDP than private sector workers in the 1997 federal election, they were more likely to vote Reform than NDP (Nevitte et al. 2000: ch. 9).

The class voting debate has also been surprisingly inattentive to the gender dimension. As Clement (1990) notes, the expanded labour force participation of women represents one of the most profound changes affecting class formation. He goes on to show that class formation is significantly different for women and men. In Canada, as elsewhere, the working class (defined relationally) is larger for women (68 per cent) than for men (50 per cent). The sectoral differences are even larger and potentially more significant. Gender drives a wedge through the Canadian working class. Men (43 per cent) are much more likely than women (14 per cent) to be in the goods sector, while women (43 per cent) are more likely than men (24 per cent) to be found in the service sector. This concentration of Canadian women in the much weaker capitalist service sector contrasts with Nordic women's strength in the state sector. Clerical and sales workers in the private sector are much less likely to be unionized and enjoy significantly lower benefits on average than other workers. The implications for class voting remain to be explored.

In 1993, the NDP lost its official party status in the wake of its dismal performance in the 1993 federal election when it gained only 6.9 per cent of the popular vote and a mere nine seats in Parliament. The party rebounded somewhat in the 1997 election, winning 11 per cent of the popular vote and 21 seats, only to fall back to 8.5 per cent of the popular vote and 13 seats in the 2000 election. Even in 1997, only 8 per cent of manual workers voted NDP while fully 29 per cent voted Reform.[16] In light of these figures, it might seem time to put an end to the class voting debate. The real issue, however, is not whether working class voters vote for 'their party', but how class plays out in electoral politics (cf. Brooks and Manza 1997). Understanding that process is arguably more urgent today than it was 30 years ago. While the future of Canada's social democratic party is in question, the new right, with its market vision of society, has seen its vote share increase from 19.4 per cent in 1997 to 25.5 per cent in 2000.[17] Meanwhile, the gap between the haves and the have-nots in Canadian society is widening. For those who resist the notion that market forces should be the ultimate arbiter over people's life chances, there is a pressing need to grasp the processes that shape voters' perceptions of their material interests and their readiness to act on them.

Notes

The research on which this chapter is based was supported by grants from the Social Sciences and Humanities Research Council of Canada and Fonds pour la formation de chercheurs et l'aide à recherche. I am grateful to Greg Saxton for his research assistance.

1. Across 10 surveys conducted between 1952 and 1962, the average score for Canada on Alford's class voting index was only 8, compared with 40 for Britain, 33 for Australia, and 16 for the United States. In his later work, he extended the time series to 1965, only to find even lower levels of class voting in the latter period.

2. Jenson explained the admitted incongruity of this essentially agrarian setting producing a party system supposedly typical of modern industrial society by drawing an analogy between the economic uncertainty and insecurity of wheat farmers dependent upon a fluctuating international market and the situation of workers in an industrialized society.

3. Fletcher and Forbes (1990) concluded that the weakness of the class cleavage at the national level reflects cross-cutting regional effects for education and occupation. They identified two distinct patterns of class voting, one east of the Ottawa River based on education and another west of the Ottawa River based on occupation. It is not clear, however, in what sense the Quebec/Atlantic pattern represented class voting given that it was the upper status groups (the more educated) who were the more likely to vote NDP.

4. Alford tried adopting a more rigorous definition of class position by combining occupation with education, income, and subjective class identifi-

cation, but in each case the level of class voting in Canada remained atypically low.

5. Their study rested on the assumption that the weakness of class in explaining party choice in Canada should not be taken to mean that class is somehow irrelevant to political attitudes in general. They suggest that class cleavages will become increasingly salient as we move from the concrete level of attitudes toward political parties and governmental institutions to the more abstract level of ideological perspectives. Even defining political views more broadly, however, there is little evidence of a strong class cleavage.

6. For a characterization of the left-right placement of the political parties in the 1990s, based on the positions taken by their supporters, see Blais et al. (forthcoming).

7. Higher levels of subjective class voting were registered within particular provinces. The highest level of provincial subjective class voting occurred in Saskatchewan, closely followed by British Columbia, Manitoba, Alberta, and Ontario. Relatively high levels of federal subjective class voting were confined to Saskatchewan, followed by Manitoba and British Columbia).

8. The possible economic criteria were people's wealth (31 per cent), income (9 per cent), how well off their family was when growing up (4 per cent), kind of work they do (3 per cent), and whether they own their own business (3 per cent).

9. As Lambert and his colleagues caution, saying that the idea of social classes does not have any meaning does not necessarily indicate a lack of comprehension. It could mean that the idea has no significance for the respondent or that it lacks reality. In either case, though, it would suggest a weak basis for subjective class voting.

10. Alford himself was careful to emphasize that his findings should not be taken to mean that class

interests do not exist in Canada or that they are politically irrelevant.

11. Schreiber (1980) found little evidence that voters were forgoing voting their 'real' preference in favour of a 'realistic' alternative. Liberal and Conservative voters were most likely to name the other (then) dominant party as their second choice and the NDP as their least preferred party. Schreiber's results are limited, however, by his failure to break this result down by class.

12. Analysis of strategic voting in the 1997 federal election indicates that about 8 per cent of those who actually preferred the NDP voted for another party (Blais et al., in press).

13. The simple statistical association, of course, risks overstating the degree of class-motivated voting. As Butler and Stokes (1969) observe, it would be as absurd to see perceived class interests in all class voting as it would be to infer perceived class interests from class differences in the time of dinner.

14. Ornstein and Stevenson (1999: 272) point to another problem with the élite manipulation argument: surveys of party activists suggest significant ideological differences both within and among parties.

15. Union members remained more likely than non-members (8 per cent) to vote NDP. These figures are taken from the 1997 Canadian Election Study on which the author was co-investigator with André Blais, Richard Nadeau, and Neil Nevitte. The data are available at www.isr. yorku.ca/projects/ces/english/download.html. Data from the 2000 Canadian Election Study were not available at the time of writing.

16. These figures are taken from the 1997 Canadian Election Study.

17. These figures are the vote shares of the Reform Party in 1997 and its successor, the Canadian Reform Conservative Alliance, in 2000.

References

Alford, R.R. 1963. *Party and Society: The Anglo-American Democracies* (Chicago: Rand McNally).

———. 1967. 'Class Voting in the Anglo-American Pol-

itical Systems'. In *Party Systems and Voter Alignments*, ed. S.M. Lipset and S. Rokkan (New York: Free Press).

Archer, K. 1985. 'The Failure of the New Democratic

Party: Unions, Unionists, and Politics in Canada', *Canadian Journal of Political Science* 18: 354–66.

Blais, A., D.E. Blake, and S. Dion. 1990. 'The Public/Private Sector Cleavage in North America', *Comparative Political Studies* 23: 381–403.

————, R. Nadeau, E. Gidengil, and N. Nevitte. Forthcoming. 'Measuring Strategic Voting in Multiparty Elections', *Electoral Studies*.

————, E. Gidengil, R. Nadeau, and N. Nevitte. Forthcoming. 'Do Party Supporters Differ?' In *Citizen Politics: Research and Theory in Canadian Political Behaviour*, ed. J. Everitt and B. O'Neill.

Blake, D.E. 1972. 'The Measurement of Regionalism in Canadian Voting Patterns', *Canadian Journal of Political Science* 5: 54–81.

Brodie, M.J., and J. Jenson. 1988. *Crisis, Challenge and Change: Party and Class in Canada* (Ottawa: Carleton University Press).

Brooks, C., and J. Manza. 1997. 'Class Politics and Political Change in the United States, 1952–1992', *Social Forces* 76: 379–408.

Brym, R.J., M.W. Gillespie, and R.L. Lenton. 1989. 'Class Power, Class Mobilization, and Class Voting: The Canadian Case'. *Canadian Journal of Sociology* 14: 25–44.

Butler, D., and D. Stokes. 1969. *Political Change in Britain* (London: Macmillan).

Buttel, F.H., and W.L. Flinn. 1979. 'Sources of Working Class Consciousness', *Sociological Focus* 12.

Clement, W. 1990. 'Comparative Class Analysis: Locating Canada in a North American and Nordic Context', *Canadian Review of Sociology and Anthropology* 27: 462–86.

Coburn, D., and V.L. Edwards. 1976. 'Objective and Subjective Socioeconomic Status: Intercorrelations and Consequences', *Canadian Review of Sociology and Anthropology* 13: 178–88.

Dawson, R.M. 1954. *The Government of Canada* (Toronto: University of Toronto Press).

Erickson, B.H. 1981. 'Region, Knowledge and Class Voting in Canada', *Canadian Journal of Sociology* 6: 121–44.

Fletcher, J.F., and H.D. Forbes. 1990. 'Education,

Occupation and Vote in Canada, 1965–1984', *Canadian Review of Sociology and Anthropology* 27: 441–61.

Gidengil, E. 1989. 'Class and Region in Canada: A Dependency Interpretation', *Canadian Journal of Political Science* 22: 563–87.

————, A. Blais, R. Nadeau, and N. Nevitte. 1999. 'Making Sense of Regional Voting in the 1997 Canadian Federal Election: Liberal and Reform Support Outside Quebec', *Canadian Journal of Political Science* 32: 247–72.

Glenday, D. 1989. 'Rich But Semiperipheral: Canada's Ambiguous Position in the World-Economy', *Review: Fernand Braudel Center* 12: 209–61.

Gold, D.A., C.Y.H. Lo, and E.O. Wright. 1975. 'Recent Developments in Marxist Theories of the Capitalist State', *Monthly Review* 27.

Horowitz, G. 1968. 'Toward A Democratic Class Struggle'. In *Agenda 1970: Prospects for A Creative Politics*, ed. T. Lloyd and J. McLeod (Toronto: University of Toronto Press).

Hunter, A.A. 1982. 'On Class, Status, and Voting in Canada', *Canadian Journal of Sociology* 7: 19–40.

Jenson, J. 1976. 'Party Systems'. In *The Provincial Political Systems: Comparative Essays*, ed. D.J. Bellamy, J.H. Pammett, and D.C. Rowat (Toronto: Methuen).

Johnston, J.P. 1981. 'Some Methodological Issues in the Study of "Class Voting": A Critique of Erickson's Analysis', *Canadian Journal of Sociology* 6: 145–56.

Johnston, W.A., and D. Baer. 1993. 'Class Consciousness and National Contexts: Canada, Sweden and the United States in Historical Perspective', *Canadian Review of Sociology and Anthropology* 30: 271–95.

Kahan, M., D. Butler, and D. Stokes. 1966. 'On the Analytical Division of Social Class', *British Journal of Sociology* 17: 122–32.

Kay, B.J. 1977. 'An Examination of Class and Left-Right Party Images in Canadian Voting', *Canadian Journal of Political Science* 10: 127–43.

Keddie, V. 1980. 'Class Identification and Party Preference Among Manual Workers: The Influence of Community, Union Membership, and Kinship', *Canadian Review of Sociology and Anthropology* 17: 24–36.

Korpi, W. 1972. 'Some Problems in the Measurement of Class Voting', *American Journal of Sociology* 78: 635–7.

Lambert, R.D., and A.A. Hunter. 1979. 'Social Stratification, Voting Behaviour, and the Images of Canadian Federal Political Parties', *Canadian Review of Sociology and Anthropology* 16: 287–304.

———, J.E. Curtis, S.D. Brown, and B.J. Kay. 1986. 'In Search of Left/Right Beliefs in the Canadian Electorate', *Canadian Journal of Political Science* 19: 541–63.

———. 1987. 'Social Class, Left/Right Political Orientations, and Subjective Class Voting in Provincial and Federal Elections', *Canadian Review of Sociology and Anthropology* 24: 526–49.

———, and J.E. Curtis. 1993. 'Perceived Party Choice and Class Voting'. *Canadian Journal of Political Science* 26: 273–86.

Langford, T. 1996. 'The Politics of the Canadian New Middle Class: Public/Private Sector Cleavages in the 1980s', *Canadian Journal of Sociology* 21: 153–83.

Lipset, S.M., and S. Rokkan. 1967. 'Cleavage Structures, Party Systems, and Voter Alignments: An Introduction'. In *Party Systems and Voter Alignments,* ed. S.M. Lipset and S. Rokkan (New York: Free Press).

Myles, J.F. 1979. 'Differences in the Canadian and American Class Vote: Fact or Pseudofact?', *American Journal of Sociology* 84: 1232–7.

———, and D. Forcese. 1981. 'Voting and Class Politics in Canada and the United States', *Comparative Social Research* 4: 3–31.

Nakhaie, M.R. 1992. 'Class and Voting Consistency in Canada: Analyses Bearing on the Mobilization Thesis', *Canadian Journal of Sociology* 17: 275–99.

Nevitte, N., A. Blais, E. Gidengil, and R. Nadeau. 2000. *Unsteady State: The 1997 Canadian Federal Election* (Don Mills, ON: Oxford University Press).

Ogmundson, R. 1975a. 'On the Measurement of Party Class Position: The Case of Canadian Federal Political Parties', *Canadian Review of Sociology and Anthropology* 12: 565–76.

———. 1975b. 'On the Use of Party Image Variables to Measure the Political Distinctiveness of a Class Vote: The Canadian Case', *Canadian Journal of Sociology* 1: 169–77.

———. 1975c. 'Party Class Images and the Class Vote in Canada', *American Sociological Review* 40: 506–13.

———. 1976. 'Mass-Elite Linkage and Class Issues in Canada', *Canadian Review of Sociology and Anthropology* 13: 1–12.

———. 1977. 'Two Modes of Interpretation of Survey Data: A Comment on Schreiber', *Social Forces* 55: 809–11.

———. 1980. 'Liberal Ideology and the Study of Voting Behaviour', *Canadian Review of Sociology and Anthropology* 17: 45–54.

———, and M. Ng. 1982. 'On the Inference of Voter Motivation: A Comparison of the Subjective Class Vote in Canada and the United Kingdom', *Canadian Journal of Sociology* 7: 41–59.

Ornstein, M.D., and H.M. Stevenson. 1999. *Politics and Ideology in Canada: Elite and Public Opinion in the Transformation of a Welfare State* (Montreal: McGill-Queen's University Press).

———, and A.P. Williams. 1980. 'Region, Class and Political Culture in Canada', *Canadian Journal of Political Science* 13: 227–71.

Pammett, J.H. 1987. 'Class Voting and Class Consciousness in Canada', *Canadian Review of Sociology and Anthropology* 24: 269–89.

Pineo, P.C., and J.C. Goyder. 1973. 'Social Class Identification of National Sub-Groups'. In *Social Stratification: Canada,* ed. J. Curtis and W. Scott (Scarborough, ON: Prentice-Hall).

Resnick, P. 1989. 'From Semiperiphery to Perimeter of the Core: Canada's Place in the Capitalist World-Economy', *Review: Fernand Braudel Center* 12: 263–97.

Schreiber, E.M. 1980. 'Class Awareness and Class Voting in Canada: A Reconsideration of the Ogmundson Thesis', *Canadian Review of Sociology and Anthropology* 17: 37–44.

Schwartz, M.A. 1974a. 'Canadian Voting Behaviour'. In *Electoral Behaviour: A Comparative Handbook,* ed. R. Rose (New York: Free Press).

———. 1974b. *Politics and Territory: The Sociology of Regional Persistence in Canada* (Montreal: McGill-Queen's University Press).

Stevenson, P. 1977. 'Class and Left-Wing Radicalism', *Canadian Review of Sociology and Anthropology* 14: 269–84.

Wilson, J. 1974. 'The Canadian Political Cultures: Towards A Redefinition of the Nature of the Canadian Political System', *Canadian Journal of Political Science* 7: 438–83.

Wright, E.O. 1976. 'Class Boundaries in Advanced Capitalist Societies', *New Left Review* 98: 3–41.

Zipp, J.F., and J. Smith. 1982. 'A Structural Analysis of Class Voting', *Social Forces* 60: 738–59

Chapter 15

Class and Politics in the Era of the Global Economy

William A. Johnston

Introduction

It may seem that the current surge of conservatism sweeping across North America and other Western countries is a moment in an endless cycle, where the rise and fall of political parties and ideologies resembles the tides. Like cycles in Parisian fashions, recent trendy designs are soon passé, but return in a generation as the latest in haute couture. So while it might appear to students, who 30 years ago were turned on by Jerry Rubin and Stokeley Carmichael, and are presently excited by Stockwell Day and George Bush, that history has just begun, and to those with a longer perspective, that history is cyclical, neither vision of history or conception of political process has much purchase on the changing nature of political and ideological dominance. The popularity of the 'New Conservatism', like that of the 'Social Democratic Vision' that preceded it, is rooted in a particular configuration of power and specific events that only has the semblance of a repetition. To be sure, it owes something to the past, but it is the product of a contested terrain that is singular and unique.

In order to understand the current attractiveness of conservatism we need to leave behind the security of the notion of cycles and undertake an exploration of the complex interrelationship among politics, ideologies, and class relations. For it is in their interaction that changes in political and ideological dominance are grounded. One site

of this complex interaction is the modern welfare state of Western Europe, Australasia, and North America. While not a uniquely privileged site, the welfare state is of interest because its development was a product of an endemic social conflict between left and right during the twentieth century and the current debates over its future tell us a good deal about the reasons for the Conservative resurgence. Consequently we will focus, first, on the conditions, collective actors, and strategies that underpinned the postwar expansion of the welfare state, and, second, on the changes in social structure and the world economy that have undone the balance of class power established in the aftermath of World War II.

The Postwar Accommodation

Following a long, bitter, and terribly destructive war, hopes for a measure of normalcy and well-being were exceedingly high. After all, this was the generation that had fought in the war, waited on bread lines during the Depression, and suffered through the scarcities of the wartime economy. Yet in the immediate aftermath of the war, much of Western Europe was involved in a struggle for sheer survival, while in North America fears of an economic collapse due to a decline in military expenditures were active in the public mind. While the Marshall Plan and the Cold War served to alleviate these problems and anxieties by providing the means to reconstruct Western Europe and to reduce the magnitude of defence cuts, the central political question facing Western publics was which sociopolitical actor had a social vision that would ensure social harmony and prosperity. In many countries voters turned to parties of the left, usually Social Democratic or Labour parties.[1] These parties were the product of a long process of working class formation that enabled them to consolidate a sizeable and secure electoral base in the working class and to articulate a social vision that had wider political appeal.

The left was able to capitalize on memories of the thirties and the sacrifices experienced in the war to advance a vision of the future that promised greater equality of incomes and opportunity, greater government intervention and ownership of the economy, increased social security, and full employment. All of this seemed possible once Keynesian economics had undermined the precepts of economic orthodoxy and opened the door to macro-economic management by the institutions of the state. The particular interests of the working class were now perceived to be in the general interests of society and a negotiated compromise between left and right seemed feasible (Przeworski 1985). In practice the mutual accommodation involved, on behalf of the left, a recognition of the necessity of a profitable and efficient private sector and, on behalf of the right, acquiescence in an enlarged welfare state and full employment policies. The notion of a 'managed capitalism' had acquired credibility and social democrats utilized this recognition to fashion a politically viable growth program. Concurrent with the changes in economic and social policy was a new configuration of élite power, whereby traditional élites were to be joined or replaced by representatives of subordinate classes. Class compromise and bargaining among the state, business, and labour were to replace the unilateral dictates of the corporate élite and the Treasury Board. For the left

the overall thrust of these policy and élite changes was to incline social and economic priorities away from the market and the profit motive toward social and collective needs.

In the aftermath of the traumas of war and depression, the social democratic vision had such a powerful political appeal that parties of the right were forced to abandon their earlier ideological orientations and advocate a Social Market economy or Progressive Conservatism. This would be primarily true of those countries where confessional parties of the right were able to maintain the loyalty of a substantial block of working-class voters and, therefore, were constrained to develop policies to encompass working-class interests. This re-orientation represented more than cosmetic change as the welfare state continued to grow even where parties of the right maintained or re-claimed office (Wilensky 1975). At this point, successful competition in the electoral marketplace demanded that right-wing parties trim their ideological sails and endorse the major social policy advances of the postwar period. The harsh rhetoric of competition, individualism, and fiscal responsibility gave way to that of nation, caring, and family.

Whatever the outcomes in the political system, and there was variability in the implantation of the social democratic vision, the political viability of this vision rested on the enhanced position of left parties and a more equal balance in the power relations between capital and labour. The extension of democratic institutions, the elaboration of a dense network of working-class institutions and a long process of working-class formation had levelled the playing field in the electoral contest between the left and right. In the ongoing social and political conflict, Labour's strengths lay in numbers, organization, institutional completeness, and a sense that it spoke for the average citizen, while Capital relied on the importance of private investment for economic growth, its identification with the powerful symbols of the nation, and the 'natural' capacity for governance of its political élite. A new balance had been established in the conflict between left/labour and right/capital and henceforth, whatever the variations in their relative power positions, the vision that the left had pioneered would influence all political parties. The breadth of that influence and the realization of the vision was affected by the capacity of the working-class organizations to elaborate social policies that enhanced working-class solidarity, the pattern of alliances with farmers and white-collar employees, and the location of the economy in the world system. Table 15.1 registers differences in the degree to which public provision had supplanted the market as a determinant of income, and as this was a key aspiration of the left, it provides us with evidence with which to assess their comparative success. Japan and the Anglo-Saxon democracies cluster around the minimum, 76 per cent, and Scandinavia and Central European democracies cluster at the maximum, 50 per cent. While there was a good deal of variation in the extent to which the left was able to implement its vision, there can be little doubt that there was a sense that social democracy appeared to be the wave of the future.

The Process of Working-Class Formation

The ascendency of the social democratic vision and the left was the outgrowth of a slow and difficult process of working-class formation that was initiated by shifts in social structure occasioned by the Industrial Revolution. With the onset of the Industrial Revolution, the shape of the class structure underwent a dramatic transformation. The stability of the old rural economy and social structure was shattered by the voracious appetites of large-scale production and the rise of the industrial working class. Over time, the industrial working class invariably broke free from the tutelage of liberalism and became an independent

Table 15.1 Market Distribution as a Percentage of Total Compensation, 1975–80

Australia	70.0
Belgium	55.0
Canada	68.0
Denmark	50.4
Germany	59.2
Japan	76.1
New Zealand	67.2
Sweden	59.0
United Kingdom	69.6
United States	71.2
Country Average	64.4

SOURCE: Griffin et al. CRSA 26(1) p. 41.

political actor, usually committed to collective ownership of the means of production or socialism. Although there were marked differences in the forms and paths that labour took to advance its cause, it became a major political force in all advanced capitalist nations during the course of the late nineteenth and twentieth centuries. The mainstay of the left was an industrial working class which was enmeshed in a multifaceted struggle with the social forces arrayed against it. The principal manifestations of this conflict were:

1. the respective rights of property and labour, especially the right of labour to organize into unions;
2. the rate of capital accumulation and the role of government in ensuring economic growth;
3. the distribution of wealth and income as these related to taxation and social insurance provision.

While centre stage was occupied by the conflict between capital and labour, this conflict was always overlaid with nonindustrial conflicts such as the separation of church and state, rural/urban issues, and the extension of democratic rights to the entire population. The capacity of labour to resolve these issues in its favour invariably increased over time and seems to have been most directly related to its racial, ethnic, and linguistic homogeneity, the salience of organized religion in the political life of the nation, and the character and rapidity of nineteenth- or early twentieth-century industrialization (Lash and Urry 1987; Korpi 1978).

Social historians have documented a process of working-class formation whereby people, enmeshed in a set of life experiences with similar problems, came to see themselves as having a collective identity and common interests in enacting significant changes in social policy and political power (Thompson 1963). For the working class, two processes were crucial. First was the elaboration of class solidarity. This was no mean feat as it involved the transformation of a mass of geographically dispersed individuals with strong cross-cutting loyalties into a coherent and purposeful political actor. And the elaboration of solidarity involved more than moral exhortation and ideological campaigns. Studies of the working class have found that centralized and encompassing trade unions, representative political parties, and the capacity to effect state policies favourable to labour were critical to the consolidation of working-class solidarity (Esping-Andersen 1985b). Second was the forging of alliances with other social forces in pursuit of political power; for it was only with political power that facilitating social policies could be legislated (Esping-Andersen 1985a). All of this was profoundly conditioned by the nature of industrialization, and the shape of the overall class structure, which affected politics by structuring the size and differentiation of the working class, by patterning the location and weight of the capitalist class, and by establishing the importance of the petite bour-

geoisie and middle strata in national life (Esping-Andersen 1985a).

To be sure, the process of working-class formation was an extended and difficult one, subject to the vicissitudes of the ongoing conflict, numerous conditioning factors, and the strength and strategies of opposing social forces. Nevertheless, it was a process that reached its zenith in most advanced capitalist countries during the course of the late 1940s and early 1950s. Over the course of the twentieth century, collective working-class solidarity had come to challenge earlier political identifications as the touchstone for political choice. Geographically, the process went furthest in the Scandinavian countries. At first the goal of the Scandinavian social democratic parties was to extend the scope and magnitude of the entitlements of the welfare state. By pursuing a solidaristic strategy to limit the role of the market in allocating resources, social democratic parties sought to engineer a virtuous circle whereby social policy advances that benefited the public had the effect of reinforcing the bases of support for these parties (Esping-Andersen 1985a). This would be accomplished through full employment, re-training, and universal access to social assistance.

Arrayed against the left were the social forces and political parties of the right. Typically, the core supporters of the right were big business, the military, permanent state bureaucrats, sectors of the rapidly expanding white-collar labour force and, depending on the strategic success of the combatants, often the agrarian and urban petite bourgeoisie. In many European countries, the right could exploit the strenuous opposition of the Catholic Church to communism to attract support from large numbers of workers. While the right was initially hesitant to forsake its ideological traditions, the potency of the social democratic vision soon compelled a re-appraisal. Henceforth the strategy of the right was to cautiously endorse the major gains of the early postwar years, but to contain the expansion within the flexible requirements of capital accumulation and profitability. Much of the subsequent conflict over the welfare state was structured by the different emphases that the political actors placed on the two goals of the welfare state. On the one hand, the welfare state was meant to provide a measure of security from the cyclical nature of market economies and, on the other, it was to decisively reduce inequality. The left stressed income redistribution and the right, security. Fortunately for the political system, the context allowed for some of both, and compromises were conceivable.

Power Resources Model

Implicit in this discussion is a conception of politics and historical process that places political outcomes in a wider ensemble of class politics and the organization of social power. In this power resources model of politics, society is seen to be structured by a series of conflicts between numerous collective actors, capital/labour, farmers/consumers, national/international corporations, over social and economic policies that impact on the distribution of rewards and benefits (Esping-Andersen 1985a; Korpi 1983). While the model is flexible enough to be appropriate to a variety of social conflicts, it usually assumes that the paramount political actors are defined by the class divisions of market societies, and that political conflict reflects differences over relative shares of the national income. In the capital/labour relation, the dynamic built into the opposition between profits and wages is the most immediate and obvious source of conflict. The two collective actors, Capital and Labour, enter into a strategic interaction that rapidly encompasses more than the wage bargain. Both soon realize that their capacity to achieve their immediate aims is contingent on all those social arrangements that condition their interaction: the extent of unionization, the national rate of unemployment, and their relation to political parties and political power. Thus

the conflict is generalized and, at certain intense moments, can assume the character of a clash over the whole social order. Collective actors outside the capital/labour divide, such as farmers, align themselves with one or the other of the political projects that originate from the contending visions. Coalitions are forged in pursuit of shared or negotiated goals in an appreciation that the successful pursuit of particular interests depends on cooperation with other social forces.

In all democratic capitalist countries, pressures for policies to alleviate the social and economic problems generated by the cyclical character of capitalist production built up during the course of the twentieth century. But, as students of politics understand, pressures are only translated into social and economic policy when collective actors with political power are in a position to affect outcomes. The broad accommodation that was realized in the advanced countries in the post-World War II period was realizable because the enhanced role of the working class in politics coincided with an unprecedented period of economic growth. The outcome of this accommodation was a vastly expanded welfare state.

The Expansion of the Welfare State

While the immediate economic future of Europe and North America in the postwar period was unclear, it soon became apparent to all that the advanced capitalist countries had entered a stage of sustained and substantial economic growth. The 20 years following World War II were ones of increasing prosperity and accelerating economic growth. Between 1950 and 1973 average real GDP increased by 4.8 per cent in the top sixteen OECD countries (Flora 1985). In the period between 1960 and 1973, average productivity per worker increased by 4.5 per cent, and real compensation per worker increased by 4.35 per annum (O'Connell 1994). Average unemployment in the advanced capitalist countries averaged 2.6 per cent, which contrasted very favourably with the average of 7.5 between 1920 and 1938 (Maddison 1991). This Golden Age, presided over by the United States, was the outgrowth of a number of factors, most significantly, liberalized world trade, government macro-economic policies that fostered domestic demand, the growth potential given by wartime devastation, and the dynamism of Fordism (Maddison 1991).

At its heart, Fordism is a system of production whose fundamental elements were assembly line production of industrial goods and rising wages that created a sizeable domestic market. Accompanying this organization of production were: a re-structuring of the working class, in terms of education, skills, and consumption; a reorganization of labour relations favouring unionization and collective bargaining; and an enlarged role for the state in economic and fiscal policy. In retrospect, it is clear that this regime of accumulation was premised on rising real wages due to higher levels of productivity and this promise was fulfilled in all advanced capitalist countries (O'Connell 1994). The consolidation of Fordism was very favourable for the implementation of the social democratic vision because of the correspondence between key elements of the vision and the central preconditions of a Fordist regime of accumulation.

The Golden Age of Fordism allowed Labour and Capital to engage in positive sum conflict that respected definite limits. Where it possessed enough political strength, Labour favoured a strategy that promoted the growth of the largest and most profitable corporations by expediting the rationalization of production in exchange for full employment policies, a portion of the increased productivity, and an augmented welfare state. Even where it was not the dominant political force, Labour was sufficiently influential to bring about social and economic policies favourable to working-class interests. Simply put, wherever one looks in the postwar period one finds a political context that is strongly conditioned by the representation of working-class goals.

The most forthright way to register the changes in the political economy of the advanced capitalist countries in the postwar period is to examine the growth of social security expenditure as a percentage of GDP/GNP. Social security expenditures exclude expenditures on education and housing but include health, family allowances, pensions, and unemployment insurance. So they underestimate the growth of the state's role in the economy as all governments substantially increased educational expenditures in the 1960s. In 1950 the average percentage of GDP in Europe was 9.2 per cent, increasing to 22.4 per cent in 1977. Social expenditures increased much faster than GDP throughout the period 1960–75. The state had come to play a critical role in the lives of its citizens and that role was expanding at an accelerated rate. Evidence of the acceleration is provided by comparing growth rates in different periods. In the five-year period between 1950 and 1955 the average rate of growth of social expenditures was 18 per cent. In the period between 1974 and 1977 the average rate of increase had jumped to 107 per cent (Flora 1985). In Scandinavia, where the left was most favourably positioned, entitlements grew to such an extent that market income as a percentage of total income was reduced to between 50 and 60 per cent of average income (Esping-Andersen 1985a). By 1981, the typical European country allocated 25 per cent of GDP to social expenditures (Jallade 1988) and it is clear that the mature welfare state had materialized in most advanced democratic countries.

Illustrations

The quantitative expansion of the welfare state and the qualitative change in the role of the state in the economy was an object of a contained struggle between the left and right in the postwar period. Certainly the conflict did not take the form projected in the *Communist Manifesto*, as compromise was the norm, and a polarization of the social structure never materialized. There were a few dramatic moments in the conflict between left and right, but the expansive Fordist economy permitted them to reach the accommodations that gave rise to the modern welfare state. While the driving political force behind the expansion of the welfare state was the left and the wider Labour movement, quantitative studies of the growth of the welfare state indicate that the relation between the power of the left and the size of the welfare state is not a simple and straightforward one (Bjorn 1979; Castles 1978; Pontusson 1988; Wilensky 1975). Although there is a broad correspondence between the power of the left and the extension of the welfare state, especially at the extremes, it is clear that a number of other factors come into play. First, the level of economic development and demographic pressures exert an independent effect. Second, the historical and cultural traditions of each country need to be acknowledged as possible sources of variation in the extent of the welfare state. Third, the peculiarities of state institutions and the structure of the party system exert an important influence. Finally, the way in which the left defines and pursues working-class interests can be of significance.

In arguing for the centrality of working-class power for the expansion of the welfare state we have relied on a general model of the postwar democratic class struggle that misses the considerable variation in the substance of the conflict and the manner in which the conflict between left and right reverberated in the political system. We begin with the variation in working-class power that is indexed in Table 15.2. Table 15.2 provides us with comparative indices of working-class power by registering the extent of unionization in the labour force, the extent of class voting, and the percentage of the national vote for the party of the left. The logic behind these measures is that union density and the size of the left vote are important factors in the attainment and exercise of working-class power. From Table 15.2, it is clear that the highest levels of working-class power were present in Scandinavia and the lowest level in the United States. Korpi's (1983) cross-classification of the components of working-class power yield five distinct categories based on level of mobilization and the degree of political control. In the high mobilization and stable political control category were Sweden, Norway, and Austria while in the low mobilization and no control category we find Ireland, Canada, and the United States.

The most dramatic exception to the relation between the power of the working class and the extent of the welfare state is Australia. As Francis Castles (1989a) points out, Australia poses a number of puzzles for a class model of politics. One of these puzzles is the fact that Australia has a strong labour movement and a residual welfare state. Australia's exceptionalism requires us to recognize that the strategic direction of the labour movement can intervene between the power of the working class and the size of the welfare state. In other words, the goals that power is directed toward are as important as the amount of power in actualizing the social democratic vision.

In order to demonstrate this we will compare Sweden and Australia in terms of the power of the working class, the strategic orientation of the left, and the extensiveness of the welfare state. This comparison will allow us to refine the general model and permit us to develop a narrative that fleshes out the historical processes that established the welfare state in these two countries. Australia and Sweden are countries where the labour movement was powerful, but their welfare regimes were quite different (Castles 1989b). In fact, in most respects the Australian welfare state is more like that of Japan, a country where the left is weak, than Sweden. The difference between Australia and Sweden is understandable if we acknowledge

Table 15.2 Comparative Indices of Working-Class Power

	Union Density 1961–76	Class Voting 1970s	Left Voting 1946–76
Australia	48	33	44
Canada	27	4	11
USA	26	18	1
Sweden	65	45	43
UK	43	35	35
Japan	28	27	28
Denmark	50	47	39
Netherlands	33	21	31
France	19	21	32

two distinctions. The first distinction is between a dominant political force and a contending political force. Swedish Social Democrats became the dominant political force in Sweden, exercising political power for close to 40 years, while the Australian Labour Party only alternated in office with the dominant Conservative party. Since the holding of office is critical to the implementation of political priorities, we would expect that this difference would impact on the type of welfare regime in the two countries. The second distinction pertains to the different strategic goals of the two movements. Swedish Social Democrats opted for a strategy of domestic compensation that called for a dense network of social programs and social agencies in exchange for wage restraint that recognized Sweden's position in the world economy and kept inflation within acceptable limits. Australia fell back on a model that tried to insulate the Australian economy from the unsettling pressures of the world market.

SWEDEN

We begin with Sweden because it is here we find the closest approximation to the Social Democratic vision. From being the Poor House of Europe in the nineteenth century, Sweden became a model of social engineering for the rest of the world in the twentieth. Studies of the development of the welfare state invariably identify Sweden as the most developed, and demonstrate that Swedish leadership was consolidated in the period following World War II (Gould 1993; Korpi 1983).

It is clear that this transformation is related to the historic compromises between Capital and Labour of the 1930s. For Labour, this compromise was an aspect of an overall political strategy that had three components:

1. a growth strategy that imagined a positive sum conflict with capital;
2. an acceleration of the maturation of capitalism by removing obstacles to productivity coupled with an insistence on re-training and re-location;
3. the establishment of a welfare state to maintain a floor on the conditions of life of the population (Pontusson 1988).

Francis Castles (1987) identifies this mix of policies as Domestic Compensation and argues that it can be contrasted with a set of policies, labelled Domestic Protection, that was pursued by the labour movement in Australia. Either policy is an adaptation to a changing world economy by a labour movement in a small vulnerable economy that is dependent on foreign trade. Domestic Compensation involves a trade-off such that adjustments to the world market involving sacrifices by the working class are compensated for by labour market policies, income maintenance, and a large public sector. Castles (1987) argues that the adoption of either strategy seems to be related to the historical traditions of the movement established at the turn of the century.

The success of the Swedish Social Democratic strategy of domestic compensation was due, in great measure, to the deficiencies of the political opposition. Swedish capital, while highly concentrated and internationally competitive, was incapable of unifying the potential forces of the right. Indeed a key element in a possible right-wing coalition, small independent farmers, was open to recruitment to the political project of social democracy. This unusual situation was conditioned by the historically strong position of the independent peasantry in Sweden's social structure, the demographic fragility and political socialization of the Swedish aristocracy, and the lateness of the industrialization, which established a labour movement that was not riven by craft, religious, and regional lines of cleavage (Anderson 1974; Korpi 1978).

A powerful working class confronted an economically strong, but politically weak, right. The struggle between the two social and political forces was brought within tolerable limits by two compromises. The first of these was an electoral coalition in 1932 between Social Democrats and farmers represented in the Centre Party. The chief elements in this agreement were protection for agricultural products and a Keynesian macro-economic strategy. The second was an extra-parliamentary agreement between the industrial capi-

tal, represented by the SAF or Swedish Employers Federation, and labour, represented in the LO or Labour Organization. Social Democrats preserved their political dominance in the 1950s and 1960s by re-configuring their alliances. In the course of the pension debate of the 1950s, they broke with the Centre Party and consolidated an alliance with the expanding white-collar sector. The pension reform equalized the pension status of all wage-earners and instituted a vast pool of investment capital in pension funds.

Social Democratic political dominance rested on three pillars: its deep implantation in a highly unionized working class to which it was closely linked; its political skill in forging alliances with other social forces; and the electoral system of proportional representation that guaranteed that Social Democrats, with well over 40 per cent of the votes, would be a major player in the coalition, while at the same time maintaining the fragmentation of the right.

The most distinguishing characteristics of the Swedish welfare state were universalism, funding from general tax revenues, an active labour market policy, and generous benefits (Gould 1993; Lash and Urry 1987). In the course of the 1950s, Sweden introduced social insurance benefits such as flat-rate old age pensions, child allowances, and an earnings-related health insurance. An earnings-related old age pension was added to the earlier pension scheme in the 1960s and along with reforms in other areas, provided the basis for a very provident welfare state. For instance, the basic old age pension is available to all regardless of contributions and an earnings-related pension typically allows retirees to obtain 85 per cent of their pre-retirement earnings. Moreover, those only covered by the basic pension are eligible for housing allowances and income supplements (Gould 1993). The medical care system is comprehensive, universal, and state dominated. Ninety per cent of the activities of the medical system are within the public sector and only 5 per cent of doctors are in private practice. In the 1980s the medical system took up 11 per cent of GDP (Gould 1993).

Social insurance policies were only one element in the reforms that the SPD government undertook during their forty years of power. Both the educational system and employment policy were subject to massive changes designed to equalize educational and employment opportunities. A fully comprehensive system of schooling was introduced in the 1960s and a Labour Market Board was established to intervene in the labour market, to provide training and allow people to adjust to changes in industrial structure. The establishment of this broad network of public services meant that public expenditures rose from 30 per cent of GDP in 1960 to 60 per cent in 1980 and social expenditures rose from less than 20 per cent in 1970 to over 35 per cent in 1988 (Gould 1993). Public sector employment represented 33 per cent of all employment in 1980 and it was the only employment sector that was growing.

AUSTRALIA

Australia was a pioneer in establishing social welfare measures and early in its history acquired the reputation of being the 'Working Man's Paradise'. This claim rested on the boom in the Australian economy between 1860 and 1891 and the fact that Australia was one of the richest countries in the world. This period of rapid growth was followed by a decided slowdown from 1891 to 1920. It was during this later period that the welfare measures were introduced. Reeling under the impact of the worldwide recession, accustomed to a high standard of living and faced with a politically weak right, a strong labour movement successfully pursued radical social policies. These included the introduction of an old age pension and the establishment of the principle of a living wage in claims that were adjudicated by arbitration courts established to resolve industrial disputes (Jones 1980).

The period between 1890 and 1930 has been characterized as colonial socialism (Butlin 1982). The core feature of colonial socialism was a centralized and intrusive state which sought to attract capital and labour through borrowing, immigration, and investment in fixed capital. As in most white settler colonies, the state played a critical role in facilitating economic growth. All classes looked to the state to secure their interests and to mediate the social conflicts that arose. Three features of Australian society facilitated this orientation. First, the political culture of Australia was democratic, egalitarian, and predisposed to radicalism (Aitkin 1986; Ward, 1958). Second, the agrarian structure was dominated by sheep farming that required substantial capital investment and employed large numbers of farm workers. Unlike continental Europe, where small farmers were often drawn to confessional parties of the right, small farmers occupied a minor place in the rural social structure. The large bloc of agricultural labourers was open to mobilization in the political strategy of the left. The first National Union of Pastoral Workers, arrayed against an authoritarian and hard-nosed bloc of Pastoralists, was drawn to the collectivist orientation of the Labour Party. Finally, a persistent shortage of labour created a favourable context for bargaining. In many respects, this early period was the high-water mark of the welfare state in Australia. Changes in the international economy, an outdated strategic vision, and the consolidation of the forces of the right were to undermine Australia's leadership role in social policy (Castles 1989b). From being a world leader in social policy, Australia became a world laggard.

The strategy of domestic defence combined protective tariffs, high wages, limits on immigration, and a minimal welfare state. This option served Australians well for an extended period of time. In 1966 Australia was the sixth richest country in the OECD (Castles 1989a). Despite this enviable record of economic growth, the Australian welfare state remained residual. The minor innovations of the 1940s and 1950s remained anchored in a welfare orientation that was set in the 1890s: flat rate and means tested. Despite the fact that Labour was in power between 1945 and 1949, the welfare state remained at a level of that of the 1900s. In the 1950s Australia ranked in the lowest quartile of OECD countries in the share of the national product spent by the public sector, and the innovations of the 1960s did little to change this ranking (Jones 1980). In 1965 Australian spending on social security was 8.2 per cent of GNP compared with 15.6 per cent in Sweden and 12.6 per cent in the UK. Between 1955 and 1970 Australia had the smallest increase in social security expenditures of all countries in the OECD.

As Castles (1989a) has pointed out the co-presence of a powerful labour movement and a minimal welfare state presents us with a puzzle. Solving the puzzle requires us to recognize the effects that different strategies to pursue working-class interests can have on the welfare state. Both Sweden and Australia are small states that have high levels of external vulnerability. The external vulnerability of small states is established by the reliance on foreign trade and the fact that domestic price levels are set in the international market. Australian labour adopted a strategy of Domestic Defence that took shape in the working-class upsurge of the 1890s. Domestic Defence is a buffering strategy that combines high tariffs, high wages, and limits on immigration. Given Australia's development, the strategy was reasonably successful for a time. However, changes in the international economic context rendered it vulnerable in the long run. Domestic Defence mitigated against a sizeable welfare state because welfare was to be insured by low unemployment and high wages rather than compensation for labour market failures. If Sweden tried to offset market forces by compensating for them, Australia sought to offset them by insulating the domestic economy

from the pressures of the world economy. The emergence of a world economy meant that insulation becomes more and more difficult and costly. Australia was seeking to defend standards and maintain domestic power relations that were continually being undermined by the shifting terrain of the international economy. The result was that by 1982 Australia had fallen to the sixteenth richest OECD nation (Castles 1989b).

It is important to recognize the critical role of the agrarian social structure in the realization of the social democratic vision, and place of the left in national politics. Despite the fact that the size of the agrarian sector was diminishing during the course of the twentieth century, in both Sweden and Australia, the role of the agrarian sector was critical in the initiation of the welfare state. In Sweden, the ability of Social Democrats to forge a coalition with the Centre Party was crucial to the initial phase of Social Democratic political dominance. In Australia, the marginal political weight of small farmers and the political dispositions of farm labourers made Australia one of the pioneers of welfare state measures, although changes in the world economy and the strategic option of the Australian left led in a different direction in the latter part of the twentieth century.

Undoing the Balance

The central impetus behind the expansion of the welfare states in the postwar period were Social Democratic/Labour parties acting in conjunction with the wider labour movement in a struggle for a more just society. Their efforts were largely rewarded because the context of the struggle was one of continuous economic growth and there was a more equal balance in the power relations between left and right. However, transformations in the world economy and social structural changes in the advanced economies were to undermine both of these circumstances and place the social democratic vision in jeopardy. Conjunctural events and evolutionary trends combined to subvert the compromise that had brought about the Golden Age and created a political space for an emboldened right.

WORLD ECONOMY

Beginning in the early 1970s, the rate of economic growth declined throughout the advanced capitalist world, while unemployment and inflation increased dramatically (Maddison 1991). The triggering events for this were the rapid increases in the price of oil in the early 1970s. The tripling of the price of oil started an inflationary spiral that led to inflation of the order of 15 per cent by 1974. What ensued was stagflation. Stagflation represented the unusual combination of unused capacity, high unemployment, and strong inflationary pressures. The average rate of unemployment in the 1980s was 8 per cent. Labour was in the difficult position of fighting for higher wages in a time of rapid inflation when the increases would contribute to higher levels of inflation in the future. Evidence indicates that they were unable to achieve the results that they had become accustomed to in the earlier period (O'Connell 1994). Averaged across the advanced industrial countries, real compensation per worker increased at a rate of 4.35 per cent per annum between 1960 and 1973. Over the next decade annual increases amounted to only .47 per cent per annum and actually declined by .77 per cent per annum between 1979–83 (O'Connell 1994). High levels of unemployment further weakened labour and generated greater demands on social programs. Exacerbating Western problems was the emergence of growth areas in the Pacific Rim and Latin America that undermined the monopoly on industrial production that the West had enjoyed since the end of the war. Industrial production was shifted from Europe and North America to the far-flung corners of the globe. An extended process of de-industrialization was occasioned in many of the pre-eminent industrial countries of the nineteenth and twentieth centuries.

The 1970s and 1980s witnessed the first synchronized world recession and the onset of stagflation. Countries concerned about their relative position in the world economy were forced to abandon the goal of full employment in order to fight inflation. The postwar expansion of the welfare state, which had been financed by a growing economy and sustainable deficits, now came under attack as financing the debt placed greater and greater constraints on public finance and demanded higher and higher levels of taxation. In a period characterized by slower economic growth and demographic pressures on social expenditures, governments were forced to increase taxes or expand the national debt. Most chose to do both, and at some point, this triggered a growing hostility toward taxation and an awareness that failure to restrain government expenditures would lead to increases in the future. Since much of the burden of taxation had been shifted onto individuals, it did not take long for calculations around the trade-off between benefits and costs to tilt in favour of reducing programs in sizeable sectors of the population.

The two most dramatic changes in the world economy in the recent period have been the movement of industrial production outside of Western Europe and North America and the freer movement of financial capital across the globe. The former has been an important contributor to the crisis of trade unionism and unemployment, and the latter has undermined Keynesian growth strategies that were premised on the capacity to set interest rates without reference to rates in the rest of the world (Glyn 1995). Technological innovations, economic trends, and government policies have combined to render financial capital extremely mobile and have greatly expanded the influence of international financial markets. Capital outflows in the 1980s were equivalent to 15 per cent of world merchandise trade in contrast to 7 per cent in the late 1970s (Frieden 1991). In 1989 foreign exchange trading averaged 650 billion dollars a day and currencies were subject to immediate pressure from financial markets if economic policy failed to reflect the priorities of capital (Frieden 1991). As Glyn observes, the mobility of financial capital tends to front-end load the negative impact on real wages of an expansionary program by generating a large initial depreciation due to falling exchange rates. Put simply, real wages fall because increases in the price of imports more than offset the reflationary effects of the expansionary program. When in office, Socialist or Labour parties have been forced to retreat from these experiments because of pressures from financial markets. Bondholders anxiously await the presentation of the budget and are ready to protect their investments by withdrawing their confidence. The inventory of countries or governments that have been forced to respect the power of international financial markets and retreat from electoral promises is a long one, including New Zealand, France, Ontario, Australia, Norway, and Sweden.

SOCIAL STRUCTURE AND REGIME ACCUMULATION CHANGES

By 1995, it was clear that the advanced countries were rapidly moving in the direction of postindustrial economies wherein service industries had greater weight than industry. In retrospect, it is also clear that there were two distinct paths to a postindustrial economy. One path, most closely approximated in Europe, involved a passage from agriculture to industry, then to postindustrialism. The other, followed by North America, Japan, and Oceania, involved a more balanced distribution between services and industry in all phases. In other words, the different paths are established by the relative weight of industry and services in the second period of economic development. The historical peak of industrialism in Europe was in the 1970s when about 40 per cent of the civilian workforce was in industry (Therborn 1991). Since that time all countries have seen their level

of industrial employment decline, although there is national variability within this broad trend (Esping-Andersen 1991). Wright and Martin's (1987) empirical examination of social structural trends in the United States concludes that the 1970s witnessed a dramatic decline in the number of working-class positions in the class structure. This reduction is one aspect of a general transformation of the social structure that has led to a decline in industrial employment, an expansion of service industries, and a heightened credentialization of the occupational structure.

It is not difficult to see the implication of this evolution for a left that relied on the support of the industrial working class. As a general trend, trade unions have been severely weakened in terms of membership and capacity for mobilization (Goldfield 1987). In the United States, union membership has declined to less than 12 per cent of the labour force. While other national union movements have not been subject to this level of marginalization, all have lost much of the power and influence accumulated in the aftermath of World War II. Even Sweden has seen a dramatic decline in the level of unionization, dropping from the high 90s to 80 per cent by 1990 (Gould 1993). Typically difficult to organize, private sector service jobs have remained outside the ambit of unionism. Public sector white-collar employees have found themselves at odds with private sector workers, trapped between an intransigent employer and a hostile, tax-paying public. Credentialized employees have often proven to be more concerned with career advancement than the politics of solidarity. In most countries, Southern Europe being the exception, Social Democratic or Labour parties witnessed a severe decline in membership and a less dramatic decline in their electoral fortunes in the 1980s.

The slow but persistent decline of organized labour, most dramatically revealed in the United States, due in part to changes in the occupational structure, are ultimately traceable to the consolidation of the post-Fordist or postindustrial economy. Post-Fordism involves production methods that place micro-electronics at the centre of the production process and expels labour from the process at a rapid rate. It disperses labour to smaller and smaller work units and requires flexible working practices that undermine the network of rules regarding the use of labour that was imposed in periods of labour ascendency. Mass production gives way to flexible production. International competitive pressures make it exceedingly difficult for unions to resist these changes, and their role in protecting working conditions is diminished. Coupled with the difficulties imposed on wage negotiations due to the high level of unemployment and the mobility of investment, unions seem less and less relevant to the dwindling industrial labour force. Labour's strength always rested on organization, mobilization, and collective solidarity that had been elaborated over centuries and it is precisely these attributes that are presently in jeopardy.

The Neo-Conservative Backlash

In the aftermath of World War II, Western societies were accustomed to rapidly increasing standards of living and government action to alleviate social and economic problems. During the course of the late 1980s and early 1990s, both of these expectations were called into question. Ever since the mid-1970s, real incomes have stagnated and economic growth has been stalled (Kenwood and Lougheed 1992; Maddison 1991). Against the backdrop of the previous 25 years it was easy, at first, to think that the new configuration was merely a hiatus between periods of sustained growth. Events were to prove this expectation wrong and, over time, the realization that we were entering a prolonged period of de-accelerated growth and a more competitive world economy began to enter public consciousness. The increasingly interdependent world economy and

the enhanced mobility of investment meant that government policies were placed under much stronger constraints than had been the case during the Golden Age. The traditional remedies of the Golden Age, national fiscal and monetary policies, had lost much of their viability and parties that were elected on platforms that promised to fulfill the postwar goals of full employment and an expanded welfare state were forced to backtrack very rapidly (Garrett and Lange 1991). The new context undermined the strategic options of the left and it became increasingly evident that the left had lost both organizational strength and strategic direction (Kitschelt 1994).

Against the backdrop of an increasingly weakened left, neoconservatism has come to dominate political discourse. The social democratic vision of the Enabling State has been dislodged by the New Right vision of the Minimal State. Neoconservatism or the New Right combines two disparate theoretical traditions by bringing together classical economic liberalism, which stressed property rights, opposition to the state, and a reliance on markets to allocate resources, and social and moral conservatism (Barry 1987; Green 1987). These two traditions are interwoven and articulated in a populist idiom that captures the attention of a public that has seen the hopes and aspirations of an earlier generation give way to the anxieties of the nineties. The message finds an audience because of the impact of the public debt on taxes, the financial fragility of social insurance programs, the much publicized abuses of the welfare system, and the impact of social change on the demographic landscape of most Western nations. These concerns are woven together in an ideological assault on the role of the state in social and economic life. Declining real incomes, job insecurity, and unemployment and social crises apparently related to the erosion of moral values have provided fertile grounds for the packaged message of the New Right.

The thesis of the New Right, that social and

economic problems have a common source in government spending, state interference, and a breakdown in values, was most powerfully embodied in the messages of Margaret Thatcher and Ronald Reagan. Thatcher's policies concentrated on weakening those social and political institutions that restricted the operation of market capitalism and instituted policies to create a bloc of stakeholders in the private sector by privatizing housing and numerous publicly owned services. Reagan's commitment to supply side economics led to cuts in social programs, provided tax breaks for the wealthy and corporations, and acted to cripple unions that operated in federal jurisdictions. The more fragmented political structure of the United States was favourable for a political strategy that encompassed single issues such as drugs, abortion, and crime control. These potent single issues allowed the New Right to augment their political coalition by opposing abortion, sexual permissiveness, and liberal social policies while endorsing the values of family and flag. Both Thatcher and Reagan sought to win political support by overlaying their economic programs with a populist message that linked them to the historical traditions of their respective countries—Thatcher by smashing the stranglehold that the Tory élite had over the party and resurrecting memories of Imperial glory by going to war with Argentina; Reagan by running against the Washington establishment, and appealing to those who felt that government had become remote, bureaucratized, and costly.

While the Conservative resurgence has proceeded furthest and has been articulated most stridently in the United States and Great Britain, the European right made significant gains in the 1980s. Early in the 1980s moderate left parties in the Netherlands, Belgium, Great Britain, and Germany suffered severe electoral reversals and had clearly lost strategic direction and intellectual energy. In Sweden, Social Democrats were able to regain office but they no longer set the policy parameters, and slowly lost support over the course of the decade leading up to their loss in the election of 1991 (Kitschelt 1994). In France, an extreme right-wing party, the National Front, capitalized on high unemployment, increases in crime, and the presence of masses of North African immigrants to gain an important place in the political arena (Hancock et al. 1993). While socialists managed to hold onto the presidency during the 1980s and returned to power in the legislative assembly in 1988, this was only possible after they had jettisoned many of their longstanding policy directions. In Germany, the Christian Democratic Party was returned to power in 1982 on the basis of promises to end the entitlement mentality and restore the traditional moral-cultural values of Germany (Hancock et al. 1993). More significantly radical or extreme right-wing parties have become a significant political force in Italy, West Germany, Austria, the Netherlands, and Switzerland. Even the Scandinavian countries have seen the emergence of extreme right-wing parties (Betz 1994). While these parties remain outside the corridors of power, their impact is not insubstantial in that they move the political spectrum to the right by forcing moderate right-wing parties to incorporate their issues.

A re-invigorated right and the changing pattern of political discourse was bound to shrink the breadth of the social democratic vision and trigger a process of political change in Social Democratic parties. Just as Conservative parties trimmed their ideological sails in the aftermath of World War II, Social Democratic parties have been forced to accommodate themselves to the new political context. Perhaps the most dramatic illustration of this phenomenon is provided by the New Zealand Labour Party. Like Australia, New Zealand had attempted to insulate itself from the vagaries of the international economy by practising a form of domestic defence. This orientation had been pioneered by the Labour Party in the 1930s and at the most general level involved the state playing an active role in promoting social justice. The familiar mix of redistributive policies, an expansive public sector, and Keynesian-type demand management strategies were combined with policies that guaranteed prices for agricultural products, provided subsidies to the export sector, protected domestic manufacture, placed limits on foreign ownership, and regulated the labour market. This mix was designed to shield the sectors of the economy from changes in the world economy in order to ensure political and economic stability.

Faced with a long-term decline, New Zealand's economic position, and a conjunctural exchange crisis, the fourth labour government undertook a series of measures that undid the assumptions that had underwritten New Zealand politics in the postwar period (Holland and Boston 1987). The measures included removing wage and price controls, opening the financial sector, floating the dollar, removing agricultural subsidies and tariffs, and reducing public expenditures. Accompanying these changes in economic policy were administrative measures that restructured government departments and installed commercial principles in all public enterprises and government agencies. These measures shattered the comfortable framework of postwar politics and represent, at this time, the most decided turn by a Social Democratic party toward the programmatic agenda of the New Right.

The Welfare State in the 1980s and 1990s

Social policy in the late 1980s and 1990s has been marked by a substantial retreat from the goals that were embedded in the social democratic vision: ending poverty, eliminating unemployment, and reducing inequality. Analyses of the early years of the downturn, 1975–84, demonstrate a variegated pattern, but one in which the majority of coun-

tries succeeded in restraining expenditures on social welfare (Abler 1988). Despite demographic pressures that should have led to increases in social expenditures, a number of countries managed to limit the increases in social expenditures to rises in GDP. As the period of slower growth persisted, pressures to reduce expenditures increased and a slow but ceaseless erosion of the welfare state took place. The erosion was engineered through a number of changes in the funding and entitlement to welfare services; among these were: (1) imposition of caps on increases to benefits; (2) introduction of user fees; (3) tightening of eligibility rules; (4) privatization of services making for a quasi-market system; (5) earnings-related benefits to replace flat-rate benefits—selectivity; and (6) direct contributions that played a larger role than general tax revenue.

Although all governments have experienced political difficulties when a frontal assault on the core of the welfare state is placed at the forefront of the political agenda, there is a growing sense that such an assault is now politically and even electorally feasible. A resurgent right has created conditions for substantial modification to health care, unemployment insurance, education, welfare, and pensions. However far these modifications go, there can be little doubt that we are seeing a shift toward a liberal welfare regime in which markets play an increasing role, and welfare provision descends toward the minimum. Increasingly, claims against the state are being displaced onto family and local communities. In Australia and Sweden, real social expenditures have been restrained to the point where they just keep pace with population growth despite demographic pressures (Graycar 1983; Soderstrom 1988). Even the Swedish Social Democratic party made a decided turn toward the agenda of the right, when in 1990 it gave priority to the fight against inflation, applied for membership to the European Community, cut medical care, and decided to continue to use nuclear power.

Conclusion

The resurgence of Conservatism has raised a large question mark over the future of the welfare state and ended social democratic hopes of reducing inequality, providing a tolerable quality of life for all citizens, and ensuring full employment. The starkest manifestation of this is the general acceptability of levels of unemployment that would have been unthinkable only 20 years ago. No more dramatic register of rise of the right and the decline of Labour and the left is possible. The battle against inflation has been waged on the backs of the unemployed and the labour movement, and it is clear that the notion of an insider/outsider economy is not a futurist's fantasy. Increasingly, economic well-being is tied to employment and ominous cleavages are developing in the social fabric. The fundamental premise of the postwar accommodation has been rendered inoperable under the onslaught of international financial capital, de-industrialization, and worldwide competitive pressures.

Things are a little less clear in regard to the core institutions of the welfare state. Up until the late 1980s and early 1990s the rhetoric of the right had outstripped its actions (Lane 1989). There was no massive reduction in the core programs of the welfare state, rather a general and determined effort to freeze or reduce the level of government expenditures with a variety of devices that erode rather than abolish the programs (Alber 1988; LeGrand 1990). Recent political events in the United States and elsewhere suggest that the stage has been set for such an assault but, until the drama has been completely acted out, any projected ending awaits confirming evidence. Whatever the future holds for those dependent on the programs of the welfare state, there can be no doubt that the coming period will witness an increased incapacity of the nation-state to ensure economic growth or a tolerable minimum for all citizens and a marked increase in economic and social inequality. While the economy and demographic context have contributed to this, it is necessary to recognize that objective circumstances only establish the limits and not the specific responses of public policy. Specific responses are entertained by political forces and are subject to the vicissitudes of political competition and electoral outcomes. For this reason, it is arguable that the fundamental political cause of our present situation is the current decline of the left and the resurgence of the right. The social democratic vision shares the fate of Social Democratic parties and it is increasingly unlikely that either can return to centre stage in the foreseeable future.

Note

Throughout this article various terms are employed to designate the manifold forms of the working-class movement. The *left* is the broadest of these terms and it encompasses Social Democratic or Labour parties, the trade union movement, and the myriad of collective organizations, such as cooperative societies, that were integral to the left in the postwar period. It is true that there was a good deal of variation in the relations among these institutions and their centrality to the political life of the nation. Probably the most important source of variation in the politics of the left would be the strength of the national Communist party. Communist parties were significant contributors to the left in a number of European countries for much of the postwar period, Italy and France being the most prominent examples. It is also the case that they were more influential than their electoral strength would lead us to expect in others, such as Sweden and Spain. While these parties maintained their ideological commitment to a revolutionary transformation of capitalism, their practical effect was to reinforce the left-wing of social democracy. Since this chapter means to capture the broad outlines of the social conflicts in the postwar period, the variety of national differences are sacrificed to the broader picture.

References

Aitkin, D. 1986. 'Australian Political Culture', *Australian Cultural History* 5:1 5–11.

Alber, J. 1988. 'Is There a Crisis of the Welfare State? Cross-national Evidence from Europe, North America and Japan', *European Sociological Review* 4(3): 181–203.

Anderson, P. 1974. *Lineages of the Absolutist State* (London: New Left Books).

Barry, N.P. 1987. *The New Right* (London: Croom Helm).

Betz, H-G. 1994. *Radical Right-Wing Populism in Western Europe* (New York: St. Martin's Press).

Bjorn, L. 1979. 'Labour Parties, Economic Growth and the Redistribution of Income in Five Capitalist Democracies'. In *Comparative Social Research,* ed. R. Tomasson (Greenwich: JAI Press), 93–128.

Butlin, N., A. Bernard, and J. Pincus. 1982. *Government and Capitalism* (Sydney: George Allen and Unwin).

Castles, F. 1978. *The Social Democratic Image of Society* (London: Routledge and Kegan Paul).

———. 1987. 'The Politics of Economic Vulnerability: A Comparison of Sweden and Australia', *Acta Sociologica* 30(3–4): 271–80.

———. 1989a. 'Introduction: Puzzles of Political Economy'. In *The Comparative History of Public Policy,* ed. F. Castles (Oxford: Oxford University Press), 1–15.

———. 1989b. 'Social Protection by Other Means: Australia's Strategy of Coping with External Vulnerability'. In *The Comparative History of Public Policy,* ed. F. Castles (Oxford: Oxford University Press), 16–55.

Esping-Andersen, G. 1985a. *Politics against Markets: The Social Democratic Road to Power.* (Princeton: Princeton University Press).

———. 1985b. 'Power and Distributional Regimes', *Politics and Society* 14(2): 223–56.

———. 1989. 'The Three Political Economies of the Welfare State', *Canadian Review of Sociology and Anthropology* 26(1): 10–35.

———. 1991. 'Postindustrial Cleavage Structures: A Comparison of Evolving Patterns of Social Stratification in Germany, Sweden, and the United States'. In *Labour Parties in Postindustrial Societies,* ed. F.F. Piven (London: Polity Press), 147–68.

Flora, P. 1985. 'On the History and Current Problems of the Welfare State'. In *The Welfare State and Its Aftermath,* eds S. Eisenstadt and O. Ahimer (London: Croom Helm), 11–30.

Frieden, J. 1991. 'Invested Interests: the Politics of National Economic Policies in a World of Global Finance', *International Organization* 45(4): 425–51.

Garrett, G., and P. Lange. 1991. 'Political responses to interdependence: what's "left" for the left?', *International Organization* 45(4): 539–64.

Glyn, A. 1995. 'Social Democracy and Full Employment', *New Left Review* 211: 33–55.

Goldfield, M. 1987. *The Decline of Organized Labour in the United States* (Chicago: University of Chicago Press).

Gould, A. 1993. *Capitalist Welfare Systems: A Comparison of Japan, Britain and Sweden* (New York: Longman).

Graycar, A. 1983. 'Retreat from the Welfare State'. In *Retreat from the Welfare State,* ed. A. Graycar (Sydney: George Allen and Unwin), 1–12.

Green, D.C. 1987. *The New Right: The Counter Revolution in Political, Economic, and Social Thought* (Brighton: Wheatsheaf Books).

Griffin, L., P. O'Connell, and H. McCammon. 1989. 'National Variation in the Context of Struggle: Postwar Class Conflict and Market Distribution in Capitalist Democracies', *Canadian Review of Sociology and Anthropology* 26(1): 37–68.

Hancock, M.D., D. Conrad, B. Peters, W. Safran, and R. Zariski. 1993. *Politics in Western Europe* (Chatham: Chatham House Publishers).

Holland, M. and J. Boston. 1987. 'The Fourth Labour Government'. In *The Fourth Labour Government: Radical Politics in New Zealand,* eds M. Holland and J. Boston (Melbourne: Oxford University Press), 1–14.

Jallade, J.-P. 1988. 'The Redistributive Efficiency of

European Welfare States: Basic Issues'. In *The Crisis of Redistribution in Western Europe,* ed. J-P Jallade (Chester: Trentham Books), 3–28.

Jones, M.A. 1980. *The Australian Welfare State* (Sydney: George Allen and Unwin).

Kenen, P. 1994. *The International Economy* (3rd edn) (Cambridge: Cambridge University Press).

Kenwood, A.G., and A.L. Lougheed. 1992. *The Growth of the International Economy: 1820–1990* (3rd edn) (London: Routledge).

Kitschelt, H. 1994. *The Transformation of European Social Democracy* (Cambridge: Cambridge University Press).

Korpi, W. 1978. *The Working Class in Welfare Capitalism* (London: Routledge and Kegan Paul).

———. 1983. *The Democratic Class Struggle* (London: Routledge and Kegan Paul).

Lane, C. 1989. 'From "Welfare Capitalism" to "Market Capitalism"', *Sociology* 23(4): 583–610.

Lash, S., and J. Urry. 1987. *The End of Organized Capitalism* (Madison, WI: University of Wisconsin Press).

LeGrand, J. 1990. 'The State of Welfare'. In *The State of Welfare,* ed. J. Hills (Oxford: Clarendon Press), 338–62.

Maddison, A. 1991. *Dynamic Forces in Capitalist Development* (New York: Oxford University Press).

O'Connell, P. 1994. 'National Variation in the Fortunes of Labour'. In *The Comparative Political Economy of the Welfare State,* eds T. Janoski and A. Hicks (Cambridge: Cambridge University Press), 218–44.

Pontusson, J. 1988. *Swedish Social Democracy and British Labour* (Cornell: Center for International Studies).

Przeworski, A. 1985. *Capitalism and Social Democracy* (Cambridge: Cambridge University Press).

Soderstrom, L. 1988. 'The Redistributive Effects of Social Protection: Sweden'. In *The Crisis of Redistribution in European Welfare States,* ed. J-P Jallade (Chester: Trentham Books), 75–144.

Therborn, G. 1991. 'Swedish Transition to Postindustrial Politics'. In *Labour Parties in Postindustrial Society,* ed. F.F. Piven (Cambridge: Polity Press), 101–23.

Thompson, E.P. 1963. *The Making of the English Working Class* (London: Penguin).

Ward, R.B. 1958. *The Australian Legend* (Melbourne: Oxford University Press).

Wilensky, H. 1975. *The Welfare State and Equality* (Berkeley, CA: University of California Press).

Wright, E., and B. Martin. 1987. 'The Transformation of the American Class Structure', *American Journal of Sociology* 93(1): 1–29.

Chapter 16

Does Class Matter? Beliefs About the Economy and Politics in Postindustrial Canada

Tom Langford

Introduction

Class is simultaneously a structuring principle of social life and a dimension of human experience. Classes are defined by the relationship that people have to the means for producing goods and services. In the capitalist mode of production there are three classes involved in ongoing relations. These classes are the capitalist or business class who own the means of production and employ workers in the pursuit of profits; the working class, who neither own the means of production nor have any authority in the process of production; and a diverse group of employees, sometimes called the new middle class, who, despite being nonowners like workers, exercise professional, managerial, or supervisory authority while on the job. A fourth class in Canadian society is the owners of small businesses, often called the old middle class, who produce goods or services utilizing primarily their own labour and the labour of family members rather than the labour of paid employees. This chapter investigates whether Canadians' beliefs about the economy and politics are patterned by their class experiences. In other words, does class matter to how Canadians look at important economic and political issues at the beginning of the twenty-first century?

The chapter is divided into four parts. The first part outlines some theoretical ideas on the class differentiation of beliefs, and the second part considers arguments in favour of the view that class is becoming less and less important as a source for economic and political beliefs. The third part examines the evidence. It summarizes the results of some of the important published Canadian research, and discusses data drawn from four national sample surveys, the most recent being the 1997 National Election Study. The conclusion suggests some possible future directions for research on the relationship between class and beliefs about the economy and politics.

Theoretical Ideas on the Class Differentiation of Beliefs

Every person is unique; therefore, beliefs about the economy and politics are to some extent idiosyncratic. However, people's beliefs are also affected by experiences they share in common with other people. Among the subjects of interest to political sociologists is the way that different social experiences, including class experiences, pattern what people believe about the economy and politics. This section outlines some of the ideas that sociologists have developed to help explain the relationship between class and beliefs.

An important source of people's beliefs in advanced capitalist societies is the dominant value system; it represents the interests of the most powerful and has become 'objectified and enshrined in the major institutional orders, thus providing the moral framework of the entire social system' (Parkin 1971: 83). Among the important economic and political elements of the dominant value system are individualism; the justification of property rights, the profit system, and market mechanisms; the presentation of inequalities of income as socially necessary; and the depiction of the state as a neutral arbiter of social conflict (Abercrombie et al. 1980: 128–40; Kluegel and Smith 1986: 71).

The dominant value system of a country provides a relatively stable influence on individuals' beliefs about the economy and politics (Kluegel and Smith 1986: 11). However, members of different classes are not equally open to the messages of the dominant value system. The business class and small businessowners should see much of their experience of making a living represented in dominant values; at the same time, small businessowners connected to cooperatives may have a critical perspective on market mechanisms, and small businessowners with small net incomes may be disenchanted with the fairness of income distribution. Conversely, the working class should be least likely to accept dominant values, although this is also a variable phenomenon. Frank Parkin has put forward an influential theory to account for: (1) when workers are likely to accept dominant values, and when they are likely to negotiate/modify those values, (2) why some workers in a country are more likely to accept dominant values than other workers; and (3) why there is much greater class differentiation of values in some capitalist countries than others.

Parkin proposes the existence of three major value systems in Western societies that influence the beliefs of workers. 'Each derives from a different social source, and each promotes a different moral interpretation of class inequality' (1971: 81). One of these value systems has already been discussed: the dominant value system. The other two are the subordinate and radical value systems. The social sources of subordinate values are the subcultures of the working-class community and large workplace (1967: 282–4); and the source of radical values is 'the mass political party based on the working class' (1971: 81–2).

The subordinate value system is 'essentially *accommodative*; that is to say, its representation of the class structure and inequality emphasizes various modes of adaptation, rather than either full endorsement of, or opposition to, the *status quo*' (1971: 88). A good example involves manual workers' evaluations of manual work. Dominant values are modified but not challenged when manual workers 'demote the social value of manual work while at the same time excluding their own particular manual occupations from this blanket evaluation' (p. 94). Overall, the subordinate value system involves two contradictory tendencies: fatalism and reluctant acceptance of one's subordinate position and support for actions such as unionization that will improve one's situation (1971: 91–2).

A key characteristic of the subordinate value system, according to Parkin, is that it is locally produced in subcultures rather than promoted by major institutions. In contrast, the dominant value system continually influences working people through the mass media and other institutions. Consequently, subordinate values are not formulated in conscious opposition to dominant values, but are developed as modifications of dominant values in light of the everyday experiences of working people. In this sense, the subordinate value system is said to represent a negotiated version of the dominant value system (1971: 92).

Workers' beliefs are drawn from both the dominant and subordinate value systems. Parkin proposes

> that which of the two frames of reference is actually drawn upon will be situationally determined; more specifically, it could be hypothesized that in situations where purely abstract evaluations are called for, the dominant value system will provide the

moral frame of reference; but in concrete social situations involving choice and action, the negotiated version—or the subordinate value system—will provide the moral framework (1971: 92–3).

A recent study supports Parkin's notion of how workers negotiate meaning: in focus group discussions, American workers utilized experiential and subcultural knowledge, along with popular wisdom and media discourse to make sense of issues such as plant closings and affirmative action (Gamson 1992: 4). Furthermore, Parkin's hypothesis that workers' use of dominant or subordinate values depends upon the abstractness or concreteness of a social situation was largely supported: 'Resource strategies among working people are heavily issue specific' (1992: 134). On the relatively abstract issues of nuclear power and Arab-Israeli conflict, workers did not usually integrate experiential knowledge with media discourse and popular wisdom, although the investigator was surprised 'to find such a substantial minority introducing experiential knowledge' in support of their focus group's shared perspective (1992: 131). This suggests that Parkin may have underestimated the scope of the subordinate value system: especially when they are required to elaborate their beliefs, many workers bring subcultural/experiential knowledge to bear on issues that are remote from their daily lives.

Parkin's theory also predicts which members of the working class are likely to have the most distinctive beliefs: workers who are well integrated into working-class subcultures (1967: 282–5). To fully appreciate the myriad of subcultural influences on a worker it is necessary to consider details of her/his current workplace experience (size of firm, presence of a union, type of labour control system, etc.) as well as the worker's class trajectory (involving the past, present, and anticipated future) and class networks (involving family, friends, and neighbours) (Wright 1989: 323–31).

The third source of workers' beliefs is the radical value system emanating from a working-class socialist party. Sixty years ago, the Communist Party of Canada (known at the time as the Labour Progressive Party) had a mass following among Canadian workers, and its rival on the left of the political spectrum, the Co-operative Commonwealth Federation (precursor of the New Democratic Party), had a socialist political platform. Such parties, argues Parkin, have a major influence 'in shaping the social consciousness of the subordinate class and in providing its members with a distinctive moral framework for interpreting social reality' (1971: 99). In Canada today, however, the socialist movement is much weaker—the Communist Party is left with fewer than a thousand members, and the New Democrats have become a middle of the road party in which socialists form a minority. As a consequence, most Canadian workers have no contact with radical interpretations of contemporary life. This contrasts with the situation in countries like France, Italy, and Sweden where left political parties maintain some mass support. We can thus hypothesize that in countries like Canada, workers' beliefs will be less differentiated from other classes than in countries like Italy.

There is a second problem with Parkin's approach that requires discussion. Given the absence of a radical value system in Canada, and the fact that the subordinate value system is conceived of as a negotiated version of the dominant value system, it would seem that dominant values exist relatively unopposed. But is this so? The value of rugged individualism is promoted throughout our culture, but a countertheme of 'you are your brother's [and sister's] keeper' also exists. William Gamson contends that 'there is no theme without a countertheme' (1992: 135) and that counterthemes are even part of media discourse on some issues (1992: 161). Counterthemes have divergent sources. Wallace Clement and John Myles argue that 'the "critical political consciousness" of North Americans, their cultural repertoire of protest and resistance, was forged in the crucible of radical democratic populism' of the early twentieth century (1994: 114). Other likely sources for counterthemes on economic issues are the union, cooperative, feminist, and environmental movements. The important implication of Gamson's research on workers' political talk is that counterthemes are much more readily available than Parkin's theory suggests. Therefore, where certain counterthemes speak more to the experiences of some classes than others, their availability should encourage the class differentiation of beliefs.

Most of the material in this section has considered how and why workers' beliefs might be different from the beliefs of other classes. We also need to consider whether the class experiences of the new middle class might generate distinctive perspectives on the economy and politics.

New middle class jobs typically require a certain amount of advance training and/or ongoing formal training. Thus, many members of this class bring professional perspectives and loyalties into their jobs. A common perspective amongst the professions is a stress on the importance of rational planning, science, and knowledge for socioeconomic advancement (Ehrenreich and Ehrenreich 1977: 22; Lash and Urry 1987: 194). Furthermore, entry into a new middle class position is often regulated by the possession of educational credentials. This allows a profession to protect the market privilege of its members by limiting the supply of trained practitioners.

Abercrombie and Urry identify the common interests of the new middle class as:

1. 'to deskill productive labourers';
2. 'to maximize the educational requirements of places within the social division of labour'; and
3. to maximize 'the income and resources devoted to education and science' (1983: 132).

The pursuit of these interests sets the new middle class against the working class, which faces a decline of both work and market situations as the power of the new middle class grows. However, the relationship between the new middle and capitalist classes is ambiguous, in part because the new middle class pursues its interests within the framework of a 'code of service' which morally ties members to the employing organization. Furthermore, although the new middle and capitalist classes are in conflict over the most important basis for the distribution of rewards (education vs. property), and the amount of the social surplus which should be devoted to the education and science sectors, there exists between them a relationship of mutual dependence defined by the goal of dominating/exploiting labour. We can thus hypothesize that the new middle class will have distinctive beliefs on issues involving knowledge, education, science, and planning, but will have beliefs much like the capitalist class on other economic and political issues.

Opinions on the Growing Irrelevance of Class

The idea that class is the primary social cleavage in capitalist societies has enjoyed widespread popularity among sociologists. 'Sociology has only one independent variable, class' is the maxim with which Erik Olin Wright began the first chapter of Class Structure and Income Determination (1979: 3). Furthermore, many sociologists have concurred with the materialist premise of Karl Marx that 'it is not the consciousness of humans that determines their being, but on the contrary it is their social being that determines their consciousness' (1976: 3). Representative of this thrust in scholarship, a recent book on the concept of class concluded 'that class relationships are the key to the analysis of the social structure in general, and economic and political life in particular' (Edgell 1993: 116). Within this class-centred, materialist tradition, sociological studies of belief systems have tended to focus on the class determination of beliefs, adding in additional explanatory variables to round out the investigation.

But not all sociologists agree that class should be the focus of sociological research on belief systems. Setting aside some of the philosophical and definitional issues in this controversy, there are four sorts of arguments against the primacy of class.[1]

AFFLUENT WORKERS
The first argument is that growing affluence over the past 50 years has blurred the social boundaries between classes. Although very wealthy and very poor people can still be found in advanced capitalist societies, most people are middle income. Furthermore, the distribution of income is more continuous than in the past. According to Robert Nisbet, both of these factors 'make it unlikely that self-conscious and mutually antagonistic groups will arise' (1972: 58). Furthermore, with affluence comes greater opportunities for leisure, and identities centred on leisure activities (for example, a homeowner, an RVer, or a professional sports team fan) may diminish or displace class identities (Clark et al. 1993: 299).

One of the best-known sociological studies of the 1960s investigated the impact of rising standards of living on male British workers' social life and political orientations. It found that 'a worker's prosperity, or lack of it, is only one element entering into the formation of his class and political awareness,' and when compared to workplace, community, and family experiences 'the effect of such purely material factors as level of income and possessions may be a relatively minor one' (Goldthorpe et al. 1968: 48). The study concluded, 'The weakness of the affluence thesis is that it fails to take account of the worker's social relationships, and particularly of the way in which they affect the *meaning* which the individual worker places on the fact of his prosperity or pri-

vation' (1968: 48). This British study thus failed to support the idea that affluence automatically remade workers as 'middle class'. Nevertheless, affluence did make for a different kind of working class—more instrumental in orientation towards work, and concerned more with family rather than community (1968: 76).

ECONOMIC CHANGES LIMIT THE IMPORTANCE OF CLASS
Class is one dimension of the structure of economic relationships. The second argument on the declining importance of class is that other dimensions of economic structure have become relatively more important as determinants of political and economic beliefs. These dimensions include economic sector (oligopoly, competitive, or state), the dependence of workers on the employing organization, the decline of manufacturing jobs and the rapid increase in both skilled and unskilled service jobs, the importance of knowledge in the production of goods and services, and the development of nonhierarchical forms of workplace organization. The last three of these dimensions are among the indicators of the shift from industrial to postindustrial economies.

Economic sector divides both the business and working classes, creating fractional interests that can be at odds with class interests. Furthermore, the sectoral fractions of each class have differential capacities to realize their interests; for example, workers in the oligopoly and state sectors are much more likely to be unionized than workers in the competitive sector (Clark et al. 1993: 301–2; Hodson et al. 1989: 194–201).

Many sociologists have viewed sectoral division as a defining structural feature of post-World War II economies and politics. For instance, Randy Hodson and co-authors write: 'Just as the epoch of competitive capitalism corresponded to the period of homogenization of labour and the polarization of class politics . . . the epoch of monopoly capitalism corresponded to the period of segmentation and the fractioning of class politics' (1989: 212). However, they believe a new source of division among workers is superseding economic sector in importance: loyalty to the employing organization. The economic restructuring of recent years, caused by intense global intercapitalist competition, understandably heightens job insecurity; in the face of this condition, workers tend to see their interests as being linked to the survival and success of their employer (1989: 205). Hodson and colleagues thus conclude:

> Not only have class politics become diluted by the fractioning of labour, but they are now diluted even further by the forging of a new structural and subjective common ground of interest between workers and employers. As the boundaries between class interests become dissipated, the terrain of political struggle shifts to broader arenas and more encompassing interests focused still around economic concerns but not defined so prominently by relations of production (1989: 213).

Occupational differentiation will dilute class politics in a way similar to employment sector and loyalty to the firm as long as people hold a distinctive occupational commitment and identity. This factor would thus seem to be particularly important for dividing the new middle class (where credentialized professional identities are very important) and in distinguishing workers with certified skills from other workers (Clark et al. 1993: 298). Perhaps more to the point for understanding working-class beliefs is the finding that occupational homogeneity strengthens the salience of class, as demonstrated by research on coal mining communities and other one-industry towns. Occupational diversity due to the shift from manufacturing to service employment therefore undercuts working-class formation even when occupation is not a particularly salient iden-

tity for workers. A factor complementary to occupational diversity may be rapid occupational change. But while Nisbet argues that 'the [postindustrial] job structure itself is too fluctuant, too mobile, to allow classes to form' (1972: 57), it is conceivable that occupational insecurity may cause some people to become sympathetic toward interpretations of economic restructuring and dislocation that are critical of corporate capitalism.

The importance of knowledge and education in postindustrial economies contributes to occupational diversity. It also puts pressure on individuals to get the education and training they need to secure and maintain a 'good' job. The race for good jobs obscures the fact that there are not enough good jobs to go around; nevertheless, participating in the race makes sense to many individuals since the better educated and trained are much more likely to attain those good jobs. Many of those partaking in this competitive process have what Nisbet calls a 'level consciousness' that runs counter to a class-based view on the economy.

> Unlike class consciousness, level consciousness makes for a high degree of individualism with respect to aspirations and life chances; it does not promote feeling of identification or collective involvement. The principal motive of the level conscious individual is to pass up and out of the level in which [s/]he finds himself. [S/]He is, so to speak, on the make (1972: 60).

Nonhierarchical forms of work organization are the third feature of postindustrial economies that has been implicated in the declining importance of class. Class formation is promoted by a rigid authority structure at work. The argument of postindustrial theorists is that this sort of an authority system is a thing of the past since firms work best when the knowledge workers of the new economy are given the autonomy to solve problems (Clark and Lipset 1991: 406). Perhaps the only difficulty with this argument is that while it sometimes applies to the workplace experiences of employed professionals (members of the new middle class), it is difficult to find very many workers who would describe their workplace as nonhierarchical.

NONECONOMIC IDENTITIES COMPETE WITH CLASS IDENTITY

Noneconomic identities are sometimes coterminous with class boundaries and, in such a case, serve to solidify class-differentiated beliefs and action. An example is a British manufacturing strike in 1966 where the workers were all of Punjabi ancestry: 'When people stopped work, even those doubting the wisdom of their leaders, what was paramount in their decision was their unity as an ethnic group and the ties of communal loyalty rather than the bonds of labour' (Marsh 1967: 53). However, noneconomic identities may also compete with class identity.

In some cases, these alternative identities are based on membership in socially defined subgroups of the population: gender, ethnicity, race, region, and religious affiliation are the most important elements of social structure that give rise to such subgroups. The class differentiation of beliefs is lessened when individuals from across the class structure utilize a common alternative identity (for example, Québécois) when selecting/developing a belief (for example, approval of NAFTA—the North American Free Trade Agreement). In other cases, the alternative identities are connected to movements that promote issues of a universalistic nature. Environmentalism and moral conservatism are two such movements (Clark et al. 1993: 313; Hodson et al. 1989: 203).

ONE-DIMENSIONAL THOUGHT AND BEHAVIOUR

A number of commentators have identified advanced capitalist societies as totalitarian in the way that people's definitions of needs are manipulated. Central to this process is the spread of mass culture and the increasing commoditization of life—the way that more and more facets of life have been turned into commodities to be bought and sold. Herbert Marcuse was one of the first theorists to systematically analyse the totalitarian side of contemporary life:

The means of mass transportation and communication, the commodities of lodging, food, and clothing, the irresistible output of the entertainment and information industry carry with them prescribed attitudes and habits, certain intellectual and emotional reactions which bind the consumers more or less pleasantly to the producers and, through the latter, to the whole. The products indoctrinate and manipulate; they promote a false consciousness which is immune against its falsehood. And as these beneficial products become available to more individuals in more social classes, the indoctrination they carry ceases to be publicity; it becomes a way of life. It is a good way of life—much better than before—and as a good way of life, it militates against qualitative change. Thus emerges a pattern of *one-dimensional thought and behaviour* in which ideas, aspirations, and objectives that, by their content, transcend the established universe of discourse and action are either repelled or reduced to terms of this universe (1964: 12).

If Marcuse's argument is correct, we can expect to observe the decline of class-differentiated beliefs on the economy and politics as capitalism's consumer culture pervades more and more facets of people's lives. An application of the 'one-dimensional society' perspective can be found in Thomas Dunk's recent study of male working-class culture in Thunder Bay. The author concluded: 'In Western capitalist nations of the late twentieth century the impediment to the development of an explicitly anti-capitalist culture may stem from the fact that there are no longer social relations which have been untouched by commoditization, and which therefore provide a model of a real alternative. . . . Subordinate classes and groups are trapped in a veritable hall of mirrors' (Dunk 1991: 160).

The Canadian Evidence

The national survey results found in Tables 16.1 and 16.2 provide an overview of the extent to which classes in contemporary Canada differ in their beliefs about the economy and politics.[2] Unfortunately, the information gathered in the 1997, 1993, and 1988 national election studies makes it impossible to separate the members of the capitalist and old middle classes. Consequently, the category 'owners' includes both of these classes.

BELIEFS ABOUT INEQUALITY AND REDISTRIBUTION

In a study of data from a 1977 national survey, William Johnston and Michael Ornstein found significant class differences on beliefs about inequality and redistribution. For example, 69 per cent of workers agreed that there is too much of a difference between rich and poor, compared to 54 per cent of managers, 50 per cent of the old middle class, and 32 per cent of the business class (1985: 380). These results are consistent with data recorded in Table 16.1. In the 1997 survey, 74 per cent of workers agreed that government should do more to reduce the income gap between rich and poor Canadians, compared to 63 per cent of owners. On the same item in the 1993 survey and on a similar item in the 1982 survey, the difference between workers and owners was also greater than 10 per cent. In both of these earlier surveys, the new middle class had a percentage which was very similar to that of own-

ers. In the 1997 survey, however, the new middle class percentage (70) was intermediate between those of owners (63) and workers (74). Further analysis indicates that concern about the income gap between rich and poor Canadians grew among both the private and public sector branches of the new middle class between 1993 and 1997 (see Table 16.1), while the level of concern of owners and workers was unchanged. Additional research is needed to establish whether this egalitarian shift in new middle-class beliefs persists in more recent surveys.

The other inequality and redistribution items reported in Table 16.1 involve beliefs about unemployment insurance (1997, 1993, and 1988 surveys) and whether working people get their fair share of what they produce (1993 and 1988). On all five items, workers stood apart from the other two classes, while owners and the new middle class had similar patterns of responses. In 1993, for example, 55 per cent of workers agreed that working people do not get their fair share of what they produce, compared to 36 per cent of owners and 33 per cent of the new middle class.

These results pose the same interpretive problem as the proverbial half-full, half-empty glass of water. Between 1977 and 1997 there is a stable pattern of class differentiation on beliefs about economic inequality and redistribution, with workers more likely to be egalitarian than the other two classes. This supports Parkin's notion that on issues with practical relevance for workers' lives, a subordinate value system (rooted in subcultural experiences) will provide an alternative frame of reference for some (but not all) workers. At the same time, the percentage differences between the working class and the other classes are very modest in size—generally in the 10 per cent to 25 per cent range, with the percentage differences between workers and the new middle class being less than 10 per cent in 1997. We can conclude that class is certainly not the only determinant of Canadians' beliefs about inequality and

Table 16.1 Beliefs About the Economy, by Class (Including Two Breakdowns by Sector, a Third by Nationality, and a Fourth by Sector and Gender)

1. Inequality and Redistribution

1997 and 1993 The government should do more to reduce the income gap between rich and poor Canadians.

	(% Agree)	
	1997	*1993*
Owners	62.9	62.3
New Middle Class	70.3	59.9
Private Sector	65.0	56.4
Public Sector	77.1	64.5
Working Class	74.3	74.2

1982 Many people in Canada receive much less income than they deserve.

	(% Agree)
Owners	59.4
New Middle Class	59.2
Working Class	71.8

1997 and 1993 If you had to make cuts would you cut unemployment insurance a lot, some, or not at all?

	(% Favouring Cuts)	
	1997	*1993*
Owners	60.7	66.3
New Middle Class	59.1	63.7
Working Class	52.3	52.4

1988 To cut their deficits, should governments make it harder to get unemployment insurance?

	(% for Make It Harder)
Owners	72.8
New Middle Class	70.1
Working Class	48.9

1993 Under the private enterprise system, working people do not get their fair share of what they produce.

	(% Agree)
Owners	36.2
New Middle Class	33.1
Working Class	55.5

1988 Working people in this country: (1) do not get a fair share of what they produce; or (2) usually earn what they deserve.

	(% Picking Option 1)
Owners	26.9
New Middle Class	26.6
Working Class	42.8

2. Trade Agreements

1993 Support for the NAFTA (North American Free Trade Agreement)

	(%)
Owners	38.1
Québécois	47.6
Other Canadians	36.2
New Middle Class	37.8
Québécois	47.3
Other Canadians	35.4
Working Class	23.4
Québécois	31.9
Other Canadians	20.7

1988 Support for the FTA (original Canada-US Free Trade Agreement)

	(%)
Owners	45.6
Québécois	46.4
Other Canadians	45.4
New Middle Class	42.6
Québécois	55.6
Other Canadians	39.1
Working Class	35.0
Québécois	40.6
Other Canadians	33.3

3. Profit Motive

1993 and 1988 If the system of private enterprise were abolished:

1. Most people would work hard anyway;
2. Very few people would do their best.

(% Picking Option 2)

	1993		1988
Owners	69.7	Owners	71.5
Women	57.8	Women	62.2
Men	74.1	Men	74.6
New Middle Class	59.7	New Middle Class	57.9
Private Sector	67.0	Private Sector	65.6
Women	45.5	Women	54.6
Men	76.8	Men	71.6
Public Sector	50.4	Public Sector	50.7
Women	43.3	Women	48.1
Men	56.8	Men	53.3
Working Class	48.6	Working Class	50.9
Private Sector	47.9	Private Sector	52.4
Women	35.0	Women	45.7
Men	57.0	Men	56.9
Public Sector	50.4	Public Sector	49.7
Women	44.7	Women	47.9
Men	56.6	Men	51.4

4. Welfare Spending

1997 and 1993 [If you had to make cuts] would you cut welfare spending a lot, some, or not at all?

(% Favouring Cuts)

	1997	1993
Owners	71.9	73.9
New Middle Class	62.2	72.9
Private Sector	67.9	75.0
Public Sector	55.5	70.6
Working Class	69.7	72.1

redistribution. Nevertheless, after conducting a multivariable study of the 1977 survey data, Johnston and Ornstein concluded that 'for a number of aspects of political ideology, including attitudes about the power and legal status of trade unions, the provision for some types of social welfare benefits, and the redistribution of income, class differences are stronger than cleavages along other lines of stratification' (1985: 385).

Parkin's theory predicts that those workers with extensive experiences in working-class subcultures will have far more distinctive beliefs on inequality and redistribution than workers lacking such experiences. Two findings from a comparative study of 1982 and 1984 national survey data lend support to this hypothesis: net of other variables, workers with a working-class family background tended to be more egalitarian than other workers; and in 1982, workers with nonworking-class spouses tended to be somewhat less egalitarian than other workers. At the same time, in neither survey was union membership a determinant of workers' egalitarian beliefs, suggesting 'that Canadian workers who belong to unions are not automatically influenced by a union subculture which shapes their views of class and the economy' (Langford 1992: 476). The study concluded, 'Canadian unions tend to have members who are highly committed to the rights of unions but not specially committed to the broader economic goals of the union movement' (1992: 478).

William Johnston and Douglas Baer investigated the effect of union membership on workers' beliefs in a comparative perspective. They found that union membership had a strong effect on workers' support for economic alternatives in Sweden, but negligble effects in both Canada and the United States (1993: 282); and that the effect of union membership on 'oppositional consciousness' was stronger in Sweden than in the other two countries. These results suggest that there is cross-national variation in both the range of beliefs and distinctiveness of beliefs found in the subculture of a union. Johnston and Baer (1993: 283–91) argue that the relative power of the working class explains cross-national differences in working-class beliefs, and that the power of a particular country's working class must be analysed in terms of the historical trajectory of class relations in that country.

A study of male manual workers in four Ontario communities pursued the problem of subcultural influences on class identification. Vincent Keddie (1980: 31–2) found that both union membership and wife's occupational status affected the likelihood of working-class identification. Seventy-five per cent of union members

identified with the working class compared to 47 per cent of nonunionists; and 85 per cent of those whose wives held low-status jobs identified with the working class compared to 48 per cent of those whose wives held high-status jobs .

While past studies suggest that subcultural experiences play a role in patterning Canadian workers' beliefs about the economy, there is a contradiction among them regarding the role of union subcultures. Furthermore, a second study of the 1977 national survey concluded that family background had relatively little impact on Canadians' beliefs about the economy (Johnston and Ornstein 1982: 207–8). More work needs to be done to identify the variety of working-class subcultures that exist in postindustrial Canada, and the impact that each tends to have on workers' beliefs and actions.

As already noted, the data in Table 16.1 do not allow us to differentiate the beliefs of capitalists and the old middle class. A special survey of Canadian corporate, state, and labour élites in the early 1980s enables us to get a picture of the beliefs of large (monopoly) and small (competitive) capitalists on inequality and redistribution. Compared to small capitalists (averaging 40 employees), large capitalists were less likely to agree that there is too much of a difference between rich and poor (22 per cent vs. 31 per cent) (Ornstein 1985: 146). This item was also part of the 1977 national survey discussed above where 50 per cent of the old middle class, 54 per cent of managers, and 69 per cent of workers agreed that the rich-poor difference was too large. This comparison demonstrates that the business class has a much different moral view of inequality in Canadian society than other classes; it shows that the difference between monopoly and competitive capitalists is relatively small compared to the difference between competitive capitalists and the old middle class. Michael Ornstein also found that competitive capitalists were more likely to support socialized medicine and government social welfare programs than monopoly capitalists (1985: 152). Nevertheless, he concludes that such differences 'should be understood in the more general context of the larger ideological differences between capital, the state, and labour. In that context, the survey provides evidence of a strong ideological consensus within the capitalist class, including big and small capital and lawyers in the largest firms. The differences among the executives of the largest corporations, who constitute the big bourgeoisie proper, are still smaller' (1985: 158).

Ornstein's study of élites indicates that any picture of the class differentiation of beliefs in Canadian society is incomplete unless the distinctiveness of the business class is included in the picture. This caveat should be kept in mind since the remainder of the chapter collapses the old middle and capitalist classes together, thus underrepresenting the class differentiation of beliefs.

The comparative research of Johnston and Baer also allows us to examine the size of the differences in beliefs among classes in Canada compared to the United States and Sweden. On measures of oppositional and alternative consciousness, Swedish workers were considerably more egalitarian/militant than American and Canadian workers; as a consequence, there were larger across-class differences in Sweden than in the other two countries (1993: 279). This finding is consistent with our expectation, based on Parkin's theory, that the class differentiation of beliefs will be greater in countries where a radical value system continues to be promoted among workers.

BELIEFS ABOUT TRADE AGREEMENTS AND THE PROFIT MOTIVE

Globalization and competitiveness are two of the buzzwords of economic discourse at the beginning of the twenty-first century. Items in the 1997, 1993, and 1988 election surveys allow us to investigate whether beliefs about these economic processes are differentiated by class.

One way that globalization has been presented is in terms of the building of multinational economic blocs. Canada formed an economic bloc with the United States in the late 1980s, and Mexico joined that bloc in the early 1990s. In 1988 there were modest class differences in support for the original Canada-US Free Trade Agreement (FTA): 35 per cent of the working class supported the FTA compared to 43 per cent of the new middle class and 46 per cent of owners. In 1993, however, there were somewhat larger class differences in support for the North American Free Trade Agreement (NAFTA): only 23 per cent of the working class favoured NAFTA compared to 38 per cent of each of the other two classes. This pattern of class differentiation was found in each of the Québécois and Other Canadians subsamples in 1993, even though the level of support for NAFTA was generally 10 per cent higher amongst the Québécois (see Table 16.1). There was no direct question on support for free trade agreements in the 1997 survey. However, respondents were asked whether they agreed that 'overall, free trade with the US has been good for the Canadian economy'. While 57 per cent of owners and 55 per cent of the new middle class agreed with this statement, only 46 per cent of the working class did so (data not in a table), demonstrating that there are persistent class differences in beliefs about trade agreements.

Promotion of the concept of competitiveness implies that humans require the motivation of profit to do their best in economic life. An item included in both the 1988 and 1993 surveys (but not in the 1997 survey) measured support for this notion of human nature. In both surveys, about half of the working class believed that 'very few people would do their best' if the private enterprise system was abolished, as opposed to about 60 per cent of the new middle class and 70 per cent of owners (see Table 16.1).

Many Canadians work for governments rather than private firms. It is reasonable to suppose that employees in the state sector will be more likely to believe that the profit motive is *not* necessary to get people to work hard. Consequently, a breakdown of class percentages by sector is presented for this item in Table 16.1. In both surveys, the level of support for the capitalist view of human nature was very similar for owners and the private sector new middle class (about two-thirds); in comparison, only about one-half of the public sector new middle class supported this view. We can conclude that sectoral processes account for most of the difference between owners and the new middle class on this item. In contrast, however, there was very little difference between the public and private sector branches of the working class, indicating that the overall distinctiveness of the working class cannot be due to sectoral processes.

Breakdowns by gender are also presented for this item (Table 16.1). For each class/sector sub-sample in 1993 and 1988, men were more likely to believe that 'very few people would do their best' if the private enterprise system was abolished. The gender gap ranges from 4 per cent to over 30 per cent. When we combine the effects of class, sector, and gender we are able to observe some large differences in beliefs. Specifically, 75 per cent of male owners in 1988 agreed with the capitalist view of human nature, compared to only 46 per cent of female private sector workers. The percentage difference between these two groups was 10 per cent greater in 1993 (74 per cent compared to 35 per cent).

In explaining the distinctiveness of workers' beliefs on the trade agreements and human motivation, we need to keep two processes in mind. First, there was considerable public debate about the trade agreements in both 1988 and 1993. As a result, counter-themes as well as dominant themes were available in public discourse. Second, as suggested by William Gamson's research, workers seem capable of applying experiential and subcultural knowledge to a much broader range of issues than the 'meat and potatoes' of everyday life.

Many workers utilize the subordinate value system as a frame of reference for assessing what motivates humans to work hard.

Finally, it is significant that the public sector new middle class, but not the private sector new middle class, differed from owners on support for the capitalist view of human nature. This suggests that sectoral cleavage is a very important dimension of new middle-class beliefs and politics (see Langford 1996).

BELIEFS ABOUT WELFARE SPENDING

In their analysis of 1977 survey data, Johnston and Ornstein found little class differentiation in perception of the legitimacy of corporate power (1985: 381, 385). This caused them to argue that working-class ideology in Canada is incomplete, a conclusion consistent with Parkin's view of the nature of workers' beliefs in a society lacking a radical value system.

Another economic issue where we might expect to find little class differentiation in beliefs is spending on welfare. The individualistic ethos of capitalist societies portrays success as the result of individual virtue and deprivation as the result of individual shortcoming. Welfare recipients have always been a stigmatized group in Canada, never more so than during the present-day conservative backlash against the welfare state. A majority of the members of all three classes are likely to see welfare as a place to cut government spending. Indeed, this was the case in 1993, with between 72 per cent and 74 per cent of each class favouring cuts to welfare (see Table 16.1). In 1997 the percentages for owners (72) and workers (70) were very similar to 1993. At least when presented in terms of eliminating government deficits, welfare spending is an issue that appears to be unconnected to workers' subordinate value system.

At the same time, there is one unanticipated finding in these data. Between 1993 and 1997 support for cutting welfare spending fell from 71 per cent to 56 per cent among the public sector branch of the new middle class, making this group quite distinctive in its views (see Table 16.1). One can hypothesize that the members of the public sector new middle class were generally more knowledgeable than other groups of the deleterious consequences of the cuts to welfare introduced by Canadian governments between 1993 and 1997, and the shift in their views reflects that knowledge. Nevertheless, given the relatively small size of the public sector branch of the new middle class in Canadian society (for instance, it constitutes only 9.5 per cent of the cases with class and sector observations in the 1997 survey), our conclusion must be that there is relatively little class differentiation in beliefs about welfare spending.

BELIEFS ABOUT CLASS

Karl Marx believed that the working class was the main agent of social change in capitalist societies. In his view, one of the necessary conditions for successful socialist action was the development of a world view among workers that emphasized the struggle between the business and working classes. This idea has motivated sociologists to investigate the subjective sense of class held by workers and the members of other classes.

A series of questions on this subject was included in the 1984 National Election Study. People were first asked, 'Does the idea of social classes have any meaning to you?' While 72 per cent of the Québécois said Yes, an affirmative response was obtained from only 52 per cent of English Canadians (Lambert et al. 1986: 385, 397). This is a large difference, and may reflect the greater importance of class discourse in Quebec than in English Canada.

The study also analysed the criteria that respondents believed were most important in distinguishing classes. Three categories of criteria were distinguished: materialist (for example, wealth), individualist (for example, smart), and ascriptive (for example, country of birth). Ronald Lambert and his co-authors had hypothesized that

'in the lower strata, people are compelled to deal with economic constraints on a daily basis, and so we might expect them to be especially sensitive to the material basis of society' (1986: 382). However, the study found that those with higher levels of education were more likely to use materialist criteria than those with lower levels of education, and white-collar workers were more likely to use materialist criteria than blue-collar workers (1986: 388–90). These findings indicate that many Canadian workers do not tend to analyse their material experiences of inequality using the concept of class. To whatever extent their practical consciousness (knowledge drawn upon in the course of everyday action) represents an understanding of class relations, their discursive consciousness (what can be said) tends to lack a class-analytical component (Giddens 1984: 7).

BELIEFS ABOUT POLITICS

The first item in Table 16.2 deals with the individual's internal sense of efficacy when dealing with politics and government. Exactly the same item was asked in the 1977 national survey studied by Johnston and Ornstein. They found that only 30 per cent of the business class believed that politics is too complicated to understand; in contrast, 73 per cent of the working class and 61 per cent of the old and new middle classes held this belief (1985. 382). The results for 1997 and 1993 are broadly similar to those for 1977, especially if we assume that owners with a university degree in the 1997 and 1993 surveys (38 and 33 per cent agreement respectively) serve as a proxy measure for the business class in the 1977 survey (30 per cent agreement). The breakdown for this item by education demonstrates that differences in the educational composition of the three classes explain much of the observed class differentiation.

The next two items in Table 16.2 concern beliefs about how government operates. In 1977 there were very modest differences among classes in believing that governments do not care 'what people

Table 16.2 Beliefs About Politics, by Class (Including Two Breakdowns by Education)

1997 and 1993 *Sometimes, politics and government seem so complicated that a person like me can't really understand what's going on.*

	(% Agree)	
	1997	1993
Owners	50.5	63.0
Grade 12 or less	64.5	81.0
Intermediate educ.	44.6	57.2
University degree	38.5	33.2
New Middle Class	42.0	56.5
Grade 12 or less	68.6	69.9
Intermediate educ.	51.6	60.7
University degree	30.3	46.8
Working Class	61.3	71.5
Grade 12 or less	69.0	79.1
Intermediate educ.	61.8	65.4
University degree	33.9	53.6

1997 and 1993 *I don't think the government cares much what people like me think.*

	(% Agree)	
	1997	1993
Owners	64.6	74.2
Grade 12 or less	78.1	76.3
Intermediate educ.	55.5	76.3
University degree	57.5	67.4
New Middle Class	55.8	68.3
Grade 12 or less	80.4	74.8
Intermediate educ.	64.7	76.2
University Degree	44.7	59.3
Working Class	70.8	79.3
Grade 12 or less	78.6	81.7
Intermediate educ.	67.8	80.3
University degree	51.2	67.5

1997, 1993, and 1988 *Quite a few of the people running the government are a little crooked.*

	(% Agree)		
	1997	1993	1988
Owners	44.5	43.7	46.2
New Middle Class	41.1	39.3	43.8
Working Class	61.0	57.3	56.0

1997 and 1993 *We could probably solve most of our big national problems if decisions could be brought back to the people at the grassroots.*

	(% Agree)	
	1997	1993
Owners	64.2	65.2
New Middle Class	58.8	61.9
Working Class	68.2	73.7

1982 *Despite its problems the Canadian system of government serves the interests of most Canadians.*

	(% Agree)
Owners	70.5
New Middle Class	68.2
Working Class	64.9

like me think' (Johnston and Ornstein 1985: 389). The same pattern existed in the 1997 and 1993 surveys; in 1997, for example, 56 per cent of the new middle class compared to 65 per cent of owners and 71 per cent of workers agreed with the statement. A breakdown by education is also reported for this item. The effect of education is somewhat smaller than on the belief about internal political efficacy.

The other item concerns beliefs about corruption in government. In 1997, 61 per cent of workers believed that 'quite a few of the people running the government are a little crooked' compared to 44 per cent of owners and 41 per cent of the new middle class. The percentages for each class in each of the 1993 and 1988 national election surveys were quite similar (see Table 16.2).

The results for the previous two items indicate that government responsiveness is a more important issue than government corruption in the minds of Canadians, and that workers tend to be more cynical about government responsiveness and honesty than the other two classes. The fourth item in Table 16.2 is a proposed solution to the perceived lack of responsiveness: grassroots decision-making. In both 1997 and 1993, the working class was most likely to support bringing political decisions to the grassroots and the new middle class was least likely to support this idea (in 1997 the percentage difference was 9, while in 1993 it was 12). The most significant aspect of these results is the high level of support in all three classes, especially the new middle class which should be committed to the application of knowledge by experts in decision-making. It might be that the vagueness of the idea of bringing decisions back to the grassroots accounts for the minimal class differentiation. Nevertheless, the results demonstrate the power of populist counter-themes in contemporary Canadian political discourse, a point analysed in detail by Clement and Myles (1994: ch. 5).

The final item in Table 16.2 measures support for the dominant value that 'the Canadian system of government serves the interests of most Canadians' (1982 survey). Parkin's theory suggests that workers should not systematically differ from the other classes on such a general statement of dominant ideology. The evidence supports Parkin's proposition since, with a difference between owners and workers of only 6 per cent and a difference between the new middle class and workers of only 3 per cent, there is less class differentiation on this item than on any of the other items in Table 16.2.

Conclusion: Some Directions for Research

Four general conclusions can be drawn from the evidence. First, class patterns Canadians' beliefs about many features of the economy and politics, although across-class differences are small or medium in size. Second, the beliefs of the new middle class are quite similar to the beliefs of owners on many issues; therefore, class differentiation of beliefs is mainly a consequence of the distinctiveness of the beliefs of workers (although Michael Ornstein's 1985 study of élites suggests that the beliefs of the business class are also quite distinct). Third, workers' beliefs tend to stand out from other classes on issues that cue their experiential and subcultural knowledge of class inequalities (for example, whether workers get a fair share of what they produce) and, to a lesser extent, on issues that are framed by a populist counter-theme (for example, faith in grassroots decision-making). And fourth, on some economic beliefs the public sector branch of the new middle class is quite distinctive from the private sector branch, with the gap between the two sectors appearing to grow during the 1990s.

But is class declining in importance as a source for beliefs about the economy and politics? The four arguments presented at the beginning of this chapter present such a decline as inexorable. However, the survey data examined in this chapter, covering the period from the late 1970s to the late 1990s, show no evidence of such a decline. Additional research is needed to determine whether the relationship between class experiences and beliefs attenuated in the first 35 years after World War II. In addition, ongoing research must monitor the trends in the class differentiation of beliefs over the coming decades. That said, we also need to be suspicious of deterministic theories of inexorable trends; at any point in time, social or political movements may raise the profile of class interpretations in public debates, thus increasing the salience of class for individuals' economic and political beliefs (Hout et al. 1993: 260).

Much research needs to be done. To this point, Canadian researchers (this author included) have failed to develop research programs that integrate qualitative and quantitative approaches in the study of the relationship between class experiences and beliefs. Integrated research programs would be capable of exploring the many dimensions of class trajectories, class networks, and subcultures that affect the development of economic and political perspectives. This type of exploration would help us to better understand both across-class and within-class differences in beliefs, thus providing a more detailed picture of processes of class formation in contemporary Canada. Integrated research programs also have the potential to unravel some of the social-psychological processes that mediate the effects of class experiences on beliefs. And most importantly, they could treat class experience as gendered and formed by social relations involving nationality, race/ethnicity, and region. Political sociology would benefit from a much more nuanced understanding of the interaction of class and other types of social inequality in the making of economic and political consciousness.

Notes

1. For instance, in a recent British debate on the future of class analysis, Holton and Turner asked 'whether the persistence of academic class discourse tells more about the metaphorical flexibility of a concept that is at once an intellectualised label and a source of social identity with dichotomic, gradational, and/or functional overtones, as it does about power and inequality in contemporary societies' (1994: 904).

2. The principal investigators of the 1997 Canadian Election Study were André Blais, Elisabeth Gidengil, Richard Nadeau, and Neil Nevitte; of the 1993 Canadian Election Study were Richard Johnston, André Blais, Henry E. Brady, Elisabeth Gidengil and Neil Nevitte; of the 1988 Canadian Election Study were Richard Johnston, André Blais, Henry E. Brady and Jean Crête; and of the 1982–83 Canadian Class Project were John Myles and Wallace Clement. All four surveys were funded by the Social Sciences and Humanities Research Council of Canada (SSHRCC). The 1982 survey data were provided by the Carleton University Social Science Data Archives, and the data from the election studies were provided by the Institute for Social Research at York University. Neither SSHRCC nor the institutions which provided the data nor the principal investigators for the surveys bear any responsibility for the analyses and interpretations presented here.

References

Abercrombie, N., S. Hill, and B.S. Turner. 1980. *The Dominant Ideology Thesis* (London: George Allen and Unwin).

Abercrombie, N., and J. Urry. 1983. *Capital, Labour and the Middle Classes* (London: George Allen and Unwin).

Clark, T.N., and S.M. Lipset. 1991. 'Are Social Classes Dying?', *International Sociology* 6: 397–410.

———, and M. Rempel. 1993. 'The Declining Political Significance of Social Class', *International Sociology* 8: 293–316.

Clement, W., and J. Myles. 1994. *Relations of Ruling: Class and Gender in Postindustrial Societies* (Montreal and Kingston: McGill-Queen's University Press).

Dunk, T.W. 1991. *It's a Working Man's Town: Male Working-Class Culture in Northwestern Ontario* (Montreal and Kingston: McGill-Queen's University Press).

Edgell, S. 1993. *Class* (London: Routledge).

Ehrenreich, B., and J. Ehrenreich. 1977. 'The Professional-Managerial Class', *Radical America* 11: 7–31.

Gamson, W. 1992. *Talking Politics* (Cambridge: Cambridge University Press).

Giddens, A. 1984. *The Constitution of Society: Outline of the Theory of Structuration* (Berkeley, CA: University of California Press).

Goldthorpe, J.H., D. Lockwood, F. Beckhofer, and J. Platt. 1968. *The Affluent Worker: Political Attitudes and Behaviour* (Cambridge: Cambridge University Press).

Hodson, R., P.G. Schervish, and R. Stryker. 1989. 'Class Interests and Class Fractions in an Era of Economic Decline', *Research in Politics and Society* 3: 191–220.

Holton, R., and B.S. Turner. 1994. 'Debate and Pseudo-debate in Class Analysis: Some Unpromising Aspects of Goldthorpe and Marshall's Defence', *Sociology* 28: 799–804.

Hout, M., C. Brooks, and J. Manza. 1993. 'The Persistence of Classes in Post-Industrial Societies', *International Sociology* 8: 259–77.

Johnston, W.A., and D. Baer. 1993. 'Class Consciousness and National Contexts: Canada, Sweden and the United States in Historical Perspective', *Canadian Review of Sociology and Anthropology* 30: 271–95.

Johnston, W.A., and M.D. Ornstein. 1982. 'Class, Work, and Politics', *Canadian Review of Sociology and Anthropology* 19: 196–214.

———. 1985. 'Social Class and Political Ideology in Canada', *Canadian Review of Sociology and Anthropology* 22: 369–93.

Keddie, V. 1980. 'Class Identification and Party Preference among Manual Workers: The Influence of Community, Union Membership and Kinship', *Canadian Review of Sociology and Anthropology* 17: 24–36.

Kluegel, J.R., and E.R. Smith. 1986. *Beliefs About Inequality: Americans' Views of What Is and What Ought to Be* (New York: Aldine De Gruyter).

Lambert, R.D., S.D. Brown, J.E. Curtis, and B.J. Kay. 1986. 'Canadians' Beliefs About Differences between Social Classes', *Canadian Journal of Sociology* 11: 379–99.

Langford, T. 1996. 'The Politics of the Canadian New Middle Class: Public/Private Sector Cleavage in the 1980s', *Canadian Journal of Sociology* 21: 153–83.

———. 1992. 'Social Experiences and Variations in Economic Beliefs among Canadian Workers', *Canadian Review of Sociology and Anthropology* 29: 453–87.

Lash, S., and J. Urry. 1987. *The End of Organized Capitalism* (Madison, WI: The University of Wisconsin Press).

Marcuse, H. 1964. *One-Dimensional Man* (Boston: Beacon Press).

Marsh, P. 1967. *Anatomy of a Strike: Unions, Employers and Punjabi Workers in a Southall Factory* (London: Institute of Race Relations).

Marx, K. 1976 [1859]. *Preface and Introduction to A Contribution to the Critique of Political Economy* (Beijing: Foreign Languages Press).

Nisbet, R.A. 1972. 'The Decline and Fall of Social Classes'. In *The Impact of Social Class: A Book of Readings,* ed. P. Blumberg (New York: Thomas Y. Crowell), 49–61.

Ornstein, M. 1985. 'Canadian Capital and the Canadian State: Ideology in an Era of Crisis'. In *The Structure of the Canadian Capitalist Class,* ed. R.J. Brym (Toronto: Garamond Press).

Parkin, F. 1971. *Class Inequality and Political Order: Social Stratification in Capitalist and Communist Societies* (New York: Holt, Rinehart and Winston).

———. 1967. 'Working-Class Conservatives: A Theory of Political Deviance', *British Journal of Sociology* 18: 278–90.

Wright, E.O. 1979. *Class Structure and Income Determination* (New York: Academic Press).

———. 1989. 'Rethinking, Once Again, the Concept of Class Structure'. In *The Debate on Classes* (London: Verso), 269–348.

Chapter 17

The Politics of Housing: Issues of Social Class and Gender

Norine Verberg

Introduction

Research suggests that the provision and the allocation of housing is a complex political process influenced by governments and government bureaucracies, business lobbies, social movements, and political protests. This chapter discusses the role of government, social movements, and ideology in the development of a predominantly market-based approach to housing provision and allocation in Western capitalist democracies, with emphasis on the Canadian experience. One question to be asked here is whether housing conditions should be understood in terms of *housing classes* or *housing status groups*. An alternative perspective would be to understand housing inequalities as part of the experience of consumption (in this case, it is housing itself that is the 'consumable'), which in turn can influence class-based political participation. As in political discourse, theorists from different schools of thought agree that the attainment of decent housing and ownership of one's home has a conservative effect in society. How and why this conservatism is presumed to occur is the matter of much debate. The chapter concludes with a review of the more recent feminist research on gender, housing, and political participation, with an emphasis on the research on women as housing activists and the way that housing inequalities and beliefs about gender have influenced women's lobbying efforts.

Although this chapter is limited to issues of social class and gender, note that the politics of housing is influenced by other factors, such as race and ethnic relations. For instance, research indicates that there are variations in housing tenure and condition by race and ethnicity (Balakrishnan and Wu 1992; Phillips and Karn 1992; Ray and Moore 1991; Rex and Moore 1967) and that ethnic residential segregation, which is sometimes associated with variations in social class, is a feature of most Canadian cities (Balakrishnan 1976; Darroch and Marston 1972/73; Rex and Moore 1967). Efforts attempting to address racial inequalities and prejudice must recognize the importance of making domestic property ownership accessible to visible minorities in nations where homeownership is the dominant tenure form (Phillips and Karn 1992).

The Political Conservatism Thesis and the Promotion of Homeownership Ideology

Homeownership may be accompanied by a distinctive pattern of beliefs about the preference of ownership as opposed to rental. *Homeownership ideology* refers to the belief that homeownership is superior to private (or public) rental housing because individual homeowners *and* society benefit in significant ways. Homeowners benefit because they accumulate wealth and achieve increased social status and personal security. Society is said to benefit—at least from the perspective of those who would like to see the 'status quo' preserved—because individual homeowners will act conservatively to protect their investment. Under this perspective, even the poorest citizens will act conservatively to protect the savings they have tied up in their home (Agnew 1981; Doling and Stafford 1989; Rakoff 1977; Sullivan 1989).

Homeownership ideology is rooted in certain urban housing reform movements developed in response to early twentieth-century urbanization, which was accompanied by widespread poverty, disease, and social and political unrest (Allen 1973; Rutherford 1979). At the turn of the twentieth century, urban populations across the country grew at an astonishing rate: in a 10-year period, Toronto's population doubled, Winnipeg's tripled, and Vancouver's quadrupled (Allen 1973). As the population of cities swelled, the housing situation became desperate. Across the country, shanty towns permeated and surrounded towns and cities and overcrowding and homelessness became commonplace. Civic officials were concerned about overcrowding in congested slums because it threatened social and political stability and reflected badly on the nation (Rutherford 1979: 375).

The housing crisis was a political crisis, and the solution was a matter of considerable debate. Some reformers proposed that the crisis was best resolved through the provision of low-cost public rental housing. Other reformers condemned this strategy as too 'socialist' and instead sought solutions within a private provision and allocation framework including incentives to builders to construct low-priced rental units and the extension of homeownership to the working class (Bacher 1993). Those who promoted homeownership as a solution to the housing crisis (and the political agitation it produced) propagated the

view that homeownership by the majority would ensure social order. To use the words of American housing reformers Lawrence Veiller and John Nolan (in the 1930s), homeownership fosters 'a conservative point of view in the working man' (quoted in *Public Opinion* 1986: 21).

The thesis that homeownership promotes conservatism has influenced the housing policies of successive governments throughout the century (Bacher 1993). While the tactic of using geographic dispersion of the working class ('breaking neighbourhoods') was occasionally employed to reduce working-class militancy, most governments supported policies aimed at winning working-class loyalty through the provision of better housing and working conditions (Esping-Andersen 1985: 179–80). American political scientists have noted that successive governments sought a political dividend in justifying housing policy, making homeownership broadly accessible (Kingston, Thompson, and Eichar 1984; Perin 1977). Echoing this dominant belief, Perin (1977: 78) suggests that '[t]hese last forty years of longer mortgage terms and easier credit may have to be regarded as a period in the history of industrialized democracy when homeownership was converted into a major social solution to the unmistakable contradiction between actual social inequalities and an egalitarian ideology'.

The Promotion of Private Housing Tenure and Homeownership by the State

In Canada and other Western nations the majority of housing is allocated through the private homeownership and rental housing markets. The key players in Canadian policy development and implementation aggressively promoted a market approach to housing provision that favoured homeownership by the majority of households and private rental provision (over and above public or social housing) for everybody else (see

Bacher 1993). Social housing, the alternative to private strategies, plays a different role in the housing mix of various countries, and the efforts of the state to affect this mix can have political ramifications (Bacher 1993; Sewell 1994). Until recently, social housing in Canada was limited to very few so-called public housing units that consisted of centrally administered, low-quality dwellings used as a solution to the housing affordability and accessibility problems of the poorest citizens. By contrast, public strategies were developed in nations such as Britain and Sweden as the preferred way to house the general population. Nonetheless, homeownership has become the dominant tenure form in most Western nations since the postwar period, with levels ranging from 50 to 70 per cent (Esping-Andersen 1985; Kemeny 1978; Saunders 1990). In Canada, the level of homeownership peaked in 1941 at 66 per cent, and since 1976, it has remained at about 62 per cent (Che-Alford 1990; Harris 1986b). The level of social or public housing has remained low in Canada (Bacher 1993; Bourne 1986; Burke 1990; Sewell 1994), and levels have declined in those nations where social housing was once a sizeable portion of the housing stock (for example, Britain) (Dunleavy 1979; Sullivan 1989).

Since 1938, when the federal government passed the *National Housing Act* (NHA) and enacted legislation to promote owner-occupation as the dominant tenure form, the level of homeownership has been influenced by federal (and provincial) housing policies (Sewell 1994: 81f). Since the early 1970s, when rising property values out-priced the accessibility of middle-income urban households to purchase homes, housing market adaptations *and* Canadian housing policies were instrumental in maintaining the homeownership level at around 62 per cent (Doyle and Hulchanski 1990). Although the housing industry responded by producing lower-priced homes and condominiums (for example, smaller units, suburban locations), Doyle and Hulchanski

(1990: 75–6) provide substantial evidence that government programs have been far more important than market strategies in maintaining the national homeownership level (that is, through the taxation system and federal and provincial housing programs)[1] (also see Bacher 1994; Miron 1988; Sewell 1994).

Internationally, housing policies have generally promoted homeownership and thereby served to shape or reinforce beliefs about the superiority of homeownership (Doling and Stafford 1989; Kemeny 1978, 1981, 1983; Sullivan 1989). In Britain, Sullivan contends that the government attempted to influence public perceptions of housing tenure as a means of gaining support for a shift from social to private housing allocation. This, he argues was part of an overall political program aimed at promoting the privatization of public assets (Bassett 1980). In the British Conservative Party discourse on housing policy throughout the 1980s, homeownership was referred to as a 'deep and natural desire', and later, as a 'social right', a theme which was reflected in the Conservative government's Right to Buy legislation (James, Jordon, and Kay 1991; Sullivan 1989). Thus, Sullivan (1989: 187) argued that 'housing tenure categories (were) ideologically constructed' in an attempt to sway public support away from public tenancy (called council housing), which, prior to 1980, accounted for approximately 32 per cent of all housing. Britain's Conservative government has since established policies that guided the sale of much of its public housing stock.

There has always been a strong lobby promoting social housing in Canada (Bacher 1993; Chouinard 1989; Sewell 1994; Skelton 1996; Wekerle 1993). It is useful here to make a distinction between *social housing* and *public housing*. Social housing is designed to provide specific target groups with housing geared to their social and economic needs (for example, dwellings managed by agencies such as the local chapters of the

Canadian Mental Health Association to provide supportive housing for ex-psychiatric patients and community-based housing developed for teenage mothers that provides on-location services including child care and social, educational, and medical services). Sewell (1994: 162–70) identifies two forms of nonprofit social housing including community-based housing (developed and run in the usual landlord-tenant format by community agencies) and cooperative housing (developed and operated by tenant committees).

By contrast, public housing is run by a central state bureaucracy and, while it typically provides affordable dwellings, it does not usually provide other services aimed at addressing the social needs of the tenants (for example, a social worker in an apartment building housing elderly women or people with physical disabilities).

Social housing has received *very* limited state support in Canada (Bacher 1993; Chouinard 1989; Sewell 1994; Skelton 1996). In part, this is because of the lobby *against* social housing. According to Sewell, some people view social housing as a 'hand-out' or a form of welfare that provides housing in a more costly way than could be provided through the private rental market. Social housing *is* assisted housing as it relies on financing from the state. Whether or not it is more costly (to taxpayers) than housing provided through the private market is a matter of some debate for, as Sewell (1994: 164) notes, 'all housing—private, public, ownership, and rental—is assisted in some way by government programs, public funds or tax expenditures.' Nonetheless, arguments against social housing are powerful because some of the rancorous images of certain public housing tenants, portrayed as a drain on the public purse, provide the imagery fitting the so-called deserving victim.

Although there has been opposition to social housing by members of the housing industry and middle-class homeowners, Bacher (1993) argues that the development of social housing in Canada was largely impeded due to the 'ingenious machinations' of W.C. Clark, deputy minister of finance between 1933 and 1953, and a few other powerful federal civil servants, including Clark's predecessors. Clark was steadfast in his promotion of a market approach to housing provision and allocation. Bacher seems convinced that W.C. Clark was not motivated to promote the economic interests of those who benefited from private housing provision, but rather by his belief that private corporations could 'plan' healthy, urban settings that would serve the best interest of everybody in the community including the poorest citizens. Bacher (1993: 14) notes that these and other ideological beliefs about the appropriate place of the private market in public life influenced the shape of housing policy at all levels of government. For instance, under the leadership of Premier Manning, Alberta's Social Credit government blocked the construction of all social housing from 1949 to 1966.

Bacher (1993) argues that the history of the social housing movement reveals the importance of the 'Red Tory' tradition in Canadian public policy development.[2] Prominent businessmen and philanthropists joined with labour and urban and housing reformers to form a 'fierce chorus of protest' against the policies of the federal government which forestalled the development of social housing. The movement successfully lobbied for amendments to the *National Housing Act* which shifted power to municipalities, thus allowing the development of social housing at the local level. The fact that there has been uneven development of social housing across the country reflects the importance of local leadership in the provision of social housing (Bacher 1993; Magnusson 1985; Skelton 1996; Wade 1994).

Government programs and legislation reflect the complexity of the housing system as well as the disparate interests of various groups. Housing policies influence the economic interests of private landlords, bankers, developers, realtors, and contractors in the housing industry. For this reason, these groups organize to exert political pressure to influence policy development (Bacher 1993; Dreier and Atlas 1995; Sewell 1994). The belief that the housing industry can serve economic goals lends support to demands made by actors in the housing industry (Skelton 1996). Renters and homeowners may have different stakes in the outcome of various policies, yet historically renters have had more issues with their landlords than with the homeowners in their neighbourhoods. (The exception is typically homeowners protesting the establishment of group homes or public housing apartments.) Dreier has studied the tenants' movement in the United States. His research indicates that renters' protests and political activities have been 'episodic' especially compared to the sustained political activities of members of the housing industry (1978: 255). Sewell (1994: 117) suggests that tenants have received less attention by policy writers because they are generally less well off than are homeowners and because they have less political leverage. In addition, elected officials and senior civil servants tend to be homeowners who do not understand the problems experienced by people who rent their dwellings. Nonetheless, governments have had to answer to rent strikes and political protests by tenants. For instance, Harris (1986a: 72) argued that the emergence of the Single Tax Movement in the nineteenth century 'gained impetus from the fact that most urban Canadians at the time were tenants'. He also cites research by Dalzell and Saywell who attributed much of the social unrest in Canada following World War I to high housing costs and housing shortages.

The role of state housing policies in the formation of the class system has been the subject of some discussion (Chouinard 1978; Dreier and Atlas 1995; Law 1994). For instance, Laws (1994) argued that, by reinforcing spatial segregation of certain groups of citizens the local state reproduces social marginalization. In her case study of deinstitutionalization in Metropolitan Toronto, Laws focused on a policy requiring the city officials to notify residents of proposals to establish a group home in their neighbourhood, thus providing residents an opportunity to intervene in the decision-making process.[3] Typically, neighbourhood groups formed to fight for zoning by-law amendments aimed at prohibiting group homes from opening in their jurisdiction. This, according to Laws, represents an instance of state policy serving more powerful urban residents who are better able to use the political process to reproduce their own advantaged social position. As a result, group homes have been largely confined to small, ghetto-like areas of the city, such as the Parkdale region in Toronto.

Housing, Social Class, and Political Participation

Housing has always been a central aspect of the Canadian class structure (Forcese 1975; Hunter 1986; Pineo 1988; Porter 1965). Social inequalities are reproduced as housing inequalities with variations in housing tenure, housing affordability, and dwelling size, condition, and location (Bird 1990; Blakeney 1992; Burke 1990; Che-Alford 1990; Filion and Bunting 1990). Who owns and who rents reflects patterns of social class (Bourne 1986; Che-Alford 1990; Harris 1986b). For instance, in 1974, those who were self-employed were far more likely to own domestic property than were white- and blue-collar workers (Harris 1986b). Similarly, in 1986, 85 per cent of households with incomes of $50,000 or more were owner-occupied compared to 74 per cent of households with incomes between $35,000 and $50,000, 57 per cent of households with incomes between $15,000 and $35,000, and 38 per cent of households with incomes less than $15,000 (Che-Alford 1990). Research by Doyle and Hulchanski (1990) shows an income-tenure polarization, whereby the proportion of lower-income Canadians who own domestic property has gradually declined over the past 20 years. This same phenomenon has occurred in Britain, where Bentham (1986) speculates that the polarization of tenure and income will continue to grow. Ironically, government policies in Canada may have played a part in this polarization. For example, prior to the 1960s, the Canadian Mortgage and Housing Corporation regarded homeownership as unsuitable for low-income households, even though many families in this income group had achieved the status without subsidies of any sort (Steele 1993: 44–5).

There has been considerable attention paid to the influence of housing on class-based political participation by neo-Marxists and neo-Weberians. Marxists and Weberians agree that social inequalities influence political participation, yet there is considerable disagreement on the relationship between class and political activism. Such questions become even more complex when the influence of housing is theorized.

Neo-Marxist Urban Sociology: The Political Incorporation Thesis

For the most part, neo-Marxists have paid little attention to the political ramification of housing and urban reform movements because they believe that social change is based solely in the relations of production (Jaret 1983: 519). In other words, what happens in the workplace (the relationship between employers and employees) is paramount, and little else matters in the long run. Those departing from this position argue that while workers' struggles originate in the workplace they become 'displaced' into the community as workers organize to secure basic necessities including decent and affordable housing (Castells 1977, 1978, 1983; Edel 1982; Harvey 1976, 1978). These urban neo-Marxists concur with other Marxists that housing conditions and housing tenure are derivatives of social class. Nonetheless, they argue that it may influence

class-based political action. Among the first to discuss the political implications of homeownership and housing reform for workers' political orientation was Frederick Engels. In *The Housing Question* (1935), Engels coined the term *the political incorporation thesis* to refer to the conservatizing influence homeownership would have on workers. Engels believed that if workers were successful in acquiring better housing and gaining access to homeownership, they would become 'incorporated' into the ideology of capitalism. Owner-occupation serves as an ideological tool in a capitalist economic system because it promotes values such as self-reliance and support for private property rights which in turn support the status quo (Agnew 1981; Bell 1992). Moreover, homeownership ideology portrays homeowners as more stable, thrifty, and better planners, and renters as transient, marginal, and disrespecting of property and property rights (Agnew 1981; Halle 1984; Perin 1977; Rakoff 1977). This sort of 'victim blaming ideology' serves to privatize discontent (Bell 1992: 175). The implication for the Marxist theory of social change is that homeownership may undermine working-class unity and collective efforts to overthrow capitalist relations of production because workers who buy houses may avoid activities, such as strikes, that disrupt the status quo.

Engels' early theorizing on the implications of 'consumption' on capitalist relations has been discussed and elaborated in a variety of ways (see Jaret 1983). Harvey (1978: 118) argued that movements designed to improve housing and urban conditions were a 'springboard for class action rather than an antidote to class struggle'. Faced with great hardship, workers organized rent strikes, occupied public buildings, and protested for or against various urban renewal schemes. In response to their demands, capitalists intervened by promoting homeownership, lowering costs of basic necessities (food, housing, clothing), and encouraging high levels of consumption in an effort to further capitalist accumulation and to preserve their dominance. Harvey (1978) goes further than most theorists, believing that the extension of homeownership to the working class was a *deliberate* goal of the capitalist class.

Research on Working-class Homeownership and Class-based Politics

Studies testing the political incorporation thesis confirm that working-class homeowners will be more involved in mainstream social and political activities and more conservative than working-class tenants (Aitkin and Kahan 1983; Butler and Stokes 1969; Dunleavy 1979; Ineichen 1972; Kemp 1978; Kingston, Thompson, and Eichar 1984; Pratt 1987; Särlvik and Crewe 1983; Peterson 1990). Australian (Aitkin and Kahan 1983) and British (Butler and Stoke 1969; Dunleavy 1979; Särlvik and Crewe 1983) research indicates that working-class homeownership is associated with electoral conservatism. During the transition from social to private housing provision in Britain, purchasers of council housing were more likely to vote for the Conservative Party than nonpurchasers (Williams, Sewell, and Twine 1987) and among union members, homeowners were more likely to vote for the Conservative Party (Peterson 1990). However, an American study using national election data produced mixed results (Kingston, Thompson, and Eichar 1984: 144–5). For instance, in 1976, but not in 1980, American working-class homeowners voted more often for the Republican presidential candidate than did renters, and homeownership interacted with length of residence to predict identification with the Republican Party. Although Pratt (1987) found that 'housing tenure is also associated with political attitudes', the pattern of results did not provide support for the political incorporation thesis as housing tenure was associated with political attitudes more often

for skilled white-collar workers and managers (13 out of 16 attitudes) than it was for skilled blue-collar workers (2 out of 16 attitudes).

Neo-Weberian Urban Sociology: Housing Classes and Political Cleavage

In Britain, several researchers observed that the spread of homeownership to more working-class households coincided with a dramatic decline of class voting (Garrahan 1977; Goldthorpe et al. 1967, 1969; Parkins 1967). To explain this *class dealignment* (whereby members of the working class shifted their vote from the Labour Party to the Conservative Party), sociologists and political scientists theorized that the status based in consumption practices *stratifies* workers and thereby erodes traditional class loyalties. In other words, affluent workers who gain social status through consumption practices may develop new beliefs about their place in the class structure and, in turn, change their political orientation (Goldthorpe and Lockwood 1967, 1969).[4] Thus, consumption practices, including whether or not one owns a home, can influence the *class self-image* of people who have similar work lives. Among American blue-collar workers, Halle (1984: 228) found that workers 'have two separate images of their place in the class structure, one referring to life at work (the "working man") and one referring to life outside work (being "middle class" or "lower middle class")'. Moreover, homeownership figured centrally in workers' conception of what it means to be middle class.[5]

Since then, neo-Weberian urban sociologists have debated the relevance of the 'consumption sphere' as the basis of a political cleavage. Housing tenure became a central aspect of that debate since Rex and Moore (1967) argued that seven housing classes arise out of the competition over scarce preferred housing (based on criterion including tenure, location, size, and condition).

They argued that 'men [sic] in the same labour situation may come to have differential degrees of access to housing and it is this which immediately determines the class conflicts of the city as distinct from those of the workplace' (1967: 274). Rex and Moore contended that Weber gave equal consideration to ownership of domestic property and ownership of the means of production in his analysis of the formation of classes. Haddon (1970) disputed Rex and Moore's conceptualization of seven housing classes, arguing that they do not represent class divisions as either Marx or Weber defined the term. Instead he proposed that the seven categories were best understood as *housing status groups*.

Although many theorists concurred with Haddon's criticisms of Rex and Moore's seven housing classes, some argued that *housing tenure* (as opposed to housing amenities) provides the basis for a distinct class formation because homeowners and tenants have different objective interests (Dunleavy 1979; Saunders 1978). In his early theorizing, Saunders (1978: 234) argued that homeownership is 'the basis for the formation of a distinct political force' because owner-occupation generates significant wealth for individual homeowners. Later, Saunders 'wish(ed) to abandon the attempt to theorize homeownership as a determinant of class structuration', arguing that any attempt to view homeowners as a property class 'overextends class theory and ultimately fails to relate class relations generated around ownership of domestic property to those generated around ownership of means of production' (1984: 206). Nonetheless, he maintained that because domestic property ownership is a means of wealth accumulation, it does provide a basis for a distinct pattern of political alignment by owners versus nonowners at the local level (over land use conflicts) and at the national level (over questions of housing policy and housing finance) (1984: 203). Thus, consumption sector theorists believe that homeownership creates a political cleavage, separate and distinct from the cleavage based in class relations, because homeownership creates a sectoral alignment based on shared interests (Dunleavy 1979; Saunders 1978, 1984, 1990; Thorns 1981).

Consumption sector theorists argue that sociologists have ignored the influence of the consumption sector on social organization and political participation (see Warde 1990). Pratt (1986) has argued that consumption choices can influence the decisions people make about where and how much to work in the paid labour force. She notes that the homeownership rates for dual-earner couples are significantly higher than single-earner couples, suggesting that women's employment patterns are influenced by couples' consumption decisions. Filion (1991) has argued that the process of gentrification (up-grading older, 'distinctive' housing stock in inner-city neighbourhoods) involves class structuration and social polarization because the homeowners, who disproportionately come from the 'new middle class', benefit at the expense of lower-income residents. He notes that although homeownership is viewed as an individual pursuit, gentrification has occurred because middle-class homeowners have acted collectively to use the political system to promote their common interests. Like other consumption sector theorists, Filion is critical of neo-Marxists for their failure to recognize that consumption can have implications for patterns of social stratification, social organization, and political participation.

There are some notable differences in the assumptions of neo-Marxists and neo-Weberians. Saunders (1990) believes that homeownership gained popularity primarily because ordinary people can and do make significant financial gains that they would not be able to earn from traditional forms of savings. This position stands in sharp contrast to many neo-Marxists who believe that workers are 'co-opted' by the provision of homeownership and that the benefits of homeownership are largely illusionary. And, as suggested above, while neo-Marxists believe that one's consumption will be determined by one's place in the class structure, consumption sector theorists believe that there is not necessarily any correspondence between the production and consumption spheres, especially as they pertain to political participation (see Warde 1990).

Research on Homeownership and Political Conservatism

Although some studies are now somewhat dated, there is considerable support provided by American researchers for the hypothesis that homeowners will have greater *political involvement at the local level*. Compared to tenants, homeowners are more knowledgeable about local affairs (Sykes 1951); more involved in community events and local politics (Alford and Scoble 1968; Steinberger 1981); more involved in neighbourhood activism (Agnew 1981; Cox 1982), make more demands on local government; and join voluntary associations and interact with neighbours more (Blum and Kingston 1984; Fischer 1982). Housing tenure appears to have a negligible effect on *political participation at the national level*, with the rather consistent exception that homeowners are more likely to register to vote and to turn out to vote at the national (Kingston, Thompson, and Eichar 1984; Pratt 1987) and state levels (Alford and Scoble 1968).

Housing tenure appears to have some effect on *partisanship*, although the results are weak and inconsistent (Kingston, Thompson, and Eichar 1984: 141; *Public Opinion*, 1986: 21). A study based on eight American Gallup Polls in 1985 indicated no difference between renters and owner on partisan identification although homeowners were more likely to describe themselves as conservative and renters were more likely to see themselves as liberal (*Public Opinion* 1986: 28). For instance, among middle-income earners,

aged 30 to 62, 42 per cent of homeowners described themselves as conservative compared to 29 per cent of renters, and 35 per cent of homeowners described themselves as traditional compared to 17 per cent of renters.

With very few exceptions, research indicates that housing tenure is not associated with *political attitudes* after the effects of other variables such as income, age, or occupational class have been controlled for (Kingston, Thompson, and Eichar 1984; *Public Opinion* 1986: 24–5). In fact, the authors of the *Public Opinion* study stated that '[i]n our examination of hundreds of survey questions for this section (attitudes on social issues), we have found no substantial difference between the attitudes of owners and renters, especially when we controlled for income'. There were only two exceptions (that is, policy issues related to homeownership or renting). Nonetheless, Blum and Kingston (1984: 169) found that housing tenure was associated with commitment to conventional values (that is, attitudes toward premarital sex, legalization of marijuana, allowing homosexuals to teach school, and abortion rights for women) and Pratt (1987: 45) found that homeowners were more conservative than renters on some conservatism measures.[6]

Using data drawn from the 1984 Canadian National Election Study, Verberg (1995) tested the political conservatism hypothesis for a national sample of Canadians. Table 17.1 shows the differences in average (mean) scores between owners and renters for a variety of political involvement and political conservatism measures. These means have been 'adjusted' to control for age, income level, and other relevant variables. The results indicate that, while homeowners were more likely to vote than tenants, homeowners and tenants did not differ in their levels of participation in federal politics or support for public institutions. Homeowners were more conservative than tenants on economic and moral matters but they did not differ in their attitudes toward

Table 17.1 The Effects of Housing Tenure on Political Involvement and Political Conservatism with MCA Controls[1]

Dependent Variables	Adjusted Means		Number of Cases	Significance of Difference[2]
	Owners	Renters		
Vote in 1984 Election[a]	.88	.81	3,306	***
Participation in Politics[b]	2.04	2.03	3,280	NS
Support for Institutions[c]	5.69	5.66	2,249	NS
Economic Conservatism[d]	1.97	1.92	2,862	***
Moral Conservatism[d]	3.73	3.60	2,793	***
Labour Rights[d]	3.13	3.11	3,014	*
Military Intervention[d]	2.65	2.64	2,544	NS

[1] **Statistical controls for:** family income, region, city size, education, gender, occupation, material satisfaction, and marital status. Age was covaried.

[2] **Significance Levels:** * = $p < .05$; ** = $p < .01$; *** = $p < .001$

[a-d] **Coding the Dependent Variables:** [a] Coded 0 (did not vote) and 1 (voted); [b] Coded from 1 (lowest participation) to 4 (highest participation); [c] Coded from 1 (lowest support) to 10 (highest support); [d] Coded from 1 (least conservative) to 5 (most conservative)

labour rights or military intervention. These findings indicate that the pattern of results for a Canadian sample are similar to the results for studies conducted abroad.

Housing, Gender, and Political Participation

In recent years, research and theorizing has focused on the housing inequalities experienced by women and the implications of gender norms and housing inequalities on women's political participation. Clearly, gender inequalities are reflected in housing inequalities (McClain and Doyle 1983; Munro and Smith 1989; Wekerle 1993). For instance, compared to men in similar family circumstances, women are far more likely to rent rather than own, to occupy smaller dwellings, to live in public or social housing, to have a housing affordability problem, and to be unsatisfied with their dwelling (that is, inadequate in terms of size and amenities) (Che-Alford 1990: 5; McClain and Doyle 1983: 73). The lower homeownership levels among single women and female lone-parents (compared to their male counterparts) reflects economic disparities rooted in gender inequalities (McClain and Doyle 1983; Munro and Smith 1989; Watson 1986) and the fact that women have experienced gender discrimination when seeking mortgage credit (Card 1980: 216). According to Card, there have been three socially acceptable models for homeownership by women until recently: (1) homeownership by separated and divorced women who remain in the family home to raise children; (2) homeownership by widows living in the marital home; and (3) homeownership by single 'spinsters' who inherit a home from the parents. In all cases, women became homeowners as a result of a family relationship. Women were not considered housing 'consumers' but instead were considered 'inheritors' of the family home. Lenders were reluctant to include wives' incomes in calculations of mortgage loans (that is, they believed women withdrew from the paid labour force once they became pregnant). And although women were important economic actors in the household, this was not reflected in the legal titles to the home, which, as Card notes, were social constructions and legal fictions.

The political struggle over the provision and allocation of housing has not been gender-neutral. This fact is reflected in a growing literature on women's political activism in tenant movements (Lawson and Barton 1980; Lawson, Barton, and Weissman Joselit 1980; Perlman Schoenberg 1980), urban reform movements (Gittel and Shtob 1980), the women's housing movement (Hayden 1981; Wekerle 1993), the 'safe spaces' movement (Klodawksy, Lundy, and Andrews 1994; MacLeod 1989), and the transition housing movement (housing aimed to support women leaving abusive relationships) (Kenny and Magnusson 1993; Peters 1990; Walker 1990).

There is a long and rich tradition of feminist theoretical concerns having to do with housing and urban planning (Eichler 1995; Hayden 1981; Peterson, Wekerle, and Morley 1978; Spain 1993; Wekerle 1980). Feminists such as Spain (1993) have argued that the home is anything but a 'haven' for women; rather, it is the site of women's oppression. Many feminists identify the private/public separation of home and public life as central to women's secondary status in society (Hayden 1981). Similarly, feminist planners have argued that the *built environment*—our homes, streets, public buildings, shopping areas, workplaces—are 'man-made' structures and institutions that reflect and reinforce the patriarchal social arrangements (MacGregor 1985).

Research on the history of women's political activism in housing and urban reform movements indicates that prevailing gender norms shaped women's activities. Although women played key roles in the tenant movements in the earlier part of the century, they were typically excluded from positions of political power because traditional gender norms defined leadership roles as appropriate for men and service roles as appropriate for women (Lawson and Barton 1980; Lawson, Barton, and Weissman Joselit 1980). Moreover, the goals defined for women volunteers during efforts to reform housing were such that women occupied a 'special sphere' in shaping the moral development of the nation through their nurturing roles as mothers. Thus, middle-class women volunteers in settlement houses set out to teach working-class women 'proper' care of children and the home (in keeping with an emerging ideology of motherhood) (Gittell and Shtob 1980). However, women soon redefined their initial goal of educating mothers and instead launched into political action to demand better conditions for poor urban residents. As Gittell and Shtob (1980) point out, many women became political leaders because their ideas about housing reform and social change were transformed by their experiences of working in poor neighbourhoods. Women's political activities expanded to include conducting surveys to document poor housing conditions, organizing the first American national conference on city planning, and enlisting working-class women in support of housing reform proposals. Women's organizations were instrumental advocates for the first public housing legislation in the United States (Birch 1978).

Not all women active in reforming housing adopted traditional, normative views of the family and women's role in the 'private' sphere of the home. Hayden's (1981) research focused on examples of social change in the organization of the household that were informed by a feminist understanding of gender relations. She argued that feminist beliefs guided American women and women's collectives throughout the century to create houses designed to 'socialize' housework (cleaning and cooking) and motherwork (child care). They did so because they believed that women's family roles in the private sphere were the basis of gender inequality. Feminist understandings of the relationship between gender norms and housing inequalities have been the impetus for much contemporary political action by women. In recent years, Canadian women have successfully lobbied the federal government for changes in housing policies to allow women's groups across the country to propose and develop social housing specifically designed to address the particular needs of certain groups of women such as teenage mothers and their children, native women, and older single women (Wekerle 1993). Activists argue that women continue to experience systematic discrimination in the housing market and that traditional housing design and allocation perpetuates traditional gender relations that disadvantage many women. Since 1986, more than 75 nonprofit cooperative housing projects have been developed and controlled by women, providing more than 1,500 units (Wekerle 1993).

The promotion of 'safe space' has been urged by women's groups concerned about violence against women in their homes and on the streets (Klodawsky, Lundy, and Andrew 1994). Since 1984 when a group of women in Metropolitan Toronto established METRAC (Metropolitan Action Committee on Public Violence Against Women) women have worked with municipalities across the country to make city streets and passageways safer for women. The Ontario Women's Directorate funded a study on sexual harassments of tenants (Novac 1992) which has been used as the basis for policy development (Klodawsky, Lundy, and Andrew 1994). Also, feminist activism has been somewhat successful in the establishment of transition houses, although there has been considerable discussion of the resistance of

the state to support feminist approaches to addressing domestic violence (Kenny and Magnusson 1993; Peters 1990; Walker 1990). Kenny and Magnusson examined the Women's House Saving Action (1985–6) in which feminists fought to save Vancouver's only transition house for battered women. The protest activities included an eight-month occupation of the transition house by women in an attempt to stop the British Columbia Social Credit government from following through on its plan to close the facility. When this failed, the movement expanded to include local, provincial, and federal lobbying efforts to establish a new, feminist-managed transition house. Although the City of Vancouver endorsed a proposal to establish another transition house that would also operate as a feminist-based advocacy centre, the province provided funding to the (presumably non-feminist) Salvation Army to provide the service. The women continued their lobbying efforts, and although they had the support of the City of Vancouver, funding was given to two other groups that would provide services to battered women from Native and immigrant communities. Kenny and Magnusson noted that, although the Social Credit government wanted to remove state support from feminist advocacy, its resistance actually expanded state support of feminist-based services for battered women (they note that even the Salvation Army had hired feminists to develop its transition program). Walker has also noted the resistance of government to endorse feminist understandings of domestic violence and the efforts to de-politicize the issue.

Although some feminists have identified 'the home', in particular the single family dwelling, as a site of women's oppression (for example, Spain 1993), others contend that women and men experience housing differently, owing to the fact that gender norms construct a private/public split (Madigan, Munro, and Smith 1990). Nonetheless, research on housing preferences indicates that both men and women prefer to own than rent, and that homeownership is a primary part of women's social identities (Saunders 1989). Some research suggests that homeownership as an 'exchange commodity' is equally important to women and men. For instance, there is a literature indicating that women's labour force participation varies by housing tenure, such that dual-earner couples are more likely to be homeowners than single-earner couples (Clark, Deurloo, and Dieleman 1994; Pratt 1986; Starkey and Port 1993). Second, researchers have documented women's activism in securing equal access to mortgage credit (Card 1980; Gelb and Lief Palley 1977). Challenges to mortgage discrimination by sex and marital status occurred in response to the lobbying efforts of women and the changing attitudes about gender roles and relations. In the United States, women's organizations formed a coalition to lobby for the passage of the Equal Credit Opportunity Act (Gelb and Lief Palley 1977). These are the few studies that consider women's political activities to promote women's homeownership, regardless of family status. Far more research explores women as advocates for alternatives to homeownership.

Conclusion

This chapter provides a brief introduction to the politics of housing. The research in the area gives one a sense that the provision and allocation of housing is a complex political process involving the competition of interests and ideas. Because shelter is a basic and fundamental need, and because of its association with wealth and perhaps wealth accumulation, housing will always remain on the political agenda. The majority of Western nations allocate housing through the private market, although the policies guiding private provision vary greatly from one nation to the next. For example, Sweden's housing policy prevents land speculation which keeps house price inflation in keeping with the average inflation rate

(Bacher 1993). If current political trends are any indication of the direction of future housing policy, then we can predict that the very slow but steady expansion of social housing in Canada will be curtailed in the near future. The degree to which social housing will be cut back will depend upon the public reactions to further cuts. Media reports of the chilling death of homeless women and men in the dead of winter make Canadians aware of growing housing disparities and the rising rate of homelessness. Political reactions in the past have depended upon the public's understanding of where to cast blame. Clearly the sway of political thought toward the political right suggests that victim-blaming themes may prevail at this time over beliefs that government is accountable for the welfare of the citizenry.

Theorists writing on housing provision and allocation hold assumptions about the *best* way to provide housing. Because of his enthusiastic support of homeownership, some of Saunders' peers have referred to him as the sociological representative of the New Right. Saunders believes that homeownership is a good thing because it distributes wealth to ordinary citizens and because it awakens citizens to their place in the political process, thereby bolstering democracy. Saunders refers to a nation where the majority of households are owner-occupied as 'a property-owning democracy'. What Saunders and other advocates of private housing provision do not adequately recognize or address is that society does not constitute a free-standing collection of economic equals. Clearly the exercise of citizenship rights—the ability to run for public office, the ability to challenge others in legal actions, the ability to exercise political rights—is effectively precluded in the absence of economic resources, which in turn are strongly tied to the ownership of property. Social theorists who are critics of government policies endorsing private provision and allocation of housing contend that the political system contributes to class structuration and social polarization. Although some research supports their claims, more attention needs to be given to how the political system in Canada influences the level of housing inequality in society and the benefits associated with various forms of housing.

Feminism has challenged many taken-for-granted assumptions about what roles women and men ought to play in public and private life. The feminist critique of housing and urban planning has inspired political action by many women to transform the built environment. Feminist challenges have led to some changes,

such as the establishment of transition houses, the development of women's housing, and access to mortgage credit. Nonetheless, housing and other policies influencing women's work and family roles continue to be gendered in ways that disadvantage women. Also, the political tide supporting conservative options on the right of centre does not bode well for feminists striving for equality. In fact, in this environment of expanding privatization, feminists will likely find it increasingly difficult to secure governmental support for social housing.

Notes

1. Some of the federal programs aimed at promoting homeownership include: the Assisted Homeownership Program (1973–8), the First Time Home Buyers Grant (1974–5), the Registered Homeownership Savings Plan (1974–85), the Residential Rehabilitation Assistance Program (since 1974), the Canadian Home Insulation Program (1974–86), the Canada Mortgage Renewal Plan (1980–3), the Canada Homeownership Stimulation Plan (1982–3), the Canada Home Renovation Plan (1982–3), and the Mortgage Rate Protection Program (since 1984) (Doyle and Hulchanski 1990: 75–6).

2. 'Red Tory' refers to Conservatives who nonetheless support social program expenditure, in contrast to the Conservatives (such as Ontario's Mike Harris) whose main social policy orientation is to cut program spending.

3. Deinstitutionalization refers to the policy overseeing the relocation of long-term psychiatric patients from public psychiatric hospitals to supportive housing in the community.

4. For some time, sociologists have recognized the relevance of consumption in communicating social differentiation (Rainwater 1974). Ownership of a single-family house is an influential assessment of status because it is associated with success, security, and stability (Agnew 1981; Perin 1977; Porter 1965; Rainwater 1974; Seeley, Sim, and Loosely 1956; Warner and Lunt 1949).

5. Two separate studies on the meaning of social class to Canadians suggest that 'what one has' is central to people's conception of social class, particularly for those in the lower strata (Grabb and Lambert 1982; Lambert et al. 1986). Theory suggests that those in the lower social strata are more likely to think of class in economic terms (that is, wealth, what one owns), whereas those in the higher social strata are more likely to think of class in more complex ways. Grabb and Lambert (1982) found that the majority of people, regardless of social background, think of class in economic terms, though more complex understandings were held by those from the higher strata. This finding was replicated by Lambert et al. (1986: 396). The only study that did a direct test of the proposition that housing tenure intervenes between social class and party preference by influencing one's subjective class self-image did not yield significant results (McAlister 1984: 518).

6. Although she does not summarize the precise pattern of results, Pratt summarized her findings as follows: 'Renters tended to be less conservative in their voting practices, to be more supportive of strikes, protests, and social welfare provisions, and to express more agreement concerning the unsatisfactory income differentials in Canada' (1986: 45).

References

Agnew, J. 1981. 'Home Ownership and Identity in Capitalist Societies'. In *Housing and Identity: Cross Cultural Perspectives,* ed. Duncan (London: Croom Helm).

Aitkin, D. and M. Kahan. 1983. 'Australia: Class Politics in the New World'. In *Electoral Behaviour: A Comparative Handbook,* ed. R. Rose (New York: Free Press).

Alford, R., and H. Scoble. 1968. 'Sources of Local Political Involvement', *American Political Science Review* 62: 1192–1205.

Allen, R. 1973. *The Social Passion: Religion and Social Reform in Canada, 1914–1928* (Toronto: University of Toronto Press).

Bacher, J. 1993. *Keeping to the Marketplace: The Evolution of Canadian Housing Policy* (Kingston: McGill-Queen's University Press).

Balakrishnan, T.R. 1976. 'Ethnic Residential Segregation in the Metropolitan Areas of Canada', *Canadian Journal of Sociology* 1(3): 481–514.

———, and Z. Wu. 1992. 'Homeownership Patterns and Ethnicity in Select Canadian Cities', *Canadian Journal of Sociology* 17(4): 389–404.

Bassett, K. 1980. 'The Sale of Council Houses as a Political Issue', *Policy and Politics* 8: 290–307.

Bell, D.V.J. 1992. *The Roots of Disunity: A Study of Canadian Political Culture* (Toronto: Oxford University Press).

Bentham, G. 1986. 'Socio-tenurial Polarization in the United Kingdom, 1959–1983: The Income Evidence', *Urban Studies* 2: 157–62.

Birch, E.L. 1978. 'Women-made America: The Case of Early Public Housing Policy', *A I P Journal* 44: April.

Bird, T. 1990. 'Shelter Costs', *Canadian Social Trends* Spring: 6–10.

Blakeney, M. 1992. 'Canadians in Subsidized Housing', *Canadian Social Trends* Winter: 20–4.

Blum, T., and P. Kingston. 1984. 'Homeownership and Social Attachment', *Sociological Perspectives* 27(2): 159–80.

Bourne, L. 1986. 'Recent Housing Issues in Canada: A Retreat from Social Housing', *Housing Studies* 3(2): 122–8.

Burke, M. 1990. 'Co-operative Housing: A Third Tenure Form', *Canadian Social Trends* Spring: 11–14.

Butler, D., and D. Stokes. 1969. *Political Change in Britain* (Harmondsford, UK: Penguin).

Card, E. 1980. 'Women, Housing Access, and Mortgage Credit', *Signs: Journal of Women in Culture and Society* 5 (3 suppl.): 215–19.

Castells, M. 1977. *The Urban Question: A Marxist Approach* (Cambridge, MA: MIT Press).

———. 1978. *City, Class, and Power* (New York: St Martin's Press).

———. 1983. *The City and the Grassroots: A Cross-Cultural Theory of Urban Social Movements* (London: Edward Arnold).

Che-Alford, J. 1990. 'Home Ownership', *Canadian Social Trends* Spring: 2–5.

Chouinard, V. 1989. 'Class Formation, Conflict and Housing Policies', *Journal of Urban and Regional Research* 13(3): 390–416.

Clarke, W.A.V., M.C. Deurloo, and F.M. Dieleman. 1994. 'Tenure Changes in the Context of Micro-level and Macro-level Economic Shifts', *Urban Studies* 31(1): 137–54.

Cox, K. 1982. 'Housing Tenure and Neighbourhood Activism', *Urban Affairs Quarterly* 18: 107–29.

Darroch, G. 1983. 'Occupation Structure, Assessed Wealth and Home Owning During Toronto's Early Industrialization, 1861–1899', *Histoire Sociale/Social History* 32: 81–410.

———, and W.G. Marston. 1972/73. 'The Social Class Basis of Ethnic Residential Segregation: The Canadian Case', *American Journal of Sociology* 77: 491–510.

Doling, J., and B. Stafford. 1989. *Home Ownership: The Diversity of Experience* (Brookfield, Vt: Gower).

Doyle, C., and J.D. Hulchanski. 1990. 'The Housing Affordability Gap in Canada: The Need For a Comprehensive Approach'. In *Housing in the 90's: Common Issues* ed. R.D. Katz (Champaign: University of Illinois Press).

Dreier, P. 1978. 'The Tenants' Movement in the United States', *International Journal of Urban and Regional Research* 8: 255–79.

———, and J. Atlas. 1995. 'US Housing Problems, Politics and Policies in the 1990s', *Housing Studies* 10(2): 245–69.

Dunleavy, P. 1979. 'The Urban Basis of Political Alignment: Social Class, Domestic Property Ownership, and State Intervention in Consumption Processes', *British Journal of Political Science* 9: 409–43.

Edel, M. 1982. 'Home Ownership and Working Class Unity', *International Journal of Urban and Regional Research* 6: 205–22.

Eichler, M. (ed.) 1995. *Change of Plans: Towards a Non-Sexist Sustainable City* (Toronto: Garamond).

Engels, F. 1935. *The Housing Question* (New York: International Publishers).

Esping-Andersen, G. 1985. 'The Housing Question'. In *Politics Against Markets: The Social and Democratic Road to Power,* ed. G. Esping-Andersen (Princeton, NJ: Princeton University Press).

Filion, P., and T. Bunting. 1990. *Affordability of Housing in Canada* (Ottawa: Statistics Canada).

———. 1991. 'The Gentrification-Social Structure Dialectic: A Toronto Case Study', *International Journal of Urban and Regional Research* 15(4): 533–74.

Fischer, C. 1982. *To Dwell Among Friends: Personal Networks in Towns and Cities* (Chicago: University of Chicago Press).

Forcese, D. 1975 *The Canadian Class Structure* (Toronto: McGraw-Hill Ryerson).

Garrahan, P. 1977. 'Housing, the Class Milieu and Middle-Class Conservatism', *British Journal of Political Science* 7: 125–36.

Gelb, J., and M. Lief Palley. 1977. 'Women and Interest Group Politics: A Case Study of Equal Credit Opportunity Act', *American Politics Quarterly* 5: 331–52.

Gittell, M., and T. Shtob. 1980. 'Changing Women's Roles in Political Volunteerism and Reform of the City', Signs: *Journal of Women in Culture and Society* 5 (3 suppl): 67–78.

Goldthorpe, J., D. Lockwood, F. Bechofer, and J. Platt.
1967. 'The Affluent Worker and the Thesis of Embourgeoisement', *Sociology* 1(1): 21–34.

———. 1969. *The Affluent Worker in the Class Structure* (Cambridge: Cambridge University Press).

Grabb, E., and R.D. Lambert. 1982. 'The Subjective Meanings of Social Class Among Canadians', *Canadian Journal of Sociology* 7(3) 297–307.

Haddon, R. 1970. 'A Minority in A Welfare State Society', *New Atlantis* 2: 80–133.

Halle, D. 1984. *America's Working Man: Work, Home and Politics Among Blue-Collar Property Owners* (Chicago: University of Chicago Press).

Harris, R. 1986a. 'Home Ownership and Class in Modern Canada', *International Journal of Urban and Regional Research* 10: 67–86.

———. 1986b. 'Class Differences in Urban Home Ownership: An Analysis of Recent Canadian Trends', *Housing Studies* 1(3): 133–46.

———, G. Levine, and B.S. Osborne. 1981. 'Housing Tenure and Social Class in Kingston, Ontario, 1881–1901', *Journal of Historical Geography* 7: 174–216.

Harvey, D. 1973. *Social Justice in the City* (Baltimore, MD: Johns Hopkins University Press).

———. 1976. 'Labour, Capital and Class Struggle Around the Built Environment in Advanced Capitalist Societies', *Political Sociology* 6: 265–95.

———. 1978. 'The Urban Process Under Capitalism: A Framework for Analysis'. In *Urbanization and Urban Planning in Capitalist Society,* ed. M. Boddy (New York: Methuen).

Hayden, D. 1981. *The Grand Domestic Revolution: A History of Feminist Designs for American Homes, Neighbourhoods, and Cities* (Cambridge, MA: MIT Press).

Hunter, A.A. 1986. *Class Tells: On Social Inequality in Canada* (Toronto: Butterworth).

Ineichen, B. 1972. 'Homeownership and Manual Workers' Life-Styles', *Sociological Review* 20: 381–412.

James, S., B. Jordon, and H. Kay. 1991. 'Poor People, Council Housing, and the Right to Buy', *Journal of Social Policy* 20(1): 27–40.

Jaret, C. 1983. 'Recent Neo-Marxist Urban Analysis', *Annual Review of Sociology* 9: 499–525.

Kemeny, J. 1978. 'Forms of Tenure and Social Structure: A Comparison of Owning and Renting in Australia and Sweden', *British Journal of Sociology* 29(1): 41–56.

———. 1981. *The Myth of Home Ownership: Private versus Public Choices in Housing Tenure* (London: Routledge & Kegan Paul).

———. 1983. *The Great Australian Nightmare: A Critique of Home Ownership Ideology* (Melbourne, Aus: Georgian House).

Kemp, D. 1978. *Society and Electoral Behaviour in Australia* (St Lucia, Queensland, Aus: University of Queensland Press).

Kenny, L., and W. Magnusson. 1993. 'In Transition: The Women's House Saving Action', *Canadian Review of Sociology and Anthropology* 30(3): 359–76.

Kingston, P., J. Thompson, and D.M. Eichar. 1984. 'The Politics of Home Ownership', *American Politics Quarterly* 12(2): 131–50.

Klodawsky, F., C. Lundy, and C. Andrew. 1994. 'Challenging "Business As Usual" In Housing and Community Planning: The Issue of Violence Against Women', *Canadian Journal of Urban Research* 3(1): 40–58.

Lambert, R.D., S.D. Brown, J.E. Curtis, B.J. Kay, and J.M. Wilson. 1986. *1984 Canadian National Election Survey Codebook*. Machine readable codebook, Dept of Sociology, University of Waterloo, Waterloo, Ontario.

———, S.D. Brown, J.E. Curtis, and B.J. Kay. 1986. 'Canadians' Beliefs About Differences Between Social Classes', *Canadian Journal of Sociology* 11(4): 379–99.

Laws, G. 1994. 'Community Activism Around The Built Form of Toronto's Welfare State', *Canadian Journal of Urban Research* 3(1): 1–29.

Lawson, R. and S.E. Barton. 1980. 'Sex Roles in Social Movements: A Case Study of The Tenant Movement in New York City', *Signs: Journal of Women in Culture and Society* 6(2): 230–47.

———, S.E. Barton, and J. Weissman Joselit. 1980. 'From Kitchen to Storefront: Women in the Tenant Movement'. In *New Spaces for Women,* eds G.R. Wekerle, R. Peterson, and D. Morley (Boulder, CO: Westview).

MacGregor, S. 1985. 'Deconstructing the Man-Made City: Feminist Critiques of Planning Thought and Action'. In *Change of Plans: Towards a Non-Sexist Sustainable City,* ed. M. Eichler (Toronto: Garamond).

McAlister, I. 1984. 'Housing Tenure and Party Choice in Australia, Britain and the United States', *British Journal of Political Science* 14: 509–22.

McClain, J. and C. Doyle. 1983. *Women as Housing Consumers* (Ottawa: Canadian Council on Social Development).

Madigan, R., M. Munro, and S.J. Smith. 1990. 'Gender and The Meaning of The Home', *International Journal of Urban and Regional Research* 14(4): 625–47.

Magnusson, W. 1985. 'Urban Politics and The Local State', *Studies in Political Economy: A Socialist Review* 16: 120–5.

Masson, D. 1984. 'Les Femmes Dans Les Structures Urbaines-Aperçu d'un Nouveau Champ de Recherche', *Canadian Journal of Political Science* 17(4): 755–82.

Miron, J.R. 1988. *Housing in Post-War Canada* (Kingston: McGill-Queen's University Press).

Munro, M. and S. Smith. 1989. 'Gender and Housing: Broadening the Debate', *Housing Studies* 4(1): 3–17.

Novac, S. 1992. *The Security of Her Person: Tenants' Experiences of Sexual Harassment* (Toronto: Ontario Women's Directorate).

Parkin, F. 1967. 'Working Class Conservatism', *British Journal of Sociology* 18: 278–90.

Perin, C. 1977. *Everything in its Place: Social Order and Land Use in America* (Princeton, NJ: Princeton University Press).

Perlman Schoenberg, S. 1980. 'Some Trends in the Community Participation of Women in their Neighbourhoods', *Signs: Journal of Women in Culture and Society* 5 (3 suppl.): 261–9.

Peters, E. 1990. *Second Stage Housing for Battered Women in Canada* (Ottawa: Canadian Mortgage and Housing Corporation).

Peterson, R., G.R. Wekerle, and D. Morley. 1978. 'Women and Environments: An Overview of an Emerging Field', *Environment and Behaviour* 10(4): 511–34.

Peterson, S. 1990. *Political Behaviour: Patterns in Everyday Life* (Newbury Park, CA: Sage).

Phillips, D. and V. Karn. 1992. 'Race and Housing in a Property Owning Democracy', *New Community* 18(3): 355–69.

Pineo, P. 1988. 'Socio-economic Status and the Concentric Zonal Structures of Canadian Cities', *Canadian Review of Sociology and Anthropology* 25(3): 421–35.

Porter, J. 1965. *The Vertical Mosaic: An Analysis of Social Class and Power in Canada* (Toronto: University of Toronto Press).

Pratt, G. 1986. 'Against Reductionism: The Relations of Consumption as a Mode of Social Structuration', *International Journal of Urban and Regional Research* 10(3): 377–400.

———. 1987. 'Class, Home and Politics', *Canadian Review of Sociology and Anthropology* 24(1): 39–57.

Public Opinion. 1986. 'Owners and Renters', *Public Opinion* 9: 21–9.

Rainwater, L. 1974. *What Money Buys: Inequality and the Social Meaning of Income* (New York: Basic Books).

Rakoff, R.M. 1977. 'Ideology in Everyday Life: The Meaning of The House', *Politics and Society* 7: 85–104.

Ray, B.K., and E. Moore. 1991. 'Access to Home-ownership Among Immigrant Groups in Canada', *Canadian Review of Sociology and Anthropology* 28(1): 1–29.

Rex, J., and R. Moore. 1967. *Race, Community and Conflict* (Oxford: Oxford University Press).

Rutherford, P. 1979. 'Tomorrow's Metropolis: The Urban Reform Movement in Canada, 1880–1920'. In *The Canadian City: Essays in Urban History,* eds G. Stelter and A.F.J. Artibise (Toronto: Macmillan), 368–92.

Särlvik, B., and I. Crewe. 1983. *Decades of Dealignment* (Cambridge: Cambridge University Press).

Saunders, P. 1978. 'Domestic Property and Social Class', *International Journal of Urban and Regional Research* 2: 233–51.

———. 1984. 'Beyond Housing Classes: The Sociological Significance of Private Property Rights and Means of Consumption', *International Journal of Urban and Regional Research* 8(2): 202–37.

———. 1989. 'The Meaning of "Home" in Contemporary English Culture', *Housing Studies* 4(3): 177–92.

———. 1990. *A Nation of Home Owners* (London: Unwin Hyman).

Seeley, J.R., R.A. Sim, and E.W. Loosely. 1956. *Crestwood Heights: A Study of the Culture of Suburban Life* (Toronto: University of Toronto Press).

Sewell, J. 1994. *Houses and Homes: Housing for Canadians* (Toronto: Lorimer).

Skelton, I. 1996. 'The Geographic Distribution of Social Housing in Ontario, Canada: Comparing Public Housing and Locally Sponsored Third Sector Housing', *Housing Studies* 11(2): 189–206.

Spain, D. 1993. 'Gendered Spaces and Women's Status', *Sociological Theory* 11(2): 137–51.

Starkey, J.L., and B. Port. 1993. 'Housing Cost and Married Women's Labour Force Participation in the 1980's', *The Social Science Journal* 30(1): 23–45.

Steele, M. 1979. *The Demand for Housing in Canada* (Ottawa: Statistics Canada).

Steinberger, P. 1981. 'Political Participation and Community: A Cultural-Interpersonal Approach', *Rural Sociology* 46: 7–19.

Sullivan, O. 1989. 'Housing Tenure As A Consumption-Sector Divide', *International Journal of Urban and Regional Research* 13(2): 183–200.

Sykes, G. 1951. 'The Differential Distribution of Community Knowledge', *Social Forces* 29: 376–82.

Thorns, D.C. 1981. 'Owner-occupation: Its Significance for Wealth Transfer and Class Formation', *Sociological Review* 29(4): 705–28.

Turner, B. 1986. *Citizenship and Capitalism: The Debate Over Reformism* (London: Allen & Unwin).

Verberg, N. 1995. 'Buying Into The System: Housing Tenure, Economic Deprivation, and Political Participation'. Ph.D. diss. (University of Waterloo).

Wade, J. 1994. *Houses for All: The Struggle for Social Housing in Vancouver, 1919–1950* (Vancouver: University of British Columbia Press).

Walker, G. 1990. *Family Violence and the Women's Movement: The Conceptual Politics of Struggle* (Toronto: University of Toronto Press).

Warde, A. 1990. 'Production, Consumption and Social Change: Reservations Regarding Peter Saunders' *Sociology of Consumption' International Journal of Urban and Regional Research* 14(1): 228–48.

Watson, S. 1986. 'Women and Housing or Feminist Housing Analysis', *Housing Studies* 1(1): 1–10.

———, and H. Austerberry. 1986. *Housing and Homelessness: A Feminist Perspective* (London: Routledge & Kegan Paul).

Wekerle, G.R. 1980. 'Women in the Urban Environment: Review Essay', *Signs: Journal of Women in Culture and Society* 5 (3 suppl.): 188–214.

———. 1993. 'Responding to Diversity: Housing Developed By and For Women', *Canadian Review of Urban Research* 2(2): 95–113.

Williams, N., J. Sewell, and F. Twine. 1987. 'Council House Sales and the Electorate', *Housing Studies* 2: 274–82.

Index

Aberhart, William, 191; and the development of the Social Credit Party, 207–10
aboriginal peoples. *See* First Nations
abortion, 22
Action Canada Network, 157, 159
affluence, and social class, 311
agency: and change, 105; definition of, 93; and political behaviour, 202
Agricultural Adjustment Administration, 84
Alberta, right-wing politics in, 189, 191, 202–15
Alberta Social Credit League, 207. *See also* Social Credit Party of Alberta
Alberta Wheat Pool, 205
American Civil War, 39
Americanized brand-name consumer: definition of, 94–6
American Revolution: as founding moment, 1, 11–12, 38
anomie (rootlessness), 95
antimodernist cultural warriors, 95–6
Australia, welfare state in, 294–5, 296, 297–8
authoritarianism, 70–1
autonomy, social and political, 4. *See also* state autonomy

baby boom (postwar) generation, 19–20
Belgium, ethnoregional movements in, 250
Bill 101 (Quebec language law), 231–2
Bill 150 (Quebec), 132, 134, 136
Bill 178 (Quebec), 51
Bloc Québécois, 187, 192, 258
borders: and borderless populations, 102–3; and the nation-state, 91–2, 101–2
Bosnia, partitioning of, 101
Bouchard, Lucien, 257
Britain: ethnoregional movements in, 250; housing policies in, 327; role in North America, 37–40
Broadbent, Ed, 230; and Bill 101, 232
Brownlee, J.E., 205

Calgary Board of Trade, 210
Canada, as product of counterrevolution, 38, 39
Canadian Alliance Party, 5, 6, 183, 188; election results, 192, 193
Canadian Charter of Rights and Freedoms, 222
Canadian Election Study (1984), 279, 281
Canadian Labour Congress (CLC), 157
Canadian Multiculturalism Act, 101
Canadian political party system: and the 1988 federal election results, 219–20
capitalism: definition of, 55; and depoliticization, 65; disorganized,

152; and Fordism, 156; and hegemony, 155–6; managed, 289; new varieties of, 98
capitalist/business class, 307, 317–18. *See also* owners
Caplan, Gerald, 223
caregivers, unpaid, 122, 123
Carr, David, 221
cartography: and borderless populations, 102–3
Centre Party (Sweden), 296, 298
Charlottetown Accord (1992), 258
childcare, 121
childhood socialization, 17–19, 28–9
childrearing values, Canadian-American differences, 44–5
Chrétien, Jean, 186
Christian Democratic Party (Germany), 302
citizenship: housing tenure and, 337–8; rights of, 116–17; and social participation, 116–17; and welfare state regimes, 119–21
civil disobedience: Canadian-American differences, 43–4
civil rights movement, 148
civil society, 4, 85; and NSMs, 143–4
class cleavages, 275
class dealignment, 331
class self-image, 331
class voting, 6, 28; evolutionary model of, 274–5; gender and, 282–3; housing tenure and, 331; measurement of, 278–9; occupational status and, 276; political parties and, 278; socioeconomic conditions and, 275; weakness of in Canada, 274, 280–1
co-constitutive relationship, 93
cognitive liberation, and social movements, 254
collective action: and framing, 150; and globalization, 198; rationality of, 143, 149; repertoire of, 148; repression or facilitation of, 147, 148; results of, 146
collective behaviour, 143
collective identity, and NSMs, 151–2
commoditization, of life, 313, 314
Common Frontiers initiative, 159
common sense, and hegemony, 156
communalism, defensive, 198
communication, and reader response theory, 221–2
communism, collapse of, 26
Communist Manifesto, The (Marx), 190
Communist Party: in Canada, 309; in the US, 147
conformity, and the consumer, 95
conscience constituents, and SMOs, 146
consciousness: and ideology, 71; and mobilization, 150
conservatism, 69. *See also* homeownership ideology
conservative: definition of, 6
Conservative Party. *See* Progressive Conservative Party of Canada

and, 307–14; gender politics and, 270–1; growing irrelevance of, 310–14; ideology and, 58; measurement of, 276–7; and NVOs, 168; political activism and, 330; political impact of, 269; populist movements and, 189, 190; self-definition of, 276–7; social participation and, 116–17; types of, 307; validity of analysis by, 270–1; voluntary organizations in Canada and, 172–3. *See also* class voting
Social Credit Party of Alberta, 189, 191, 205, 206–10; and anti-socialism, 212; compared with the CCF in Saskatchewan, 212–13; provincial marketing board of, 209; and registration covenants, 209
Social Credit Party of Quebec. *See* Créditistes
Social Darwinism, 97
Social Democratic Party (Sweden), 295, 296, 298, 302, 303
social equality *versus* inequality, 70, 71. *See also* inequality and redistribution
socialism: colonial, in Australia, 297; definition of, 55; and PM culture, 23; and Saskatchewan voters, 211–12
socialization, and schools, 93
social movement organization (SMO), 145, 146
social movements, definition of, 5
social organizations, and mobilization, 145
social structures, and the individual, 62–3, 93–4
social transformation, nature of, 4–5
society-centred analysis, and welfare states, 119
socioeconomic status (SES), 168; and voluntary organizations, 168, 171–3, 176–7, 179
sociological imagination, 94
sociology, and postmodernism, 85–6
sovereignty. *See also* Quebec
sovereignty, definition of in Quebec, 242–5
sovereignty-association: and the PQ, 239; support for, 245–8
sovereignty-partnership, 256
Spain, ethnoregional movements in, 250
stagflation, 299
state: definition of, 79–81; influence over policy, 2
state autonomy, 81–2; intstrumentalist approach, 82; structuralist approach, 82, 83
state capacity, 119
state-centred analysis, of welfare states, 118–19
state-centred theory, 84–5
statism, in Canada, 37, 39, 48–9
status quo and ideology, 56–7
strategic interaction and SMOs, 147
structural functionalism, 113–14
structure, definition of, 93
structure/agency debate, 92–100; and alternative futures, 105–6
subjective well-being. *See* life satisfaction
Swankey, Ben, 205
Sweden: distribution of power resources in, 117–18; welfare state in, 294–7, 298
Switzerland, 250
system and lifeworld, theory of (Habermas), 152–4
systems of government: Canadian-American differences in, 39–40; legitimacy of, 64–7

Taylorism, 156
teledemocracy, 197
television: and social capital, 13
tenants: housing policies and, 329; political attitudes of, 333–4
Thatcher, Margaret, 302
Theory of Collective Behaviour, The (Smelser), 143

Theory of Communicative Action, The (Habermas), 152
Three Worlds of Welfare Capitalism (Esping-Andersen), 120
Thunder Bay, male working-class culture in, 313–14
Tilly, Charles, 147
Touraine, Alain, 151
trade unions. *See* labour unions
tribalism, 103, 198; and Quebec, 104–5
troubles (structure/agency), definition of, 94

unemployment, and the decline of welfare state, 299, 304
United Empire Loyalists, 38
United Farmers of Alberta (UFA), 203, 204, 205
United Farmers of Canada (UFC) (Saskatchewan section), 210
United Farmers of Manitoba, 204
United Farmers of Ontario, 204
United States: as product of revolution, 38, 39
universalism, of Swedish welfare benefits, 296
use leases, for farm land, 211
US National Recovery Administration, 84
utilitarianism, 99

value systems: dominant, 57–8, 307–9; radical, 57, 58, 309; subordinate, 57, 58, 66, 308–9
Vancouver: housing for battered women, 336; SMOs in, 147, 157
violence, and the late-modern state, 96–7
voluntaristic structures, 81
voluntary organizations (VO), 5, 164–80; Canadian-American differences in membership, 171, 178; English-French Canadian differences, 166–7; involvement in, Canadian-American differences, 42, 166; political protest and, 173–4, 177, 179; Quebeckers and, 50; socioeconomic status and, 168, 171–3, 176–7, 179. *See also* new voluntary organizations
voter response theory, 221–2

wars, low-level, 91
wasted votes, in Canadian elections, 280–1
water, and conflict, 103, 106
Waters, Stan, 192
welfare spending, class beliefs about, 316, 319–20
welfare state, 3, 7; contradictions and crises, 114–15; definition of, 65–6, 110, 112; democracy and capitalism, 116–17; development in Scandinavia, 291, 293; eligibility for benefits, 120–1; expansion of, 292–304; feminist analysis of, 123–5; functionalist explanations of, 112–14; mass mobilization and, 115; post-World War II emergence of, 288–90; racism and, 124; state-centred analysis of, 110–19; in the US, 115, 118–19
welfare-state capitalism, 152
welfare state regimes, 119–21; gender and, 121–3; types of, 120–1
Williams, Fiona, 124
Wilson, Elizabeth, 123–4
women, in the working class, 270–1
Women and the Welfare State (Wilson), 123–4
Wood, Henry Wise, 203
working class: changes to, 139–40; class identification and, 317; power resources of, 118; social policy development and, 289–92, 293; value systems of, 308–10; women and, 270–1. *See also* labour
World Trade Organization (WTO), 147
World Values Study, 12
World Values Survey (1991–2), 169

Yugoslavia, ethnoregional movements in, 250